Myer Myers, *Two Torah Finials* (cat.63)

Myer Myers

JEWISH SILVERSMITH
IN COLONIAL NEW YORK

David L. Barquist

with essays by

Jon Butler and Jonathan D. Sarna

YALE UNIVERSITY ART GALLERY

in association with

YALE UNIVERSITY PRESS

New Haven and London

This catalogue is published on the occasion of the exhibition *Myer Myers: Jewish Silversmith in Colonial New York,* organized by the Yale University Art Gallery. Planning for the exhibition was supported in part by the National Endowment for the Humanities, a Federal agency, the Connecticut Humanities Council, and the Maurice Amado Foundation. The catalogue was supported by generous contributions by The Paul and Elissa Cahn Foundation, the Roy J. Zuckerberg Family Foundation, and Mr. and Mrs. Bernard G. Palitz. The exhibition and its accompanying programs were supported by generous contributions from the Maurice Amado Foundation, the Decorative Arts Society, Mr. Robert M. Rubin, Mr. and Mrs. Philip Holzer, Mr. and Mrs. E. Martin Wunsch, S.J. Shrubsole, Inc., an anonymous donor, and a bequest of Mrs. Lelia M. Wardwell.

NATIONAL ENDOWMENT FOR THE
HUMANITIES

Time for Ideas
The programs for the Connecticut Humanities Council

Design: Greer Allen
Color Separations: Professional Graphics
Printing & Binding: CS Graphics

The paper in this book meets the guidelines for permanence and durability of the Committee on Production Guidelines for Book Longevity of the Council of Library Resources.

Yale University Art Gallery, New Haven
September 14-December 30, 2001

Skirball Cultural Center, Los Angeles
February 20–May 26, 2002

Henry Francis du Pont Winterthur Museum, Delaware
June 20–September 13, 2002

For
Patricia E. Kane
AMICITIAE PIGNUS PRO BENEFICIIS RECEPTIS

Cover illustrations,
two objects by Myer Myers
FRONT:
Dish Ring (cat. 79)
BACK:
Teapot (cat. 1)

Half-title illustration,
Largeworker's workshop, detail from pl. I, "Orfèvre Grossier," in Denis Diderot, *Encyclopédie; Recueil des Planches,* vol. 8, Paris, 1751–65. The Beinecke Rare Book and Manuscript Library, Yale University, New Haven.

Contents

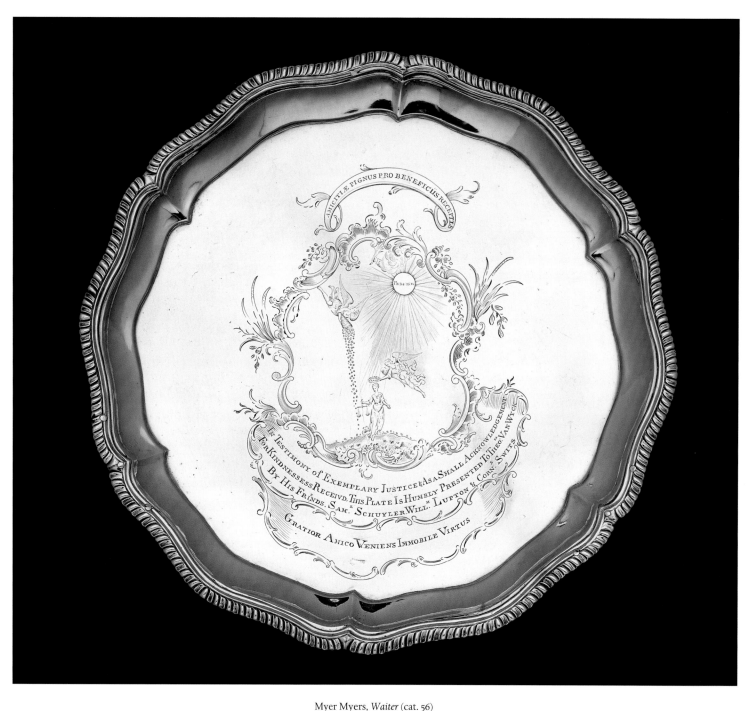

Myer Myers, *Waiter* (cat. 56)

Director's Foreword

We are very pleased to present *Myer Myers: Jewish Silversmith in Colonial New York*, the first exhibition and publication in half a century to make a detailed study of the career of one of America's greatest craftsmen. His outstanding work in silver and gold is presented here in the larger contexts of the Jewish community, the silversmith's trade, and his network of patrons. Given the ties many of these patrons had to Yale University, as well as Myers's seven-year residence in nearby Norwalk and Stratford, Connecticut, it is fitting that this exhibition should open in New Haven during the year that marks the tercentennial of Yale's founding.

David L. Barquist, Associate Curator of American Decorative Arts, organized the exhibition and wrote the catalogue. In the acknowledgments, David thanks the many colleagues, both at Yale and elsewhere, who were instrumental in the realization of this exhibition and publication. I want to underscore our appreciation for their important contributions.

We are proud to share *Myer Myers* with the Skirball Cultural Center, Los Angeles, California, and the Henry Francis du Pont Winterthur Museum, Winterthur, Delaware. Our thanks to the staffs of both museums, particularly vice president Adele Lander Burke and curator Grace Cohen Grossman at the Skirball and director Leslie G. Bowman, curator Donald L. Fennimore, and director of exhibitions Felice Jo Lamden at Winterthur.

For their generosity in sharing such precious objects, we are indebted to the fifty-nine lenders that have made this exhibition possible. Mr. Robert M. Rubin, B.A. 1974, initiated this project with a grand and crucial gesture of patronage. Planning for the exhibition was supported in part by the National Endowment for the Humanities, a Federal agency, the Connecticut Humanities Council, the Maurice Amado Foundation, and an endowment fund established with a National Endowment for the Arts challenge grant. The catalogue was supported by generous contributions by The Paul and Elissa Cahn Foundation, the Roy J. Zuckerberg Family Foundation, and Mr. and Mrs. Bernard G. Palitz. The exhibition and its accompanying programs were supported by generous contributions from the Maurice Amado Foundation, the Decorative Arts Society, Mr. and Mrs. Philip Holzer, Mr. and Mrs. E. Martin Wunsch, S.J. Shrubsole, Inc., and an anonymous donor. Fittingly, this project was also made possible by a bequest of Lelia M. Wardwell, who was Myer Myers's great-great-great-granddaughter, as arranged by her son, the late Allen Wardwell, B.A. 1957, a loyal and longtime member of the Art Gallery's Governing Board.

JOCK REYNOLDS
The Henry J. Heinz II Director
Yale University Art Gallery

Preface

Of all the media that Francis P. Garvan collected, silver was the one he loved best, and that proclivity has influenced scholarship on the subject at the Yale University Art Gallery. *Myer Myers: Jewish Silversmith in Colonial New York* follows in a long tradition of silver studies at the Art Gallery. When Garvan's collection of artifacts, ranging from furniture, ceramics, glass, textiles, and metalwork, came to Yale in 1930, it included approximately 1,000 pieces of early American silver. At the time of his gift to Yale, Garvan arranged for the University to hire as assistant curator John Marshall Phillips, whose field of expertise was early American silver. During his tenure, Phillips honed the collection and made significant acquisitions so that Yale's collection of early American silver is generally regarded as the best in the nation. The efforts of subsequent curators and the generosity of many donors have amplified both the depth and breadth of Yale's collections of early American silver. Important among these donors are Josephine Setze, who established a endowed fund to acquire early American silver for the John Marshall Phillips Collection, and Carl R. Kossack, who with his family donated more than 7,000 pieces of early American silver to Yale. In the last quarter century, the chronological range has been expanded up to the present, and now the collection contains more than 8,500 objects, ranging in date from the 1650s to the twenty-first century.

The study of American silver at Yale has benefited from the papers of early scholars housed at the Art Gallery, the most significant group of which were the papers of Francis Hill Bigelow of Cambridge, Massachusetts. An early and preeminent scholar of the subject, Bigelow had assisted Garvan in assembling his silver collection. John Marshall Phillips's knowledge and passion for early American silver enabled him to establish a bond with Bigelow, who was compiling research notes for a biographical dictionary of early American silversmiths. Following Bigelow's death, these notes passed to Phillips, who continued to refine and amplify them over the course of the next twenty years. In addition to Bigelow's research notes, the curatorial offices at the Art Gallery house and care for other notes of pioneer scholars of American silver whose efforts focused largely on identifying the earliest American silversmiths. The silver research notes of Theodore Salisbury Woolsey, a Yale University professor of international law, are housed there. Woolsey was among the first collectors of early American silver. His article, "Old Silver," was published by *Harper's Magazine* in 1896. His alphabetical files on early American silversmiths underscore the need that he and other collectors perceived for a "really useful and practical hand-book of domestic plate." In addition, the research material compiled by George Munson Curtis of Meriden, Connecticut, and used in his *Early Silver of Connecticut and Its Makers* (1913), also resides at the Art Gallery, as do the files that Maurice Brix used to publish his *List of Philadelphia Silversmiths and Allied Artificers, from 1682 to 1850* (1920), as well as the research notes of Hermann Frederick Clarke (1882–1947) for his biographies *John Coney, Silversmith 1655–1722* (1932), *Jeremiah Dummer, Colonial Craftsman & Merchant 1645–1718* (1935), and *John Hull, A Builder of the Bay Colony* (1940). These papers are a rich resource that the curators draw on continually in American silver research. This resource is also amplified by more than sixty original documents, fifty tools and pieces of equipment, and one hundred drawings relating to the silversmiths' trade donated in large part by Stephen G.C. Ensko, Mr. and Mrs. Joseph Link, Robert Ramp, and Dorelle Moulton Tanner. In addition, through the gift of the Barra Foundation, William Core Duffy, and Dr. Benjamin A. Hewitt, the University acquired the papers of the eighteenth-century Boston silversmith Zachariah Brigden that are housed in the Beinecke Rare Book and Manuscript Library.

At the time of his gift, Garvan was not only procuring a curator with expertise in early American silver, but also planning to have his silver collection published. He hired the renowned English scholar E. Alfred Jones to write a catalogue. Jones was preeminent in the field of American silver, having authored the monumental publication, *The Old Silver of American Churches* (1913). This compilation of the early silver owned by churches in the original thirteen Colonies remains an encyclopedic and invaluable tome because the objects it records were often commissioned from local silversmiths and thus are important touchstones for identifying the marks of American silversmiths. Jones had also authored a survey, *Old Silver of Europe and America* (1928), just prior to his engagement by Garvan to write the catalogue of the Yale collection. Jones produced a draft of the catalogue, but for reasons that are unclear it was never published. It was not until 1970 that the University finally produced a formal catalogue of the silver collection. That two-volume work by Kathryn C. Buhler and Graham Hood, *American Silver: Garvan and Other Collections in the Yale*

University Art Gallery, was the first of the comprehensive catalogues of silver collections in museums that appeared in the later twentieth century.

The Art Gallery also has a long tradition of organizing exhibitions in the field of American silver. To celebrate the tercentennial of the founding of Connecticut, Phillips organized "Early Connecticut Silver" in 1935. His largest effort, however, followed four years later with "Masterpieces of New England Silver." The advent of World War II and Phillips's untimely death in 1953 brought his productive career to an end and marked the beginning of a hiatus in the tradition at Yale of exhibitions addressing American silver. It was not until 1963 that the Art Gallery mounted another important exhibition in this field, "American Gold 1700–1860," organized by Peter Bohan. The pace quickened in subsequent years. Charles F. Montgomery initiated and Barbara McLean Ward and Gerald W.R. Ward carried out the ambitious exhibition "Silver in American Life," co-organized with the American Federation of Arts, which traveled to twelve venues throughout the country from 1979 to 1982. To acknowledge the gift of the early American silver collections of Carl R. Kossack and his family, David Barquist, Aline Zeno, and I mounted "American Silver from the Kossack Collection" in 1988. "First Masters of American Silver: The Craft of the Silversmith in Colonial Massachusetts," was held in 1996 to honor the publication of *Colonial Massachusetts Silversmiths and Jewelers*, the biographical dictionary begun earlier in the century by Bigelow and Phillips that was completed by me and a team of other contributors. Each of these exhibitions has attempted to expand the panoply of works and makers and to develop new perspectives on the nature of the silversmiths' trade.

Myer Myers: Jewish Silversmith in Colonial New York is the first instance in which the Art Gallery has presented a major monographic exhibition on an early American silversmith. It also introduces a new collaboration between the Art Gallery and the Department of the History of Art, since David Barquist undertook the research for this exhibition in working for his doctoral degree under the direction of Edward J. Cooke, Jr., the Charles F. Montgomery Professor of Decorative Arts. Barquist's study rests on a foundation of traditional scholarship in which the circumstances surrounding the creation of these objects has been probed through close study of the artifacts, surviving documents, and patrons. From that careful reading of the evidence, and with the help of the contextual introductory essays, this volume attains a new standard in the study of an individual silversmith and provides a fuller understanding of the makers and patrons of silver in Colonial New York.

PATRICIA E. KANE
Curator of American Decorative Arts

Smallworker's workshop and store, detail from pl. I, "Orfèvre Bijoutier," in Denis Diderot, *Encyclopédie; Recueil des Planches,* vol. 8, Paris, 1751–65. The Beinecke Rare Book and Manuscript Library, Yale University, New Haven.

Acknowledgments

This exhibition celebrates the life and work of Myer Myers, an American Jew who became the most significant silversmith of his generation in New York City. He left a legacy of some of the most extraordinary silver objects to have been made in Colonial America, and the most exciting aspect of this project has been to bring together so many of them with related works of art. I would like to express my personal gratitude to the lenders for their generosity in parting with such precious objects for the exhibition's lengthy tour. I also add my thanks to those of Jock Reynolds to the agencies, foundations, and individuals who provided financial support for both the exhibition and catalogue.

The staffs at many libraries and other collections of records have been tremendously helpful in researching this subject: Liana C. Lupas, American Bible Society; Abigail Schoolman, American Jewish Historical Society; David Beasley, Goldsmiths' Company Library, London; Leslie Fields, The Gilder-Lehrman Collection, Morgan Library; Anne Jaap van den Berg, Nederlands Bijbelgenootschap, Haarlem; James Foltz, New York State Archives; Kenneth Cobb, New York City Municipal Archives; and the staffs of the Historical Society of Pennsylvania, Municipal Archives of Amsterdam, New-York Historical Society Library, New York Public Library, and Division of Old Records, Surrogate's Court, New York City. At Yale University, I would like to thank the staffs of the Divinity, Geology, and Sterling Memorial Libraries, with special mention of Beverly Lett, Art and Architecture Library; Elisabeth Fairman, Curator of Rare Books, Yale Center for British Art; Vincent Giroud and Patricia Willis, Beinecke Rare Book and Manuscript Library; and Joan Sussler, Lewis Walpole Library.

Many individuals have been generous in providing me with access to Myers's silver and other objects, providing leads and information, or engaging in thoughtful discussions: Ellenor Alcorn, Theodore and Barbara Alfond, Rabbi Arnold Mark Belzer, Elizabeth F. Berdell, Robert W. Brinckerhoff, Clarissa Burnett, Mrs. Henry M. Burrows, Paul and Elissa Cahn, Helen and Peter Du Bois, Kevin Faughnan, Elizabeth Pratt Fox, Rita Gans, Raymond Horowitz, Philip and the late Ann Holzer, John D. Kernan, the late Carl Kossack, Stephen Lerman, Mr. and Mrs. Calmon Mendel, Ruth J. Nutt, Ann J. Prouty, Joseph B. Rosenblatt, Iris and the late Seymour Schwartz, Lita Solis-Cohen, Virginia Sullivan, Drs. Richard Weiss and Sandra Harmon-Weiss, Nancy Van Meter and Richard P.W. Williams,

Mrs. Herman W. Williams, Jr., E. Martin Wunsch, and Roy J. Zuckerberg. Jennifer Boudreaux, William B. Bradley, William Core Duffy, Robert Jackson, Frank Levy, James McConaughy, Carl Nordblum, Jeanne Sloane, Seth A. Thayer, Kevin Tierney, Phyllis Tucker, Laura Verlaque, and Michael Weller have shared information and brought objects to my attention. Allison E. Ledes, editor of the Magazine *Antiques* made many helpful suggestions and recommendations. Ubaldo Vitali offered thoughtful insights into techniques and conserved many of the objects. Some individuals have preferred to remain anonymous, so I offer my wholehearted thanks to them without mentioning them by name.

I owe many colleagues at museums and other institutions my gratitude for their time and assistance in research and examination: Susan Faxon, Addison Gallery of American Art; Wesley G. Balla, Tammis K. Groft, and Diane Shewchuk, Albany Institute of History and Art; Ellen G. Smith, American Jewish Historical Society; Judith Barter and Jennifer Downs, Art Institute of Chicago; M.B. Munford, Baltimore Museum of Art; Kathleen B. O'Connor and Michael K. Brown, Bayou Bend Collection, Museum of Fine Arts, Houston; E. Deane Turner and Kathy Kaasch, The Brick Presbyterian Church, New York; Kevin Stayton and Robert Thill, Brooklyn Museum of Art; Alexis Goodin, Michael Agee, and Nancy Spiegel, Sterling and Francine Clark Art Institute; John D. Davis and Janine E. Skerry, Colonial Williamsburg; Marilyn H. Pettit, Sarah Weiner, and Joceyln K. Wilk, Columbia University; Rita Slom and David Bazarsky, Congregation Jeshuat Israel; Rabbi Marc Angel, Rabbi Ira Rohde, and Susan Tobin, Congregation Shearith Israel; Sarah Cash, The Corcoran Gallery of Art; P. Andrew Spahr, Currier Gallery of Art, Manchester, New Hampshire; Olive B. Graffam, Daughters of the American Revolution Museum; James Tottis, Detroit Institute of Arts; Deborah McCracken Rebuck, The Dietrich American Foundation; Gail F. Serfaty, Diplomatic Reception Rooms, U.S. Department of State; Timothy Anglin Burgard and Patricia Junker, Fine Arts Museums of San Francisco; David Pultz, First Presbyterian Church, New York; Dorothy Moss, Greenfield Village and the Henry Ford Museum; Diana Larsen and Alvin L. Clark, Jr., Harvard University Art Museums; Amy Meyers, Henry E. Huntington Library and Museum; Leslie Bowman, Donald L. Fennimore, Felice Jo Lamden, and Anne Verplanck, Henry Francis du Pont Winterthur Museum;

Amanda Lange and Edward Maeder, Historic Deerfield; Kathleen Eagen Johnson, Historic Hudson Valley; Tom Beckman, Historical Society of Delaware; Kathryn Potts, The Jewish Museum; Rabbi Albert Gabbai and Ruth Hoffman, Kahal Kadosh Mikveh Israel; Ann Smith Finn, Mattatuck Museum; Morrison H. Heckscher, Peter Kenny, Ellin Rosenzweig, and Frances G. Safford, The Metropolitan Museum of Art; Catherine Futter, Minneapolis Institute of Arts; Jeannine Falino, Museum of Fine Arts, Boston; Deborah Depehdahl Waters, Museum of the City of New York; Doris Bowman, Jennifer Oka and the late Rodris Roth, National Museum of American History; Stephen Frank, National Museum of American Jewish History; Margaret K. Hofer, Jennifer Jensen, and Kimberly Terbush, New-York Historical Society; John L. Scherer, New York State Museum; Anne Cassidy and Bruce Naramore, New York State Parks, Recreation, and Historical Preservation; Beatrice Garvan, Jack Lindsey and Martha C. Halpern, Philadelphia Museum of Art; Derek Dreher and Judith M. Guston, Rosenbach Museum and Library; Julie Emerson, Seattle Art Museum; David Conradsen, Saint Louis Art Museum; Nancy Berman and Grace Cohen Grossman, Skirball Cultural Center; B. Schlessinger Ross, The Society of Friends of Touro Synagogue; Kathleen Betts, Society of the Cincinnati; Howard Miller, Elie Pinkersoff, and Miriam Rodriguez Pereira, Spanish and Portuguese Jews' Congregation, London; Carol Lovell, Stratford (Connecticut) Historical Society; Roger Berkowitz, Toledo Museum of Art; Nancy E. Richards, Tryon's Palace Historic Sites and Gardens; David Park Curry, Virginia Museum of Fine Arts; Thomas Denenberg and Jason Busch, Wadsworth Atheneum Museum of Art; David Brigham and Nancy Swallow, Worcester Art Museum; Gabriel M. Goldstein, Yeshiva University Museum.

The exhibition and its catalogue have benefited greatly from the observations of two groups of consultants who offered their expertise. Focus Groups funded by the Connecticut Humanities Council were ably led by Daryl K. Fischer and included William S. Ayres, Elin Schoen Brockman, Hildegard Z. Cummings, Ann Smith Finn, Lois Goglia, Jennifer Hoffman Lee, and Roberta Friedman. Two panels funded by the National Endowment for the Humanities sparked lively discussions between Ellenor Alcorn, Gretchen Townsend Buggeln, Jenna Weissman Joselit, Neil D. Kamil, together with Yale University professors Edward S. Cooke, Jr., Paula E. Hyman, and Jules D. Prown. Susan Schussler and Patterson B. Williams also offered valuable insights into conservation requirements and educational programming.

My deepest gratitude is due to Beth Carver Wees, formerly of the Sterling and Francine Clark Art Institute and now at The Metropolitan Museum of Art. As the curator responsible for two major collections of Myers's silver, she has been a stalwart friend and unfailing in her willingness to share ideas and objects and help with logistics. I am also greatly indebted to independent scholar Robert B. Barker of London, England for his insightful reading of the entire manuscript, which has saved the author from embarrassment and the reader from many inaccurate or unclear passages.

My parents and many friends have offered heartfelt support, moral and otherwise, in the hours of need, and I hope they know how much they have meant to me. I would particularly like to thank Sandra J. Markham, a stalwart supporter of this enterprise from the beginning, who has provided accommodations, references, and research in addition to proofreading the entire manuscript. Martin Berger made it possible to examine private and public collections in the Buffalo area and helped with translations of Hebrew. Nancy R. Marshall, Beth E. Miller, Dr. Fiona E. Karet, and Janet M. Koszalka provided much appreciated help with last-minute research and proofreading.

For both the exhibition and catalogue, I have been fortunate to work with individuals whose superior skills have improved and refined my research and provided the reader and visitor with superbly ordered experiences: catalogue editor Sheila Schwartz, catalogue designer Greer Allen, and exhibition designer Stephen Saitas. Their unfailing good humor and friendship have meant much to me during the process of putting together this magnificent catalogue and exhibition. I am also grateful to Professors Jon Butler and Jonathan Sarna for their essays that offer broader contexts for understanding Myers's life and work. The catalogue has also benefited from the beautiful photography of Richard Goodbody, the skillful typesetting of John Moran, and the contributions of Patricia Fidler, Charles Grench, Mary Mayer, and Judy Metro of Yale University Press.

This project developed out of my dissertation in the History of Art department at Yale, and from its inception I have been grateful to my advisor, Edward S. Cooke, Jr., for his enthusiastic support, careful readings, and above all his constant good humor. Jules D. Prown gave the dissertation a thoughtful reading that provided many helpful observations. I also benefited greatly from discussions with Jon Butler.

In the Yale University Development Office, Charles T. Clark, Dennis Danaher, and Usha Pashi have all helped with successful fundraising for this project. At the Yale University Art Gallery, almost every one of my colleagues has helped with this project, and I thank them for their cheerful assistance. I would particularly like to thank Jock Reynolds for his support as well as Antoinette Brown and Bernice Parent in the Director's Office; Associate Director Louisa Cunningham and Charlene Senical, Mary Anne Tomlinson, and Maria Zawadowski in the Business Office; Associate Director Kathleen Derringer and Robert Pranzatelli; Susan Frankenbach and especially L. Lynne Addison in the Registrar's Office; Mary Kordak, Ellen Alvord, Daphne Deeds, and the late Janet Saleh Dickson in Education; Alex Contreras, John ffrench, Carl Kaufman, and Janet Zullo in Photography and Digitization; Burrus Harlow, Clarkson Crolius, and their unsurpassed installation team of Peter Cohen, Stuart Lane, Richard Miller, David Norris, and Nancy Valley; Howard el-Yasin for his help with the catalogue; Mark Aronson, Anne O'Connor, and especially Patricia Garland in Conservation; John Pfannenbecker and Kevin Bradley in Security; and curators Suzanne Boorsch, Helen Cooper, and Susan Matheson.

In the department of American Decorative Arts, I am ever grateful to Joanne Thompson, Museum Assistant, for her meticulous and gracious execution of a myriad of tasks relating to the exhibition and catalogue. Nancy Yates has been a superb problem-solver. Marcia Brady Tucker and Rose Herrich Jackson Fellows Shelley Hagen, Brendan Walsh, Karen Wight, and Kristina Wilson helped with research, as did Fred Murphy and the late Florence M. Montgomery. The late Marion F. Sandquist did much of the support work during the planning stage, and Sylvia Grinder took over on short notice. Bursary student Noah Chesnin tracked down many references in New York newspapers. Special thanks are due to Research Fellow Christopher Sterba, who undertook much of the research into the histories of ownership of these objects. His amazing abilities as a researcher and genealogist have informed many of these entries and given us the context for Myers's work. I owe him a tremendous debt.

It has been my greatest privilege to work at the Art Gallery for the past twenty years under the guidance of Patricia E. Kane. Her superb connoisseurship and scholarship in the field of early American silver have set the standard for examining and evaluating records and objects. Her unwavering support in facing the challenges that such a project engenders has been of inestimable help to me in bringing the catalogue and exhibition to completion.

DAVID L. BARQUIST
Associate Curator
American Decorative Arts

Lenders to the Exhibition

Albany Institute of History and Art, New York

American Jewish Historical Society, New York City and Waltham, Massachusetts

The Art Institute of Chicago

Beinecke Rare Book and Manuscript Library, Yale University, New Haven

Elizabeth F. Berdell

David M. Brinckerhoff, Nelson F. Brinckerhoff, Peter R. Brinckerhoff, Robert W. Brinckerhoff, and their families

Robert W. Brinckerhoff

Brooklyn Museum of Art, New York

The Burrows Collection, courtesy of the Sterling and Francine Clark Art Institute, Williamstown, Massachusetts

Paul and Elissa Cahn

Clermont State Historic Site, New York State Parks, Recreation, and Historic Preservation, Clermont, New York

Columbia University in the City of New York

Congregation Jeshuat Israel, Newport, Rhode Island

Congregation Shearith Israel, New York

The Corporation of the Brick Presbyterian Church in the City of New York

The Currier Gallery of Art, Manchester, New Hampshire

The Detroit Institute of Arts

William B. Dietrich

Helen and Peter Du Bois

Fine Arts Museums of San Francisco

The First Presbyterian Church, New York

E. Norman Flayderman

Mrs. Jerome T. Gans

Greenfield Village and the Henry Ford Museum, Dearborn, Michigan

Harvard University Art Museums, Cambridge, Massachusetts

Henry Francis du Pont Winterthur Museum, Delaware

Historic Deerfield, Inc., Deerfield, Massachusetts

Historic Hudson Valley, Tarrytown, New York

Historical Society of Delaware, Wilmington

Philip Holzer

Kahal Kadosh Mikveh Israel, Philadelphia

Lewis Walpole Library, Farmington, Connecticut, a department of Yale University Library

The Metropolitan Museum of Art, New York

The Minneapolis Institute of Arts

Museum of Fine Arts, Boston

Museum of the City of New York

The New-York Historical Society

Eric Noah

Ruth J. Nutt

Philadelphia Museum of Art

The Rosenbach Museum and Library, Philadelphia

Sheila S. Scott

Toledo Museum of Art, Ohio

Tryon Palace Historic Sites and Gardens, New Bern, North Carolina

Nancy Van Meter and Richard P.W. Williams

Virginia Museum of Fine Arts, Richmond

Wadsworth Atheneum Museum of Art, Hartford, Connecticut

Worcester Art Museum, Massachusetts

Yale University Art Gallery, New Haven

Barbara and Roy Zuckerberg

8 private collections

Notes to the Catalogue

DATES from sources that used the Hebrew calendar have been converted to the Gregorian calendar throughout the text; the dates in the original document are given in the notes. Dates prior to 1752 are given as New Style.

CATS. 1–104 are by Myer Myers; objects marked by the partnership of Halsted and Myers are so designated.

All OBJECTS were made in New York City unless otherwise indicated.

DIMENSIONS are given in inches with centimeters in parentheses; weights are recorded in troy ounces with grams in parentheses. "Scratch wt." refers to a weight scratched onto a given object's underside; these have been recorded if they appear to date from the eighteenth century. No weight is given when the silver elements of an object account for less than half of its gross weight.

Information on MARKS, INSCRIPTIONS, ARMORIALS, and PROVENANCE are provided only for objects by Myer Myers.

The MARKS referred to in the entries are illustrated and described in Appendix I. The Mark illustration number identifies the catalogue number of the object from which the photograph was taken.

All INSCRIPTIONS are in Roman capitals unless otherwise indicated.

Under PROVENANCE, the names of the original owners are given when known; subsequent owners have been recorded if they are referred to in the inscriptions or mark a significant change in ownership.

NOTE REFERENCES in the essays and entries are abbreviated for all but infrequently cited manuscript sources; full citations appear in the Bibliographical Abbreviations.

The NAMES OF NEWSPAPERS in Colonial America were not always consistent with regard to spelling and punctuation. The names are given here as they appear on the masthead of the issue cited.

Fig. 1. David Grim, *A Plan of the City and Environs of New York* (cat. 143).

The New York World of Myer Myers

Jon Butler

Myer Myers was a most fortunate artisan, not least in the decision made by his parents to settle in a still infant New York in the 1720s. The town— yet another place of exile for European Jews— proved a felicitous choice, especially for their son. New York's persistent cultural pluralism and booming economy fueled Myers's success into the 1770s. The city's population growth, religious pluralism, swelling economy, and burgeoning artisanal energy made Myers's talents more valuable than they would have been in many other places, including other towns in British America. Even the downturn in business Myers faced in the 1780s and 1790s demonstrated how his prospects always had been tied to New York.

New York bore an international flavor throughout the colonial era, from its origins as New Amsterdam in 1626 to the founding of the American republic. Never a place for utopian experimentation or reclusive piety, New Amsterdam existed for commercial purposes to further Dutch international trade, a New World outpost in the already far-flung seventeenth-century Dutch empire. But the city's trade and crucial position as gateway to massive territories to the north and west, filled with furs and rich with land, also made it an object of irresistible English desire. That desire surfaced with military force in September 1664, when four English warships appeared in the New Amsterdam harbor and forced the Dutch to surrender the town and colony. New Netherland and New Amsterdam now became New York, named for James, Duke of York, brother of the English monarch Charles II.[1]

Whether New Amsterdam or New York, the city was a complex and anomalous place. Above all, it was a town that harbored ethnic, racial, religious, and cultural minorities from the 1690s on, a composition that attracted refugee Jews like Solomon Myers, who arrived sometime before his son Myer's birth around 1723. Even as early as 1703, New York had no national, ethnic, or religious majority. About 40 percent of its residents were Dutch, 30 percent were English, a little less than 20 percent were African (most of them slaves), 10 percent were French Huguenots, with a small scattering of Jews (already enough to form a synagogue), Germans, Walloons, Scots, Irish, and other Europeans. When the United States took its first federal census in 1790, the city still remained without a clear ethnic or religious majority; its lists of nationalities and religions were longer than they had been in 1703, yet Africans still comprised more than 10 percent of the town's population, even though many had fled during the Revolution.[2]

New York's diversity from the 1660s to the 1760s brought tension over race as well as over ethnicity and religion. Throughout the eighteenth century, Africans easily comprised between 15 and 20 percent of the population, and Europeans feared those they enslaved. In 1712, a small group of Africans in New York revolted; three Englishmen, three French Huguenots, two Dutch men, one Walloon, and one German were murdered in a night of bloody mayhem. In the days after the revolt failed, six Africans committed suicide while being interrogated by British authorities, and within two weeks the British had hanged nineteen Africans for their alleged roles in the revolt. In 1741, unexplained fires and rumors of a possible "Negroe conspiracy," perhaps not unlike the conspiracy that had created South Carolina's bloody but failed Stono Rebellion in 1739, sent New York's Europeans into a frenzied search for plots and conspirators. In several weeks of court hearings and accusations, which recalled the witch trials a half-century earlier in Massachusetts, 150 Africans and twenty-five Europeans went to jail, eighteen Africans and four Europeans were hung, another thirteen Africans were burned, and seventy more were packed off to the West Indies.[3]

Tensions also characterized relations among Europeans, especially in the decades before Solomon Myers arrived in New York. Dutch bitterness against the English conquest of 1664 boiled over in the so-called Leisler Revolt of 1689, led by a staunch German Calvinist, Jacob Leisler, to protest James II's Catholicism and protect Dutch Calvinist interests against the English. Dutch-English antagonism reached new heights when the English Governor Henry Sloughter not only ordered Leisler hanged but also disemboweled, decapitated, and quartered, displaying Leisler's head on a post to remind Dutch residents of treason's consequences. The tension, often palpable, continued well into the 1710s. And it was not helped by the passage of the Ministry Act in 1693, which provided government funds for religion. But the funds went to New York's small Church of England congregations, not to the city's much better attended and far more powerful Dutch Reformed Church.[4]

Yet most Europeans, including Jews, experienced far greater tolerance in New York than in the Old World cities they came from. Dutch-English tension generally abated after 1720, while French Huguenots faced only minor, almost nonexistent, opposition. Jews sometimes did have serious problems. In 1737, the politician William Smith successfully petitioned the New York Assembly, on explicitly anti-Semitic grounds, to disallow the Jewish votes recently cast in the Assembly elections; ten years later, thugs defaced markers in New York's two Jewish cemeteries, the first of which dated from the 1650s.[5]

Despite such incidents, Jews remained relatively free in this New World town. Both before and after the 1737 election, Jews voted without apparent incident. They openly pursued a wide variety of trades without restriction or residential segregation. And no known opposition arose to the construction of a new synagogue in the 1730s or to the increasing prominence of Jews in New York's religious life. When Congregation Shearith Israel held a traditional Hebrew prayer service in September 1760 to commemorate the British capture of Montreal during the French and Indian Wars, the New York printer William Weyman published the service in a small pamphlet "translated into English, by a friend to truth." Whether for Jews, French or Dutch Protestants, or several varieties of English Protestants, life in New York was an improvement on the discrimination, hostility, and even violence that religious difference still generated throughout much of Enlightenment Europe.[6]

Marriage—intermarriage specifically—offered one especially visible, sometimes painful, measure of colonial New York's practical toleration and pluralism among Europeans. At one extreme, New York's Dutch proved especially clannish, both before and long after the Leisler Revolt. Well into the 1730s, almost no Dutch men took English or French Protestant wives, an obvious attempt to preserve Dutch homogeneity. Although a sixth of Dutch women married English and French Protestant husbands, their own flexibility pointed up the persistent practice of most Dutch residents, women and men alike, of using marriage to maintain ethnic cohesion and solidarity.[7]

In contrast, French Protestants intermarried so frequently that Huguenots disappeared as a religious and national group in New York. Most arrived in the city as refugees from France after Louis XIV initiated a massive persecution of Protestants in the 1680s, notably by revoking the Edict of Nantes, which had guaranteed limited Protestant worship since 1598. Yet even in their first decades in New York, 40 percent of Huguenot refugees married English or Dutch spouses, and by the 1740s more Huguenots married outside their own ethnic and religious boundaries than chose French spouses. The consequences for Huguenot cohesion proved disastrous. Most of these mixed couples joined Dutch Reformed, Church of England, Presbyterian, Baptist, and even Quaker congregations, and New York's shrinking French Church barely struggled on; it finally closed during the Revolution.[8]

There is little evidence about how mixed marriages were viewed in eighteenth-century New York. Exceptional are several letters written in 1743 by Abigail Franks, the wife of Jacob Franks, one of New York's prominent Jewish merchants, that detailed her distress at the surreptitious marriage of her daughter Phila to Oliver DeLancey, son of the wealthy Huguenot merchant and politician Stephen DeLancey. Among Jews, tension had already emerged over marriages between Spanish or Portuguese Jews (Sephardim) and German-speaking Jews from Central and Eastern Europe (Ashkenazim). But nothing equaled Abigail Frank's anguish when her daughter eloped with DeLancey, shattering family and religion simultaneously: "My Spirits was for Some time Soe Depresst that it was a pain to me to Speak or See Any one. . . . My house has bin my prison."[9] That Phila Franks and Oliver DeLancey could even consider marrying—and did—suggests that New York's pliant environment could produce the liberal effects that parents rightly feared.

New York's babble of languages, an inevitable product of a remarkable ethnic and national diversity, gave way to a growing dependence on English as the town's commonly spoken language, though not without protest. Before 1740 especially, many European New Yorkers and Africans clearly were bilingual, trilingual, and more in various rudimentary ways, at least in speech and for some in reading and writing. Yet it was not without reason that the mid-eighteenth-century New York politician and essayist Robert Livingston wrote at mid-century that "in all the British colonies, as the knowledge of the English tongue must necessarily endure, so every foreign language . . . must, at length, be neglected and forgotten." Especially in New York, Livingston well caught the drift toward English as the city's most common tongue amidst so many languages. French Protestants not only left their churches because they married English and Dutch spouses, but also because they and their children simply lost their acquaintance with the French language. New York's Dutch residents, too, gradually adopted English, even though they still only married within the Dutch community. The Reverend Gualtherus Du Bois worried in 1748 that widespread neglect of the Dutch language accounted for the sparse attendance at Dutch Reformed Church services; by the 1760s the church hired an English-speaking minister to bring non-Dutch-speaking "Dutch" residents back into the congregation.[10]

New York may have become increasingly monolingual in Myer Myers's lifetime, but in the sphere of religion, pluralism reigned, relentlessly paralleling the city's expanding ethnic, national, and racial heterogeneity. When Governor Thomas Dongan assessed New York in 1687, he expressed bewilderment at the chaos: "Here bee not many of the Church of England; few Roman Catholicks; abundance of Quakers preachers men and Women especially; Singing Quakers, Ranting Quakers, Sabbatarians; Antisabbatarians; Some Anabaptists[;] some Independents; [and] some Jews." In short, Dongan wrote, "of all sorts of opinions there are some, [while] the most part [are] of none at all."[11]

New immigrants and divisions among old ones accelerated religious pluralism in New York, which outstripped anything found in a single European city. This pluralism took visible form in a welter of religious buildings. By the 1720s, when Solomon Myers arrived in New York, the city had added new buildings for its Church of England, Dutch Reformed, French Protestant, Baptist, and Presbyterian congregations; the new synagogue on Mill Street, Congregation Shearith Israel, was constructed in 1730 for the growing Jewish population. In a flurry of building, a dozen churches were built or enlarged between 1750 and the Revolution, including construction of a new Presbyterian church in 1768. By the time of Myer Myers's death in 1795, New York contained at least twenty-five functioning congregations from eleven different religious groups— Episcopalian, Dutch Reformed, Presbyterian, Quaker, Baptist, Lutheran, Moravian, Universalist, Methodist, Roman Catholic, and Jewish— not to mention those worshipers who met in homes.[12]

Many of these people were drawn to New York by the city's episodic yet strongly expanding economy, which produced the urban wealth and specialization that ultimately supported hundreds of eighteenth-century urban artisans like Myer Myers. This economy had its deepest roots in the region's agricultural expansion. Before and after the Revolution, New York's economy depended on the export of agricultural products and furs to pay for the import of consumer goods. The dramatic tenfold growth in New York Colony's rural population between 1720 and 1790 bore strong results for the city's trade. Imports ballooned from £45,000 to over £500,000 between 1720 and 1770, while exports— foodstuffs, timbers, and furs— rose from £20,000 to over £80,000 in the 1770s, a trade deficit paid for by rapidly expanding credit from London sources. The greatest rise in New York's imports and exports occurred between 1750 and 1770, fueled by dramatic population and economic expansion, and enriched by the merchants, farmers, and landholders who could support the silversmiths and other fine craftsmen crowding into New York.[13]

New York's wealth, including the wealth of its leading urban families, rested on a unique agricultural base. From the Dutch settlement into the mid-eighteenth century, New York's leading families not only had merchant interests, but also held massive, unprecedented acreage on both sides of the Hudson River to the north of the city and then to the far west. Accompanied by charges of corruption and bribery, leading families acquired thousands of acres of rich New York land through grants or "gifts" made in the 1690s and early 1700s by New York governors. The Heathcotes, Livingstons, Morrises, Philipses, Schuylers, and others obtained hundreds of thousands of acres which they then leased to tenants who paid rents, not unlike European farmers. The practice drew criticism. Richard Coote, Earl of Bellomont and New York governor between 1699 and 1701, wryly observed, "What man will be such a fool as to become a base tenant to Mr. Delius, Colonel Schuyler, [and] Mr. Livingston . . . when for crossing Hudson's river that man can for a song purchase a good freehold in the Jersies." Still, several thousand immigrants found leasing profitable in the eighteenth century. It was common in counties such as Dutchess, north of the city, and profited the great families, many of whom also patronized urban artisans like Myer Myers for objects with which to furnish their mansions in the town of New York.[14]

New York's economic growth stimulated an urban economy of real complexity and sophistication that itself fed on newly arrived immigrants and an internally generated labor supply. Even by the 1720s, when Solomon Myers arrived in New York, the town supported many specialized crafts and trades— shoemakers, weavers, hatters, tailors, seamstresses, coopers, and carpenters, as well as cabinetmakers, silversmiths, and goldsmiths. But the number and range of specialized crafts ballooned almost spectacularly after mid-century. By the late 1780s, as Myer Myers attempted to resurrect his silver business after the Revolution, New York supported an amazing array of trades, not only the old ones but such new entrepreneurs as bird sellers, chocolate merchants, sign painters, clockmakers, painters and glaziers, a ship breadmaker, combmakers, milliners and wigmakers, glovemakers, musicians, portrait painters, a bellowmaker, even a bookbinder. They all prospered and expanded in a markedly growing economy both in the city and throughout the countryside, especially after 1750.[15]

New York obtained its workers from two sources. The first group comprised the substantial number of immigrants, including those with skills used by artisans like Myers. In addition, prosperity and an absence of imperial regulation allowed New York to develop highly successful local apprentice systems in the fine crafts. These furnished skilled labor as well as successors for aging masters and became the foundation on which entrepreneurially inclined workers started their own local shops. Had the British authorities chosen to restrict apprentice systems, New World craftsmen would have been dependent on London-trained workers. But no restrictions were ever imposed, perhaps in the mistaken impression that the American crafts paled in comparison to their Old World counterparts.[16]

Such a comparison could not have been more misguided. In New York, as in the other colonial ports, the local apprenticeship systems allowed both immigrants and native-born men and women to learn valuable crafts and trades without ever journeying across the Atlantic. Ethnicity or religious identity played important roles in apprenticeship for some New Yorkers. Huguenot silversmiths often took Huguenot children as apprentices, even though Huguenots exhibited relatively little

Fig. 2. Simeon Soumaine, *Sugar Dish*, New York, 1738–45. Silver.
Yale University Art Gallery, New Haven; Mabel Brady Garvan Collection.

ethnic loyalty in marriage. Nevertheless, there was a flexibility in personal relations and business that would have been unusual in Britain or on the Continent. In this environment, Myer Myers was able to train as a silversmith in New York, even though there were no Jewish silversmiths with whom he could apprentice. Whether as a matter of indifference or fascination, Myers's Judaism did not bar his own apprenticeship or prevent him from employing non-Jewish apprentices and workers, native-born or immigrant.[17]

New York's developing fine crafts production became one of the city's notable achievements. Colonists everywhere, New Yorkers included, imported many fine goods from London. In the 1730s, one New Yorker reported that "tea and china ware cost the province, yearly, near the sum of £10,000."[18] But New Yorkers also bought fine objects from local makers, not merely because their prices were cheaper but because local craftsmen, including craftsmen trained locally, increasingly produced exceptionally fine goods.

New York's most prominent fine craftsmen worked in silver. The Huguenot immigrant Simeon Soumaine arrived in the 1690s after being trained in London, where Huguenots were among the renowned silversmiths, and emerged in the 1710s as one of several major silversmiths in New York. Soumaine did not copy the ornate style of his London teachers, but instead often produced work of elegant simplicity, such as his sugar dish of 1738–45 (fig. 2), which is regarded as one of the finest pieces of pre-Revolutionary American silver. Soumaine and other Huguenot silversmiths in New York— Charles Le Roux, Peter Quintard, and John Hastier— took apprentices, including Huguenot children, to help them in

their shops and to continue their increasingly profitable trade in an increasingly wealthy town. For Soumaine, the move to America proved dramatically fortunate. In the 1690s and early 1700s, he was among New York's poorest taxpayers. But between 1710 and his death in the 1730s, assessors ranked Soumaine in the top 10 to 20 percent of the town's taxpayers, signaling the prosperity that could be won by a skilled, persistent craftsman in colonial New York.[19]

Fine cabinetmakers also prospered in colonial New York, although historians know less about them than about their counterparts in Philadelphia and Newport. Craftsmen such as Gilbert Ash, Thomas Burling, Joshua Delaplaine, and Andrew Gautier, as well as more common chairmakers such as Jonas Colon and William Gillicker, were among many who produced furniture and chairs in a city with a growing demand for goods and the capacity to fill the demand. Thomas Burling made superb tables and dressing bureaus, of a quality competitive with work by Philadelphia and Newport makers (all of which now bring enormous prices as antiques). By 1795, the city's chairmakers were producing in such volume that they could export five thousand Windsor chairs to the West Indies.[20]

The productivity of New York's silversmiths and cabinetmakers bespoke a strongly consumer-oriented market that extended to civic life generally, including politics. Myers knew this firsthand because his two best-known clients, the Livingston family and the Anglican minister Samuel Johnson (cat. 126; not to be confused with the London literary critic), were among the central figures of this market. The Livingstons included the lawyer, newspaper editor, and leading Presbyterian layman, William Livingston, as well as his brothers Philip (cat. 129) and Robert (cat. 127), and the latter's son Peter (cat. 34). Samuel Johnson was a well-known clergyman and infamous Connecticut apostate who had abandoned Puritanism at Yale in the 1720s. Myers's skill in maintaining clients at such opposite ends of the New York political spectrum testifies to the flexibility of the city's eighteenth-century politics and to Myers's personal ingenuity. Tumultuous charges of graft, bribery, and corruption rang through New York politics up to the Revolution and far beyond. They reflected a highly charged, personal politics that revolved around great family alliances, whose bitter and often byzantine disputes became direct models for the "factions" Alexander Hamilton excoriated in his famous essay in the *Federalist Papers*, originally published in the *New York Packet* in November 1787.[21]

From the early eighteenth century to well past the Revolution, New York's greatest families maneuvered family connections and personal relationships to shape society and politics alike. The Alexanders, DeLanceys, Livingstons, Morrises, Philipses, and Smiths dominated political dialogue and elections to the New York City Council and the New York Assembly across six decades, often with tumult and rancor. Governor George Clinton alleged in 1752 that Oliver DeLancey (the man who had married Phila Franks in 1743), won elections "by the numbers . . . [he] horsewhipped."[22]

The Livingstons headed one of eighteenth-century New York's most important family factions. Moderate "Whigs," they attacked the cronyism, venality, and conspiracies associated with Britain's Tory party and New York's Tory-associated governors. They used the rhetoric of "liberty," an increasingly volatile term in New York and colonial politics after 1750. They opposed the concept of the divine right of rulers and tyranny in general, blame for which they laid on their opponents' doorstep.[23]

William Livingston and Samuel Johnson clashed openly in New York's newspapers, which were more numerous than those published in Britain. The *Independent Reflector*, edited by Livingston, John Morin Scott, and William Smith, Jr., devoted itself almost exclusively to politics. It took London's *Tatler* and *Spectator* as its models, and Livingston and his editors attacked their opponents on a wide variety of issues, especially the sale of political offices and public and private immorality among New York officials. One of the *Independent Reflector*'s most famous attacks took place in 1753 in connection with the proposed creation of King's College (later Columbia University). Supporters of the school planned to install another of Myer Myers's clients, Reverend Samuel Johnson, the Puritan apostate, as its head. The newspaper belittled Anglicans and Johnson as "Vendors of Jargon, gloomy Imposters, devout System-Mongers, and spiritual Conjurers." Even without the college, Anglicans had created a colony "overrun with Priest-craft and every Office userp'd by the ruling Party." Johnson's Anglican supporters fought back in the *New-York Mercury*, ridiculing Livingston's claim that the coexistence of many religions was preferable to the alleged truth of one. If all religions were equal, Johnson and his Anglican supporters charged, the result would be "a Scene of Confusion" and "dreadful Convulsions." Only the hegemony of the Church of England, which an Anglican-dominated King's College could ensure—would keep everything in "balance."[24]

Yet if New York politics forced tradesmen like Myers to tread carefully among factious clients, it also opened windows of opportunity, especially when family conflicts arose. Peter Livingston purchased silver from Myer Myers (cat. 34) and probably arranged for the purchase and donation of three silver communion or collection plates (cat. 32) for the Presbyterian church. But his relationship with his father, Robert Livingston, was crossed with anger and grief. Peter overspent, despite or because of his taste for silver, and went bankrupt in 1771. His father rescued him to preserve family respect. But in a new will he abrogated Peter's rights as eldest and forced Peter to share the family's vast New York properties with his younger brothers. Craftsmen like Myer Myers sold their goods to all these disputing New Yorkers, weaving their way among

internal family disputes, as with the Livingstons, and among the colony's multifarious political thickets, as in the Anglican-Presbyterian conflict. Principle seems not to have hindered either production or consumption.[25]

The swelling economy and population that benefited silversmiths and energized New York politics also produced an expansive, often equally agitated public culture between 1740 and 1770. New York tavern life exploded at least as rapidly as its population. Taverns ranged from cheap and thoroughly disreputable one-room "establishments," which dispensed alcohol and violence in equal measure, to larger taverns whose entertainment extended from impromptu brawls and cockfights to exotic caged bears and tigers. Women operated some taverns, usually assuming ownership from deceased husbands. The best-known taverns—the Black Horse Tavern, Kings Arms Tavern, D'Honneur's Tavern, and Fraunces Tavern (the latter now rebuilt at its original location on Prince Street in lower Manhattan)—joined the Exchange Coffee House, Tontine Coffee House, and the Merchants Coffee House as centers of commerce and politics. New York Assembly committees conducted public and private business at D'Honneur's Tavern in the 1730s, and John Jay and other patriotic politicians wrote the Colony's strongly worded attack on the 1774 Intolerable Acts at the Merchants Coffee House.[26]

Clubs and fraternal associations populated New York's "better" taverns and coffee houses. Often, they bore ethnic, language, and even religious identities, not only in New York but elsewhere. By mid-century, Charleston's elite had organized fifteen clubs and associations for Scots, Huguenots, Welsh, Irish, and German residents. New York had clubs for English, Dutch, French, Scottish, and Irish residents. By the 1730s, New York also hosted a Masonic lodge, and by the 1750s this lodge was sponsoring other Masonic lodges in the New York Colony.[27]

Elite emphasis on social organization produced institutions with distinct public significance. New York's first circulating library was the New York Society Library, a private club formed in 1754 modeled on Benjamin Franklin's Library Company of Philadelphia. New York's fire companies, first authorized in the 1730s, were also organized as fraternal associations that competed for the right to extinguish fires even as buildings burned. Other public services suffered under competing claims to authority. The town fitfully enlarged its port facilities, usually after bitter arguments over public rights versus private monopolies. New York lacked a road department until 1764, and paved streets existed only in the city's wealthiest areas. Sewers were nonexistent or problematic. Residents regularly disposed of human wastes in the East and Hudson Rivers, and a storm sewer enlarged in 1747 never worked properly, becoming a cesspool of fetid water and human and animal wastes.[28]

The quality of housing depended entirely on wealth and

became increasingly problematic for the poor as New York grew. Throughout the colonial period, housing existed everywhere throughout the town, right down to the wharves that lined the rivers. From the 1720s to the Revolution, housing became scarcer and more expensive, especially for laborers and the poor. Although the Maryland traveler Dr. Alexander Hamilton reported in 1744 that most New York houses featured brick construction, a more careful examination would have revealed many flimsy wood buildings vulnerable to fire, usually occupied by the city's poor laborers and their families. Two, three, even four families inhabited quarters originally meant for one because they could not afford New York's increasingly stiff rents, a pattern that continued well past the Revolution.[29]

Housing for the wealthy and upper-middle classes, however—those who constituted Myer Myers's clients—became more luxurious and more ornate during Myers's lifetime. David Clarkson constructed a handsome home surrounded by gardens on Great George Street. The Walter Franklin mansion on Cherry Street served as George Washington's first residence after his election as president, and a large house built by Alexander McComb on Broadway in 1786 served as Washington's second home in New York. William Walton's mansion on Pearl Street, built in 1754 from bricks imported from the Netherlands, stood three stories high and 50 feet wide, with spacious drawing rooms on either side of its entrance. Wall Street contained a series of distinguished homes that occupied wide, deep lots and formed a fitting preview to the new town hall built between 1745 and 1747, which Pierre L'Enfant enlarged in 1789 to become Federal Hall, the seat of the new government.[30]

Wealth and poverty shaped New York politics as much as it determined where people lived. In the 1730s, Governor Lewis Morris and his faction openly appealed to poorer voters in municipal elections by promising to create a new almshouse and poorhouse, issue paper currency to ease the money shortage, and construct new fortifications to provide military protection as well as jobs. In the 1760s, several of the Colony's political factions, including the Livingstons, appealed explicitly to the poor and the laborers among voters; the DeLanceys, the Livingstons' bitter opponents, charged that the Livingstons were openly approaching "Journey-man Carpenters Solliciting Votes" and offering "to give Money to their Box."[31]

The Revolution highlighted and momentarily resolved at least some of New York's complexities and tensions. From the Stamp Act Crisis of 1765 to the rush to independence between 1774 and 1776, tensions about wealth, poverty, and class merged into anti-Parliamentary and anti-monarchical protest. Popular leaders such as Isaac Sears and Alexander McDougall, whose language and manners strongly revealed their working-class origins, proved as wily as the Colony's more aristocratic politicians in maneuvering New York politics. In 1766, tenant farmers in Dutchess County revolted against their wealthy landlords, marching on New York City to destroy the landlords' townhouses. But the Sons of Liberty, headed by Sears and McDougall, remained silent despite pleas for help, and the governor's militia ended the farmers' revolt. But in other instances throughout the 1760s and early 1770s, Sears and McDougall deftly led their group in raucous anti-British protests. In 1775, Sears simply seized the keys of New York's customs collector, Andrew Elliot, to close the entire port in one of the first acts of the American Revolution.[32]

The Revolutionary War itself proved disastrous to the city. Washington's defeat and near capture at the Battle of Brooklyn in August 1776 led to the British occupation of New York in September. Then, on September 21, a major fire burned through most of the city along the Hudson River, including Trinity Church, the seat of the Church of England in New York, as well as the city's Dutch Reformed and Lutheran churches, and another fire on August 3, 1778 destroyed more of the city. Enormous numbers of New Yorkers fled. Lucky exiles such as Myer Myers established rudimentary businesses elsewhere, Myers in Connecticut. Others scraped by, some modestly so, some all but starving. Tories, their supporters, and those who cared not at all about the war and merely remained in New York, did little better. Throughout the British occupation, the town was a shell of its former self—and not only because of the destruction caused by the fires. Throughout the long British occupation, New York remained a Loyalist refugee bastion that could not sustain itself without massive British imports or help from troops, who harassed nearby farmers to feed hungry city dwellers. Lord Cornwallis's loss at Yorktown in 1781 merely changed the direction of departures from the city, as 40,000 British Loyalists scurried to reach Britain or Canada.

Patriotic New Yorkers rushed to greet a triumphant General Washington on Evacuation Day, November 25, 1783, as he entered the city from the north while the last British troops sullenly rowed to their ships in New York Harbor. But even the most vociferous patriot understood that the Revolution had brought more than political independence. The disastrous British occupation and the new demands of freedom destroyed the world pre-Revolutionary New Yorkers had shaped and which many believed they had fought to preserve.[33] New Yorkers, like all Americans, now scrambled to find new markets, new credit, and new trading partners for exports and imports. They also took time to settle political scores. A New York Assembly dominated by radical and angry patriots stripped property from Tories, prevented them from holding public office, and forced sales of confiscated Tory lands and estates. And New Yorkers, led by the enormously successful Alexander Hamilton, debated the creation of a new federal government, as well as national economic policies about tariffs, paper currency, and the repayment of war debts.[34]

Artisans such as Myer Myers had more personal concerns. Whether they had been patriots or Loyalists, the disappearance of the pre-Revolutionary world brought an end to their successful enterprises. In Providence, for example, numerous merchants and tradesmen active before the war vanished by the 1780s, never to reappear. A New York merchant wrote in 1785 that "many of our new merchants and shopkeepers set up since the war have failed. We have nothing but complaints of bad times."[35] Of course, some old clients simply died, as had Myer Myers's client Samuel Johnson by 1772. Many had experienced grievous economic losses during the British occupation, some fleeing and languishing elsewhere, some suffering under the British. Many never recovered. And new residents migrating to the city in search of opportunity did not necessarily flock to old merchants and artisans. Instead, they patronized younger artisans or newcomers like themselves, all eager to make a place in a town remade by the Revolution and now the nation's capital. As a result, the immediate post-Revolutionary economic decline fell with particular harshness on older, displaced artisans and merchants.

In the last decade of Myers's life, New Yorkers—artisans and merchants, laborers, landlords, freed and enslaved Africans—struggled intensely over their own political and economic destiny. The city, state, and nation belonged to them now more than ever before. And the difficult post-Revolutionary circumstances seemed to steel the resolve of New Yorkers. As one observer described the arrival of Washington in New York City in November 1783, the British troops "with their scarlet uniforms and burnished arms, made a brilliant display," while Washington's troops "were ill-clad and weather-beaten, and made a forlorn appearance." But "they were our troops, and as I looked at them, . . . my heart and my eyes were full."[36]

Myer Myers probably took little consolation in the fact that the Revolution which brought about his economic decline and that of his fellow artisans after 1780 had also created a new, independent nation, centered on New York. But he could not have been unaware that his career and life—as a silversmith, as an apprentice who trained apprentices, as a tradesmen who negotiated around faction and personal intrigue, and as a Jew—had always been shaped by the city in which he lived, a city whose tolerance, energy, and enthusiasm for things beautiful made his success possible.

NOTES

1 Kammen 1975, pp. 71–72.
2 Goodfriend 1975, p. 139; Jackson 1995, p. 921, s.v. "Population."
3 Kammen 1975, pp. 213–14, 283–86; Davis 1985; Horsmanden 1971; Szasz 1967.
4 Kammen 1975, pp. 121–26, 136–37, and Murrin 1990, both superseding Reich 1953.
5 Kammen 1975, p. 240; Faber 1992, p. 99; Hershkowitz/Meyer 1968, pp. 4–5 n. 12, 116–118 n. 4.
6 Faber 1992, pp. 84–106.
7 Goodfriend 1991, pp. 92–99.
8 Butler 1983A, pp. 158–60, 187–89.
9 Abigail Franks to Naphtali Franks, June 7, 1743, in Hershkowitz/Meyer 1968, p. 117.
10 Balmer 1989, pp. 141–44; the quotation from Robert Livingston is on p. 142.
11 "Governor Thomas Dongan's Report to the Committee of Trade on the Province of New-York, dated 22d February, 1687," in O'Callahan 1849–51, I, p. 186.
12 Butler 1990, p. 177; Butler 2000, pp. 27, 195; Burrows/Wallace 1999, p. 209.
13 Vickers 1996, pp. 234–35; McCusker/Menard 1985, pp. 189–97.
14 Richard Coote, quoted in Fox 1926, p. 116. For a positive view of New York's tenant farming, see Kim 1978. Dissatisfaction with the system brought substantial protests in the decades before the American Revolution; see Kim 1978, pp. 281–415, Lynd 1962, Lynd 1968.
15 See the lists of residents and occupations drawn from New York City tax lists from 1703 and 1789 in Rothschild 1990, pp. 185–204, 205–27.
16 Butler 2000, pp. 74–75.
17 Butler 2000, pp. 74–75; Jackson 1995, p. 1070, s.v. "Silver."
18 Breen 1994, p. 456.
19 Butler 1983A, pp. 178–83. For a parallel case of a later Dutch craftsman, see Smith 1950.
20 Stott 1995. See the listings for Jonas Colon and William Gillicker in the 1789 roster of city occupants and taxpayers printed in Rothschild 1990, pp. 205–27, and Sack 1987.
21 Bonomi 1971; Tully 1994, pp. 51–60.
22 Clinton, quoted in Tully 1994, p. 245.
23 Ibid., pp. 213–36.
24 Klein 1963, pp. 1–50, 276; Tully 1994, pp. 137–38.
25 Kierner 1992.
26 The best study of colonial taverns is Conroy 1995. On taverns in New York, see Butler 2000, p. 172; Burrows/Wallace 1999, p. 124; Jackson 1995, pp. 74, 248.
27 Butler 2000, pp. 173–74; Bullock 1996, pp. 46–47; Jackson 1995, p. 667.
28 Butler 2000, p. 168; Bridenbaugh 1938, pp. 160, 319; Bridenbaugh 1955, p. 237; Burrows/Wallace 1999, pp. 184–85.
29 Butler 2000, pp. 146–48. The best study of laborers' housing in the colonial period is Smith 1981.
30 Many of the buildings are described in Smith 1889, pp. 5–52; regrettably, there is no adequate study of eighteenth-century New York City architecture.
31 Quoted in Bonomi 1971, p. 244; see also pp. 229–78, on pre-Revolutionary politics. Burrows/Wallace 1999, pp. 179–81; Butler 2000, pp. 95–96.
32 On New York in the Revolution, see Countryman 1981; Ranlet 1986; Burrows/Wallace 1999, pp. 223–64; Mason 1966.
33 Burrows/Wallace 1999, pp. 259–60.
34 For general histories of the economic effects of independence, see Matson 1996, pp. 337–62; McCusker/Menard 1985, pp. 351–77; Appleby 1984.
35 John Thurman, quoted in Smith 1889, p. 5.
36 Quoted in Burrows/Wallace 1999, p. 260.

Colonial Judaism

Jonathan D. Sarna

Refugees from the Inquisition

The Judaism that began to grow in mid-seventeenth-century colonial America was rooted in the soil of the Iberian peninsula. Wherever they lived, Jews who traced their roots back to the Iberian peninsula came to be known as Sephardic Jews, or Sephardim, from the biblical name Sepharad (Obadiah 1:20), which they understood to mean Spain. They distinguished themselves from the Jews of the Germanic lands, known as Ashkenazic Jews or Ashkenazim, based on the biblical name Ashkenaz (Jeremiah 51:27), associated with Germany. Sephardim developed many distinct rites, practices, traditions, and foodways, and the language of their faith, including words for sacred objects and occasions, appropriated Spanish and Portuguese terms. Culturally, too, Sephardim stood apart from their Northern coreligionists: because there were no ghettos in Spain or Portugal, Sephardim had lived among non-Jews, absorbing Iberian values, and learning to appreciate secular knowledge. Yet their collective consciousness had also been seared by memories of cruel expulsions and Inquisitional terror. These experiences shaped the worldview of the Sephardim, underscoring the instability of diaspora life and the fragility of worldly success.[1]

Sephardic Crypto-Jews, forced converts who were outwardly Christian but inwardly Jewish, along with those who escaped Iberia from the fifteenth century onward in order to resume the open practice of Judaism under more favorable regimes, identified as members of a somewhat vaguely defined "Portuguese Jewish Nation."[2] This Nation, something of an imagined community, was nevertheless rooted in a common place and culture. Tangled webs of association and kinship, common memories of persecution, and a shared devotion to the maintenance of the Sephardic heritage and tradition bound its members together. Embracing practicing Christians of Jewish origin as well as strict Jews, the Nation emphasized the tribal aspects of Judaism, the ties of blood and peoplehood; religion remained a secondary element in this collective identity. The seismic questions posed by this separation of religion from ethnicity— questions concerning the authority of religion in Jewish life, the definition and boundaries of Judaism, and whether Judaism, like post-Reformation Christianity, could be practiced in a multiplicity of ways— would continue to rattle Jews throughout the modern period.[3]

Amsterdam is where these questions first came to the fore. The young Calvinist republic of the Netherlands, newly independent of Spain and bitterly antagonistic toward the Holy Inquisition, emerged as a vibrant center of world trade in the seventeenth century and became a magnet for Crypto-Jews who sought economic opportunities in a more tolerant religious environment. Synagogues, a Jewish school, and Jewish printing houses opened in Amsterdam, where most Jews settled, with the result that those who had previously practiced Jewish rituals underground were now able to openly embrace their ancestral faith and resume living as Jews in the sunlight (fig. 4). But conflicts concerning Jewish religious authority, intellectual and spiritual freedom, and the relationship between practicing Jews and those who still preferred to keep their Jewish ancestry secret plagued the Jewish community. In some cases, they resulted in painful excommunications, such as that of the philosopher Baruch Spinoza in 1656. Economically, however, the community expanded and thrived. As early as the 1630s, one study shows, Jews of Iberian descent were responsible for as much as 8 percent of the Dutch Republic's total foreign trade.[4]

In 1630, when Holland captured the colony of Pernambuco in Brazil from the Portuguese (aided, it was alleged, by Crypto-Jews seeking revenge on their former persecutors), Jewish communal life on the Amsterdam model became possible for the first time in the New World. The Dutch West India Company, which governed the colony as a profit-making venture for its investors, actively sought to attract enterprising Jews to its new dominion. The Company had learned to value Jewish merchants as stimulators of industry and trade— not to mention that Jews already spoke the local language (Portuguese) and were connected through ties of kinship and trade with Portuguese *conversos* who had settled there. In secret instructions, the West India Company explicitly ordered the chief of its expedition to grant Jews liberty on a par with Roman Catholics: "No one will be permitted to molest them or subject them to inquiries in matters of conscience or in their private homes."[5]

Recognizing the region's great economic potential, Jews flocked to Pernambuco, establishing in the city of Recife and its environs a community that, at its peak in the 1640s, had 1,000–1,450 Jews— between a third and a half of Dutch Brazil's

Fig. 3. Interior of Touro Synagogue, completed 1763, Newport, Rhode Island.

total civilian white population.[6] The community included ordained rabbis, an active synagogue, and two Jewish schools—more than any North American Jewish community would be able to claim for another two hundred years. Most significantly, the Jews of Dutch Brazil enjoyed rights unmatched by any other seventeenth-century Jewish community in the world. "Treat and cause to be treated the Jewish nation on a basis of equality with all other residents and subjects in all treaties, negotiations and actions in and out of war without discrimination," the States General of the United Netherlands ordered.[7]

Some six hundred Jews remained in Recife when Portuguese troops recaptured the province on January 26, 1654. Jews as well as Protestants lost everything and were given three months to leave. Those Jews who could find safe passage set sail for Amsterdam. There they asked Dutch officials for protection and begged assistance from the city's well-organized community of Jews. Other refugees searched for New World havens. By April 26, 1654, all openly professing Jews had left Brazil. Short-lived as it was, a mere twenty-four years, this first organized Jewish community in the New World was nevertheless of considerable significance. At a time when most of Europe's Jews still lived highly restricted and traditional lives, Recife offered an alternative vision, one based on legal equality and commercial opportunity. Protestants, Catholics, and Jews coexisted in Recife, albeit somewhat uneasily, and Jews practiced their religion conspicuously and traded lustily. Long before the forces of enlightenment and emancipation brought about comparable changes in the lives of German and Eastern European Jews, market forces in the New World triumphed over traditional prejudices and created a climate where Jewish life could develop and thrive.

In Pernambuco's wake came a series of three events that transformed Jewish life on both sides of the Atlantic.[8] First, Sephardic Jewish merchants in Holland, seeking to strengthen trade links with the Caribbean weakened by the loss of Recife, stimulated the return of Jews to England, abetted by Manasseh ben Israel, a leading rabbi, mystic, and scholar in Amsterdam. In 1655, Manasseh went to England to petition Oliver Cromwell for the readmission of Jews, who had been expelled in 1290. The rabbi infused the return with millennial significance, seeing it as a harbinger of Israel's redemption. No formal readmission of Jews took place, but informally Jewish settlement was permitted. By 1695, London was home to eight hundred Jews and a vital center of Sephardic trade between Europe and the New World.[9]

The second event was the establishment by Sephardic Jews of new Jewish settlements in the West Indies to replace Recife. The most significant of these, the Dutch communities of Curaçao (1659), Cayenne (1659), and later Surinam (which passed to Dutch rule in 1667), beckoned Jews with promises of religious liberty and civic equality that more than matched what Recife had offered. Prospective Jewish settlers in the Jewish-sponsored colony in Cayenne, for example, were promised "freedom of conscience with public worship, and a synagogue and school," as well as "all Liberties and Exemptions of our other colonists as long as they remain there."[10]

The third event was surely, in the eyes of contemporaries, least important: a new Jewish settlement was also established at the remote Dutch colony of New Netherland. There, in September 1654, a boatload of bedraggled Recife Jewish refugees—twenty-three of them an old record suggests, but this number is now disputed—sailed into the port of New Amsterdam and requested permission to remain.[11]

Later generations, looking back, celebrated these refugees as "the Jewish Pilgrim Fathers,"[12] but they were in fact nothing of the sort. The English Pilgrims who sailed into the harbor at Plymouth, Massachusetts, in 1620 migrated voluntarily as Puritan religious separatists seeking a colony of their own where they could worship, work, and live together according to the tenets of their faith. By contrast, the Jews who arrived in 1654 came involuntarily, penniless, and in need of refuge. They did not want a colony of their own, but rather permission to reside among the local residents and conduct trade. Moreover, at least according to one historian, women and children dominated the group; only four among them, he claims, were actually "fathers."[13] If they were not "Pilgrim Fathers," however, the refugees did initiate the first Jewish communal settlement in North America.

Piety vs. Profit

The Jews who arrived in 1654 were not the first Jews in English-speaking North America. Back in 1585, the Roanoke colony's metallurgist and mining engineer was a Jew named Joachim Gaunse, and thereafter a small number of other Jews, mostly intrepid merchants bent on trade, made brief stops at American ports to conduct business.[14] What distinguished the refugees of 1654 was precisely their desire to settle down and form a community, to "navigate and trade near and in New Netherland, and to live and reside there."[15]

New Amsterdam in 1654 was among the New World's most diverse and pluralistic towns. By the time the Jewish refugees arrived, the clergy of the dominant Dutch Reformed Church were already deeply agitated, feeling that their legal prerogatives as the colony's only recognized faith were being usurped.[16] Peter Stuyvesant, the dictatorial director-general of New Netherland and himself an elder of the Reformed Church and the son of a minister, sought to promote morality and social cohesion by enforcing Calvinist orthodoxy while rooting out nonconformity. When Lutherans petitioned for permission to call for a minister and organize a congregation, he

A. Le Cadan Berescid } ou Époux de la Loy, representant les Rois   SIMCHA TORA   la Loy, le dernier jour de la fête des Cabanes : Le Cadan Tora est
B. Le Cadan Tora ······ }   ou   celui qui la finit, le Cadan Berescid, est celui qui la recommence.
   d'Israël qui etoient obligez de commencer, et de finir la Lecture de IOYE pour la LOY.   CC. Deux Parnassins .

Fig. 4. Bernard Picart, *Synagogue des Juifs Portugais à Amsterdam*, from *Cérémonies et coutumes religieuses de tous les peuples du monde*,
Amsterdam, 1723. Yale Center for British Art, New Haven; Paul Mellon Collection.

was relieved that his superiors in Amsterdam turned them down. He forced them to worship in private; some were even subjected to fines and imprisonment.[17]

When the Jews arrived, Stuyvesant sought permission from Amsterdam to keep them out altogether. The Jews, he explained, were "deceitful," "very repugnant," and "hateful enemies and blasphemers of the name of Christ." He asked the directors of the Dutch West India Company to "require them in a friendly way to depart" lest they "infect and trouble this new colony." He warned in a subsequent letter that "giving them liberty we cannot refuse the Lutherans and Papists." Decisions made concerning the Jews, he understood, would serve as precedents and determine the colony's religious character forever after.[18]

Forced to choose between their economic interests and their religious sensibilities, the directors of the Dutch West India Company back in Amsterdam voted with their pocketbooks. They had received a carefully worded petition from "the merchants of the Portuguese [Jewish] Nation" in Amsterdam that listed a number of reasons why Jews in New Netherland should be permitted to stay there.

One argument doubtless stood out among all the others: the fact that "many of the Jewish nation are principal shareholders." Responding to Stuyvesant, the directors noted this fact and referred as well to the "considerable loss" that Jews had sustained in Brazil. They ordered Stuyvesant to permit Jews to "travel," "trade," "live," and "remain" in New Netherland "provided the poor among them shall not become a burden to the company or to the community, but be supported by their own nation." After several more petitions, Jews secured the right to trade throughout the colony, serve guard duty, and own real estate.[19]

Just as Stuyvesant had feared, the economic considerations that underlay these decisions soon determined policy for members of the colony's other minority faiths as well. "We doubt very much whether we can proceed against [these faiths] rigorously without diminishing the population and stopping immigration which must be favored at a so tender stage of the country's existence," the directors admonished in 1663 after Stuyvesant banished a Quaker from the colony and spoke out against "sectarians." "You may therefore shut your eyes, at least not force people's consciences, but allow every one to have his own belief, as long as he behaves quietly and legally, gives no offense to his neighbor and does not oppose the government."[20]

Expedience thus became the watchword in cosmopolitan New Amsterdam, though it lived in constant tension with the established Dutch church. The priority of economics proved fortunate for the refugee Jews and the small group of immigrants from Holland who joined them. They benefited from their ties to powerful merchants of the "Hebrew Nation" back in Amsterdam and drew sustenance from the struggles of other minority faiths in the colony, whose efforts were linked to their own. Ultimately, though, the rights Jews battled hardest to obtain and maintain were civil rights, not religious ones. Public worship, while desirable and available to Jews in Recife and Amsterdam, was not a religious requirement. Granted the right to settle and trade, they consented to worship in private.

Preserving and Maintaining Jewish Life

The far more difficult challenge facing New Amsterdam's nascent Jewish community—one that American Jews would confront time and again through the centuries—was how to preserve and maintain Judaism itself, particularly with their numbers being so small and Protestant pressure to conform so great. From the earliest years of Jewish settlement, a range of responses to this challenge developed. At one extreme stood Solomon Pietersen, who in 1656 became the first known Jew on American soil to marry a Christian. While it is not clear that he personally converted, the daughter that resulted from the marriage, named Anna, was baptized in childhood.[21]

Asser Levy stood at the other end of the spectrum. An Ashkenazic Jew from Vilna who had briefly sojourned in Amsterdam and perhaps Brazil, he arrived in New Amsterdam in 1654 totally impoverished but deeply committed to the maintenance of his faith. He enjoyed considerable success as a butcher ("excused from killing hogs, as his religion does not allow him to do it"), merchant, and real estate entrepreneur. Among the Jews who immigrated to New Amsterdam in 1654 he was the only one who stayed, maintaining a home in the city until his death in 1682. As Dutch rule waned, the Sephardic Jews departed for colonies with more sun and promise; by 1654, the Levys were the only known Jewish family in town. Yet the inventory of Asser Levy's estate suggests that he resolutely observed at least the principal rituals of his faith, including the Sabbath and Jewish dietary laws, within the precincts of his own home. His life epitomized both the many hardships entailed in being a Jew in early colonial America and the possibilities of surmounting them.[22]

One spur to the maintenance of Jewish communal life was the need for a burial ground—fear of death, as it were, promoting a communal spirit. Early American Jews, among them refugees from Recife, the Inquisition, and from other calamities and persecutions, had learned from experience that life was fragile. They knew that religious hatred, as well as the diseases and misfortunes common to all humanity, might strike them down at any time. As early as July 1655, three Jews acting in the name of all others in New Amsterdam petitioned the "Worshipful Director General and Council . . . to be permitted to purchase a burying place for their nation." They certainly "did not wish to bury their dead . . . in the common burying ground," which was Christian. Jews and Christians in Europe (and for that matter in Recife) had regularly buried their followers apart, maintaining in death the separate religious identity so strongly felt in life; the petition to continue this hallowed practice proved uncontroversial. The Jews were granted "a little hook of land" outside the city for a burial place. The location of that land has long since been forgotten, but not its significance as the Jews' first municipally recognized religious turf. It offered Jews the spiritual serenity of knowing that when they died they would be buried within their faith. It also encouraged group loyalty, since burial in the "little hook of land" could be denied those who violated Jewish communal norms. Even when the exigencies of life drew individuals away from their people and their faith, the mystery of death often brought them back. By 1682, Joseph Bueno de Mesquita had purchased a different burial plot "for the Jewish nation in New York," and this remained in use (once it was enlarged in 1729) for one hundred and fifty years.[23]

A second and even more important spur to the creation and maintenance of Jewish communal life in New Amsterdam was the arrival late in 1655 of Abraham de Lucena, a Sephardic merchant, bearing a Torah scroll, garbed in a "green veil, and cloak and band of India damask of dark purple color, borrowed from the synagogue in Amsterdam." In colonial North America, as elsewhere, the presence of a Torah scroll served as a defining symbol of Jewish communal life and culture, of Jewish law and lore (fig. 5). It created a sense of sacred space: the presence of a Torah elevated a profane parlor into a cherished place of holiness and the private home in which Jews worshiped into a hallowed house of prayer. The return of the green veiled Torah to Amsterdam in about 1663 signified that the community had scattered: the *minyan*, the prayer quorum of ten males over the age of thirteen traditionally required for Jewish group worship, could no longer be maintained.[24] The subsequent reappearance of Torah scrolls in the city under the British was a sign that the community had been reestablished and private group worship resumed.[25]

In an effort to promote tranquility and commerce, the British, who established their authority in New York in 1664, scrupulously maintained the religious status quo, according Jews the same rights (but no more) as they had enjoyed under the Dutch. The operative British principle, for Jews as for other social and religious deviants from the mainstream, was "quietness." When in 1685 the approximately twenty Jewish families in town petitioned for the right to worship in public, which London's Jews had enjoyed since 1657, they were summarily refused; "publique Worship," they were informed, "is Tolerated . . . but to those that professe faith in Christ."[26] Years later, long after these restrictions had been lifted, many Jews continued to look upon "quietness" as a principle conducive to Jewish group survival. Their instinct, rooted in a history most no longer recalled, was to keep their Judaism as private as possible.

Public worship became available to Jews without any fanfare or known change in the law around the turn of the eighteenth century, just about the time when New York's first Quaker Meeting House was erected, and before the Baptists and Catholics had opened churches in the city. Based on assessment lists, Leo Hershkowitz believes that he can date with great precision the moment of transition from covert worship in a private home to overt worship in a rented house: "The renting of the synagogue must have taken place between December 28, 1703 . . . and February, 1704." Even if the real date was more like 1695, as other scholars insist, it was in the early eighteenth century that the synagogue drew up its constitution and commenced keeping records.[27] For the next 125 years, the synagogue dominated Jewish religious life in New York.

The Synagogue-Community

The synagogue and organized Jewish community in colonial America became one and the same—a synagogue-community—and as such it assumed primary responsibility for preserving and maintaining local Jewish life. The synagogue-community descended from the *kehillah*, the distinctive form of communal self-government that characterized Jewish life in the Middle Ages. Although it drew upon Jewish communal patterns going back to Spain and Portugal, it now defined community in terms of the synagogue. It governed its members much like a Protestant church governed its parish, thereby promoting discipline while avoiding the appearance of a Jewish "state within a state."[28]

The synagogue established in New York was located in a small rented house on Mill Street, today South William Street, but then popularly known as Jews Alley. The congregation's official name became Kahal Kadosh Shearith Israel ("the holy congregation remnant of Israel"). Like most New World synagogues of the time, its name hinted at the promise of redemption—"I will surely gather the remnant of Israel," said the prophet Micah (2:12); "I will put them together . . . as the flock in the midst of their fold." The name Shearith Israel thus recalled the widespread belief that the dispersion of Israel's remnant to the four corners of the world heralded the ingathering.[29] The synagogue closely resembled its Old and New World counterparts in assuming responsibility for all aspects of Jewish religious life: communal worship, dietary laws, life-cycle events, education, philanthropy, ties to Jews around the world, oversight of the cemetery and the ritual bath, even the baking of matzoh and the distribution of Passover *haroset* (a mixture of ground nuts, fruits, spices, and wine used as part of the seder ritual.) The advantages of this all-encompassing institution were, from a Jewish point of view, considerable: it promoted group solidarity and discipline; evoked a sense of tradition as well as a feeling of kinship toward similarly organized synagogue-communities throughout the Jewish world; and improved the chances that even small clusters of Jews, remote from the wellsprings of Jewish learning, could survive from one generation to the next.

Looming large among the values espoused by the synagogue-community were tradition and deference. At Shearith Israel, various prayers, including part of the prayer for the government, continued to be recited in Portuguese; the congregation's original minutes were likewise written in Portuguese, even though only a minority of the members understood that language and most spoke English on a regular basis. Portuguese was the language of the community's founders and of the Portuguese Jewish Nation scattered around the world.[30] In matters of worship, too, Shearith Israel closely conformed to the traditional *minhag* (ritual) as practiced by Portuguese Jews in Europe and the West Indies. Innovations were prohibited; "our duty," Sephardic Jews in England (writing in Portuguese) once explained, is "to imitate our forefathers." On a deeper level, Sephardic Jews believed, as did the Catholics among whom they had for so long lived, that ritual could unite those whom life had dispersed.[31] This goal often proved difficult to realize. One cynical observer, Manuel Josephson, writing in 1790, complained that "our North American Congregations . . . have no regular system . . . they have continually remained in a state of fluctuation." He blamed the small numbers and "frequent mutability" of local Jews, and grumbled that even the readers who chanted the liturgy "collected some materials from one & another And patched up a system of ceremonies of his own, which will be followed during the time he remains in office, but no sooner another one succeeds, some new customs & formalities will be introduced." What American synagogues needed, he proclaimed, was to emulate European congregations where, "Custom & ceremonies even the most minute [are] reduced to a regular system, from which they do not deviate on any account."[32]

Deference formed part of Sephardic tradition as well. Worshipers expected to submit to the officers and elders of the congregation, which were entirely lay-dominated. As in most religious and political institutions of the day, power was vested in men of means. At Shearith Israel, governing authority rested in the hands of the *parnas* (president or warden), assisted by a small number of officers and elders who constituted the *mahamad* or *adjunta* (council). These were usually men of wealth and substance who took on the burden of communal leadership out of a sense of *noblesse oblige*. *Yehidim* (members), generally men of status who materially supported the congregation, made most of the important decisions; they were the equivalent of "communicants" in colonial Protestant churches. The rest of the worshipers, including all women, occupied seats but held no authority whatsoever.

No Jewish religious authority of any kind in colonial America possessed sufficient status to challenge the authority of the laity. Neither Shearith Israel, nor any of the synagogues subsequently established prior to the Revolution ever hired a *haham* (sage, the title given to a rabbi in the Sephardic community), nor did rabbis regularly grace American pulpits until 1840. Sermons, when they were delivered at all, were offered by visitors or by the officiating (unordained) reader. London's Sephardic synagogue had considered it "necessary and imperative . . . to have a Haham," and appointed one in 1664, just seven years after that congregation's founding, to "instruct us and teach the observance of the most Holy Law." In the New World, the Jewish communities of Recife, Curaçao, Surinam, Barbados, and Jamaica all enjoyed the religious leadership of a *haham* at various times in the seventeenth and eighteenth centuries.[33] In New York, lack of members and funds partly explains why Shearith Israel did not follow suit, but the practice of local churches was probably more important. Only about a fourth of the Christian congregations in the province of New York enjoyed full-time pastors in 1750, and even the Anglicans failed to appoint a bishop to oversee their flock.[34] The absence of a religious authority thus did not demean Jews in the eyes of their neighbors. Moreover, the diversity of the city's Jewish community, which by the mid-eighteenth century embraced Sephardim and Ashkenazim from many different locales, would have made the task of finding an appropriate *haham* difficult if not impossible. To compensate, the officiating *hazan* (cantor-reader), in addition to chanting the liturgy, assumed many of the ceremonial functions that a *haham* might otherwise have performed. But with all the respect that non-Jews showed the *hazan*, insiders knew that he was still only a religious functionary subject to the *parnas*.[35]

Colonial American synagogues also differed from their European and West Indies counterparts in their relationship to the state. In Sephardic communities as diverse as Bayonne (France), Curaçao, and the Virgin Islands, synagogue leaders looked to the government to buttress their authority. The leaders of Curaçao's congregation, for example, were constitutionally empowered under various circumstances to seek "the intermediation of the Honorable Governor should all other means fail."[36] In other communities, fear of the state justified extraordinary extensions of Jewish communal power. Concern for "our preservation" led synagogue leaders in London, for example, to demand the right to have "revised and emended" any book written or printed by any local Jew in any language.[37] No such clauses, however, appear in any known American synagogue constitution. In the religiously pluralistic colonial cities where Jews principally settled, local governments (at least in the eighteenth century) extended a great deal of autonomy to churches and synagogues and rarely intervened in their internal affairs. As a result, synagogue leaders, like their church counterparts, found it necessary to rely on their own authority.

Fig. 5. Bernard Picart, *Manière d'exposer la Loy au peuple, avant que de commencer à la lire*
(detail) from *Cérémonies et coutumes religieuses de tous les peuples du monde*,
Amsterdam, 1723. Yale Center for British Art, New Haven; Paul Mellon Collection.

In the North American colonies, therefore, punishments for wayward congregants remained within the purview of the religious community, a practice parallel to church forms of discipline. The ultimate authority available to the synagogue-community was the power of the *herem*, or excommunication. The anathematized person lost all rights within the Jewish community and was treated as if he were dead. This punishment, however, was threatened far more often than it was actually invoked, for its effectiveness in a society where Jews and Christians mixed freely was highly questionable.[38] More commonly, therefore, punishments entailed fines, denial of synagogue honors, and, most effective of all, threatened exclusion from the Jewish cemetery. Even these punishments required some degree of communal consensus. The leaders of Shearith Israel found this out the hard way in 1757 when they attempted to crack down on outlying members of the congregation who were known to "dayly violate the principles [of] our holy religion, such as Trading on the Sabbath, Eating of forbidden Meats & other Henious Crimes." The *adjunta* darkly threatened these violators with loss of membership and benefits, including that "when Dead [they] will not be buried according to the manner of our brethren." But six months later, in the face of opposition from congregants (and, presumably, a drop in donations), they decided to "reconsider," quoting Isaiah's call to "open the gates" for a "nation that keeps faith" (Isaiah 26:2).[39] Synagogue-communities thus may be said to have patrolled "the edges" of irreligious behavior, much as Jon Butler shows New England congregational parishes of the time did. It was more important, they knew, to blazon the possibility of censure than to pursue every accusation.[40]

What really sustained the colonial synagogue-community was not so much discipline as a shared consensus concerning the importance of maintaining Judaism and its central values. Shearith Israel's new Mill Street Synagogue, consecrated in 1730 (see cat. 143), reflected this consensus in its very architecture and design. Never before had North American Jews built (or even owned) a synagogue, so this was their first opportunity to shape the urban landscape. Since the completion of Trinity Church by the Anglicans in 1696, a slew of competing houses of worship had been built, including a French Church, a Dutch Church, a Lutheran Church, and a Presbyterian Church. These opulently designed buildings, with large spires and towers, had transformed and sacralized the city's skyline, displaying for all to see the Colonists' burgeoning material success (fig. 1, cat. 143).[41] Jews had likewise achieved material success (the house of Lewis M. Gomez, for example, was assessed at nearly ten times the value of the frame building that Jews had previously rented as their house of worship), but the new synagogue building as finally constructed privileged tradition over external display. It focused attention on the interior of the synagogue, designed in classical Sephardic fashion, while keeping the exterior comparatively simple. The architectural message was that Jews should practice discretion on the outside, and not draw excessive attention to themselves, while glorying in their faith on the inside, where tradition reigned supreme.

Seating arrangements in the new synagogue underscored the power of deference. They mirrored social and gender inequalities within the community and reinforced religious discipline. The congregation assigned a "proper" place to every worshiper and each seat was assessed a certain membership tax in advance. Members of the wealthy Gomez family thus enjoyed the most prestigious seats and paid the highest assessments. Others paid less and sat much further away from the Holy Ark. Women, in accordance with Jewish tradition, worshiped upstairs in the gallery, removed from the center of ritual action below (figs. 3, 4). In Amsterdam, Recife, and London, few women attended synagogue services, so there was little need for designated seating. In New York, however, where Protestant women frequented church, Jewish women attended synagogue much more punctiliously, and seats had to be assigned to them. Since the women's section was small, disputes over status and deference abounded—so much so that a special area was eventually reserved just for the elite women of the Gomez clan.[42]

An additional source of tension at Shearith Israel and throughout colonial Judaism stemmed from the ever-growing number of Ashkenazic Jews in North America, immigrants from Central and Eastern Europe whose traditions, background, and worldview diverged markedly from those of the founding Sephardim. In Europe and the West Indies, Sephardim and Ashkenazim worshiped apart. They formed two Jewish communities, married among themselves, and coexisted uneasily. Jews in New York, by contrast, worshiped together, as they had in Recife, with the Sephardim exercising religious and cultural hegemony. This practice continued despite the fact that Ashkenazim formed a majority of the Jewish population as early as 1720,[43] in part because the Sephardim had arrived first and enjoyed higher status. An additional explanation is economic: Curaçao's wealthy Sephardic congregation had threatened to stop assisting the New Yorkers unless they agreed not to allow the German Jews "any More Votes nor Authority than they have had hitherto."[44] Nevertheless, Ashkenazim did come to exercise considerable authority within Shearith Israel's new synagogue, serving as officers slightly more often, according to Eli Faber's calculation, than the Sephardim. Jacob Franks, an Ashkenazic Jew, was a perennial leader of the congregation, and Gershom Mendes Seixas (fig. 6), its most important and beloved colonial-era *hazan*, was the product of mixed Sephardic-Ashkenazic parentage—as were a growing number of other colonial Jews.[45] Sephardic traditions still held, but Iberian blood ties had less and less significance. Religious connections gradually became the dominant force among the Sephardim and Ashkenazim of diverse origins who worshiped together in New York, and power slowly shifted to the Ashkenazim.

The synagogue-community structure of Shearith Israel served as the model for other organized Jewish communities that took root in the American colonies: Savannah (1733), Newport (1750s), Charleston (1750s), and Philadelphia (1760s). All of them developed in tidewater settlements, with mixed urban populations, where Jews found economic opportunity and a substantial measure of religious toleration. Newport and Philadelphia, the two communities most closely connected to New York, had witnessed several attempts to organize and establish regular synagogue worship, dating back in Newport to the seventeenth century. Success came only in the second half of the eighteenth century, however, as the number of Jews in the American colonies increased, approaching one thousand, and colonial cities prospered. Shearith Israel extended help to these fledgling congregations, and both followed its lead in organizing as a synagogue-community, embracing Sephardic tradition, and welcoming Jews of diverse origin, including Ashkenazim, into their midst. Jews in Philadelphia prior to the Revolution never got beyond the stage of worshiping in private homes or rented quarters, since they lacked the money and the confidence to invest in a permanent house of worship. The wealthy Jews of Newport, by contrast, with financial assistance from Jews in New York, London, and the West Indies, built a beautiful synagogue, the oldest still surviving in North America, which they dedicated in 1763 (fig. 3). Ironically, and not for the last time in Jewish history, the Newporters who placed too much confidence in the security of their surroundings would soon be disappointed, while the Philadelphians who placed too little confidence in them were pleasantly surprised.

The Compartmentalization of Colonial Jewish Life

Synagogue-communities, as they developed in the major cities of colonial America, bespoke the growing compartmentalization of eighteenth-century American Jewish life into Jewish and worldly domains. Unlike synagogues in Amsterdam, London, and Recife, colonial synagogue-communities did not tax commercial transactions, censor what Jews wrote on the outside, or punish members for deviant personal beliefs (as opposed to public expressions of ritual laxity) or for lapses in individual or business morality. Instead, like the neighboring churches, they confined their activities to their own sphere, disciplining some religiously wayward congregants with fines and loss of religious privileges, but leaving commercial and civil disputes, even those that pitted one Jew against another, to the lay authorities. Some Sephardic Jews went so far as to employ different names in each realm, recalling their former double identities as Crypto-Jews. The renowned Newport merchant Aaron Lopez, for example, inscribed his business

Fig. 6. *Gershom Mendes Seixas*, New York, c. 1790. Watercolor on ivory. Museum of the City of New York; Gift of Annie Nathan Meyer.

ledgers with his Portuguese baptismal name, Duarte. In the synagogue, he was always known as Aaron.[46]

The social club founded by Newport Jews in 1761 similarly reflected compartmentalization. "Conversation relating to synagogue affairs" was, if not totally prohibited, severely regulated within the club's portals. The very existence of such an institution, a place for low-stakes cardplaying, supper, and imbibing every Wednesday evening in winter, indicates that Jews led bifurcated lives, complete with rules, institutions, and customs that kept synagogue life and general life distinct.[47]

The problem for early American Jews was that central Jewish observances—maintaining the Sabbath on Saturday, celebrating Jewish holidays in the fall and the spring, and observing Jewish dietary laws—blurred the boundaries that the separation of realms sought so scrupulously to maintain and engendered painful conflicts between the demands of Jewish law and the norms of the larger society in which Jews moved. Refusing to work on the Jewish Sabbath effectively meant working five days instead of six, since local "blue laws" prohibited work on Sunday, the Christian Sabbath. Jewish holidays similarly conflicted with the workaday world of early America. Jewish dietary laws—a complex system of forbidden foods, separation of milk and meat, and special laws for slaughtering and preparing ritually acceptable animals— made both travel away from home and social interactions outside of Jewish homes difficult.

Early American Jews found no easy solutions to these dilemmas. Religious laxity there was aplenty, just as Todd Endelman found among English Jews of the time,[48] but there were also those who managed to weave Judaism into the fabric of their daily existence. Indeed, the most striking feature of Jewish life in the colonial period was its diversity, a spectrum ranging all the way from deep piety to total indifference. Ignorance of Jewish law and the absence of rabbinical authority partly account for this diversity. The small community of Jews in North America consisted of merchants, not scholars, and though some had studied traditional Jewish texts in Europe, none is known to have possessed even the rudiments of an adequate Jewish library. Advanced adult Jewish education was not seriously promoted by the synagogue-community. Indeed, Isaac Pinto of Shearith Israel admitted in 1766 that even Hebrew, the language of the Bible and the prayerbook, was "imperfectly understood by many, by some, not at all." Precisely for this reason, he undertook to translate the Sabbath and High Holiday prayers into English (cat. 144). Dependent on translations and received traditions, rather than on thoroughgoing knowledge of Jewish law, colonial Jews negotiated the gap between Judaism and American life with a combination of intuition and expedience.

When it came to the Sabbath, for example, the wealthy Aaron Lopez "rigidly observed . . . Saturday as holy time," closing his business from Friday afternoon to Monday morning. Over the three-year period for which we have records, none of his ships left port on a Saturday.[49] Many surviving colonial Jewish letters also reflect strict Sabbath observance. One, for example, ends abruptly with the comment "Sabbath is coming on so fast," for once the sun set on Friday, writing was prohibited.[50] Visiting New York in the middle of the eighteenth century, the Swedish naturalist Peter Kalm heard that the city's pious Jews "never boiled any meal for themselves on Saturday, but that they always did it the day before, and that in winter they kept a fire during the whole Saturday" (to avoid lighting a fire on the Sabbath, which was prohibited, fires were lit before sundown on Friday).[51] On the other hand, Kalm also heard reports of Jewish ritual laxity. Indeed, evidence that Jews were trading on the Sabbath and traveling in violation of its commandment to rest abound— so much so that, as we have seen, Shearith Israel once threatened wayward members who violated the Sabbath with excommunication.[52] The most revealing of all accounts of Jewish Sabbath observance in the colonial period, however, comes from a missionary to the Delaware Indians named David McClure. Sometime in 1772,

he spent a weekend in Lancaster, Pennsylvania, and went with a business order on Saturday to the home of Joseph Simon, a prominent local Jewish merchant (see cat. 139):

[Simon] *said, "Gentlemen, today is my Sabbath, & I do not do business in it; if you will please to call tomorrow, I will wait on you." We observed that the same reasons which prevented his payment of the order on that day would prevent our troubling him the day following [Sunday]. We apologized for our intruding on his Sabbath, & told him we would wait until Monday. He replied, you are on a journey, & it may be inconvenient to you to wait. He went to call in his neighbor, Dr. Boyd, & took from his Desk a bag, laid it on the table & presented the order to the Dr. The Doctor counted out the money and we gave a recipt. The Jew sat looking on, to see that all was rightly transacted, but said nothing, & thus quieted his conscience against the rebuke of a violation of his Sabbath.*[53]

The dilemma of Simon, torn between his Sabbath, his business, and what he saw as common courtesy, very much reflected what many an observant American Jew of his day experienced. Simon's use of a surrogate to solve the problem, however, failed to impress: "he might as well have done the business himself," McClure groused. But what made Jewish life among the Gentiles so difficult was that every solution would likely have been wrong; often Jewish law and American life simply proved irreconcilable.

Jewish holidays posed similar problems. When Jews abstained from work on their holidays they knew that their Christian neighbors, employers, and competitors did not. Nevertheless, the autumn holidays surrounding the Jewish New Year, especially the high holidays of Rosh Hashanah and Yom Kippur, as well as the spring holiday of Passover, were widely observed— perhaps because they came but once a year and carried deep religious and social meaning. Colonial Jews living in outlying areas often visited communities with synagogues at these times in order to renew their ties with fellow Jews and to revitalize their faith. Isaac Solomon, although he had a Christian wife, traveled all the way from Halifax to Shearith Israel in New York for the New Year's holidays in 1755.[54] As on the Sabbath, however, the demands of secular business sometimes clashed with the requirements of faith. On one occasion, the Philadelphia merchant Barnard Gratz (cat. 138) was busy in western Pennsylvania negotiating a treaty with the Indians around the high holidays. Although his brother hoped that he would be home "before Rosh Hashono," in fact he had to send for his high holiday prayerbook and worship alone. Two years earlier, Gratz had greatly distressed his non-Jewish partner, William Murray, by taking off from work on the Jewish holiday of Shavuot. "Moses was upon the top of a mount in the month of May— consequently his followers must for a certain number of days cease to provide for their families," Murray complained in apparent exasperation. [55] His sense of disbelief

Fig. 7. Bernard Picart, *La circoncision des Juifs Portugais*, from *Cérémonies et coutumes religieuses de tous les peuples du monde*, Amsterdam, 1723. Yale Center for British Art, New Haven; Paul Mellon Collection.

underscored the problems Jews faced in maintaining their rituals in an alien environment and explains why some compromised their rituals, or abandoned them altogether.

Dietary laws, of course, presented even greater difficulties for colonial Jews. It was not always easy to find kosher-slaughtered meat, especially for Jews living in isolated communities. Moreover, the laws of *kashrut* were supposed to be observed at all times, even outside the home. They were intended to prevent precisely those kinds of social interactions with non-Jews that commerce and neighborly relations demanded. For those wishing to observe the dietary laws—to eat only kosher meat and avoid mixing dairy and meat products at the same meal—eating at the home of a Gentile friend or business associate was an enormous challenge. Eighteen-year-old Naphtali Franks, who had recently moved from New York to London, faced this challenge in 1733. His mother, Abigail Franks, assuming the voice of religious authority in her family—how common a role this was for a colonial Jewish woman is unclear—"strictly injoyn[ed]" her son to follow the dietary laws faithfully, warning him in a letter "Never [to] Eat Anything . . . Unless it be bread & butter" at any home, Jewish or non-Jewish, "where there is the Least doubt of things not done after our strict Judiacall Method."[56] Some colonial Jews kept the faith by serving as their own ritual slaughterers; wealthier Jews would hire immigrants to slaughter meat for them, and to teach their children the rudiments of Judaism on the side. Many, however, compromised their ritual observance when kosher food was unavailable. One report from New York claims that Jews on the road, especially if they were young, "did not hesitate the least" about eating pork "or any other meat that was put before them." A Lancaster Jew apologetically explained that he violated dietary laws because he was poor and could not "afford . . . to keep a Person to kill for me."[57] Some labored to uphold the dietary laws wherever they were, others quickly abandoned them. Still others maintained a double standard—one for home and one for outside—that effectively mirrored the bifurcated world which they inhabited.

For all the diversity that characterized the ritual life of colonial American Jews, at least two bedrock principles continued to unite them: their commitment to Jewish peoplehood and their belief in one God. Peoplehood, the feeling of kinship that linked Jews one to another, obligated them to assist Jews around the world and set them apart from everybody else. Bonds of Jewish peoplehood were essentially tribal in nature, rooted in faith, history, and ties of blood. They began for males with circumcision (fig. 7), a rite that colonial Jews maintained (if not necessarily on the traditional eighth day of life) better than they did any other Jewish ritual with the possible exception of the rite connected to death. Ritual circumcision records (fig. 8) demonstrate that even Jews far removed from major settlements and traditional Jewish life continued to circumcise their children—and if necessary adults too.[58] In 1767,

when Aaron Lopez spirited his half-brother and family out of Portugal, saving them "from the reach of Barbarous Inquisition," he arranged for them to obtain what he called, significantly, "the Covenant which happily Characterize us a peculiar Flock."[59] Circumcision, he understood, defined Jews as "peculiar" by permanently distinguishing them from their uncircumcised neighbors, what Barbara Kirshenblatt-Gimblett has felicitously called "the cut that binds."[60]

The other bedrock principle that underlay colonial Jewish life was even more fundamental than the first: belief in one supernatural God—no Jesus, no Holy Spirit. References to the Divine power alone abound in colonial Jewish correspondence, from stock phrases like "whom God protect" to heartfelt prayers for life, health, and prosperity. Aaron Lopez once consoled the bankrupt Hayman Levy by referring to "the decrees of a just [and] wise Ruler, who directs all events for our own good."[61] A member of the Gomez family expressed his belief in God through an original prayer, recorded in his ledger, beginning "Be merciful to me, O Lord. Forgive my iniquities."[62] Belief in God may also be inferred from mentions of weekday prayer with *tallit* (prayer shawls) and *tefillin* (phylacteries used in prayer), from calculations concerning the coming of the Messiah (anticipated dates included 1768 and 1783), and from the practice recorded in July 1769 by Newport's Reverend Ezra Stiles (cat. 133) in which Jews during thunderstorms threw open doors and windows while "singing and repeating prayers . . . for meeting Messias"—a practice apparently inspired by the mystical belief that Jews were soon to be spirited away upon a cloud to Jerusalem.[63] Some American Jews, to be sure, were less spiritually inclined. "I cant help Condemning the Many Supersti[ti]ons wee are Clog'd with & heartily wish a Calvin or Luther would rise amongst Us," Abigail Franks famously wrote in a 1739 letter to her son, Naphtali. But she remained a believing and observant woman. Eight years later, she consoled Naphtali upon the death of his first-born child, terming it "the Will of that Divine Power to wich all must submit."[64]

While these private beliefs and practices defined colonial Jews religiously and distinguished them from their Christian neighbors, social interactions in trade, in the street, and wherever else Jews and Christians gathered inevitably blurred these distinctions. The majority of American Jews resided in religiously pluralistic communities with people of diverse backgrounds and faiths, including many who had themselves experienced religious persecution. Perhaps for this reason, they felt more comfortable interacting with Christians than Jews did in most parts of the world—so much so that we know of Jews and Christians who joined forces in business, witnessed each other's documents, and socialized in each other's homes. Jews certainly faced continuing bouts of prejudice and persecution on account of their faith (see cats. 148, 149); legally speaking, in most American colonies, they remained second-class citizens,

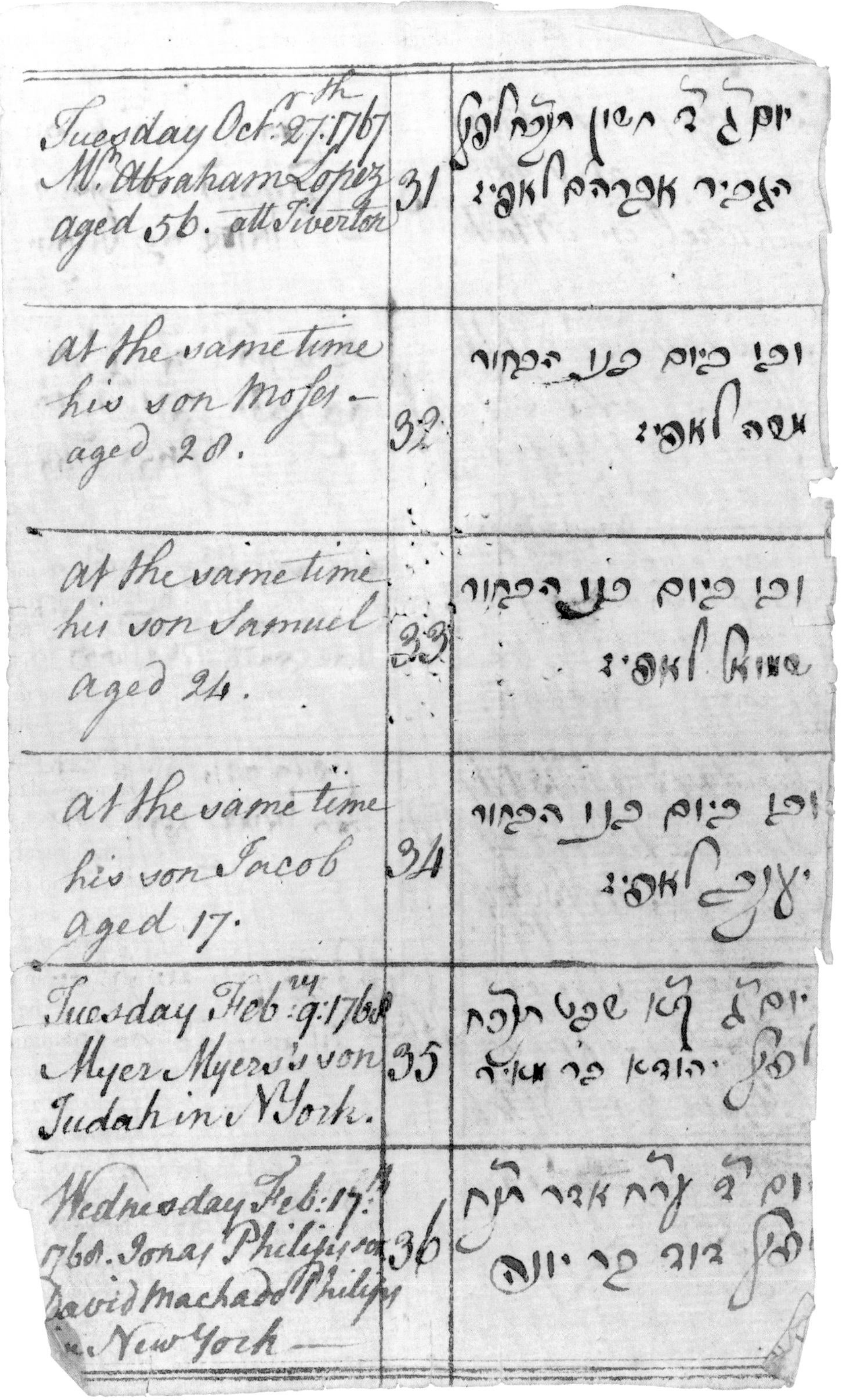

Tuesday Oct. 27.ʳ.ᵗʰ 1767 Mr. Abraham Lopez aged 56. att Tiverton	31	יום ג' ד' חשון תקכ"ח אברהם אלבז אב"י
at the same time his son Moses — aged 28.	32	ובו ביום בנו בכור משה אלבז
At the same time his son Samuel aged 24.	33	ובו ביום בנו שמואל אלבז
At the same time his son Jacob aged 17.	34	ובו ביום בנו יעקב אלבז
Tuesday Feb.ʳʸ 9. 1768 Myer Myers's son Judah in N. York.	35	יום ג' ך"א שבט תקכ"ח יהודה בן מאיר מיערש
Wednesday Feb: 17.ᵗʰ 1768. Jonas Philips's David Machado Philips in New York —	36	יום ד' כ"ט שבט תקכ"ח דוד מאכאדו יונה פיליפש

Fig. 8. Abraham Abrahams, page from circumcision register, New York and elsewhere, 1756–81. American Jewish Historical Society, New York City and Waltham, Massachusetts.

barred from holding public office or even, in some cases, from voting. But from the very beginning of Jewish settlement, Jews and Christians also fell in love and married, an alarming development from the point of view of the Jewish community. It was also a sure sign of Jewish acceptance— particularly since only a small number of the Jews who intermarried converted to Christianity.

Estimates of Jewish intermarriage in the colonial period range from 10 to 15 percent of all marriages, with men intermarrying more frequently than women, and those living far from their fellow Jews more likely to marry out than those who lived within or in proximity to a Jewish community. Available statistics leave many questions unanswered, chief among them whether the rate rose or fell over time. Still, the numbers are far lower than for some other religious groups of the day. New York City's French Huguenots, to take an extreme case, experienced an intermarriage rate between 1750 and 1769 that exceeded 86 percent![65] Colonial Jews mostly dealt with intermarriages on an ad hoc basis. When Phila Franks married the wealthy Huguenot merchant Oliver DeLancey in 1742, her pious, grief-stricken mother, Abigail, withdrew from the city and in traditional Jewish fashion resolved never to see her daughter again, "nor Lett none of ye Family Goe near her." Her more politic husband, however, demurred: "Wee live in a Small place & he is Related to ye best family in ye place," he explained, and tried to promote reconciliation.[66] As a rule, intermarried Jews did sooner or later drift away from the Jewish community, but there were exceptions. David Franks, for example, continued to maintain close social and economic ties to Jews. Benjamin Moses Clava was buried as a Jew. Samson Levy and Michael Judah had their non-Jewish children ritually circumcised.[67] Caught between two realms that they strove mightily to keep separate, colonial Jews vacillated. Once again, Jewish law and American life proved difficult to reconcile.

Accommodation to America

On the eve of the American Revolution, Judaism remained all-but-invisible to most colonists. No more than one American in a thousand was Jewish, only five cities had significant Jewish populations, and only New York and Newport boasted synagogue buildings. America's Jewish communities paled in comparison with those of Curaçao, Surinam, and Jamaica. Each of those West Indies communities had more Jews in the mid-eighteenth century than all of the North American colonies combined. If Judaism was a minor American religion, however, it was by no means inert. To the contrary, as it accommodated to its new American setting it underwent changes that mirrored in significant ways the transformations experienced by other American faiths with far larger populations.

First and foremost, American Judaism adapted—and con-tributed—to the pluralistic character of American religious life, already evident in major cities such as New York, Newport, and Philadelphia. Whereas in so many other diaspora settings Judaism stood all alone in religious dissent, in America it shared this status with other minority faiths. It was the only organized non-Christian religious community, to be sure, but by no means the only one with a sad history of persecution and oppression. From the beginning, as we have seen, colonial leaders explicitly linked Jewish economic and religious rights in North America to those of other minority faiths. Indeed, the very term Jews used to define their community was influenced by American religious pluralism. If early on they were, in the Sephardic tradition, members of the Jewish or Portuguese "Nation," by the eve of the Revolution they more commonly spoke of themselves as members of a "religious society," on the model of parallel Christian religious societies, such as the Society of Friends. When Ezekiel Levy was hired in 1774 to serve as ritual slaughterer, reader, and teacher in Philadelphia, his contract was thus with the "Jewish Society," of that city not, as earlier contracts read, with the "Jewish Nation." Later, in 1783, when New York Jews wrote a formal letter of welcome to Governor George Clinton, they used the same term. Revealingly, they juxtaposed "the Society, we Belong to" with "other Religious Societies," as if to underscore that Judaism stood on an equal footing with all the rest.[68]

The second characteristic of American Judaism that reflected the larger population was that it too became increasingly diverse and pluralistic. The 1790 United States Census recorded Jews who had been born in England, France, Germany, Holland, Poland, Portugal, and the West Indies, as well as in the American colonies, a mix that properly reflects the composition of the late colonial Jewish community.[69] The Sephardic form of Judaism predominated, as it always had in North America, but the preponderance of colonial Jews were actually Ashkenazim or of mixed background; "pure" Sephardim represented a vanishing breed. As a result, the synagogue-community functioned as something of a melting pot, its diversity echoing that of many a colonial city. This diversity carried over into congregational life. Notwithstanding the help and support that Shearith Israel, the "mother congregation" of America's synagogues, provided its more recent counterparts, it exercised no real authority over them, for even fledgling congregations jealously guarded their prerogatives. American Judaism thus developed along staunchly congregationalist lines, characterized by increasing multiformity, with each synagogue functioning as an autonomous entity.

Finally, Judaism on the eve of the Revolution was largely confined to two settings, the synagogue and the home, leaving a large public space in between where Jews and Christians interacted. The effort to compartmentalize, as we have seen, caused significant strains—hardly a surprise, since Judaism, like Christianity, was designed to govern all aspects of life, not just selected spheres. By the latter decades of the eighteenth century, the kind of communal discipline that the synagogue-community exercised was no longer possible, and the reach of its leadership was severely limited. Just how limited may be seen from a draft constitution proposed by Congregation Mikveh Israel of Philadelphia in 1798. The traditional language initially proposed warned any out-of-town Jew who came to the synagogue "occasionally or on holy days" but failed to contribute to the congregation's support that his name would be erased from its books, he would not be interred in its cemetery, and no officer or member would be allowed to assist at his burial. That threat, however, was crossed through in the original document. The amended text, more in keeping with the congregation's more delimited sphere of power, simply warned that such a person would "not be entitled to any mitzvas [sic], provided notice thereof be first given him."[70]

The American Revolution would transform American Judaism. Where colonial Judaism represented a modification of earlier patterns, an accommodation to a new setting, independence and the ensuing changes in society recast Judaism altogether. A Jewish religious revolution took place that overthrew the synagogue-communities and replaced a monolithic Judaism with one that was much more democratic, free, diverse, and competitive. In the half-century following independence, a new and distinctively *American* Judaism emerged.

NOTES

1 Means 1971, XIV, col. 1171; Zimmels 1976.
2 The term, according to Haim Beinart (1992, p. 58), originated among the Portuguese, who employed it against Crypto-Jews "in a tone of hatred and contempt." *Conversos* (converts) transvalued the term. To belong to the "people of the nation" became for them "a sign of honor and distinction."
3 Kaplan 1986, pp. 166ff.
4 Vlessing 1991, p. 62.
5 As quoted in Wiznitzer 1960, p. 57.
6 Wiznitzer 1960, pp. 128–30; Emmanuel 1962, p. 41.
7 Bloom 1934, p. 105; Emmanuel 1955, pp. 43–46.
8 Yerushalmi 1982.
9 Israel 1989; Kaplan 1992.
10 Oppenheim 1907, p. 184; Yerushalmi 1982, pp. 184–89.
11 Hershkowitz 1993.
12 Wiznitzer 1954; Krauskopf 1906.
13 Wiznitzer 1954, p. 92.
14 Feuer 1987.
15 Emmanuel 1955, p. 51.
16 Rink 1994.
17 Bonomi 1986, p. 25.
18 Oppenheim 1909, pp. 4, 5, 20.
19 Ibid., pp. 8–37.
20 Corwin 1901–16, I, p. 530.
21 Marcus 1970, I, pp. 216–17; III, p. 1226.
22 Oppenheim 1909, pp. 24, 25, 35, 36; Hühner 1900; Stern 1974; Hershkowitz 1990.
23 Pool 1952, pp. 7–12, 25.
24 Emmanuel 1955, pp. 17–23, 56.
25 For evidence of privately held seventeenth-century Torah scrolls in New York, see Hershkowitz 1990, p. 22, and Pool 1952, p. 188. For Torah scrolls in Savannah, Georgia, see Stern 1965, p. 247; for Lancaster, Pennsylvania, Brener 1976, p. 232; and for Reading, Pennsylvania, Trachtenberg 1944, p. 31.
26 Oppenheim 1909, p. 33; Schappes 1971, p. 19.
27 Hershkowitz 1964, p. 408; Marcus 1970, I, p. 402.
28 Wiznitzer 1958; Swetschinski 1980, pp. 337–66; Bodian 1985, pp. 12–13. The Ashkenazic community in Amsterdam established its own congregation in 1635; see Kaplan 1989, p. 29.
29 Wiznitzer 1956, p. 48 n. 41, suggests that the name refers to the "remnant of Israel" that survived from Recife in 1654 and to the use of this phrase in a depiction of Recife's fall by Isaac Aboab de Fonseca. Jacob R. Marcus, however, cites documents from the early 1720s suggesting that the congregation's original name was Shearith Yaakob ("remnant of Jacob"); see Marcus 1969, pp. 44–45.
30 Salomon 1995. Ladino, or Judeo-Spanish, written in Hebrew letters, was only spoken by the Sephardim of the Ottoman Empire.
31 Barnett 1931, p. 3; Salomon 1979, pp. 18–29.
32 *Lyons Collection* 1920, pp. 187–88.
33 Barnett 1931, p. 15; Loker 1991, p. 41.
34 Pointer 1988, pp. 13–15.
35 Grinstein 1945, pp. 84–87; Marcus 1970, II, pp. 928–34; Marcus 1990, pp. 132, 282.
36 Emmanuel/Emmanuel 1970, p. 544; Cohen n.d.; Nahon 1992, p. 348.
37 Barnett 1931, p. 11.
38 Kaplan 1993, p. 103.
39 The minutes of the *adjunta's* decision are reprinted in *Lyons Collection* 1913, pp. 74–76.
40 Butler 1990, pp. 173–74.
41 Ibid., pp. 113–16.
42 Sarna 1991; Wiznitzer 1954, p. 17; Barnett 1931, p. 4; Pool/Pool 1955, p. 44.
43 Marcus 1969, p. 50; Pool 1952, pp. 169–73.
44 *Lyons Collection* 1920, p. 4.
45 Faber 1992, p. 64; Stern/Angel 1976.
46 Chyet 1970, p. 173.
47 Marcus 1970, II, p. 1023; Gutstein 1936, pp. 170–72; Kaplan 1986.
48 Endelman 1979, pp. 132–35.
49 Gutstein 1936, p. 132; Chyet 1970, p. 158.
50 Marcus 1990, p. 265.
51 Handlin 1949, p. 32.
52 Grinstein 1945, p. 334; Marcus 1970, II, pp. 956–57.
53 Beam 1901, pp. 108–09. See Brener 1976, p. 243, for McClure's account.
54 Godfrey/Godfrey 1995, p. 77.
55 Wolf/Whiteman 1956, pp. 73–74. For other holidays, see Marcus 1970, II, pp. 978–83.
56 Abigail Franks to Naphtali Franks, July 9, 1733, in Hershkowitz/Meyer 1968, pp. 7–8.
57 Wolf/Whiteman 1956, p. 64; Stern 1963, p. 185; Handlin 1949, p. 32.
58 Stern 1967, pp. pp. 24–35, 49–51.
59 Aaron Lopez to Ab'm Abraham, September 6, 1767; Aaron Lopez to Isaac Da Costa, September 17, 1767. Both letters reprinted in Broches 1942, pp. 61–62.
60 Kirshenblatt-Gimblett 1982.
61 Marcus 1990, p. 15.
62 Marcus 1970, II, p. 947.
63 Oles 1958, p. 115; Marcus 1970, II, p. 952; Rivkind 1937, p. 70; Dexter 1901, I, p. 19; Scholem 1973, pp. 594–95 (I owe this last reference to Jonathan Schorsch).
64 Hershkowitz/Meyer 1968, p. 66; Hershkowitz 1969, p. 224.
65 Stern 1958, p. 85; Marcus 1970, III, p. 1232; Butler 1983, p. 187.
66 Hershkowitz/Meyer 1968, pp. 116–25.
67 Stern 1958, pp. 94–97; Marcus 1970, III, pp. 1225–35; Godfrey/Godfrey 1995, p. 294 n. 14.
68 Marcus 1990, p. 104; Schappes 1971, p. 67.
69 Rosenwaike 1960.
70 Marcus 1990, pp. 129–30.

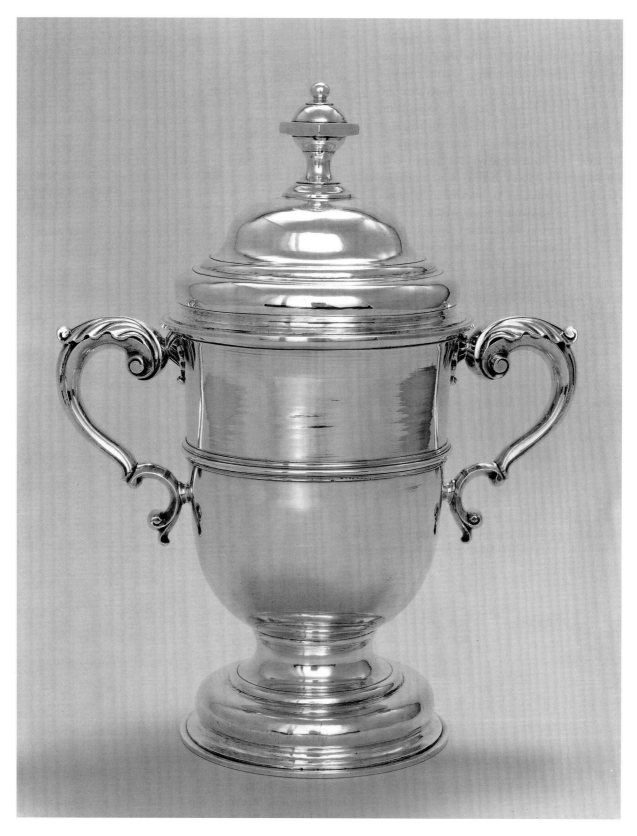

Fig. 9. Myer Myers, *Standing Cup*, New York, 1755–65. Silver.
The Art Institute of Chicago; Gift of Mrs. Philip D. Sang in memory of Philip D. Sang.

"That Noted and Proficient Mechanic": The Life and Career of Myer Myers

Born in New York in 1723, the son of a Jewish shopkeeper, Myer Myers became the city's leading silversmith during the late Colonial period. From the mid-1750s into the 1770s, his workshop produced some of the finest American silver in the Rococo style. A good deal of Myers's personal life is documented through the extraordinary number of original records preserved by his congregation, Shearith Israel ("Remnant of Israel"), founded in 1654 and still in operation today. As for his fifty-year career as a silversmith, however, no workshop accounts and few letters or other documents have been discovered. The 380 objects that survive with his marks provide the primary evidence for examining his career, with the caveat that the extant objects may not be representative of the workshop's production as a whole because of the vagaries of survival.

Myers's success as a silversmith was the result of his talents not only as a craftsman but also as an entrepreneur who marshaled the skills of other craftsmen and specialists. As a Jew and thus an outsider in the craft, he may also have been more inclined than his Christian competitors to seek out new business opportunities and explore innovative strategies. He formed, for example, the first formal partnership in New York between two silversmiths, worked closely with at least one immigrant European silversmith, and developed relationships with other New York craftsmen that allowed him to increase his share of the market.

This idea of the craftsman as entrepreneur contradicts the traditional image found in the literature, wherein the preindustrial silversmith proudly creates individual objects of beauty. But it accords with more recent scholarship concerning the silversmith's role as banker, retailer, and manager of complex networks of craftsmen and trade. Scholars have begun to investigate the subject of silversmithing in terms of production, structure and specialization of labor, and other economic matters. Barbara McLean Ward's studies of the silversmith's trade in Colonial Boston established both the hierarchical organization of the trade and the relationship of master craftsmen to the journeymen, specialists, and jobbers who were the primary laborers.[1] Similar studies in England have proved that the "maker's mark" was often the mark of a retailer and also defined the role of the jobbers and specialist craftsmen who had been largely anonymous save for mention in the surviving documents.[2]

Using the organization of the silversmith's trade in London and Paris as a model, Ward proposed the categories of largeworkers, smallworkers, and jewelers to describe the different types of silversmiths working in Colonial Boston.[3] At the top of this hierarchy were a few of what Ward termed "merchant-artisans," trained largeworkers who operated sizable workshops, employed apprentices and journeymen, and outsourced additional or specialized work to the local network of jobbers, jewelers, and specialist craftsmen. Merchant-artisans were craftsmen who had achieved a certain level of renown and were favored by leading patrons.[4] Largeworkers, as the name implies, made hollow-ware objects; some operated retail stores, whereas others worked primarily as jobbers for the retailers. Smallworkers made flatware and small pieces of hollow ware and in urban centers worked primarily as jobbers. Jewelers, who specialized in evaluating and setting stones, operated retail stores, sometimes of considerable size. Ward noted that in Boston the boundaries among these categories were fluid, particularly given the absence of guilds or any controlling legal authority in the Colonies. Most of these craftsmen, if they worked with or retailed precious metals, referred to themselves as "goldsmiths," a term used synonymously with silversmith.

Myer Myers was a paradigm of Ward's "merchant-artisan." Based on his 380 extant objects, his workshop must have been the largest in New York from the mid-eighteenth century to the outbreak of the Revolutionary War; in quantity, his extant output exceeds that of any other New York maker working before the war. A survey of this output indicates that he primarily was a largeworker, since two-thirds of his surviving production was hollow ware. The forms that he made most frequently were canns (28), tankards (24), sugar dishes (23), and waiters (21). He also made a considerable number of such expensive hollow-ware forms as coffeepots (14) and sauceboats (12) as well as routine forms such as milk pots (15). Like all eighteenth-century silversmiths, he marked and sold flatware, the most widely owned form of silver. Of the 380 objects, 140, or more than one-third were spoons, ladles, or sugar tongs. He marked very few buckles or pieces of jewelry and very few small objects such as boxes or salts.

This production is consistent with the output of a merchant-artisan. Precise production are not available for other New York craftsmen, but Myers's output can be compared to that of such major Boston merchant-artisans as Jacob Hurd (517 surviving objects) and Benjamin Burt (319 surviving objects). Myers's younger and best-known Boston contemporary, Paul Revere, Jr., whose extant objects number 1,014, tops them all.[5] Burt's production is strikingly similar to Myers's, particularly the high numbers of canns (48) and tankards (39). Fewer coffeepots (5), milk pots (6), and sugar dishes (5) survive with Burt's marks, but there are more porringers (44), beakers (18), teapots (17), and casters (12), which may reflect regional preferences in New England for certain forms. One-fourth, or 76, of the total represents flatware. Like Myers, Burt did not mark many pieces of jewelry or small objects.

Myers's workshop produced two principal types of silver objects. His renown, in his own time as well as today, was due to his ability to execute high-style custom order work for the wealthiest patrons. His workshop was one of the few in New York during the third quarter of the eighteenth century that supplied such labor-intensive, richly ornamented forms as candlesticks, bread baskets, covered jugs, and cruet stands, not to mention unique productions such as Torah finials. Such bespoke work required special castings or ornamental work by specialist craftsmen such as engravers, chasers, or piercers. Many of these specialists were immigrants and thereby became agents of change, bringing their familiarity with current styles in London or Continental Europe. Moreover, the wealthy clients who commissioned special work were more likely to be familiar with current forms and styles in England, either by travel or owning imported silver.

Most of the previous scholarship on Myers has focused on this type of object, particularly the unique or exceptional examples. Stylistic change was most evident in large hollow ware and other commissioned forms. In addition to these commissioned, style-conscious forms, however, Myers's shop from the mid-1750s produced larger numbers of less expensive work to generate a steady income. There was a greater demand from a larger, less affluent clientele for modest forms such as canns, milk pots, sugar dishes, and flatware. The quantities that survive indicate that such objects probably were made for retail sale in the store rather than on commission. The style of routinely produced objects changed relatively little over time. The limited style variations over time may represent standardized forms that were easier and less expensive to produce.

Requiring only about 5 troy oz. of silver, milk pots were the archetypal inexpensive silver object, what Robert Barker has aptly called the "entry level" piece of silver hollow ware.[6] Charles Oliver Bruff advertised in 1767 that he charged 24 shillings for making a milk pot, 11 shillings less than a sugar dish and only 4 shillings more than his charge for making a "Soop-spoon."[7] Cat. 5 is the earliest example of the three-foot form to survive with Myers's marks; at least nine other examples are known. This quantity of survivals suggests that they were a form produced routinely in Myers's workshop for ready sale. They also exhibit considerable uniformity over time: a milk pot of 1755–65 (cat. 11) shows only subtle differences from one made in 1784–85 (cat. 95). Aside from its engraving, cat. 11 is also identical to a milk pot marked by Halsted and Myers between 1756 and 1766 (cat. 12). The majority of the objects marked by the partnership of Halsted and Myers were small, simple forms that could be produced relatively inexpensively and in quantity for sale in a retail store.

Canns were another less expensive form of hollow ware. By the mid-1750s, Myers's workshop produced canns in a graceful bellied shape with a double-scroll handle and a leaf grip. A cann (cat. 29) engraved in 1755–65 as part of a set with a tankard (cat. 28) had the additional embellishments of a shell ornament at the juncture of the handle and the body, as well as a more sculptural scroll terminal to the handle's lower end. The same details are found on a pair of canns made for Charity Johnson between 1754–58 (cat. 22). These details may have represented an extra cost rather than an earlier date, however, as a cann without these features (cat. 39) is contemporary, if not earlier.

At least twenty-four canns of this type survive from Myers's workshop. They frequently were made in pairs as well as to accompany tankards, which survive in similar numbers. Their cost was less than a third of the price of a tankard. The quantity and stylistic uniformity of the majority of Myers's canns strongly suggest that they were sold as ready-made objects. A cann made 1765–76 (cat. 87) was owned by John Stevenson of Albany, who married Magdalena Douw about 1771. Samuel and Susannah Cornell purchased an identical cann, probably between 1770 and 1776 (cat. 77).

Over a third of Myers's surviving output is flatware, primarily spoons, and most of those made in his workshop during the Colonial period follow the same pattern: a handle with an upturned, rounded end and a short, faint midrib, and a double drop at the juncture of the handle and the bowl (see cat. 4). This uniformity again suggests that flatware of this type was a stock item available for ready sale in Myers's store. Because the majority of Myers's spoons are in this one pattern, they can be dated apart only by provenance and mark.

Biographical Background

Like many Jews in pre-Revolutionary New York, Myers's private and professional lives generally remained separate. One cannot, however, track the development of his career without understanding his family background and kinship ties in the Jewish communities of New York and other Colonial cites.

As a Jew, Myer Myers's life was inextricably interwoven with the history of Jews in New York and of Congregation Shearith Israel in particular. Founded in 1654, it was the oldest and largest Jewish community in Britain's North American Colonies, although it had numbered only about two hundred and fifty members during the later Colonial period and never accounted for more than 1 percent of the city's total population (p. 22). Myers served as one of the heads of the congregation from early adulthood, and was renowned as a leader of the Jewish community no less than as a craftsman.

Jews were one of the smallest minorities in Britain's American Colonies. Their limited numbers made it inevitable that the ties of common religious observance would be strengthened by those of kinship, often on multiple levels. The family into which Myers was born in 1723 quickly extended beyond New York to include Jews from communities in Newport, Philadelphia, and elsewhere. For many Jews, including Myers, religion and kinship created a network of economic support and business opportunities, just as it did for other minority groups.[8] In an era when kin relationships were often a primary means of economic advancement, Myers benefited not only from his own two advantageous marriages, but also from those of his own and his spouses' siblings.

No contemporary record has survived of Myer Myers's birth date. A family register written in 1847 recorded it as 1723, which accords well with subsequent events in Myers's life.[9] Myer Myers was the son of Solomon Myers (c. 1699–1743) and his wife, Judith (1696–1773), the daughter of Joseph (family name unknown). Solomon Myers was neither a native New Yorker nor born a British subject, for in 1723 he took the oath of allegiance required of residents who had immigrated to British colonies from places outside the Empire.[10] In 1740, he qualified for naturalization under the Act of Naturalization passed by Parliament that same year, which permitted foreign Protestants, Quakers, and Jews certain rights of inheritance, of owning property, and of conducting civic and commercial activity in the American Colonies.[11] This act conferred on Jews in America greater rights than their counterparts in Britain enjoyed (cat. 148).

Solomon and Judith Myers's ancestry is uncertain. The 1847 family register stated that they were "from Holland."[12] However, no birth or marriage records for either of them could be found in Amsterdam, where the majority of Dutch Jews lived. Perhaps Solomon Myers, having been born elsewhere in Northern Europe, sailed to New York "from Holland" or from one of the Dutch colonies in the West Indies. Evidence suggests that Solomon Myers was of Ashkenazic background. Unlike most Sephardim, he did not have a family surname, and to suit the British legal tradition of patriarchal family names, he followed Ashkenazic practice and adopted his father's given name for this purpose. In the earliest minute book of Congregation Shearith Israel, his name was set down interchangeably as Solomon Myers and "Selomo bar Meyr" (Solomon the son of Myer); thus the silversmith was named twice over for his paternal grandfather.[13] Moreover, Myer Myers and most of his siblings married Ashkenazim.

In 1723, "Solomon Meyers, Shop keeper" paid a fee to register as a Freeman of the Corporation of New York City, thereby gaining the right to conduct retail trade, hold public office, and vote for representatives to the Assembly, which had the power to approve taxes.[14] Theoretically, Freeman status was for merchants or artisans engaged in retail sales, although the City could confer the privilege as an honor (cat. 115). Evidence of Solomon Myers's business activities dates from 1737, when he was sued for the substantial sum of £86 by the executors of the estate of Moses Levy, a wealthy merchant with whom he may have had business dealings.[15] He was also indebted to the estate of the merchant Abraham Isaacks for a note of hand in the amount of £25.8.6, which remained unpaid as late as 1750.[16] By the time he took the oath of naturalization in 1740, Myers was described as a "merchant," implying involvement in shipping as well as retail business.[17]

Solomon Myers must have achieved at least some degree of social standing and financial success. He held elected office as "a Jew" at least twice, as Constable for the Montgomery Ward in 1731 and again for the South Ward in 1736.[18] His sons Myer and Joseph were trained as silversmiths, one of the most prestigious artisinal professions in the eighteenth century; his third son, Asher, was a coppersmith (p. 48). Three of his four daughters married successful merchants, which likewise indicated that they came from a financially prosperous background: Sloe married the merchant Hayman Levy in 1751 with a dowry of £300, and, in a double ceremony in 1766, Rebecca married Solomon Maraché and Rachel married Moses Michael Hays (cat. 42).[19] Myer Myers would have personal, congregational, and business interactions with these men throughout his life.

In 1738, Solomon was recorded as a head of household in the city's South Ward.[20] At that time his family probably was living in a house in Stone Street, described three years later as "lately Occupied by Mr. Soloman Myers, opposite to Mr. Lynsen, the Baker."[21] The house was one block away from Shearith Israel's synagogue in Mill Street (cat. 143). Like his sons after him, Solomon was an active member of the congregation. He regularly made donations to Shearith Israel, although over the course of a decade the amounts remained in the lowest range of contributions. In 1728 he contributed 12 shillings toward the purchase of a burial ground, for which the higher contributions ranged from £1 to £7.10.0, and in 1739 he contributed 5 shillings, the lowest of any donations, toward building a wall around the burial ground.[22]

On June 16, 1730, Solomon Myers was appointed the congregation's shohet and bodek ("slaughterer" and "searcher"), who was responsible for killing or inspecting all meat consumed by the congregation according to Jewish dietary laws.[23] Myers's annual salary for this position began at £20 and rose to £40 shortly before his death in 1743, and included such perquisites as "Eight Cord of Nutwood and passover Cakes [*matzoh*] for his family."[24] Such enticements may have made this menial job a desirable sinecure for men engaged in the uncertainties of trade. Jacob Marcus has referred to the position of *shohet* in Colonial New York as "the last resort of the incompetent . . . the first resort of the impoverished," but Myers was praised for "his indefatigable Pains & other reasons," and it does not appear that he pursued this calling full-time.[25] In European communities, moreover, the *shohet*'s responsibilities were equated with those of the rabbi, because both helped the congregation observe their covenant as Jews.[26]

Solomon Myers died on October 9, 1743, when his eldest son was about twenty years old. The date of his death is confirmed by the entry in a 1758 "Livro dos Miseberagh," or listing of memorial prayers offered by the congregation, for "Selomoh Bar Myer" on Tishri 21 (October 9).[27] The previous month, on September 18, he had been granted a raise in salary from £30 to £40, "as paid by some former parnassim & now by the Consent of the Adjuntos." Four days after his death, on October 13, the sum granted to his widow was reduced: the members of Shearith Israel voted "to allow his Widow Judith Myers and Family Thirty Pounds annually and Massoth [*matzoh*] on account of the Synagogue— and Eight Cord Wood."[28]

The earliest documentary reference to Myer Myers appears in the minutes of Shearith Israel for March 6, 1742, which record his offering of 1 shilling; his father donated £3.10.0.[29] This record supports the birth date of 1723, since he would have been eighteen or nineteen years old in 1742 and probably still an apprentice, unable to make a larger offering. The donation may have marked Myers's entry into adult membership of the congregation, as "any member of this Congregation that's above 18 Years of age that refuses to give his attendance att the ajunta of the Kaal when properly sumend thereto shall pay the sum of Twenty Shillings Currency of New York for every time he omits coming."[30] At about the age of twenty-one, on July 12, 1744, Myers witnessed the will of the Jewish merchant Joshua Isaacs; two of his fellow witnesses were Jacob and Samuel Pinto, brothers of the silversmith Joseph Pinto and the author Isaac Pinto (cat. 144).[31]

In 1747, at age twenty-four, Myer Myers was named one of the *yehidim*, or adult male members, of Shearith Israel.[32] Throughout the later 1740s and early 1750s, he was a regular contributor to the congregation, although in every instance his offerings, like those of his father, were at the low end of the range of contributions. His first donation after becoming a Freeman, on September 14, 1746, was 8 shillings toward a "publick and free subscription to buy wood" for the congregation to dispense to the poor.[33] In April 1747, he was assessed an annual tax of £2.6.8 as a member of the *yehidim* to "Injoy all the rights of a Jehid and be capable of serving for Parnas or ajunto." Myers's assessment was the lowest of six rates, the

highest being £14.[34] On October 5, 1750, the congregation recorded the rates paid by individuals for their seats in the synagogue; Myers paid £1.6.0, the other options being £4, £2.9.0, and 15 shillings.[35]

Training and Early Career, 1738–53

On April 29, 1746, Myer Myers "Goldsmith" and thirteen other men, including "John Zenger Printer," appeared before Mayor Stephen Bayard and the Mayor's Court and were "Sworn Freeman and Ordered to be Registered."[36] Myers registered as a Freeman without paying a fee, a privilege granted to individuals who had completed a seven-year apprenticeship in New York City.[37] Myers's apprenticeship had followed the traditional pattern. A statute of 1711 required apprenticeships to last for a term of seven years, usually commencing when boys were about fifteen years old.[38] Thus Myers's apprenticeship would have begun in 1738 and ended in 1745, one year before he was sworn as a Freeman. The new city charter in 1731 no longer specified length, although documented apprenticeships to New York silversmiths after this date usually lasted seven years. In 1741, Myers's contemporary Elias Pelletreau was apprenticed to the silversmith Simeon Soumaine for seven years.[39]

No extant records identify the silversmith to whom Myers was apprenticed. His subsequent career indicates that he trained with a largeworker, and there were about fifteen independent silversmiths working in New York between 1738 and 1745 for whom hollow-ware objects have survived.[40] Kin relationships and ethnic background were principal factors in determining the choice of a master, since apprentices lived in his household, but as the first Jew in New York to train as a silversmith Myers had to look outside the Jewish community.

When Myers registered in New York as a "Goldsmith" in 1746, he was in fact the first native Jew within the British Empire to have had formal training and establish himself as a working, retail silversmith since the incorporation of the Worshipful Company of Goldsmiths in 1327. In part because of the traditional association of Jews with usury, most European countries had maintained laws prohibiting Jewish residents from working with precious metals. In the Netherlands, as part of the larger strategy of allowing Jews to live and worship freely while maintaining strict legal separation, Jews could be apprenticed to silversmiths, but the Amsterdam craft guilds specifically prohibited membership by Jews, who were also prohibited from operating retail stores.[41] Membership in the London Goldsmith's Company, which required swearing an oath on the Christian Bible and recognizing the sovereign as head of the Church, was limited largely to Protestants. For the same reason, Jews could not become Freemen of London and thereby sell their work at retail. Despite these restrictions, by the eighteenth century some Jews were working as silver-smiths in both cities, and a few, such as Abraham Lopez de Oliveyra and Moses Jacobs, registered marks in London.[42]

For a Jewish silversmith in America, however, the prospects were different. Myers, born in 1723, was the earliest to establish himself, but by the mid-1760s, both immigrant and native Jews had taken up the silversmith's trade—two of them immigrants in the Southern Colonies and at least four native-born Jews in New York. Unlike Myers, none of these craftsmen made any objects that can be identified today with certainty. Most if not all of the native New Yorkers probably served apprenticeships with Myer Myers (pp. 35–36). The best-documented immigrant silversmith was Isaiah Isaacs (1747–1806), an Ashkenazic Jew from Germany who had settled in Richmond, Virginia, by April 1769 and identified himself as a "silver smith," but after the Revolutionary War shifted his focus to mercantile activities and described himself in his will as a "merchant."[43] Another Jewish immigrant working as a silver-smith was Jacob Moses (d. 1785), who arrived in Savannah, Georgia, before April 1768 and advertised with his partner, William Sime, as "Goldsmiths and Jewelers from London. . . . They intend carrying on their business in all its branches, as they have brought proper tools for that purpose." Sime was working independently by the beginning of 1769, and no other documents connect Moses to silversmithing.[44] In New York City, a "Mr. Judah, Silver Smith" was mentioned in a 1774 advertisement by the immigrant silversmith Lewis Fueter, who had taken over Judah's former house, but no further information on this silversmith has been found.[45]

Myers's earliest work demonstrates his familiarity with styles popular in New York during the second quarter of the eighteenth century, when he served his apprenticeship, and offers clues as to his master's possible identity. He made no purely Dutch forms, such as a brandywine bowl, probably because such objects were out of fashion after the mid-1740s. A few objects by Myers, including a teapot (cat. 1), tankard (cat. 2), and cann (fig. 12), all struck with his earliest mark, were typical examples of the hybrid Anglo-Dutch tradition found in New York. The cann, with its relatively straight sides and a shallow, almost square bottom, is an English form of the 1720s that remained popular in New York into the 1750s but was infrequently made elsewhere in the Colonies by that date.[46] Peter Van Dyck and Bartholomew Le Roux II, as well as Adrian Bancker and Henricus Boelen, made similar canns.[47]

Myers's best work from before 1755, however, was informed by a thorough understanding of the simplified, late Baroque style made popular by immigrant Huguenot silversmiths in London during the 1720s and 1730s. By the date of Myers's apprenticeship, the Huguenot style was less specifically associated with one ethnic group and had become the dominant fashionable style in English, Dutch, and American silver.[48] Sev-

Fig. 10. Myer Myers, *Waiter*, New York, 1746–55. Silver. Present location unknown; stolen from The Historical Society of Pennsylvania, Philadelphia.

eral New York silversmiths of Dutch ancestry, who had been trained within the Dutch tradition, produced sophisticated if less ambitious objects in this international "Huguenot" style.

Nevertheless, if the forms and style of Myers's early work are the best evidence for identifying his master, the Huguenot Charles Le Roux (1689–1745) would appear to be the most likely candidate. Le Roux and his brother-in-law Peter Van Dyck (cat. 105) had inherited the workshop tradition established by Charles's father, Bartholomew Le Roux I, the first non-Dutch silversmith working in New York. Charles Le Roux was the proprietor of a large, productive workshop, and unlike Van Dyck he is known to have trained a number of apprentices: his son Bartholomew II, Peter Quintard, Jacob Ten Eyck, and possibly Ten Eyck's cousins Tobias and Lucas Stoutenburgh.[49] Le Roux also held numerous posts in city government and was rewarded with considerable official patronage, including commissions for engraving copper plates for currency, for a silver oar for the Vice Admiralty Court, and for a gold freedom box.[50]

The range of forms and quality of workmanship and design that Myers demonstrated early in his career as a largeworker are matched more closely in the production of Le Roux's workshop than in the work of other New York silversmiths. One outstanding example is a small waiter (fig. 10), made for David and Margaret Franks and bearing the mark Myers used between 1746 and 1755.[51] Its square shape and indented corners

ultimately derive from London waiters by Benjamin Pyne, Paul Crespin, and Paul de Lamerie.[52] Le Roux made two similar square waiters between 1735 and 1740 that represent the earliest American examples of this form.[53]

Myers's two-handled standing cup (fig. 9) of 1755–65 reinforces the conclusion that he had learned the necessary skills and sense of design from a local master of the Huguenot style like Le Roux.[54] Baroque versions of the form have been identified most closely with the leading Huguenot silversmiths working in London.[55] One of five known cups of this type made in New York during the Colonial period, the other four were made by craftsmen of Huguenot ancestry: two in 1720–30 by Charles Le Roux, and the other three in 1740–60 by Bartholomew Le Roux II (fig. 11) and Elias Pelletreau.[56] The grandest form of presentation plate in the American Colonies for most of the eighteenth century, Myers's standing cup may have been commissioned for the 1764 marriage of Petrus Stuyvesant (1727–1805) and Margaret Livingston (1738–1818).[57]

Myers's standing cup also illustrates a close relationship between some of his early work and silver marked by Charles Le Roux's son, Bartholomew Le Roux II. The cups by Myers and the younger Le Roux are particularly close in both their overall form as well such details as the double-scroll handles with curled-leaf grips. Other objects demonstrate considerable similarity. Both a waiter (cat. 3) and sauceboat (cat. 6) by

Myers have almost identical counterparts marked by Bartholomew Le Roux II. This close relationship of their silver reinforces the conclusion that Myers trained with Charles Le Roux.

Little work survives from Myers's earliest years as an independent craftsman. Charles Le Roux died at age fifty-six in 1745, the year Myers would have completed his training, and it is possible that Bartholomew Le Roux II asked Myers to assist him for a few years. Myers had established himself as an independent maker by 1754, the last year that the earliest surviving object with his mark could have been made (cat. 1). His first workshop may have been the one located opposite the Meal Market, on the intersection of Wall and Queen (now Pearl) Streets. How long he was at this location is unclear; the earliest reference records his removal from the site in August 1754.[58]

Scant documentary evidence survives from Myers's first years of activity as a silversmith. There are records of two suits he filed in the Mayor's Court, which was the New York court that heard common plea cases, primarily for debt or personal damages. On September 1, 1747, he filed suit against a Thomas Jones, but for reasons that are unclear Jones was not served with the writ.[59] The following year, Myers obtained an order to arrest a John Sutton in a suit for £19, presumably in default of a loan, although possibly for nonpayment of a commission.[60]

Fig. 13. Cat. 2 (detail).

Fig. 11. *Left,* Bartholomew Le Roux II, *Standing Cup,* New York, 1739–63. Silver. Henry Francis du Pont Winterthur Museum, Winterthur, Delaware; Bequest of H.F. du Pont, 1969.

Fig. 12. *Right,* Myer Myers, *Cann,* New York, 1746–55. Silver. Courtesy A.S. Rau Antiques, New Orleans.

Myers began his career at a propitious time. Unlike New England, New York had prospered economically during England's wars of the 1740s with Spain and France, the latter known in the Colonies as King George's War.[61] Myers's earliest identified patrons included Thomas Barnes (cat. 7), who apparently had profited handsomely as a privateer during the war; David Franks (cat. 4), who was embarking on a career in Philadelphia as an overseas merchant as international trade revived; and Samuel Prince (cat. 5), then at the beginning of his career as a joiner in Flushing, Long Island.

SPECIALIST CRAFTSMEN

Engraving was a basic skill for any working silversmith, since simple block initials recording ownership were usually placed on precious-metal objects. These served to identify the object if it was lost or stolen, as numerous newspaper advertisements attest. These engraved initials were referred to in the eighteenth century as the "marks" on the piece whereas what today is called the maker's mark, which was struck with a punch, was referred to as the "stamp." Myers undoubtedly would have learned rudimentary engraving as part of his apprenticeship. For more decorative engraved monograms or other ornament, however, he and most silversmiths of his generation employed skilled specialists.

Myers's reliance on specialist engravers can be documented as early as 1753. He clearly had considered it worthwhile to pay for the transatlantic passage of at least one such craftsman so that he could offer customers engraving in the latest English style. On April 9, 1753, Myers's first newspaper advertisement offered £3 reward for a runaway, an indentured "English servant Man, named, Lewis Meares, between 24 and 25 years old . . . and a jeweller and engraver by trade."[62] Myers may have found this craftsman through the Mears family of New York, his future in-laws, although whether Lewis Meares was a relative or even Jewish remains unknown.

Decorative engraving ornament appeared on Myers's silver throughout his career, and a series of stylistic changes is noticeable. The earliest examples reveal an additional connection to the workshop of Charles Le Roux, reinforcing the theory that Myers trained with him. Le Roux was either a skilled engraver or employed one in his workshop, since on November 15, 1734, he received the commission to engrave the new bills of credit for the Colony of New York; his plate for the arms of New York remained in use until 1771.[63] The mirror cypher "JEH" on Myers's earliest surviving tankard (cat. 2; fig. 13) is surrounded by a zigzag border that closely resembles similar borders on two waiters and a tankard marked by Le Roux.[64] It is possible that Myers called upon the same specialist who had worked for Le Roux to execute this ornament, since the cypher— a dense, tightly interwoven design with a knot of lines and foliate embellishments at its center— is in an early eighteenth-century style.

The mirror cypher "DMF" engraved on David and Margaret Franks' waiter (fig. 10) was the work of a different craftsman. Its symmetry complements the object's Baroque geometry. Influenced by such London publications as Samuel Sympson's *A New Book of Cyphers* (1726), the design of the cypher is looser, with an open center and a simple linear frame. The foliate embellishments are confined to the outside edges of the design. The same engraver executed at least two other cyphers, "SB" and "JFM" for tankards of 1750–65 by Myers.[65]

Rapid Expansion, 1753–65

A fortuitous combination of circumstances in the mid-1750s spurred the growth of Myers's business, and in the years between 1753 and 1765, his production increased considerably in quantity and quality. His shift to the Rococo style in the mid-1750s was concomitant with an equally dramatic change in his patronage, which expanded to include the city's military, political, and social leaders, among them the wealthiest patrons of their generation. This change in the class of patrons was in turn coeval with the Seven Years' War (1756–63), which brought a new affluence to New York, the headquarters of the British army in North America as well as a principal battle-ground. New York benefited economically from the sudden influx of money and munitions from Great Britain, and leading merchants, including Lewis Morris II (cat. 18), made fortunes provisioning the British army.[66] The value of English imports rose to their highest peak during this period, and the city's population increased, surpassing Boston as the second-largest city after Philadelphia.[67] William Smith, Jr., later observed, "Our affluence, during the late war, introduced a degree of luxury in tables, dress, and furniture, with which we were before unacquainted."[68]

The first personal circumstance to benefit Myers's career occurred about 1750–52, when he married his first wife, Elkaleh (b. c. 1730–1765). She was the daughter of Samuel Myers Cohen and, presumably, his first wife, Rachel (Asher) Levy.[69] In the minute books of Shearith Israel during the 1740s, her family name has been consistently recorded as "Myers Cohen," and thus the record of a debt of £2 owed the congregation by "Elkela Myers" in June–July 1750 may indicate that she had already married the silversmith by that date.[70] Myer and Elkaleh Myers's first son, Solomon (1753–1791), was born on November 30, 1753, so the marriage must have taken place no later than that same year. Over the ensuing twelve years, they had four more children: Samuel (cat. 140), Joseph (1758–1817), Rachel (1760–1761), and Judith (cat. 96).[71] Myers's marriage

would later cement his relationships with two of the most prominent Jewish families in Philadelphia: Elkaleh's sister Richea married the Philadelphia merchant Barnard Gratz (cat. 138) in 1760, and her sister Rebecca married the Philadelphia merchant Mathias Bush four years later.

Elkaleh was an advantageous match for an ambitious young craftsman, providing what must have been a substantial dowry. Her father, Samuel Myers Cohen, had been a wealthy merchant in the transatlantic trade.[72] He had also immediately preceded Solomon Myers as *shohet* for Shearith Israel, resigning in May–June 1730.[73] Over the course of his life, he made several significant gifts to the congregation, including £3.18.0 for the first synagogue in 1728 and £1.8.0 for constructing a wall around the burial ground in 1737, both amounts being three times Solomon Myers's contributions. At his death in 1743, Myers Cohen bequeathed £25 "to and for the use of the Synagogue now frequented and belonging to the People called Jews and whereof at present am a Member."[74] He left a large estate, with individual bequests of £100 and £200 to his niece and brother, respectively, mourning clothes to each of the four executors, and seven mourning rings "of the Value of forty shillings sterling." The bulk of his property, including silver plate and Negro slaves, was divided equally between "my beloved wife Rachel and my four Daughters namely Elkaley Hiah Rebecca and Richa . . . to be put at interest for their maintenance and education until each shall marry or arrive at the age of eighteen years which shall first happen."[75]

The money from their marriage must have enabled Myer and Elkaleh Myers to lease a large double house in King (now Pine) Street that they ultimately purchased ten years later.[76] The house had belonged to the "Chirurgeon" John Dupuy, and the purchase provided another, perhaps coincidental, connection to Huguenot silversmiths.[77] The property was rented and eventually sold to Myers by the heirs of Dr. Dupuy, among whom were two Philadelphia Huguenot silversmiths: Daniel Dupuy and his nephew John David.[78] John's father, Peter David, had been apprenticed in New York to fellow Huguenot Peter Quintard.[79]

According to a description of the King Street house at the time it was offered for sale, the lot size was substantial: "thirty four feet front and rear, and seventy eight feet deep, containing every conveniency necessary to a family."[80] In contrast, the house rented by Myers's brother Asher in 1757 was 22 feet wide, the standard width of an urban house, with a side hall and one chamber across the front.[81] In 1735, the London silversmith George Wickes accommodated his family, workshop, and retail store in one house 19 feet wide and 32 1/2 feet deep; in 1744, he leased a second house for his workshop with a frontage of 18 feet 10 inches and a depth of 33 feet 4 inches.[82] Both halves of a divided house 38 feet wide were purchased in 1742 by Jacob Hurd, who similarly housed his family and workshop within the same building.[83] Thus Myers's King Street house was roughly the same size as Wickes's two houses combined and bespoke the considerable ambitions of this young craftsman. Presumably it had a central hall and was intended to provide separate quarters for Myers's family, his workshop, and perhaps a retail store.

Between the mid-1750s and mid-1760s, Myers appears to have focused on building his workshop into the largest and most important in New York. No records survive for any court cases during this time. Together with the merchant David Hays, the paternal uncle of Moses Michael Hays, in May 1763 Myers borrowed £220 from Abraham de Peyster.[84] This money may have been for a business venture, or it may have been in preparation for the purchase of the King Street house and lot, which Myer and Elkaleh Myers purchased on July 5, 1764 for £1,000.[85] Myer and "Elcaley" Myers then leased the house two days later to Evert Byvanck in a transaction that functioned somewhat like a mortgage.[86]

By the late 1750s, Myers had also advanced to a position of importance in Shearith Israel. On November 9, 1758, in his role as *parnas residente*, or vice president, he was one of four "Trustees of the Jewish Congregation" who signed the deed purchasing for £500 a house and 25 x 86-foot lot in Mill Street adjoining the synagogue from the baker Cornelius Clopper and his wife, Catherina Keteltas; Myers himself contributed £3 toward the purchase.[87] The following year he took up his first appointment as *parnas*, or president.[88]

PARTNERSHIP WITH BENJAMIN HALSTED

It was more than a good marriage, however, or the vicissitudes of war among European powers that led to Myers's prosperity as the only Jewish silversmith in New York. With a sense of entrepreneurship unknown among craftsmen in Colonial New York, Myers developed business strategies that ensured his success, precisely because they broke with long-established practices. New York silversmiths had belonged to closely knit craft networks determined largely by kinship, religion, or ethnicity. Kristan McKinsey's study of the Le Roux and Van Dyck families documents the importance of these relationships in the lives of artisans.[89] About 1756, Myers altered this pattern by entering into a partnership with Benjamin Halsted (1734–1817). The formation of such a partnership and, in general, Myers's expansion of his professional associations beyond the Jewish community were clearly necessitated by the challenge of finding financial and craft support in the absence of any family of fellow Jews in the same profession. Earlier New York silversmiths, connected by ties of kinship or religious affiliation, apparently had no need of formal partnerships, despite the fact that the very nature of silversmithing, with its costly materials, expensive, specialized tools, and labor-intensive techniques, encouraged the sharing of equipment and talent. In Boston, a few silversmiths established partnerships, beginning with John Hull and Robert Sanderson, Sr., in 1652, but none are recorded in New York before that of Halsted and Myers. And the only subsequent New York partnerships during the Colonial period all involved immigrant English jewelers: Simeon and William Coley in 1766, Bennett and Dixon in 1772, and Whitehouse and Reeve in 1774–75.[90]

Beyond the innovation of their partnership, Halsted and Myers were responsible for at least one other invention: the new kind of mark they devised to identify their wares. Each of the earlier Boston makers working as partners had struck his individual mark on the same object. In contrast, Halsted and Myers used one mark that combined the initials of their surnames, separated by an ampersand, a device that would become typical in the nineteenth century but, in the mid-1750s, represented the first use anywhere in the American Colonies (Appendix I, MARKS 11 and 12). A "N-York" mark (MARK 11A) also appears on one object with their first partnership mark as well as on two objects with a second H&M mark.[91] This use of a city mark, like that of the H&M partnership mark, is one of the earliest instances of a type of mark that became popular in the later eighteenth and nineteenth centuries.

Despite ample documentation, the dates of the partnership and biographical facts about Halsted have been given incorrectly in many references. Halsted was baptized on February 17, 1734, in Elizabeth, New Jersey. His parents were John T. Halsted and Susannah Blanchard, who were married in 1727. His father was from Hempstead, Long Island, but moved to Essex County, New Jersey, where he was denominated "Esquire" in local records, implying significant wealth.[92] In 1756, Halsted turned twenty-two and would have completed his training. However, Halsted never registered as a Freeman, which suggests he may not have served or completed an apprenticeship as a craftsman.[93]

A beginning date of about 1756 for the partnership is supported by the earliest documented work to survive bearing the marks of their partnership: a coffeepot stand (cat. 21) and a sugar dish (cat. 23) made for Charity Johnson between 1756 and 1758. A tankard (cat. 15) made for Wessel and Maria Van Schaick could also have been made in 1756 or shortly thereafter. Documents and two newspaper advertisements from the 1760s amplify the partnership's range of activities. Two receipted bills of sale from 1760 have survived (Appendix II, nos. 1, 2). The first, dated July 1, was issued to Catherine Schuyler for a substantial order that totaled £82.19.9 and comprised a plain waiter, a pair of chased sauceboats, and a cruet stand. On October 24, 1760, an otherwise unidentified "Mrs Levengston" was given a receipt "in fool" by Benjamin Halsted himself in the amount of £5.8.10 for a soup spoon and a pair of salt shovels. An even wider range of silver, jewelry, and other fancy goods was described by the partners in their newspaper advertisement of November 10, 1763.

MYERS, & HALSTED, Gold Smiths, Have removed to the lower End of King-Street, at the House of Mr. John Bell, Where they continue to make, all kinds of work, in gold and silver, and have to sell, a neat assortment of ready made plate, chased and plain; diamond rings, garnet hoops, and broaches in gold, crystal buttons and ear-rings, in ditto, silver, ivory, and wood etwees, tooth pick cases, and smelling bottles; cases of silver handled knives and forks, best spare blades for ditto, glasses for silver salts, cut cruets for table equipages, and an assortment of tools, for watch and clock makers.[94]

How long the partnership continued after 1763 is uncertain. Less than one year later, on July 5, 1764, the partners moved again, to "the Store House of Mr. Elias Desbroses, where Messers. Phenix and Broom lately kept Store, being the next Corner to Mr. Henry Cuyler."[95] In his will of 1778, Desbrosses mentioned "the lot, house and store fronting King, Queen and Dock Streets," which would have been around the corner from Myers's King Street house.[96] Since Halsted and Myers placed only these two newspaper advertisements, in November 1763 and July 1764, scholars have assumed, incorrectly, that the partnership lasted less than one year.

Halsted and Myers may have ended their partnership in 1766. On October 22, 1765, Halsted was married in Trinity Church to Elizabeth Tredwell (1744–1812), the daughter of Thomas Star Tredwell.[97] On September 17, 1766, Benjamin Halsted, having "followed the business some time in New-York," announced his partnership with his younger brother, Matthias Halsted, as "Gold and Silver-Smiths" in Elizabeth, New Jersey. They advised potential customers that "any orders for work being left at Mr. Thomas Star Tredwell's, at Burling's-slip, New-York, will come safe to hand."[98]

Although this documentary evidence points to a dissolution of Benjamin's partnership with Myers by 1766, at least one object with the first "H&M" mark (MARK 11) as well as at least two objects with a second "H&M" mark (MARK 12) can be dated to around 1770 (cats. 42, 60, 61). Moreover, Matthias Halsted advertised without his brother beginning in 1769, an indication that their association in New Jersey had ceased. Perhaps Benjamin Halsted returned to New York or had continued his financial connection with Myers's shop.

Halsted's role within the partnership with Myers is uncertain. Only about twenty objects survive with the partnership's marks, a surprisingly low number for at least eight years of association during a very active period in Myers's career. Although scholars traditionally have assumed that all objects made during the partnership's duration would be marked with the partnership's marks, during these years, both Myers and Halsted were also making or selling silver that they marked with their individual maker's marks. The Jones sword (cat. 16) and Meserve sauceboats (cat. 17), made in 1756–58 during the first years of their partnership, bear only Myers's marks. Silver marked by Benjamin Halsted alone that can be dated to the partnership period is rare, but his independent activity was documented by an ill-fated commission in 1763 for "a Set of Silver Buttons for a Suit of Clothes" from Andrew Bowne of Shrewsbury, New Jersey.

They were made exactly to his Directions; and when he came to fetch them, he seemed perfectly pleased with them. Three Weeks afterwards he called on me, and desired I would take them back. I represented to him how unsaleable Things made after another's Whim were; and that before I found a Person of his Taste, Years might elapse. He then offered me a Dollar; which I refusing, he grew passionate, and went away in the greatest Anger.[99]

After an exchange of letters, Bowne published "A Premonition to those Gentlemen that may hereafter have an Occasion to employ a Silver-Smith, to beware of that Villain BENJAMIN HALSTED; lest they be bit by him, as I have been." Anticipating Bowne's advertisement, Halsted announced in the same newspaper: "I am resolved to sue him immediately for Scandal."[100] Halsted's partnership with Myers was never mentioned in the course of these numerous public exchanges, perhaps because of a semi-independent partnership agreement, or perhaps because their partnership had already ceased by August 1764, when the details became public.

Although the partnership's 1760 bill of sale to Catherine Schuyler and the 1763 advertisement mention chased objects and elaborate forms, the majority of the surviving hollow ware marked by Halsted and Myers are small or relatively plain examples of routine shopwork (cats. 12, 45). Their flatware is equally generic, with the standard upturned, rounded end handles with a faint midrib and molded double-drop characteristic of New York City (cat. 42).[101] Even on objects made contemporaneously for the same patron, Charity Johnson, the partnership marked a sugar dish (cat. 23) and coffeepot stand (cat. 21), but not the larger and more expensive coffeepot (cat. 20), which was marked by Myers alone. The Johnson coffeepot stand is the only extant object with the partnership mark and cast and chased ornament in the Rococo style. Myers apparently wished to be identified as the exclusive maker of such stylish objects.

More perplexing is the fact that identical objects, apparently produced in the same workshop at the same time, could be marked by the partnership or by either Myers or Halsted alone, such as the two milk pots (cats. 11, 12). A punch strainer with a feathered handle marked by Benjamin Halsted appears to be almost identical to a punch strainer recorded as by Halsted and Myers, and may be an example of contemporaneous work that Halsted marked separately from the partnership.[102]

Even the partnership's most impressive objects, such as the tankard (cat. 15) or coffeepot (cat. 14), have similar counterparts marked by Myers alone (cat. 31). There is also the unexplained circumstance of a cann (cat. 40) that was marked originally with the partnership mark and deliberately overstruck with Myers's individual surname mark.

Benjamin Halsted's most likely contribution to his partnership with Myers was not as a craftsman but as a source of capital, since he was born into and married into prominent mercantile families. Objects marked by the partnership would have been productions in which Myers and Halsted had a joint financial interest, in terms of materials, labor, or perhaps the customer. Given Halsted's career after the Revolutionary War as a retail jeweler (p. 66–67), it seems most likely that he served as the manager of the retail side of the business, providing Myers with the time and financial stability to create the outstanding work he made during those years.

WORKSHOP PERSONNEL

Myers's partnership with Halsted coincided with an increase in the shop's production, and their moves in 1763 and 1764 probably were required by an increased workforce that needed larger accommodations. The separation of the workshop from Myers's home may also have been a response to the increased size of his family— now five children— along with apprentices and at least one slave. The ever-increasing production of Myers's shop during the Colonial period must have been supported by a number of apprentices and journeymen. None of Myers's sons appears to have trained as a silversmith with his father. At age eleven, his son Samuel (cat. 140) signed a receipt dated April 25, 1766, recording Nicholas Bayard's payment of 16 shillings for "making a new bowl to a Soup Spoon" (Appendix II, no. 4), but as Samuel's sister later recalled, he "early took up trade of a merchant."[103]

Myers's most important working relationship within his family may have been with his brother, Joseph Myers, who was also trained as a silversmith. Unfortunately, little information concerning Joseph's life has survived. He was born no later than 1732, as his name was included on the list of seat rates in the Mill Street Synagogue for October 1750.[104] During his older brother's first term as *parnas* in 1759, Joseph Myers entered his name in the minute book as one of the *yehidim*.[105] Although in 1761 he was chosen for the honor of *hatan bereshith* ("bridegroom of the beginning"), the reader who commenced the annual cycle of readings from the Torah, Joseph never served as *parnas* of Shearith Israel, unlike his brothers Myer and Asher.[106] One possible explanation is that Joseph was not economically independent. He apparently never married; his name was included among Solomon and Judith Myers's children in the 1847 family register, but without any life dates or further details, an indication that he had not produced descendants.[107]

The only contemporary reference to Joseph Myers as a craftsman was in a letter dated November 20, 1758 from the New York immigrant merchant Uriah Hendricks to his father Aaron Hendricks in London:

Dear father I have Recommed to you Jos. Myers a worthy Honest young man a Native of this place being Related to the franks familly & of worthy Parents whom I Beg youll Entertain at your home for my sake as he being an Entire Stranger at your Place tho' he has Recommendations to the franks familly & c. he is a working Silver Smith by Trade & comes to purchase Some things in his way & c. I Believe he Brings with him about £600 or £700 Ster^g Belongin to him & familly his Companion Named Sol^n Marache comes Likewise Trading voyage. . . .[108]

Solomon Maraché would become Joseph's brother-in-law, marrying his sister Rebecca in 1766.

Hendricks's tantalizing reference to Joseph being in London in 1758 for the purpose of acquiring "Some things in his way" and having the significant sum of £600–700 that belonged to him "and family" prompts speculation that Joseph was acting on behalf of his brother, whose recent marriage, partnership with Halsted, and the wartime economic boom had provided funds to expand his business. It is tempting to further imagine that Joseph spent much, if not all, of his career working as a silent partner for his brother, although no evidence for this relationship has survived. None of the extant receipts or bills of sale from Myer Myers mention Joseph or were signed by him. No silver marked by this "working Silver Smith" has been identified.

Joseph Myers's death date is not recorded. From 1769 to 1780, the tax lists of Lancaster, Pennsylvania, included a Joseph Myers whose profession was recorded as "silversmith" in 1771. Myer Myers's brother was still alive in July 1773, when Sampson Simson left him a mourning ring in his will.[109] Three references in 1787 to a Joseph Myers in New York may refer to him or his nephew, Myer Myers's son of the same name, born in 1758. The 1787 insolvency record for Benjamin Halsted, listed "Myer & Joseph Myers" together as a principal debtor, implying a partnerlike association.[110] A Joseph Myers paid 7 shillings for his seat in the synagogue at the end of 5547 (August 1787), and an account of offerings made to the *sedaka* (synagogue funds) of Shearith Israel during the first quarter of 5548 (1787) included the more substantial contribution of £2.12.0 from a Joseph Myers.[111] In each instance, the identity of this individual cannot be determined with certainty.

No records survive for any apprentices to Myer Myers, although it is possible to identify a few highly likely candidates. The most probable group includes four or five younger Jews from New York who described themselves as silversmiths between about 1750 and 1765. The only firm evidence of these younger men's careers comes from newspaper advertisements and other documents; no surviving silver objects can be attributed with certainty to any of them. Their small number is nevertheless an extraordinary percentage of a community of no more than 250 individuals. So far as can be determined, these five were, together with Myers himself, the only Jews who might have apprenticed as silversmiths in British North America, including Philadelphia, during the Colonial period. Myers's operation seems to have been the catalyst for the young New Yorkers' choice of profession, and these younger men would have had the added advantage of serving their time with a master whose household observed their religious holidays and dietary laws.

Samson Mears, born around 1740, was a cousin of Myers's first wife, Elkaleh.[112] If he served an apprenticeship with Myers, Samson would have been in the workshop between about 1755 and 1762; during those years, his older sister Caty married Asher Myers, and his sister Joyce became Myer Myers's second wife. Mears set up shop immediately upon completing his time, advertising on November 29, 1762, that "he intends to carry on the gold and silver-smith's business, after the newest and neatest fashion; and all commands he is favoured with, will be executed with the most thankful dispatch."[113] However, Mears never registered as a Freeman, and he did not remain a craftsman for very long. By the 1770s, he was working as an agent for Aaron Lopez of Newport and, like his father, became a West Indies merchant (p. 44).[114] In 1787, with Andrew Ten Eyck, Myers inventoried and appraised the estate of Ten Eyck's maternal uncle, Andrew Breestead, in whose house Samson Mears had set up shop in 1762.[115]

Myers probably trained both Benjamin Etting (d. 1778) and Andrew Hays (1742–1835), who gave their profession as "Goldsmith" when they registered together as Freemen on February 8, 1769.[116] As a New York Jew who became a silversmith, Etting probably was apprenticed to Myers, but little is known of Etting other than his parents' names and his date of death. Andrew Hays was a first cousin of both Moses Michael Hays and Jochabed (Hays) Pinto, wife of Joseph Pinto. Andrew, born in 1742, would have been apprenticed to Myers between about 1759 and 1766. No subsequent information survives concerning either man's activity as a craftsman. Etting died in 1778 in Norwalk, Connecticut, where Myers and other Jewish refugees from New York were living.[117] Apparently a Loyalist, Andrew Hays moved to Montreal at some point before 1778, when he married Brandele Abigail David and became an elder of Montreal's congregation, also named Shearith Israel.[118] He apparently lived in Montreal until his death; his name never appears in New York directories or the United States Census. Hays visited New York in May 1784, when he made a loan of £15 to Ephraim Hart that became grounds for a suit for £200 in

1786.[119] An "AH" mark on spoons made after 1780 has been attributed to Hays, but after the Revolutionary War he was never recorded as a silversmith in Canada.[120]

Like Samson Mears, Joseph Pinto (c. 1735–1798) never registered as a Freeman, which may indicate that he did not serve a formal apprenticeship. He was the son of the *shohet* and chandler Abraham Pinto and his wife, Sarah, and in 1765 married Jochabed Hays, sister of Myers's brother-in-law Moses Michael Hays (cat. 42).[121] Although Pinto subsequently described himself as a "Silversmith, at his Shop in Bayard-Street," evidence for his career as a working craftsman is scarce. James H. Halpin noted among the silver listed as stolen in March 1767 from Rebecca (Michaels) Hays, Pinto's mother-in-law, "1 Silver Coffee-Pot, no Mark, Maker's Name I,P" that possibly may have been made by Pinto.[122] However, in neither of his two newspaper advertisements did Pinto state that he took orders for custom work, a standard feature of most silversmiths' notices. The first, on October 30, 1758, offered for sale "Men's Shoe, Knee and Stock Stone Buckles; Women's Shoe and Girdle, do. Silver Watches, chased Silver Milk Pots, Stone Rings."[123] Three years later, Pinto offered a much wider range of silversmith's products:

a very fine silver chas'd turene, dish and spoon; chas'd and plain stands, full furnished; chas'd candlesticks, coffee and tea pots, sugar dishes, slop bowls and sauceboats, chas'd and plain pint and half pint mugs, salvers of different sizes, and milk pots, salts and pepper casters, and marrow spoons, cases with silver handled knives and forks, silver watches, silver and plated spurs, chas'd and plain whistles, gold headed canes, locket buttons set in gold, shoe, knee, and girdle buckles, and a variety of stone rings.[124]

Given the absence of any solicitation for commissions or of surviving objects that conclusively can be attributed to him, it seems probable that Pinto was primarily a retailer of precious metal goods that were imported or made by other New York craftsmen.[125] The similarity of Pinto's 1761 advertisement to the list of wares that Halsted and Myers advertised two years later (p. 34) suggests that Pinto might have retailed wares made in Myers's workshop. Aside from his two advertisements, Pinto was not described as a silversmith in any other documents, and his listings in the New York city directories between 1786 and 1797 did not include a profession.

STYLES AND SPECIALIST CRAFTSMEN

By the mid-1750s, Myers was producing silver in an assured version of the Rococo style that had emerged in England and Europe during the 1730s. Some of Myers's earlier works, among them the sauceboat (cat. 6), had included Rococo elements such as double-scroll handles with a leaf grip. In 1754, Myers had ordered "kink" wood handles for coffeepots, teapots, and milk pots (presumably a covered pot for hot milk, a form unknown in Myers's surviving silver) from the cabinet-maker Joshua Delaplaine.[126] Beginning in the mid-1750s, Myers's silver output was completely transformed into the Rococo idiom. Simple, geometric forms became curvilinear, "double-bellied" bodies on coffeepots and sugar dishes (cats. 20, 23); there are also two "bellied" tankards with double-scroll handles and domed covers ascribed to Myers's shop.[127] Cast shells on borders and handle junctures, as seen on the covered cup (fig. 9), replaced symmetrical scroll ornaments. Engraved ornament likewise featured Rococo elements in the frames (figs. 16–18). Instead of the smooth, uniform surfaces of the earlier objects, Myers's Rococo silver was enlivened by rich contrasts of textures, seen in both the chased surfaces of the cast elements and in the shading of the engraving.

During these years, for certain special commissions Myers began to place his mark in distinctive ways that suggests a confident self-promotion. On the set of four candlesticks (cats. 35, 36), his initials mark is placed on the sockets, an uncommonly visible location, as candlesticks were usually marked on the underside. In the early 1750s, Myers apparently was the first silversmith in New York to use a surname mark, a form more recognizable than initials (Appendix I, MARK 8). On the snuffers (cat. 38), his surname mark was struck on the outside surface of the cutting blade, where any right-handed user would see it, rather than on the inside, where English snuffers usually were marked.

Cast ornament forms a major element in Myers's interpretation of the Rococo during this time. In part, this technique allowed him to make direct copies of English objects, as for the set of candlesticks made for Catherine (Livingston) Lawrence (cats. 35, 36). Casting patterns may also have been a specialty of his workshop. Barbara Ward observed that the close similarity between cast decorative elements and cast objects such as candlesticks in Baroque-style Boston silver may be explained by the presence of a few silversmiths who specialized in casting.[128] A similar relationship exists between cast elements of Myers's silver and work by younger New York silversmiths, including a coffee urn by Ephraim Brasher with identical handles to Myers's covered jugs (cats. 26, 27), a coffeepot and stand by Cary Dunn that have identical castings to Myers's versions (cats. 21, 47), and a porringer by Otto Paul de Parisien (cat. 111) with a handle made from the same pattern as Myers's (cat. 46).[129] Moreover, the cast elements—spouts, finials, and S-shape handles—are strikingly similar on coffeepots and covered jugs by Myers (cats. 26, 27, 31) and coffeepots and flagons by the New York pewterers John Will and his son Philip (fig. 14).[130] The close relationship of all these cast elements may indicate communication and emulation among a group of craftsmen in related trades, or it may indicate that Myers's larger workshop specialized in making casting patterns that

Fig. 14. Philip Will, *Flagon*, New York or Philadelphia, 1763–87. Pewter. Henry Francis du Pont Winterthur Museum, Winterthur, Delaware.

Fig. 15. Cat. 26 (detail).

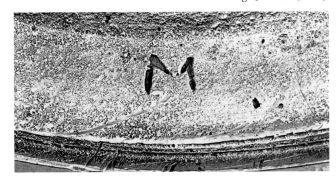

were used by other craftsmen. The circular foot rings on two objects by Myers, a covered jug (cat. 26) and a punch bowl (cat. 54) have the letter "M" incised in the patterns, perhaps to identify Myers's workshop as the source when they were lent to other craftsmen (fig. 15).

As he had from the beginning of his career, Myers turned to specialists for ornamental engraving. Many of the skilled engravers working in New York during the later Colonial period were metalworkers who practiced engraving as a side-line. The beautiful engraving on a tankard by the New York silversmith John Hastier probably was a specialty of his workshop, since in February 1739 he was unsuccessfully approached to engrave copper plates for counterfeit currency.[131] The pewterer Joseph Leddel, Jr., advertised in 1752 that he "also Engraves on Steel, Iron, Gold, Silver, Copper, Brass, Pewter, Ivory or turtle-Shell in a neat Manner, and reasonably," and both silver and copper objects engraved by him are known.[132] James Poupard, an immigrant from London, worked as both silversmith and engraver. In February 1776, he billed Philip Schuyler for engraving crests "on 4 pieces of his Plate" and coats of arms "on 2 Silver sauceboats," as well as for repairing a piece of silver.[133]

There were some engravers during the second half of the eighteenth century who advertised in New York as full-time specialists. The majority were immigrants. The best known was the Englishman Henry Dawkins, who had trained in London and worked in New York between 1754 and 1757 and again between 1774 and 1780; he advertised in 1755 that "he engraves in all sorts of mettals."[134] Other immigrants from England included John Hutt, "from London," who advertised in 1773 that he "Engraves Coats of Arms, Crests and Cyphers on Plate," and William Bateman, who "has had the honour to do work for the first nobility and gentry in London to their satisfaction."[135] Some engravers in New York came from Continental Europe, including John Anthony Beau from Geneva and Joseph Simons, "Seal-Cutter and Engraver, from Berlin," who advertised in 1763:

[He] engraves Coats of Arms, Crests, Cyphers, on the Plate, &c. Those Gentlemen and Ladies that please to send their Escutcheons, may depend upon having them done after the Manner of the Herald's office, and as neat as in any Part of England.[136]

The immigrant specialist engravers brought with them knowledge of the latest European styles. The engraving on New York silver during the second half of the eighteenth century was strongly influenced by English models. English design books for monograms or cyphers were imported into the Colonies: Joseph Richardson, Sr., gave Samuel Powel of Philadelphia 5 shillings to buy for him in London "An alphabet Cypher book to Ingrave by and a book of Drafts to Draw by and a book to Ingrave Snuff boxes."[137] Imported English objects with engraved ornament may also have influenced American engravers.

There were a few native-born engravers working in New York. Elisha Gallaudet had the longest career, active from 1756 to the time of the Revolutionary War.[138] In August 1767, like John Hastier thirty years earlier, he was contacted by would-be counterfeiters to engrave plates for them; more legitimate commissions came in 1771 from the Colony of New York for new bills of credit and in 1776 from the Albany Committee of Correspondence for Promissory Notes.[139] Gallaudet's sole documented commission to engrave silver was for a group of four medals for the Literary Society in New York in 1767.[140]

Although the level of artistry of engraved decoration on New York silver is high, its cost was very low relative to the cost of the object it adorned. Poupard charged Schuyler only 1 shilling sixpence for engraving each crest and 3 shillings for each coat of arms; routine decoration such as borders of flowers (cats. 53, 60) probably cost about the same. In New York throughout the second half of the eighteenth century, the engraver's contribution seems to have been valued consistently at about 20 percent of the silversmith's, with engraving accounting for about 5 percent of the finished object's total cost. In an undated bill of about 1760–65, John Heath billed Pierre Van Cortlandt £5.4.1 for making a punch bowl and £1 for the engraving, out of a total cost of £20.1.8.[141] A five-piece tea set made by Daniel Bloom Coen in 1792 cost £12.8.0 for "making" and £2.14.0 for "Engraving the whole"; the total value of the completed set would have been about £46.[142]

In trying to associate the work of a particular engraver with Myers's workshop, it is important to bear in mind that some engraving, particularly when it seems atypical, may represent a subsequent commission from the owner rather than engraving done at the time of the object's manufacture. If, on the other hand, there are several contemporary objects from Myers's workshop engraved by the same hand, it is likely that Myers subcontracted the work to the engraver. An unpublished waiter by Myers engraved with the Onderdonk arms is the only coat of arms on a piece of Myers's silver not executed by either of his specialist engravers and may represent an addition ordered by the owner.[143]

Beginning about 1755, Myers engaged a single craftsman for engraved armorials and monograms on important pieces of hollow ware. This engraver had a thorough understanding of the Rococo style from printed sources that first appeared in England during the early 1730s and in Boston as early as 1745.[144] The finest examples of his early work are the armorials on two contemporaneous objects: a tankard with the Livingston arms (cat. 28, fig. 16) and a covered jug with the Clarkson arms (cat. 27, fig. 17). This engraver also executed the Dunscomb coat of arms and a monogram on a tankard marked by Elias Pelletreau of Southampton, Long Island.[145] The overall design of all three armorials is almost identical, with shellwork frames overlapped by leaves. Characteristic details include a leaf overlapping the arms at their right (or sinister) side, the large flower issuing out of the frame at the left side, and the shelf of fruit and flowers at the upper right. The execution is tight and detailed, and certain mannerisms are present on all three

Fig. 16. Cat. 28 (detail).

Fig. 17. Cat. 27 (detail).

armorials: the relatively thin, even outlines of the design; the long, sharp hooks at the ends of leaves and "raffles"; and the use of closely spaced, even strokes for shading the shell forms.

This engraver or his workshop also executed crests, monograms, and other decorative engraving on Myers's silver that exhibited the same stylistic features as the contemporaneous coats of arms. The same workshop engraved the Livingston crest and motto on the cann (cat. 29) made *en suite* with the Livingston tankard as well as the unidentified crest and motto on a contemporary waiter from Myers's workshop.[146] This craftsman also engraved the latter crest on a caster made by Elias Pelletreau.[147] At least one monogram on Myers's silver of this period can also be attributed to this engraver: the "SSC" on the coffeepot made about 1756 for Samuel and Susannah Cornell (cat. 19, fig. 18). It exhibits the same shell frame defined by evenly spaced strokes of uniform thickness and the same sharp, hooked ends on the leaves. A virtually identical "MD" monogram appears on the cover of the Pelletreau tankard that this engraver embellished with the Dunscomb arms.

This engraver's work on objects marked by both Pelletreau and Myers may indicate that he operated an independent workshop in New York, but it is also possible that he worked in association with Myers. There is at least one documented instance of a specialist engraver working in a New York silversmith's shop. John Anthony Beau advertised in 1769–70 for commissions through the silversmiths Daniel and Lewis Fueter: "He engraves and does all Sorts of chasing Work, at the most reasonable Rates. Whoever will favour him with their Commands, are desired to apply to Mr. Lewis Fueter."[148] However, it may also be possible to identify the engraver of the armorials on Myers's and Pelletreau's silver as Elisha Gallaudet. Myers's association with this one engraver can be dated to the mid-to-late 1750s, when Gallaudet first started working in New York. He may well have been introduced to Myers by Otto Paul de Parisien, who served as godfather to two of Gallaudet's children, and could have been connected to Pelletreau, a fellow Huguenot, through Pelletreau's cousin by marriage, William Ustick, who acted as his agent in New York.[149] Gallaudet's 1761 bookplate for Jeremias Van Rensselaer exhibited the same overall design as the armorials as well as the same tight execution, with shading lines of even thickness (fig. 19). It should be noted, however, that the design was derived from English Rococo prototypes available to more than one craftsman, such as Matthias Lock's engravings of about 1746.[150]

Fig. 18. Cat. 19 (detail).

Fig. 19. Elisha Gallaudet,
Bookplate of Jeremias Van Rensselaer,
New York, 1761. Engraving.
Historic Cherry Hill, Albany, New York.

DANIEL CHRISTIAN FUETER

Myers's ability to create objects in the English Rococo style was due not only to specialist craftsmen, perhaps immigrants, but also to his close relationships with an immigrant silversmith, the Swiss Daniel Christian Fueter (1720–1785). Fueter probably had more impact on Myers than any other silversmith. Born and trained in Bern, Fueter had fled to London in 1752 after a failed political coup and entered a mark at Goldsmith's Hall on December 8, 1753.[151] According to Ian M.G. Quimby's study of Fueter's life and career, he had joined the Moravian Church in England, and together with fellow Moravians sailed to New York in the spring of 1754. He announced upon his arrival that he made "all sorts of gold and silver work, after the newest and neatest Fashion."[152] Fueter was naturalized in New York on July 31, 1765, as a silversmith and member of "Unitas Fratrum" [*sic*], or Moravian Church.[153]

The arrival in New York of a European-trained silversmith who had worked in London must have been of intense interest to Myers. The timing was fortunate as well, since by 1754 Myers was expanding his own workshop and output. The two men were almost exactly the same age, and Fueter's status as both a political refugee and a member of a religious minority may have strengthened their professional bond. If Myers had learned Yiddish, he might have been able to communicate with this German-speaker, although Fueter had lived in London and by 1767 was capable of writing a letter in excellent English (p. 47). Fueter clearly had close connections to the Jewish community in New York. In addition to his two-year association with Myers, discussed below, he announced in July 1769 "that he is removed into the House of Mrs. Pinto . . . in Bayard-Street."[154] His landlady was Sarah Pinto, mother of the silversmith Joseph Pinto, whose store had been at the same address.[155]

These two silversmiths may have initially formed a reciprocal relationship because they were outsiders in a city dominated by local craft dynasties. Myers's and Fueter's obvious talent and success during the later 1750s and early 1760s then seems to have contributed to the erosion of this traditional system, as patrons sought them instead of second- or third-generation craftsmen such as Richard Van Dyck (fig. 28) or Bartholomew Le Roux II (fig. 11), who were less active as craftsmen than their forebears.[156]

During Fueter's years of residence in New York, his career frequently overlapped with Myers's. They shared several important patrons, including William Samuel Johnson (cats. 52, 108) and Mary (Thong) Livingston (cats. 30, 107). Both craftsmen made Indian trade silver for Sir William Johnson, general superintendent of Indian affairs in North America; Fueter made two sets of medals in 1760 and 1764 for presentation to Indian allies of the British.[157] Robert B. Barker has observed that Fueter and Myers may have shared casting patterns, since the feet on Fueter's cruet stand (cat. 106) appear to be made from the same pattern as the lower handle juncture on Myers's covered jug (cat. 27).[158]

More important, certain similarities in Fueter's and Myers's silver may document a significant interchange of techniques and traditions that benefited both craftsmen. They clearly shared an ambition and ability to produce forms more commonly made in or imported from England, such as bread baskets (cat. 78), cruet stands (cats. 91, 106), and scalloped dishes (cat. 52), and theirs are among the only surviving examples of these forms marked by Colonial New York silversmiths. Sufficient differences exist between their versions of these forms to rule out the likelihood that one craftsman made them all. Fueter may have been something of a catalyst to Myers, demonstrating in his work a wider range of possibilities than Myers had seen previously in New York. At the same time, Myers's familiarity with local traditions may have influenced Fueter's versions of a New York-style tankard (cats. 15, 108) and a teapot that is almost identical to cat. 1.[159] It is also possible that Myers or another silversmith supplied Fueter with these typically New York objects to mark and sell. Although Fueter never adopted a surname mark, he did use a "N:York" mark like Halsted and Myers, whose partnership coincided almost exactly with Fueter's residence in New York (Appendix I, MARK IIA).

IMPORTED ENGLISH SILVER

Another significant influence on Myers's work was English silver imported into New York. The boom economy during the Seven Years' War enabled New Yorkers to acquire English silver in higher quantities than they had earlier. Robert Barker's research in the English Customs Export Records has revealed that for the twenty years between 1746 and 1765, an average of 1,487 oz. per year of wrought plate was exported to New York, as opposed to about half that amount in previous years. The supply and demand fluctuated considerably during this time, with the highest peak between 1759 and 1762, during the Seven Years' War; the largest amount, 5,368 oz., was exported in 1761.[160] The silver Catherine Schuyler purchased from Halsted and Myers in July 1760 (Appendix II, no. 1), which may have been imported, totaled just under 100 oz. for four objects, and thus 215 such objects would equal the total quantity exported from London to New York in 1761. While representing a sharp increase, these amounts, as Ellenor Alcorn has observed, accounted for only a small fraction of the silver produced in London at this time.[161]

The London trade was organized into a complex network of workshops that specialized in specific forms or techniques, permitting production of high-quality objects on a larger scale than was possible in the Colonies.[162] Most of the surviving English silver objects with histories of ownership in New York are the work of specialists in specific forms that probably were acquired by the patrons or importers from retail silversmiths instead of the makers. A cruet stand of 1754–55 (cat. 121), probably imported and purchased by David Clarkson during the Seven Years' War, is a typical example of this form from a maker, Samuel Wood, who specialized in such production.

A few of the English objects with histories of ownership in New York represented more expensive wares than typical London production, often Rococo objects with chased ornament that would have been difficult for most New York silversmiths to reproduce. A punch bowl of 1754–55 by William Grundy (cat. 120) has elaborate cast and chased decoration that was not uncommon in London but rarely duplicated by the craftsmen available in the Colonies. In 1761–62, Colonel Philip Schuyler purchased in London for his new home in Albany a "Chased Cup and Cover" weighing 93 oz. 13 dwt., two pairs of "Chased Candle sticks & Nozells" weighing 137 oz. 7 dwt., and a "Chased Snuffer pan" weighing 12 oz. 13 dwt., undoubtedly because chased forms such as these would have been difficult to have made in New York.[163]

The English silver imported into New York impacted Myers's work in several ways. Imported objects represented competition to his workshop, particularly if sold by merchants or retail silversmiths without his overhead. Myers, however, seems to have engaged in a reciprocal relationship with these imports: the quality and breadth of his own production was both inspired by and dependent on the quality and range of imported forms sold and owned in New York. Commissions for unusual forms stemmed from patrons' desires to emulate the objects they had seen in other homes, and Myers's success depended on his ability to provide style-conscious patrons with objects that evoked what was perceived as the London mode. In some instances, he used English objects as models to copy as best he could, as with his cruet stand or bread basket (cats. 78, 91). It is also possible that the Torah finials made in London by Gabriel Sleath for the Barbados synagogue served as the model for Myers's Torah finials (cats. 63–65).

In other instances, Myers could duplicate imported English objects by using them to make casting patterns for both objects and ornamental elements. In at least one case, he was commissioned to make an exact copy of an English waiter and undoubtedly cast the border from the original (cat. 119). Once he had a casting pattern, Myers creatively used the castings: a foot from a cruet stand or epergne was used as the lower juncture of the handle on one of Myers's covered jugs (cat. 27). Casting also allowed Myers to make duplicates of costly, specialized forms such as candlesticks (cats. 8, 9, 35, 36); the pattern for one pair preserves the hallmarks of the English original (cats. 35, 36).

Some of these English objects may have came through Myers's workshop for repair, whereas others may have come into his retail store as payment or resale as second-hand objects (cat. 122). Myers may also have imported English silver to sell at retail. Joseph Myers's trip to London in 1758 to "purchase some things in his way" with the considerable sum of £600–700 may have been to acquire silver objects for resale, perhaps in his brother's retail store.[164] An English cann has Myers's marks struck over the original hallmarks, suggesting that it was sold though his store.[165] The Philadelphia silversmith Joseph Richardson, Sr., imported large quantities of English wares, particularly small and inexpensive forms.[166]

Since the mid-1750s, Myer Myers had likewise offered for sale small silver and gold objects and other small luxury goods that were either imported from England or made locally by smallworkers or jewelers. From May 1755 to December 1758, he purchased some of these wares from an unidentified Jewish merchant in Philadelphia.[167] On June 2, 1755, Myers was debited for £1.18.1 for "3 Silver Seals No. 34, 35" and "11 thimbles Silver" purchased in May "per Mr. Mendiz."[168] By August of the same year, Myers had purchased an extensive assortment of jewelry and small fancy goods amounting to £18.7.6:

1 Card Bristol Ston Buttons	*1.10.0*
1 Dᵒ Studs	*1.10.0*
1 Doz fish Skin Ink potts	*0.16.0*
3 Doz Whatch Springs	*4.19.0*
3 Gold Rings wᵗ Stones	*3.0.0*
3 Dᵒ Dᵒ	*2.14.0*
3 Dᵒ Dᵒ	*1.2.6*
1 smalling bottle wᵗ S[ilve]r top	*0.6.0*
1 Doz & 2 Aggat Buttons	*0.15.0*
1 Doz Gilt Seals	*0.8.0*
1 Pʳ Gold Dabbs Earrings	*1.15.0*
1 Pʳ pinch Back Earrings	*0.2.0*[169]

His transactions with this Philadelphia merchant probably stemmed from their connection as fellow Jews, rather than from any lack of availability of such wares in New York. In an undated transaction, Myers supplied "1 pʳ Seals" as partial payment for £4.9.5 worth of "Sund[rie]s" from Barnard and his brother Michael Gratz.[170] Similar small luxury items continued to be part of Myers's business into the 1760s, perhaps because of Benjamin Halsted's connection to the retail jewelry trade.

PATRONAGE

Myers's patrons for Rococo style objects in the mid-1750s and 1760s included political, military, financial, and social leaders. The Earl of Loudon (fig. 20, cat. 17) was commander-in-chief of the British army in North America in 1756–58 and would have provided a conspicuous example for Colonial administrators to emulate. The Reverend Samuel Johnson (cat. 126) was the founding president of King's College in 1754. David Clarkson (cat. 27) and Lewis Morris II and III (cat. 18) were powerful and wealthy landowners and merchants. Foremost among Myers's patrons during this period were members of the Livingston family, most notably Robert Livingston, Jr., along with his siblings and cousins (cats. 28–39).

The Reverend Samuel Johnson and his first wife, Charity (Floyd) Nicoll, were among Myer Myers's most important early patrons. Together they owned or commissioned at least nine pieces from his shop: a coffeepot, stand, three sugar dishes, pair of canns, large dish, and covered jug (cats. 20–26, 52). A graduate of Yale (class of 1714), Samuel Johnson left the Congregational Church in 1722 and was ordained in England as an Anglican minister. He founded the first Anglican church in Connecticut (Christ Church, Stratford) in 1723, and in 1754 he was appointed founding president of King's College (now Columbia University), the first Anglican college in the northeast. His wife, Charity, the widow of her cousin Benjamin Nicoll, was the older sister of Nicoll Floyd, who owned a teapot (cat. 1) by Myers, and the daughter of the wealthy landowner Colonel Richard Floyd and his wife Margaret Nicoll of Mastic, Long Island.[171]

Samuel's position as a minister and college president, as well as Charity's substantial means and family connections, put the Johnsons at the center of a circle of prominent Anglican merchants and landowners. The objects they commissioned from Myers after their arrival in New York in 1754 indicated a lavish lifestyle, displaying both their wealth and sophistication, and they may well have served as models for their peers. Johnson would have known David Clarkson as a founding trustee of King's College, and their similar covered jugs (cats. 26, 27) offer evidence of a reciprocal emulation of styles of entertaining as well as choice of silversmith. Johnson was also connected to Lewis Morris II (cat. 18), baptizing his daughter Catherina in Trinity Church on March 2, 1757.[172] Morris's son from his first marriage, Lewis Morris III, had married Mary Walton, whose sister was married to another prominent Anglican, David Johnston (cat. 98), who later patronized Myers.

Myers's clientele came from both sides of the political divide, as evidenced by the patronage of the Livingston family—Whigs who represented the Tory Samuel Johnson's fiercest opponents (p. 5). Few families in Colonial New York rivaled the wealth and political power that had accrued to the

Fig. 20. John Faber, Jr., after Allan Ramsay,
*The Right Honble the Earl of Loudon
in the Regimentals of His Highland Regiment*,
London, 1753. Mezzotint. Henry E. Huntington Library,
Museum and Gardens, San Marino, California.

Livingstons by the middle of the eighteenth century. The basis for the Livingston fortune in America was provided by Robert Livingston (1654–1728), an archetypal immigrant-entrepreneur, who married Alida (Schuyler) Van Rensselaer, a wealthy widow from the Dutch oligarchy in Albany. He accumulated political appointments as well as tracts of land in what are now Columbia and Dutchess Counties; in 1686, the latter were consolidated into a patent for 160,000 acres, thenceforth known as Livingston Manor.[173] By the middle of the eighteenth century, the Lord of Livingston Manor was entitled to

rents and other perquisites from tenants as well as a seat in the General Assembly.

In 1749, Robert Livingston, Jr. (cat. 127) succeeded to the title of Third Lord of Livingston Manor and, like his father and grandfather, traded as a merchant and developed the Manor's resources with lumber and grist mills, profiting handsomely during the Seven Years' War.[174] Although it cannot be determined that Robert and his first wife, Mary Thong (cat. 128), inspired their relatives' patronage of Myer Myers, they were at the head of an extended family that clearly favored Myers with important hollow-ware commissions. Robert Livingston, Jr.'s siblings and cousins, as well as their children, commissioned more than twenty-five of the objects that survive from Myers's shop, ranging from sets of spoons (cats. 33, 34, 101) to tankards and canns (cats. 28–30) to candlesticks and snuffers (cats. 35, 36, 38). These objects provide the largest body of documented work by Myers for a single family group. The silver that Myers made for the Livingstons between about 1750 and 1765 included many objects in the Rococo style that attest to the family's affluence as well as to their desire to display it. A traditional form such as the tankard (cat. 28) made for Robert R. and Margaret Livingston was enriched with lavish Rococo engraving surrounding the family coat of arms. The snuffers and tray (cat. 38) made for Robert Gilbert Livingston and the set of candlesticks made for his cousin Catherine (Livingston) Lawrence (cats. 35, 36) were among the most elaborate versions of these forms made in the American Colonies.

In addition, the Livingstons' example apparently had considerable influence on their extended family and political and business associates. John Stevenson (cat. 87) was a business associate of Philip Livingston (cat. 129). The Livingstons were prominent members of the Presbyterian Church, and a significant group of Myers's patrons were Presbyterians, including Robert, Jr.'s son Peter R. Livingston (cats. 32, 34), William and Thomas Smith (cat. 55), Ennis Graham, and Daniel McCormick (cat. 51). The complexities of church membership among dissenting Protestants, as well as the identification of leading Presbyterians with Whig politics (p. 5), may indicate a stronger connection to political alliances than religious affiliation. William Smith, Jr., a leader of the Whig party and brother of Thomas Smith, was married to Janet Livingston, the sister of Margaret Livingston, who married Peter R. Livingston. In ongoing political disputes between mercantile and landed interests in New York, the Livingstons were allied closely with the Morris family, who also patronized Myer Myers (cats. 18, 48).[175]

The role of all these major figures, Tory and Whig, Anglican and Presbyterian, in shaping the style of Myers's silver of this period appears to have been significant. A few of his commissions were specifically related to military events, or to relationships formed during wartime (cats. 16, 17). The influx of both British officials as well as British goods during these years may have inspired a greater desire to emulate the fashions of London. Most important, however, the wealth generated by the war could be expressed through the cast forms and ornament that required more metal and thus more money. During these years, Myers made the largest and heaviest objects that survive from his shop: the standing cup (fig. 9, 76 oz.) and covered jug (cat. 27, 59 oz.). Other objects were part of large sets that represented equally significant amounts of silver: Catherine (Livingston) Lawrence's four candlesticks (cats. 35, 36) rep-

resented a combined weight of at least 80 oz., and Robert R. and Margaret Livingston's original set of matching tankards and canns (cats. 28, 29) had a combined weight of about 100 oz. The scale, weight, and cast Rococo ornament of the silver Myers produced during this period clearly was intended as an explicit statement of his patrons' wealth.

New York's Leading Silversmith, 1765–76

The mid-1760s marked the beginning of changes in Myers's personal life and business affairs. In 1764, he extended his financial reach beyond the silversmith trade when he and two partners invested in the Spruce Hill Lead Mine in Connecticut. Two years later, Benjamin Halsted moved from New York to New Jersey, and his partnership with Myers may have ended. At this same time, Myers appears to have engaged in business relationships with a number of younger silversmiths, probably in an effort to expand his market.

Myers's personal world was also remapped in these years. On August 23, 1765, one year after purchasing the King Street house, Elkaleh Myers died. Myers and his wife had already suffered the loss of their daughter Rachel, who had died on August 8, 1761, just two months after her first birthday and nine months before the birth of her sister Judith. As a working widower with four children age three through twelve, Myers would have been unlikely to remain unmarried, particularly in the small Jewish community. Within two years, on March 18, 1767, he married Joyce Mears (1737–1824), Elkaleh's first cousin and the younger sister of his brother Asher's wife, Caty.[176] This second marriage, like Myers's first, would further strengthen an existing business association. In 1768, Joyce's sister Sarah married the merchant Solomon Simson, whose brother Sampson was Myers's partner in the Connecticut lead mine (see below).[177]

Joyce Mears probably brought smaller financial benefits to the marriage than had Elkaleh Myers Cohen. Joyce was the daughter of the West Indies merchant Judah Mears, who had been born in London and lived in Guadeloupe, and Jochabed Michaels.[178] Mears moved to New York before August 7, 1728, when he made his first donation to Shearith Israel, and in 1738 he became a Freeman of New York as a merchant.[179] His gifts to the congregation in 1728 were in the lower middle range, although the amounts were more than double Solomon Myers's contributions.[180]

On February 2, 1768, Myer and Joyce Myers had their first child, Judah, who was circumcised by Abraham Abrahams on February 9, 1768 (see fig. 8), but died within a year.[181] Over the next nine years, they had seven more children: Richea (1769–1837), Moses Mears (1771–1860), Samson Mears (1772–1803), the twins Aaron and Miriam (1774–1775), Rebecca (1776–1836), and Benjamin (1778–1835).[182] Following the birth of the twins on

December 27, 1774, Joyce Myers apparently suffered a physical or nervous breakdown that required treatment by Dr. Peter Middleton, who also attended the twins until their death in August 1775.[183]

Other residents of the King Street house during these years included "a Negro Wench, named Daphne," who ran away in May 1767.[184] Daphne almost certainly was a house servant and may have arrived as the property of Elkaleh or Joyce. Myers's widowed mother, Judith, may also have lived with his family. Dr. Middleton's ledgers record different treatments for "Ms. Judie" in September 1772 and February 1773.[185] Leo Hershkowitz assumed this individual was Myers's daughter Judith, but she was ten years old at this time, and the treatments were more typical of those administered to adults: on September 11, 1772, Middleton administered an emetic and a bolus (a rose petal and rhubarb syrup used as a purgative). Moreover, Judith Myers died on February 19, 1773, precisely at the time when one series of Middleton's treatments end, suggesting he had attended her in her last illness.[186]

Two documents survive from January 1772 that provide a rare glimpse into the state of Myers's own health. Middleton's ledgers record that he attended the craftsman from January 9 onward, prescribing treatments for an illness that Hershkowitz interpreted as dysentery.[187] However, in a letter of January 26, which accompanied the delivery of Torah finials to Michael Gratz (cats. 65, 66), Myers wrote, "I am still Confined with my Sore arm & Rheumatism and am writing in pain . . ." (Appendix II, no. 6).

All through these years of deaths, illnesses, and childbirths, Myers's production as well as his market continued to expand and his economic interests diversify. With the British victory in the Seven Years' War in 1763, land in northern New York and New England that previously had served as a buffer zone between the French and the English became open for settlement. In June 1763, Myer Myers received grants of land in adjoining townships laid out as Underhill and Westford, New Hampshire (now Vermont). Other New Yorkers among Myers's fellow grantees were his brother-in-law Solomon Maraché, his patron William Sackett (cats. 71, 72), Isaac Adolphus, and Andrew Ten Eyck.[188] Grantees were required to clear and farm five acres within five years, and it is likely that Myers acquired this land as an investment for subsequent resale.

THE SPRUCE HILL LEAD MINE

During the mid-1760s, Myers also invested in a lead mine located in a granite ridge, known in the eighteenth century as Spruce Hill, on the west side of the Shepaug River in Woodbury township (now Roxbury), Connecticut. The site was a 66 x 12-rod tract granted as a mine on August 30, 1762, to the

brothers Abraham and Israel Brownson of Woodbury, who were farmers and blacksmiths.[189] The Brownsons divided their lot into sixteen shares, and sold them in both whole and fraction pieces for £100 per share.[190] Among the shareholders was Benjamin Stiles, a third cousin of Ezra Stiles (cat. 133) and a nephew of the Reverend Samuel Johnson (cat. 126).[191] Benjamin Stiles's first cousin, William Samuel Johnson (fig. 32) was also a shareholder.

For Myers, the mine seems to have been a financial venture rather than a source of precious metal for silversmithing. Although silver is found together with lead sulphide, or galena, the deposits of galena at this site were small. All the surviving documents relating to the mine consistently and exclusively refer to it as a lead mine, but perhaps because two silversmiths became involved with the project, there has been considerable confusion in subsequent histories as to the mine's purpose.[192]

Myers's involvement may have come about through a variety of connections. One of his partners in this mine (and fellow elder of Shearith Israel), Sampson Simson, had interests in several mines, including one in Westchester, New York, leased in 1771 from Frederick Philipse, and a lead mine in Middletown, Connecticut.[193] Shareholder William Samuel Johnson was Myers's patron during the 1760s, and other patrons were involved in mining, such as Robert Livingston, Jr. (cat. 127), who had inherited one iron forge on Livingston Manor and built a second, both supplied with ore from a mine in Salisbury, Connecticut.[194] Moreover, American silversmiths had been interested in mines since the 1650s, when Robert Sanderson, Sr., of Boston formed a mining company.[195] The New York silversmith Cornelius Kierstede, together with two fellow New Yorkers, leased land for mining copper in Mount Carmel and Wallingford, Connecticut, in 1722 and settled in nearby New Haven two years later.[196]

Myers may also have become interested in mining because of his skills as a metal refiner. Only a few of the largest merchant-artisan silversmiths in Colonial Boston had mercury and touchstones in their inventories, which led Barbara Ward to conclude that only these large workshops undertook refining to supply themselves as well as other craftsmen.[197] Myers apparently achieved renown as a refiner. In the spring of 1775, the Connecticut Assembly appropriated £500 for establishing a smelting operation at a lead mine in Middletown and appointed a committee to search for lead refiners. After traveling to New York, New Jersey, and Pennsylvania, Benjamin Henshaw reported to the Assembly on June 30, 1775:

I treated with Mr. Otto Parasein [Parisien] and Mr. Myer Myers with whom both I had some conversation before I left New York and find Mr. Parasein will come and oversee the work at £150 York currency per annum and Mr. Myers for £200 yr per annum, and those charges paid up here. . . . The character of the two aforemen-

tioned Gentlemen are that they are honest and skillfull in the pro-
fession of gold and silversmith, but Mr. Myers has much the prefer-
ence in regard to refining metals, and by some Gentlemen, is much
preferred.[198]

Other New York silversmiths involved as metal refiners, including Parisien as well as Daniel Christian Fueter, were from Northern Europe, as were Jews involved in mining and refining in America, including Michael and Barnard Gratz (cat. 138) in Pennsylvania and the "Gold & Silver Refiner" Isaac Moses in Georgia.[199] This suggests a tradition of expertise in mining or metal refining among some Ashkenazic Jews. In light of the fact that Myers and both his brothers pursued careers as metalsmiths, it is possible that their father, Solomon Myers, had some training in this field, although there is no evidence that he ever worked as a refiner or craftsman. It is also possible that Myer Myers learned metal refining from either Parisien or Fueter.

On April 3, 1764, Myers, Simson, and a third partner, tobacconist George Trail, signed a forty-two-year lease for three-quarters of the Brownsons' tract, "lately laid out and recorded to us . . . [and] already opened and dug upon."[200] The partnership was responsible for mining operations and building appropriate structures, and the Brownsons would receive one-eighth of all ore produced at the mine for the first twenty-one years, presumably to be redistributed in some form among the mine's shareholders.

The mine brought Myers into a formal business relationship with Daniel Christian Fueter in 1765, when he was hired to manage the mine. Like Myers, Fueter was skilled as a metal refiner; he mentioned in his newspaper advertisements that "he also gilds Silver and Metal, and refines Gold and Silver after the best Manner, and makes Essays on all sorts of Metal and Oar," or that he performed "refining in the exactest Manner."[201] On April 25, 1765, a year after signing their lease, Myers and his partners, "the Owners of the Lead Mine upon Spruce Hill," hired Fueter to be the superintendent, requiring him "to live conveniently near the mine."[202] The records of the Moravian Congregation mention Fueter's move to Connecticut in December 1765, although the mining he was supposed to be supervising had begun shortly after his hiring in April. His account for the year between July 1, 1765 and July 26, 1766, the height of the operations, details the expenditure of £275.19.6 to build a furnace, board the workmen, and purchase supplies, including ten gallons of rum.[203] According to an 1831 account, the company carried out an extensive exploration of the site, working not only on the outcrop but also halfway down the hill.[204] Between November 1765 and November 1766, the company employed a total of seventeen miners, thirteen laborers, two slaves, and a German blacksmith.[205]

The mine never yielded anything close to the partners'

expectations, and they began to suffer financial difficulties. Presumably to raise additional funds, Myers sold a "one sixteenth part of Spruce Hill Lead Mine" on November 27 to Michael Gratz for £45.6.6.[206] One year after Gratz made his investment, on November 23, 1766, Myers wrote Gratz as "so much a Philosopher in disappointments" (Appendix II, no. 5). Myers and his partners were trying to sell their lease, and he reported that "we have two strings to our Bow." Both an agent for "One of the Richest Companies of Mines in London" as well as "Mr. Housenclever," undoubtedly Peter Hansenclever, who owned iron smelting furnaces in New York and New Jersey, had taken samples of the lead ore for testing.[207] No further offer from London or Hansenclever is recorded, although Hansenclever remained in contact with both men. In January 1772, "by Mr. Hausenclever," Myers dispatched a letter to Gratz, although its subject is unknown (Appendix II, no. 6).

In his letter of November 1766, Myers had informed Gratz that the Company had rejected Hansenclever's previous offer of £1,000 because "that is not one third of our cost." This claim that the partners had expended over £3,000 in developing the mine is borne out by Myers's request that Gratz send him £240 as "a sixteenth," presumably the amount of debt that the owner of a sixteenth share would be responsible for, thereby making the total debt £3,840. He concluded his plea: "Were I not in the greatest want, would not ask you for your part but must make a large payment in ten or twelve days; your assistance will near do it" (Appendix II, no. 5).

On March 13, 1767, Myers's brother Joseph wrote to the Woodbury, Connecticut, lawyer Benjamin Stiles on behalf of "My Brother and Mr. Sampson [Simson]" with reference to "our affairs at Spruce Hill."

Sir, I have been informed that Mr. [Thomas] Rowe is in town and will leave it to morrow and tho' I have been waiting for an opportunity to answer your favour ever since I received it, this offer [comes?] so sudenly that I can only inform you that I have communicated your proposals to some Gentlemen who have not yet given me their determination. The ill success s^d mining has met with for some time past makes them timorous, but hope shall be able to let you know their full determination in my next.

I have been told that your other mine is likely to prove good, on which account beg leave to congratulate you. My Brother and Mr Samson join me in thanks for your kind offer of friendship in regard to our affairs at Spruce Hill and we shall be glad to have it in our power of rendering any service in return.

I am with much esteem, Sir, Your Most Hbl Serv. Joseph Myers[208]

By the fall of 1767, the "ill success" Joseph Myers mentioned obliged the partners to cease mining and settle their accounts. On October 19, 1767, Fueter wrote from Woodbury:

I have disburst most of the debts contracted for the Co. And the draft from Mr. Meyers has been a great help . . . but I am greatly behind hand to my good friends Messers Von Vleck, Barton, Bemper & Gen at New York, which makes me many uneasie hours. . . . Beg you to settle my accounts with my son Lewis and let him have the balance due me.[209]

Fueter apparently remained in Connecticut for almost another year, returning to New York late in 1768. To satisfy a £12 debt from Israel Brownson, Fueter had seized a parcel of land adjoining the Spruce Hill mine, presumably his residence. On October 13, 1769, five days before his return to Switzerland, Fueter quit claim the land to Myers for £12.[210]

Records from the later 1760s and early 1770s, particularly those for a number of lawsuits between 1769 and 1771, suggest that Myers was experiencing financial difficulties during these years, possibly brought on by his investment in the mine. Moreover, the size of his workshop and the number of objects being made for ready sale would have required a constant supply of silver that Myers may have been forced to purchase with borrowed funds.[211] He had been loaned £200 by the carman Henry Shafer on February 6, 1765, and in 1771, the executors of Shafer's estate sued Myers for debt; the court ordered him to repay the loan in addition to £8.6.9 in damages and costs.[212] In November 1770, Myers was sued for the same amount, £200, by the merchant Joseph Reade, who lived across King Street from Myers's house. On July 6, 1769, one Joseph Smith sued Myers for £41.16.0. Five months later, on November 30, 1769, the landowner Nicholas W. Stuyvesant sued him for £25. Like the Shafer suit, these other cases, particularly Reade's, probably were for defaulted loans.[213] Additional evidence indicates that Myers was borrowing money: on August 20, 1772, he executed a bond to the Loyalist landowner and merchant John Wetherhead for £203.15.1 and 3 farthings. Wetherhead assigned the bond to the Ulster County land surveyor William Cockburn, and in 1774 Myers made a payment of £27.12.0 on the bond to Cockburn.[214]

Another possible sign of financial trouble at this time was an advertisement of July 8, 1773, announcing that Myers's house and lot in King Street were for sale.[215] He apparently had difficulty disposing of the property, and in late August he announced: "If the above house should not be disposed of by the first of September, it will be sold at public Vendue at the Coffee-House."[216] No such sale was ever advertised, however, and as of September 23 it was still described as "the house of Mr. Myer Myers" when the house next door was put up for auction by Myers's fellow silversmith John Burt Lyng.[217]

Myers's business problems did not affect his increasingly prominent role at Shearith Israel during the decade preceding the Revolutionary War. In 1764, he served his second term as *parnas*, followed by a third term six years later.[218] Together

with his brother-in-law Solomon Simson and the wealthy merchant Daniel Gomez, he signed a bond in 1772 holding the Mill Street property in trust for the congregation. Three years later, on February 5, 1775, the congregation voted to appoint Myers a "Future Trustee" of all real estate belonging to Shearith Israel.[219] In a less official capacity, he served in 1774 as an executor of the will of his "good friend" Isaac Adolphus, who was married to Charity Hays, the paternal aunt of Moses Michael Hays.[220]

Myers devoted his community service to his congregation; unlike his father and brother Asher, he never held a civic office. He did become a Freemason in the 1760s. Jews had been Masons in England as early as the 1710s, and during the Colonial period they joined lodges in Georgia, South Carolina, Virginia, Maryland, Pennsylvania, Connecticut, and Rhode Island.[221] King David's Masonic Lodge, the first exclusively Jewish lodge in the American Colonies, was established in New York on February 17, 1769 by Provincial Grand Master George Harison. The founding warrant named "our Worshipful and well beloved Brother Moses M. Hays" as Master and Myer Myers and Isaac Moses (cat. 141) as Senior and Junior Wardens, respectively.[222] No records survive to document Myers's previous membership in the Masons, but as Harison's reference to Hays implied one, presumably the other two officers had been Masons as well. King David's Lodge was short-lived in New York; in 1780, during the Revolutionary War, Moses Michael Hays moved it to Newport, where it was assimilated into St. John's Lodge.[223]

Myers's interest in the Masons may have stemmed from his ambitions as a craftsman. As Edith Steblecki has pointed out, Freemasonry's emphasis on honesty and ethical principle would be beneficial to the reputation of a silversmith working in precious metals.[224] However, unlike Paul Revere, Jr., almost half of whose Boston patrons were fellow Masons, Myers had few wealthy clients who were active Masons.[225] The most prominent was Daniel McCormick, who commissioned a pair of gold shoe buckles (cat. 51). A gold snuffbox marked by Myers may have been made for a fellow member of King David's Lodge (cat. 50). But Myers's role as a Mason may have provided him with other types of contacts: both his doctor, Peter Middleton, and William Malcolm, from whom he purchased merchandise in the 1780s, were prominent Masons.[226]

WORKSHOP PERSONNEL

The location of Myers's workshop during these years is uncertain. He may have remained in the space leased from Elias Desbrosses beginning in July 1764. In June 1771, he put up for auction a 22-foot-wide house and lot on Elbow Street, where he may also have operated his workshop.[227]

The identities of apprentices or other craftsmen associated

with Myers during these years cannot be ascertained, but his increased volume of production indicates the assistance of others. Dr. Middleton charged Myers for treating an otherwise unidentified "Andrew Barnsley" between 1771 and 1775, and as Middleton's other charges were all for members of Myers's family, Leo Hershkowitz suggested that Barnsley may have been an apprentice or journeyman living in Myers's household.[228] However, no subsequent record for a silversmith or any individual by that name resident in New York has been located. In 1796 and 1797, a Benjamin "Lusada" was listed as a silversmith in the New York City directory.[229] If this is the Benjamin Louzada who was the son of Moses Louzada and nephew of Aaron Louzada of New York, he would have been born no later than 1750 and trained between about 1765 and 1772.[230] Myers presumably would have been his master, as Benjamin was a first cousin of Myers's second wife, Joyce. No advertisements or other information on Louzada's work as silversmith have been found.

Another slave recorded as belonging to Myers, named Tom, was treated by Dr. Middleton at the King Street home between 1771 and 1775.[231] As an adult male slave of an urban craftsman, Tom might have been trained to assist in the workshop. In 1758, John Hastier advertised for a runaway "lusty well-set Negro Man, named Jasper . . . [who] understands the Silversmith's Trade."[232] At least two Philadelphia silversmiths, John Bayly in 1763 and George Christopher Dowig in 1770, offered for sale male slaves "which can work at the Silversmith Trade."[233] Southern silversmiths such as William Faris of Annapolis and Alexander Petrie of Charleston owned male slaves who were highly valued for their skills as silversmiths.[234] In 1784, the silversmithing skills of one slave apparently were shared by Myers's former partner Benjamin Halsted and other silversmiths:

Eight Dollars Reward. Ran-Away from the subscriber, a negro man, named JOHN FRANCES, *but commonly called* JACK: *he is about 40 years of age . . . speaks good English, by trade a goldsmith. . . . Said negro was carried to New York and left in charge of Mr. Ephraim Brasher, goldsmith, from whom he absconded, and returned to me after skulking about this city for a considerable time. . . . Whoever takes up said negro and delivers him to John Le Telier, goldsmith in Market street, or to the subscriber in New York, shall have the above reward, and all reasonable charges paid.*
BENJAMIN HALSTED [235]

As a brazier, Myers's youngest brother, Asher, may also have assisted Myers with certain tasks. The cast brass crowns on the Torah finials made by Myer Myers (cats. 63, 64, 100) as well as the pair of brass candlesticks Myer Myers engraved in 1787 (cat. 142) possibly could have been made or supplied by his brother. Asher was sworn a Freeman of the City as a "Brazier" on September 30, 1755.[236] Documentary information relating to his career indicates that he made or sold a wide variety of copper-alloy objects. In 1769 and 1770, he was paid £100.14.6 for supplying two bells for City Hall and one for the jail as well as £20.5.6 for "Soddering the flatt Copper Roof of the City Hall."[237] In the account book of the New York City pewterer Henry Will, Asher was credited in 1772 for "2 Copper Scale Bowls" that cost £1.11.6, and in 1774 for "1 Sawspan" that cost 18 shillings and "mending a wash Kettle" for 5 shillings, although he was also billed in 1772 for "a Copper Cover" that cost 17 shillings.[238] His "Braziers Work to the Water Works in 1775," amounting to £45.15.10, was not paid for by the city until April 9, 1788, one year before his death on May 7, 1789.[239] During his time in Norwalk, Connecticut, Asher was also working: his brother-in-law Samson Mears requested from Philadelphia in February 1779 "about fifty wt of sheet copper to send Mr. Asher Myers."[240] No copper or copper-alloy objects marked by Asher Myers have survived, if he ever used a mark. His New York workshop was continued in the 1790s by his sons Judah and Sampson Myers.[241]

MYER'S WORKSHOP: PRODUCTION AND STYLE

Although the number and identity of the workers in Myers's shop cannot be determined, there are other ways of confirming the increased production of the shop between 1765 and the Revolutionary War. Marks provide one form of evidence. Over half of Myers's surviving production is marked with surname MARK 9, which cannot be conclusively documented to use prior to the second half of the 1760s (Appendix I). Given that only a relatively small number of these objects can be dated, in terms of style, to the last decade of his life, and his production during the Revolutionary War was necessarily limited, approximately 125 of his 380 extant objects can be ascribed to the eleven years between 1765 and 1776. Moreover, a survey of these objects indicates an increase not only in the workshop's overall production, but specifically in the less expensive forms more likely to be made for ready sale. Some of this work, such as the chased sugar dishes and milk pots, involved skilled labor, but nevertheless seems to have been made in quantities equal to that of the plain alternatives. Barbara Ward observed a shift about 1750 toward a higher production of ready-made silver objects by Samuel and Thomas Edwards of Boston.[242] A similar strategy could have informed Myers's workshop's production prior to 1765, but the objects have not survived to prove or disprove the hypothesis.

Myers continued to make exceptional, labor-intensive, commissioned objects during this period, and indeed the objects for which he is perhaps best known today— the pierced-work Torah finials, cake basket, and dish ring— all date to this period. Moreover, on certain special commissions after 1765 he further refined the placement of his surname mark in such a way that it functioned as a "signature," something marks in England were never intended to do (Appendix I). On the Van

Fig. 21. Cat. 55 (detail).

Wyck waiter (cat. 56), his surname mark was struck as part of the engraved inscription, and on the dish ring (cat. 79), two strikes of his surname mark were given equal prominence with the owners' monogram. These unusually prominent locations indicate his pride in his work.

Myers's increased production may have been in part a response to the restrictions on imports from England. After the mid-1760s, the importation of English silver became a highly charged political issue. Beginning in 1768, a succession of boycotts and non-importation agreements relating to English goods greatly reduced the quantities of English silver exported to the Colonies. For retail silversmiths in New York, particularly jewelers, these agreements jeopardized their livelihood. Simeon Coley and Thomas Richardson, both jewelers from London, were threatened by mobs of patriotic New Yorkers in July and September 1769, respectively, for flouting the ban on selling imported goods.[243] However, for workshops like Myers's, capable of large-scale production, these restrictions may have had a positive impact on the demand for their wares, both wholesale and retail.

During the decade preceding the outbreak of the American Revolution, Myers's interpretation of the Rococo shifted from the sculptural ornament of the 1750s to more delicate effects, in response to less flamboyant interpretations of the Rococo style in England and Europe as the more restrained Neoclassical style grew in popularity. The majority of Myers's waiters are simple hexagonals (cat. 57), less complicated than their earlier counterparts (cats. 3, 10). Their narrow, gadrooned rims, replacing the cast borders with rich textural contrasts favored

in the preceding decade, followed London waiters and plates of the 1760s.[244] Narrow gadrooned borders also appeared on Myers's milk pots, sugar dishes, and bottle stands at this time (cats. 75, 76, 81). Finials on coffeepots were reduced in scale and rendered in delicate relief (cat. 47). This emphasis on more delicate effects and abstract patterns in Myers's silver was most splendidly realized in the chased and pierced objects produced at this time (cats. 78–80, 85, 86). An aesthetic inspired by pierced work seems to have permeated cast elements of Myers's silver as well: the cast handles of an openwork pattern closely related to pierced work appeared on two porringers (cats. 45, 46).

SPECIALIST CRAFTSMEN: ENGRAVERS

Specialist craftsmen, particularly chasers and piercers, played an even more important role in the creation of silver in Myers's shop than they had in the previous decade. About 1765, a different engraver took over the execution of armorials and monograms on major commissions from Myers's workshop. His work ranks among the finest engraving found on Colonial American silver. Two magnificent examples are the Smith arms on a punch bowl (cat. 55, fig. 21) and the allegorical scene and surrounding frame on the Van Wyck waiter of 1768 (cat. 56, fig. 22). In contrast to the earlier armorials, the overall design of these is looser and less confined, with foliage fanning outward from the frame. The scale of the frame is smaller in relation to the design, and the scrolls forming it are clearly separated from the shellwork, with no overlapping leaves. The

Fig. 22. Cat. 56 (detail).

Fig. 23. Cat. 57 (detail).

execution, though looser and with less detailed forms, is superb. Deep lines and sharp cuts accent some areas of the design; instead of the evenly spaced, regular shading lines, alternating thick and thin lines create a more lively pattern. This craftsman also used a considerable amount of crosshatching to contrast light and shaded areas. The style is very similar to printed designs published in England in the 1760s, such as the *New Book of Ornaments*, published in 1762 by the otherwise unidentified P. Baretti.[245]

On Myers's silver of the early 1770s, what appears to be the same engraver's style underwent further development toward an increasingly looser execution and more abstract forms. His rendition of the Philipse arms on a pair of waiters (cat. 57, fig. 23) has the same thick and thin shading lines seen on the Smith arms, but the overall execution is more rapid, and outlines in particular are rendered in staccato strokes. An even more abstracted frame surrounds the inscription on the waiter commissioned from Myers by Maria Van Beverhoudt (cat. 59, fig. 24). The elements of the design have been turned into abstract forms, although the use of thick and thin lines and the nervous energy of the execution indicate that it is from the same hand or workshop. Both the Philipse and Van Beverhoudt waiters also exhibit a greater concentration of heavy strokes and detail on the right side of the design.

Crests and monograms executed by this craftsman or his workshop display the same loosening of technique and abstraction of detail found on the later coats of arms. The Goelet crest on a small waiter (cat. 58) was executed by this workshop during the late 1760s or early 1770s, as were crests on

another pair of waiters by Myers.[246] The "DR" monograms found on the silver purchased for Dorothea (Remsen) Brinckerhoff about 1772 (cats. 85, 86, 122), exhibits the same nervous energy and staccato touches found on the Van Beverhoudt and Philipse waiters.

This engraver executed decoration on silver by several of Myers's competitors, including Ephraim Brasher and John Heath (cat. 109), which suggests he may have worked as an independent craftsman rather than as an employee of Myers's workshop.[247] It is possible that this engraved decoration on Myers's silver of the late 1760s and early 1770s represented a later stylistic development of the same craftsman who executed the Livingston and Clarkson armorials, although enough differences exist to suggest that they were the work of different individuals. The later engraving work does not resemble any work by Elisha Gallaudet, particularly the 1767 set of Literary Society medals (p. 38). The figures and other details of these medals are reminiscent of, but not identical to, those found on Myers's Van Wyck waiter of 1768 (cat. 56).

Myers relied on these specialists to execute only the most elaborate decorative engraving on his silver. This was the typical practice for leading London silversmiths such as Paul de Lamerie, who repeatedly used the same highly skilled craftsman to engrave major commissions, whereas the routine engraved decoration shows a wider variety of hands.[248] Myers, too, did not use these skilled craftsmen exclusively, particularly for less demanding tasks such as crests and monograms. In the later 1760s and early 1770s, another engraver created several elaborate monograms on silver from Myers's workshop,

Fig. 24. Cat. 59 (detail).

Fig. 25. Cat. 78 (detail).

including the "SSC" on the bread basket (cat. 78, fig. 25) and the "AB" on the waiter (cat. 83, fig. 26). Both of these monograms exhibit minimal shading, and small dots are used to accent the main strokes of the letters where they form additional tendrils. The same absence of shading pervades the "AB" monogram's frame, whose symmetrical format and regular, even strokes are very different in character from the nervous, asymmetrical, dramatically shaded frames on the Van Wyck or Philipse waiters. The frame's design is strikingly similar to the frame enclosing the scene at the top of a presentation certificate engraved in Philadelphia for Sir William Johnson in 1770 by Henry Dawkins (fig. 27). Dawkins had returned to New York by 1774, and it is possible that he was the craftsman who engraved Myers's waiter. Like Myers, Dawkins was a Freemason.[249]

CHASERS

Unlike engraving, chasing was practiced in Myers's workshop for a relatively brief period. Chasing was a purely ornamental technique, serving no practical purpose for identifying ownership, and its popularity in both England and America waxed and waned as styles changed over the course of the eighteenth century. The rich, sculptural effects created by this technique were a perfect means of realizing Rococo ornament.

Chased ornament in the Rococo style seems to have become popular in New York during the economic boom of the later 1750s and persisted until the Revolutionary War. A "large chaced Salver wt. about 49 oz." was reported stolen in 1757, and one year later Joseph Pinto offered "chased Silver Milk Pots" at his shop (p. 36).[250] Much of this chased silver undoubtedly was imported, such as the chased milk pot identified as "English make" that was stolen in 1762.[251] "A Variety of neat chas'd silver coffee pots with cases" headed a Captain Jacobson's list of silver and fancy goods "just imported" from London in April 1765.[252] Surviving pieces of English silver with chased ornament and histories of ownership in New York confirm the popularity of chased Rococo decoration beginning in the mid-1750s (cats. 120, 121). A tea kettle and stand, coffeepot, and pair of tea caddies with Rococo chasing, all made in London in 1762–63, were purchased by Samuel and Judith (Crommelin) Verplanck, presumably for their return to New York in 1763 after their marriage in the Netherlands two years earlier.[253] A large two-handled cup with similar Rococo chasing, marked by the London silversmith Francis Crump in 1762–63, belonged to Isaac and Elizabeth (Peachman) Gouverneur, who were married in 1777.[254]

The earliest documented Rococo chasing on silver marked by a New York silversmith is the flat-chased ornament on a bowl made before 1756 by Richard Van Dyck for Benjamin and Abigail (Taylor) Woolsey of Connecticut and Dosoris, Long Island (fig. 28).[255] This was about the same time that Rococo chasing appeared in Philadelphia on silver by Philip Syng, Jr., and Joseph Richardson, Sr., but several years after Boston silversmiths began employing it in the mid-1740s.[256] A craftsman who apparently was associated with the Van Dyck workshop

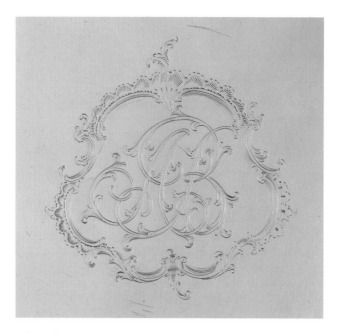

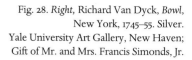

Fig. 28. *Right,* Richard Van Dyck, *Bowl,*
New York, 1745–55. Silver.
Yale University Art Gallery, New Haven;
Gift of Mr. and Mrs. Francis Simonds, Jr.

Fig. 26. Cat. 83 (detail).

Fig. 27. Henry Dawkins, *Presentation Certificate* (detail),
Philadelphia, 1770. Engraving, restrike from original copperplate.
The New-York Historical Society.

executed the chasing on the Woolsey bowl. Identical chasing appears on three other objects marked by Van Dyck: an undocumented bowl and tankard as well as a tankard that was presented to the Woolseys' daughter-in-law after her marriage in 1742.[257] This chaser's distinctive style does not resemble that on other New York or London silver. Kathryn Buhler compared his work to chasing on contemporaneous Irish silver.[258] Similarly dense, finely rendered flat-chasing is found on silver made in Dublin as well as Edinburgh and Glasgow in the early 1740s, and it is possible that the chaser was an immigrant from Ireland or Scotland.[259]

Although such chased ornament was popular among New York customers, it never became common on silver made in the city during the later Colonial period. Some customers probably declined to have commissioned objects chased because of the additional cost. The pair of chased sauceboats that Catherine Schuyler purchased from Halsted and Myers in 1760 was priced at 18 shillings per ounce, whereas the "plain Silver Waiter" was priced at 16 shillings per ounce (Appendix II, no. 1). In 1767, Myer Myers prepared an estimate for Sir William Johnson for a silver soup tureen that cost "if plain,

£53.15s, and, if chased, £67 10s," a difference of almost £14, or an additional 25 percent, to the cost of an unornamented object.[260]

Chasing may also have been uncommon on New York silver because it required specialized craftsmen. In her work on Boston silversmiths of the later Colonial period, Patricia Kane concluded that the technique of chasing had survived as a residual skill in that city, even though chasing was virtually absent from Boston silver for almost thirty years.[261] Chasing probably had continued more actively in New York, in part because of the persistence into the 1730s of traditional Dutch forms with chased ornament, such as Jacob Boelen's "Cup with two twisted Ears chas'd with Scutcheons" stolen in 1733, forms made by craftsmen of Huguenot as well as Dutch ancestry.[262] The Baroque quality of the bold, symmetrical chasing found on a teapot made after about 1755 by John Moulinar may represent the work of a chaser who had learned his craft through the residual local tradition.[263]

Unlike their counterparts in Boston, Myers and other New York silversmiths could also draw on a number of immigrant craftsmen who specialized in chasing, many of them from

Continental Europe, where this type of ornament was more common. The earliest was the silversmith Daniel Christian Fueter, whose newspaper advertisements specifically mentioned chasing. Another immigrant silversmith who advertised chasing was Otto Paul de Parisien, a French Huguenot by ancestry, although he came to New York in 1756 from Berlin. The following year he stood as godfather in the French Church for the son of engraver and fellow Huguenot Elisha Gallaudet.[264] Parisien, a "French Protestant," was naturalized on January 18, 1763, with Gallaudet as one of the witnesses for his seven years' residency.[265] On January 31, 1769, Parisien paid the Freemanship fee, since he had not served his apprenticeship locally, as a "silversmith."[266] His whereabouts during the Revolutionary War are unknown. By 1785, he had returned to New York and was listed in the directories as a "silversmith" until 1797, working in partnership with a son between 1789 and 1790.[267]

Parisien apparently was trained as a chaser, since his newspaper advertisements repeatedly mentioned this skill, although no piece of chased silver by him is known to the author. In 1763, he stated that he "undertakes chasing any Piece of old Plate," and six years later he offered to supply potential patrons "with all Kinds of wrought Plate, either chased or plain, according to any Pattern they shall please to send or direct; and by doing the Work in the best and neatest Manner, and at the cheapest Rates."[268] He may have served Myers's shop as a specialist outworker, at least during his first seven years in New York. It was not until two months after his naturalization in 1763 that he placed his first newspaper advertisement, describing himself as "from Berlin," when in fact he had already lived in New York for the requisite seven years.[269]

Other immigrant chasers worked in New York during these years. Between 1757 and 1763, Michael De Bruss advertised in New York that he performed "Curious Chasing or other Raised Work, in general, on Gold and Silver Watch-Cases, Snuff-Boxes, & c."[270] The best-known of these advertisements appeared in 1769, when Fueter advertised "Mr. John Anthony Beau, Chaiser, from Geneva, works with him; where Chaising in general, viz. Snuff Boxes, Watch Cases, & c. & c. is done in the best and cheapest Manner."[271] Beau only worked in New York for about three years; by 1772 he announced his arrival in Philadelphia as "A CELEBRATED CHASER" and offered to dec-

Fig. 29. Cat. 72 (detail).   Fig. 30. Cat. 63 (detail).

orate "watch-cases, coffee and tea pots, sugar-boxes, cream-pots, &c. in the genteelest and newest taste."[272]

Myer Myers offered chased silver for sale as early as 1760, when Halsted and Myers sold Catherine Schuyler a pair of chased sauceboats (Appendix II, no. 1). In their detailed 1763 advertisement (p. 34), Halsted and Myers noted that they kept for sale "a neat assortment of ready made plate, chased and plain." It is not known if these pieces were made in the workshop or imported; no chased objects survive with either mark used by the partnership.

The extant objects with chased decoration in the Rococo style that can be credited to manufacture in Myers's workshop all probably date after 1765. These include four pairs of Torah finials (cats. 63–66), a teapot (cat. 68), two bowls (cats. 69, 70), two matched sets of sugar dishes and milk pots (cats. 71–74), a sugar dish associated with a matching, unmarked milk pot (cats. 85, 86), two unmatched sugar dishes (cats. 67, 75), and an unmatched milk pot (cat. 76). These objects exhibit considerable stylistic cohesion, despite having ornament by different chasers. They have exaggerated inverted pyriform silhouettes, with broad midsections tapering to narrow extremities and diminutive bases, and many feature gadrooned borders. Nineteen of them also bear the same mark, MARK 9 (cat. 86 is unmarked). Such similarities suggest that these objects were made within a relatively short period of time, probably in the later 1760s and early 1770s. The documented examples include a sugar dish and milk pot with matching chased decoration (cats. 71, 72) purchased from Myers by William and Anna (Lawrence) Sackett, but the exact date is uncertain. The only chased objects from Myers's workshop with precise dates of manufacture are another sugar dish and milk pot made for Dorothea (Remsen) Brinckerhoff between 1772 and 1776 (cats. 85, 86) and Torah finials delivered to Philadelphia in 1772 (cats. 65, 66).

The chased ornament on silver from Myers's workshop was executed by a number of specialists. Much as he did with engravers, Myers employed at least four different chasers. The teapot and one bowl (cats. 68, 69) were executed by one chaser. The other bowl (cat. 70) and a sugar dish (cat. 85) are unique examples of different chasers' work for Myers. One pair of Torah finials (cat. 66) and a sugar dish (cat. 67) have a distinctive style of spiral fluting that may represent a single craftsman's handiwork.

As with engravers, Myers's relationship with one particular chaser seems to have lasted longer than with any of the others. This craftsman, who decorated twelve of the extant pieces, had a distinctive style (figs. 29, 30). Details that recur in his work include long, scrolled leaf forms with blunt, curled ends; smaller leaves with curled, pointed ends, usually clustered around flowers; a somewhat heavy-handed use of round punches to define the curls in the leaves or edges of petals; flowers with recessed, textured (often crosshatched) centers; meandering lines of small dots across the surface of shells; and trails of diminishing dots defining veining in the foliage. With the exception of the Torah finials, this chaser developed different designs for the ornament on different objects, although all his designs are centered on long, gently flowing lines.

A comparison of this craftsman's work to London chasing of the 1750s and 1760s reveals his indebtedness to contemporary London silver for his patterns of scrolls, shells, and flowers (cats. 120, 122).[273] But unlike these objects, the ornament on Myers's silver was executed as flat chasing rather than repoussé work. His chaser's ornament was linear in quality, with a limited range of depth and textural contrasts. All these characteristics relate to chasing found on contemporary silver made outside London, in both Scotland and Ireland.[274] Further evidence, discussed below (p. 56), suggests that this chaser may have been an Irish immigrant.

The conclusion that this craftsman's work for Myers dates to the mid-1760s or later is corroborated by chasing he executed for other New York silversmiths. He chased the ornament on a sugar bowl with a less exaggerated pyriform shape by John Burt Lyng, which could have been made as early as 1761, when Lyng registered as a Freeman, although in 1773, Lyng owned a house and lot in King Street next door to Myers's house.[275] He also chased a three-piece tea set marked by Pieter de Riemer that dates after 1763, when de Riemer completed his apprenticeship.[276] The same chasing appears on the milk pot matching a sugar dish marked by William Gilbert that was made after 1766 and may have been supplied by Myer Myers (cat. 113).

PIERCERS

The specialist ornament with which Myer Myers is most frequently associated today is pierced work. A relatively small number of pierced objects have the mark of Myers's workshop, including three pairs of Torah finials (cats. 63–65), a bread basket (cat. 78), a dish ring (cat. 79) and two pairs of bottle stands (cats. 80, 81). All these pierced objects bear the same mark, MARK 9, which is also the only mark used on the objects with chased decoration. Also like the chased objects, the pierced objects probably were produced in Myers's workshop within a relatively short period of time. The only securely dated object with piercing is a pair of Torah finials delivered to Congregation Mikveh Israel in 1772 (cat. 65).

Piercing was a slow and difficult technique, usually undertaken after a piece of hollow ware was raised, so it was generally entrusted to skilled specialists who would not compromise the labor already expended in raising the form. Unlike engraving and chasing, the techniques used in England for piercing silver changed significantly over the course of the eighteenth century. The pierced components of Baroque-style objects were fashioned with a hammer and chisel to strike out the open sections (fig. 30). By the middle of the century, piercing files and fretsaws were used to cut away the open parts of the design (cat. 123). Both these hand methods were superseded after 1770 by the fly press, which used pressure and steel dies to stamp out the patterns.[277]

The handcraft piercing techniques required significant time and skill, so that prior to mechanization, pierced work became a distinct sub-specialty within the silversmith's trade in London. Robert Barker's research has revealed that the eighteenth-century craftsmen who specialized in pierced work tended to form a discrete group in each generation, closely interconnected by their own apprenticeships to a related group of masters from the previous generation. For example, in London, the specialist piercers and basket makers Henry Bailey, Henry Green, Samuel Herbert, and William Plummer were all apprenticed to Edward Aldridge I.[278] Silversmiths with large retail operations, such as George Wickes or the successor firm of John Parker and Edward Wakelin, relied on these specialist workshops to supply them with pierced objects.[279]

No specialist piercers are known to have operated an independent workshop in Colonial America, but a few craftsmen trained as piercers clearly were active in New York during the third quarter of the eighteenth century. New York silversmiths marked virtually all the surviving pierced silver in the Rococo style made in Colonial America. In addition to the pierced objects from Myers's workshop, Daniel Christian Fueter marked a bread basket with an elaborate pierced pattern between 1754 and 1769, and John Heath marked pierced salts (cat. 110).[280] Moreover, Myers's former partner Benjamin Halsted and his brother Matthias advertised for sale in 1766 "a few silversmith's tools" that included "piercing, riffling and common files."[281] No piercing files described as such appeared in any surviving inventories of tools owned by Boston makers, although the jeweler John Codner had a "Small Spring Saw."[282] Joseph Richardson, Sr., of Philadelphia ordered pierced silver objects from London in the 1760s, but the earliest pierced objects bearing a Richardson mark were made by his sons after the Revolutionary War.[283]

Like chasing, the technique of chisel-piercing would have existed in New York as a residual skill, since the covers of Baroque casters as well as chafing dishes had elaborate pierced elements; Peter Van Dyck and Adrian Bancker both made these forms.[284] However, American-made pierced objects are rare, probably because of the highly organized, large-scale production of them in England. Imports of pierced objects to New York are well documented (cat. 123). This raises the question of whether any of Myers's pierced objects may have been imported and then marked by him. At least two pairs of salts that resemble salts by the London specialists David and Robert Hennell were marked in the 1760s by the New York silversmith John Heath (cat. 110).

A close examination of Myers's pierced silver, however, suggests that most of it was made in his workshop rather than imported and then marked by him. These objects were fabricated using a variety of piercing techniques. The Torah finials were chisel-pierced, and the dish ring, bread basket, and two pairs of bottle stands were saw-pierced. Chisel-piercing was not used by the majority of the large-scale London shops from the 1750s onward. Moreover, when compared to the high standard of contemporary London work, the design and execution of the piercing on Myers's Torah finials, as well as on the bread basket and dish ring, seem tentative, with relatively small piercings and occasional errors in laying out the design (fig. 31).

The three pairs of Torah finials (cats. 63–65) offer additional evidence that the piercing was done in Myers's shop. In these works, the chisel-pierced sections were also ornamented with chasing (fig. 30). These are the only instances known to the

Fig. 31. Cat. 78 (detail).

author of the two techniques being executed in combination on any piece of American Colonial silver, including other work by Myers. This combination was characteristic of Baroque-style objects made in England and the Continent during the late seventeenth and early eighteenth centuries, including the Sleath Torah finials that may have served as the models for Myers's work (see cats. 63–65). But chasing over piercing was uncommon on London pierced work in the Rococo style, which suggests that the craftsman or men who executed it had trained outside of the capital. The chasing on the Torah finials appears to be by the same artisan who ornamented the majority of chased domestic objects made in Myers's workshop; the continuous, flowing design is typical of his work, as are the flowers with recessed, textured centers and the long leaves with rounded, curled ends. The piercing was done with a chisel, a technique closely related to chasing, and the fluency with which the piercing and chasing work together on Myers's Torah finials strongly suggests that they were created by a single craftsman.

As noted, the chaser who worked in association with Myers in the late 1760s and early 1770s may have been an Irish immigrant, and there is stronger evidence for identifying the piercer as an immigrant. Not only does his chasing style relate to Scottish and Irish work, but the dish ring, a rare form in English silver, was common in Ireland during the second half of the eighteenth century (cat. 79). One group of Irish dish rings in the Rococo style features designs entirely chased over the pierced work.

The origin of the two pairs of identical bottle stands (cats. 80, 81) is less certain. They were made by a different piercer, who created a more delicate, openwork pattern than those found on the bread basket or dish ring. His pierced work is more accomplished and very carefully finished, with no saw marks easily visible. Although these bottle stands may have

been made in Myers's workshop, the quality of their execution, particularly in comparison to Myers's other pierced silver, raises the possibility that they were English imports that Myers marked and sold.

JEWELERS AND GOLD CHASERS

The only extant goldwork with Myers's mark also dates to this period. The fabrication of gold jewelry and related objects in urban centers tended to be the work of specialists. In her study of the organization of the silversmith's trade in Colonial Boston, Barbara Ward made the distinction between small-workers, who made objects such as spoons, boxes, and buckles and tended to work as jobbers for larger silversmiths' workshops, and jewelers, who set gemstones and worked in enamel and tended to make their living as retailers.[285] The Boston jeweler Daniel Boyer, for example, sold gold rings to a number of Boston silversmiths and in turn retailed silver flatware and routine silver hollow ware made by others, which he stamped with his own marks.[286]

Six examples of gold objects marked by Myers survive: a snuffbox (cat. 50), a pair of shoe buckles (cat. 51), and three mourning rings (cats. 48, 49, and one now missing).[287] These gold objects form a relatively homogeneous group. All bear the same initials mark, MARK 6, and most can be dated to the 1760s.[288] The Panet and Morris mourning rings are both dated 1764, and the pair of buckles probably was made between 1765 and 1770. The missing mourning ring was made following Philip Philipse's death on May 9, 1768. As discussed below, the snuffbox may have been made in connection with the founding of King David's Masonic Lodge in 1769.

Documentary sources provide additional information concerning gold jewelry made in Myers's workshop or sold by him during the later 1760s. On March 24, 1766, Nicholas Bayard paid Myers £15.16.4 "for his own accot. & on accot. of a gold seal delivd Miss Ann Burk" (Appendix II, no. 3). A second, undated receipt recorded Myers "making a pair gold buttons" for which he received "7 grains gold" (the smallest unit of measure in the Troy scale) for Evert Bancker, Jr. (Appendix II, no. 7). Rosenbaum published the latter document with the date 1767, although the source for her information is uncertain.[289] These buttons may be one of the two pairs of gold "sleeve buttons" bequeathed by Evert Bancker to his son Abraham, who also inherited a mourning ring marked "MM," although this "MM" may refer to the decedent's initials rather than the craftsman's stamp.[290] Less ambiguous is the "plain Gold Ring, Maker's name M.M. the owner's name R.A. both inside," advertised as lost in New York in 1781.[291] In a November 1766 letter to Michael Gratz, Myers informed him that "I have sold one of your rings for 40 1/2 dollars" (Appendix II, no. 5), an object Gratz had apparently consigned to him; its high cost suggests it was set with precious stones.

Myers, like his counterparts in Boston, probably relied on specialist jewelers to supply him with gold rings, as the surviving examples all have enamel decoration and one was set with stones (cat. 49). As Martha Gandy Fales pointed out, New York City in the later Colonial period had more documented, independent jewelers than either Boston or Philadelphia. As with chasers and engravers, the majority of these were immigrants from London, including Charles Dutens in 1751, Simeon Coley in 1766, James Bennett in 1768, Thomas Richardson in 1769, and Jeremiah Andrews, William Bateman, Henry Hart, and the partners Whitehouse and Reeve in 1774.[292] Myers may have benefited from contacts with Ashkenazic Jews who worked as jewelers on both sides of the Atlantic. A jeweler named Henry "Miers" of London wrote a letter in Yiddish to Barnard Gratz in 1763 offering smallwork "steel or p.b. [pinchbeck], or tin or other wares for women's use, hats, bonnets, ribbons, gores or necklaces, wash [presumably gold wash] goods or earrings."[293] Jacob Marcus identified as Jewish the Henry Hart who advertised in New York in 1775 that he "MAKES and SELLS all kinds of JEWELRY."[294] Although he was not a member of the Hart family of New York, he possibly may have been related to the family of Judah Hart, a silversmith and rabbi in Portsmouth, England.[295]

Over the course of his career, Myers engaged one or more specialist jewelers to work in his shop. The Englishman Lewis Meares, who ran away from his service in 1753, was "a jeweller and engraver by trade" (p. 31). At least two other New York silversmiths engaged jewelers to work in their shops during the later Colonial period. In 1746, Thauvet Besly advertised the arrival of Peter Lorin from London, who later worked independently in New York as a jeweler.[296] Shortly after his arrival in New York in 1763, Charles Oliver Bruff was "provided with jeweller's, one from London and another from France."[297] Myers's partner Benjamin Halsted may have been responsible for expanding this aspect of Myers's operation during their partnership. Their advertisement in 1763 included "diamond rings, garnet hoops, and broaches in gold, crystal buttons and ear-rings, in ditto" (p. 34). The partnership lasted into the mid-1760s, and Myers maintained business dealings with Halsted well into the 1780s, when Halsted was working as an independent retailer of jewelry (pp. 66–67).

Snuffboxes and buckles, forms more commonly made by a smallworker rather than a jeweler, required a chaser to execute their ornament. Gold chasers constituted a separate trade from silversmiths in London, as the small scale and specialized skills of their work allowed them to operate independently.[298] In both London and Amsterdam, the craft of gold chasing was dominated by German-speaking artisans, and it is therefore not surprising to find that the Swiss immigrants Daniel Christian Fueter and his son Lewis Fueter worked together with John Anthony Beau of Geneva from 1769 to 1772.[299]

It is possible that Otto Paul de Parisien, who had emigrated from Berlin, worked for Myers in a similar capacity. Parisien's advertisements indicate that he sold gold jewelry in addition to silver hollow ware, although these trades usually were separate. In 1765, Parisien reported the theft of a box containing nine rings, presumably gold, set with a variety of precious stones, including diamonds, emeralds, rubies, garnets, and "a Saphio."[300] There is no indication that he had made these particular rings, but in 1792 he informed customers "that he continues to make all sorts of large plate after any pattern given him, and all kinds of gold lockets, pins and rings; Also, executes the most elegant devices in hair, chases, gilds and tries ores on reasonable terms."[301] Perhaps his training as a chaser included gold chasing; as noted above, craftsmen from Germany were associated with the kind of gold chasing done on snuffboxes in London.

RELATIONSHIPS WITH OTHER SILVERSMITHS

The increase in Myers's production after 1765 apparently induced him to reach a larger share of the local market by retailing his work through other silversmiths, primarily craftsmen who lacked large workshops for producing hollow ware. Other than extant objects, little documentation survives to permit speculation regarding this practice. Based on similarities of their silver, Myers appears to have supplied hollow ware to the silversmith William W. Gilbert (cat. 134). Like Benjamin Halsted, Gilbert apparently came from a relatively affluent background. He was the son and namesake of William Gilbert and Aeltie (Verdon) Gilbert, and his paternal grandfather, also named William Gilbert, had been a prosperous baker and salt-measurer who in his will left a house and lot to each of his five children.[302] William W. Gilbert's marriage to Catherina Cosine (cat. 135) provided him with additional wealth.

Gilbert never registered as a Freeman, perhaps indicating that he may not have completed an apprenticeship, and the documentary evidence that survives for his career suggests that he primarily was a retail silversmith who sold objects made by others. He was operating a retail store by August 1770, when "some Villains broke into the Shop of Mr. Gilbert, Silver-Smith in the Broad Way, and robb'd the same of near two Hundred Pounds, in Plate & c."[303] Even allowing for an inflated valuation, £200 worth of silver and related merchandise was a large amount for a twenty-four-year-old craftsman to have on hand, particularly one for whom few large or specialized objects survive. In that same year, moreover, Gilbert purchased for £10.11.3 "a Parcel of Pewter ware" and "London pewter" weighing 62 pounds from the pewterer Henry Will, a quantity that must have been bought for resale.[304] He was listed as a silversmith in the 1786 New York directory and as chairman of the Gold and Silver Smith's Society in 1787, but his profession in the latter year was replaced by the title

"Esq[uire]."[305] In the 1790 census, he owned four slaves, and beginning the following year, the firm of William W. Gilbert and Son was listed in the city directories as "merchants."[306] By this time he had also begun a career in politics, serving as an alderman for the Dock Ward (1782–88), in the State Assembly (1788–93 and 1803–08), and in the State Senate (1809–12).

About thirty-five silver objects marked by Gilbert survive, including two small bowls (cat. 114), three canns, and a waiter. Over one-third of the remainder are milk pots and sugar dishes, and another third are flatware. Gilbert's few large pieces of hollow ware were a pyriform teapot in the Colonial style and two teapots in the Neoclassical style (cat. 116).[307] This high percentage of routine forms suggests that Gilbert may have retailed silver made by working craftsmen, his brother-in-law Ephraim Brasher among them.[308] Several objects by Gilbert in the Rococo style were not only identical to objects marked by Myers, but they were also engraved and chased by the same specialist craftsmen (cats. 53, 72, 113, 114), suggesting that Gilbert was marking and selling objects that originated in Myers's workshop. A cann and waiter marked by William Gilbert was engraved with the Bayard crest by the specialist engraver who worked for Myers after 1765, and these routine forms as well as the decoration may have been executed in Myers's workshop.[309]

Myers may well have supplied silver to other silversmiths in New York, although their retail careers are less well documented than Gilbert's. Only about twenty objects with marks by Parisien have survived, despite his forty years of activity as a craftsman; the objects include hollow ware such as tankards as well as flatware and jewelry.[310] An inverted pyriform coffeepot marked by Parisien descended in the McEvers family together with a pair of candlesticks by Myers (cat. 8), and its cast elements are identical to those on coffeepots by Myers.[311] Parisien also marked a porringer (cat. 111) with a handle made with the same casting pattern as examples marked by Myers and Halsted and Myers (cats. 45, 46). If Parisien worked primarily as a specialist outworker or jeweler, it seems plausible that Myers had supplied these objects.

Cary Dunn was another New York silversmith who may have retailed objects made in Myers's workshop. Dunn's first son was baptized in the Presbyterian Church on June 10, 1759, indicating that Dunn himself was born about 1735.[312] He paid for his Freemanship as a "Goldsmith" on October 29, 1765, which suggests that he had not been apprenticed in New York; his advertisement in 1774 acting as an intermediary for a group of immigrants "from the North of Scotland" suggests that he may have been a Scottish immigrant.[313] The scant documentary evidence suggests that Dunn worked as a jeweler: a 1775 bill of sale charges Philip Schuyler £7.4.0 for "Making" nine gold mourning rings, in addition to the £7.7.0 for the gold.[314] Dunn's directory listings in partnership with his son during the later 1780s and 1790s were as "gold-smiths and jewellers, hard-

ware store."[315] Few examples of large hollow ware by Dunn survive, and, as noted on p. 37, a coffeepot and stand marked by him are identical to examples made by Myers. Dunn also marked a porringer with a handle cast from the same pattern as cats. 45 and 46, and a sugar dish with chased Rococo ornament similar to that on Myers's silver has been published as Dunn's work.[316] Dunn may have made these objects using casting patterns or a specialist chaser from Myers's shop, but as a jeweler it seems more plausible that he was retailing hollow ware made by Myers. Myers's relationship with a jeweler such as Cary Dunn may well have been reciprocal, with Dunn supplying jewelry to Myers's retail store.

PATRONAGE

In the decade leading up to the Revolutionary War, Myers continued to attract wealthy and influential patrons. Thomas Smith (cat. 55) served in the second Provincial Congress and Samuel Cornell (cat. 131) was a supporter of Governor William Tryon, but overall there were fewer figures from the political and military elite. Theodorus Van Wyck (cat. 56), and Abraham and Dorothea (Remsen) Brinckerhoff (cats. 136, 137) all belonged to important mercantile families. Some patrons represented the second generation of families who had been his clients in the previous decade. Peter R. Livingston undoubtedly chose Myers as a silversmith because of his parents' patronage (cats. 32, 34). Philena Barnes, daughter of Thomas Barnes, may have been the customer for a bowl (cat. 53). William Samuel Johnson (fig. 32), the surviving son of Samuel and Charity Johnson, inherited all the silver his parents purchased from Myers. But in at least two instances (cats. 26, 52), he may have commissioned objects himself. If so, his taste directly emulated that of his parents, perhaps not surprising considering that he had married the daughter of his father's second wife and followed his father as president of Columbia University. A parallel situation exists in the Johnsons' patronage of the Stratford silversmith Robert Fairchild. He had made a sauce spoon for Charity Johnson before her move to New York in 1754, and subsequently made a chafing dish for either William Samuel Johnson when he returned to Stratford in 1747 or for Samuel Johnson after his retirement in Stratford in 1763.[317]

One patron who may have connected to Myers through Freemasonry was Sir William Johnson. Johnson was general superintendent of Indian Affairs in North America and had been created a baronet for his part in routing French forces at the Battle of Lake George. His only documented purchases from Myer Myers, none of which have survived, were made in 1767, two years before the founding of King David's Lodge, but at a date when Myers may already have joined the Masons (p. 47). On February 22, George Croghan, Johnson's agent with the Indians, submitted an account listing "20 silver

Fig. 32. Thomas McIlworth,
William Samuel Johnson,
New York, 1761. Oil on canvas.
Smith College Museum of Art,
Northampton, Massachusetts.

medals" from Myer Myers costing £39.19.10 1/2.[318] On April 24, Johnson was sent Myers's bill to John Wetherhead, Johnson's agent in New York City, "for tablespoons."[319] More aristocratic in intention was an estimate he received from Myers in April 1767 for making a five-quart tureen, a form unknown in surviving American Colonial silver.[320]

Johnson and Myers have been linked with a Masonic commission by a letter of February 11, 1767 from John Wetherhead. Now destroyed, the letter was summarized in 1909 as "mentioning the *Annual Register* and some jewels which he sends; also inclosing Myer Myers's bill."[321] This has been interpreted in some sources to mean that Myers supplied Johnson with Masonic jewels.[322] However, at the founding ceremony for St. Patrick's Lodge in Johnstown on May 23, 1766, the minutes recorded "Sr. Wm Johnson being invested with the Badges of

his Office [Master] as well as the rest of the Officers," indicating that jewels or "Badges" were in the Lodge's possession one year before Wetherhead's letter.[323] The "jewels" mentioned by Wetherhead may have been gems rather than Masonic badges, and the bill could have been for either the medals or tablespoons. The unmarked silver jewels for the Master, Senior Warden, and Junior Warden now owned by St. Patrick's Lodge No. 4 do not appear to be Myers's work.[324]

If the Johnsons and Livingstons were responsible for Myers's most significant commissions in the later 1750s and early 1760s, Samuel Cornell and his wife, Susannah Mabson, were his most important patrons of the later 1760s and early 1770s. Born in Flushing, Long Island, in 1732, Cornell left New York when he was about twenty-five years old and settled in New Bern, North Carolina, where in 1756 he married Susannah Mabson, the daughter of Arthur Mabson of New Bern.[325] Cornell's successful career as a West Indies merchant and landowner paralleled and supported his political ambitions. He became a leading financial supporter of Governor William Tryon, who in 1770 appointed him to the Provincial Council.[326] During the Revolutionary War, Cornell not surprisingly was a staunch Loyalist, and his extensive landholdings in North Carolina were attainted as Tory property by the Patriot government.

With the exception of the Torah finials, the silver that the Cornells commissioned from Myers has probably played the greatest role in establishing Myers's subsequent reputation as a silversmith. Cornell may have come to patronize Myers through his cousin Martha (Cornell) Thorne, who had acquired a sugar dish from Myers around 1754 (cat. 13). At the time of their marriage in 1756, Samuel and Susannah Cornell purchased a coffeepot (cat. 19) from Myers that is identical in its style and marks to Charity Johnson's coffeepot of 1754–58 (cat. 20). All the silver acquired from Myers by the Cornells subsequently has been dated to the time of their wedding,[327] but in fact, the Cornells returned to Myers about a decade later to commission a more substantial group of silver: a cann, bread basket, dish ring, and pair of bottle stands (cats. 77–80). Myers's dish ring and bottle stands are the only extant Colonial American examples of these forms; the bread basket is one of the few American-made examples of this form from the Colonial period. These forms are also exceptionally rare examples of pierced silver in the Rococo style. As an assemblage of table silver, they evoke the opulent lifestyle that Samuel and Susannah Cornell enjoyed before the American Revolution. Cornell was an ambitious, largely self-made man, and his political and personal aims required great self-aggrandizement.

More conventional forms for dining and drinking tea or coffee were acquired from Myers by Abraham Brinckerhoff and his wife, Dorothea Remsen, around the time of their marriage on December 17, 1772, which united two long-established New York families of Dutch ancestry. In the seventeenth century, both the Brinckerhoffs and Remsens had settled farms in Flushing, Long Island. By the eighteenth century, the younger generations of both families had moved to New York City to pursue mercantile careers. Abraham was the son of the merchant Joris (or George) Brinckerhoff and his second wife, Marytie Van Deursen, who were married in 1741; Dorothea was the daughter of the merchant Peter Remsen and Jannetje de Hardt.

Abraham's sister Lucretia, who had married Jacobus Lefferts, Jr., in April 1772 and acquired a waiter from Myers's shop (cat. 82), may have influenced the Brinckerhoffs' choice of Myers. The silver that Abraham and Dorothea purchased from Myers is distinctive in a number of ways. There seems to have been a division between the objects that each spouse bought at the time of the marriage, since the sauceboats (cat.

84) and waiter (cat. 83) are engraved with Abraham's initials and the tea wares (cats. 85, 86, 122) and a ladle with Dorothea's; no objects bearing both their initials are known to the author. Within Myers's surviving work, the Brincker-hoff/Remsen silver also represents a large group acquired within a relatively short period of time, presumably no earlier than 1772 nor later than Myers's removal from New York in the summer of 1776. It seems unlikely that unmarried individuals in their twenties would have acquired such impressive objects prior to their engagement, particularly since they chose complementary forms. The different chasing on the sugar dish and milk pot (cats. 85, 86) may represent hasty production by different workmen in Myers's shop in order to meet a deadline, although it is also possible that the two objects were not made or acquired at same time. Typical of Myers's work from the early 1770s, the silver owned by Abraham Brinckerhoff and Dorothea Remsen was more traditional than the contemporaneous silver commissioned by Samuel and Susannah Cornell, perhaps because it was commissioned by a couple whose wealth was largely inherited.

These high-style objects that Myers made for his Christian clients, modeled on and in some cases cast from English prototypes, contrast dramatically with the examples of his work owned by his Jewish patrons. The surviving domestic objects Myers made for his fellow Jews were, without exception, small or routine forms.[328] Even Jews who owned substantial pieces of silver seem to have obtained modest objects from Myers. David and Margaret Franks owned silver by Paul de Lamerie, possibly received as wedding gifts, but they acquired only a small waiter (fig. 10) and a salt shovel (cat. 4) by Myers. Among the impressive array of silver hollow ware stolen in 1767 from Rebecca (Michaels) Hays, the widow of Judah Hays and mother of Moses Michael Hays, the only objects with Myers's mark were six tablespoons:

1 Two-Quart Silver Tankard, marked I, H, R.
1 Large Silver Punch Bowl, with two Handles.
3 Silver Porringers, marked M, M, K.
1 Silver Sugar Castor, marked M, M, K.
2 Pair of Round Silver Salts, with Feet, marked I, H, R.—
    And one odd do. [ditto] marked in the same Manner.
1 Small Silver Salver, without any Mark.
6 Table Spoons, marked B, H. Maker's name Myers.
1 Pair of Diamond Rings, with Drops.
1 Silver Coffee-Pot, no Mark, Maker's Name I, P.
    And a Silver Tea-Pot.[329]

The £1.16.9 that Myers had received on her account from Moses Hays on March 15, 1765 may have represented payment for that set.[330] Similarly, silver stolen from Isaac and Rachel Seixas in 1754 lists only "two large Silver Table Spoons, mark'd with the Cypher I R S, Maker's Name M M" among their small collection of silver.[331]

The six tablespoons stolen from Rebecca Hays undoubtedly were similar— if not identical— to three surviving tablespoons from another set made for Jewish clients (fig. 33). They are in the standard pattern produced in Myers's workshop and indistinguishable from spoons made for Livingstons (cats. 33, 34). These three spoons descended from Elkaleh "Nellie" Bush (1772–1830), who in 1792 married Dr. Moses Sheftall (1769–1835) of Savannah, Georgia.[332] Struck with MARK 4, the spoons were made before about 1765 and presumably were acquired by Moses or Elkaleh Sheftall's parents. Elkaleh's parents, the Philadelphia merchant Mathias Bush (1722–1790) and his second wife, Rebecca Myers Cohen, whom he married in 1764, are the most probable original owners; Rebecca was the sister of Myer Myers's first wife.[333] Moses Sheftall's parents, Mordecai Sheftall of Savannah and Frances Hart of Charleston, South Carolina, who married in 1761, are less likely candidates.[334]

If the Bush provenance is correct, these spoons demonstrate the complex interplay of religious, business, and kin ties in Myers's relationship to his Jewish patrons. Some of his Jewish clients in Philadelphia may have acquired their Myers objects as payment for financial transactions that began in the mid-1750s, when Myers was expanding his business (p. 42). These dealings may have been part of an informal system of mutual financial support among fellow Jews, involving loans of money that supported the craftsman's growing enterprise, although they could also have been for goods that Myers acquired to sell at retail. In 1756, he was paid £13.6.9 "per order on M.B.," presumably Mathias Bush.[335] Two years later, Barnard Gratz paid Myers £11.12.7 on behalf of the Lancaster, Pennsylvania, merchant Joseph Simon for "sd. Myers' order."[336] Elkaleh Sheftall's set of tablespoons as well as a cann (cat. 40) that Gratz apparently owned date to this period and could have satisfied Myers's debts. Both Bush and Gratz could also have received these objects as gifts when they married into Myers's family, both men marrying sisters of Myers's first wife, Elkaleh. Similarly, the sauce spoon (cat. 42) owned by Moses and Rachel (Myers) Hays could have been a gift from the silversmith to his sister and brother-in-law. As a working craftsman, Myers could not have given away costly pieces of hollow ware.

The modest forms and simple style of these objects also say much about the status of Jews in Colonial America. Jews had little reason to feel they were either part of British society or able to exert control over their Christian peers (cats. 148, 149). A similar emphasis on plainness was typical of synagogue buildings in both London and New York (cat. 143).[337] This desire to maintain a low public profile may have influenced their choice of household furnishings as well. Many Jewish patrons were affluent enough to afford silver hollow ware but may have wanted to observe an aesthetic of restraint.

Overall, Myers's commissioned silver between 1765 and 1775 shows evidence of restraint from even his wealthiest clients.

Fig. 33. Myer Myers, *Tablespoon* (one of three), New York, 1755–65. Silver. Private collection.

Certain large-scale forms, such as coffeepots and tankards, were made to the same scale and weight as earlier counterparts. In other cases, such as the Van Wyck and Brinckerhoff waiters, routine forms were customized with engraving. Nothing has survived from this decade on the scale of the standing cup or covered jugs. One of the heaviest extant objects is the bread basket weighing 41 oz. (cat. 78). Some large objects are lighter in weight than their dimensions suggest: the dish ring (cat. 79) weighs only 14 oz. The replacement of cast ornament with chasing and piercing not only suited the Rococo aesthetic but also reduced the amount of metal needed for the finished objects. These considerations clearly inspired David Clarkson, Jr., who in the 1750s had commissioned the substantial covered jug (cat. 27) from Myers, to send to London in 1767 for "a handsome silver bread basket, open work. . . . I would have it light and thin, so as to cost but little money, with the crest, a griffin's head, upon it." When he received the basket, Clarkson praised it "as I desired it might be, very light and very pretty."[338]

This restraint on the part of Myers's patrons after 1765 probably reflects the depression and currency shortages in the New York economy that followed the boom of the war years.[339] Victory in 1763 left Great Britain with a large debt and the burden of administering and protecting new territories in North America.[340] Mercantile activities in the decade before the Revolutionary War were hampered further by a series of boycotts of British goods, beginning with that initiated by the Sons of Liberty in 1765 in response to the Stamp Act. This patriotic emphasis on American versus imported goods may have benefited American craftsmen and inspired Myers's increased production, although the merchants who were the principal clients of silversmiths would have suffered a significant loss of income. Dean Failey observed a steady decline in the value of Elias Pelletreau's silver production during this period, from £300 in 1765 to £130 in 1774.[341]

Refugee: The Revolutionary War Years, 1776–83

Myers's activities as a silversmith and entrepreneur came to an abrupt halt during the summer of 1776, when New York became a battleground. His support for the Patriot cause had been evident as early as the previous summer, when he was approached about supervising the refining of lead ore needed to cast bullets in Middletown, Connecticut (pp. 45–46). On September 27, 1775, both Myers and his brother Asher attended the last quarterly meeting of the *yehidim* of Shearith Israel to be recorded prior to the outbreak of war.[342] On April 13, 1776, George Washington arrived in New York, making the city his headquarters. With the British advancing, the majority of the Jews made immediate plans to flee. Myers's family had moved to Norwalk, Connecticut, by April 26, 1776, when his daughter Rebecca was born there. In July 1776, after Myers had vacated

New York, the Patriot government removed lead weights from window sashes, in a house described as Myers's property, in order to melt the lead down for bullets.[343] There is a record of Myers filing suit in New York City on August 13 for £19 against one Thomas Hun; either he had an attorney file in his place or he returned briefly to the city, which by then was under siege.[344] The British commander, Sir William Howe, had landed troops on Staten Island in June and July, drove the American forces from Brooklyn in August, and captured Manhattan on September 15, 1776.

As a minor port on Long Island Sound, Norwalk appeared to be a safe haven. Myers's younger brother-in-law and presumed apprentice, Samson Mears, who also moved to Norwalk, observed, "I don't apprehend much danger here from the enemy . . . they will have greater objects to attend to than this insignificant place."[345] A few Jewish families had settled in Connecticut prior to the Revolutionary War.[346] According to the recollections of Myers's eldest daughter, Judith, as later transmitted by her widower, Jacob Mordecai, the family was "agreeably settled" in Norwalk.[347] On May 2, 1778, Myers's thirteenth child, Benjamin, was born there. That Myers remained active as a craftsman during these years is documented by the survival of one teaspoon (cat. 93), made for Hannah (Finch) Benedict of Norwalk.

As a fifty-three-year-old refugee with a wife and at least six dependent children living with him, Myers was not able to fight as a soldier, but he actively supported the Patriot cause. On October 16, 1776, he appeared before Thomas Fitch, Justice of the Peace in Norwalk, along with one Peter Betts, to offer testimony against the Loyalist New Haven merchant Ralph Isaacs concerning a conversation they overheard "at a public house in said Norwalk":

And these Deponents say that from the Conversation and Declaration of sd Ralph Isaacs it evidently appeared that he was of the opinion that Wherever the British Troops should pass the people there would readily submit to them and that said Isaacs's whole Conversation was very Discouraging with respect of Success on the Continental side.[348]

Despite its seeming lack of importance, Norwalk's location left it vulnerable to raids by British ships from Huntington Bay on Long Island. Myers and his brother Asher, as well as three other Jews, were among seventy-one residents who signed a petition of October 14, 1777 to the Connecticut Assembly, asking that an armed sloop of six or eight guns patrol the shoreline.[349] Their fears were well-founded, for on July 11, 1779, a force commanded by General William Tryon sailed across the Sound and attacked the town. According to Myers's daughter Judith, the residents fled "with such things only as were of the first necessity," and the British burned Norwalk in their wake.[350]

The raid left the Jews without homes or means of support.

Samson Mears wrote immediately afterwards to his business associate, the wealthy merchant Aaron Lopez of Newport:

And altho we were closely employed till the hour of the Sabbath, we were obliged (from the difficulty of procuring teams) to leave a considerable part of furniture and other valuable effects in our respective dwellings, that has to the great distress of some of our families been consumed with the houses, and is most extensively felt by Myer and Asher Myer[s] and M[oses]. Isaacs, the two former being deprived of a very considerable part of their tools.

In this reduced situation we were going from house to house soliciting a shelter, and happy we were to get into the meanest cot. . . . Judge of our situation when a room about twelve feet square contd between twenty and thirty persons, old and young, from Friday to Sunday morning.[351]

Lopez immediately responded with an offer of supplies and financial assistance, which both Myer and Asher Myers declined:

Although their losses have been severe, they are yet blesst with some means of making necessary provisions for their families, and therefore hope their refusal to a part will not be accepted as a slight to your favour, but purely from a conscentiousness that they do not stand in that need of it as some others.[352]

In October 1779, the brothers signed a petition to the Connecticut General Assembly requesting abatement of taxes due to their losses in Tryon's raid, which was granted the following May.[353]

After the burning of Norwalk, Myers and his family moved further east on the Connecticut shoreline to Stratford. From the beginning of the conflict, a *minyan* of Jews— the quorum of ten men required for communal worship— including Gershom Mendes Seixas, had lived in Stratford.[354] Stratford was also the home of William Samuel Johnson, who was both Myers's patron and an investor in the Spruce Hill Lead Mine.[355] According to a nineteenth-century source, Myers and his family lived "on the hill in the rear of the Levi Curtis [sic] homestead."[356] The Curtiss house, which still stands on the Upper Green, belonged in the eighteenth century to Levi's father, Stephen Curtiss, and was adjacent to the property of their cousin Nehemiah Curtiss.[357] Beginning in August 1781, Nehemiah Curtiss recorded accounts with "Mr Miars the Jew," primarily for foods such as apples, corn, geese, mutton, "viel," and beef but also for "my mare to Ride to fairfeild."[358]

Jeanette Rosenbaum incorrectly stated that Myers spent the last two years of exile in Philadelphia, basing her claim on his contributions to a new synagogue for Congregation Mikveh Israel, particularly the "Offerings at the Synagogue" in Philadelphia on April 15, 1782, when Myer Myers was recorded making a contribution of 12 guineas.[359] However, Myers's name never appears among those present at any meetings of Mikveh Israel between March 24, 1782 and September 27,

1783.[360] It is possible that Myers made a brief visit to Philadelphia in April 1782, although a contribution could also have been made in his name by his brother Asher or his daughter Judith. It is also possible, if less likely, that the Myer Myers who contributed to the building fund was not the silversmith but the West Indies merchant Myer Myers (b. after 1753–1791), a younger brother of Moses Myers of Norfolk, Virginia, and a distant cousin of Joyce (Mears) Myers.[361]

The accounts with Nehemiah Curtiss place Myers in Stratford during the years 1779–83, as do two additional sources. The first is Myers's daughter Judith. In reminiscences addressed to her children, she asserted that Myers remained in Stratford for the duration of the conflict:

Your grandfather then settled at Stratford where he continued the remainder of the war and your mother by the desire of her brother yore Uncle Samuel then a resident in the West Indies came with some female friends to Philadelphia where she resided until peace enabled her to return to the habitation of her father in New York.[362]

In 1783, "Myer Myers of Stratford in the County of Fairfield" petitioned the Connecticut General Assembly as the "only surviving Partner to the late Partnership of Symson Symson Myer Myer and George Trail." A deed for land in Woodbury, presumably connected with the Spruce Hill Lead Mine, had been sold to them by one Charles Scott but had been improperly recorded, and Myers successfully requested that the deed be declared valid.[363]

Despite the loss of tools in Tryon's raid, Myers continued to work as a silversmith in Stratford. Extant objects by Myers with histories in the town include a tankard (cat. 94) and spoons.[364] Myers himself may have engraved the "DS" monogram on the tankard's cover (fig. 34), as it seems unlikely that he would have had access to any specialist engravers. The style of the monogram is derived from unshaded designs of the type published in London in the 1760s, although the overall configuration of the letters as well as the motif of an elongated bead flanked by foliage are identical to the "SD" monogram published in the 1750 edition of Samuel Sympson's *A New Book of Cyphers.*[365] This reliance on or recollection of an old-fashioned source is perhaps not surprising for a fifty-six-year-old silversmith accustomed to having the best specialists in New York execute such work.

At Stratford, Myers had the assistance of a younger New York silversmith, John Burger (cat. 117). Burger's marriage in New York to Sarah Baker had been recorded on January 20, 1767, indicating that he was born no later than about 1745.[366] He was first identified as a silversmith on April 25, 1775, when he signed a receipt for a musket issued by the City of New York from the Royal Arsenal, following news of the Battles of Concord and Lexington.[367] Burger apparently worked with Myers in Stratford beginning in 1779. Upon his return to New

York City in 1784, Burger announced:

As he carried on business but a few months before the evacuation in 1776, his friends and the public had not an opportunity of knowing his abilities; but he doubts not but he will be able to give general satisfaction, having since had five years experience with that noted and proficient mechanic Mr. Myer Myers.

N.B. He regulates all gold coin, and gives cash for old gold and silver.[368]

The implication that his time with Myers had improved his abilities suggests that Burger had served his apprenticeship with someone else.

The Postwar Years, 1784–95

The Revolutionary War made it difficult for Myers to reconstruct his career as the leading silversmith in New York. His workshop had been closed and his network of specialist craftsmen had scattered during the British occupation of New York. Only a few silversmiths had remained in the city, most notably Charles Oliver Bruff and Lewis Fueter, both of whom departed with the British troops in 1783.[369] Myers's attempts to reestablish his business were further hampered by a shortage of patrons, many of whom suffered from the postwar depression and widespread shortages of money.

The British army had evacuated New York City on November 23, 1783. Myers and Nehemiah Curtiss "Seteled all Book Accounts" on November 24, and Myers and his family returned to New York shortly thereafter. On December 9, 1783, he was present at a meeting of the *parnassim* of Shearith Israel and was elected one of three members to present an address in January 1784 to the new Governor of New York, General George Clinton.[370] The leadership of Congregation Shearith Israel remained in the hands of those who had served before the war, undoubtedly in an attempt to restore stability as quickly as possible. On June 17, 1784, in response to an act of the New York State Legislature that required the reincorporation of existing corporate entities, a majority of the congregation reelected as their trustees the same men who had held the office in 1775: Myer Myers, Hayman Levy, Solomon Simson, Isaac Moses, Solomon Myers Cohen, and Benjamin Seixas (cat. 145).[371] On July 25, 1784, the deed for a house and lot adjoining the synagogue was reentered into the city's land records, with Daniel Gomez, Joseph Simson, Jacob Franks and Myer Myers acting on behalf of the congregation.[372]

The locations of Myers's residence and workshop in the first four years after his return cannot be established. It is not known if he returned to live in the King (soon to be renamed Pine) Street house, if indeed it still belonged to him. No record of its sale by Myers or his family has survived. In the later 1780s and early 1790s, he apparently was a tenant rather than an owner of property, and no acquisitions are listed for him in the

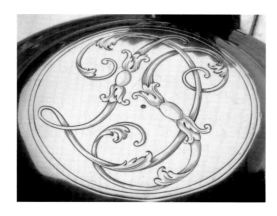

Fig. 34. Cat. 94 (detail).

land records. In 1787, the second New York City directory listed his home address at 29 Broad Street.[373] Myers had rented this property beginning June 1 from the attorney Joseph Winter and apparently had difficulty paying his rent. On October 16, 1787, Winter sued Myers for £12.10.0 for "the use Occupation and Enjoyment of one Messuage and Dwelling House with the Appurtenances . . . for the Space of three months." Myers failed to appear before the Mayor's Court on December 18, and on January 8, 1788, a jury that included fellow silversmith William G. Forbes awarded Winter £6.19.0 in damages and costs in addition to the back rent.[374] The 1789 and 1790 directories gave Myers's address as 29 Princess (now Beaver) Street, at the corner of Broad Street, which probably was the same residence.[375]

The first United States Census of 1790 listed the sixty-seven-year-old Myer Myers as a head of family in the Dock Ward, living with four white females (presumably his wife, Joyce, daughters Rebecca and Richea, and possibly a house servant) and one white male under sixteen years (probably his twelve-year-old son Benjamin).[376] By this time, Myers's older children had reached adulthood (cats. 96, 140). His address in the 1791 city directory was 14 Pearl Street, where he remained until 1794, when he was listed at 17 Pearl Street.[377] None of the directories gave more than one address for Myer Myers, indicating that he lived at the same location as his workshop.

STYLE, SPECIALIST CRAFTSMEN, AND PATRONAGE

Myers found himself confronted with the need to work in a new aesthetic, for the Revolutionary War coincided with the introduction of the Neoclassical style in America. Indeed, the war has served historians as the point of demarcation between the Rococo of the Colonial period and the Neoclassical style of the new Republic.[378] Myers's workshop seems to have made the shift, without difficulty, since his sugar tongs of 1784–86 (cat. 97) reveal an immediate familiarity with Neoclassical forms and ornament. In the last decade of his career, Myers produced an urn-shaped sugar dish (cat. 104) and hooped tankards (cats. 98, 99) that represented a stylistic as well as a technical break with his work from the Colonial period. The tankards were made from flattened and seamed sheet metal, which would have required a rolling mill. Myers may not have invested in such expensive equipment and simply had the metal fabricated by someone else, like the silversmith Joel Sayre, whose 1818 estate sale included "1 rolling mill" and "Large plating [mill] 3 rollers" for creating and ornamenting sheet metal.[379] The reeded moldings applied to Myers's Neoclassical tankards likewise may have been executed by another craftsman, such as the wood and ivory turner James Ruthven, who "hooped" mugs for the silversmith Hugh Wishart in 1803.[380]

Once Myers had returned to New York, he again entrusted the decorative engraving on his silver to leading specialists, as evidenced by the abrupt shift in objects produced after the war to Neoclassical-style engraving. One engraver executed the Hamilton arms on a pair of pint tankards (cat. 99, fig. 35). His technique consisted of short, tight, highly controlled strokes with sharp contrasts between shaded and unshaded areas. The only engraving that may be by Myers's own hand are the Hebrew inscriptions on the candlesticks at Shearith Israel that he was paid for in 1787 (cat. 142).

Other Neoclassical silver marked by Myers was distinguished by the use of engraving today known as "bright cut," an English innovation of the late 1770s, where deep gouges cut at an angle create patterns that catch light and produce a sparkling effect. The earliest documented use of bright-cut engraving in America appears on the borders of Samuel Johnson's 1784 Freedom box, engraved by Peter Maverick (cat. 115).[381] Myers was not slow to adopt bright-cut decoration, which is found on the 1784–86 sugar tongs from his workshop (cat. 97). His use of bright-cut engraving, however, was restricted almost exclusively to flatware. His only surviving hollow ware with bright-cut decoration is a pair of Torah finials that are richly ornamented with bright-cut engraving of chains of husks, garlands of leaves and flowers, and a variety of intricate, abstract borders composed of different-sized dots and gouges (cat. 100, fig. 36). The identical motifs appear again on John Burger's sugar urn (cat. 117) as well as on silver from the later 1780s and 1790s by Ephraim Brasher, Daniel Bloom Coen, Ezekiel Dodge, Jabez Halsey, and William Gilbert, which suggests the work of a single craftsman or shop.[382]

The majority of Myers's patrons after the Revolutionary War had connections to those from the prewar era. A few, like David and Magdalen Johnston (cat. 98), belonged to the same generation as patrons of the 1750s and were related to them as well. Others, like Edward and Mary (McEvers) Livingston (cat. 101), were the children of parents who had supported Myers during the Colonial period. Phoebe Lewis of Stratford, Connecticut, apparently purchased a set of teaspoons from Myers

Fig. 35. Cat. 99 (detail).

after his return to New York; as the surviving teaspoon is ornamented with bright-cut engraving, it presumably postdates Myers's period of residence in Stratford.[383] Fellow Jews, particularly his relatives, also continued to buy his work (cats. 88-90). Overall, however, Myers's decreased output indicates a smaller number of patrons and fewer wealthy or prominent names. Without commissions from the rich people who became the style setters of the new "Republican Court" in New York, Myers's silver from this period consisted primarily of modest, routine forms or was restrained in its scale and ornament.

PRODUCTION AND CHANGES IN THE SILVERSMITH'S TRADE

Myers attempted to reestablish himself as a largeworker and merchant-artisan. Based on surviving objects that can be dated by style or provenance to the Federal period, however, the output of his workshop during the last decade of his life never returned to the prewar level, undoubtedly because he could not reassemble a large work force or the financial wherewithal to maintain such an operation. His output during the postwar years may also have been restricted by the new nation's perilous economic conditions, which affected other craftsmen and merchants as well. Elias Pelletreau's business, which had begun to decline in the mid-1760s, continued to suffer in the postwar years: in 1795, the total value of his silversmith's work was only £68.14.4.[384] Both Myers's son-in-law Benjamin Mordecai and his former partner Benjamin Halsted were declared insolvent in 1786 and 1787 (see below and cat. 96). But the decrease in Myers's work may also have been affected by his age; he was sixty years old when he returned to New York after having lived as a refugee for seven years.

The small output from Myers's shop and its stylistic restraint may also reflect a change in the postwar years to retail rather than craft activity. This shift, in turn, reflects a trend in the new Republic away from the merchant-artisan toward the pure merchant. Myers's listings in the New York directories gave his profession as "goldsmith" until 1794 and 1795, when he was listed as "clock and watch-maker." Although this change may have been in error, it may also have reflected a new emphasis on retailing silver, jewelery, and other fancy goods such as clocks and watches. In 1785, William Malcolm sued Myers for £55 for "divers Goods wares and Merchandizes" that Myers had purchased from him, perhaps for resale.[385] When Benjamin Halsted went bankrupt in 1787, Myers was indebted to him for £140, possibly for jewelry and other luxury items he had purchased to resell.

Although Myer Myers may have been unable to reestablish himself as a merchant-artisan on the same scale after the Revolutionary War, he clearly continued to be held in high regard by his peers. In 1785, the newly formed Gold and Silver Smith's Society elected Myers its first chairman (fig. 37).[386] The Society probably was a social club that represented the old guard of silversmiths who followed the pre-Revolutionary, traditional techniques and hierarchical organization of the trade, with the master largeworker at the top. Myers's seniority may have won him the election as chairman; the only other member born in the 1720s was Samuel Johnson. A number of the members were former associates of Myers, including Halsted, Gilbert, Parisien, and Dunn. Like Myers, and perhaps under his influence, most of the members had adopted surname marks as well as "N-York" marks prior to the Revolutionary War (see Appendix I, MARK IIA). Paul von Khrum has surmised that the otherwise unknown Daniel "Chene" listed as a member in 1786 was a misspelling of Daniel Bloom Coen, who appears on the membership list in 1787.[387]

Significant by their absence from this group were most of the younger silversmiths who began working after the Revolutionary War, including Jeronimus Alstyne, Simeon Bayley, Philip Dally, Garret Schank, Andrew Underhill, Thomas Underhill, John Vernon, and Daniel Van Voorhis. These craftsmen formed several short-lived partnerships among themselves and represented a distinct group. One key to understanding the difference between them and the members of the Gold and Silver Smith's Society may be found in the withdrawal of William G. Forbes from the organization after 1786. Although no reasons are documented for his resignation, Forbes' career set him apart from the other, older members of the Society—who remembered when merchant-artisans like Myers had dominated the craft. Forbes, by contrast, belonged to the network of younger craftsman who sold their products to retailers or, in his case, purchased finished silver pieces for resale. Joseph and Teunis DuBois as well as Garret Schank and John Vernon supplied Forbes with silver.[388] He became the patriarch of a family that would control much of the retail trade in the early years of the nineteenth century, including his brother Abraham, sons John W. and Colin Van Gelder, and Abraham Forbes's apprentice Garret Eoff.[389]

Benjamin Halsted's career after the Revolutionary War more clearly illustrates these changes. Halsted may have been operating as a retail silversmith after his move to New Jersey in 1766 (p. 34), and after the war he operated primarily, if not exclusively, as a retailer of silver or jewelry. Evidence from this period suggests that he himself did not make much of the considerable amount of flatware or few pieces of hollow ware in the Neoclassical style that bear his mark (cat. 118). His whereabouts after about 1770 and during the Revolutionary War are not documented. He may have spent the war in Philadelphia, since immediately afterwards the war he opened a store in that city. Although he called himself a "gold and silversmith," an advertisement of August 1783 lists what must have been largely imported goods:

BENJAMIN HALSTED, GOLD and SILVERSMITH, has just opened shop in Arch Street, between Second and Third streets, on the north side, and has for SALE, the following articles, on very low terms, viz. ELEGANT paste, silver, plated, gilt and metal shoe, knee, and stock buckles; silver bottle slides, ditto salts and shovels, ditto soup, table, gravey, sauce, pap and tea spoons, ditto tongs, ditto punch strainers and ladels, ditto chamber candlesticks; silver'd hangers; silver and ivory handled table and dessert knives and forks, with or without cases, ditto carvers, ditto common.

A grand assortment of JEWELLERY, viz. Handkerchief pins and runners, lockets, bracelets, broaches, finger rings, earrings, sleeve buttons, &c.

Silver and gilt watches, gold, silver and common watch chains and seals; gold stock buckles and thimbles; china plates, bowls, and cream jugs; gold scales and weights; silver, steel and metal spectacles; paste hair sprigs, pins and stay hooks, paste and plain combs; buckle and tooth brushes, pen knives, scissars, books, lancets in cases, childrens gilt and silver whistles and bells, thimbles, very fine and common spy glasses, cap and hat pins, watch glasses, brass and iron wire, borax, bibles, testaments, common prayers, psalters, spelling books, primmers and horn books, a few religious and history ditto, a variety of small, entertaining and improving books for children, with a variety of other articles too tedious to mention.[390]

He operated this store in Philadelphia until his return to New York in 1786, when he opened a store selling the same range of flatware and jewelry at 13 Maiden Lane.[391] On April 14, 1787, he was declared insolvent. A minutely detailed inventory was made of his possessions, including the contents of his store as well as personal property and wearing apparel.[392] But the inventory lists no tools or materials for fabricating either silver or jewelry, with the exception of "16 lb of brass Wire, 15 lb of

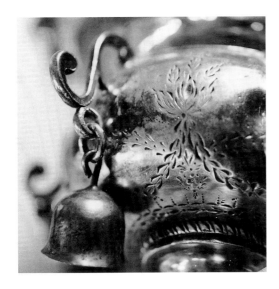

Fig. 36. Cat. 100 (detail).

Gold and Silver Smiths's Society, meets on Wednefdays, at the houfe of Walter Heyer.
MYER MYERS, Chairman,
Members,---Samuel Johnſon,
William Gilbert, Eſq; , Broadway,
Otto De Perrizang,
William Forbes, 88, Broadway,
John Burger, 207, Queen-ſteeet
Daniel Chene,
Cary Dunn,
Benjamin Halſted, 13, Maiden-lane
Ephraim Braſher, 1, Cherry-ſtreet.

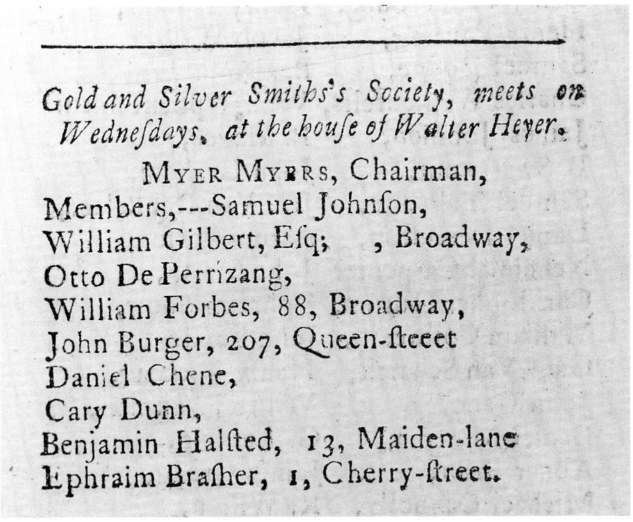

Fig. 37. David Franks, *The New-York Directory*, p. 69 (detail). New York, 1786. The New-York Historical Society.

Iron binding Wire," although he had also offered such materials for retail sale in Philadelphia. The inventory consisted of a large selection of jewelry and fancy goods, similar to those advertised in Philadelphia: silver teaspoons, tea tongs, and salt shovels; silver, gold, and stone-set jewelry; watches, watch-chains, keys, and seals; pins, razors, spyglasses, flatware, and other small metal goods; and numerous books.

The debtors and creditors listed in the insolvency papers indicate that at least some of Halsted's business was as a wholesale supplier of jewelry and fancy goods to retailers. "Myer & Joseph Myers" headed his list of debtors for £140 worth of goods, presumably for items Myers acquired for resale. Halsted was also in debt to the mercantile firm of Samuel and Moses Myers in Richmond (see cat. 140) in the amount of £46.4.11. His largest creditors were those individuals who presumably had sold him his stock: his brothers John and Matthias for £600 and £211, respectively, and two New York merchants, Blanck Bieaus's estate (£200) and Joseph Browning (£2,150.10.0). The only craftsman listed among his creditors was Ephraim Brasher, whom he owed the small sum of £5.3.0, perhaps for a piece of silver Brasher had supplied. Halsted and Brasher apparently shared the services of the slave John Frances, and Halsted may have sold wares made for him by Frances (p. 48).

Halsted somehow managed to settle his debts—and settle them quickly: three months later, in June 1787, he reopened his Maiden Lane shop. But he cut back significantly on the range of fancy goods offered for sale. An advertisement that month mentions no jewelry, offering only "silver tea spoons for one shilling per doz."[393] During the early 1790s, Halsted decided to specialize in the manufacture of thimbles. On August 30, 1794, he placed the following advertisement:

Thimble Manufactory. BENJAMIN HALSTEAD [sic] Respectfully informs his Friends and the Public in general, that he still continues carrying on the Gold and Silversmiths business, No. 67 Broad street; he has brought the manufactory of Gold, Silver and Pinchbeck Thimbles with steel tops to great perfection, and thinks he could make a sufficient quantity to supply the United States. Citizens, consider your interest, and encourage American Manufactures. Those imported are of the slightest kind, I will engage that one of mine, will do more service than 3 of them, and I know by experience, that imported ones of the quality of mine cost 18 shillings per doz. and could not be sold by 25 per cent. as low as mine. Every dealer in this article will soon find the advantage of keeping Halsted's Thimbles, and have the satisfaction of knowing that he does his customers justice.—Silver and steel Bodkins, Tooth and Ear picks by the Doz. or Single.[394]

After 1794, the making of thimbles seems to have dominated the business of Halsted and his sons John and David.[395] His listings in the city directories changed from "silversmith and thimble manufacturer" to simply "thimble manufacturer." At least one of Halsted's thimbles has survived.[396] He continued to retail some gold jewelry, as documented by his purchase in 1799 from the wholesale jeweler Epaphras Hinsdale of Newark, New Jersey.[397]

Halsted's shift to from retail trade to manufacturing echoes that of the younger silversmith John Burger, who had worked with Myers in Stratford and returned to New York in 1784 (p. 63). Although he may have made a cann owned by Thomas and Mary Arden, also patrons of Myers (cat. 97), he seems to have set himself up as a wholesale supplier to retail silversmiths (cat. 117).[398] Burger's postwar career— as well as Halsted's— reflects the changes taking place in the structure of the silversmith's trade during the early Republic. The Colonial trade dominated by merchant-artisans was giving way to a trade where working craftsmen supplied jewelers and other retail establishments. Labor was devalued in favor of the mercantile side of enterprise, a widespread trend in American handicrafts at this time.[399] From 1797 to 1813, the silversmith Teunis DuBois, working in Freehold, New Jersey, supplied flatware and occasional small pieces of hollow ware to eighteen different New York retailers. With one exception, his largest sales were all to customers identified as "merchants," who accounted for half of his clientele; only three were gold and silversmiths.[400] The same trend affected the trade in New York City, where as early as the 1810s, a majority of working silversmiths no longer operated retail stores, but supplied finished goods to large retailers such as Baldwin Gardiner, whose training was as a shopkeeper, not as a craftsman.[401]

THE JEWISH COMMUNITY

Even as Myers's professional fortunes declined, he remained a senior member of the Jewish community, continuing to serve in various leadership capacities at Shearith Israel. In July 1784, he was "Reelected to the Chair" of a meeting of trustees.[402] Between 1785 and 1787 he served two terms as *parnas*.[403] Presumably in that capacity, his name was included in 1786 on a list of individuals owing £24 rent to the estate of William Brownejohn, for a stable in Mill Street.[404] This stable would have been adjacent to the residence of the *hazan* (cantor-reader); the location of Myers's home in that year is uncertain, although in 1787 he was living only one block away on Broad Street.

Not surprisingly for a man in his sixties, Myers devoted much of his time during these years to activities on behalf of the burial ground. On May 7, 1784, he was one of those who represented the congregation in the purchase of a lot adjacent to the existing burial ground from the merchant and sugar refiner Isaac Roosevelt and his wife, Cornelia Hoffman.[405] Five years later, Myers made an agreement with cartmen to grade the entrance of the burial ground for £42.10.0.[406] He was also a founding member of a burial society, the *Hebra Gemiluth Hasadim*, in 1785 (cat. 142).

To judge by the surviving records, Myers's financial situation never recovered after the Revolutionary War. No slaves were recorded as living in the household by the 1790 Census, perhaps an indication of diminished means. In addition to the rent owed to Joseph Winter in 1787, he may have been the "M: Myers" who owed 17 shillings to Charles Cox in 1788.[407] In May 1789, the lawyer Pierpont Edwards of Connecticut sued

Myers for "trespass" and £20 damages, apparently the same case for which a warrant was signed ordering Myers's arrest on August 9, 1792.[408] A list of debts to Shearith Israel, drawn up on March 27, 1787, named Myer Myers as the third largest debtor, owing £19.8.0.[409] His son-in-law Jacob Mordecai, declared insolvent only four months previously, owed the greatest amount, £24.23.6 (see cat. 96). Solomon M. Myers, the silversmith's eldest son, owed a debt of £3.4.6.[410] To make matters worse, some of Myers's prewar debts still were active; in 1790 he made a deposition before Richard Morris in the case of Cockburn vs. Wetherhead (p. 47).[411] Another loose end from before the war was Myers's forty-two-year lease on the Spruce Hill Lead Mine. On May 25, 1792, Myers and his brother-in-law Solomon Simson, who had inherited his brother Sampson's share in 1773, sublet their lease to James Holmes II of Salisbury, Connecticut, who unsuccessfully attempted to mine and smelt iron ore.[412]

The record of Myers's activities at Shearith Israel indicates that he remained involved in the affairs of the congregation up to his death at age seventy-two. In 1792, he paid £6 for three years' rent for his seat in the synagogue and an additional £2 "for Son Benjⁿ," who was fourteen. Myers's own seat rate was in the middle range: the highest rate was £12, whereas his twenty-year-old son "Sampson" paid £4 for his seat.[413] On February 2, 1794, Myer Myers visited the Hebrew school with Isaac Moses and Alexander Zuntz and found "that the Scholars then attending make good progress in Learning."[414]

Myer Myers died in New York sometime between March 20 and June 17, 1795, the second quarter of 5555. For the third quarter of 5555, his name was recorded as "Myer Myers Decd" under a list of bills collected on behalf of Shearith Israel.[415] In 1847, his death was recorded erroneously by his granddaughter Julia Mordecai as December 12, but this in fact was the end date (Kislev 30) of the first quarter of 5556, when the remaining bill of £1.6.6 was listed under "Widow M. Myers."[416] No will written by Myers has survived, and no administration of his estate was recorded.[417]

John Burger's reference to Myer Myers as "that noted and proficient mechanic" suggests of the high regard in which Myers's craftsmanship was held throughout his career. As the leading merchant-artisan in late Colonial New York, Myers had created some of the most impressive works in silver to be made in America. His ability to rise to the top of his profession unquestionably resulted from his skill and his innovative business strategies. His religious community also had profound implications for his life and his career as a craftsman. His family, particularly that of his first wife, provided him with significant connections and financial resources. Throughout his career, his fellow Jews, who were also his kinsmen, provided him with patronage and financial support. The leading role he played in New York's Jewish community paralleled his role as a master artisan. Although he left no written statements concerning his craft, Myers offered a subtle indication of his own view of his abilities and status as a craftsman in the way he marked certain objects. They bespeak his pride, as a Jew and a craftsman, in an extraordinary achievement.

NOTES

1 Ward 1984.
2 Barr 1980; Hare/Snodin/Clifford 1990.
3 Ward 1984, pp. 131–33; Kane 1998, p. 9.
4 Ward 1984, pp. 131–32; Kane 1998, p. 9; Ward 1990, pp. 132, 134.
5 Kane 1998, s.v. "Burt, Benjamin," "Hurd, Jacob," and "Revere, Paul Jr."
6 Barker 1996, p. 8.
7 *The New-York Mercury*, April 20, 1767, as cited in Gottesman 1936, p. 33.
8 Wolf 1994.
9 Mordecai 1847, p. 46.
10 Scott 1975, p. 48.
11 Rosendale 1893; Hollander 1897, pp. 104–05, 109–10, 116; Hühner 1905, p. 6; Wolfe 1963, p. 136; Hershkowitz 1976, p. 15.
12 The earliest source for genealogical information on the family was provided by Myer Myers's granddaughter Julia Mordecai (1799–1852), the child of Myers's daughter Rebecca (1776–1863) and her husband, Jacob Mordecai (1762–1838). Julia's "Family Register" (Mordecai 1847) presumably was based on oral history from her grandmother, who died in 1824, as well as her own mother, who was still alive when the document was written. See also *MCCNY-1*, IV, pp. 70–74, 345–47, 351.
13 KKSI-MB1, p. 14, "Selomo bar Meyr"; p. 19, "Selomo Meir."
14 De Lancey 1885, pp. ix–xiii, 44–46, 104; Hershkowitz 1976, p. 18.
15 Samuel J. Oppenheim Papers, AJHS, cited in Rosenbaum 1954A, p. 58.
16 "Inventory of the personal Estate of Abraham Isaacks," p. 5; Isaacks family papers, AJHS.
17 Hühner 1905, p. 6.
18 *MCCNY-1*, IV, pp. 74, 346, 351.
19 Mordecai 1847, pp. 61–64; Stern 1991, pp. 104, 159, 184, 217; Pool 1952, p. 324. The *ketubah* (marriage certificate) mentioned by Pool was in the Lyons Collection, AJHS, but could not be located for the present study.
20 O'Callaghan 1849–51, IV, p. 271.
21 *The New-York Weekly Journal*, May 25, 1741, p. 4.
22 KKSI-MB1, p. 13 (Elul 2, 5488); KKSI-MB1, p. 25 (Sivan 13, 5499); see also Pool 1952, p. 28. Solomon Myers also pledged a donation of £1.10.0 toward the purchase of the lot for the original synagogue building on October 18, 1728 (Cheshvan 15, 5489), at a time when the higher contributions ranged between £10 and £20.
23 KKSI-MB1, p. 17 (Rosh hodesh Tammuz 5490).
24 Ibid., p. 40.
25 Marcus 1951, pp. 211, 219.
26 Mintz/Deitsch 1997, pp. 54–70.
27 "Livro dos Miseberagh," p. 3.
28 KKSI-MB1, pp. 80 (Elul 29, 5503), 84 (Tishri 25, 5504).
29 Ibid., p. 70 (Adar 30, 5502). Rosenbaum 1954A, p. 28, stated that the earliest reference to Myer Myers in the congregation's records was in 1737, but the present author has been unable to locate this reference.
30 KKSI-MB1, p. 95.
31 MCNY, doc. 42.173; Hershkowitz 1966B, pp. 68–71.
32 KKSI-MB1, p. 97.
33 Ibid., p. 92 (Tishri 11, 5506).
34 Ibid., pp. 96–97.
35 Ibid., p. 115 (Tishri 5, 5511).
36 NYCMCMB, vol. for August 24, 1742–February 7, 1749, p. 377.
37 De Lancey 1885, p. xii.
38 Waters/McKinsey/Ward 2000, I, p. 20.
39 Failey 1971, p. 3.

40 Two additional makers working at this time can be ruled out by the dates of their careers: Peter van Inburgh died only two years into the period of Myers's apprenticeship, and Nicholas Roosevelt did not register as a Freeman until 1739, at which point only would he have been permitted to take apprentices.
41 Michman-Melkman 1972, p. 55; Morgenstein/Levine 1981–82, pp. 7–8; Bloom 1937, pp. xvi–xvii, 31.
42 Grimwade 1990, pp. 490, 559.
43 Ezekiel/Lichtenstein 1917, pp. 13–16; Marcus 1970, II, p. 538; Stern 1991, p. 126.
44 Stern 1991, p. 194; Cutten 1958, pp. 92, 102. In July 1769, Moses received a grant of 100 acres of land near Augusta, and in 1780 he was licensed to sell liquor in Savannah. It is possible that Jacob Moses was related to a gold and silver refiner named Isaac Moses, who had arrived in Savannah from Hanover, Germany, in 1758. The latter's indenture was purchased by Mordecai Sheftall. See indenture between Isaac Moses and Edward Somerville, London, May 19, 1758, M.A. Levy Collection, Keith Read Manuscript Collection, University of Georgia, Athens; see also Marcus 1970, II, p. 538. This Isaac Moses is not recorded in Stern 1991.
45 *Rivington's New-York Gazetteer*, May 12, 1774, p. 3. Judah never registered as a Freeman and was not naturalized between 1740 and 1769; nor can he be identified with any member of the Judah family in New York.
46 Stratton 1975, p. 27, illustrates a cann made in London by Thomas Mason in 1722–23. Myers's cann has a history of ownership by Abraham Ten Broeck (1734–1810) of Albany, but its style and Myers's mark indicate that it originally belonged to the previous generation. Both Ten Broeck and his wife, Elizabeth Van Rensselaer were descended from Dutch families in Albany. See Christie's 2000, lot 322; Runk 1897, p. 59.
47 *Glen-Sanders Collection* 1966, no. 61; Waters/McKinsey/Ward 2000, I, nos. 13, 78; Skerry/Sloane 1992, pl. III.
48 Hayward 1959, pp. 3–4.
49 Buhler 1956, pp. 23–24, suggested that Bartholomew Le Roux I began as the Stoutenburghs' master, but he could not have taken Tobias as an apprentice, since Tobias was only thirteen at the time of Bartholomew's death in 1713.
50 Waters/McKinsey/Ward 2000, I, p. 35.
51 This salver, formerly in the Historical Society of Pennsylvania, has been missing since the early 1980s. Rosenbaum 1954A, p. 66, reproduces what apparently is the mark on this object, although it cannot be verified by comparison; the mark is very similar to the one identified as MARK 1 in the present study.
52 Clayton 1985, p. 129, figs. 5–7; Hartop 1996, nos. 84–85, 87, 93.
53 Buhler/Hood 1970, II, nos. 611–12; Lindsey 1999, nos. 209, 246.
54 Engraving has been buffed from the upper half of the cup's body, the present finial is probably a later replacement, and both the cover and foot possibly were ornamented at one time with chasing that subsequently has been removed.
55 Hayward 1959, pp. 31–34.
56 For a discussion of this group, see Belden 1967. The second cup by Charles Le Roux is described but not illustrated in Phillips 1937, p. 8. An earlier style covered cup bears the marks of Charles Le Roux's father, Bartholomew Le Roux I; Puig et al. 1989, no. 180. Pelletreau was sworn as a Freeman in 1750, and Dean Failey has suggested that during the first years of Pelletreau's career he probably had a legacy of New York City patrons from the silversmith Simeon Soumaine, to whom he had been apprenticed and who had died in 1750; Failey 1971, pp. 4–5. The Van Cortlandt arms were engraved on Pelletreau's cup, but the specific members of the family who commissioned it have not been identified.
57 When the cup was sold in 1961, its ownership was linked to Petrus and Margaret Stuyvesant's daughter Elizabeth (1775–1854), who married Colonel Nicholas Fish (1758–1833) in 1803, and by descent to an unspecified great-great-granddaughter, who consigned it to auction; Parke-Bernet 1961, p. 59. Another possibility is that Nicholas Fish inherited this cup from his parents, Jonathan and Elizabeth (Sackett) Fish, who

were married in 1750; Fish 1929, pp. 40–42. They owned a set of table-spoons by Halsted and Myers with upturned, midrib handles and the initials "F/JE" engraved on the back; one spoon from this set was owned by the New York City dealer S.J. Shrubsole in January 1998.

58 *The New-York Weekly Mercury*, August 12, 1754, p. 3. The Meal Market shop was taken over in September 1754 by Rowland De Paiba, an importer of silver and jewelry who subsequently advertised silver and jewelry imported from London to be sold "at the late shop of Mr. Myer Myers, goldsmith, opposite the Meal Market"; *The New-York Mercury*, June 16, 1755, p. 3.

59 NYCMCMB, vol. for August 24, 1742–February 7, 1749, p. 553. Without file papers for this case, the identity of this Thomas Jones remains uncertain, as there were several individuals in New York by this name in 1747.

60 Notes from Writ Book, 1746–54, Samuel J. Oppenheim Papers, AJHS, cited in Rosenbaum 1954A, p. 58. Neither the Writ Book cited by Oppenheim nor any file papers for this case have survived. The identity of this John Sutton is unknown.

61 Nash 1979, pp. 176–78.

62 *The New-York Mercury*, April 19, 1753, p. 3.

63 Newman 1990, p. 253.

64 Buhler/Hood 1970, II, no. 611; Lindsey 1999, no. 209; Waters/McKinsey/Ward 2000, I, no. 41. None of these objects has a mirror cypher; the waiters both have coats of arms, and the device inside the border on the tankard's cover was erased and replaced with a later monogram.

65 The "SB" tankard is reprod. in Christie's 1993, lot 125; the purported history of ownership by Samuel Bush is incorrect. The "JFM" tankard is at NYHS; see Rosenbaum 1954A, p. 93.

66 Kammen 1975, pp. 330–32; Nash 1979, pp. 233–46.

67 Kammen 1975, pp. 278–79.

68 Smith/Kammen 1972, I, p. 226.

69 Malcolm Stern recorded Elkaleh's mother as Samuel's second wife, Rachel Michaels, whom he married in or after 1733, perhaps because Julia Mordecai gave Elkaleh's birth date as 1735; Mordecai 1847, p. 46; Stern 1991, p. 223. If Rachel (Michaels) Myers Cohen was indeed her mother, Elkaleh would have been no more than twenty when her first son was born. Her father's will names her first in the list of his daughters, implying that she was the eldest. Since both of his wives were named Rachel, it is possible that Elkaleh's maternity was confused in the later records.

70 KKSI-MB1, p. 111 (Sivan 5510).

71 Mordecai 1847, p. 46; Stern 1991, p. 217.

72 NYCPR-2, liber 15, pp. 103–04. Samuel Myers Cohen had written his will on August 4, 1741, "being now bound on a voyage to England and considering the Danger of the Seas and certainty of Death."

73 Ibid., p. 103; Pool 1930, p. 71; KKSI-MB1, p. 36 (Sivan 5490).

74 KKSI-MB1, p. 14; NYCPR-2, liber 15, pp. 103–04.

75 NYCPR-2, liber 15, pp. 103–04.

76 *The New-York Mercury*, August 12, 1754, p. 3.

77 NYCLR, liber 37, pp. 325–26.

78 Quimby/Johnson 1997, p. 355.

79 *Indentures* 1909, pp. 148–49, 166; Lindsey 1999, p. 189, no. 210.

80 *Rivington's New-York Gazetteer*, August 26, 1773, p. 4.

81 *The New-York Mercury*, May 2, 1757, p. 3.

82 Barr 1980, pp. 31, 49–52.

83 Kane 1998, pp. 30–31.

84 Indenture between David Hayes [sic] and Myer Myers and Abraham De Peyster, May 2, 1763, NYHS. An indenture was the generic name for a written legal agreement.

85 NYCLR, liber 37, pp. 325–30; Wetmore et al. 1863, p. 15.

86 Lease from Myer and "Elcaley" Myers to Evert Byvanck, July 7, 1764, AJHS. Several merchants by the name of Evert Byvanck were active in New York at this time, and it is not clear which of them took the lease on the Myers's house.

87 NYCLR, liber 35, pp. 72–75; Wetmore et al. 1863, p. 15.

88 Pool/Pool 1955, p. 502.

89 Waters/McKinsey/Ward 2000, I, pp. 13–37.

90 *The New-York Gazette or the Weekly Post-Boy*, September 11, 1766, as cited in Gottesman 1936, p. 37; *The New-York Journal or The General Advertiser*, August 6, 1772, p. 3; *Rivington's New-York Gazetteer*, September 29, 1774, p. 3; *The New-York Journal or The General Advertiser*, May 4, 1775, p. 3.

91 An unusual ladle with a shell-shaped bowl attached to a turned wood handle in The Metropolitan Museum of Art, inv. 27.28, is struck with both MARK 11A and MARK 12. Although the marks appear to be genuine, the authenticity of this object is uncertain. It bears the engraved inscription "The Gift of Frederick de Peyster, Esqr."

92 Williams 1949, p. 51. I am grateful to Dwight F. Halsted of Akron, New York, for supplying extensive genealogical information on his forebears.

93 Ernest Currier stated that Halsted registered as a Freeman in 1764, but no evidence for this assertion has been found; Currier 1938, p. 67. This information was repeated in Darling 1964, p. 95.

94 *The New-York Gazette or The Weekly Post-Boy*, November 10, 1763, p. 3.

95 *The New-York Gazette or The Weekly Post-Boy*, July 5, 1764, p. 3.

96 NYCPR-1, liber 37, p. 58–60; information on Desbrosses is from Stevens 1867, pp. 27–34.

97 Williams 1949, p. 51. The Halsteds had eight children: Elizabeth (b. 1766), Susannah (b. 1771), Margaret (b. 1773), Sarah Tredwell (b. 1774), David B. (b. 1776), John Thomas (b. 1777), Benjamin, Jr. (b. 1780), and Harriet (b. 1782). I am indebted to Dwight F. Halsted for this information.

98 *The New-York Gazette or The Weekly Post-Boy*, September 18, 1766, p. 3.

99 *The New-York Gazette or The Weekly Post-Boy*, September 6, 1764, p. 1.

100 *The New-York Gazette or The Weekly Post-Boy*, August 16, 1764, p. 3.

101 In addition to cat. 42, the author has examined two Halsted and Myers ladles with silver handles, and five tablespoons, of which three belong to one partial set.

102 The Halsted punch strainer is at the Philadelphia Museum of Art; Williams 1949, p. 50, fig. 18. The Halsted and Myers punch strainer was illustrated in Norman-Wilcox 1954, p. 50, fig. 8. Its current location is unknown to the present author, so an accurate comparison to the Halsted example cannot be made.

103 Mordecai 1796, n.p.

104 KKSI-MB1, p. 115 (Tishri 5, 5511). No rate is recorded next to Joseph's name.

105 Ibid., p. 139.

106 KKSI-MB2 (Elul 28, 5521).

107 Mordecai 1847, p. 45. The order in which Myer Myers and his siblings are recorded in Julia Mordecai's register may not reflect the actual chronology of their births. Joseph, listed third, certainly was older than Asher, as was their sister Sloe, born in 1728.

108 Uriah Hendricks Letterbook, 1758–59, p. 26, Hendricks Papers, NYHS.

109 Brener 1976, p. 224; Gerstell 1972, p. 85; NYCPR-1, liber 29, pp. 44–46.

110 NYCIR-1, box 13, Halsted file.

111 Minutes of the Trustees, April 6, 1784–December 18, 1799, p. 103 (Elul 16, 5547), Archives of Congregation Shearith Israel, New York; "Account of the Monies rec'd for Offerings," first quarter 5548, Lyons Collection, box 1, file 50, AJHS. The Joseph Myers in both these documents may also have been the physician Joseph Hart Myers (1758–1823), although it is not certain that he was living in New York at this time; Stern 1991, p. 221.

112 Stern 1991, p. 190.

113 *The New-York Mercury*, November 29, 1762, p. 4.

114 Stern 1991, p. 190.

115 "An Inventory of the Estate of Andrew Breestead Deceased," June 15, 1787, Joseph Downs Manuscript and Microfilm Collection, The Henry Francis du Pont Winterthur Museum. For Ten Eyck and Breestead, see NYCPR-1, liber 28, pp. 499–500; for Mears, see *The New-York Mercury*, November 29, 1762, p. 4.

116 De Lancey 1885, p. 225. Hays's elder brother, Michael Solomon Hays, became a Freeman seven months later as a "Watchmaker"; De Lancey 1885, p. 227, and Stern 1991, p. 106.

117 Stern 1991, p. 67.

118 Ibid., pp. 46, 106; Marcus 1959, pp. 106–11.

119 NYCMCR, Parchment 206 H-2; the Judgment for this suit was filed on January 22, 1787, case 132.

120 Darling 1964, p. 98; Belden 1980, p. 220; Traquair 1940; Langdon 1960; Langdon 1970.

121 Stern 1991, p. 251.

122 Hammerslough 1965, p. 109. The theft of the Hays silver was reported in *The New-York Gazette*, April 6–13, 1767, p. 4.

123 *The New-York Mercury*, October 30, 1758, p. 2.

124 *The New-York Mercury*, October 26, 1761, p. 2.

125 Halpin published a ladle with an "I·P" mark as by Joseph Pinto, but this may be a mark of the London smallworker and hiltmaker James Perry, who registered six similar marks between 1765 and 1773; see Hammerslough 1965, pp. 106–09, and Grimwade 1990, no. 1582, pp. 118, 620. The crest engraved on the ladle is that used by the Stuyvesant family. There is no supporting provenance that connects this ladle to manufacture or ownership in New York City.

126 Delaplaine 1753–56, p. 34.

127 Both tankards were recorded with the mark "MM in cartouche," possibly MARK 3 (see Appendix I). Unfortunately, neither tankard could be located for this study. One was formerly in the YUAG collection, inv. 1930.1299, but was deaccessioned in 1948. The other was formerly in the Addison Gallery of American Art, Andover, Massachusetts (Rosenbaum 1954A, pp. 133–34), but was stolen in 1968.

128 Ward 1984, p. 147.

129 Barter et al. 1998, no. 99; Hammerslough 1958, p. 94; Waters/McKinsey/Ward 2000, I, no. 24.

130 Herr 1995, pp. 86–87. John Will's flagon is on loan to YUAG from the Woodbridge (Connecticut) Historical Society, inv. ILE1999.1.1; Montgomery 1978, fig. 4–42.

131 Scott 1953, pp. 42–44; Buhler/Hood 1970, II, no. 617.

132 *Supplement, The New-York Gazette Revived in The Weekly Post-Boy*, March 23, 1752, as cited in Gottesman 1936, p. 104. For silver and copper objects engraved by Leddel or his father, see Skerry/Sloane 1992; Fennimore 1996A, no. 191.

133 James Poupard, bill to Philip Schuyler, February 1, 1776, Schuyler Papers, NYPL. Poupard led a peripatetic life: he arrived in Philadelphia in 1772 and worked there until at least 1774, before moving to New York and by 1780 to Quebec, where he advertised "imported silver and plated work" for sale; Prime 1929, pp. 26, 86; Langdon 1960, p. 81. He apparently returned to Philadelphia around 1785 and moved back to New York around 1790; Darling 1964, p. 143.

134 *The New-York Mercury*, October 20, 1755, p. 4. For an account of Dawkins's career, see Heckscher/Bowman 1992, pp. 39, 52–54.

135 *Rivington's New-York Gazetteer*, June 24, 1773, p. 3; *The New-York Gazette and The Weekly Mercury*, November 7, 1774, p. 2.

136 *The New-York Gazette or The Weekly Mercury*, May 9, 1763, as cited in Gottesman 1936, pp. 13–14.

137 Fales 1974, fig. 24.

138 Waters/McKinsey/Ward 2000, I, pp. 133–35.

139 Scott 1953, p. 126; Newman 1990, pp. 258–61.

140 Waters/McKinsey/Ward, I, no. 26.

141 Buhler/Hood 1970, II, p. 137; the bill is reproduced in Ward/Ward 1979, p. 75.

142 Waters/McKinsey/Ward 2000, II, p. 300. Coen's bill for the service amounted to £20.16.6, but the client supplied almost three-quarters of the silver required to make the set, amounting to roughly another £26.

143 The waiter is in the collection of Ruth J. Nutt. The Onderdonck arms are: argent, a lion rampant sable; Matthews 1965, p. 165.

144 *Rococo* 1984, pp. 50–55; Kane 1998, pp. 92–94.

145 Waters/McKinsey/Ward 2000, I, no. 55.

146 Buhler 1972, II, no. 506.

147 Pulos/Schwartz 1959, fig. 13.

148 *The New-York Journal or The General Advertiser*, December 20, 1770, p. 4.

149 Failey 1971, p. 5.

150 Heckscher 1979, pl. 14–15; see also Heckscher/Bowman 1992, pp. 2–3.

151 Largeworker's Register vol. B2, p. 18, Library of the Worshipful Company of Goldsmiths, London.

152 Quimby/Johnson 1995, p. 230.

153 Wolfe 1963, p. 144. Fueter's name was misspelled "Tueter" in the original record, so it was not picked up in previous examinations of this source.

154 *The New-York Gazette and The Weekly Mercury*, July 31, 1769, p. 3.

155 Stern 1991, p. 251, gives Abraham Pinto's date of death as circa March 1797, but the *ketubah* for Joseph's Pinto's marriage to Jochabed Hays, dated November 6, 1765, names Joseph as "son of the late distinguished married man Abraham Pinto"; archives of Congregation Shearith Israel, New York, cited in Pool 1952, p. 310.

156 Waters/McKinsey/Ward 2000, I, pp. 32–34.

157 Buhler/Hood 1970, II, pp. 135–36, nos. 718–19.

158 In conversation with the author, May 2000.

159 Ensko 1948, p. 61; the same photograph in Stow 1950, p. 43.

160 Heckscher/Bowman 1992, p. 75; Robert B. Barker to the author, May 21, 2000. I am indebted to Robert Barker for his thoughtful examinations of the English export records for this period as well as for his willingness to share this research with me.

161 Alcorn 2000B, p. 3.

162 Hare/Snodin/Clifford 1990, p. 27.

163 "Invoice of Sundries Sent to America," pp. 2–3; undated manuscript, Schuyler Papers, NYPL. Schuyler's trip to London is discussed in Cunningham 1955, p. 4, and Gerlach 1964, pp. 32–33.

164 This observation was made by Robert B. Barker.

165 Private collection, reprod. in *Antiques*, 149 (January 1996), p. 86.

166 Fales 1974, pp. 210–19.

167 See Daybook 1755–69. Samuel Oppenheim (1913) determined that the merchant was Jewish, sinced five-sixths of his transactions were with Jews, and the word for Passover was written in Hebrew in an entry for July 12, 1755. Oppenheim proposed David Franks (cat. 4) as the owner, but this seems unlikely because there are numerous transactions with Franks in the book.

168 Daybook 1755–69, p. 6.

169 Ibid., p. 17.

170 Gratz 1757–62B, n.p.

171 NYCPR-1, liber 9, pp. 486, 492–95.

172 De Lancey 1876, p. 18.

173 Kierner 1992; Bonomi 1971, pp. 71–74.

174 Bonomi 1971, pp. 71–74; Kierner 1992, pp. 7–8.

175 Bonomi 1971, pp. 69–75.

176 Notebook no. 1, p. 350, Lyons Collection, box 7, AJHS; the marriage date recorded by Lyons is Adar II 17, 5527. Joyce's mother, Jochabed (Michaels) Mears, was the sister of Rachel (Michaels) Myers Cohen, the second wife of Elkaleh's father, Samuel Myers Cohen; as noted above (n. 69), Elkaleh's maternity is uncertain.

177 Stern 1991, pp. 104, 120, 190, 193.

178 Ibid., p. 190.

179 De Lancey 1885, p. 136.

180 Together with Nathan and Isaac Levy, Mears contributed £3 toward the purchase of land for the burial ground, and two months later Mears donated £2.10.0 to buy the lot for the Mill Street Synagogue; KKSI-MB1, pp. 13 (Elul 2, 5488), 25.

181 Abrahams 1756–81, no. 35 (Shebat 21, 5528).

182 The birth of "Richa" Myers was recorded on Sivan 5, 5529 and Moses Mears Myers on Tevet 28, 5531 ("Livro dos Miseberagh," pp. 62–62v). Moses's circumcision was recorded on Shebat 6, 5531 (January 21, 1771); Abrahams 1756–81, no. 50.

183 Hershkowitz 1981, p. 466. The birth dates given for Myers's children by Hershkowitz are incorrect. Peter Middleton, a Tory, was appointed Deputy Grand Master of New York during the Revolutionary War; Singer/Lang 1981, p. 31.

184 *The New-York Mercury*, May 4, 1767, as cited in Rosenbaum 1954A, p. 54.

185 Hershkowitz 1981, pp. 465–66.

186 Stern 1991, p. 217.

187 Hershkowitz 1981, p. 464.

188 Batchellor 1895, pp. 510–14, 537–40.

189 Hull 1966, pp. 5–6.

190 Shepard 1831, p. 312.

191 Dexter 1885–1912, I, p. 653; Cothren 1854, pp. 697–99.

192 Shepard 1831, pp. 312, 314, first asserted that the proprietors were seeking precious metals, such as silver. The actual history was clarified in Hull 1966, pp. 3–4, 10.

193 Marcus 1970, III, p. 1497.

194 Piwonka 1986, pp. 37–40.

195 Kane 1998, p. 883.

196 Curtis 1913, p. 48.

197 Ward 1984, p. 147.

198 Connecticut State Archives, Revolutionary War Series I, vol. 1, part 2, doc. 246, Connecticut State Library, Hartford. As had been Myers's own experience with lead mining, the committee eventually determined that "the manufacture of said ore was unprofitable to the State." In 1778, the Assembly ordered the discontinuation of further smelting of lead ore at the mine; Hinman 1842, p. 313.

199 Marcus 1970, II, p. 670; indenture between Isaac Moses and Edward Somerville, London, May 19, 1758, M.A. Levy Collection, Keith Read Manuscript Collection, University of Georgia, Athens.

200 George Trail was sworn a Freeman of New York City as a "snuff maker" on September 27, 1769; De Lancey 1885, p. 227, and Scott 1969, p. 136.

201 *The New-York Gazette or The Weekly Post-Boy*, May 27, 1754, p. 3; *The New-York Gazette, and The Weekly Mercury*, July 31, 1769, p. 3.

202 Hull 1966, p. 8.

203 Ibid., p. 9.

204 Shepard 1831, p. 315.

205 Spruce Hill Lead Mine, account book, Litchfield Historical Society, Litchfield, Connecticut.

206 Receipt, New York, November 27, 1765, Gratz Manuscripts, case 8, box 14, Historical Society of Pennsylvania, Philadelphia.

207 Kauffman 1966, p. 22.

208 Spruce Hill Mine Papers, private collection.

209 Hull 1966, pp. 9–10.

210 Woodbury Land Records, vol. 22, p. 32, Woodbury Town Hall, Connecticut. I am indebted to Edward S. Cooke, Jr., for this reference.

211 The Boston silversmith Jacob Hurd experienced similar financial problems between 1745 and 1755; see Kane 1998, p. 583.

212 NYCMCR, Parchment 143 C-4.

213 The Writ Book recording these suits apparently no longer survives; they were recorded in the Samuel J. Oppenheim Papers, AJHS, cited in Rosenbaum 1954A, p. 58.

214 Myer Myers, Deposition to Richard Morris, June 4, 1790, AJHS; Palmer 1984, p. 920; Zimm et al. 1946, I, p. 26.

215 *Rivington's New-York Gazetteer*, July 8, 1773, p. 3.

216 *Rivington's New-York Gazetteer*, August 26, 1773, p. 4.

217 *Rivington's New-York Gazetteer*, September 23, 1773, p. 3.

218 KKSI-MB2 (Tishri 4, 5524); Rosenbaum 1954A, p. 33; Pool 1955, p. 502.

219 Pool 1930, p. 53; Rosenbaum 1954A, p. 42.

220 Hershkowitz 1966, pp. 119–22; see also *The New-York Journal; or the General Advertiser*, October 6, 1774, p. 4.

221 Smith/Tatsch 1937, pp. 21–26.

222 Coen 1954–55.

223 Gutstein 1936, pp. 193–94.

224 Leehey et al. 1988, pp. 121–22.

225 Ibid., pp. 125–26.

226 Singer/Lang 1981, p. 31; Franks 1786, p. 130.

227 *The New-York Gazette; and The Weekly Mercury*, May 20, 1771, p. 3.

228 Hershkowitz 1981, pp. 466–67.

229 Low 1796, p. 114; *Longworth's* 1797, p. 234.

230 Stern 1991, p. 179; see also Pool 1952, pp. 239–40.

231 Hershkowitz 1981, pp. 462–63.

232 *The New-York Gazette or, the Weekly Post-Boy*, May 15, 1758, p. 1.

233 *The Pennsylvania Journal and Weekly Advertiser*, March 10, 1763, p. 3; *The Pennsylvania Gazette*, July 5, 1770, as cited Prime 1929, p. 60.

234 Pleasants/Sill 1930, p. 266; Burton 1991, pp. 79, 107–08.

235 *The Pennsylvania Packet*, May 1, 1784, p. 3.

236 De Lancey 1885, p. 183.

237 MCCNY-1, VII, pp. 164, 172, 227.

238 Fennimore 1996B, n.p. (pp. 2v–3r of original).

239 MCCNY-2, I, p. 363; Stern 1991, p. 217.

240 Samson Mears to Aaron Lopez, February 23, 1779, as cited in Marcus 1949, p. 42.

241 *New-York Directory* 1790, p. 74; *Longworth's* 1797, p. 256; for Judah and Sampson Myers, see Stern 1991, p. 217.

242 Puig et al. 1989, pp. 73–74.

243 *The New-York Chronicle*, July 13–20, 1769, p. 95; September 14–21, 1769, p. 167.

244 McFadden/Clark 1989, nos. 14–16.

245 Friedman 1975, p. 68, pl. 155–59.

246 Flynt/Fales 1968, pp. 91–92. The Rococo cartouche and flanking foliage were executed at the time the waiters were made; the original heraldic devices were later erased and replaced with the crest of the Cecil family, presumably after these waiters had migrated to England. Henry Flynt purchased them from the English collector Lionel Crichton in July 1956.

247 Monograms with characteristic surrounds are found on at least two objects by Brasher: a tankard (Waters/McKinsey/Ward 2000, II, no. 135) and a coffee urn at The Art Institute of Chicago (Barter et al. 1998, no. 33).

248 Oman 1978, pp. 91, 100.

249 Reid 1938–39, pp. 100–03.

250 *The New-York Gazette or the Weekly Post-Boy*, January 31, 1757, as cited in Gottesman 1936, p. 51.

251 *The New-York Gazette or, the Weekly Post-Boy*, August 16, 1762, as cited in Gottesman 1936, pp. 51–52.

252 *The New-York Mercury*, April 29, 1765, p. 4.

253 Heckscher/Bowman 1992, p. 75; Ver Planck 1892, p. 152.

254 The Gouverneur cup is at NYHS, inv. 1984.57ab. For information on the owners, see Pelletreau 1907, I, p. 162; Johnson 1939, p. 137; Hoffman 1899, p. 516.

255 Now at YUAG, inv. 1981.21; see "Woolsey Bowl" 1943; Dwight 1873, p. 144.

256 *Philadelphia* 1976, no. 44; Fales 1974, pp. 79, 82, 87–89; Kane 1998, pp. 94–96.

257 Flynt/Fales 1968, p. 64; Buhler/Hood 1970, II, nos. 647–48.

258 Buhler/Hood 1970, II, p. 93.

259 Wees 1997, no. 54; Finlay 1956, pl. 67, 88.

260 Day 1909, p. 351.

261 Kane 1998, pp. 94–95.

262 *The New-York Gazette*, October 1–8, 1733, as cited in Gottesman 1936, p. 31; Waters/McKinsey/Ward 2000, I, no. 64.

263 Buhler/Hood 1970, II, no. 651.

264 Waters/McKinsey/Ward 2000, I, p. 134.

265 Wolfe 1963, p. 143.

266 De Lancey 1885, p. 222.

267 Von Khrum 1978, p. 98.

268 *The New-York Gazette*, March 14, 1763, p. 3; *The New-York Journal; or, The General Advertiser*, February 9, 1769, p. 3.

269 *The New-York Gazette*, March 14, 1763, p. 3.

270 *The New-York Gazette or The Weekly Post-Boy*, December 19, 1757, p. 2.

271 *The New-York Gazette, and The Weekly Mercury*, July 31, 1769, p. 3.

272 *The Pennsylvania Packet and The General Advertiser*, July 13, 1772, p. 1.

273 Similar patterns appear on a set of tea canisters and a sugar box by Samuel Herbert and Company of 1751–52 as well as on a teapot by

Thomas Whipham and Charles Wright of 1763–64, and a tea canister of 1774–75 by Matthew Boulton and James Fothergill of Birmingham. The first two are in the Victoria and Albert Museum, London, inv. M24:1-2B-1945 (tea canisters and sugar box), M43-1993 (teapot); the Boulton and Fothergill tea canister is reprod. in Delieb/Roberts 1971, p. 95.

274 For similar chasing on Irish silver, see Teahan 1979, pls. 5, 26; Davis 1992, nos. 32, 36; Wees 1997, no. 89.

275 Buhler/Hood 1970, II, no. 727; von Khrum 1978, p. 83; *Rivington's New-York Gazetteer*, September 23, 1773, p. 3.

276 Waters/McKinsey/Ward 2000, I, no. 23.

277 Rowe 1965, p. 54.

278 I am grateful to Robert B. Barker for discussing his research into the Aldrige group with me.

279 Barr 1980, p. 61; Wees 1997, p. 189.

280 Buhler 1972, II, no. 504.

281 *The New-York Gazette or The Weekly Post-Boy*, September 18, 1766, p. 3.

282 Kane 1998, pp. 312, 1061–63, 1073.

283 Fales 1974, pp. 166, 175–77, 186–87.

284 Buhler/Hood 1970, II, no. 588; Puig et al. 1989, no. 191; Waters/McKinsey/Ward 2000, I, no. 79.

285 Kane 1998, pp. 9, 19–24.

286 Ibid., pp. 86–87, 193–95.

287 A mourning ring made for Philip Philipse was stolen from the New York antiques dealers Ginsburg and Levy in the 1960s and remains unlocated; it was illustrated and recorded in Rosenbaum 1954A, p. 116, pl. 6, and Bohan 1963, pp. 21, 43, no. 105.

288 The Philipse mourning ring appears to be struck with MARK 6 (Rosenbaum 1954A, pl. 6).

289 Rosenbaum 1954A, p. 37.

290 Smith 1966, pp. 204–05, 207, lists F and G.

291 *The Royal Gazette*, November 17, 1781, p. 2.

292 Fales 1995, pp. 66–70.

293 Henry Miers to Barnard Gratz, London, Adar 19, 5523 (March 4, 1763), Gratz Papers, AJHS. Translation provided by AJHS.

294 *New-York Journal or the General Advertiser*, March 9, 1775, p. 3; Marcus 1970, II, p. 539, III, p. 1469.

295 Stern 1991, p. 101. Two of Judah Hart's other sons came to New York in the 1830s.

296 *The New-York Weekly Post-Boy*, November 10, 1746, as cited in Gottesman 1936, p. 30.

297 *The New-York Gazette or The Weekly Post-Boy*, June 9, 1763, as cited in Gottesman 1936, p. 33.

298 *Rococo* 1984, pp. 127–28.

299 *The New-York Gazette or, The Weekly Mercury*, July 31, 1769, p. 3.

300 *The New-York Mercury*, May 20, 1765, p. 2.

301 *The Diary; or Loudon's Register*, August 15, 1792, p. 1.

302 Rasmussen 1991, pp. 69–70.

303 *The New-York Gazette or Weekly Post-Boy*, August 27, 1770, as cited in Gottesman 1936, p. 44.

304 Fennimore 1996B, n.p. (pp. 3v–4r of original).

305 Franks 1786, p. 55; Franks 1787, pp. 16, 48.

306 Population schedules, first census (1790), New York, IV, p. 116, National Archives, Washington, D.C.; Duncan 1791, p. 48; Duncan 1795. p. 84.

307 I am indebted to Paul Cushman of New York for his carefully researched inventory of Gilbert's work; a copy is in the silversmith research files, American Arts Office, YUAG.

308 For the relationship between Gilbert and Brasher, see Waters/McKinsey/Ward 2000, II, p. 289.

309 Waters/McKinsey/Ward 2000, II, nos. 191–92.

310 Parisien marked at least two tankards, one of which, "a Silver Tankard, that holds about a quart, made by Mr. Parisien, having his stamp at the bottom" was stolen from Philip Kissick in September 1778; *The Royal Gazette*, September 9, 1778, p. 2. Another tankard by Parisien is in the Henry E. Huntington Library, Museum and Gardens, San Marino, Cali-

fornia, Gift of the Wunsch Americana Foundation. Flatware and jewelry by Parisien is recorded in *Checklist* 1968, s.v. "Parisien."

311 The teapot was owned by the dealers Robert Jackson and Ann Gillooly, Doylestown, Pennsylvania; the coffeepot is reprod. in *Maine Antique Digest*, 26 (February 1998), p. 10-A.

312 Christening records of the First and Second Presbyterian Churches, New York, 1722–87, fiche 1002749, *International Genealogical Index* (microfiche), Salt Lake City, Church of Jesus Christ of Latter-Day Saints, 1984.

313 De Lancey 1885, p. 211; *Rivington's New-York Gazetteer*, January 27, 1774, p. 4.

314 Cary Dunn to Colonel Philip Schuyler, January 28, 1775, Library, Albany Institute of History and Art. I am grateful to Chief Librarian Sandra J. Markham for bringing this bill to my attention.

315 Duncan 1791, p. 38; see also Von Khrum 1978, p. 42.

316 The porringer is in NYHS, inv. 1954.163; for the sugar dish, see Norman-Wilcox 1954, p. 50, fig. 8.

317 Buhler/Hood 1970, I, no. 340. The later engraved inscription records the gift of this chafing dish from William Samuel Johnson (1859–1937) to William Harmon Beers (d. 1949), the son of his wife, Caroline Ryder (Gatley) Beers and her first husband (see cats. 22–25).

318 Flick 1927, p. 265.

319 Day 1909, p. 353, no. 125. Johnson also has been erroneously identified as the patron of a pair of Neoclassical pint tankards that Myers made well after Johnson's death; Larus n.d., p. 6.

320 Day 1909, p. 351.

321 Ibid., p. 344, no. 47.

322 Rice 1964, p. 13.

323 Minute book of St. Patrick's Lodge No. VIII [now No. 4], n.p.; see *St. Patrick's Lodge* 1966.

324 I am grateful to Kirk D. Swineheart for bringing these jewels to my attention and am especially indebted to Wade Wells of St. Patrick's Lodge for making the jewels and the Lodge's records available to me.

325 Cornell 1902, p. 190.

326 Dill 1955, pp. 128–54; Powell 1981, pp. 661, 740.

327 Hood 1971, pp. 131–32; Heckscher/Bowman 1992, p. 122.

328 A few unlocated objects by Myers confirm this pattern. Rosenbaum recorded a ladle with an initials mark and a turned wood handle owned by Samuel and Richea (Gratz) Hays, who were married in 1794, and which therefore was probably inherited from a previous generation; Rosenbaum 1954A, p. 113. A pedestal-base milk pot descended from Solomon and Rachel (Gratz) Moses, who were married in 1806 and therefore also inherited it from their parents, all patrons of Myers: Isaac and Reyna Moses and Barnard and Richea Gratz; Rosenbaum 1954A, p. 110.

329 *The New-York Gazette*, April 6–13, 1767, p. 4. It seems likely that the "BH" described as engraved on these spoons was a typographical error in the newspaper for "RH." Some of this silver apparently was inherited from Rebecca's parents, Moses and Katherine (Hachar) Michaels.

330 Judah and Moses Michael Hays, receipt book H, 1763–66, no. 59, Virginia State Library, Richmond.

331 *The New-York Gazette or The Weekly Post-Boy*, March 18, 1754, p. 4.

332 The spoons descended to Moses and Elkaleh Sheftall's great-great-granddaughter; Stern 1991, pp. 5, 28, 267, 278.

333 Stern 1991, p. 223. Mathias Bush was Myers's relative twice over: his first wife, Tabitha Mears, was the paternal aunt of Myers's second wife.

334 Mordecai Sheftall was a merchant, but his primary contacts seem to have been in England and the West Indies rather than in New York; Sheftall 1984, pp. 71–73; Stern 1991, pp. 98, 267.

335 Gratz 1757–62A, p. 33.

336 Daybook 1755–69, p. 50.

337 Jamilly 1999, p. 7.

338 *Clarksons* 1876, pp. 217–18.

339 Nash 1979, pp. 246–50, 312–25.

340 Kammen 1975, pp. 332, 357–59.

341 Failey 1971, pp. 106–08.

342 KKSI-MB2 (Tishri 3, 5536).

343 Knight 1901, pp. 64–66.

344 Notes from Writ Book, 1773–76, Samuel J. Oppenheim Papers, AJHS, cited in Rosenbaum 1954A, p. 58. Three different men named Thomas Hun, all first cousins and grandsons of Thomas Harmense Hun, lived in New York at this time; see Talcott 1883, pp. 93–97.

345 Samson Mears to Aaron Lopez, April 28, 1779, in Marcus 1949, p. 45.

346 Marcus 1951, pp. 174–76.

347 Mordecai 1796, n.p.

348 Connecticut State Archives, Revolutionary War Series I, vol. 5, doc. 427, Connecticut State Library, Hartford; Dexter 1885–1912, II, pp. 699–701; Marcus 1949, pp. 18–20, 23. Although as early as 1903, Hühner (1903, p. 88) observed that "The Isaacs family, while not Jews, are repeatedly referred to as of Jewish descent," this error was perpetuated in a 1927 genealogy that described Isaacs as "of Hebraic lineage"; see New Haven Genealogical Magazine, 4 (1927), p. 909. Isaacs in fact was a lifelong member of the Church of England, and his wife, Mary Perit, was the great-granddaughter of Pierre Perit, the first Huguenot minister in New York; Dexter 1895–1912, VI, pp. 699–701. See also Marcus 1949, p. 20 n. 8: "He will have to be considered a non-Jew"; and Stern 1991, p. 126: "There is nothing to show that Ralph was Jewish."

349 Connecticut State Archives, Revolutionary War Series I, vol. 8, doc. 82, Connecticut State Library, Hartford.

350 Mordecai 1796, n.p.

351 Samson Mears to Aaron Lopez, July 30, 1779, in Marcus 1951, p. 172.

352 Samson Mears to Aaron Lopez, October 8, 1779, in Marcus 1949, p. 47.

353 Connecticut State Archives, Revolutionary War Series I, vol. 15, doc. 265, and vol. 18, doc. 269, Connecticut State Library, Hartford.

354 Marcus 1951, p. 160.

355 Marcus 1949, p. 27; Stern 1991, p. 251.

356 Two Hundred 1890, p. 108.

357 James H. Linsely, A Plan of Stratford, 1824 (printed map); Stratford Historical Society, Connecticut. On this map, Nehemiah Curtiss's house is labeled as the property of his son, Freeman Curtiss. For Stephen, Levi, Nehemiah, and Freeman Curtiss, see Curtiss 1903, pp. 77, 86.

358 Nehmiah and Freeman Curtiss Account Book, 1779–1856, p. 33, Stratford Historical Society, Connecticut. I am indebted to both Edward S. Cooke, Jr., and Hiram Tindall for bringing this account book to my attention.

359 Rosenbaum 1954A, pp. 45–46; the offerings are recorded as being made on "Ros hodes Iyar."

360 KKMI-MB, Nisan 9, 5542-Elul 30, 5543. See also Rosenbach 1909, pp. 11–12, in which Myer Myers is listed as a contributor but not as a member of the congregation.

361 The younger Myer Myers was the son of Hyam Myers (d. c. 1801) and Rachel Louzada (d. 1790), whose paternal uncle Aaron Louzada was married to Blume (Michaels), the sister of Joyce Myers's mother, Jochabed; Stern 1991, pp. 179, 193, 218. Born in New York, he had moved with his parents to Montreal by 1763 and apparently lived in Charleston, South Carolina, after the Revolutionary War. In November 1786, "Myer Myers Junr of Charleston" was listed among Jacob Mordecai's largest debtors, owing £614.17.7 3/4; NYCIR-2, box 1786–87, file 42. He presumably also was the Myer Myers who, on May 6, 1785, received a loan of 3,960 Dutch guilders from the New York merchant Nicholas Low in exchange for one-half interest in the schooner Count DeGrasse, bound for Tortola and Dominica; Nicholas Low, Certificate of sale, New York, May 6, 1785, Kane American Autograph Collection, Henry E. Huntington Library, Museum and Gardens, San Marino, California. Hope Spencer discovered this certificate and kindly brought it to my attention. Myer Myers the merchant died unmarried on April 5, 1791, in Les Cayes, Haiti, where there was a small Jewish community; Loker 1983, pp. 138–39.

362 Mordecai 1796, n.p.

363 Labaree 1943, pp. 222–23.

364 A "Hanoverian" pattern tablespoon, struck twice with MARK 9 and engraved with the initials "L/GM," was found in an outbuilding of an old Stratford house in the 1960s. It may have been made for George Lewis and Mary Wheeler, who were married in 1758; Orcutt 1886, pp. 1239, 1334; this spoon is in the collection of Mrs. Todd Lovell, who kindly brought it to my attention. A "silver spoon; sleeve buttons, said to be beryl, set in silver, made by Mier Miers, a Jew goldsmith" were catalogued in Two Hundred 1890, p. 108, no. 106. A teaspoon made for Phoebe Lewis of Stratford probably postdates Myers's residence in the town (see n. 383 below).

365 Friedman 1975, p. 68, pl. 151; Sympson 1750, p. 28.

366 Marriage Licenses 1860, p. 55.

367 Stephens 1950, p. 17. Muster and Pay Rolls 1915, pp. 500, 502–03, lists three different individuals named John Burger as recipients of muskets but does not record their professions.

368 The New York Paquet and The American Advertiser, January 1, 1784, p. 4.

369 Pleasants/Sill 1941; Langdon 1968; Quimby/Johnson 1995, p. 255.

370 KKSI-MB2 (Kislev 14, 5544).

371 Appointment of Trustees, Sivan 28, 5544, Lyons Collection, box 2, file 111, AJHS.

372 "Inventory of papers in chest," Lyons Collection, box 2, file 116, AJHS.

373 Franks 1787, pp. 26–27.

374 NYCMCMB, 1787–89, pp. 75, 93, 135. The Judgment in this case was signed on January 21 and filed on February 8, 1788; NYCMCR, case 269.

375 New-York Directory 1789, p. 65; New-York Directory 1790, p. 74.

376 Population schedules, first census (1790), New York, IV, p. 57, National Archives, Washington, D.C.

377 Duncan 1791, p. 92; Duncan 1792, p. 97; Duncan 1793, p. 111; Duncan 1794, p. 134; Duncan 1795, p. 156.

378 Montogmery/Kane 1976, p. 32.

379 Waters/McKinsey/Ward 2000, I, p. 49.

380 Ibid., p. 46.

381 Rowe 1965, p. 76; Stephens 1950, p. 95.

382 Buhler/Hood 1970, II, nos. 692, 729; Waters/McKinsey/Ward 2000, II, nos. 143, 194; Darling 1964, p. 66; Phillips/Parker/Buhler 1955, p. 89; Decatur 1941, p. 61.

383 The teaspoon is at the Stratford Historical Society, inv. 4483. The donor, Harriet Greenleaf (Plant) Moles, was the great-great-great granddaughter of Phoebe Lewis (1765–1842) and her husband, William Augur Tomlinson (b. 1763), also of Stratford, whom she married in 1786; Orcutt 1886, pp. 1238, 1313. The spoon is engraved with the script monogram "PL" and is struck once with MARK 9.

384 Failey 1971, pp. 68, 108–11, 171.

385 Mayor's Court Records, New York (microfilm), reel 2, frames 123–27, AJHS. Malcolm was represented by his attorney, Aaron Burr, who had served in Malcolm's regiment during the Revolutionary War; Kline et al. 1983, I, pp. lxii–lxiii; II, pp. 1193–94.

386 Von Khrum, pp. ix–x.

387 Ibid., p. 28.

388 Laidlaw 1988, pp. 25–32.

389 Waters 2000, p. 361.

390 The Pennsylvania Gazette, August 27, 1783, p. 3.

391 Franks 1786, p. 33.

392 NYCIR-1, box 13, Halsted file.

393 The New-York Packet, June 8, 1787, p. 3.

394 The Diary; or, Evening Register, August 30, 1794, p. 4.

395 Von Khrum 1978, pp. 61–62.

396 Sickels 1967, p. 372, fig. 5.

397 Hamilton 1995, p. 171; for Hinsdale, see Williams 1949, pp. 96–98.

398 Burger also held a number of civic offices, including Coroner and Regulator of Clocks and in 1787 served as deputy chairman of the Society of Mechanics and Tradesmen. See MCCNY-2, III, p. 378; VIII, p. 733; Franks 1786, p. 77; Waters/McKinsey/Ward 2000, II, pp. 293–94.

399 Gilje/Rock 1992, p. 4.

400 Laidlaw 1988, esp. p. 36, table 2.

401 Waters 2000, pp. 359–63; Waters/McKinsey/Ward 2000, I, pp. 47–49.

402 KKSI-MB2 (Tammuz 29, 5544).

403 Pool/Pool 1955, p. 503.

404 "Rent Roll of the Estate of W^m. Brownejohn deceased," AJHS.

405 NYCLR, liber 44, p. 184.

406 Pool 1952, p. 75.

407 NYCIR-1, box 5, Cox file.

408 *Mayor's Court Records, New York* (microfilm), reel 3, frames 46–47; reel 5, frames 1–2; AJHS. The present author was unable to locate the original documents in NYCMCR.

409 "List of Debts Due to the Sedaka," Nisan 8, 5547, Lyons Collection, box 2, file 91, AJHS.

410 Ibid.

411 Myer Myers, deposition to Richard Morris, June 4, 1790, AJHS

412 Hull 1966, p. 14.

413 "Sales of the Mens Seats in Synagogue," August 26, 1792, Lyons Collection, box 2, file 113, AJHS.

414 "Report of the Committee respectg School," Adar I 2, 5554, Lyons Collection, box 2, file 75, AJHS.

415 "Bills Rec^d of Mr Lazarus," second quarter 5555 to first quarter 5556, Lyons Collection, box 3, file 112, AJHS. The second quarter of 5555 was between Adar 29 and Sivan 30.

416 Mordecai 1847, p. 46.

417 A tombstone in the burial ground previously identified as Myer Myers's (Phillips/Phillips 1894, p. 257) was probably that of Manuel Myers (1727–1799), who in his will directed "my said Executrix and Executor shall cause a Tomb Stone to be erected for me to the value of Ten pounds . . . at least"; NYCPR-2, liber 42, pp. 496–500; Pool 1952, pp. 280–81.

Catalogue
of the Exhibition

Silver
by
Myer Myers

Cats. 1–104

1

Teapot, 1746–54

Silver with wood handle, h. 7½ (19.1), w. 8½ (21.6), diam. base 3⅛ (7.9), diam. rim 2¾ (7), gross wt. 21 oz. 11 dwt. (670g)

MARK 1 once on underside of body

INSCRIPTION: "F/N*T" engraved on underside of body

PROVENANCE: Nicoll Floyd (1705–1755) and Tabitha Smith (1704–1755), who were married in Smithtown, Long Island, in 1730; by descent to William Floyd II, by whose heirs sold at auction in 1982.[1]

Private collection

This teapot is the earliest documented object to bear Myers's mark as an independent craftsman; the initials engraved on the underside indicate that it was made prior to Tabitha (Smith) Floyd's death on January 17, 1755; her husband died two months later.[2] By the early 1750s, teapots of this pyriform shape were out of fashion in England, where they had been popular during the first quarter of the eighteenth century. This form was most frequently made in the American Colonies by New York City craftsmen, including Henricus Boelen, Thauvet Besley, and Peter Van Dyck (cat. 105), and remained popular into the 1760s.[3] Daniel Christian Fueter marked an example between 1754 and 1769.[4] Subtle influences of the Rococo style can be perceived in Myers's use of a broader spreading foot and the more exaggerated curves of the outline.

Nicoll Floyd was a prosperous landowner in Mastic, Long Island. In 1744, his wife inherited half of the estate of her father, Jonathan Smith of Smithtown, Long Island, which included substantial landholdings in Suffolk County.[5] Like many of Long Island's landowning families, the Floyds were conservative in their choice of household furnishings.[6] Dean Failey characterized their son William Floyd as "interested in fashion, but . . . tempered by his upbringing on rural Long Island and his limited exposure to urban influences."[7] The Floyds' patronage of Myers may have provided the craftsman with his connection to Nicoll's sister, Charity (Floyd) Nicoll Johnson, who became one of Myers's most important patrons during the mid-1750s (cats. 20–23).

1 Sotheby's 1982A, lot 197B.
2 *Abstracts* 1892–1906, III, p. 440. Jones 1907, p. 194, incorrectly gives Nicoll Floyd's date of death as 1752. Floyd signed his will on March 5, 1755. It was not proved until February 8, 1757; NYCPR-1, liber 20, p. 188.
3 Buhler/Hood 1970, II, nos. 593, 595, 620.
4 The Fueter teapot is illustrated and described in Quimby/Johnson 1995, pp. 231–32, no. 193. It has been published erroneously as by Myer Myers in Ensko 1948, p. 61, and Stow 1950, p. 43.
5 NYCPR-1, liber 15, pp. 276–80; *Abstracts* 1892–1906, IV, p. 19.
6 Failey 1976, pp. 68–74.
7 Ibid., p. 68.

2

Tankard, 1746–55

Silver, h. 7⅞ (20), diam. base 5¹¹⁄₁₆ (14.4), diam. rim 4½ (11.4), wt. 38 oz. 6 dwt. (1192g)

MARK 1 twice at rim, flanking handle (one double-struck)

INSCRIPTION: "JEH" (mirror-cypher monogram) engraved on cover

PROVENANCE: unknown prior to 1925, when Francis P. Garvan acquired it from the New York branch of the London silversmiths and antiques dealers Crichton Brothers.

Yale University Art Gallery, New Haven; Mabel Brady Garvan Collection

Although the original owners of this tankard are unidentified, it can be dated to the earliest years of Myers's career. It bears the same mark as the Floyd teapot (cat. 1). Like this teapot, as well as a cann with the same mark (fig. 12), the tankard follows a New York model of the second quarter of the eighteenth century. Unlike contemporary tankards made in England and New England, the New York model retained the broader proportions, plain body, and flat cover of seventeenth-century versions of the form. Tankards with similar thumbpieces, base moldings, and handle terminals were made in New York between 1725 and 1740 by John Hastier and between 1745 and

1760 by Nicholas Roosevelt; the Hastier example has a mirror cypher engraved on its cover similar to that found on Myers's tankard (fig. 13).[1] Other examples of Myers's earliest silver engraved with mirror cyphers include a waiter (fig. 10) and a set of tablespoons with the same mark.[2]

Myers made another tankard identical to this example in size and in most of its details, save for additional beading on the drop below the hinge.[3] As indicated by the initials engraved on the handle, it was owned originally by the New York merchant Ennis Graham and his first wife, Sarah Man, between their marriage in 1747 and Sarah's death prior to 1763.[4] The Graham tankard bears Myers's MARK 2, which appears on other early silver by him (cats. 3, 4).

1 Buhler/Hood 1970, II, nos. 618, 643.
2 The tablespoons are in the Wadsworth Atheneum Museum of Art, Hartford, inv. 1977.73A-F.
3 Rosenbaum 1954A, p. 132; reprod. in Rosenbaum 1954B, p. 127.
4 The cover was later engraved with the script monogram "EEG" when Graham married his second wife, Elizabeth Wilcox, in July 1763; "Trinity Church Marriages 1746–1861," fiche 0882993; Harrison 1981, pp., 166–67; "Pedigree of John Collins Daves," Society of the Cincinnati, Washington, D.C.

3

Waiter, 1746–55

Silver, h. 1⅛ (2.9), diam. 7⅝⁄₁₆ (18.6), wt. 11 oz. 8 dwt. (355g) (scratch wt. 11 oz. 15 dwt.)

MARK 2 twice, once on upper surface of one foot and once on underside

INSCRIPTION: "B/S★R" engraved on underside; "G" (script) added later on front; "PG/MJS/CAS" (script) added later on underside

PROVENANCE: original owners ("B/S★R") probably from the family of Maria E. Bocking (1735–1779), first wife of David Grim, the antiquarian (cat. 143); to their son, Philip Grim ("G" and "PG"; b. before 1779–d. before 1826); to his daughter, Maria Isabel ("MJS"), who married George Stevens Schermerhorn; to their son, Charles A. Schermerhorn ("CAS"); to his daughter, Constance (Schermerhorn) Skillin, the donor in 1937.[1]

The New-York Historical Society; Gift of Constance Schermerhorn Skillin

Like many of Myers's earliest works, this waiter, with its segmented border and hoof feet, is derived from London prototypes of the 1730s.[2] Many of these have six repeats in the border, whereas the five used by Myers permit a looser and more dynamic outline. Myers's version is similar in size and design to examples made in New York between 1744 and 1762 by Bartholomew Le Roux II and between 1756 and 1769 by Thomas Hammersley.[3]

1 The Royal Gazette, October 9, 1779, p. 3; GRSNS, II (1916), p. 35; III (1923), p. 39; NYHSQ, 22 (January 1938), p. 34. The waiter possibly could have been owned in the family of David Grim's second wife, Mary Barwick, whom he married on December 24, 1781, although her parents did not have these initials; Marriage Licenses 1860, p. 19.
2 Davis 1976, no. 130.
3 Waters 2000, I, no. 39; Buhler/Hood 1970, II, no. 677.

2

3

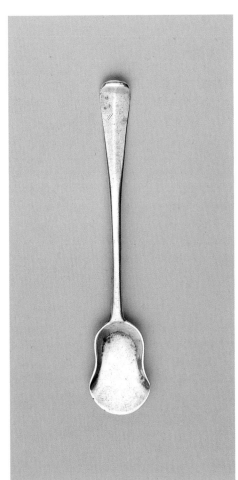

4

4

Salt Shovel, 1746–55

Silver, l. 3⅝ (9.2), wt. 5 dwt. (5g)

MARK 2 twice on back of handle

INSCRIPTION: "F/D M" engraved on back of handle

PROVENANCE: possibly David Franks (1720–1794) and his wife, Margaret Evans (1720–1780); subsequent history unknown until acquisition by the present owner.

Collection of Barbara and Roy Zuckerberg

Almost a third of Myers's surviving output is flatware, primarily spoons, and most of those made in his workshop during the Colonial period follow the same pattern as this one: a handle with an upturned, rounded end and a short, faint midrib, and a double drop at the juncture of the handle and the bowl. Today known as "Hanoverian," this style of spoon was first introduced in England at the beginning of the eighteenth century and remained popular in both England and America until the 1760s.[1] Because the majority of Myers's spoons are in this one pattern, they can be dated only by provenance and mark.

Although the history of this salt shovel is not documented, the initials engraved on it are those of David Franks and his wife, Margaret Evans, who were married in 1743. Franks was a Jew, the son of Jacob Franks and Bilhah Abigail Levy of New York. Despite his marriage to a Christian, he never renounced his religion, although his children were all baptized in the Church of England.[2] David and Margaret Franks owned a small waiter by Myers engraved with a mirror cypher of their initials (fig. 10) that descended in the family through their daughter Abigail (see cat. 99).[3] Given their patronage of Myers early in his career, it seems plausible that they also acquired this salt shovel from him.

Moreover, like other domestic silver by Myers owned by Jewish clients, the salt shovel is a modest object that would have been made for ready sale in Myers's retail store. Nicholas Roosevelt offered "salts and shovels" for sale in 1769.[4] A pair of salt shovels costing 10 shillings was listed on Halsted and Myers's 1760 bill to "Mrs. Levengston" (Appendix II, no. 2). It offers a dramatic contrast to the tea kettle, waiter, bread basket, and bowl with sumptuous chased Rococo ornament made in 1742–45 for David and Margaret Franks by Paul de Lamerie, apparently as wedding gifts from David's London relatives.[5]

1 Clayton 1971, p. 278.
2 Morais 1894, pp. 35–36.
3 The waiter was donated to the Historical Society of Pennsylvania by the Franks' great-great-great-great-granddaughter, Lena Cadwallader Evans; Stern 1991, pp. 75, 79–80.
4 The New-York Gazette and the Weekly Mercury, January 30, 1769, p. 3.
5 Dennis 1968, figs. 1–5; Hartop 1996, no. 77.

5

5

Milk Pot, 1751–65

Silver, h. 4¼ (10.8), w. 3¹⁵⁄₁₆ (10), d. 4¹⁄₁₆ (10.3), wt. 4 oz. 4 dwt. (130g)

MARK 8 once on underside

INSCRIPTION: "P/S R" engraved on underside

PROVENANCE: Samuel Prince (1727–1778) and Ruth Carman (b. 1729), who were married in Trinity Church, New York, on April 24, 1751; by descent to their granddaughter Susan Winter, who married John I. Plume; by descent in the family until sale at auction in 1988.[1]

Private collection

Requiring only about 5 troy oz. of silver, milk pots were modest, inexpensive forms that could be produced routinely in workshops such as Myer Myers's. Charles Oliver Bruff advertised in 1767 that he charged 24 shillings for making a milk pot, 11 shillings less than a sugar dish and only 4 shillings more than his charge for making a "Soop-spoon."[2] At least nine examples of this three-foot form survive with Myers's marks. The bold, symmetrical scrolls flanking the legs on this example indicate that it was a relatively early example of the form. This object is also one of the earliest to be struck with Myers's first surname mark (see Appendix I, MARK 8).

Inexpensive silver objects such as this were within the financial means of a successful craftsman like the cabinetmaker Samuel Prince. Although born in New York City, Prince apparently began working as a joiner in Flushing, Long Island, where a number of his children were born in the 1750s. There were several prominent patrons of Myers's from Flushing, including the Cornell family (cat. 13). By 1762, Prince had returned to New York, where he worked until his death.[3] He was described posthumously by his apprentice Thomas Burling as "a conspicuous character in his way, and esteemed one of the first workmen in this city."[4]

1 Christie's 1988, p. 43, lot 73. "Trinity Church Marriages" 1746–1861, fiche 882993; NYCPR-1, box 48, file 2883; Plumb 1893, pp. 44–45.
2 *The New-York Mercury*, April 20, 1767, as cited in Gottesman 1936, p. 33.
3 Prince signed a bond for John Lybourne on February 8, 1762, and his son Samuel Junior was born in New York on May 29 of the same year; Scott 1969, p. 86, and Prince 1899, p. 116.
4 *Loudon's New-York Packet*, January 24, 1785, p. 1.

6

Sauceboat

ORIGINALLY ONE OF A PAIR, 1750–65

Silver, h. 4⅝ (11.7), w. 7¼ (18.4), d. 4⅛ (10.5), wt. 12 oz. 14 dwt. (395g) (engraved wt. on underside: "ozˢ/25¾ yᵉ pʳ.")

MARK 8 once on underside, double-struck

INSCRIPTION: "B/T P" engraved on underside

PROVENANCE: unknown prior to sale at auction in 1982, when catalogued as "property of a descendant of the original owner."[1]

Private collection

The block capital initials engraved on the underside are the same as those on cat. 7, made for Thomas and Phebe Barnes. Also like the punch bowl, the weight is engraved rather than scratched on the underside. Given that both objects bear marks used by Myers early in his career, it is possible that the sauceboat and its now-unlocated mate were made originally for the same patrons.

Sauceboats were introduced into England in the second decade of the eighteenth century, and examples with three feet first appeared during the 1730s.[2] The double-scroll handle with leaf grip and the scroll legs above hoof feet are found on London examples from the early 1750s.[3] In comparison to cats. 17–18, the arrangement of the feet on this sauceboat gives more balance to the overall design than the unstable silhouette of the more Rococo versions. This stability is reinforced by the symmetrical ornaments on either side of the feet, evocative of Baroque scrolls seen on Myers's early waiter (fig. 10) and milk pot (cat. 5). This style of sauceboat was a popular among Myers's patrons, as evidenced by two additional examples with the same knee ornaments.[4] A sauceboat of the same design was marked by Bartholomew Le Roux II prior to 1763.[5]

1 Christie's 1982, lot 46.
2 Clayton 1971, pp. 231, 241, fig. 482.
3 Jackson 1911, II, p. 823.
4 Burke 1979, p. 14; Sotheby's 1991, lot 111.
5 Christie's 1983A, p. 25, lot 68.

7

7

Punch Bowl, 1746–63

Silver, h. 4 (10.2), diam. base 4⁵⁄₁₆ (11), diam. rim 8¹¹⁄₁₆ (22.1), wt. 25 oz. 11 dwt. (795g) (engraved wt. on underside "ozs/26")

MARK 3 once on inside bottom

INSCRIPTION: "B/TP" engraved on underside

PROVENANCE: Thomas (d. 1763) and Phebe (d. 1788) Barnes; by Phebe's will, dated November 3, 1785, "my Gold Watch and my large Silver Punch Bowl" bequeathed to her daughter Phebe (Barnes) Tolmie (d. 1795).[1] Subsequent ownership uncertain; Phebe Tolmie bequeathed "one Silver milk Pot" to her unmarried sister Philena, "my wearing Apparel & Jewels" to her niece Pheba Cummings, and the remainder of her estate to her nephew David Harris.[2] Exhibited during 1940s at The Metropolitan Museum of Art from "the Collection of Miss Ahline Jones"; sold in 1949 by the dealers James Graham and Sons of New York, acting as an agent for "a descendant of the original owners, Thomas and Phoebe [sic] Barnes," to the collector Waldron Phoenix Belknap, Jr., whose collection was donated to The New-York Historical Society at his death in 1949.[3]

The New-York Historical Society; Gift of Mrs. Waldron Phoenix Belknap, Sr., The Waldron Phoenix Belknap, Jr., Collection

Thomas and Phebe Barnes may have been significant early patrons of Myer Myers. If all the surviving objects by Myers engraved with the initials "B/TP" were theirs, they owned a sauce spoon (cat. 41) and a pair of sauceboats (cat. 6) in addition to this punch bowl. Both the bowl and spoon are substantial forms in size and weight, with little embellishment. The sauceboat is equally solid but reflects a greater awareness of the late Baroque style. A smaller bowl of c. 1765–76 (cat. 53),

also by Myers, apparently descended together with the sauceboat and may represent the family's continuing patronage of Myers; its engraved initials "PB" could stand for either Phebe or her unmarried daughter Philena.[4] This later bowl may reflect the younger generation's taste for lighter forms and richer ornament.

Simple but substantial objects probably suited Thomas Barnes. In his will, he gave his profession as "mariner," although he in fact was commander of the sloop *Elizabeth*, a privateer that attacked and pillaged French and Spanish vessels, a dangerous but highly lucrative business.[5] During the first year of Seven Years' War, the Earl of Loudon estimated that French prizes seized by New York privateers amounted to £200,000.[6] At the time of his death, Barnes owned several Negro slaves, a house and several lots on Cherry Street along the East River, as well as a house and twenty acres of land in Westchester and woodland on Throgs Neck.[7]

1 NYCPR-1, liber 40, pp. 177–81. In this will, Phebe Barnes referred to her unmarried daughter as "Philinda"; as noted in the text, her sister called her "Philena."

2 *Marriage Licenses* 1860, p. 17; NYCPR-1, liber 41, pp. 547–51.

3 James Graham, Jr., to Waldron Phoenix Belknap, Jr., April 27, 1949, object files, NYHS.

4 Christie's 1982, lot 45.

5 *Abstracts* 1892–1906, IV, p. 21.

6 Kammen 1975, p. 330.

7 NYCPR-1, box 35, folder 1626; *Abstracts* 1892–1906, VI, pp. 209–10.

8

Two Candlesticks, 1750–65

Silver

A. h. 8¹⁄₁₆ (20.5), w. base 4½ (11.4), wt. (without nozzle) 15 oz. 4 dwt. (472g)

B. h. 8 (20.3), w. base 4½ (11.4), wt. (without nozzle) 14 oz. 18 dwt. (464g)

MARK 8 four times on underside of base

PROVENANCE: uncertain until Catherine Augusta McEvers (1795–1868), who in 1814 married Hugh McCulloch Birckhead (1788–1853); by descent to their great-grandson, by whom consigned to auction in Baltimore in 1997.[1]

Private collection

1 Rutledge 1945, p. 121; Barnard 1931, p. 311.

8-9.1. George Roupell, *Peter Manigault and His Friends* (detail), Charleston, South Carolina, c. 1760. Ink and wash on paper. Henry Francis du Pont Winterthur Museum, Winterthur, Delaware.

9

Two Candlesticks, 1750–65

Silver

A. h. 8 (20.3), w. base 4½ (11.4), wt. 16 oz. 14 dwt. (520g)

B. h. 7¾ (20), w. base 4½ (11.4), wt. 17 oz. 17 dwt. (555g)

MARK 8 four times on underside of base

PROVENANCE: uncertain before about 1900, when owned by George Thornburgh Macaulay Gibson of Baltimore; to his daughter, Sara Thornburgh (Gibson) Lynde; to her daughter, by whom consigned to auction in 1974.[1]

Private collection

Silver candlesticks were a costly extravagance in eighteenth-century America. Only the most affluent New Yorkers purchased such objects, as exemplified by Myers's set of four candlesticks, made for Catherine (Livingston) Lawrence (cats. 35,

36). Myers undoubtedly cast the present two pairs from contemporary English silver or even brass candlesticks of this characteristic late Baroque form, on which the nozzle, baluster, and base were ornamented with Rococo shells. These four are very close to a pair made in London by the specialist candlestick maker John Cafe in 1753–54.[2]

One can imagine these candlesticks at the center of convivial evenings like the one depicted by Roupell (8-9.1). Because both pairs were owned subsequently in Baltimore, they may originally have formed one set of four. The original patron can be tentatively identified based on the provenance for the first pair. Catherine (McEvers) Birckhead was the daughter of Guilian McEvers and Elizabeth LeRoy, who were married in 1793. The style and marks of these candlesticks indi-

9

cate that they were commissioned by the previous generation of the family, and all of Catherine Birckhead's grandparents were probable patrons of Myer Myers. The most likely prospects are Elizabeth LeRoy's parents, Jacob LeRoy (1727–1793) and his second wife, Catherine Rutgers, who were married in 1766. Jacob's first wife, whom he married in 1755, had been Catherine's sister Cornelia Rutgers. Cornelia and Catherine were the daughters of Harman Rutgers, the brother of Elsje (Rutgers) Marshall (see cat. 49); their brother Anthony was LeRoy's business partner.[3]

Jacob LeRoy's initials were engraved on a pair of canns by Daniel Christian Fueter (now in a private collection) that descended together with the Myers candlesticks to his grand-daughter Elizabeth (LeRoy) McEvers and through the Birck-head family, so it is possible that the candlesticks also origi-nally belonged to Jacob LeRoy. However, Guilian McEvers came from an equally affluent family. He was the son of the New York merchant Charles McEvers, who in 1763 married Mary Verplanck.[4]

1 Sotheby's 1974, lot 1030. The candlesticks did not sell and subsequently were purchased by the dealer S.J. Shrubsole; *Fifty Years* 1986, no. 69.

2 Sotheby's 1973, lot 92.

3 Pelletreau 1902, II, pp. 140–41; Evans 1901, p. 405; Wright 1902, p. 54; Crosby 1886, pp. 86–87; Robison/Bartlett 1917, p. 186. A connection to Myers after the fact was established when Elizabeth (LeRoy) McEvers's half-brother, Herman LeRoy, married Hannah (Cornell), the daughter of Samuel and Susanna (Mabson) Cornell (see cats. 19, 78).

4 Verplanck 1892, p. 104.

10

Waiter, 1755–65

Silver, h. 1¼ (3.2), diam. 12 (30.5), wt. 27 oz. 16 dwt. (865g)

MARK 6 twice on upper surface

ARMORIAL/INSCRIPTION: Bedford arms (argent, three bears' gambs vert couped erect within a bordure azure) and crest (a bear's gamb of the field) added on front after 1871 (see Provenance);[1] "GJB" (script) added c. 1800 on front (see below)

PROVENANCE: James Parker (1714–1770) and his wife, Marie Ballareau (b. 1711); to their daughter Jane (c. 1746–1831), who in 1772 or 1773 married Gunning Bedford, Jr. (1747–1812); to their daughters Anna Maria (1775–1835) and subsequently Henrietta Jane (1788–1871), who bequeathed it to Judge Gunning S. Bedford, Jr. (1837–1894), the son of her second cousin: "a silver waiter with the initials GIB thereon which belonged to my par-ents and to have the Bedford Coat-of-Arms inscribed thereon."[2] Subse-quent ownership unknown until about 1951, when the New York dealer Robert Ensko sold it to the Dover, Delaware, collector Jessie Harring-ton; bequeathed in 1965 to the Delaware Art Museum; transferred to the Historical Society of Delaware in 1987.[3]

Historical Society of Delaware, Wilmington; Acquired by Exchange with the Delaware Art Museum, Bequest of Jessie Harrington

This is one of the largest and heaviest waiters from Myers's workshop, and its scale and richly chased, cast border and feet are typical of his early silver in the Rococo style. It follows a standard pattern for English waiters of the 1750s and 1760s, including examples by John Swift of 1753–54 and Ebenezer Coker of 1763–64.[4] Myers's MARK 6 is found on similar cast objects from this time period, including the set of candlesticks made for Catherine (Livingston) Lawrence (cats. 35, 36). Myers's workshop produced at least one larger and three smaller versions of this style of waiter, including cat. 21, and two of them can be dated prior to 1759.[5]

The large script monogram is atypical of the engraving found on Myers's work of any period as well as of engraving on New York silver in general. It closely resembles the large-scale, foliate script found on Philadelphia and Wilmington sil-ver made after the Revolutionary War.[6] Its delicate, almost schematic quality is very similar to the engraving found on a tea service of about 1806 made by the Wilmington silversmith Thomas McConnell, which suggests that the monogram may have been added in Delaware after the Bedfords inherited the waiter.[7]

Given the waiter's probable date of manufacture around 1760, the most likely original owners were Jane (Parker) Bed-ford's parents, the printer James Parker and his wife, Marie (Ballareau) Parker, who were married about 1740. Parker was the leading printer of his generation in New York, succeeding William Bradford as Public Printer from 1743 to 1760; by the late 1750s, he was the most active printer in the Colonies and in 1756 he was appointed comptroller and secretary of the Colo-nial post offices.[8] Myers and Parker presumably were well acquainted, as the silversmith advertised in Parker's *New-York Gazette* between 1753 and 1771.

1 Bolton 1964, p. 12. It is not certain that the tinctures on these arms were rendered correctly.

2 Waters 1984, p. 59; see also Rosenbaum 1954A, p. 119.

3 Conrad 1900, pp. 8–10; *DAB*, II, p. 123; Harrison 1980, pp. 131–35; Klett 1996, pp. 687–88; obituary, *New York Tribune*, October 30, 1893, p. 2; *National Cyclopedia of American Biography*, 9 (1907), p. 361; accession file 1987.20.3, Historical Society of Delaware.

4 Davis 1976, no. 137; Lomax 1992, no. 55.

5 The larger waiter, which is 15 13/16 in. in diameter and originally weighed 50 oz. 9 dwt., is at The Art Institute of Chicago, inv. 1987.174. The smaller waiters are at NYHS, inv. 1969.28, and the Museum of Fine Arts, Boston; Buhler 1972, II, no. 506. The latter waiter was made for Elizabeth (Stillwell) Wraxall Maunsell in 1756–59. It was engraved with her maiden initials, indicating that it probably was made about the time of her first marriage in 1756, perhaps from part of the legacy of £200 she received from her father, Richard Stillwell in 1743; NYCPR-1, box 24, will 428. Presumably she would not have reverted to her maiden initials after the death of her first hus-band, Peter Wraxall, in 1759 (NYCPR-1, box 32, will 1274; Smith/Kammen 1972, II, p. 295) or her subsequent marriage in 1763 to John Maunsell (Statham 1920, II, p. 540). Her will was proved in New York on November 6, 1815; NYCPR-1, liber 52, pp. 537–41.

10

6 Characteristic examples are found on objects marked by the Philadelphia silversmiths Joseph Anthony, Jr. (Quimby/Johnson 1995, no. 310), Daniel Dupuy (Garvan 1987, p. 76), Joseph Lownes (Quimby/Johnson 1995, no. 391), Joseph and Nathaniel Richardson (Fales 1974, pp. 168–90, esp. figs. 150, 155, 159), and the Wilmington silversmiths Thomas Byrnes and Bancroft Woodcock (Waters 1984, pp. 68–69) and Jesse Zane (Quimby/Johnson 1995, no. 517).

7 Quimby/Johnson 1995, no. 408.

8 Smith/Kammen 1972, II, p. 291; *DAB*, XIV, pp. 226–27; Kammen 1975, p. 245.

11
Milk Pot, 1755–65

Silver, h. 5⁵⁄₁₆ (13.5), w. 4⁹⁄₁₆ (11.6), d. 3¼ (8.3), engraved wt. 7 oz. (218g)

MARK 4 once on underside

INSCRIPTION: "HLS" (mirror cypher) engraved on front; "S/HL" and "7:oz" engraved on underside

PROVENANCE: unknown prior to sale at auction in 1949 as property of a "N.Y. Private Collector" with the notation that it has been acquired from the dealer Charles Woolsey Lyon; subsequent ownership uncertain until sale at auction by the estate of Norman Norell in 1972, when purchased by the Brooklyn Museum.[1]

Brooklyn Museum of Art, New York; H. Randolph Lever Fund

The "HLS" cypher engraved on this milk pot is typical of the style of one engraver Myers employed during the 1750s. His cyphers are extremely linear, with no defined foliate details, so

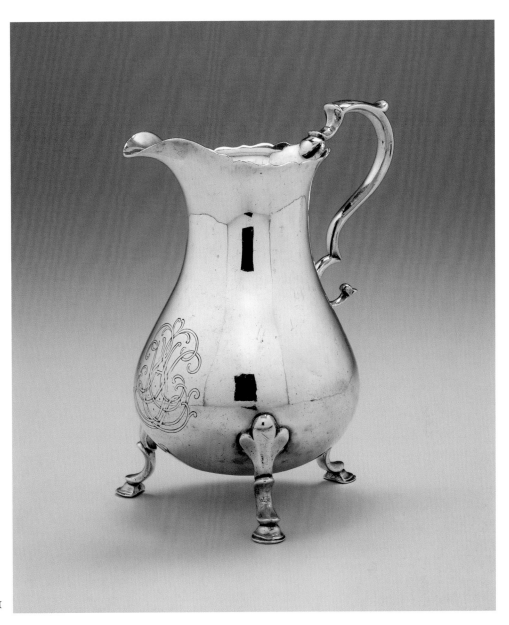

11

individual letters are relatively easy to distinguish. The terminal scrolls at the lower end of the cypher are "stacked" in a somewhat repetitious manner. Two additional objects from Myers's workshop, a tankard and a waiter, were engraved by the same craftsman with "HK" or "HKC" cyphers, apparently for the same client.[2] Unfortunately, none of the original owners of these objects is known, so they cannot be dated precisely, although all three bear the same Myers mark, MARK 4, which he used between about 1755 and 1765 (Appendix I). The waiter has a border that is almost identical to the Peaston waiter of 1747–48 (cat. 119), which likewise suggests a date in the 1750s.

11.1

1 Parke-Bernet 1949, lot 312; Sotheby's 1972, lot 142.
2 The tankard is reprod. in Conradsen 1999, no. 38; the waiter in Christie's 2000, lot 325. According to the consignors of the waiter, it had descended from the Chapman family.

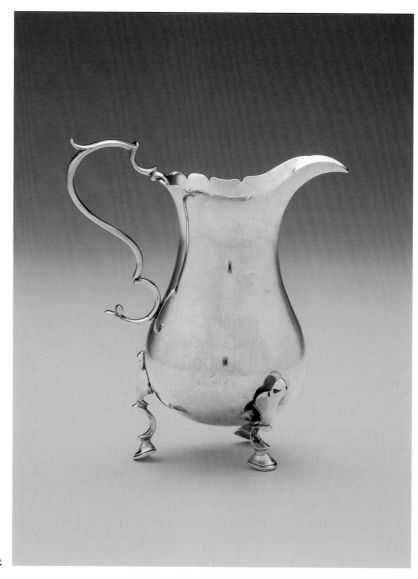

12

12

Milk Pot, 1756–66

Silver, h. 4 ¹¹⁄₁₆ (12), w. 4³⁄₁₆ (10.7), d. 2½ (6.3), wt. 4 oz. 5 dwt. (132.7g)

MARKS 11 and 11A once each on underside

INSCRIPTION: "R/WS" and "M TE" (conjoined) engraved on underside

PROVENANCE: original owner uncertain; to Allen Rabineau (1808–1893) and his wife, Mary Frances Zabriskie (1810–1863); to their great-granddaughter, Elizabeth (Penny) Hart; to her niece Patricia (Kramer) Welte, the donor.[1]

Museum of Fine Arts, Boston; Gift of Patricia Kramer Welte

Like the majority of the objects marked by the partnership of Halsted and Myers, this milk pot represents a small, simple form that could be produced relatively inexpensively and in quantity for sale in a retail store. Identical milk pots were marked by Myer Myers (cats. 11, 95) and Benjamin Halsted working independently, perhaps at the same time that they were partners.[2] The surviving silver from the Colonial period with Halsted's mark comprises similar small, routine forms and supports the conclusion that he was a smallworker, jeweler, or retail silversmith.[3]

1 Patricia Welte to Jeannine Falino, Oaxaca, Mexico, January 23, 1990, accession file, Museum of Fine Arts Boston. A presentation pitcher by Baldwin Gardiner with the same provenance is at the Museum of the City of New York; Waters/McKinsey/Ward 2000, II, no. 181.

2 The Halsted milk pot is in The Newark Museum, reprod. in *Pulse of the People* 1976, pp. 242–43, no. 406.

3 These silver pieces include a salt with shell ornaments (The Newark Museum, reprod. in *Pulse of the People* 1976, p. 243, no. 407) and a cann with a leaf grip, purportedly marked by Halsted, known to the author only through an undated and unprovenanced photograph in the Silversmith Maker's files in the American Arts Office, YUAG.

13

Sugar Dish, c. 1754

Silver, h. 4⅜ (11.1), diam. base 2¹¹⁄₁₆ (6.8), diam. rim (of bowl) 4³⁄₁₆ (10.6), wt. 8 oz. 18 dwt. (277g)

MARK 8 once on underside of bowl and once on top of cover

INSCRIPTION: "MC" engraved on underside of bowl; "John Hobart Warren/from his Mother's Estate/Dec 23d 1879" engraved on front of bowl

PROVENANCE: Martha Cornell (1732–1783), who married William Thorne in 1754; by descent to their great-great-great-great-granddaughter, Janet (Ingersoll) Miller, the donor in 1991.[1]

Philadelphia Museum of Art; Gift of Mr. and Mrs. John A. Miller

This sugar dish probably was made about 1754, the year of Martha Cornell's marriage to William Thorne. It is almost identical to the three sugar dishes made contemporaneously for the Johnson family (cats. 23–25), and together they indicate that this relatively simple form was a standard production piece in Myers's workshop. Martha may also have owned an equally generic milk pot with the same block initials "MC" engraved on its underside.[2] The marks on the two objects are

contemporaneous, and the fact that the marks are not the same reinforces the idea that the objects were not made as a set or commission.

Martha (Cornell) Thorne, was the first cousin twice over of both Samuel Cornell (cat. 131) and Mary (Cornell) Pell (cat. 95); their fathers were three of the sons of Thomas Cornell and their mothers were also siblings, the daughters of Charles Doughty and Elizabeth Jackson of Queens County.[3] Martha and Samuel were close in age, whereas Mary was approximately twenty years younger. About two years after Martha acquired this sugar dish, her cousin Samuel Cornell's greater wealth and social ambitions would be made dramatically evident at the time of his own marriage in 1756 by the sumptuous coffeepot engraved with a Rococo monogram that he commissioned from Myers (cat. 19).

1 Accession file 1991-91-1, Philadelphia Museum of Art.
2 The Detroit Institute of Arts, inv. 35.36. The underside of this milk pot is struck with Myers's mark 4 and engraved with the initials "M*C."
3 Cornell 1902, pp. 155, 166–67, 169; Doty 1912, p. 282.

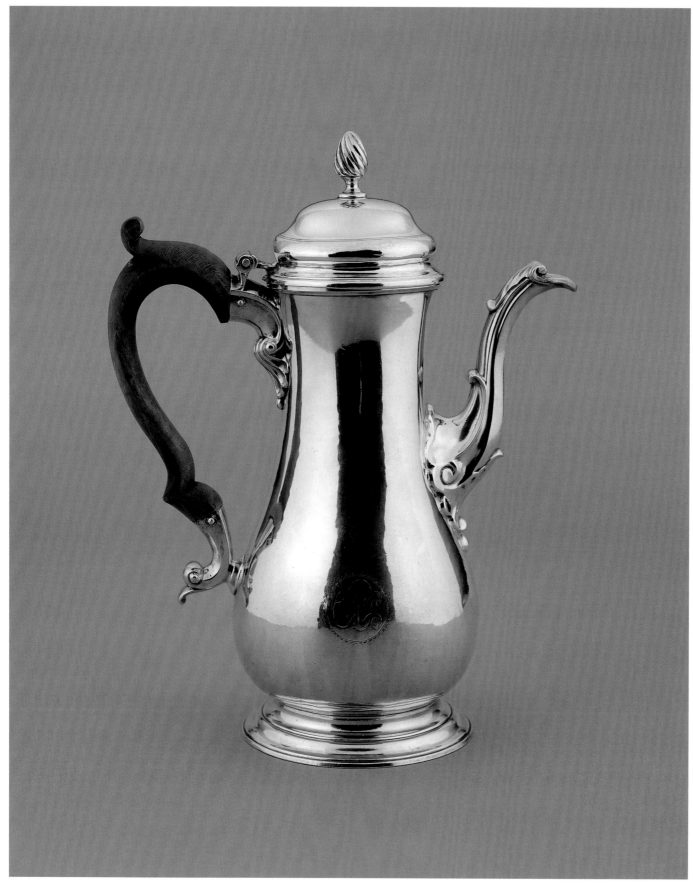

94 MYER MYERS

14

HALSTED AND MYERS

Coffeepot, 1756–66

Silver with wood handle, h. 10⅞ (27.6), w. 8½ (21.6), diam. base 4⁷⁄₁₆ (11.3), diam. rim 3¼ (8.3), gross wt. 30 oz. 9 dwt. (947g) (scratch wt. 29 oz. 7 dwt.)

MARK 11 once on underside

INSCRIPTION: "RAV" (script) engraved on left side; "CVJ" monogram added c. 1800 to right side

PROVENANCE: unknown prior to sale at auction in 1985, when catalogued as from the Boston dealer Gebelein Silversmiths.[1]

Collection of Ruth J. Nutt

This coffeepot is one of the few surviving pieces of large hollow ware marked by Halsted and Myers (see also cats. 15, 60). Presumably a commission, it raises the question of what distinctions existed within Myers's workshop between similar objects with his mark and work marked by the partnership (pp. 34–35). Like cat. 60, the coffeepot's spout and handle sockets were cast using the same patterns Myers used for an object he marked alone, a coffeepot in a private collection made between 1750 and 1765.[2]

1 Sotheby's 1985, lot 49.
2 Christie's 2001, lot 342.

15

HALSTED AND MYERS

Tankard, 1756–66

Silver, h. 7⅜ (18.7), w. 8 (20.3), diam. base 5⁵⁄₁₆ (13.5), diam. rim 4⅝ (11.7), wt. 36 oz. 10 dwt. (1135g) (scratch wt. 37 oz. 9 dwt.)

MARK 11 once on underside of body

INSCRIPTION: "WMVS" (cypher monogram) engraved on cover; "GWVS" (script) added c. 1800 to front of body; "Francis P. Garvan Jr." (script) added c. 1950 on underside; "WVS" scratched on underside

PROVENANCE: Wessel Van Schaick (1712–1783) and Maria Gerritse Van Schaick (1718–1797), who were married in 1743; to their son, Gerrit Wessel Van Schaick ("GWVS"; 1758–1816); subsequent ownership unknown until the New York City collector R.T.H. Halsey, who loaned it in 1909 to The Metropolitan Museum of Art; purchased by Francis P. Garvan in 1929 and donated to the Yale University Art Gallery; returned to his widow, Mabel (Brady) Garvan, who gave it in 1948 to their son, Francis P. Garvan, Jr.; sold at auction by his widow in 1979.[1]

Private collection

This tankard is the largest and most impressive piece of hollow ware known to survive from the Halsted and Myers partnership. It represents a continuation of the eighteenth-century New York tankard form, with the same scrolled thumbpiece and baluster-shape drop seen on cat. 2, but updated with such Rococo details as a double-scroll handle and a front edge on the cover shaped into reverse curves. Myers independently marked at least seven tankards of identical design during the period 1750–65, including cats. 28 and 30.[2] The "WMVS" monogram on the Van Schaick tankard is simpler and more stylized than those executed by Myers's favored engraver during this time, particularly in the use of a dotted line instead of a shell frame. The horizontal shading is similar to the monogram on the "BRG" cann of c. 1760 (cat. 40).

Wessel Van Schaick was a merchant in Albany, the son of Anthony Van Schaick and his wife, Anna Catherine Ten Broeck, the paternal aunt of Christina (Ten Broeck) Livingston (cat. 130).[3] Van Schaick's tankard may have been purchased with a legacy from his parents' estates, since they died in the same year. This circumstance might explain the choice of a New York City maker for the tankard: if monies from debts due the estates were forthcoming from New York, a tankard engraved with Wessel's and Maria's initials may have provided a safer means of transport to Albany than currency. For other pieces of their household silver, including a chased teapot of c. 1770 and a large serving spoon of c. 1775, Van Schaick and his wife patronized their kinsman Jacob Gerritse Lansing of Albany.[4]

1 Reynolds 1911, III, p. 993; Metropolitan 1909, II, p. 107, no. 354; "Yale Exchange for Monteith," photograph album, no. A884.C73.HF354, American Arts Office, YUAG; Sotheby's 1979, lot 381.
2 Rosenbaum 1954A, p. 133 (Vandervoort, Murray, and L/IGS tankards); Christie's 1993, lot 125; an eighth, unpublished tankard was in the collection of Dr. and Mrs. Philip Cornwell in 1954; Adolph S. Cavallo to Mrs. Robert Rosenbaum, New York, June 3, 1954, Brooklyn Museum of Art archives.
3 Runk 1897, p. 55. Van Schaick described himself as "of the city of Albany, merchant" in his will dated December 16, 1782; Albany Probate Records, file AV136, NYSA.
4 Rice 1964, pp. 28, fig. 34, pp. 32, fig. 44. The serving spoon was made by Lansing in partnership with Henry Van Vechten. The Van Schaicks and Lansing were related through the marriage of the Van Schaicks's great-aunt Gerrtje (Van Schaick) Coster to Lansing's grandfather Johannes Gerritse Lansing in 1678; Reynolds 1911, III, p. 992; Reynolds 1914, III, p. 1436.

15.1

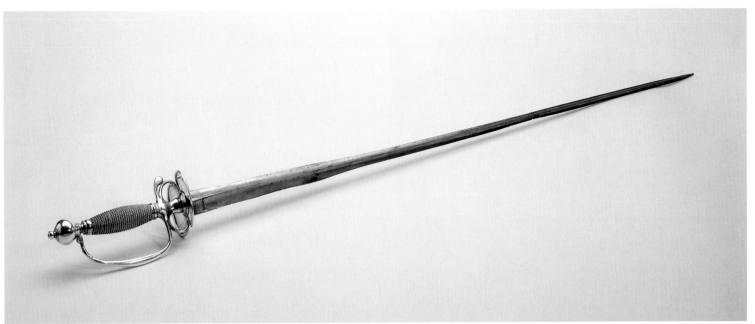

16

Small Sword (Colichemarde), 1757–58

Silver and steel, l. 36¼ (92.1); h. (of handle) 6⅛ (15.6), w. 3½ (8.9)

MARK 4 once on the knuckleguard near the pommel

INSCRIPTION: "Capt.ⁿ John Hulot/to David Jones Jun.ʳ" engraved on underside of shellguard

PROVENANCE: presented by Captain John Hewlett ("Hulot"; 1702–1790) to David Jones, Jr. (1737–1758); subsequent ownership uncertain, although described as "still in possession of the family" in 1907.[1] No further information until purchase in 1944 by the collector Philip Medicus; purchased from him in 1954 by the Boston collector Mark Bortman; to his daughter, Jane (Bortman) Larus.[2]

Private collection

Captain John Hewlett of East Woods (now Woodbury), Long Island, was the commander of a Long Island regiment formed in 1758 to fight the French in Canada. He presented this sword to his first lieutenant, David Jones of Hempstead, Long Island. In August 1758, the regiment fought in a successful campaign that captured Fort Frontenac on Lake Ontario, but on the return trip Jones died of disease near present-day Rome, New York.[3] Jones was unmarried, and the subsequent history of his sword is unknown. It may have passed to his nephew and namesake David Jones, who inherited from Lieutenant David's father, Judge David Jones, "my small Frontenack Gun with the initial Letters of my Son Davids name writt upon a silver plate on the Stock of said Gun."[4]

Silver-hilted small swords were not intended as weapons; rather, they were popular signs of status. George Roupell's drawing of Peter Manigault entertaining a group of friends in Charleston, South Carolina, about 1760 (8-9.1) shows several men wearing swords at the dining table in a domestic interior.

During the 1760s and 1770s, numerous silversmiths and jewelers in New York offered for sale ready-made "neat small swords," including Charles Oliver Bruff, Simeon Coley, Stephen Reeves, and Nicholas Roosevelt.[5] Silver hilts were relatively inexpensive: in 1775, Elias Pelletreau charged £2.18.4 for a silver hilt weighing 6 oz. 5 dwt., with an additional £2 "to fashioning & Scabbard & Cleaning Blade," making the sword equal in cost to a cann or porringer.[6] Nevertheless, swords were treated as important heirlooms for male descendants, even for men who did not have military careers. In 1775, the New York merchant Dirck Brinckerhoff left to his children "each, a piece of plate as they shall choose, to be unto them for a Remembrance," but reserved to his only son George "my fowling piece with my name engraved on the barrel, and my case of pistols, and my silver hilted sword, and my Mother of Pearl Powder horn, set in silver."[7]

1 Jones 1907, p. 99.

2 Medicus 1944, p. 342. Bortman lent the sword to the Museum of Fine Arts, Boston, in August 1954; file S.E. 2180, "Jewish Tercentenary Exhibition" records, Museum of Fine Arts, Boston.

3 Jones 1907, pp. 98–99, 335.

4 NYCPR-1, liber 30, pp. 31–49. This David Jones was the nephew of Captain David Jones, the eldest son of Judge David Jones's daughter Mary (b. 1743), who married her first cousin, Thomas Jones; Jones 1907, p. 64, and Floyd-Jones 1906, p. 28.

5 The New-York Gazette and The Weekly Mercury, June 19, 1775, as cited in Gottesman 1936, p. 35; The New-York Mercury, October 5, 1767, as cited in Ibid., p. 37; The New-York Gazette and The Weekly Mercury, October 7, 1776, p. 4; The New-York Gazette and The Weekly Mercury, January 30, 1769, p. 3.

6 Failey 1971, p. 156.

7 NYCPR-1, liber 30, p. 49.

17

Pair of Sauceboats, 1756–58

Silver:

A. h. 4 $^{11}/_{16}$ (11.9), w. 6 $^{7}/_{8}$ (17.5), d. 3 $^{7}/_{8}$ (9.8), wt. 11 oz. 15 dwt. (365g)

B. h. 4 $^{7}/_{8}$ (12.4), w. 7 $^{1}/_{8}$ (18.1), d. 3 $^{13}/_{16}$ (9.7), wt. 11 oz. 8 dwt. (355g)

MARK 5 once on underside of body (on each)

ARMORIAL/INSCRIPTION: British Royal crown above "G II R" engraved on right side of each; "From the Right Honble the Earl of Loudon/Commander in Chief of His Majestys Forces in North America/To Colonel Nathaniel Meserve [misspelled "Merserve" on B] of New Hampshire/in Testimony of His Lordships Approbation/of his Good Services at Fort Edward in the year 1756" engraved within a scalloped surround on left side of each

PROVENANCE: presented by John Campbell (1705–1782), fourth Earl of Loudon, to Nathaniel Meserve (c. 1705–1758); subsequent history unknown before mention in April 1869, without name of owner; by 1954 owned by Lawrence Larkin.[1]

Private collection

These elegant sauceboats bear an early Myers mark. Although similar to cat. 6, including the identical handle casting, these sauceboats reveal a greater awareness of Rococo style, especially in the design of the rim, the somewhat clumsy shell ornaments above the feet, and the arrangement of the feet, which provides a more open, asymmetrical silhouette. In addition to cat. 18, Myers made another pair of this design at a somewhat later date.[2] Myers's sauceboats are closely related to English sauceboats of the 1750s, including examples marked by William Grundy in 1753–54.[3]

The engraved inscription records these sauceboats as a gift from the Earl of Loudon (fig. 20), who in July 1756 was sent to New York City as commander-in-chief of all British forces in North America, a post he held until Lord Pitt recalled him early in 1758.[4] The recipient was Colonel Nathaniel Meserve, a carpenter and shipwright from Portsmouth, New Hampshire. Meserve had served previously with distinction in the 1745 siege and capture of the French fortress of Louisburg on Cape Breton Island (now Nova Scotia), designing special sledges for hauling cannon and mortars. In the Seven Years' War, he was commissioned as the commander of New Hampshire regiments that served under Loudon during the 1756–57 campaigns in upstate New York, including the one at Fort Edward on the

18

Hudson River. In 1758, Meserve was made captain of a special "Comp[an]y of Artificers"—110 carpenters who were sent from Portsmouth to participate in the retaking of Louisburg. Unfortunately, ninety-two of the men became infected with smallpox, among them Meserve and his son, who both died of the disease at Louisburg.[5]

Meserve's surviving correspondence with Loudon indicates that in 1756–57 he moved about from Fort Edward to Boston, Deerfield, and Northfield, Massachusetts, as well as Albany, Flushing, and New York City. He served the earl in a variety of capacities, primarily finding skilled carpenters and ordering tools, but also arranging for troop transport and paying for gunpowder and firewood.[6] In November 1756, Loudon wrote Governor Benning Wentworth of New Hampshire: "[I] beg leave to Repeat to you the Obligation we be under to that Gentleman, for the Skill, Activity, & Zeal, he on every Occasion shewed for the Service, and the real use he was of in it."[7]

1 Tuttle 1869, p. 202; Rosenbaum 1954A, p. 120.
2 These later sauceboats, with Myers's mark 9, subsequently were engraved

with the crest of the Chrystie family and may have had beading added to their rims. The sauceboats are in the Harvard University Art Museums, inv. 1999.306.17.1-2, from an auction of Chrystie family heirlooms in 1949; Parke-Bernet 1949, lot 308.
3 Jackson 1911, II, p. 823.
4 The standard study of Loudon's North American career is Pargellis 1933; see also *DAB*, XI, p. 428.
5 Tuttle 1869; *DAB*, XII, p. 577; "List of the Dead and Missing," October 30, 1758, Loudon Papers, The Henry E. Huntington Library, Museum and Gardens, San Marino, California.
6 Correspondence, Loudon Papers, ibid.
7 The Earl of Loudon to Governor Benning Wentworth, Albany, New York, November 21, 1756, Loudon Papers, ibid.

18

Pair of Sauceboats, 1746–65

Silver, h. 4⁷⁄₁₆ (11.3), w. 7⅛ (18.1), d. 4³⁄₁₆ (10.6), wt. 13 oz. 17 dwt. (430g) each

MARK 3 twice on underside of each

INSCRIPTION: "LM" engraved on underside of each

PROVENANCE: Lewis Morris III (1726–1798), who married Mary Walton (1727–1794) in 1749; by descent to their great-great-great-great granddaughter.[1]

Private collection

Since 1937, family history has connected the initials engraved on the undersides with Lewis Morris III, who represented New York in the Continental Congress and signed the Declaration of Independence.[2] Lewis III graduated from Yale College in 1746 and returned home to help manage the Manor of Morrisania—five hundred acres in "Bronck's land" north of the Harlem River, patented by his grandfather, Lewis Morris I, who served as Chief Justice of the Supreme Court of the Province of New York and subsequently first Royal Governor of New Jersey. In 1749, Lewis III married Mary Walton, the daughter of Jacob and Maria (Beekman) Walton; like her sister Magdalen (see cat. 98), Mary received £1,000 at her marriage.[3] As a young couple from spectacularly affluent backgrounds, Morris and his bride may well have purchased such opulent tableware when setting up their own home.

However, it is also possible that the initials refer to Lewis's father, Lewis Morris II (1698–1762), a judge of the Admiralty Court in New York, who became the second Lord of Morrisania in 1746. In that same year, he married his second wife, Sarah Gouverneur, the daughter of Nicholas Gouverneur. The sauceboats could have been ordered from the newly established Myers in celebration of either event.[4] A mourning ring made for Lewis II's brother Robert in 1764 was also commissioned from Myers (cat. 48).

These sauceboats are almost identical to those commissioned by the Earl of Loudon (cat. 17), with handles and feet cast using the same patterns as well as the clumsy chased shell forms at the juncture of feet and body. As one of the leading Anglican landowning families in New York, the Morrises must have become acquainted with Loudon while he was in America. Lewis Morris III's younger brother, Staats Long Morris, married Lady Catherine Gordon, daughter of the second Earl of Aberdeen and widow of the third Duke of Gordon, both Scottish peers whom Loudon must have known.[5]

1 Spooner 1907, pp. 220, 223; Stillwell 1903–32, IV, pp. 36, 42–43, 53.
2 Miller 1937, p. 22, no. 207; see also Rosenbaum 1954A, p. 120.
3 *Abstracts* 1892–1906, VII, pp. 178–81, XI, pp. 116–17.
4 De Lancey 1876; Stillwell 1903–32, IV, pp. 14–34.
5 De Lancey 1876, p. 17.

19
Coffeepot, 1756–60

Silver with wood handle, h. 12½ (31.8), diam. base 4⅞ (12.4), diam. rim 3⅛ (7.9), gross wt. 37 oz. 19 dwt. (1180g)

MARK 8 once on underside of body, double-struck

INSCRIPTION: "SSC" (script) engraved on side; "Samuel Cornell/ 1756—to/Susan Mabson" added later above monogram

PROVENANCE: Samuel Cornell (1731–1781) and Susannah Mabson (1732–1778); to their daughter Hannah (1760–1818), who in 1786 married Herman LeRoy (1758–1841); to their great-great-grandson, Edward A. LeRoy III (b. 1895), the donor in 1980.[1]

Museum of the City of New York; Gift of a descendant, Edward A. LeRoy

Unlike the more spectacular pierced objects that they acquired from Myers in the 1770s, the Cornells apparently purchased this coffeepot at the time of their marriage in 1756. The coffeepot is typical of Myers's earliest versions of this double-bellied form, of which at least two additional examples survive, including cat. 20.[2] Exhibiting the same broad proportions, these coffeepots feature similar large, floral finials and identical spouts, with a ruffle-frame cartouche on the front, a sculptural shell form at the spout's juncture with the body, and a small leaf at the top opening. A contemporary coffeepot by Francis Crump of London of 1756–57 has a similar spout and somewhat taller proportions.[3] The monogram of the Cornells' initials (fig. 18) was executed by the specialist engraver Myers used in the middle and later 1750s for the coats of arms on the Livingston tankard (cat. 28) and Clarkson covered jug (cat. 27).

1 Pelletreau 1907, II, p. 141; Cornell 1902, pp. 190–91, 215; *GRSNS*, I, p. 100; obituary for Edward A. Leroy, *The New York Times*, December 12, 1913, p. 11; *Harvard Class* 1966, pp. 267–68.
2 The third example was included in Metropolitan 1909, II, no. 413a, and is presently in a private collection.
3 Davis 1976, no. 84.

20
Coffeepot, 1754–58

Silver with wood handle, h. 11¾ (29.8), diam. base 4⁷⁄₁₆ (11.3), gross wt. 34 oz. 2 dwt. (1061g) (scratch wt. 32¾ oz.)

MARK 8 once on underside of body

INSCRIPTIONS: "C I" engraved on underside of body; "1725" and "I/WS&A/1772" added later on underside of body, as was "S.W.J. 1819, W.S.J. 1856, S.W.J. 1883, W.S.J. 1895/W.S.J. TO COLUMBIA UNIVERSITY" on underside of foot

PROVENANCE: Charity Johnson ("CI"; 1692–1758); to her son William Samuel Johnson (1727–1819) and his wife Ann (Beach) Johnson (1729–1796; "I/WS&A"); to their son Samuel William Johnson ("S.W.J. 1819"; 1761–1846); to his son William Samuel Johnson ("W.S.J. 1856"; 1795–

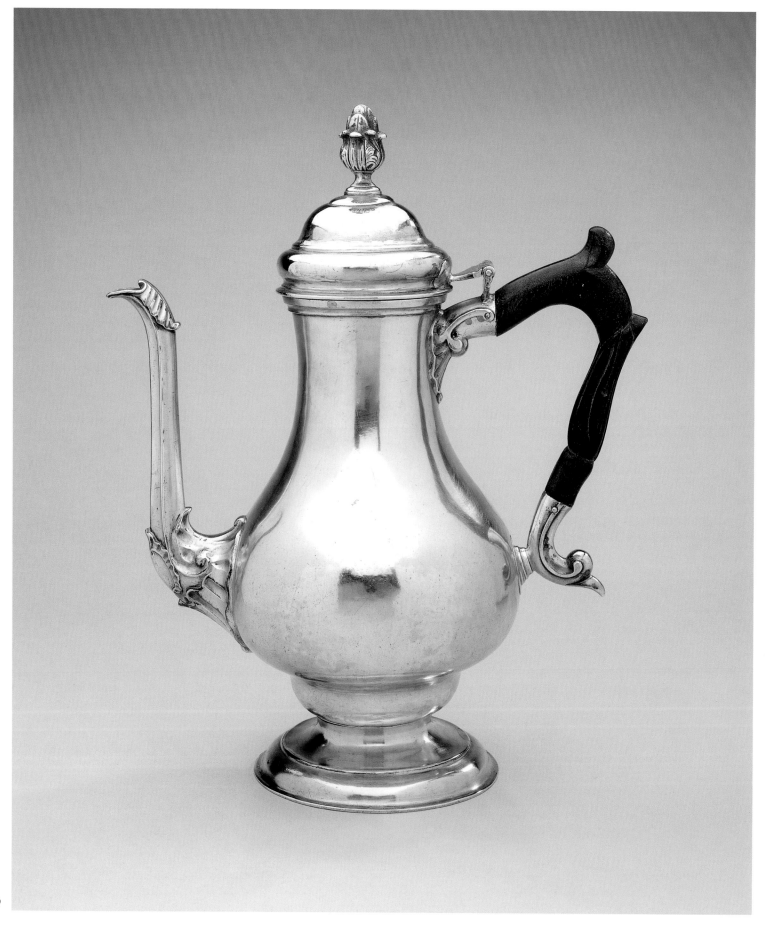

102 MYER MYERS

21

1883); to his son Samuel William Johnson ("S.W.J. 1883"; 1828–895); to his son William Samuel Johnson ("W.S.J. 1895"; 1859–1937), the donor in 1935.[1]

Columbia University in the City of New York; Gift of William Samuel Johnson

This coffeepot, its matching stand (cat. 21), and a pair of canns (cat. 22) can be dated between Samuel and Charity Johnson's arrival in New York from Stratford, Connecticut, in April 1754 and Charity's death four years later, on June 1, 1758.[2] All four objects had Charity's initials "CI" engraved on their undersides, indicating that they were purchased with money that Charity had independently of her second marriage. On September 1, 1754, Myer Myers paid the cabinetmaker Joshua Delaplaine 9 s. for a "kink Coffee pot handle," and it is tempting to identify this as the original wood handle for Charity Johnson's coffeepot; the present handle is a replacement.[3]

1 Thomas 1939; Talcott 1984, pp. 714–16; obituary for William Samuel Johnson, *The New York Times*, March 4, 1937, p. 23.

2 Talcott 1984, p. 714.

3 Delaplaine 1753–56, p. 34.

21

HALSTED AND MYERS

Coffeepot Stand, 1756–58

Silver, h. 1 1/16 (2.7), diam. 7 (17.8), wt. 7 oz. 11 dwt. (235g)

MARK 8 twice on underside, one double-struck, and mark 11 once on underside

INSCRIPTION: "CI" engraved on underside

PROVENANCE: Charity Johnson (see cat. 20); subsequent ownership unknown until 1936, when donated by the collector Edsel Ford to the Henry Ford Museum.

Greenfield Village and the Henry Ford Museum, Dearborn, Michigan

This exquisite small waiter undoubtedly was made as the stand for cat. 20, having the same engraved initials as well as Myers's MARK 8. Small waiters frequently were intended to serve as stands for coffeepots and teapots, thereby protecting tables from drips. The finely chased shells and bold scrolled border of the Halsted and Myers stand give it a lively presence equal to that of larger waiters (cat. 10). It is modeled on contemporary English versions, including one of similar size and design made in 1758–59 by the specialist London maker Richard Rugg.[1]

This stand is the only surviving object with a Halsted and

22

Myers mark with cast and chased ornament of this quality. It is also the only object on which both Myers's surname mark and MARK 11 of his partnership with Benjamin Halsted are visible, thereby confirming the latter mark as one used by the partnership. The rationale of marking the stand with the partnership's mark and the coffeepot with Myers's mark alone is uncertain (p. 34). Charity Johnson may have been unaware of the marks or their meaning.

1 McFadden/Clark 1989, no. 13.

22

Cann, 1754–58

Silver, h. 4⅝ (11.7), diam. base 3³⁄₁₆ (8.1), diam. rim 3⁹⁄₁₆ (9), wt. 11 oz. 18 dwt. (370g)

MARK 8 once on underside

INSCRIPTION: "C I" engraved on underside; "I/WS*A" and "W.S.J. to E.E.F./1930" added later on underside

PROVENANCE: Charity Johnson to her son William Samuel Johnson and his wife Ann (Beach) Johnson (see cat. 20); descent as in cat. 20 to William Samuel Johnson (1859–1937); given and inscribed by him in 1930 to his step-granddaughter Elizabeth Endicott Farley.

Collection of Elizabeth F. Berdell

At least twenty-four canns from Myers's workshop survive. They frequently were made in pairs, and this example had a mate that was published in 1961.[1] They also were made in sets with tankards (cats. 28, 29), which survive in similar numbers.

The quantity and stylistic uniformity of the majority of Myers's canns indicates that they were sold as ready-made objects. Some of Myers's earlier canns had the embellishments of a shell at the handle's upper juncture with the body and an articulated scroll at the handle's end, both seen on this example.

1 Kernan 1961, p. 339. See Rosenbaum 1954A, p. 105, and pl. 9 (p. 75), where the cann is illustrated but incorrectly identified as that from the collection of John D. Kernan which originally belonged to Robert and Mary Livingston (see cat. 30). In a conversation with the present author in October 1999, John D. Kernan said he could find no records concerning his purchase of the Johnson cann in 1947 or its subsequent disposal; he apparently had sold it by 1963, when it was advertised by Whimsey Antiques in *Antiques*, 84 (August 1963), p. 131. The cann's present whereabouts are unknown.

23

HALSTED AND MYERS

Sugar Dish, 1756–58

Silver, h. 4⁹⁄₁₆ (11.6), diam. base 2¹¹⁄₁₆ (6.8), diam. rim (of bowl) 4³⁄₁₆ (10.6), wt. 8 oz. 17 dwt. (275g)

MARK 11 once on underside of body of bowl

ARMORIAL / INSCRIPTION: Johnson crest (a demi-lion couped holding a mullet in the dexter gamb, gules) and motto "Audacitur" (*sic*, boldly) engraved on side of bowl; "I / SC" engraved on underside of base

PROVENANCE: Samuel and Charity Johnson ("I/SC"; see cat. 20); subsequent ownership unknown prior to acquisition by the Boston collector Mark Bortman by 1953.[1]

The Burrows Collection; on long-term loan to the Sterling and Francine Clark Art Institute, Williamstown, Massachusetts

This sugar dish is the only object in the Johnson group to be engraved with an armorial as well as both Samuel's and Charity's initials. The scroll containing the motto resembles others engraved on Myers's silver of this period (cat. 29). The crest chosen by the Johnsons most closely resembles one recorded for the Ewing family of New Jersey and Pennsylvania, although lion crests were used by English families named Johnson.[2] Their son William Samuel Johnson used a bookplate with the coat of arms "argent a chevron gules between three lions' heads couped crowned," so perhaps the lion crest related to the lions in these arms.[3]

1 *Early American* 1953, no. 46; silver research files, YUAG.
2 Bolton 1964, p. 57; Fairbairn 1992, p. 262, pl. 33, 120. *Early American* 1953, no. 46, and Rosenbaum 1954A, p. 136, recorded the crest on this sugar dish as Ewing.
3 Bolton 1964, p. 92. The crest and motto used with these arms were an eagle rising or and "Per aspera ad astra" ("Through hardship to the stars").

24

Sugar Dish, 1758–65

Silver, h. 4³⁄₁₆ (10.6), diam. base 2⁵⁄₈ (6.7), diam. rim (of bowl) 4⁵⁄₁₆ (11), wt. 9 oz. 13 dwt. (300g)

MARK 8 once on top of cover and once on underside of bowl

INSCRIPTION: "I/WS*A" and "Ex dono Pat.ˢ honorand.'S.J.[script]" engraved on outside of rim of bowl; "MI" and "W.S.J TO A.B.F" added later on underside of bowl

PROVENANCE: Samuel Johnson (cat. 126) to his son William Samuel Johnson and his wife Ann (Beach) Johnson (see cat. 20); either to their daughter Mary (1759–1783) or to William's second wife, Mary (Brewster) Beach (d. 1827); subsequent descent as in cat. 20 to William Samuel Johnson (1859–1937); given and inscribed by him to his step-granddaughter Alice Barrett (Farley) Williams; by gift to the present owners.[1]

Collection of Nancy Van Meter and Richard P.W. Williams; on long-term loan in honor of Alice B.F. Williams to The Corcoran Gallery of Art, Washington, D.C.

As the only child of Samuel and Charity Johnson's marriage to have issue, William Samuel Johnson (fig. 32) eventually inherited most if not all of his parents' silver. The objects marked with only Charity's initials (cats. 20–22) may have passed to him upon her death in 1758, whereas the sugar dish marked with both her initials and her husband's (cat. 23) presumably remained in Samuel's possession until his death in 1772. However, Samuel appears to have presented his son and daughter-in-law with this sugar dish by Myers (or the funds to buy it), as the inscription engraved on its rim, visible when the bowl is uncovered, pays tribute to William and Ann Johnson's "honored father." The mention of only "SJ" in the inscription suggests that Samuel Johnson made the gift after Charity's death in 1758 but before his remarriage, to Ann's mother, in 1761. The block initials "MI" refer to either William and Ann Johnson's daughter Mary or to William's second wife, Mary (Brewster) Beach, whom he married in 1800, the widow of his first wife's brother Abijah.[2] At the date either Mary would have received the dish, such initials would have been old-fashioned, particularly the barred "I," although it is in keeping with the "I/WS&A" William and Ann Johnson had added to the coffeepot and cann (cats. 20, 22).

This sugar dish is identical to cat. 23, which bears the mark of Halsted and Myers. It is not certain why different marks appear on identical objects made contemporaneously in the workshop that were acquired by the same clients (p. 34). Like the cann (cat. 22), these sugar dishes were routine products made for ready sale (see cat. 13).

1 I am greatly indebted to Mrs. Hermann Warner Williams, Jr., for her recollections of her step-grandfather and his silver, as well as for detailed information on the provenance of these objects.
2 Orcutt 1886, II, p. 1127.

23

24

25

Sugar Dish, 1754–65

Silver, h. 4³⁄₁₆ (10.6), diam. base 2⁵⁄₈ (6.7), diam. rim (of bowl) 4⁵⁄₁₆ (11), wt. 9 oz. 13 dwt. (300g)

MARK 8 once on top of cover and once on underside of bowl

INSCRIPTION: "W.S.J TO C.J.F" added later on underside of bowl

PROVENANCE: possibly Samuel Johnson (cat. 126); descent presumably as in cat. 20 to William Samuel Johnson (1859–1937); given and inscribed by him to his step-granddaughter Caroline J. (Farley) White-law, by whom sold in 1973.

Collection of Ruth J. Nutt

Samuel Johnson may have purchased this sugar dish as a gift for his other son, William (1730–1756), who died unmarried. It is a similar form to cat. 24 and bears the same MARK 8.

26

Covered Jug, 1755–65

Silver, h. 9⁷⁄₈ (25.1), w. 8¼ (21.0), diam. base 4¾ (12.1), diam. rim 3½ (8.9), wt. 45 oz. 3 dwt. (1405g) (scratch wt. 45 oz. 9 dwt.)

MARK 8 once on underside of body

INSCRIPTION: "VP" script monogram added later on front below spout; "M" cast into underside of foot (fig. 15)

PROVENANCE: probably Samuel and Charity Johnson (see cat. 20); by descent to their granddaughter Elizabeth Johnson (1763–1789), who married Daniel Crommelin Verplanck (1762–1834); by descent in the Verplanck family to Jeanette (Verplanck) Etting (b. 1849), until at least 1921; subsequent ownership unknown until acquired by the Henry Ford Museum from a Mrs. McKinley in 1964.[1]

Greenfield Village and the Henry Ford Museum, Dearborn, Michigan

Although there are no initials to confirm the jug's original owners, the overall style and Myers's MARK 8 indicate that it was made between 1755 and 1765. This substantial, impressive form, with cast and chased Rococo ornament, is consistent with other objects Myers made for Charity Johnson in the

25

1750s, such as her coffeepot and matching stand (cats. 20, 21). Robert Barker has observed that the elaborate casting at the handle's upper juncture with the body was cast from the foot of an English epergne, such as examples marked by William Cripps in 1756–57 and 1759–60, Samuel Courtauld in 1758–59, and a Dublin version of 1745.[2] The same casting is found on the closely related covered jug made by Myers for David Clarkson, Jr. (cat. 27)—which offers a further connection to Samuel Johnson, since Clarkson was both a trustee of King's College as well as one of the prominent members of the Church of England in New York. As a leading Anglican minister who had been ordained at Oxford University, Johnson would have been likely to commission a covered jug, a form frequently presented as a ceremonial gift to English bishops.[3] The present jug is somewhat less successful in its design than Clarkson's, in part because the same cast elements had to be adapted to a smaller object, 2 inches shorter and originally weighing 8 troy oz. less than cat. 27.

Family history further supports the ownership of this jug by either Samuel Johnson or his son William. The "VP" monogram engraved on the front dates from after the Revolutionary War and may have been added in 1785, when William and Ann Johnson's daughter Elizabeth married Daniel Crommelin Verplanck. One of Daniel Verplanck's descendants called him "a great collector of silver," but also specifically mentioned "that [silver] brought to the family by the Johnson and Walton marriages," of which this would be the only Johnson example that can now be identified.[4]

1 Lent by Mrs. Etting to an exhibition at the Pennsylvania Museum (now the Philadelphia Museum of Art) in 1921; see Woodhouse 1921, p. 27, no. 158, and Stern 1991, p. 67.
2 Jackson 1911, II, facing p. 925; Davis 1976, no. 114; Clayton 1985, p. 165, fig. 14; Bennett 1972, p. 111.
3 Brown/Schwartz 1996, p. 76.
4 Ver Planck 1892, p. 193.

108 MYER MYERS

27

Covered Jug, 1750–65

Silver, h. 11¾ (29.8), w. 9½ (24.1), diam. base 5⁷⁄₁₆ (13.8), diam. rim 4¼ (10.8), wt. 52 oz. 10 dwt. (1633g) (scratch wt. 59 oz. 9 dwt.)

MARK 8 once on underside

ARMORIAL: Clarkson arms (argent on a bend engrailed sable three annulets [or]) and crest (an eagle's head erased between two wings addorsed) engraved on side of body[1]

PROVENANCE: David Clarkson, Jr. (1726–1782) and Elizabeth French (1724–1808), who were married in 1749; to their daughter Anna Margareta, who married Garrit Van Horne (1758–1825) in 1784; by descent to their great-great-great-grandson, George Willoughby Moke, second Baron Norrie, by whom consigned to auction in 1978 and again in 1980.[2]

Private collection

Covered jugs were used in eighteenth-century England to serve alcoholic beverages at table, particularly for ceremonial meals at religious or corporate institutions. In several instances, the form was referred to as a "decanter."[3] Few American covered jugs made for domestic rather than ecclesiastical use survive, and the two marked by Myers are the only examples from New York. As a teenager, David Clarkson, Jr., spent eight years being educated in England, and this form as well as the coat of arms engraved on it may have been intended to emulate aristocratic models he observed during that time.

The commission for a covered jug also may be related to David Clarkson's position as a founding trustee of King's College (now Columbia University) in New York. The only other covered jug marked by Myers (cat. 26) may have belonged to the college's first president, Samuel Johnson (cat. 126).

The close similarity of the Clarkson and Johnson covered jugs suggests that they were contemporary and reflects Myers's reuse of casting patterns. Clarkson's covered jug is larger in every dimension, and originally it weighed exactly 8 oz. more, in part because of the additional enrichments of the thumbpiece and the shell at the lower handle juncture. The handle and the upper shell on both examples appear to be identical. The Rococo castings used for the shell forms at the handle's junctures with the body were taken from English models; the upper handle juncture was cast from the foot of an epergne, and the lower handle juncture apparently was cast from the same pattern used to make the feet of Daniel Christian Fueter's cruet stand (cat. 106).

The engraver who executed the superb coat of arms and crest (fig. 17) on Clarkson's covered jug was also responsible for the armorial on a tankard and cann (cats. 28, 29) and a monogram on a coffeepot (cat. 19) that were made contemporaneously in Myers's workshop. Characteristic of his technique is the use of even, tightly spaced, short strokes. His careful renditions of different tinctures, or the engraved representations of different colors, indicates his familiarity with the conventions of heraldry. He may have owned an English book of heraldry that allowed patrons to identify arms for him to copy, as did the Boston silversmith and engraver Nathaniel Hurd.[4] In 1774, the English immigrant William Bateman informed potential customers that he had brought to New York "a book of heraldry which contains some thousand of names, where gentlemen who want their arms engraved by him, and do not know them, may search the book gratis."[5]

Clarkson and his wife enjoyed an opulent lifestyle. This covered jug, weighing over 50 troy oz., or five times the weight of a cann, was a sumptuous statement of their wealth. In addition, an inventory made of the silver in their possession at the time of Clarkson's death in 1782 listed forty-five pieces of hollow ware and several sets of flatware. Among the objects that survive are the cruet set made by Samuel Wood of London (cat. 121) and a large waiter by William Grigg of New York.[6]

The Clarksons' extended kinship group included many of Myers's patrons. Elizabeth (French) Clarkson was the daughter of Philip French and his first wife, Susanna Brockholst, the daughter of Anthony Brockholst, Lieutenant Governor of New Jersey.[7] On her mother's side, she was a first cousin of Philip Philipse (cat. 57), and on her father's side, she was a first cousin of John Reade, who married Catherine Livingston (cat. 38); in 1769, David Clarkson was a witness to the will of John's father, the merchant Joseph Reade.[8] Elizabeth (French) Clarkson's sister Susanna married William Livingston, another Governor of New Jersey, founding trustee of King's College, and younger brother of Robert Livingston, Jr. (cat. 127).

1 Bolton 1964, p. 35, citing the bookplate of David Clarkson, Sr.
2 NYCPR-1, box 53, file 3536; *Clarksons* 1876, I, p. 282, and foldouts; Spooner 1907, pp. 280–81; *Burke's* 1975, pp. 1986–87; Sotheby's 1978, lot 403; Sotheby's 1980, lot 179.
3 Brown/Schwartz 1996, pp. 75–76.
4 Kane 1998, p. 617.
5 *The New-York Gazette and The Weekly Mercury*, November 7, 1774, p. 2.
6 *Antiquarian Society* 1977, pp. 158–59.
7 French 1940, pp. 29–30.
8 NYCPR-1, box 43, file 2403.

28

Tankard, 1755–65

Silver, h. 7⅞ (20) w. 8¼ (21), diam. base 5¼ (13.3), diam. rim 4¼ (10.8), wt. 37 oz. (1156g)

MARK 4 once on underside

ARMORIAL / INSCRIPTION: Livingston coat of arms, crest, and motto engraved on front. Arms: Livingston quartering 1) Callendar and 2) Hepburn quartering Magill (first and fourth quarters, argent three gillyflowers within a tressure flory counter flory [Livingston]; second quarter, 1 and 4 gules on a chevron argent a rose of the field between two lions passant of the same [Hepburn], 2 and 3 azure three martlets [Magill]; third quarter sable a bend between six billets argent [Callendar]. Crest: a ship of three masts, top sails set. Motto: "Prestat opes sapientia" ("Wisdom surpasses wealth").[1] "L/RM" and "No. 2" engraved on underside; "ML" (script) added on cover in early nineteenth century

PROVENANCE: probably Robert R. Livingston (1718–1775; cat. 124) and his wife, Margaret Beekman (1724–1800; cat. 125), who were married in 1742; presumed descent to either their son Robert Livingston (1746–1813) or their daughter Margaret (Livingston) Tillotson (1749–1823); to either Robert's granddaughter Maria Livingston (1800–1830) or Margaret's son John C. Tillotson (1791–1867), who were married in 1816; the initials "ML" could stand for either Margaret or her niece Maria.[2] Subsequent ownership unknown prior to acquisition by the West Hartford, Connecticut, collector Philip Hammerslough between 1970 and 1973.[3]

Wadsworth Atheneum Museum of Art, Hartford, Connecticut; Philip H. Hammerslough Collection

This tankard was part of a set of table silver made in Myers's workshop that included a second tankard as well as a cann (cat. 29), which probably also had a mate. Such a set would have been an impressive display of its owners wealth: Elias Pelletreau charged £19.11.6 for a tankard weighing 4 troy oz. less than the present example in 1765 and £3.4.5 for a "1/2 pint Cup wt. 5 oz 3 dwt 18 gr" in 1775, which would make the total cost of Myers's set over £45.[4] The tankards' form followed Myers's standard model of the later 1750s and early 1760s, which was similar in most details to his earlier tankards (cat. 2) with the exception of a double-scroll handle. The spectacular armorials (fig. 16) are by the specialist engraver Myers used during this period for his most important commissions (pp. 38–39). Not surprisingly, given the complicated quartering in the Livingston arms, some of the tinctures were depicted incorrectly: the gillyflowers of Livingston should be gules, and the bend and billets of Callendar should be or.[5]

Although these arms and the initials indicate that the original owner was a member of the Livingston family, the tankard's precise history of ownership remains somewhat uncertain. The matching tankard and cann were sold at auction in 1972 with a group of eight English and New York silver objects "formerly in the Collection of the Livingston family," and the sale catalogue identified the initials on the tankard as those of "Robert R. and Margaret Livingston" (cats. 124, 125).[6]

However, when the collector Philip L. Hammerslough published the present tankard in 1973, he named Robert and Margaret's son, "Chancellor" Robert R. Livingston (1746–1813) and his wife, Mary Stevens (1752–1814), as the original owners.[7] Unfortunately, no records of Hammerslough's source for this information survive. These associations with the Clermont branch of the Livingston family, as well as the date of Myers's mark and the engraving, indicate that the most likely original owners were Robert and Margaret Livingston, since their son Robert did not marry Mary Stevens until 1770.

One distinctive detail of the tankards and their matching cann is the motto "Prestat opes sapientia" engraved on each of them. Most eighteenth-century descendants of the first Lord of Livingston Manor used his motto "Spero meliora" ("I hope for the best") as well as his crest of a ship.[8] However, mottos as well as crests were not associated with specific coats of arms and could be altered by individual family members. Aside from these two tankards and the cann, the only other use of this motto by a Livingston family member in the eighteenth century was by Peter R. Livingston (cats. 32, 34), whose bookplate, engraved in Boston by Nathaniel Hurd, included "Prestat opes sapientia" beneath the Livingston coat of arms.[9] A teakettle and porringer associated with Peter R. Livingston were also engraved with this motto.[10] The present author has been unable to locate a bookplate or other heraldic material associated with Robert R. Livingston, but his son Chancellor Robert Livingston's bookplates featured the motto "Spero meliora," which makes him an unlikely candidate for the tankard's original owner.[11]

1 For the arms, see Bolton 1964, p. 103.
2 Hawley 1989, p. 328.
3 Hammerslough/Feigenbaum 1973, pp. v–vi, 2.
4 Failey 1971, pp. 144, 155.
5 For a detailed discussion of the origins and variations of Livingston family heraldry, see Livingston 1910, pp. 489–507.
6 Sotheby's 1972, lots 86–87. The tankard (lot 86) in this sale had had a spout added in the early nineteenth century. The initials on the cann (lot 87) were not noted or identified.
7 Hammerslough/Feigenbaum 1973, p. 2.
8 Bolton 1964, p. 103. See Livingston 1910, pp. 505–06, for a discussion of mottos associated with Livingston arms. The crest of a demi-Hercules and motto "Si je puis" ("If I can"), used from the sixteenth century onward by the Lords Livingston of Callendar in Scotland, was adopted by several American Livingstons in the nineteenth century.
9 A second state of this bookplate, altered for Peter R. Livingston's son Peter William Livingston, changed the motto to "Spero meliora"; see French 1939, pp. 118–19, pl. 26.
10 Sotheby's 1972, lots 84, 88. See further discussion under cat. 34.
11 For Chancellor Robert Livingston's bookplate, see Stephens 1950, p. 101, nos. 159–61. One of them is illustrated on the cover of Walworth 1982. Since the bookplate's engraver, Peter Maverick, was not born until 1755, it is unlikely that his bookplates were executed for Judge Robert Livingston, who died in 1775.

29

Cann, 1755–65

Silver, h. 4¹¹⁄₁₆ (11.9), w. 4⅞ (12.4), diam. base 3⁹⁄₁₆ (9), diam. rim 3⅛ (7.9), wt. 11 oz. 8 dwt. (355g)

MARK 8 once on underside of body

ARMORIAL/INSCRIPTION: Livingston crest (a ship of three masts, top sails set) and motto ("Prestat opes sapientia" ["Wisdom surpasses wealth"]) engraved on front; "L/R*M" engraved on underside

PROVENANCE: probably Robert R. Livingston (1718–1775; cat. 124) and his wife Margaret Beekman (1724–1800; cat. 125); descent presumably as cat. 28, but specific ownership unknown until sale at auction in 1972 as "formerly in the Collection of the Livingston family."[1]

Harvard University Art Museums, Cambridge, Massachusetts; Bequest of David Berg

The armorials and initials engraved on this cann, as well as its contemporaneous mark, indicate that it was acquired as part of a set with the preceding tankard. It is nevertheless identical in style and size to other canns made in Myers's workshop for ready sale (cats. 22, 39) and as such cost less than a third of the probable price of the tankard. Because the tankard had a mate, it seems likely that this cann also was made as one of a pair.

1 Sotheby's 1972, lot 87.

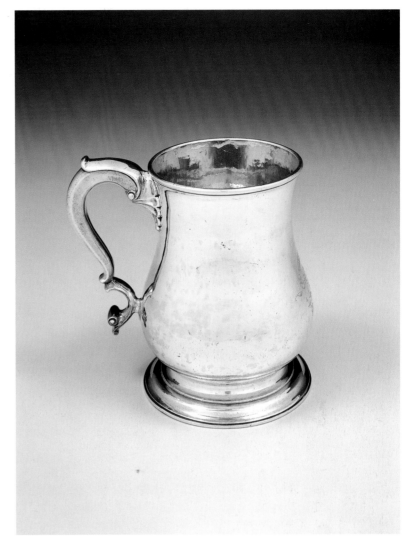

29

30

Tankard, 1750–65

Silver, h. 7¼ (18.4), diam. base 5¼ (13.3), diam. rim 4⁷⁄₁₆ (11.3), wt. 31 oz. 15 dwt. (927g)

ARMORIAL/INSCRIPTION: arms, crest, and motto of Livingston (see cat. 28) added c. 1900 on front, with "Robert and Mary Thong Livingston/Married 1731" below; "M/R*L" engraved on handle below hinge

MARK 8 once on underside

PROVENANCE: Robert Livingston, Jr. (1708–1790; cat. 127) and Mary Thong (1711–1765; cat. 128), who were married in 1731; by descent in the family of Robert's cousin Margaret (Livingston) Stuyvesant (1738–1818) to Stuyvesant Fish, the donor in 1941.[1]

Museum of the City of New York; Gift of Stuyvesant Fish

Robert Livingston, Jr., inherited Livingston Manor in 1749, and this tankard and a coffeepot (cat. 31) may have been commissioned when he took up residence in the Manor House. Tankards such as this example frequently were accompanied by canns. A cann by Myers, likewise engraved with the initials "M/RL" and struck with his MARK 8, apparently was made contemporaneously for the same patrons.[2] The tankard and cann may each have had mates and formed a large set like that made by Myers for Robert Livingston's cousin Robert R. Livingston (cats. 28, 29). The arms and inscription engraved on the front of this tankard about 1900 may have replaced older, worn engraving; any trace of earlier armorials was removed when the surface was buffed.

1 Fish 1929, pp. 48–49, 69; Waters/McKinsey/Ward 2000, I, pp. 170–71.
2 Collection of John D. Kernan; Rosenbaum 1954A, p. 105. Kernan received it as a gift from Nancy DeWitt (Pell) Osborne, the daughter of James Duane Pell, who also owned a sauceboat by Myers; ibid., p. 120. The initials "CD" are scratched on the underside. A spout was added to the cann in the nineteenth century.

30

31
Coffeepot, 1750–65

Silver with wood handle, h. 11¾ (29.8), diam. base 4⅞ (12.4), gross wt. 38 oz. 10 dwt. (1198g) (scratch wt. 38 oz. 6 dwt.)

MARK 8 once on underside

PROVENANCE: probably Robert Livingston, Jr. (1708–1790; cat. 127) and Mary Thong (1711–1765; cat. 128); to their son John Livingston (1750–1822); by descent in his family to Emeline (Cornell) Hopkins Livingston by 1954; to her son Henry H. Livingston (b. 1918), by whom sold at auction in 1988.[1]

Collection of Paul and Elissa Cahn

Although this coffeepot has no identifying initials, its direct descent in the family would suggest Robert and Mary Livingston as its original owners. It features a similar cast finial and the identical spout as on the coffeepots made in the mid-1750s for Charity Johnson (cat. 20) and Samuel and Susannah Cornell (cat. 19), but is a simpler shape than their exuberant double-bellied forms. This restraint, if not conservatism, seems characteristic of the taste of the third Lord of Livingston Manor and his wife.

1 Rosenbaum 1954A, p. 108; Sotheby's 1988, lot 244.

32

Set of Three Alms Basins, 1761–65

Silver, h. ¹⁵⁄₁₆ (2.4), diam. 10¹⁄₁₆ (25.6) each, wt. A. 13 oz. 5 dwt. (412.5g), B. 14 oz. 17 dwt. (460.6g), C. 13 oz. 13 dwt. (423.8g)

MARK 8 once on underside of brim on each

INSCRIPTION: "EX DONO PETER R: LIVINGSTON" engraved on brim of each

PROVENANCE: presented by Peter Robert Livingston (1737–1794) to the First Presbyterian Church, New York.

The First Presbyterian Church, New York

This set may represent Myers's only extant commission for Christian church silver. Alms basins became a significant piece of Protestant church plate after the Reformation. The 1662 edition of the Book of Common Prayer directed that offerings be collected in a "decent bason," and during the remainder of the service these basins frequently were placed upright on the altar table in the place of a cross or crucifix.[1] Alms basins were included in each of the services of plate presented to Trinity Church in New York by William and Mary, Anne, and George III.[2] These London-made examples were larger versions of domestic dishes, with narrow, beaded rims. An alms basin made in New York for Trinity Church by George Ridout in 1747 has the unmolded rim seen on Myers's set.[3] The relatively small size and plain rims of Myers's basins became typical for alms basins at the end of the eighteenth century; a set of ten similar basins by a number of makers was donated in 1791 to the First Reformed Dutch Church of New York.[4]

The donor of these basins, Peter Robert Livingston, was the eldest surviving son of Robert and Mary (Thong) Livingston (cats. 127, 128). In 1758, he married his third cousin Margaret Livingston, the daughter of James Livingston and Maria Kierstede.[5] During the 1760s, he sat in his father's seat in the General Assembly, and in 1761 he began his first four-year term as a trustee of the Presbyterian Church in New York, with which his family was closely associated.[8]

No record of Livingston's gift of these basins has been located in the records of the First Presbyterian Church, although Myers's MARK 8 indicates that they probably were made during Livingston's first term as trustee.[7] It is possible that the dishes were made at this time for Livingston's personal use and donated to the congregation at a later date. In their efforts to demystify church rituals, dissenting Protestant sects used vessels of secular rather than distinctly sacred forms, which enabled members of the congregation to donate domestic objects for sacred purposes.[8] Although silver dishes would have been extremely uncommon in eighteenth-century New York households, Peter Livingston was renowned for his lavish lifestyle, and could have ordered such plate.[9] His extrav-

agance eventually forced him into bankruptcy in 1771, when Robert R. Livingston (cat. 124) observed:

Cousin Robert is quite unfortunate in his children. His eldest son goes up in the Spring to live at the Manor & his good & generous father will be obliged to advance eleven thousand pounds for him after which [Peter] will not be worth one groat.[10]

It is possible that these dishes were donated to the church after Livingston's bankruptcy and removal from New York. The inscriptions show evidence of being engraved over scratches and other wear on the basins' surfaces, although they may have become worn and been recut at a later date.

The engraved inscriptions are significant because they are simple lettering rather than the armorials frequently found on New England church silver during this period. Perhaps the basins' inscriptions were influenced by the Livingston family's Whig politics, which was closely tied to fellow members of the Presbyterian Church (p. 5). Armorials would have suggested acceptance of a social hierarchy based on English aristocratic models; their absence, a commitment to equality of membership within the church. Peter Livingston had some of his domestic silver engraved with a crest, although his set of tablespoons by Myers bore only initials.[11]

1 Gilchrist 1967, pp. 72, 98–99.
2 Jones 1913, pp. 332–34.
3 Warren/Howe/Brown 1987, no. 27.
4 Now the Collegiate Church; Jones 1913, pp. 330–31.
5 Livingston 1910, pp. 558, 562.
6 Trustee Minute Book, 1717–75, p. 138, Presbyterian Historical Society, Philadelphia.
7 The Trustee Minutes, which are largely concerned with financial matters, contain no record of this gift. A more likely source of information would be the Session Minutes, but unfortunately none survive prior to 1765.
8 Gilchrist 1967, pp. 55, 71–72, 110–11; Ward 1988, p. 5.
9 Livingston 1910, pp. 483–84; Kierner 1992, p. 155.
10 Quoted in Kierner 1992, p. 155.
11 Among the silver objects associated with Peter R. Livingston and engraved with a crest are a silver tea kettle on stand, made in 1757 by Daniel Piers of London, and a porringer by Henricus Boelen; Sotheby's 1972, lots 84, 88.

32

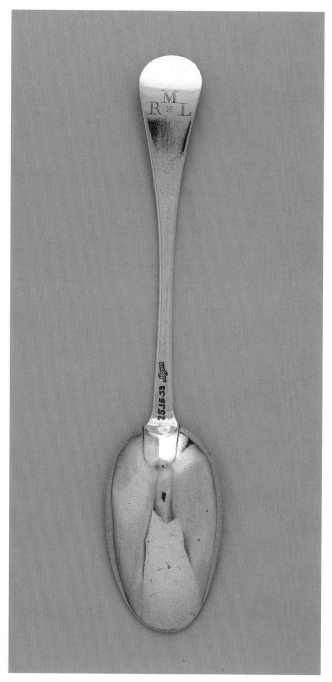

33

34

33

Tablespoon, 1755–65

Silver, l. 8³⁄₁₆ (20.8), wt. 1 oz. 19 dwt. (60g)

MARK 10 once on back of handle

INSCRIPTION: "M/R*L" engraved on back of handle

PROVENANCE: probably Robert Livingston, Jr. (1708–1790; cat. 127) and Mary Thong (1711–1765; cat. 128); by descent or purchase to Alfred Duane Pell, the donor.

The Metropolitan Museum of Art, New York; Bequest of Alfred Duane Pell, 1925

34

Tablespoon
ONE OF FIVE, 1765–76

Silver, l. 7³⁄₁₆ (18.3), wt. 1 oz. 6 dwt. (40g)

MARK 9 once on back of handle

INSCRIPTION: "L/P·M" engraved on back of handle

PROVENANCE: Peter R. Livingston (1737–1794) and Margaret Livingston (1738–1809), who married in 1758; subsequent history unknown until sold at auction in 1972, when these Livingstons were identified as the original owners.[1]

Collection of Philip Holzer

Although it was bequeathed to The Metropolitan Museum Museum of Art without any history of ownership, cat. 33 may have been made for Robert and Mary (Thong) Livingston. The spoon bears a third Myers surname mark, MARK 10, which to date has not been found on any firmly documented work by him (Appendix I). However, the spoon's simple pattern is typical of Myers's flatware and consistent with the silver associated with the Livingstons. The tankard and cann made for them by Myers (see cat. 30) were engraved with their initials in the atypical arrangement "M/RL," which was also used on the pipe lighter owned by Robert's brother Philip Livingston (cat. 37). Although Kathryn Buhler suggested that the practice of positioning the wife's initial above the husband's was exclusive to Albany, the same arrangement was used not only by Myers in New York, but also in 1763 by Elias Pelletreau in Southampton.[2]

The theory that cat. 33 was originally owned by Robert and Mary Livingston is supported by the connections of the spoon's donor, Alfred Duane Pell, to the Livingston family. His wife, Cornelia Livingston Crosby, was related to Robert's brother Philip as well as to Robert Gilbert Livingston (cat. 38), through her maternal great-grandparents, Philip's daughter Sarah and Robert's nephew, the Reverend John H. Livingston, who were married in 1775.[3] Alfred Duane Pell may have been more directly related to Robert and Mary Livingston through their daughter Maria, who married James Duane (see cat. 107), although no connection can be proven; Robert and Mary Livingston's cann descended in the Duane family.[4] Pell was also a collector of English silver, and it is possible that he acquired this spoon because of these family connections.[5]

Cat. 34 has a more secure history of ownership by Robert and Mary Livingston's son Peter (cat. 32). It originally was part of a set from which at least four others survive.[6] Peter's choice of Myers as the silversmith as well as the spoons' style may have been influenced by his parents' prior patronage.

1 Sotheby's 1972, lot 85.
2 Rosenbaum 1954A, p. 132; Failey 1971, p. 39.
3 Livingston 1910, p. 552; Lawrence 1932, pp. 34, 52–55; obituary for Jane Murray Livingston Crosby, *The New York Times*, May 26, 1911, p. 13; obituary for Mrs. Alfred Duane Pell, *The New York Times*, August 18, 1938, p. 20.
4 Livingston 1910, p. 545; Walworth 1982, p. 69.
5 Obituary for Alfred Duane Pell, *The New York Times*, March 8, 1924, p. 11; Avery 1925, pp. 69, 71–72.
6 One spoon is in The Art Institute of Chicago, Gift of Mr. and Mrs. Allen Wardwell in honor of David Hanks, inv. 1973.557. This may be the same spoon owned in 1954 by Mrs. Wendell P. Colton; Rosenbaum 1954A, p. 125. A pair of spoons from this same set was formerly owned by Jeanette Rosenbaum, who purchased them from John D. Kernan in 1953; Rosenbaum 1954A, p. 125, and Jeanette Rosenbaum to Charles Nagel, May 26, 1953, Decorative Arts Department, exhibition files, Brooklyn Museum of Art.

35

Two Candlesticks
FROM A SET OF FOUR, 1755–60

Silver

A. h. 10¹⁄₁₆ (25.6), w. base 5⁷⁄₁₆ (13.8), w. nozzle 2⁷⁄₈ (7.3), wt. 19 oz. 12 dwt. (610g)

B. h. 9⁷⁄₈ (25.1), w. base 5½ (14.0), w. nozzle 2¹³⁄₁₆ (7.1), wt. 20 oz. 5 dwt. (630g)

MARK 6, twice on each candlestick, once on socket and once on flange of nozzle

INSCRIPTION: "THE GIFT Of PETER & SARAH V:ⁿ BRUGH To CATHA:ᴱ LIVINGSTON" engraved on underside of each

PROVENANCE: Catherine (Livingston) Lawrence (1733–1807); by bequest in her will dated April 7, 1807: "I bequeath to Louisa E.F. Patterson Wife of my Grand Nephew John W. Patterson one pair of my Silver candlesticks . . . & the other pair of Silver Candlesticks I leave to my Niece Lady Mary Watts." The latter pair by descent to Mary's great-great-grandson, DeLancey Watts; by sale or gift to Inglis Griswold (d. 1957), by whom sold to Francis P. Garvan in 1936.[1]

Yale University Art Gallery, New Haven; Mabel Brady Garvan Collection

1 NYCPR-1, liber 47, pp. 97–104. Mary (Alexander) Watts was the daughter of Catherine's older sister Sarah and Major General William Alexander, who styled himself "Lord Sterling," hence the reference to his daughter as "Lady Mary"; see Lawrence 1932, pp. 17–18.

36

Two Candlesticks
FROM A SET OF FOUR, 1755–60

Silver

A. h. 10¹⁄₁₆ (25.6), w. base 5³⁄₈ (13.7), wt. 19 oz. 6 dwt. (600g)

B. h. 10⅛ (25.7), w. base 5⁷⁄₁₆ (13.8), wt. 20 oz. 16 dwt. (647g)

MARK 6, twice on each candlestick, once on socket and once on flange of nozzle

INSCRIPTION: "THE GIFT Of PETER & SARAH V:ⁿ BRUGH TO CATHA:ᴱ LIVINGSTON" engraved on underside of each

PROVENANCE: Catherine (Livingston) Lawrence; by bequest as described in cat. 35 to Louisa Patterson, whose husband was the grandson of Robert and Mary (Thong) Livingston (cats. 127, 128); subsequent ownership unknown until 1972, when offered for sale by the dealer Harry Arons of Ansonia, Connecticut.[1]

The Metropolitan Museum of Art, New York; Sansbury-Mills Fund, 1972, 1977

This set of four candlesticks was made for Catherine (Livingston) Lawrence, the youngest child of Philip Livingston, the second Lord of Livingston Manor, and his wife Catharina Van Brugh.[2] As indicated by the engraved inscriptions, the set

120 MYER MYERS

was funded by a legacy from Catherine's maternal grandparents, Pieter Van Brugh, who served three terms as Mayor of Albany, and his wife, Sarah Cuyler. As their youngest grandchild, Catherine may have received a special remembrance in the wills of one of her grandparents, who died in the early 1740s. The candlesticks undoubtedly were not commissioned until Catherine reached adulthood and most likely date to the first years of her brief marriage to John Lawrence in 1759. It seems unlikely that she would have reverted to her maiden name for the inscription after becoming a widow.

Such sets of silver candlesticks were owned by only the wealthiest American patrons. The amount of silver required to cast them and the special chasing needed to finish their details would have made this set among the most costly products of Myers's workshop. The "2 pr Chased Candlesticks & Nozells" sent to New York from London by Philip Schuyler at the same time that Myers made this set weighed 137 troy oz. 7 dwt. and were valued at £43.10.0.[3] Using the same calculation, Myers's set, which now weighs about 82 troy oz., would have cost Catherine about £26. As noted earlier (pp. 41–42), Myers cast these candlesticks using an English silver candlestick for the pattern; the hallmarks on the English stick were picked up in the casting and deliberately filed off (35.2). Candlesticks in this style were popular in England during 1750s and 1760s; among the many silver examples are a pair marked by the specialist candlestick maker John Cafe in 1751–52 and 1752–53 that were owned by Samuel Cary of Charlestown, Massachusetts.[4] Identical examples were also made in paktong.[5]

Myers apparently felt some pride in this set. He struck his mark on the socket of each candlestick, where it is in full view; most English and American candlesticks were marked on the undersides. This is one of the earliest instances of Myers striking his mark in a prominent and unconventional location, using his silversmith's mark as a signature (see also cats. 38, 56, 79). On the candlesticks, Myers used his smallest initials mark

so that it would register clearly on the curved surface of the socket.

Catherine Lawrence's decision to have Myers make a set of candlesticks undoubtedly was influenced by the sets owned by other members of her family. Pieter and Sarah Van Brugh owned a superb pair in the Baroque style made in New York about 1750 by the English immigrant George Ridout.[6] The "1 pr. largest chased candlesticks" owned by Robert and Catherine (McPhaedres) Livingston (cat. 38) weighed 39 oz. 3 dwt., about the same as one pair from Catherine Lawrence's set.[7] Another member of the family owned a pair of elaborately chased Rococo candlesticks made in London by William Cafe in 1763–64.[8] Even without the legacy from her grandparents, Catherine Lawrence had the means to afford such luxuries. John Lawrence was a wealthy merchant; in his will dated August 11, 1761 and proved September 25, 1764, he left his widow the enormous legacy of "the use and interest" of £5,000, all his real estate, £1,000 "at her own disposal," interest on £3,000 for life, two slaves and "all my household furniture and plate," as well as "as much money as I had with her in Marriage . . . [and] all the Estate that was left her by her father Philip Livingston Esq."[9]

1 Correspondence in accession file 1936.148, American Arts Office, YUAG; *Antiques*, 101 (January 1972), p. 121.

2 Lawrence 1932, pp. 15–18.

3 "Invoice of Sundries Sent to America," pp. 2–3, undated manuscript, Schuyler Papers, NYPL.

4 Alcorn 2000A, no. 104. Additional examples by the Cafe family are illustrated in Davis 1976, no. 17, and Lomax 1992, no. 173.

5 An eighteenth-century paktong candlestick in this pattern is in the Louisiana State University Museum, Baton Rouge.

6 Buhler/Hood 1970, II, no. 694.

7 New York Supreme Court of Probates Records, box 10, Inventories and Accounts, 1666–1822, NYSA.

8 This pair is now in the Burrows Collection; on long-term loan to the Sterling and Francine Clark Art Institute, Williamstown, Massachusetts, inv. TR182/81.

9 NYCPR-1, liber 24, pp. 481–86.

35.1

35.2

37

Pipe Lighter, 1750–65

Silver with wood handle, h. 1⅞ (4.8), l. 10⅞ (27.6), diam. rim 4⅛ (10.5), gross wt. 6 oz. 4 dwt. (193g)

MARK 8 once on underside

INSCRIPTION: "C/P*L" engraved on underside

PROVENANCE: Philip Livingston (1717–1778, cat. 129) and Christina (Ten Broeck) Livingston (1718–1801, cat. 130); to their grandson, Henry Alexander Livingston (1776–1849); by descent in the family until sale at auction in 1983.[1]

Collection of Ruth J. Nutt

A pipe lighter was filled with lighted charcoal to supply a modicum of heat and a means of lighting pipes or candles without resorting to the fireplace. Unlike chafing dishes, which kept plates warm at the table, pipe lighters were designed to burn uncovered since they had no openings to supply oxygen to the charcoal fire.[2] The term "silver pipe lighters," which Kathryn Buhler observed in the 1763 advertisement of silver imported by Edmund Milne of Philadelphia, probably referred to this form.[3] It was an extremely uncommon form in both English and American silver, and most of the surviving American examples were made in New York City. Adrian Bancker and Thomas Hammersley marked pipe lighters; there are two additional versions by Myers with double-bellied bottoms and

scalloped rims.[4] In September 1754, Myers paid the cabinet-maker Joshua Delaplaine 6 s. for "2 Chafing dish [handles]," which would have been identical to the handle on this object.[5]

The scallop shells at the juncture of the legs and basin are a more successful adaptation of English Rococo designs than those found on Myers's sauceboats (cats. 17, 18). This may indicate that the pipe lighter was slightly later in date, although the spiral-pattern feet are cast from the same pattern Myers used for the feet on a waiter made for Elizabeth (Stillwell) Wraxall Maunsell between 1756 and 1759 and on the snuffers tray made contemporaneously for Robert Gilbert Livingston (cat. 38).[6] As noted in cat. 33, the unusual arrangement of the Livingstons' initials was found on other pieces of New York silver, including pieces made by Myers for Philip's brother Robert.

1 Piwonka 1986, pp. 60–61; Lawrence 1932, pp. 24–26, 52–55; Christie's 1983B, lot 60.
2 Clayton 1971, p. 199.
3 Rosenbaum 1954A, p. 114; the advertisement appeared in *The Pennsylvania Journal and Weekly Advertiser*, December 15, 1763, p. 1.
4 Clayton 1971, p. 199; Buhler/Hood 1970, II, no. 680; Rosenbaum 1954A, pl. 5, p. 115; Christie's 1993, lot 124.
5 Delaplaine 1753–56, p. 34.
6 Buhler 1972, II, no. 506; see cat. 10 for a discussion of the Maunsell waiter's history.

38

Candle Snuffers and Tray, 1750–65

Silver

Snuffers, h. 1½ (3.8), l. 6⁷⁄₁₆ (16.4), wt. 3 oz. 6 dwt. (103g)

MARK 8 once on outside face of cutting blade

Tray, h. 2⁷⁄₁₆ (6.1), w. 7³⁄₈ (18.7), d. 3¾ (9.5), wt. 9 oz. 17 dwt. (306g)

MARK 8 twice on underside, one double-struck

INSCRIPTION: "L," "RGL," "IR," and "C Reade" (script), all scratched on underside of tray

PROVENANCE: Robert Gilbert Livingston ("RGL"; 1713–1789) and his wife, Catherine McPhaedres (1722–1792); possibly the set listed in Catherine's 1792 estate inventory as "1 Do [ditto, snuffers dish] (& best snuffers)" weighing 12 oz. 9 dwt. and valued at £8.5.4; to their daughter Catherine (Livingston) Reade ("C Reade"; 1756–1829), who married John Reade ("IR"; 1745–1808); in her 1830 estate inventory as "1 pair Snuffers & Stand" weighing 14 5/8 oz. (possibly the avoirdupois weight?); by descent to her great-great-grandson, Lynde Catlin (1876–1949), who sold them in 1936 to Francis P. Garvan.[1]

Yale University Art Gallery, New Haven; Mabel Brady Garvan Collection

Snuffers were required for trimming the wicks of lighted candles prior to the invention of self-consuming wicks about 1820, but silver versions of this form were a rare and costly exception. Because sharp cutting blades were needed, snuffers usually were made wholly or in part of steel by specialist makers.[2] David Clarkson, Jr.'s, inventory of 1782 included only a silver "snuffer pan," probably because the accompanying snuffers were not made of silver. Sets of silver snuffers and stands were known in Colonial New York. Robert and Catherine Livingston's daughter, Helena (Livingston) Hake, owned two sets of candle snuffers and matching trays made in London in 1765–66.[3] Philip Schuyler's purchase of two pairs of chased silver candlesticks from the London silversmiths Theed and Pickett in 1760 was accompanied by a pair of snuffers and "Chased Snuffer pan" from Stafford Briscoe that weighed a total of 15 oz. 12 dwt. and cost £6.18.0; the pan accounted for £5.7.6 of the total.[4] Myers's set now weighs 14 oz. 5 dwt. and probably cost about the same as Schuyler's set.

Robert Gilbert Livingston, grandson of the first Robert Livingston (see cats. 127, 128) through the latter's youngest son, Gilbert Livingston, denominated himself "gentleman" and was a prosperous dry goods merchant who owned extensive property in Manhattan, Long Island, and Dutchess County. He and his wife Catherine (McPhaedres) Livingston owned an enormous quantity of plate. The 1792 inventory of Catherine Livingston's estate listed seventy-eight pieces of silver hollow ware, with almost every form associated with dining, drinking tea and alcohol, and lighting, including three silver snuffer trays.[5] Robert and Catherine also had more opulent taste in silver than the majority of their Livingston kin. Many of the

objects in Catherine's estate were described as "chased" or "flowered," including a large salver, slop bowl, two milk pots, two sugar dishes, a "teaspoon dish," three pairs of candlesticks, and five pairs of salts. Extant objects from this group include the Rococo punch bowl by William Grundy (cat. 120), a richly ornamented pair of salts by the London silversmith Edward Wood, and a pair of scalloped dishes by George Ridout.[6]

Myers's snuffers and tray follow English models of the third quarter of the eighteenth century. The scissors-shape snuffers, with three stud feet and a box to contain the severed wick, has blades shaped into opposing S-curves and handles composed of C-scrolls.[7] The sumptuous tray is embellished with cast and chased Rococo scrollwork and shell forms. Similar English examples are known, but the only comparable tray marked by a Colonial American silversmith is an example with the same dimensions and an identical cast border made by Philip Syng, Jr., of Philadelphia.[8] The two trays are so similar, aside from variations in finishing the cast elements, that their castings may have been taken from the same English prototype, or they may have been made by a specialist craftsman who moved between New York and Philadelphia. The only distinguishing feature of Myers's tray are the spiral-shell feet, which he cast using the same pattern for the feet on the pipe lighter (cat. 37) and on a waiter.[9]

As with Catherine Lawrence's candlesticks, Myers apparently felt that this set was of sufficient significance to place his mark in an unusually prominent location. His earlier surname mark, MARK 8, was struck on the outside of the snuffers' cutting blade, where it would be seen whenever the snuffers were used. English snuffers were normally marked on the inside of the blade.

1 The snuffers and tray have been erroneously published as being part of a set with four candlesticks made for Catherine (Livingston) Lawrence (cats. 35, 36) in Hood 1971, p. 157; Montgomery/Kane 1976, p. 195; Ward/Ward 1979, p. 155. For the correct history, see NYCPR-1, liber 40, pp. 256–67; New York Supreme Court of Probates Records, box 10, Inventories and Accounts, 1666–1822, NYSA; Dutchess County Probate Records, file no. 3193, October 4, 1830; Caroline A. Catlin to John Marshall Phillips, April 25, 1937, object file 1936.137, American Arts Office, YUAG.

2 Clayton 1971, p. 262.

3 The Metropolitan Museum of Art, New York; Gift of Frederic Ashton de Peyster, inv. 46.33.2-5. The maker's mark is W.T in an oval, which may be a mark of the London silversmith William Tuite (act. c. 1755–73); Grimwade 1990, p. 276, nos. 3901–02.

4 "Invoice of Sundries Sent to America," pp. 2–3; undated manuscript, Schuyler Papers, NYPL.

5 New York Supreme Court of Probates Records, box 10, Inventories and Accounts, 1666–1822, NYSA.

6 Waters/McKinsey/Ward 2000, I, nos. 57, 98.

7 Clayton 1971, p. 262.

8 Davis 1976, no. 30; Heckscher/Bowman 1992, no. 86.

9 Buhler 1972, II, no. 506.

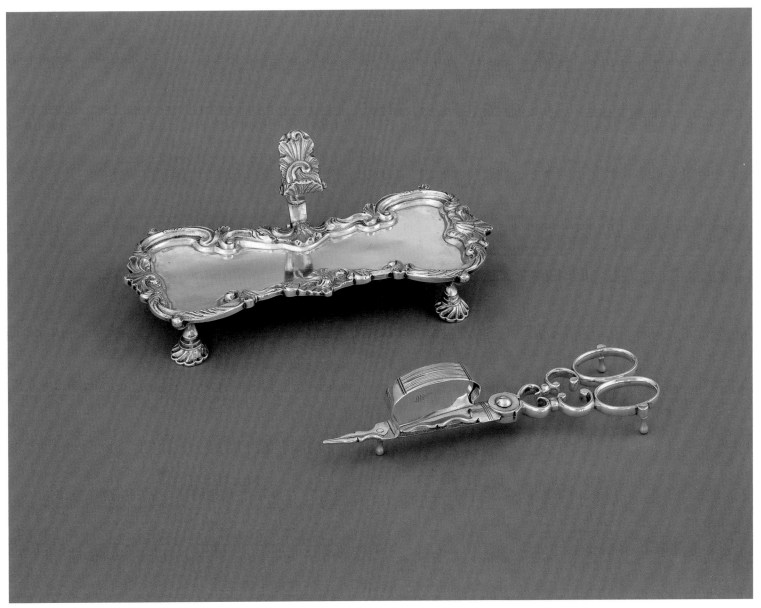

38

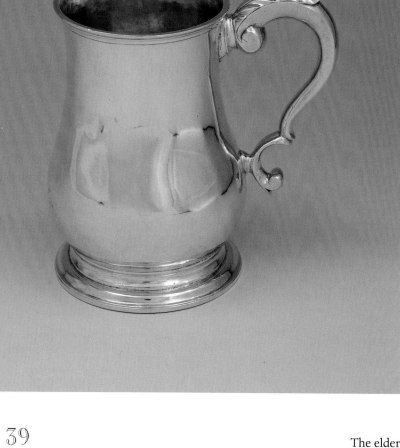

39

Cann, c. 1750–60

Silver, h. 5¼ (13.3), diam. base 3⅜ (8.6), diam. rim 3³⁄₁₆ (8.1), wt. 10 oz. 19 dwt. (340g)

MARK 3 once on underside

INSCRIPTION: "M/AS" engraved on underside; "CLR" (script) added later on front

PROVENANCE: Andries Meyer and his wife, Susanna McPhaedres (1713–d. before 1770), who were married before 1750; to their niece, Catherine (Livingston) Reade (see cat. 38); by descent to her great-great-granddaughters, Helen S. (Dudley) Braman, Laura Dudley, and Fanny Dudley, the donors in 1943.[1]

Museum of the City of New York; Gift of the Misses Dudley and Mrs. Helen Stuyvesant Braman

The elder sister of Catherine (McPhaedres) Livingston (cat. 38) owned this cann. As a simple, routine form, it contrasts with the costly snuffers and tray owned by Catherine and may indicate the difference in wealth between the sisters' husbands.

1 Susanna (McPhaedres) Meyer was deceased by February 21, 1770, when her mother Helena wrote her will, and three of her own children had married by that date; NYCPR-1, liber 36, pp. 528–32. For the family genealogy, see Kinkead 1954, pp. 178–79, and Waters/McKinsey/Ward 2000, I, pp. 163–64.

40

MYER MYERS; HALSTED AND MYERS

Cann, 1760–70

Silver, h. 5¼ (13.3), diam. base 3⅝ (9.2), diam. rim 3⁵⁄₁₆ (8.4), wt. 14 oz. 3 dwt. (440g)

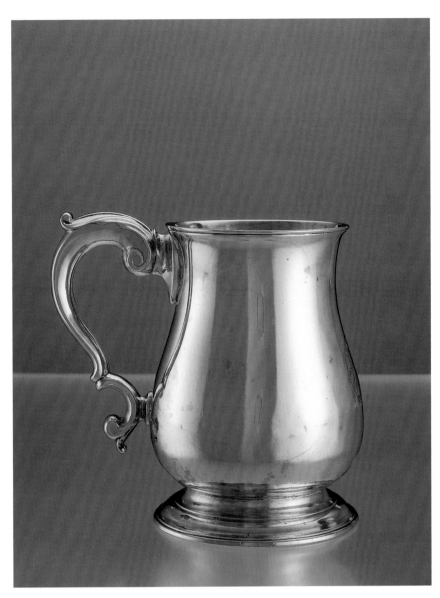

MARK 9 twice on underside, one double-struck, the other overstriking MARK 11

INSCRIPTION: "BRG" (script) engraved on front of body

PROVENANCE: possibly Barnard Gratz (1738–1801) and his wife, Richea Myers Cohen (1731–1801); subsequent ownership unknown until 1976, when acquired by the New York City dealers Bernard and S. Dean Levy.

The Burrows Collection; on long-term loan to the Sterling and Francine Clark Art Institute, Williamstown, Massachusetts

This cann is struck twice with Myers's MARK 9, one overstriking the Halsted and Myers partnership MARK 11. Since Myers's other surname mark and the partnership mark were struck independently on at least one object (cat. 21), it is not certain why the latter mark was obliterated here. Nor can it be determined if these two marks are contemporary or if the cann was an unsold, stock item in Myers's store with an earlier Halsted and Myers mark that he overstruck at the time it sold.[1] However, the partnership seems to have continued in some form after Halsted's move to New Jersey in 1766 (p. 34).

Although this cann has no documented history, the initials in the engraved monogram are those of Barnard and Richea Gratz. Given their close connections to Myers and his first wife (see cat. 138), it seems plausible they owned it. Like other objects from Myers's workshop owned by fellow Jews, the cann is a modest form that was customized with the owners' engraved initials or monograms. The restrained style of this engraving is similar to that on a bowl Myers made between 1765 and 1776 (cat. 54).

1 Another cann is recorded with the mark of Halsted and Myers, originally made for Elias Boudinot of Elizabeth, New Jersey; "Jewish Community" 1980, p. 14.

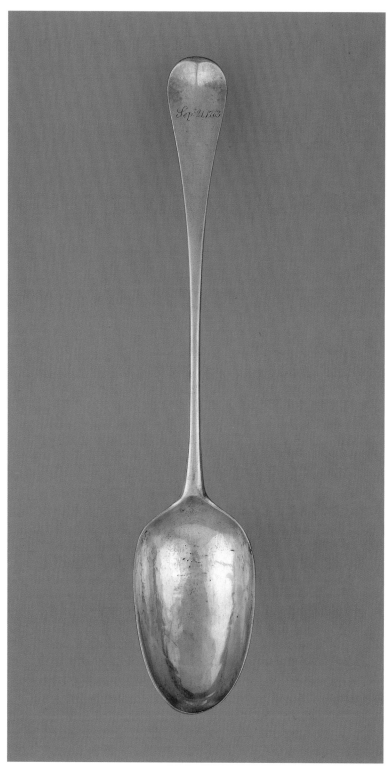

41

41

Sauce Spoon, 1765–76

Silver, l. 15¼ (38.7), wt. 5 oz. 19½ dwt. (186g)

MARK 9 twice on back of handle

INSCRIPTION: "B/T*P" engraved on back of handle; "Sept. 21, 1763" added on front of handle, probably in late nineteenth or early twentieth century

PROVENANCE: possibly Thomas (d. 1763) and Phebe (d. 1788) Barnes; subsequent ownership unknown prior to the collector Lincoln N. Kinnicutt of Worcester, Massachusetts, by 1913; to Dr. and Mrs. Roger Kinnicutt, the donors in 1954.[1]

Worcester Art Museum, Massachusetts; Gift of Dr. and Mrs. Roger Kinnicutt

Large spoons such as this example and cats. 42–43 were called "sauce spoons," "ragout spoons," or even "soup ladles" in contemporary sources.[2] Given its high price of £4.18.10, the "Soop Spoon" listed on Halsted and Myers's bill of October 1760 (Appendix II, no. 2) probably was a large spoon of this type and not a spoon for individual dining.

The block capital initials engraved on this spoon are also found on a punch bowl and sauceboat (cats. 6, 7) by Myers. The punch bowl is documented as belonging to Thomas and Phebe Barnes of New York, and this spoon is in the same simple style. However, Myers's MARK 9 on this spoon has not been found on firmly documented objects dating earlier than about 1765, by which time Thomas Barnes was deceased, so this identification of the initials remains problematic (see Appendix I).

1 *Exhibition* 1929, no. 230; object files, Worcester Art Museum.
2 Snodin 1982, p. 38.

42

HALSTED AND MYERS

Sauce Spoon, c. 1766

Silver, l. 15⅝ (39.7), wt. 7 oz. 2 dwt. (220g)

MARK 11 twice on back of handle

INSCRIPTION: "H/MR" engraved on back of handle

PROVENANCE: possibly Moses Michael Hays (1739–1805) and Rachel Myers (1738–1810), who were married on August 13, 1766; subsequent ownership unknown prior to 1980, when purchased by the dealers Bernard and S. Dean Levy of New York.[1]

Collection of Eric Noah

The identification of this spoon's original owners as Myer Myers's younger sister Rachel and her husband is bolstered by the fact that, like other silver owned by Myers's relatives, this relatively simple spoon was a standard pattern made in the workshop. A ladle with a nearly identical handle, featuring the same wide rounded end, short midrib, and sharply tapered, long midsection, bears the same mark of the Halsted and Myers partnership.[2] The Hays' wedding occurred in the same year that Halsted moved to New Jersey and his partnership with Myers may have ended (see p. 34), so perhaps the spoon was a gift of a recently made stock item.

If the history is correct, this Colonial period spoon offers a striking contrast to the elaborate Neoclassical forms Moses and Rachel Hays commissioned after the Revolutionary War, when they became significant patrons of Boston silversmiths, most notably Paul Revere, Jr. Among the twenty-five orders they placed with Revere between 1783 and 1792 were such objects as teapots, sauceboats, a milk pot, a set of wine cups, and numerous spoons ornamented with bright-cut engraving.[3] Some of these objects were purchased as gifts for their daughters Judith, Rebecca, and Sarah, two of whom married sons of Myer Myers (cat. 140). Hays's patronage of Revere undoubtedly stemmed from their association as Masons of the Grand Lodge of Massachusetts and as partners in the founding of the Massachusetts Mutual Fire Insurance Company.[4] However, Hays may have returned to Myers to commission a pair of Torah finials that descended in their family (cat. 100).

Moses Michael Hays was born in New York and spent much of his life as a West Indies merchant. He married Rachel Myers in a double ceremony, the other couple being Myer and Rachel's youngest sister Rebecca and Solomon Maraché.[5] By 1770, the Hays family had moved to Newport, Rhode Island, where Hays went bankrupt in 1771. He reestablished himself but left Newport in advance of the British in 1776, ultimately settling in Boston in 1782. His postwar affluence resulted from his role as one of the founders of the Massachusetts Bank in 1784 and three different fire and marine insurance companies in the 1790s.[6]

1 "Jewish Community" 1980, p. 14.
2 This ladle, engraved with the unidentified block initials "T/P*E," measures 14 1/2 in. in length and weighs 5 oz. 9 dwt. It is in the collection of Eric M. Hellige, who kindly brought it to my attention.
3 Objects purchased from Boston silversmiths by Moses and Rachel Hays are identified in Kane 1998, pp. 474, 808, 813, 825–26, 830, 838–41, 845, 898. In addition to Revere, the Hayses owned silver by Stephen Emery and William Simpkins; Kane 1998, pp. 474, 898. See also Bortman 1954; Conger/Rollins 1991, p. 345; Christie's 1992, pp. 92–95.
4 Leehey et al. 1988, pp. 125–26.
5 Stern 1991, pp. 104, 184, 217.
6 Sarna/Smith 1995, pp. 34–39. The reference here to Hays being admitted as a Freeman of New York in 1769 is erroneous, Moses Hays being confused with Andrew Hays (p. 000).

43

Sauce Spoon
ONE OF A PAIR, 1765–76

Silver, l. 11⁷⁄₁₆ (29.1), wt. 3 oz. 10 dwt. (109g)

MARK 9 twice on back of handle

PROVENANCE: unknown prior to March 1935, when purchased, together with its mate, by Francis P. Garvan from the New York dealer Robert Ensko.[1]

Yale University Art Gallery, New Haven; Mabel Brady Garvan Collection

An elegant Rococo expression, the scrolled end on the handle of this spoon recalls the carved terminals on contemporaneous armchairs. Introduced in England about 1745, at the height of the Rococo style, this pattern enjoyed its greatest popularity there during the 1760s; but it was never popular in New York. In America, it was found primarily on ladles and large spoons made in the Philadelphia region; in 1763, the Philadelphia silversmith Edmund Milne advertised "fluted and polished sauce-spoons, with scroll heads."[2] This pattern was also known by the name "Onslow," supposedly after Arthur Onslow, Speaker of the House of Commons.[3]

1 "Lists of Silver and From Whom Bought," Garvan Papers, box 26, file 8, Library, Albany Institute of History and Art.
2 *The Pennsylvania Journal and Weekly Advertiser*, December 15, 1763, p. 1. Ladles with "scrolled heads" were made about 1770 by William Faris of Annapolis, Maryland (Quimby/Johnson 1995, no. 346) and about 1790 by Joseph Richardson, Jr., of Philadelphia (Fales 1974, p. 194, fig. 176).
3 Jackson 1911, II, pp. 528–29; Clayton 1971, p. 279.

44

Ladle, 1765–76

Silver, l. 14½ (36.8), wt. 4 oz. 17 dwt. (150g)

MARK 9 twice on back of handle

ARMORIAL: unidentified crest (a lion rampant) engraved on front of handle

PROVENANCE: unknown prior to sale at auction in 1982, when catalogued as "property of a Danish private collector."[1]

Private collection

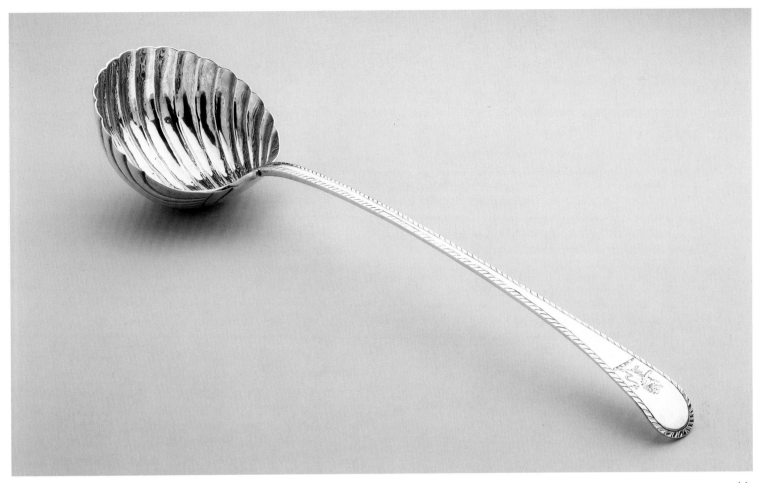

44

44.1

In the early 1750s, a new pattern of flatware was first introduced in England, with a downturned end on the handle and a
molded tip and faint midrib on the underside.[2] Today known
as "Old English," this pattern was called "turn'd back" in London during the 1760s, when it became extremely popular.[3] The
decorative border was known as "gadrooned" or "feathered"
in the eighteenth century.[4] A newspaper advertisement of
1779, placed after Myers had fled the city, described the theft of
"Ten Silver Tea Spoons, some of them plain, the rest
gadrooned, all made by Myers, late of New-York, and marked
as well with his mark."[5] A set of five gadrooned teaspoons by
Myers has survived.[6] The same gadrooned border is found on
the crossguard of a hunting sword marked by Myers (44.1), and
both gadrooned borders and fluted details appear on contemporary hollow ware from Myers's workshop in the Rococo
style (cat. 76).

1 Sotheby's 1982B, lot 234.

2 Jackson 1911, II, pp. 529–30; Clayton 1971, p. 279.

3 Snodin 1982, p. 47.

4 Wees 1997, p. 479.

5 *Royal Gazette*, November 13, 1779, as cited in Gottesman 1954, p. 71.

6 Collection of Ruth J. Nutt; reprod. in Rosenbaum 1954A, pl. 24, fig. B.

44.1 Myer Myers, *Hunting Sword* (detail), New York, 1765–76.
Silver, ivory, and steel. Private collection.

45

HALSTED AND MYERS

Porringer, 1756–66

Silver, h. 2 (5.1), l. 8¼ (21), diam. rim 5³⁄₁₆ (13.2), wt. 8 oz. ¾ dwt. (250g)

MARK 11 on underside of bowl

INSCRIPTION: "S/ER" engraved on top of handle

PROVENANCE: unknown prior to 1937, when loaned to an exhibition at the Museum of the City of New York by Mr. and Mrs. Bernard H. Cone of New York; subsequent ownership uncertain prior to sale at auction in April and November 1981.[1]

The Burrows Collection; on long-term loan to the Sterling and Francine Clark Art Institute, Williamstown, Massachusetts

1 Miller 1937, no. 153, reprod. p. 54; Sotheby's 1981A, lot 391; Sotheby's 1981C, lot 177. Probably using the information from the 1937 exhibition catalogue, Kathryn Buhler recorded the porringer in Rosenbaum, but without crediting an owner; Rosenbaum 1954A, p. 136. It was not included in the Brooklyn Museum exhibition of the same year, suggesting that its owner was not known at that time.

46

Porringer, 1765–76

Silver, h. 2 (5.1), l. 7⅜ (17.8), diam. rim 4¹³⁄₁₆ (12.2), wt. 8 oz. (247g)

MARK 9 inside bottom of bowl

INSCRIPTION: "Johanna Abeel" (script) engraved on upper surface of handle

PROVENANCE: Johanna Abeel (1764–1810), who married Leonard Bleecker in 1783; subsequent ownership unknown until acquisition by Francis P. Garvan prior to 1930.[1]

Yale University Art Gallery, New Haven; Mabel Brady Garvan Collection

At least four porringers with handles cast from the same distinctive pattern are known, marked by Myer Myers and New York silversmiths associated with him, Otto Paul de Parisien (cat. 111) and Cary Dunn.[2] The interlaced pattern centered on a lozenge shape relates to Myers's silver from the later Colonial period, such as his dish ring of 1770–76 (cat. 79), as well as to pierced chair splats and carved pediment moldings of New York furniture of the same era.[3]

Cat. 45, marked by Halsted and Myers, is potentially the earliest of the four, although it is identical to example marked by Myers alone. In 1937, John Marshall Phillips published the latter porringer as a christening gift to Johanna Abeel in 1764, although the source of his information is uncertain.[4] Johanna was the daughter of James Abeel and Gertrude Neilson of New York City, who were married in 1762. The Abeel family

was sufficiently affluent to afford such an extravagant gesture; Johanna's father was an iron merchant in New York City and also inherited land in the Albany region.[5] Phillips's dating would be supported by the Halsted and Myers example, which could have been contemporaneous.

It may be more likely, however, that the Johanna Abeel porringer was acquired at the time of her marriage to the New York merchant Leonard Bleecker on November 23, 1783. Like the Cornell milk pot (cat. 95), this porringer may have been a piece of unsold stock that Myers still had in his possession, or Johanna Abeel may have purchased it secondhand. It seems highly unlikely that Myers would still have had a casting pattern used twenty years earlier, although he could have used an earlier porringer to recreate it.

Little documentation exists for the practice of presenting porringers as christening gifts in the eighteenth century. As Anthony N.B. Garvan pointed out, the majority of initials engraved on early New England porringers were for married couples rather than individuals, suggesting that "the valuable silver porringer was like the silver tankard, principally a mark of status shared by a man and wife and not a functional weaning appliance."[6] Both the Halsted and Myers and Parisien porringers bear initials of married couples. A porringer with a handle cast from this same pattern, marked by Cary Dunn, was presented to Mary (Alsop) King by her father, John Alsop, supposedly for the birth of her first son in 1788, but could also have been a gift at the time of her marriage to Rufus King in 1786. Dunn may have cast the handle from one of the earlier porringers, or his porringer may have been owned by the Alsop family before the War. A porringer marked by John Burger has a history of being a christening present to Elizabeth Van Cortlandt in 1787, but it too could have been acquired at the time of her marriage in 1810.[7]

1 Pearson 1872, p. 13; Dwight 1903, p. 234; Duyckinck 1908, pp. 79, 180–81; Vedder 1927, pp. 60–63; "Family Register" 1975, p. 235.
2 The Dunn porringer is in NYHS, inv. 1954.163.
3 Downs 1952, nos. 149, 224. This observation was first made by Martha Gandy Fales, who mentions a porringer with this type of handle by Andrew Billings; Fales 1970, p. 139.
4 Phillips 1937, p. 9.
5 Duyckinck 1908, pp. 180–81; Gottesman 1936, pp. 203, 213, 219; Vedder 1927, pp. 60–63.
6 Garvan 1958, p. 548.
7 Waters/McKinsey/Ward 2000, II, no. 139.

46

45

47

Coffeepot, 1765–70

Silver with wood handle, h. 12¼ (31.1), w. 9½ (24.1), diam. base 4⅞ (12.4), diam. rim 3³⁄₁₆ (8.1), gross wt. 40 oz. 3 dwt. (1249g) (scratch wt. 39 oz. 8½ dwt.)

MARK 9 twice on underside of body

INSCRIPTION: "K/L*C" engraved on underside of foot; "RCC" (script) engraved on side of body, probably later eighteenth century

PROVENANCE: probably unidentified members of the Koecks (Cocks) family with the initials "K/L*C"; to Robert Cocks, who in 1764 married Catherine Ogden ("RCC"); to their son Robert (b. 1769), who married Mary Lee; to their great-great-granddaughter Julia (Whiteridge) Bergland (b. 1902); to her son, by whom consigned to Phyllis Tucker Antiques of Houston in 1996, from whom purchased by the Virginia Museum in 1997.[1]

Virginia Museum of Fine Arts, Richmond; Museum Purchase, The Floyd D. and Anne C. Gottwald Fund

Requiring over 30 troy oz. of silver, coffeepots were one of the largest hollow ware forms made in eighteenth-century New York. Although equivalent in weight to quart tankards, coffeepots survive from Myers's workshop in fewer numbers—fourteen coffeepots versus twenty-four tankards, perhaps because they cost more to make. The double-bellied shape would have required more labor to fabricate, and more cast elements were used. A double-bellied sugar dish engraved with the same initials "K/LC" and struck with Myers's MARK 9 apparently was purchased by the original owners of this coffeepot.[2]

The cast elements on Myers's coffeepots provide a means of dividing them into three chronological groups. The earliest dates from about 1750–65 (cats. 19, 20, 31). A second group of coffeepots, including the present example, dates to about 1765–70. The spout is more curved, with a ruffled leaf form on the front, scrolls on the shaft, and a larger leaf at top. All three examples in this group have a flat piece of silver cut in a lozenge shape at the juncture of the lower end of the handle with the body of the pot. The finials are smaller than those on the earlier group and are pinecones or spirals.

The present example and an almost identical coffeepot at the Museum of the City of New York both date to the 1760s; the latter is engraved with the original owner's initials "C:C," probably for Cornelia Crooke, who married Gabriel William Ludlow in 1764.[3] Identical castings for the spout and handle mounts appear on a coffeepot marked by Cary Dunn that was owned by John Jay and his wife, Sarah Van Brugh Livingston, the daughter of William Livingston and niece of Robert, Philip, and Catherine Livingston (cats. 35, 36, 127, 129).[4]

What probably is the latest group of coffeepots to be made by Myers during the Colonial period consists of three examples that are more vertical in appearance, with a smaller belly and a smaller spout, positioned higher on body. The spout, richly ornamented with stylized scroll and leaf forms, closely resembles London coffeepots of the 1760s.[5] The bases have a small diameter. None of this group is documented, but the verticality of the design and stylized ornament would suggest a date of 1770–76.[6] No surviving coffeepots by Myers can be dated to after the Revolutionary War, possibly because the form is rare in New York during the early Federal period.

1 Miller 1912, p. 130; *Baltimore* 1912, II, pp. 275–80. When Julia Bergland presented the coffeepot to her son, she told him, apparently mistakenly, that it had descended from the Custis family of Virginia; she was a direct descendant of Major John Custis, a cousin of Daniel Parke Custis, the first husband of Martha (Dandridge) Custis Washington. No couples with the initials K/L*C or RCC were found in the Custis genealogy, for which see Upshur 1904.
2 Sotheby's 1986B, lot 395.
3 Waters/McKinsey/Ward 2000, I, no. 48. This coffeepot descended in the family of Gabriel and Catherine Ludlow's niece, Catherine Ludlow (d. 1849), who in 1791 married General Jacob Morton (1762–1836); to their great-granddaughter Caroline Shippen (1869–1961); to Wendell Davis, a collateral descendent of Jacob and Catherine Morton. See Pelletreau 1907, II, p. 387, and Cutter 1913, I, p. 30; Gordon 1919, pp. 141–46; Roney 1940, pp. 123–26.
4 Waters/McKinsey/Ward 2000, I, no. 24.
5 Banister 1965, pl. 95; see also cat. 122.
6 These coffeepots are in the collections of Historic Deerfield (Flynt/Fales 1968, p. 90), The Saint Louis Art Museum (Rosenbaum 1954A, pl. 14), and Winterthur (Quimby/Johnson 1995, no. 230).

48

Mourning Ring, 1764

Gold with white enamel, diam. ⁹⁄₁₆ (1.4), wt. less than 1 oz.

MARK 6 once inside

INSCRIPTION: "ROBERT·HT/MORRIS·ESQ·/OB: 27 JAN·/1764·AE 51"

PROVENANCE: unknown prior to the present owner

Collection of Eric Noah

In the eighteenth century, mourning rings were made as tokens of remembrance for friends and relatives of a deceased person. Usually the estate covered the cost of these rings, and many individuals left detailed lists of recipients in their wills. In January 1775, the New York silversmith Cary Dunn billed Philip Schuyler £14.11.0 for making "9 Gold Mourning Rings," presumably commissioned in memory of John Bradstreet, who in his will of September 1774 had left such arrangements to Schuyler, his executor.[1] This custom was social rather than religious and was followed by Jews as well as Christians. Myer Myers and his brothers Asher and Joseph were bequeathed mourning rings in the 1773 will of Sampson Simson, Myers's partner in the Spruce Hill Lead Mine (p. 45).[2]

This ring was made in memory of Robert Hunter Morris (1713–1764), who suddenly died at a dance in Shrewsbury, New Jersey. He had never married, and the now-worn white enamel background for the lettering traditionally signified a child or unmarried person.[3] The ring may have been commissioned by Morris's nephew, Lewis Morris III, who also owned a pair of sauceboats by Myer Myers (cat. 18). Shortly after Lewis Morris I was appointed Governor of New Jersey in 1738, his twenty-five-year-old son Robert was named Chief Justice of the Province, a position Robert would retain until his death. He also inherited his father's considerable estates in East Jersey. Not surprisingly, Robert Morris spent much of his career promoting the interests of the landholders in both New Jersey and New York as well as seeking a position of greater power. In 1754, after five years of political maneuvering in England, Morris won the appointment as Governor of Pennsylvania from the Penn family, but his open conflict with the Assembly forced his resignation two years later.[4] One of his principal opponents was Benjamin Franklin, who wrote in his *Autobiography*: "But he was so good-natur'd a Man, that no personal Difference between him and me was occasion'd by the Contest, and we often din'd together."[5]

1 Invoice from Cary Dunn to Colonel Philip Schuyler, New York, January 28, 1775, Library, Albany Institute of History and Art, New York. I am grateful to Chief Librarian Sandra Markham for bringing this invoice to my attention and supplying additional information on Bradstreet. For Bradstreet's will, see Loring 1862.
2 NYCPR-1, liber 29, pp. 44–46.
3 Bohan 1963, pp. 44–45.
4 De Lancey 1876, pp. 16–18; Lefferts 1907; *DAB*, XIII, pp. 213–15, 225–26; Spooner 1907, pp. 220–23.
5 Franklin 1964, pp. 212–13.

48   49

49

Mourning Ring, 1764

Gold with black enamel and paste stones, diam. ¾ (1.9), gross wt. 2 dwt. (3g)

MARK 6 once inside

INSCRIPTION: "A:MARIA/PANET/OB:19 May/1764··AE:33·"

PROVENANCE: unknown prior to donation in 1931 by Cornelia E. Marshall, presumably a collateral relative of Anna Maria (Marshall) Panet.

Museum of the City of New York; Gift of Miss Cornelia E. Marshall

This ring was made in memory of Anna Maria (Marshall) Panet (1731–1764), who was baptized in the Reformed Dutch Church on October 6, 1731, the daughter of John Marshall and Elsje Rutgers. One of the witnesses at her baptism was her maternal grandfather, the wealthy brewer and landowner Harman Rutgers.[1] On May 2, 1752, Anna Maria married

Johannes Panet of the Danish colony of St. Thomas, who was naturalized in New York ten years later as a "gentleman."[2] Little is known of Johannes Panet's life in New York; he was still living in the city in September 1772, when he was granted a water lot in the East River, as were his relatives Hendrick Rutgers and Eva (Rutgers) Provoost, two other children of Harman Rutgers.[3] Since Panet and his wife had no children, he bequeathed his real and personal property in New York to his wife's relatives, Susannah Marshall, Ann Burke, and Mary Burke.[4]

This marriage furthered the close connection between Panet and two other patrons of Myer Myers, Maria (Van Beverhoudt) Barclay (cat. 59) and her stepfather, the merchant Nicholas Bayard, to whom the Marshalls were closely associated, if not related. Susannah Marshall left bequests of land to both Thomas Duncan and Andrew D. Barclay, the eldest sons of Maria and her sister, Margaretta (Van Beverhoudt) Duncan; in her will, Susannah described Maria's son Andrew as "my God-Son."[5] Ann Burke, one of the beneficiaries of Panet's will, received a gold seal supplied by Myers in 1764 and paid for by Nicholas Bayard (Appendix II, no. 3).

1 Wright 1902, p. 16; Crosby 1886, pp. 86–87; Robison/Bartlett 1917, p. 186.
2 Purple 1890, p. 185; Wolfe 1963, p. 142.
3 *MCCNY*-1, VII, p. 374.
4 Waters/McKinsey/Ward 2000, I, p. 162.
5 NYCPR-1, liber 41, pp. 62–82; Moffat 1904, pp. 106–07.

50

Snuffbox, c. 1760–70

Gold, h. 1 (2.54), diam. 2⅜ (6), wt. 2 oz. 11 dwt. (80g)

MARK 6 four times on exterior of bottom and four times on interior of cover

PROVENANCE: unknown prior to 1963, when owned by Harry Burke of Philadelphia.[1]

The Metropolitan Museum of Art, New York; Mr. and Mrs. Marshall P. Blankarn Gift, 1966

Snuff, a powdered form of tobacco inhaled through the nose, was a fad that swept through Europe during the eighteenth

century. Since the 1670s, gold snuffboxes had been significant presentation objects, commemorating such occasions as marriages and diplomatic exchanges. Clare Le Corbeiller observed that the use of gold boxes in the shape and size of snuffboxes to present the Freedom of a city, such as cat. 115, probably derived from this precedent.[2]

Specialist gold chasers ornamented European gold snuffboxes and watchcases. A few European craftsmen trained as gold chasers came to New York in the Colonial period (p. 57), including Michael De Bruss, who advertised "Curious Chasing or other Raised Work, in general, on Gold and Silver Watch-Cases, Snuff-Boxes, & c."[3] For the Rococo cartouche on the underside of this snuffbox, Myer Myers relied on the chaser he used most frequently to ornament his silver. The design is flat-chased rather than repoussée-chased, and this craftsman's characteristic meandering lines of small dots, scrolled leaf forms with rounded, curled heads, and heavy-handed use of dots to define edges are apparent. The cover plaque, which is inset in the box, appears to be the work of a different craftsman. His work in relief and use of a variety of punches to define different textures and patterns reveals his familiarity with the techniques of European gold chasing, although it falls far short of the superb workmanship found on the finest examples. In London, chased plaques such as this were produced by specialists as component parts of hollow ware as well as jewelry, and this example may have been imported.[4]

The biblical scene represented on the cover is David's first meeting with King Saul:

Wherefore Saul sent messengers unto Jesse, and said, Send me David thy son, which is with the sheep. And Jesse took an ass laden with bread, and a bottle of wine, and a kid, and sent them by David his son unto Saul. And David came to Saul, and stood before him: and he loved him greatly; and he became his armor-bearer (I Samuel 16: 19–21).

Aspects of the scene rendered on the snuffbox, including the canopy with lambrequins and Saul's theatrical gesture, strongly suggest that the composition was copied or adapted from a Renaissance print. As Richard Edgcumbe has noted, a reliance on earlier prints for figure subjects was typical of English gold chasers of the mid-eighteenth century.[5] The relatively rare representations of this episode are found in engravings, such as one by the sixteenth-century Dutch artist Maerten van Heemskerck. Heemskerck's composition shares such features as David's twisting pose, seen from the back, and Saul seated under a canopy, extending his arm.[6]

A member of King David's Masonic Lodge, of which Myers was a charter officer in 1769 (p. 47), could have commissioned this unusual subject. The two prominent columns in the background may represent the two pillars of King Solomon's Temple, a central Masonic image.[7] The scene of David approaching Saul's throne with sacrificial animals also relates to Masonic rituals. Perhaps this snuffbox was commissioned as a fraternal gift from one member of the lodge to another. There is, however, no overtly Masonic symbolism, and in the absence of any history of ownership this suggested origin remains a matter of conjecture.

1 Bohan 1963, no. 15.
2 Le Corbeiller 1966, p. 17.
3 *The New-York Gazette or The Weekly Post-Boy*, December 19, 1757, p. 2.
4 Oman 1970, p. 18.
5 *Rococo* 1984, p. 127.
6 Veldman/Luijten 1993, no. 95.
7 Silvestro/Franco 1976, p. 49.

51

Pair of Shoe Buckles, 1765–70

Gold and steel, each h. 1¾ (4.4), w. 2⁵⁄₁₆ (5.9), gross wt. 1 oz. 9 dwt. (45g)

MARK 6 twice on underside of each

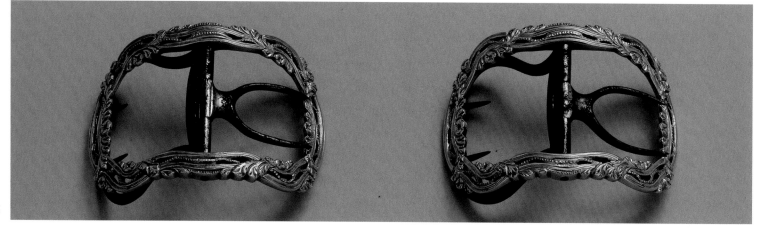

INSCRIPTION: "The Gift of Rob.ᵗ Arcdeckne Esq. to Dan.ˡ McCormick" engraved on underside of each

PROVENANCE: Daniel McCormick (1742–1834); subsequent ownership unknown until April 1935, when one buckle acquired by Francis P. Garvan from the dealer Robert Ensko; ownership of the second buckle unknown until sold at auction in 1981.[1]

Yale University Art Gallery, New Haven; Mabel Brady Garvan Collection and Gift of Mr. and Mrs. Philip Holzer

Unlike the chasing found on Myers's silver or even the preceding snuffbox, the superb chasing on these buckles undoubtedly was executed by a jeweler accustomed to working on a small scale. The buckles' openwork design and delicately rendered flowers and beading are consistent with the taste for pierced work and narrow, gadrooned borders found on Myers's work beginning about 1765 (p. 49).

Robert Arcedeckne (d. after 1768) was a member of an Irish family from County Galway that had settled in Saint Catherine, Jamaica, in the 1710s. His uncle, Andrew Arcedeckne, was a merchant, landowner, and barrister in Saint Catherine and served as Attorney General for Jamaica and as a member of the Colonial Assembly.[2] The *Pennsylvania Gazette* reported in 1757 that a French privateer had taken a ship belonging to "Andrew Arcedeckne, Esq." after it had sailed from Jamaica.[3] Andrew Arcedeckne, who died in 1763 without legitimate heirs, divided his large estate between two illegitimate children and his nephew Robert, but the will was challenged on grounds of his senility.[4] It has not been possible to find further information on Robert Arcedeckne except that his own will was signed in Saint Catherine on April 3, 1768.[5]

The recipient of Arcedeckne's gift, Daniel McCormick, was a prominent attorney in New York City, although he paid for his Freemanship in 1769 as a "Gentleman" rather than as a lawyer.[6] He was born in Ireland, presumably of Scotch-Irish ancestry, as he was a member and trustee of the First Presbyterian Church as well as a president of St. Patrick's Society.[7] Many of his business relationships were with fellow Irishmen and Presbyterians, such as the historian and Loyalist William Smith.[8] It is possible that McCormick received his gift from Arcedeckne, another Irishman, in gratitude for legal assistance provided, perhaps at the time of Arcedeckne's inheritance from his uncle. The gift may well have been transmitted in the form of gold coins, which McCormick then had made into the buckles.

Such opulence apparently was in character for McCormick, who was later described as "one of the most polished gentlemen in the city."[9] Between 1790 and 1792, he built a 40-foot-wide brick house on Wall Street. In reminiscences of the early 1800s, Joseph Scoville depicted McCormick clinging to the elegance of the *ancien regime,* exemplified by these gold shoe buckles:

Mr. McCormick was a glorious sample of the old New Yorker. . . . the only gentleman who continued to reside in his own house, in the good old fashioned style. He never changed his habits. He stuck to short breeches and white stockings and buckles to the last. He wore hair-powder as long as he lived, and believed in curls. . . . He gave good dinner parties, and had choice old wines upon the table. . . . He owned large landed property, and when he died was very rich.[10]

McCormick never married, and his will made numerous large bequests to relatives, friends, and the First Presbyterian Church. The only object mentioned specifically was "my best gold snuff box," which he left to Thomas William Moore.[11]

1 "Lists of Silver and from Whom Bought," Garvan Papers, box 26, file 8, Library, Albany Institute of History and Art; Sotheby's 1981B, lot 508.

2 Metcalf 1965, p. 93.

3 *The Pennsylvania Gazette,* March 3, 1757, as cited in "The Pennsylvania Gazette 1728–1800," *srch.accessible.com* (website), item 20381.

4 Lewis 1972, p. 46. I am indebted to Robert Barker for this reference and for many insights into Colonial Jamaica.

5 Livingston 1909, p. 21. The original document could not be located for the present study.

6 De Lancey 1885, p. 222.

7 Barrett 1889, II, pp. 248–52, 257, 264–65, 281–82, 343, 380.

8 Settlement of Account between William Smith and Philip Schuyler, March 14, 1793, Schuyler Papers, Household and Personal Accounts, box 2, Manuscripts and Archives Division, NYPL.

9 Barrett 1889, II, p. 249.

10 Ibid., pp. 252–53.

11 NYCPR-1, liber 71, pp. 368–74.

52

Dish, 1763–76

Silver, h. 2⁵⁄₁₆ (7.5), diam. 12³⁄₈ (31.4), wt. 30 oz. 11 dwt. (950g)

MARK 9 twice on underside

PROVENANCE: probably Samuel Johnson (cat. 126) or his son William Samuel Johnson and his wife, Ann (Beach) Johnson (see cat. 20); descent as in cat. 20 to William Samuel Johnson (1859–1937), the donor.

The Metropolitan Museum of Art, New York; Gift of William Samuel Johnson in memory of his wife, Carrie G. Johnson, 1926

The history provided with this dish at the time of its donation to The Metropolitan Museum of Art identified its original owner as Samuel Johnson, although Myers did not begin using MARK 9 until about 1765, two years after Johnson had retired as president of King's College in 1763 and returned to Stratford, Connecticut (see Appendix I). The scalloped rim also relates to a bowl (cat. 53) and the shapes of waiters (cat. 57) Myers made after 1765. The dish possibly could have been made for William Samuel Johnson, although its large size and impressive form are consistent with the opulent table silver owned by the father. Like the covered jug (cat. 26), the form of this dish suggests the Anglophilic character of its patron. Low dishes with scalloped edges were introduced in England beginning in the 1690s and enjoyed continuous popularity into the

1760s.[1] Smaller versions of this form apparently were used for desserts, hence the twentieth-century term "strawberry dishes"; the larger examples may have had more general uses.[2]

Surviving examples of this form by silversmiths working in the American Colonies are extremely rare and primarily by New York makers. Much smaller versions were made by the immigrant George Ridout for such Anglophile patrons as Catherine (McPhaedres) Livingston (cats. 38, 120) and Philip and Margaret Philipse.[3] Significantly, Daniel Christian Fueter made the only other scalloped dish of comparable size to Myers's.[4] As noted (p. 41), Fueter seems to have inspired many of the rare forms made by Myers, who may have wanted to best his colleague with this example. Fueter's dish is 2 inches smaller in diameter and has the sixteen scallops most commonly found on English examples, whereas Myers's dish has twenty-four segments.[5]

1 See, for instance, the set of five dishes made by Lewis Mettayer in 1714–15; Hackenbroch 1969, no. 133. An example marked by Paul de Lamerie in 1724–25 has the twenty-four scallops found on Myers's dish; Hare/Snodin/Clifford 1990, no. 44.
2 Hare/Snodin/Clifford 1990, p. 122.
3 Waters/McKinsey/Ward 2000, I, no. 57; Buhler/Hood 1970, II, no. 696.
4 Historic Deerfield, Inc., inv. L-1-1977; 10 1/8 in. diam., wt. 23 oz. 14 dwt.
5 Hare/Snodin/Clifford 1990, p. 85.

53

Bowl, 1765–76

Silver, h. 3¾ (9.5), diam. base 3 (7.62), diam. rim 6⅝ (16.7), wt. 12 oz. 10 dwt. (389g) (scratch wt. 12 oz. 19½ dwt.)

MARK 9 twice on underside of body

INSCRIPTION: "PB" (script) engraved on outside

PROVENANCE: unknown prior to sale at auction in 1982, as "the property of a descendant of the original owner."[1]

Yale University Art Gallery, New Haven; Gift of Mr. and Mrs. Philip Holzer

Stylistic elements of this bowl represent a late interpretation of the Rococo style, particularly the delicate engraved decoration, subtly scalloped rim, and high pedestal foot. The "PB" monogram may refer to the widow Phebe Barnes (d. 1788) or her unmarried daughter, Philinda or "Philena," who was still living in 1795. The bowl was consigned to auction in 1982 with an earlier sauceboat by Myers engraved with the initials of Phebe and Thomas Barnes (see cats. 6, 7, 41).

1 Christie's 1982, lot 45.

54

Punch Bowl, 1765–76

Silver, h. 3⅞ (9.8), diam. base 4¾ (12.1), diam. rim 8⅞ (22.5), wt. 23 oz. (715.3g)

MARK 9 once on underside

INSCRIPTION: "SC" (script) engraved on outside; "M" cast into underside of foot

PROVENANCE: Sarah (Cock) Coles (1749–1798); by descent in the family to Townsend Scudder, Jr. (1865–1960); by sale by his widow, Alice (McCutcheon) Scudder, to the uncle of the couple by whom consigned to auction in 1998.[1]

Private collection

This punch bowl was made for Sarah (Cock) Coles, the only child of Daniel Cock of Musketa Cove, Long Island. Her mother was Daniel's second wife, Sarah Rushmore, who had died before 1766, when Daniel married his third wife, Susannah Youngs. The silver bowl therefore may have been made for Sarah with a legacy from her mother, perhaps in 1765, the year Sarah was married to a fellow Quaker, Jacob Coles.[2] The "SC" monogram would thereby identify both the donor and owner of the bowl.

The monogram's linear quality, with no shading and a simple, circular frame, offers a striking contrast to the elaborate

54

Rococo engraving on objects made in Myers's workshop at this time (cats. 55, 83). Although this conservatism may reflect the more sober taste of Quaker farmers in rural Long Island, engraved ornaments and monograms composed of unshaded outlines became a fashionable alternative in the 1760s to richly textured Rococo engraving (p. 63).

1 Christie's 1998, lot 88. Cox 1912, pp. 21–25; Jones 1907, pp. 308–15, 344; *NCAB* 1958, p. 58.
2 Cox 1912, pp. 21–22.

55

Punch Bowl, 1765–76

Silver, h. 4⅛ (10.5), diam. base 4⁹⁄₁₆ (11.6), diam. rim 8¹³⁄₁₆ (22.4), wt. 26 oz. 10 dwt. (825g) (scratch wt. 26 oz. 18 dwt.)

MARK 9 three times on underside

ARMORIAL/INSCRIPTION: Smith arms (argent three broken lances erect in fess, a chief chequy or and gules), crest (a sea lion) and motto ("Mens sibi conscia recti" ["A mind conscious of its own recti-

tude"]) engraved on front.[1] "The Gift of a number of the Presbyterian Congregation of New York to their Second Church Feb. 5ᵗʰ 1791" (script) engraved on outside beneath rim, presumably in 1791.

PROVENANCE: probably Thomas Smith (1734–1795); purchased in 1791 for the Second Presbyterian Church, New York.

The Corporation of the Brick Presbyterian Church in the City of New York

As with the tankard made for the Livingston family (cat. 28), the magnificent armorials (fig. 21) engraved on this bowl are those of a leading New York family, but they do not conclusively identify the original patron. This coat of arms and crest were used by the Smith family, among whose most prominent members in the Colonial period were Judge William Smith (1697–1769) and his brother the Reverend John Smith (1702–1771), as well as William's son, the historian William Smith, Jr. (1728–1793).[2] Charles Bolton recorded a Thomas Smith as the only one of his family to adopt the motto found on this bowl, although Bolton did not identify the specific Thomas Smith or the source of his information. The most likely candidate seems to be Thomas Smith (1734–1795), a

younger son of Judge William Smith. Thomas's father, uncle, and brothers all used these arms with other mottos; his own son Thomas Smith, Jr. (d. 1815) had a bookplate engraved by Peter Maverick in the 1790s with the same arms and the motto, "Nec aspera terrent" ("We fear no hardship").[3]

Thomas Smith was an attorney of independent wealth who styled himself "Esquire." His father, Judge William Smith, was the lawyer who successfully defended John Peter Zenger in the famous libel case brought against him in 1735. His brother William Smith, Jr., was a founding member of the Sons of Liberty in New York, although he opposed breaking all ties with Great Britain and eventually became the Chief Justice of Canada. Both Thomas and his brother were prominent members of the Presbyterian Church in New York.[4] Thomas Smith served as a trustee of the church together with Peter R. Livingston, who donated three alms basins by Myers to the congregation (cat. 32), and both Smith and Livingston were among the trustees who petitioned the City to establish the Second Church in 1766.[5]

The engraved armorials are among the finest to be found on New York silver of the Colonial period. As discussed elsewhere (pp. 49–50), this engraving was executed by the same craftsman who worked on equally impressive commissions from Myers's shop, including the Van Wyck and Philipse waiters (cats. 56, 57). His design for the Rococo frame was derived from printed sources published in London by Matthias Lock in the 1740s (some of which were reissued in the later 1760s) and P. Baretti in 1762.[6] Elisha Gallaudet had engraved the Smith arms on a bookplate for William Smith, Jr., the brother of Myers's patron, with a very different, Baroque surround.[7] The style of the punch bowl's engraving as well as the date range of Myers's MARK 9 indicate that this bowl was manufactured after 1765. Smith may well have commissioned this punch bowl after his father's death in 1769, when he inherited large properties in New York and New Jersey. The elaborate arms may have been a tribute to a legacy from his father. Moreover, at this same time, Smith entered politics and also was a founding member of "The Moot," a debating club for Whig lawyers that existed between about 1770 and 1774.[8] One is tempted to imagine this punch bowl at the center of a scene like that depicted by Roupell (8-9.1). Thomas was elected a deputy to the second Provincial Congress in November 1775.

Four years before Thomas Smith's death, this punch bowl took on a more pious purpose. On March 3, 1791, the Session Minutes of the Presbyterian Church in New York recorded: "Coll. Stevens informed the session, that he and some other Gentlemen, had purchased a silver bason for the use of baptizing children in the new church, which they had presented to said congregation for this End."[9] A later history of the Brick Church recorded, "It was in common use for this purpose for over a hundred years."[10] Colonel "Stevens" apparently was John Stephens, a longtime member of the church who had served with Smith as trustee before and after the Revolutionary War. In the Colonial period, pieces of household silver frequently were bequeathed to churches after the deaths of their owners, although it was less common for them to be bought secondhand. Smith's lifelong connection to the Presbyterian Church suggests that he may have sold the bowl to them directly. However, Thomas Smith had moved from New York City in 1775 to property inherited from his father in Haverstraw, a town on the Hudson River. Three years later, during a raid by British soldiers, he was robbed of all his plate "and other Things to a large Amount."[11] Perhaps his punch bowl reappeared in New York City after the war, when Stephens bought it.

1 Bolton 1964, pp. 151–52.
2 Ibid. William Peartree Smith (1698–1801), a first cousin of Judge William Smith, also used these arms with the motto "Deus nobis haec otia fecit" ("God hath given us these things in tranquility"). Identical renditions appeared on his bookplate engraved by Thomas Johnston as well as on a silver waiter Smith commissioned from Jacob Hurd; Johnston may also have engraved the waiter. See Allen 1894, p. 45, and Kane 1998, pp. 81–83, 601.
3 Allen 1894, pp. 45, 282–83; Stephens 1950, p. 104; Sabine 1958, I, p. iv.
4 DAB, XVII, pp. 352–53, 357–58; McLachlan 1976, pp. 122–25.
5 Knapp 1909, p. 20.
6 Heckscher 1979, pl. 14–15; Friedman 1975, pl. 155–57.
7 Reprod. in Sabine 1958, I, p. iv.
8 McLachlan 1976, pp. 122–25.
9 "New York Presbyterian Church Session Book," 1765–1808, p. 111, Presbyterian Historical Society, Philadelphia.
10 Knapp 1909, p. 81. The Second, or "New Church," as it was known in the eighteenth century, was part of the same congregation and ministry as the First Church; it acquired the name Brick Church about 1799, when the Third Church was constructed; Knapp 1909, pp. 26–27.
11 Koke 1973, p. 38.

56

Waiter, c. 1768 (illustrated in color on p. vi)

Silver, h. 1¼ (3.2), diam. 12⅟₁₆ (30.6), wt. 28 oz. 6 dwt. (881g)

MARK 9 once on upper surface, within engraved border

INSCRIPTION (on front): "AMICITIAE PIGNUS PRO BENEFICIIS RECEPTIS" ("A pledge of friendship for kindness received") engraved within scroll above central cartouche; "PS:34:15.VE" engraved in sun within central cartouche; "IN TESTIMONY of EXEMPLARY JUSTICE & AS A SMALL ACKNOWLEDGEMENT/FOR KINDNESSESS RECEIVD. THIS PLATE IS HUMBLY PRESENTED TO THEO:ʳˢ VAN WYCK/BY HIS FRINDS [E added above I]. SAM.ᴸ SCHUYLER. WILL.ᴹ LUPTON & CORN.ˢ SWITS" engraved directly below central cartouche; "GRATIOR AMICO VENIENS IMMOBILE VIRTUS" ("Steadfast virtue [is] more welcome coming from a friend") engraved below previous inscription.

PROVENANCE: Theodorus Van Wyck (1718–1776); by descent to his great-great-great-great-great-great grandson, Philip Van Rensselaer Van Wyck III (b. 1955), by whom consigned to auction in 1994.[1]

Collection of Paul and Elissa Cahn

Although the form of this object is one of Myers's standard hexagonal waiters, its engraved inscriptions and allegorical scene make it an extraordinary example of presentation silver from Colonial New York. It was made for Theodorus Van Wyck, a New York City merchant and landowner descended from Dutch forebears who settled in Long Island. In 1741, Van Wyck's younger sister Margretta had married Brandt Johannese Schuyler, who died in 1752, leaving her with four children: Johanna, Catherine, Samuel, and Anne Elizabeth. As an executor of Schuyler's will, Van Wyck assumed responsibility as a trustee for his nephew and nieces, even after his sister married Anthony Ten Eyck in 1760.[2]

From its inception, this waiter was associated exclusively with men. It was presented to Theodorus Van Wyck by his nephew Samuel along with William Lupton and Cornelius Swits(e), the respective husbands of Johanna and Catherine.[3] Anne Elizabeth was not included among the presenters apparently because she had not yet married. The date presumably was 1768, when Samuel reached his majority and the year before Anne Elizabeth married John J. Bleecker.[4] Moreover, in his will, Van Wyck bequeathed to his eldest son, Abraham, "my large Dutch family Bible also my large Silver Salver or waiter which was presented unto me by my friends Samuel Schuyler William Lupon [sic] and Cornelius Swits," thereby conferring upon the waiter the status of an heirloom in the traditional sense of a property indivisible from a family name or title, that is, something inherited only by male heirs.[5] The waiter descended through eight generations of first-born male heirs bearing the surname Van Wyck.

Van Wyck's description of the "waiter which was presented to me" implies that it was commissioned by the donors and

56

56.1

given as a finished object, rather than as a gift of money that Van Wyck used to purchase an object. In this regard, the word "plate" in the English inscription may be significant. In eighteenth-century English, "plate" meant an object made of silver, but it also referred to the flat sheet of metal that received engraved or etched images or text.[6] The present feet on the waiter are later additions, riveted through the front, and the considerable wear on the waiter's underside indicates that it originally did not have feet. Myers's mark may have been struck on the front because of the absence of feet. Given that the waiter originally had a flat bottom, "plate" can be read with a double meaning that emphasizes the engraved inscriptions and ornament, the object's most extraordinary feature; in London, pulls occasionally were taken of the engraved ornament on waiters.[7] It also suggests that the waiter, unlike most Colonial American silver, may never have been intended to serve a practical purpose, but to stand upright on a sideboard.

The engraving was executed by the specialist craftsman who created the finest engraved coats of arms on objects made contemporaneously in Myers's workshop (pp. 49–50). Textural contrasts achieved with crosshatching and tapered shading strokes are typical of his style (fig. 22). The loose execution of the frame with heavy accent lines contrasts further with the delicately rendered scene inside. Rather than a coat of arms, which would have been more consistent with its heirloom status, a complicated allegorical scene and series of inscriptions in Latin and English were devised. The classical imagery and the use of Latin indicate that the person who designed it had a formal education. A similar use of emblematic figures and Latin inscriptions appears on a medal engraved by Elisha Gallaudet in 1767 for the Literary Society in New York at King's College.[8] This confirms the address of the waiter to male viewers, since such decoration would have been incomprehensible to anyone without a grounding in Latin or classical imagery, including most women. The English inscription translates the Latin to some extent, but it offers little gloss on the allegorical scene, which was conceived as an amplification of the written inscriptions.

Below the figure of Justice holding the scales are the words "exemplary Justice," referring to Theodorus Van Wyck. The accompanying figures may also be read as emblems. An angel on high pours coins out of a cornucopia, symbolizing *Liberalitas*, or generosity. Both the palm branch held by the hand in the clouds and the laurel wreath placed by another angelic figure on Justice's head were emblems of *Premio,* or reward.[9] Thus Van Wyck's virtuous dealings and generosity with his sister's children are rewarded by this waiter.

A more specifically religious explication may be offered by the reference in the sun to Psalm 34:15: "The eyes of the Lord are upon the righteous, and his ears are open unto their cry"; the figure of Justice in this context would be the righteous person. The angel crowning her also holds a shield, referring to verse 7: "the angel of the Lord encampeth round about them that fear him, and delivereth them." The coins falling from the cornucopia refer to verse 9: "O fear the Lord, ye his saints: for there is not want to them that fear him."

Double meanings or hidden allusions were popular in eighteenth-century allegories, and it seems likely that Myers manipulated these emblems to make reference to himself as the creative force behind the object. In this reading, the coins falling from the cornucopia are the silver used to make the waiter, and they fall into the silversmith's balance used to calculate the weight and value of the metal. The Justice figure becomes an embodiment of the silversmith or craftsmanship, with the palm and laurel being accolades for Myers's achievement. At the very bottom of the engraved decoration, Myers struck his surname mark, MARK 9—made part of the inscription by being enclosed within the frame. The mark is immediately below the Latin phrase "Steadfast virtue [is] more welcome coming from a friend," so Myers the craftsman is identified as the virtuous friend. Although exceptional in American or English silver of this period, a deliberately self-referential positioning of Myers's marks occurs on several of his most significant objects (cats. 38, 79), and this waiter is certainly among them.

Figural engraving of this type was uncommon in American silver of the Colonial period, although the majority of precedents can be found in New York. These examples date to midcentury or earlier. A snuffbox made by Bartholomew Schaats between 1708 and 1758 was engraved with the death of Pyramis and Thisbe.[10] The scene of a fire that threatened Trinity Church in 1750 is engraved on a bowl by Adrian Bancker made from a share of the reward given to the men who saved the building.[11] The closest parallels to the Van Wyck waiter are the elaborate anti-Jacobite allegories engraved in 1750 on a tankard and cann as well as the figures of Justice and Truth engraved in 1751 on a copper sundial by the New York pewterer Joseph Leddel, Sr., or his son Joseph Leddel, Jr.[12]

1 Sotheby's 1994, lot 611.
2 Van Wyck 1979, p. 97. I am indebted to David Conradsen for locating a copy of this source and to Paul Cahn for sharing it with me.
3 These marriages took place in September 1761 and January 1762, respectively; Conradsen 1999, p. 117.
4 Van Wyck 1979, p. 97.
5 NYCPR-1, liber 37, p. 137.
6 Johnson 1754, s.v. "plate."
7 Oman 1978, pp. 74–78, 91–94.
8 Waters/McKinsey/Ward 2000, I, no. 26. As noted (p. 50), Gallaudet does not appear to be the engraver who executed the Van Wyck waiter.
9 Among the many examples are those in Ripa 1988, II, pp. 12–14, 126–27.
10 Christie's 1986, lot 86.
11 Safford 1983, p. 43.
12 Skerry/Sloane 1992; Fennimore 1996A, no. 191.

57

Pair of Waiters, 1770–76

Silver, h. 1⅛ (2.9), diam. 7¹³⁄₁₆ (19.8) each; wt. A. 11 oz. 8 dwt. (355g), B. 10 oz. 19 dwt. (340g)

MARK 9 twice on underside of each

ARMORIAL: Philipse arms ([azure] a demi-lion ducally gorged argent and ducally crowned [or]) engraved on front[1]

PROVENANCE: Frederick Philipse (b. c. 1752–d. 1827); by descent to his great-great grandson, Warburton Gouverneur Iselin, by whom sold to the New York dealers Ginsburg and Levy in 1954.[2]

The Burrows Collection; on long-term loan to the Sterling and Francine Clark Art Institute, Williamstown, Massachusetts

The engraving on these waiters (fig. 23) was executed by the same craftsman or workshop as cat. 55 but exhibits the characteristics of his later style, after about 1770: nervous outlines, thick and thin shading lines, and staccato cuts. Unusually for this engraver, the tincture of the Philipse family coat of arms was rendered incorrectly; the ground should be azure, indicated by parallel horizontal lines. Additionally, the coronet from which the demi-lion rises should be a ducal coronet with five strawberry leaves rather than a marquis's coronet of three leaves alternating with pearls.[3]

These waiters have been associated in previous publications with Philip Philipse and his wife Margaret Marston, who were married in 1751. Philip Philipse was the younger brother of the last Lord of Philipsburg Manor and in his own right held one-third of the original patent, inherited from his great-uncle.[4] He and his wife possessed a substantial collection of silver, including a waiter of this same size by Bartholomew Le Roux II, a marrow scoop by Charles Le Roux, a pair of canns by George Ridout, and pair of tablespoons by Simeon Soumaine.[5] All of these objects are in a late Baroque style and date to the early 1750s, when the Philipses were married; they also bear their initials "P/P*M" as well as the Philipse crest. Myers was chosen to provide a mourning ring in memory of Philip Philipse, who died in 1768.[6]

The absence of initials on Myers's waiters, as well as the later style of their form and engraving, may indicate that they were made for Philip and Margaret Philipse's only son, Frederick. Within a year of Phillip's death, Margaret married the Reverend John Ogilvie, so it would be unlikely for her to have ordered waiters with her deceased first husband's coat of arms.[7] An Anglophile who died while living in England, Frederick Philipse may have chosen the marquis's coronet for the arms on these waiters as a witty reference to his "rank" within the family (as the son of a younger son), since a marquis is below a duke in precedence. The earliest documentary reference to the waiters is among the plate listed in Frederick's 1829 estate inventory, together with the Soumaine tablespoons.[8]

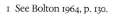

57

1 See Bolton 1964, p. 130.

2 Pelletreau 1907, I, pp. 163–64.

3 A correct rendition of the Philipse arms and motto was engraved on a waiter of 1763–64 made by Richard Rugg of London; Butler 1983B, no. 209.

4 NYCPR-1, liber 26, pp. 326–28; Glenn 1900, pp. 277–78.

5 Winchester 1947, p. 391; Waters/McKinsey/Ward 2000, I, nos. 39, 42, 58. The Soumaine tablespoons (now in the Burrows Collection) originally had belonged to Philip Philipse's maternal aunt, Mary Brockholst. Margaret Philipse's parents, the merchant Nathaniel Marston and Mary Crooke, also owned a substantial amount of plate by mid-century makers such as William Anderson, Tobias Stoutenburgh, and George Ridout.

6 Bohan 1963, p. 43, no. 105. The present location of this ring is unknown; it was stolen from Ginsburg and Levy about 1970.

7 Abstracts 1892–1906, VII, p. 183.

8 This inventory and an account book of Philip Philipse were in the possession of Warburton Gouverneur Iselin in 1954; information courtesy Bernard and S. Dean Levy.

58

Waiter, 1765–76

Silver, h. 1 (2.5), diam. 6½ (16.5), wt. 6 oz. 9 dwt. (200g)

MARK 9 twice on underside

ARMORIAL: Goelet crest (a swan) engraved on front[1]

PROVENANCE: possibly Peter Goelet (1727–1811) and Elizabeth Ratsey (1734–1769); subsequent ownership in the family uncertain until the waiter was discovered c. 1950 in a house built by Robert Goelet (1841–1899) and Harriette Louise Warren (1854–1912), who were married in 1879.[2]

Private collection

Judging by at least twelve examples that survive, small five- and six-sided waiters with a narrow gadrooned border were a routine production of Myers's workshop. In 1760, Halsted and Myers's charge for a "plain Silver waiter" was calculated at 16 shillings per ounce, 2 shillings less than for hollow ware such as a cruet stand or sauceboats (Appendix II, no. 1). The present waiter was customized by the engraved crest of the Goelet family on a Rococo bracket. Although its original owners are not documented with certainty, its subsequent history in the

Goelet family suggests that it belonged to Peter Goelet and Elizabeth Ratsey, who were married in 1755. In his will, Peter Goelet directed that "as my Plate is chiefly family Plate the same together with my books be disposed of by my Executors to and amongst my Children and Them only."[3]

1 Bolton 1964, p. 68.
2 *GRSNS*, I (1905), pp. 66–67.
3 NYCPR-1, liber 49, pp. 448–94. For subsequent generations of the family, see Van Pelt 1898, III, pp. 33–35, and *GRSNS*, 1 (1905), pp. 66–67.

59

Waiter, 1770–72

Silver, h. 1⁵⁄₁₆ (3.3), diam. 7⁷⁄₈ (20), wt. 12 oz. 2 dwt. (376g)

MARK 9 twice on underside

INSCRIPTION: "Liefde Gift Van/de Jongvrouw Anna/Maria Hultin/Von [*sic*]/Beverhoudt" engraved on front

PROVENANCE: commissioned by (Anna) Maria Van Beverhoudt (1750–1791); subsequent ownership unknown prior to acquisition by the Philadelphia collector and antiques dealer Philip H. Rosenbach.

The Rosenbach Museum and Library, Philadelphia

The engraved cartouche surrounding the inscription (fig. 24) on this waiter is in a looser version of the style seen on cat. 57. Dutch inscriptions are found on very few pieces of eighteenth-century New York secular silver; by the mid-1760s, Dutch had been superseded by English even for services in the Reformed Dutch Church.[1] This is the only instance of a Dutch inscription in Myers's work. Maria Van Beverhoudt was born into a New York family of Dutch ancestry and was baptized as Maria in the Reformed Dutch Church; her parents were Johannes Van Beverhoudt and Margaritie Langemach, his second wife.[2] Since the inscription memorialized this waiter as a "loving gift from Miss Anna Maria Hultin Van Beverhoudt," it probably was made before her marriage in 1772 to the Anglican merchant James Barclay in Trinity Church.[3] It may have been commissioned with the substantial legacy that Maria Van Beverhoudt received at age twenty upon her mother's death in 1770. When the widow Margaritie Van Beverhoudt married the merchant Nicholas Bayard on December 2, 1755, she signed articles of agreement that stated Bayard "should be entitled to all of her real and personal estate," with the proviso that "the said Margaritie should have full power to make her will, and to give to her children £2,400, being part of her personal estate." Her will of May 26, 1758 divided this sum as equal bequests to her son Barendt Langemach Van Beverhoudt and her daughters Maria and Margaret, naming as executors her deceased husband's sons from his first marriage and "my good friend Johannes Pannel" (Panet; see cat. 49).[4] As Maria's brother

Barendt had died in 1768, and no codicil was made to her mother's will, she and her sister presumably each received the substantial legacy of £1,200.

Maria Van Beverhoudt's patronage of Myers may have been influenced by her stepfather, Nicholas Bayard, who in 1766 bought a gold seal from Myers and also had a spoon repaired in the workshop (Appendix II, nos. 3, 4). The choice of Dutch for the waiter's inscription may represent an assertion of Maria Van Beverhoudt's ethnic heritage as she assimilated into an English family, but it may also indicate that the recipient was someone who spoke Dutch more fluently than English—perhaps Johannes Panet. It is possible that Maria presented him with this waiter in gratitude for services he performed following her own father's death, much like the waiter given to Theodorus Van Wyck (cat. 56). Panet clearly maintained a close relationship with the Van Beverhoudt children and may have served as a kind of guardian; in 1767, he was named an executor when Maria's brother Barendt wrote his will. Barendt also made bequests to "the 2 Churches and Hospital in St. Thomas," where Panet had lived previously.[5]

1 *Catalogue of American Portraits* 1974, I, p. 437.
2 Wright 1902, p. 159.
3 Moffat 1904, pp. 106–07; Robison/Bartlett 1917, pp. 247–48.
4 NYCPR-1, liber 27, pp. 350–52. "Margaretta" Van Beverhoudt was referred to as the "late wife" of Thomas Duncan in Susannah Marshall's will of September 14, 1789; NYCPR-1, liber 41, pp. 62–82.
5 NYCPR-1, box 40, file 2163.

60

HALSTED AND MYERS

Teapot, 1766–70

Silver with wood handle, h. 6¼ (15.9), w. 9¾ (24.8), diam. base 2¹⁵⁄₁₆ (7.5), gross wt. 18 oz. 1 dwt. (562g)

MARKS 12 and 11A, each struck once on underside of body

INSCRIPTION: "I I" engraved on underside of foot

PROVENANCE: unknown prior to 1954, when owned by the collectors Mr. and Mrs. W. Edwin Gledhill of Santa Barbara, California.[1]

Fine Arts Museums of San Francisco; Bequest of Elaine Henderson

Exhibited in New Haven only

This teapot marked by Halsted and Myers is very similar to an example marked by Myers alone (cat. 68), with the spouts and handle sockets cast from the same patterns. Typical of objects marked by the partnership, its engraved decoration is much simpler than the elaborate and more expensive chased ornament found on Myers's teapot. It is possible that the foliate engraving around the shoulders of this teapot was added later, but its close similarity to the loose technique of the engraver of

58

59

Myers's Van Beverhoudt waiter (cat. 59) may indicate another engraver from the same workshop. Significantly, the more skilled craftsman worked on the flat surface of the waiter marked by Myers, where the engraving would be more visible, whereas a less skilled artisan was assigned the border on the teapot, which would have been noticed but perhaps not "read" in the same way as an inscription or coat of arms.

1 Norman-Wilcox 1954, p. 50, fig. 8; *Old English* 1962, p. 3, no. 25.

61

HALSTED AND MYERS

Covered Jar, c. 1769

Silver, h. 5⅝ (14.3), diam. base 1⅝ (4.1), diam. rim 1⅜ (3.5), wt. 4 oz. 13 dwt. (145g) (scratch wt. 4 oz. 13 dwt.)

MARK 12 once on underside of body; MARK 11A twice on outside of base

INSCRIPTION: "MS" engraved on underside of body; script "G" added c. 1800 to outside of body

PROVENANCE: Miriam (Simon) Gratz ("MS"; 1749–1808; cat. 139) of Lancaster and later Philadelphia; to her daughter Rachel, who married Solomon Moses (see cats. 88–90); to their great-granddaughter Kathleen Matilda Moore (b. 1886), who died unmarried.[1]

Private collection

The original purpose of this diminutive but graceful object remains an enigma. Kathryn Buhler published it as a tea caddy, undoubtedly because of its resemblance to baluster-shape porcelain tea caddies of the mid-eighteenth century.[2] Small, covered tea caddies of this baluster shape were also a specialty of Dutch silversmiths working in Haarlem in the eighteenth century, although most had fluted or richly chased surfaces: extant examples are by Jacob Groeneweg of 1731 and Florianius van der Hoeff of 1766.[3] The majority of surviving American silver tea caddies were made in a boxlike shape, however, and English baluster-shape caddies were usually of a larger size to complement matching sugar dishes. A pair of elaborately chased tea caddies of this small size and same shape, with London hallmarks for 1743–44, has been published.[4]

Miriam (Simon) Gratz was from a family that took great pains to observe Jewish rituals in the inland town of Lancaster, Pennsylvania (p. 18). It is thus possible that this object was made as a *b'samim*, a container for the sweet spices that were blessed and smelled during *havdalah*, the ceremony concluding the Sabbath or other holy days.[5] Two holes, now filled, in the cover may have allowed users to smell the spices while keeping the cover in place, so that the jar could be passed without spilling the contents.[6] The 1750 estate inventory of Abraham Isaacks of New York included "1 [Silver] Spice Box" valued at

£1.10.0, and there are references to the form in the homes of other eighteenth-century American Jews.[7] Noting the absence of English silver spice boxes in the more distinctive tower form during the eighteenth century, Arthur Grimwade identified two "ordinary domestic silver casters" that had been used by English Jews for this purpose, one by Samuel Wood of c. 1750 and another dated 1753–54.[8] Baluster-shape spice boxes that resemble casters but are identified as spice boxes by engraved inscriptions were used in the United States and Europe during the nineteenth century, although no earlier examples are known to the present author.[9]

If this speculation as to the covered jar's purpose is correct, it would be the only American-made piece of domestic silver Judaica that can be identified from the Colonial period. Its simple design and modest size speak eloquently to the modesty of the Simon and Gratz families' aspirations with regard to domestic display. The objects made for Sabbath and *havdalah* celebrations, rituals that took place in the home rather than the synagogue, were specifically connected to women, and Joseph Simon may well have purchased the jar from Halsted and Myers for his daughter when she married and set up housekeeping. Although he lived in Lancaster, Simon had long-standing business connections with Myers; in an undetermined year between 1757 and 1762, Barnard Gratz recorded "Rec^d Novr 16 of Mr Jo^s Simons £11.14.4 Phild^a ["Jersey" crossed out] money for acc^t Myer Myers order on him for £12.13.10 York curr^y."[10]

1 Stern 1991, pp. 87, 138, 209.
2 Buhler 1956, no. 221; Rosenbaum 1954A, p. 137; *American Silver* 1960, no. 133. For ceramic examples, see Walkling 1985, figs. 9–10, 12.
3 Rijksmuseum, Amsterdam, inv. BK-14839 and BK-NM-7883, respectively.
4 Clayton 1971, fig. 621. For more typical tea caddies, see De Castres 1977, pp. 36–43, and Clayton 1985, pp. 163, 220.
5 Kanof 1975, p. 54; Keen 1991, p. 64.
6 The present ring handle appears to be a later addition, as indicated by the difference between the present weight and the scratch weight.
7 Inventory of Abraham Isaacks, p. 1, AJHS. The 1833 inventory of the estate of Judith Hadassah (Jacobs) Myers of New York included one silver spice box valued at $3.10, AJHS.
8 Grimwade 1955, p. 8. The casters are both at The Jewish Museum, London; Barnett 1974, nos. 417, 435.
9 A baluster-shape spice box dated Sivan 15, 5629 (May 25, 1869) by Francis W. Cooper of New York is in The Jewish Museum, New York, inv. F4439. A similar form, dated 1876, from the Jewish community in Leeuwarden, and another that was given by the Society Tiferet Bacharim to the Jewish Community in Assen in 1890 are both in the Joods Historisch Museum, Amsterdam. An undated pewter spice box of this form is in the Jüdisches Museum, Vienna, inv. 642.
10 Gratz 1757–62B, n.p.

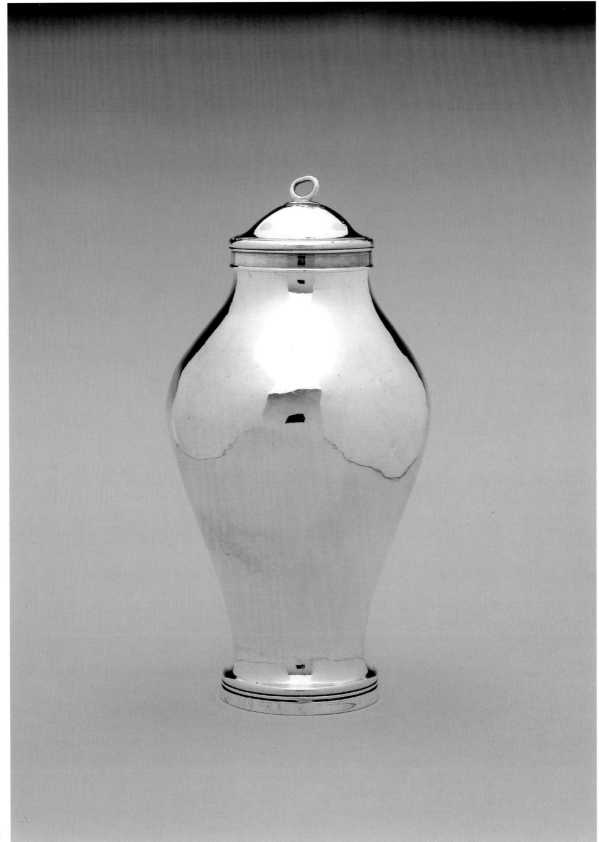

61

62

Circumcision Shield, 1765–76

Silver, 2⅝ x 1½ (6.7 x 3.8), wt. 18 dwt. (28.3g)

MARK 9 once on upper surface

PROVENANCE: probably Moses Seixas (1744–1809); by descent to his great-grandson, Naphtali Taylor Phillips (b. 1868).[1]

American Jewish Historical Society, New York City and Waltham, Massachusetts; Captain N. Taylor Phillips Collection

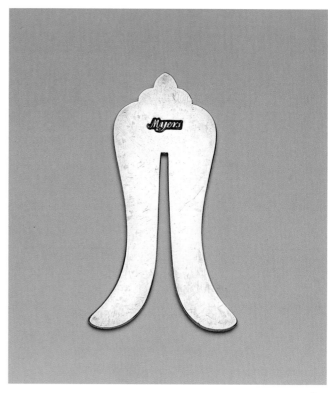

62

Aside from the five pairs of Torah finials (cats. 63–66, 100), the only surviving object for public Jewish ritual by Myer Myers is this circumcision shield. The circumcision of male children on the eighth day after birth was one of the most important covenants between God and Israel (p. 20). In 1733, the founding members of the Jewish congregation in Savannah, Georgia, brought with them from London "a Safertora with two Cloaks and a Circumiscion box . . . for the use of the Congregation, that they intend to Establish."[2]

A plate from Bernard Picart's *Cérémonies et coutumes religieuses* of 1723 shows a *berit milah*, a circumcision, that must have been similar to those in eighteenth-century America (fig. 7). The operation was performed by a *mohel*, or circumciser (E, in Picart's image), and the child was presented to a *minyan*, or quorum of ten men, and held during the operation by his *sandak*, or godfather (C). The foreskin was pulled through the slit in the shield, which the *mohel* holds in his right hand, protecting the glans of the penis from the cutting edges of the knife. Jewish women (B) did not witness the ceremony, although Picart showed Christian women present. At the conclusion of the operation, the *mohel* blessed wine (held by F) and recited a prayer in which the boy's name was given.

As with his Torah finials, Myers followed a traditional form for the shield. The shape of an inverted lyre was in use from at least the seventeenth century and was recorded in illustrations from Picart (62.1) as well as in the circumcision register used by Bernard Jacobs, a *mohel* in the Lancaster, Pennsylvania, area in the 1760s.[3] Other implements, seen in Picart's plate, included the knife with two sharpened edges and a rounded tip, a flask containing styptic powders for healing the cut, and trays for holding plasters and receiving the foreskin. These implements were to be used only for circumcisions and in Europe frequently were made of precious materials. Myers's shield is the only extant object from the circumcision ritual with a definite history in eighteenth-century America, although it was donated to the American Jewish Historical Society as part of an incomplete set of implements (lacking a knife) of different dates, contained in a box labeled by a London trunkmaker, Dudley Johnson.[4]

The shield apparently belonged to the Newport merchant and banker Moses Seixas, who in the 1770s occasionally served

Newport's congregation, Yeshuat Israel, as a *mohel*, after learning to perform circumcisions from Abraham Abrahams (fig. 8).[5] Seixas also served as *parnas* (president) and by the late 1790s had become custodian of the Torahs and finials of Yeshuat Israel after regular services ceased (cats. 63–65). His younger brother, Gershom Mendes Seixas (fig. 5), served Shearith Israel in New York not only as *hazan* but also as a *mohel* in the early 1800s. According to at least two later sources, the shield was "made for Moses Seixas of Newport, Rhode Island," although more recently, it has been published with the less specific provenance of "the Seixas family of New York."[6] The set was donated by a direct descendant of Moses Seixas who had inherited a collection of Seixas family heirlooms.

The importance of this ceremony to eighteenth-century Jews is reinforced by another silver object Myers made to accompany a circumcision, a silver medal to commemorate the circumcision of Moses Etting Hays in 1789. Now unlocated, it was recorded in a drawing by Jacques Judah Lyons in the 1870s (62.2). The Hebrew inscription around the letter for God on the medal's obverse translates: "I Elchanan bar Abraham raised my hands in the holy covenant to circumcise the boy/Moshe bar David on Monday 5th day of the month Tishri this being the 13th day since his birth." Lyons interpreted the conclusion of this second line as standing for the year 5544, an error for 5549; he interpreted the letters on the reverse as signifying the number 41, "the number of children thus far named by this *Mohel*."[7]

62.1 Bernard Picart, *Instrumens qui servent à la circonsision*, from *Cérémonies et coutumes religieuses de tous les peuples du monde*, Amsterdam, 1723. Yale Center for British Art, New Haven; Paul Mellon Collection.

62.2 Jacques Judah Lyons, *Drawing of a Circumcision Medal*, New York, c. 1870.
Ink on paper. American Jewish Historical Society, New York City and Waltham, Massachusetts.

62.1

62.2

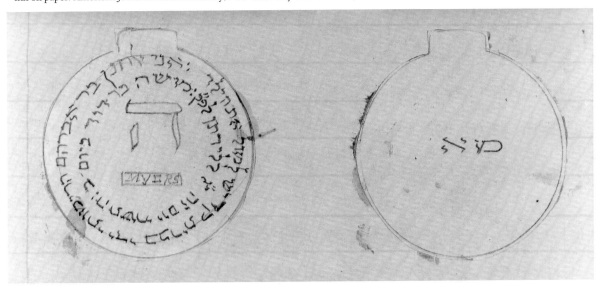

1 Stern 1991, pp. 154, 165, 244, 263, 276.

2 Levi Sheftall, "Diary of Jews in Savannah," p. 2, Marion Abrams Levy Collection, Keith Read Manuscript Collection, University of Georgia Library, Athens.

3 *Encyclopedia Judaica*, V, p. 570; Stern 1991, p. 132; Mittelman 1998, p. 61.

4 Reprod. in Brilliant/Smith 1997, p. 16.

5 Gutstein 1936, pp. 131–32; Marcus 1970, II, p. 988.

6 Schoenberger 1953, p. 2; "Exhibition" 1954, p. 1, no. 6; Brilliant/Smith 1997, pp. 14, 16.

7 *Lyons Collection* 1920, pp. 383–84. Moses Hays died unmarried, and in the 1870s this medal belonged to his nephew, David Solis Hays; Stern 1991, p. 104. The present author's attempts to trace its ownership further have proved unsuccessful. I am grateful to Martin Berger and especially Joseph Mayer for their assistance in translating the inscription.

63

Two Torah Finials, 1765–76

(illustrated in color in frontispiece)

Silver and brass with parcel gilding

A.(open crown): h. 13 (33), diam. base 1¼ (3.2), gross wt. 18 oz. 16 dwt. (585g)

MARK 9 once horizontally on shaft near base

B.(closed crown): h. 14⅜ (36.5), diam. base 1⁵⁄₁₆ (4.9), gross wt. 16 oz. 14 dwt. (520g)

MARK 9 once vertically on shaft near base; mark on one bell attributed to Stephen Hedges (dates unknown), London¹

INSCRIPTION: "NEWPORT" engraved on shaft parallel to mark

PROVENANCE: with Shearith Israel by 1833 and probably earlier; see below.

Congregation Shearith Israel, New York

Exhibited in New Haven only

1 Hedges registered the mark on this bell on September 1, 1759; Smallworkers' Register, vol. C3, p. 34, Worshipful Company of Goldsmiths, London.

64

Two Torah Finials, 1766–76

Silver and brass with parcel gilding, h. 14½ (36.8), diam. base 1⁵⁄₁₆ (3.3) each, gross wt. A. 21 oz. 17 dwt. (680g), B. 22 oz. (685g)

MARK 9 once perpendicular to base on shaft of A., parallel to base of shaft on B.

INSCRIPTION: "NEWPORT" engraved on shaft of A.

PROVENANCE: with Congregation Yeshuat (now Jeshuat) Israel by about 1780 and probably earlier; see below.

The Touro Synagogue, Congregation Jeshuat Israel, Newport, Rhode Island

65

Pair of Torah Finials, 1765–76, possibly 1771–72

Silver and brass with parcel gilding, h. 14¼ (36.2), diam. base 1⁵⁄₁₆ (3.3), diam. center sphere 5¼ (13.3) each, gross wt. A. 27 oz. (840g), B. 26 oz. 14 dwt. (830g)

MARK 9 once on each shaft

PROVENANCE: possibly the Torah finials commissioned for Congregation Mikveh Israel and delivered by Myers in January 1772; see below.

Kahal Kadosh Mikveh Israel, Philadelphia

Torah finials, or *rimonim,* were removable ornaments placed over the upper end of the rollers of the Torah scroll. As readings from the Torah were the central part of every service, the Torah's importance was emphasized from ancient times by covering the scroll with silk mantles and ornamenting the staves with silver and gold decorations. Removable Torah finials had appeared by the twelfth century.¹ A detail from a plate in Bernard Picart's *Cérémonies et coutumes religieuses* of 1723 (63-65.1) shows an eighteenth-century Dutch Torah adorned with finials and the typical flared mantle of Sephardic tradition. After removing the mantle and before reading the Torah, the reader raised the scroll with the finials still on the staves (fig. 4); and an accompanying ringing of the bells would have focused the congregation's attention. As an elder of his congregation, Myers would have served as a reader of the Torah; at age thirty, he was chosen for the honor of *hatan Torah* ("bridegroom of the Torah"), the man who performed the final reading in the annual cycle.²

Unlike Protestant church silver, which was modeled self-consciously on domestic forms to demystify worship, Myers's Torah finials followed centuries-old designs for elaborate sacred objects. Maimonides decreed that "the decorative silver and gold pomegranates that are made for a Torah scroll are considered sacred articles," which could not be sold except to buy a Torah.³ Myers made these three pairs of finials with three stacked, flattened spheres ornamented with six bells attached to addorsed C-scroll brackets, terminating in crown finials. Each element of this design had its origins in biblical and other sacred texts. The three spherical sections resemble Sephardic Torah finials, with spheres representing pomegranates, hence the name *rimonim,* which means "pomegranates."⁴ One scholar has proposed that the seeds in dried pomegranates functioned in ancient times as a natural rattle.⁵ The earliest surviving European finial, made in Spain during the later fifteenth century, has pierced spherical sections above and below the central tower form, on which hang the bells.⁶ Pomegranates had additional iconographic significance. The two great brass pillars in the porch of the Temple in Jerusalem had capitals with "pomegranates . . . two hundred in rows round and about" (I Kings 7:18–20) as a symbol of fruitfulness. Moreover, the rollers of the Torah scroll were called *Eẓ Ḥayyim* ("Tree of Life"), a reference to Proverbs 3:13, 18: "Happy is the man that findeth wisdom, and the man that getteth understanding. . . . She is a tree of life to them that lay hold upon her." As Guido Schoenberger observed, the pomegranates on the Torah finials therefore could be interpreted as the fruits of the Tree of Life.⁷

The gilded bells that sounded the removal and return of the Torah to the Ark were a literal transposition of the gold bells on the High Priest Aaron's robe:

And beneath upon the hem of it thou shalt make pomegranates of blue, and of purple, and of scarlet, round about the hem thereof; and bells of gold between them round about: a golden bell and a pomegranate, a golden bell and a pomegranate, upon the hem of the robe round about. And it shall be upon Aaron to minister; and his sound shall be heard

63

63.1

when he goeth in unto the holy place before the Lord, and when he cometh out, that he die not (Exodus 28:33–35).

The original bells on Myers's Torah finials probably were English or Dutch imports, made by specialist smallworkers. In 1954, Rosenbaum, in reference to the pair of Torah finials at Shearith Israel, recorded that "some bells bear a Dutch stamp"; these are no longer present.[8] One English bell survives in place on this pair and may represent a restoration for bells lost during the turmoil of the Revolutionary War (see below). The bell bears a sovereign's head duty mark for 1786–1820 and what may be the maker's mark of the London smallworker Stephen Hedges (63.1).

The crown at the top of each finial serves as the "Crown of the Law," an emblem of worldly power reinforcing the absolute authority of the Torah. Tom Freudenheim connected the use of crowns to a passage from the *Mishnah*: "Rabbi Shimon said: There are three crowns: the crown of Torah, the crown of priesthood, and the crown of kingship; but the crown of a good name excels them all."[9] Individual crowns had been used to ornament the Torah since at least the eleventh century.[10] According to Rafi Grafman, it was a Dutch innovation of the seventeenth century to combine the crown with Torah finials, which usually took the form of a Baroque

church tower.[11] Crowns were almost always added to Torah finials made during the eighteenth century in England, the Netherlands, and Germany.[12] The gilded brass crowns on Myers's New York and Newport Torah finials were cast from the same patterns, and may have been supplied by his brother Asher (p. 48).

Only Mikveh Israel's pair of Torah finials lacks crowns. Their absence raises the possibility that the finials originally had crowns that became damaged and were replaced. Freudenheim has noted the similarity of the Philadelphia pinecones to Myers's coffeepot finials, and the crowns on Myers's other two finials have small pinecones at their tops.[13] However, the large size of the Philadelphia pinecones and the style of the spiral-pattern disks below them more closely resemble furniture mounts of the early nineteenth century. Moreover, pinecone finials atop the Torah staves evoked the thyrsus of the Bacchae in Greek mythology and would have been in keeping stylistically if not iconographically with the severe Egyptian-classical synagogue designed by William Strickland that Mikveh Israel dedicated in 1825.[14]

As noted above, Torah finials with pierced spherical elements were a traditional Sephardic form, as in those made by Abraham de Oliveyra for London's Hambro Synagogue in

156 MYER MYERS

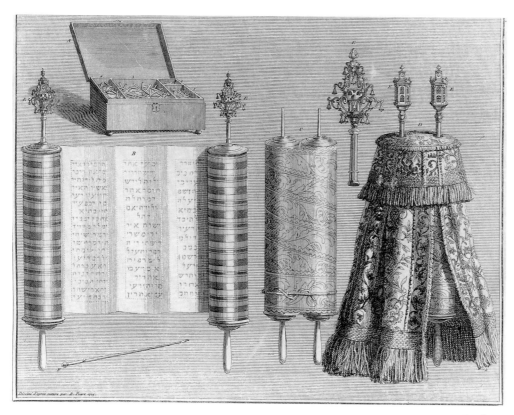

63-65.1

1724.[15] The closest precedent for Myers's design is a pair of Torah finials made in London by Gabriel Sleath in 1719–20 for Congregation Nidhe Israel in Bridgetown, Barbados (63-65.2). The design and decoration of Sleath's Torah finials strongly resemble Baroque secular objects with the same pierced and chased ornament, particularly English and Dutch perfume burners that range in date from the 1670s to the 1710s (63-65.3).[16] Although it is unlikely that Myers knew of these earlier perfume burners, the strong mercantile connections between Barbados and New York make it probable that either he or someone in New York had seen the Sleath finials firsthand, since any Jews traveling to Barbados would have worshiped at the synagogue in Bridgetown. There were active connections between the Bridgetown and New York congregations: in 1729, four members of the Barbados congregation contributed £22.13.0 toward the construction of the Mill Street Synagogue, and in 1737 the widow of Mordecai Burgos, who had died while visiting New York and was buried in the cemetery, donated £40 for a wall around the burial ground.[17] Myers's finials are a Rococo variation on Sleath's Baroque model, with its strict gradation in size and ornament organized into self-contained panels. Myers's composition, with the largest sphere at the center, is more dynamic, and the pierced and chased patterns form a continuous flow around the sphere.

The close similarities among the Newport, New York, and Philadelphia finials indicate that they were made within a short period of time. The same chaser appears to have made the pierced spheres, all of which follow nearly identical patterns (pp. 55–56; fig. 30). Stylistically, the flowing, floral patterns of the chasing resemble Myers's secular work of the late 1760s and early 1770s (cats. 75, 76). This date is supported by the only documentation connected to any of the Torah finials, a letter written by Myers in January 1772 to Michael Gratz in Philadelphia, concerning delivery of one pair to Mikveh Israel: "Mr. Aarons is kind enough to take the *rimonim* with him, which hope he will deliver you, and that they may meet your, and the Contributers Approbation" (Appendix II, no. 6). It is not certain if Myers's letter refers to cat. 65 or to a second pair (cat. 66), or possibly to both.

Myers's reference to "Contributers" indicates that members of the Philadelphia congregation had commissioned the Torah finials for their new synagogue. The choice of Myers to make the Torah finials was logical given his close relationship to the Gratz family and other members of Philadelphia Jewish community (p. 61). He had also been involved in procuring a Torah for Mikveh Israel, as Barnard Gratz (cat. 138) related in a letter of October 1771 to one of his associates in London:

In Regard the sefer [Torah] *have only to say & to lett you know that we have the one you mentiond to me that Did Belong to Mr Jonas Philips from new York from Mr Myers as Mr Philips ordered for which you will Be kind enough to Pay Mr Philips for it, I suppose he will not charge too much for it, as he asked me But 7 guenes I think for it, But shuld he ask somthing more Now you must pay him*[.] *Mr Myers of new York I heard told sombody, he thinks it will be 9 guenes but hope Mr Philips will lett it goe for the Price he asked me for it, as above, However I live this to you to agree with him*[.] *you need not to send the silver yod I*

63-65.2   63-65.3

mentioned to you before as we had one made a present for the shul *from New york, & shuld be glad if you would be kind enough after Paying Mr Philips for the* sefer *& if mony enough in your hands you would pay Mr Jacob Barnett 75/0 sterling for some* tefillin *he sent me hear.*[18]

The identification of "Mr. Myers" with the silversmith seems likely: not only had he been commissioned to provide the Philadelphia congregation with Torah finials, but he had given testimony for Phillips's naturalization the preceding April.[19] The tantalizing reference in Gratz's letter to a "silver *yod . . .* made a present . . . from New York" raises the possibility that Myers had also made a torah pointer, although no *yod* marked by Myers is known to survive.[20]

No records survive to document when the Torah finials at either Shearith Israel or Yeshuat Israel were commissioned by or donated to the congregation. Shearith Israel had Torahs from the earliest years of its existence, many of them placed on loan by members or by other congregations (p. 13). A meeting of the *parnassim* (officers) on September 11, 1765 recorded the complicated protocol of choosing which Torah should be used for the weekly reading:

It is further agreed for the sake of Peace, that the Sepharim [Torahs] *shall be taken out in their turns according to the following regulation to say—Each Sepher* [Torah] *to read in the proper days for two weeks (Holy days excepted) beginning with those belonging to the Congregation[,] according to the seniority of the owners of each Sepher or failure of the same the the* [sic] *Hazan to pay a fine of Twenty shillings.*[21]

Myers originally may have made the Torah finials now at Shearith Israel for one of these privately owned Torahs. Considerable evidence survives regarding ownership of Torah finials in New York, particularly in the wealthy Gomez family (see cat. 145). In his will of December 24, 1730, Luis Moses Gomez bequeathed to his eldest son, Mordecai Gomez "one pare of Silver Adornements for the five Books of Moses weying [weighing] Thirty nine ounces or thereabouts in full satisfaction of his being my Eldest Son."[22] Mordecai's younger brother Daniel Gomez purchased his own Torah finials, crediting Isaac Levy Maduro of Curaçao in 1744 for "Silvor romonims."[23] Ten years after their father's death, in a will dated May 3, 1750, Mordecai Gomez gave to his eldest son, Isaac, "Five Books of Moses and one pair of silver ornaments thereto belonging, weighing about 30 ounces," apparently a different set from the one he had received.

Many of these privately owned Torahs became the property of the congregation by gift or bequest. Seven years after the opening of the Mill Street Synagogue, the widow Rachel Luis bequeathed £10 "to buy a Shefer Tora for the use of the Kall Kados [*Kahal Kadosh*, "holy congregation"] Sherith Ysraell."[24] A pair of silver Torah finials engraved with the date 5497 (1736–37) survives at Shearith Israel and originally may have belonged to the Torah purchased with Luis's bequest. The Torah itself no longer exists, but in 1860 Jacques Judah Lyons recorded a dedicatory inscription of 5497 on one roller of a Torah then in the synagogue.[25] In 1794, Benjamin Judah of New York presented Shearith Israel with "A Taba Cloth—

Sepher Mantle & Roller with their ornaments; silver and Green tissue ground, bound with a Silver Orris & c."[26] In the same year, another Torah with black rosewood staves was deposited at the synagogue by Ephraim Hart and was later purchased from his widow.[27]

During the British occupation of New York, Torahs belonging to Shearith Israel, presumably with their ornaments, had been taken by the *hazan* Gershom Mendes Seixas, who after the war requested reimbursement of £6.3.2 "for transporting the Sepharim & Chest belonging to the K.K." [*Kahal Kadosh*], first from New York to Stratford, Connecticut, and later to Philadelphia.[28] One scroll owned by Shearith Israel remained in the Mill Street Synagogue, together with another belonging to the Loyalist Uriah Hendricks. Two British soldiers broke into the building in 1777, desecrated these scrolls, and stole the two pairs of finials.[29]

As in New York, the Torah finials in Newport originally may have been private commissions that were loaned or donated to the congregation. There were close connections between Yeshuat Israel and Shearith Israel; Myer Myers was *parnas* of Shearith Israel in 1759 when "Freewill offerings" amounting to £149.0.6 were raised toward the building of a synagogue in Newport. When the Touro Synagogue opened in 1763, Shearith Israel lent it three Torahs, including one that had been deposited in New York by the Jews of Savannah, Georgia.[30] Individual members of the New York congregation had also made "offerings of Furniture, & Ornaments towards this pious undertaking."[31] It is possible that cat. 64 was a gift or accompanied a Torah from New York at this time, although the finials more probably date from the later 1760s or early 1770s. In his description of a service at the Touro Synagogue in 1773, Ezra Stiles (cat. 133) made no mention of finials on the Torahs, although this pair may well have been in use by that date.

At some point, the word "NEWPORT" was engraved on one finial in cats. 63 and 64. The two thus engraved presumably formed a single pair that belonged to the Newport congregation, but subsequently became intermixed with a pair belonging to Shearith Israel; in other words, each congregation now owns one finial originally from the Newport pair and one finial originally from the New York pair. As in New York, most of the Jews in Newport fled the city prior to British takeover in 1776, but unlike New York, the community never returned in large numbers. After the war, the Touro Synagogue was used only occasionally as a house of worship, and in 1818 it was reported to the *parnassim* of Shearith Israel:

For a great number of years past there has not been service in the synagogue in Newport and the Seapharim have been deposited in the house of the late Mr. Moses Seixas [cat. 62] of that place for more than twenty years and now under the charge of his Widow and son Mr. Benjamin Seixas.[32]

However, it was not until 1833 that the four Torahs (and presumably their ornaments) were transferred to Shearith Israel "for safekeeping in our place of worship until they should be required for the use of the Newport shool [*shul*]."[33] At this time, "NEWPORT" may have been engraved on each finial in Yeshuat Israel's pair to distinguish them from the nearly identical pair already at Shearith Israel. If this scenario is correct, we may thereby infer that both pairs were in their respective congregation's possession before 1833. The Torahs and Torah finials were returned from New York in 1883, and the congregation in Newport was rechartered as Jeshuat Israel in 1894.[34] By this time, however, the distinction between these pairs had been forgotten, resulting in the present arrangement.

Myers's Torah finials are unique examples of eighteenth-century American Jewish religious silver. They are also among the most extraordinary precious-metal objects produced in Colonial America. Large in scale, imbued with symbolism, and virtuoso in technique, they represent the grand ambitions of both the craftsman and his religious community.

1 Grafman/Mann 1996, p. 9.

2 KKSI-MB1, p. 127.

3 Maimonides 1990, p. 184.

4 Keen 1991, pp. 28–29, no. 8; Schoenberger 1953, p. 3, figs. 1, 6.

5 Barnett 1974, p. 25.

6 Cathedral Treasury of Palma de Majorca; reprod. in Grafman/Mann 1996, fig. 9.

7 Schoenberger 1953, p. 3.

8 Rosenbaum 1954A, p. 100.

9 *Mishnah* 1987, p. 125; Freudenheim 1965, p. 3.

10 Grafman/Mann 1996, p. 11.

11 Ibid., pp. 42–43.

12 See Torah finials from these countries in Grimwade 1955 and Grafman/Mann 1996.

13 Freudenheim 1965, p. 3.

14 Wolf/Whiteman 1957, pp. 365–66; Tatum 1961, p. 86; reprod. Pool/Pool 1955, facing p. 413.

15 Grimwade 1955, pp. 6–7 n. 1, fig. 3.

16 An English perfume burner dated 1677–78 is illustrated in Jackson 1911, I, fig. 255; for another undated English example, see Oman 1970, fig. 74. A Dutch perfume burner of 1714 is illustrated in Den Blaauwen 1979, no. 99.

17 Pool/Pool 1955, p. 415.

18 Barnard Gratz to Michael Samson, October 15, 1771, Etting papers, oversize folder, Historical Society of Pennsylvania, Philadelphia. Words in Roman type are in Hebrew in the original document.

19 Pool 1952, p. 193.

20 A *yod*, formerly in the collections of Alfred Lenssen and the Stevens Institute of Technology, Hoboken, New Jersey, was analyzed at the Winterthur Museum and determined to be of twentieth-century date.

21 KKSI-MB2 (Elul 25, 5525).

22 Hershkowitz 1966A, p. 362.

23 Account with Manuel Levy, 1743–44, loose page from Daniel Gomez Ledger, Lyons Collection, AJHS. These Torah finials were valued at "112.5.3"; the currency appears to be pistoles rather than pounds.

24 Hershkowitz 1966A, p. 356.

25 Pool/Pool 1955, pp. 109–10, 113–14, reprod. opposite p. 124.

26 Benjamin Judah to the Trustees of Congregation Shearith Israel, June 10, 1794, Lyons Collection, AJHS.

27 Pool/Pool 1955, p. 110.

28 Notebook no. 4, pp. 140–41, Lyons Collection, box 7, AJHS.
29 *Lyons Collection* 1913, p. 216.
30 Friedman 1946, pp. 50–52; Pool/Pool 1955, pp. 420–21.
31 Moses Lopez to Joseph Simpson and Samuel Judah, Newport, July 25, 1762, Lyons Collection, AJHS.
32 Pool/Pool 1955, p. 421.
33 Ibid., p. 422.
34 Ibid.; Gutstein 1936, p. 271.

66

Pair of Torah Finials, 1765–76, possibly 1771–72

Silver and brass, each h. 12⅞ (32.7), diam. base 1³⁄₁₆ (3), diam. body 4⅛ (10.5), gross wt. A. 14 oz. 6 dwt. (445g) B. 14 oz. 3 dwt. (440g)

MARK 9 twice on shaft near base on each

PROVENANCE: possibly the Torah finials commissioned for Congregation Mikveh Israel and delivered by Myers in January 1772; see below.

Kahal Kadosh Mikveh Israel, Philadelphia

This pair of Torah finials is unlike the other four pairs made by Myers, which followed a traditional Sephardic form with spherical sections (cats. 63–65, 100). The present pair's bulbous shape, accentuated with spiral fluting and equally evocative of the pomegranate, apparently was inspired by Ashkenazic models from Northern Europe. Related examples were made in eighteenth-century Germany, including a pair marked by the Nuremberg silversmith Johann Samuel Beckensteiner (66.1).[1] It is tempting to speculate that Otto Paul de Parisien, who had immigrated to New York from Germany, might have been familiar with Torah finials of this design, since German examples were made by Christian silversmiths. However, given that Ashkenazic Jews were almost equal in numbers to Sephardic Jews in both New York and Philadelphia (pp. 16–17), it seems more likely that Myers knew of German models through the local Jewish community. At one time the present pair of Torah finials was entirely gilded.[2]

The date at which these Torah finials came into Mikveh Israel's possession is uncertain. Myers's letter to Michael Gratz of January 1772 (Appendix II, no. 6) may refer to this pair, or to cat. 65, or to both; as noted (p. 156), Myers's reference to "Contributers" indicates that the finials being delivered had been a commission from a committee of Mikveh Israel's members rather than a private client. The spiral fluting on this pair of finials relates to a sugar dish from Myers's workshop (cat. 67); on the finials, the design is reversed, with the fluting articulating rather than framing the swelled midsection. The sugar dish and all Myers's Torah finials are struck with his MARK 9, which suggests that they are contemporaneous.

1 Schoenberger 1953, pp. 7–8; Grimwade 1955, p. 7 n. 1; Grafman/Mann 1996, nos. 264–65.
2 Janice Carlson, Analytical report no. 4065, March 20, 2000, The Winter-

66.1

66.1 Johann Samuel Beckensteiner, *Torah Finials*, Nuremberg, c. 1750. Silver with parcel gilding. The Jewish Museum, New York; Gift of Dr. Harry G. Friedman.

thur Museum Analytical Laboratory. I am indebted to Ruth Hoffman, archivist of Kahal Kadosh Mikveh Israel, for sharing a copy of this report with me.

67

Sugar Dish, 1765–76

Silver, h. 6¹⁄₁₆ (15.7), diam. base 3 (7.6), diam. rim 4⅝ (11.7), wt. 10 oz. 6 dwt. (320g) (scratch wt. 10 oz. 14 dwt.)

MARK 9 twice on underside of body

ARMORIAL: crest (a lion rampant) engraved on outside of body below rim

PROVENANCE: unknown prior to sale before 1954 by the dealer Israel Sack to the Newport, Rhode Island, collector Cornelius C. Moore; by bequest to Salve Regina College, by whom sold at auction in 1986.[1]

Private collection

The spiral fluting that distinguishes this sugar dish was exceptional in Myers's workshop. Although he used spiral patterns

67

in the design of a bread basket (cat. 78) and a milk pot (cat. 76), his only other objects with repoussé chasing forming sculptural, spiral flutes are the pair of Torah finials made for Congregation Mikveh Israel in Philadelphia (cat. 66), which probably were contemporary and possibly made by the same craftsman. On these objects, the silver is worked very thinly, atypical of Myers's usual workshop practice. The fluting on the sugar dish is located at its top and bottom, leading the eye toward the projecting center. This form of chased decoration was uncommon on silver made in Colonial America.

Spiral fluting, however, was popular both in England and Continental Europe from the early 1730s into the 1770s, and was particularly popular in England in the later 1750s and early 1760s.[2] Spiral fluting similar to that on Myers's sugar dish is found on a silver tea kettle made by the London silversmith Daniel Piers in 1757 that was acquired by Myers's patron Peter

R. Livingston (cats. 32, 34) after his marriage in 1758.[3] This object may well have influenced Myers's sugar dish, particularly as the Livingston crest and motto on the teakettle appear to have been engraved by Myers's preferred engraver of the time. Daniel Christian Fueter may also have provided the inspiration for this ornament in Myers's work. Chased spiral fluting appears on his gold whistle of 1761–64 (cat. 107), and cast or stamped spiral fluting is applied to a pair of candlesticks he made following Swiss models.[4]

1 Sotheby's 1986A, lot 149.
2 English examples are reprod. in Jackson 1911, I, p. 308, II, pp. 968, 970, 985, 987; Oman 1965, pls. 144, 146; Wees 1997, nos. 195, 205–07, 292; Puig et al. 1989, no. 84. Dutch examples are reprod. in Den Blaauwen 1979, nos. 125, 135; De Lorm 2000, nos. 80, 95, 112, 116.
3 Sotheby's 1972, lot 84.
4 Quimby/Johnson 1995, no. 195.

68

Teapot, 1765–76

Silver with wood handle, h. 6⅝ (16.8), w. 9¾ (24.8), diam. base 3¼ (8.3), gross wt. 19 oz. 2 dwt. (594g)

MARK 9 once on underside; a possible second strike may be covered by solder

PROVENANCE: unknown prior to sale at auction in Boston in 1997.[1]

Collection of Mrs. Jerome T. Gans

1 Grogan 1997, lot 881.

69

Bowl, 1765–76

Silver, h. 4⅜ (11.1), diam. base 3⁹⁄₁₆ (9), diam. rim 6⅝ (16.8), wt. 12 oz. 11 dwt. (390g) (scratch wt. 13 oz. 14½ dwt.)

MARK 9 once on underside

PROVENANCE: unknown prior to 1954, when owned by the dealer Morris Cohon of Englewood, New Jersey; by whom sold in the same year to the dealer Lawrence Fleischman of Detroit; by whom sold to The Detroit Institute of Arts in 1969.[1]

The Detroit Institute of Arts; Founder's Society Purchase, Gibbs-Williams Fund, with additional funds from K.T. Keller, Mrs. Russell Alger, and anonymous donors

The teapot is the largest piece of domestic silver with chased decoration to survive from Myers's workshop. The same chaser who executed its ornament also ornamented the bowl (cat. 69). The design on both objects is identical, down to the acanthus leaves at the base, which suggests that they originally were made to match.[2] The pattern features a cartouche framed by C-scrolls with feathers issuing from the top on one side, with a cartouche framed by a shell on the opposite side (69.1). The cartouches are flanked by stiffly rendered stems of leaves that terminate in flowers; below these stems are thick and relatively flat C-scrolls with curled ends and flowers in the middle. In contrast to the chaser who ornamented most of Myers's silver (cats. 71–76), this craftsman used cuts rather than dots to punctuate the edges of his leaves, and he favored a textured background for the design that shifted direction when interrupted by raised elements.

Matching pieces of tea equipage appeared in England as early as the 1710s, but the earliest surviving examples made in the American Colonies date a generation later.[3] The most common forms made in Myers's workshop were similarly decorated or engraved sets of milk pots and sugar dishes (cats. 71–74). Teapots ornamented to match other forms were extremely rare in Colonial New York silver; the best-known example is one marked by Pieter de Riemer after 1763.[4]

The bowl probably was intended to function as the "slop bowl" of a tea service. Slop bowls were used to receive the dregs of cold tea from a cup before the cup was refilled. Martha Fales pointed out that the Philadelphia silversmith Joseph Richardson, Sr., used this term in his accounts to refer to all bowls of the size and weight of this example.[5] An earlier, lavishly ornamented bowl of the same type made by the London silversmith Paul de Lamerie in 1744–45 was owned by Myers's patrons David and Margaret Franks of Philadelphia (cat. 4).[6] Myers made another bowl of identical size and design (cat. 70), as well as a pedestal bowl of the same size that probably served the same purpose (cat. 53).

1 Rosenbaum 1954A, p. 103.
2 The bowl had initials or arms in one cartouche that have been erased. On the teapot, the dot-and-diaper pattern in the cartouches is a later addition, suggesting that there originally was a monogram or coat of arms that was covered over.
3 Clayton 1971, p. 308; Fales 1974, figs. 35a and 54, 53 and 61.
4 Waters/McKinsey/Ward 2000, I, no. 23.
5 Fales 1974, pp. 95–96.
6 Hackenbroch 1969, no. 184; Dennis 1968, pp. 637–38, fig. 5.

69.1   Alternate view

68

69

70

70.I

70
Bowl, 1765–76

Silver, h. 4 1/16 (10.3), diam. base 3 3/4 (9.5), diam. rim 6 7/8 (17.5), wt. 13 oz. 4 dwt. (405g) (scratch wt. 13 1/2 oz.)

MARK 9 on underside

INSCRIPTION: "RC" (script) engraved in cartouche on front; "S:B" engraved on underside; "FCL from CL/Oct 8th 1868" added on underside

PROVENANCE: unknown prior to the present owner.

Collection of Ruth J. Nutt

This is the only piece of silver marked by Myer Myers to survive with chasing by this craftsman, whose robust execution and broadly defined forms are atypical of the relatively flat and more detailed chasing found on the workshop's silver. The fact that the chased ornament occupies almost exactly the same position on both this bowl and cat. 69 suggests that they were made at the same time in the workshop and given to different chasers to complete. If such a scenario is correct, Myers

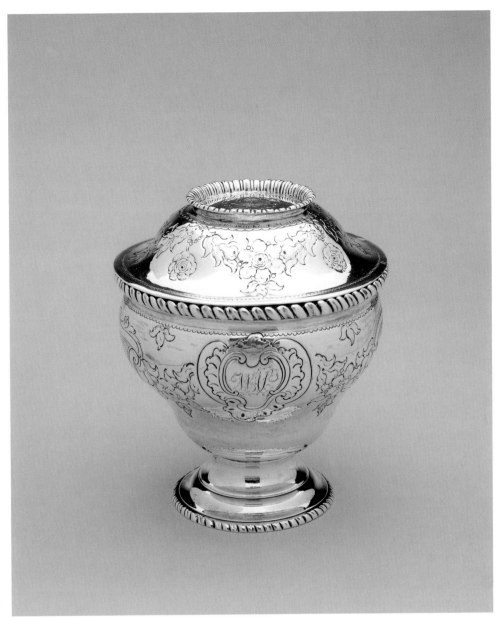

71

had at least two specialist chasers working at one time. In contrast to cat. 69, the pattern is a band of continuous C-scrolls interwoven with garlands of flowers, and the execution is more sculptural, with higher raised elements and deeply impressed lines. The chaser used a large oval punch to define the outside edges of forms, and outlined the inside edges of shells with tightly spaced rows of small dots (70.1). Both this design and style of execution are less sophisticated approximations of the chased decoration found on contemporary London silver, such as the coffeepot of 1761–62 by Robert and William Peaston (cat. 122). The Peaston coffeepot may have been engraved in Myers's workshop about 1772 to match cats. 85–86 or retailed by him, and it could have served as a model for the chaser of this bowl.

71
Sugar Dish, 1765–76

Silver, h. 5⅛ (13), diam. base 2¹³⁄₁₆ (7.1), diam. rim 4⁵⁄₁₆ (11), wt. 10 oz. 3 dwt. (315g)

MARK 9 once on underside of body, and twice on inside of cover

INSCRIPTION: "WAS" (script) engraved in cartouche on front

PROVENANCE: William Sackett (1727–1801) and Anna Lawrence (1731–1798), who were married in 1749; to their son, John Sackett (1755–1819); to his great-great-great-grandson, Bertram John Lawrence Ainsworth; by sale to the present owner in 1975.[1]

Private collection

1 Weygant 1907, pp. 40, 72, 129–30, 193; Louise H. Ainsworth to "whom it may concern," October 24, 1975, private collection.

72

72

Milk Pot, 1765–76

Silver, h. 4¹⁵/₁₆ (12.5), w. 4¹⁵/₁₆ (12.5), diam. base 2³/₁₆ (5.6), wt. 5 oz. 19 dwt. (185g)

MARK 9 once on underside of body

INSCRIPTION: "WAS" (script) engraved in cartouche on front; "A·L ["L" changed to "S"]/P·L" engraved on underside of foot

PROVENANCE: William and Anna (Lawrence) Sackett (as in cat. 71); apparently to Patience (Riker) Lawrence, the wife of Anna's nephew John Lawrence (1758–1817) ("A.L/S to P.L"); subsequent ownership uncertain until 1969, when sold at auction as "property of a Florida private collector;" purchased by the antiques dealers Ginsburg and Levy.[1]

The Burrows Collection; on long-term loan to the Sterling and Francine Clark Art Institute, Williamstown, Massachusetts

1 Lawrence 1858, p. 92; Parke-Bernet 1969, lot 124.

72.1

73

Sugar Dish, 1765–76

Silver, h. 5⅛ (13), diam. base 2⅞ (7.3), diam. cover 4⁵⁄₁₆ (11), wt. 9 oz. 18 dwt. (308.6g)

MARK 9 twice on underside of bowl, both double-struck

INSCRIPTION: "HVW" engraved on underside of foot

PROVENANCE: unknown prior to sale at auction with its matching milk pot (cat. 74) in 1991.[1]

Collection of William B. Dietrich

1 Sotheby's 1991, lot 115.

74

Milk Pot, 1765–76

Silver, h. 5⁵⁄₁₆ (13.5), w. 4⅝ (11.7), diam. base 2¼ (5.7), wt. 4 oz. 14 dwt. (146.6g)

MARK 9 once on underside of body

INSCRIPTION: "HVW" engraved on underside of foot

PROVENANCE: unknown prior to sale at auction with its matching sugar dish (cat. 73) in 1991.

Collection of William B. Dietrich

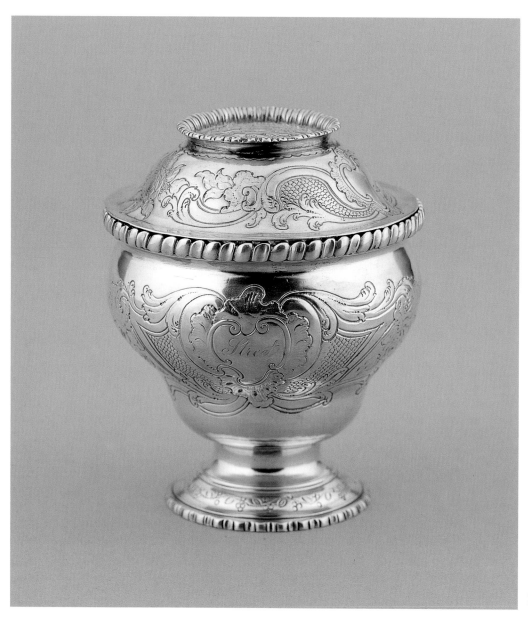

75
Sugar Dish, 1765–76

Silver, h. 5¼ (13.3), diam. base 2¹³⁄₁₆ (7.1), diam. rim 4⁵⁄₁₆ (11), wt. 9 oz. 18 dwt. (308g) (scratch wt. 10 oz. 3 dwt.)

MARK 9 once on underside of body, double-struck

INSCRIPTION: "Street" added to front of bowl in the nineteenth century

PROVENANCE: unknown prior to acquisition by the present owner.

Collection of Ruth J. Nutt

76
Milk Pot, 1765–76

Silver, h. 5⁹⁄₁₆ (14.1), w. 4⅜ (11.1), diam. base 2¼ (5.7), wt. 5 oz. 9 dwt. (170g)

MARK 9 once on underside of body, triple struck

INSCRIPTION: "TMS" engraved on front of body

PROVENANCE: unknown prior to publication in 1948 by the dealer Stephen Ensko; subsequent history uncertain prior to ownership by the New York dealers Ginsburg and Levy, who advertised it in 1964; advertised again by the successor firm Benjamin Ginsburg in 1976; purchased by The Art Institute of Chicago in 1990.[1]

The Art Institute of Chicago; Gift of the Antiquarian Society

Two surviving sets of milk pots and sugar dishes with matching chased decoration, as well as two now-unmatched objects,

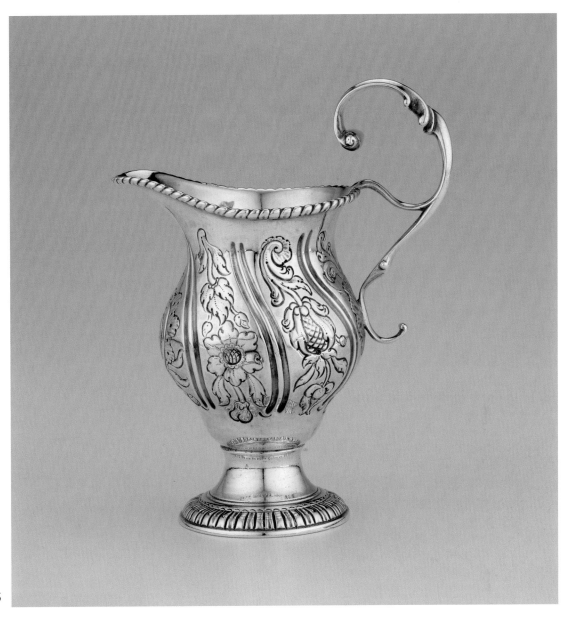

76

indicate that Myers's workshop produced such pieces in some quantity and perhaps for ready sale. In 1763, Halsted and Myers advertised that they "have to sell, a neat assortment of ready made plate, chased and plain" (p. 34). These advertised wares may have been imported, but the extant chased objects form a cohesive group that indicate production in Myers's shop. Details of the objects reveal that his workshop was producing them from component parts. All but one of the chased milk pots have the same distinctive cast handle with an upward spiral pattern, and all but one of the sugar dishes have fluted ring handles on covers. Neither of these features was found commonly on English sugar dishes or milk pots of this inverted pyriform shape, whereas both handles seem to have been pop-

ular in New York City during the decade before the Revolutionary War. Plain examples are recorded by Ephraim Brasher, William Gilbert, John Heath, and Elias Pelletreau, in addition to chased examples by Myers and Peter de Riemer.[2] Myers also made unchased versions of both these sugar dish and milk pot forms.[3]

These objects were also chased by the same specialist craftsman who executed the ornament on the majority of chased objects made in Myers's workshop (p. 54; figs. 29, 30). Together, they illustrate this specialist's inventiveness as a designer, since he rarely followed the same pattern for his decoration. The design vocabulary used for one sugar dish (cat. 75) makes it one of his most richly embellished works. The cast ring handle on the cover is surrounded with a scalloped border, and the base has a wavy vine of dots and circles. The ornament on both the bowl and cover is centered on two cartouches, connected by long scrolls and raffles with a continuous garland of flowers and foliage beneath. The fish-scale pattern appears on another sugar dish (cat. 74), on which a different design was composed with only one cartouche and a series of alternating C-scrolls and shells with flowers placed as accents.

On cat. 76, the chaser worked with assurance to create one of the finest pieces of silver in the Rococo style to survive from Myers's workshop. Unlike cat. 67, the spiral fluting is flat-chased as a pattern, framing sprays of leaves and flowers. This design reveals the craftsman's awareness of Dublin as well as London models, including a bowl by Samuel Walker of c. 1750, tea caddies of 1765–66, and another tea caddy by Parker and Wakelin of 1774–75.[4] The downward spiral on the body complements the upward spiral of the handle, a unique variant of this distinctive design, creating a sense of motion and counter-balanced forms characteristic of the best Rococo silver. The floral ornament was designed to add a sense of stability to the body's "double-bellied" shape, with the largest flowers placed on its widest part. This chaser's skill as a craftsman is particularly evident in his subtle manipulation of the centers of flowers and the use of very fine dots to articulate the leaves and petals.

These chased sets seem to have been popular, despite the fact that the chased decoration would have increased the cost by as much as 25 percent over plain versions (p. 52). Only one set in this group is documented to its original owners. Cats. 71 and 72 were owned by William and Anna (Lawrence) Sackett of Newtown (now Elmhurst), Long Island, who both were from wealthy landowning families that included other patrons of Myer Myers. Anna was the sister of John Lawrence, husband of Catherine Livingston (cats. 35, 36); William was a first cousin Elizabeth (Sackett) Fish, who may have owned the covered cup (fig. 9).[5] This set may have been purchased with the substantial legacy Anna received from her father, the landowner John Lawrence of Newtown, in August 1765.[6]

1 Ensko 1948, p. 91; *Antiques*, 86 (December 1964), p. 657; *Antiques*, 110 (November 1976), p. 865.

2 Sugar dishes are reprod. in Miller 1937, no. 58, and Wadsworth 1945, no. 72. Milk pots are reprod. in Buhler/Hood 1970, II, no. 671; Failey 1976, p. 181; Warren et al. 1998, no. M51. Chased examples of both forms by de Riemer are reprod. in Waters/McKinsey/Ward 2000, I, no. 23.

3 Quimby/Johnson 1995, no. 232; *Antiques*, 110 (December 1976), p. 1164.

4 Ticher 1972, pls. 55a–b; Jackson 1911, II, pp. 968, 970. I am grateful to Robert Barker for bringing the Walker bowl to my attention.

5 Weygant 1907, p. 33.

6 NYCPR-1, liber 25, pp. 108–10.

77

Cann, 1770–76

Silver, h. 4 1/16 (10.3), diam. base 2 15/16 (7.5), diam. rim 2 13/16 (7.1), wt. 8 oz. 12 dwt. (268g)

MARK 9 twice on underside

INSCRIPTION: "SSC" (script) engraved on front

PROVENANCE: Samuel Cornell (1731–1781; cat. 131) and Susannah Mabson (1732–1778); subsequent ownership unknown prior to acquisition by the West Hartford, Connecticut, collector Philip Hammerslough before 1953.

Wadsworth Atheneum Museum of Art, Hartford, Connecticut; Philip H. Hammerslough Collection

All of the silver acquired from Myers by Samuel and Susannah Cornell has been dated to the time of their wedding in 1756.[1] In fact, only cat. 19 appears to have been purchased in the later 1750s. About a decade or so later, the Cornells returned to Myers to commission a significant group of silver objects. These pieces may have been acquired following Cornell's appointment to the Governor's Council in 1770, as the style of the pierced objects suggest they were made in the early years of that decade. The Cornells' purchases at this time also included an enormous London waiter of 1765–66 by Richard Rugg (77.1). Its large engraved monogram of their initials is similar to that engraved on this cann, the most modest among their purchases. The bread basket (cat. 78) was engraved with a monogram following a similar pattern, although it does not appear to have been executed by the same engraver.

1 Hood 1971, pp. 131–32; Heckscher/Bowman 1992, p. 122.

77.1

77

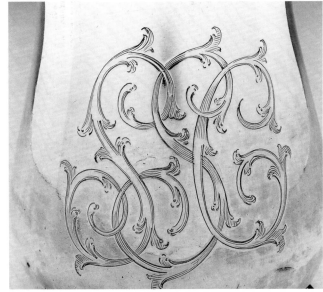

77.2

77.1 Richard Rugg, *Waiter*,
London, 1765–66.
Silver.
Tryon Palace Historic
Sites and Gardens,
New Bern, North Carolina.

78

Bread Basket, 1770–76

Silver, h. (to handle) 11¼ (28.6), h. (rim of basket) 4⅛ (10.5), w. 14½ (36.8), d. 11½ (29.2), wt. 41 oz. 3 dwt. (1280g)

MARK 9 once on underside

INSCRIPTION: "SSC" (script) engraved on inside bottom; "Wedding present given/Mrs. Herman LeRoy (Hannah Cornell)/19th October 1786" added later on underside

PROVENANCE: Samuel Cornell (1731–1781) and Susannah Mabson (1732–1778); to their daughter Hannah (1760–1818), who in 1786 married Herman LeRoy (1758–1841); by descent in the family to their great-great-granddaughter, Mary Augusta McCagg (b. 1895), by whom sold to The Metropolitan Museum of Art.[1]

The Metropolitan Museum of Art, New York; Morris K. Jesup Fund, 1954

Together with the following dish ring and bottle stands (cats. 79, 80), this pierced bread basket evokes the opulent lifestyle that Samuel and Susannah Cornell enjoyed before the American Revolution. Their bread basket is one of the few American-made examples of this form from the Colonial period, another being by Daniel Christian Fueter. As noted (p. 41), Fueter's bread basket may have inspired Myers's version, although Myers's basket is in a later style and probably was not made until after Fueter returned to Switzerland in 1769. The same craftsman who executed the Torah finials (cats. 63–65) may have done the piercing on Myers's basket, although he used a saw to pierce the basket, rather than the chisel used on the finials. Perhaps because this craftsman was trained as a chaser, his technique on the basket was somewhat unsure, and he had laid out and begun one section before he had to shift the design over (fig. 31).

The design of this basket follows London models with beaded, spiral ribs separating different pierced patterns that were made from the mid-1760s through the 1770s. English baskets with such features as the high foot formed from a pierced band, narrow gadrooned rim and base moldings, and feather-edge, geometric handle, date to the early 1770s.[2] The gadrooned rim on Myers's basket, its stylized shells, as well as its engraved monogram (fig. 25) may well have been influenced directly by the similar details on the Cornells' Rugg waiter of 1765–66 (77.1).

Most of the bread baskets owned in America were imported from or purchased in England. Silver baskets of this size apparently were an English innovation without Continental precedent. Examples were made beginning in the early seventeenth century, and by the middle of the eighteenth century they were being manufactured in large quantities by London workshops that specialized in their production.[3] Although these baskets were used to hold a variety of foods, fruits, and flowers, in English silversmith's accounts they were almost invariably referred to as "bread baskets."[4]

A number of Myers's patrons owned imported bread baskets. Shortly after their marriage in 1743, David and Margaret Franks (cat. 4) acquired a bread basket of 1744–45 by the renowned London silversmith Paul de Lamerie.[5] Catherine (McPhaedres) Livingston (cat. 38) owned a substantial bread basket weighing 51 oz. 2 dwt that was valued at £34.1.0 in her 1792 estate inventory.[6] In 1767, David Clarkson (cat. 27) asked a fellow merchant in London to procure "a handsom silver bread basket, open work . . . I would have it light and thin, so as to cost but little money."[7] Philip Schuyler (cat. 81) also owned a basket that may have been imported; the silversmith James Poupard charged him 8 shillings in 1776 for "Mending a Large Silver basquet of flowers In 24 different places."[8]

1 Pelletreau 1907, II, p. 141; *Harvard College* 1899, pp. 49–50; *Harvard Class* 1934, p. 170.
2 English baskets with these features include examples made by Edward Aldrige I in 1770–71 (Wees 1997, no. 107), William Plummer in 1772–73 (Argentum 1986, p. 8), William Plummer in 1773–74 (Puig et al. 1989, no. 90), as well as epergne baskets by Emick Romer in 1770–71 (Wees 1997, no. 121).
3 Kaellgren 2000, pp. 941–44.
4 Barr 1980, p. 130; Kaellgren 2000, p. 941; Puig et al. 1989, p. 89; Wees 1997, p. 189.
5 Dennis 1968, pp. 636–38.
6 New York Supreme Court of Probates Records, box 10, Inventories and Accounts, 1666–1822, NYSA.
7 *Clarksons* 1876, pp. 217–18. This may be the "large" bread basket that appeared in the inventory of David Clarkson's silver; ibid., p. 283.
8 Invoice, James Poupard to General Schuyler, February 1, 1776, Schuyler Papers, NYPL. The basket repaired by Poupard possibly may be the heavily repaired English basket of 1768 that descended in the Schuyler family and now is owned by the Schuyler Mansion in Albany; Cunningham 1955, no. 84.

79

Dish Ring, 1770–76

Silver, h. 4⁵⁄₁₆ (11), diam. base 8⅞ (22.5), diam. rim 7¾ (19.7), wt. 14 oz. 6 dwt. (445g)

MARK 9 twice on exterior flanking central monogram

INSCRIPTION: "SSC" (script) engraved on front

PROVENANCE: Samuel Cornell (1731–1781) and Susannah Mabson (1732–1778); to their daughter Elizabeth (1764–1854), who in 1783 married William Bayard, Jr. (d. 1826); to their great-great-great-granddaughter Justine Van Rensselaer (Barber) Hooper, by whom sold to Francis P. Garvan in 1936.[1]

Yale University Art Gallery, New Haven; Mabel Brady Garvan Collection

The only extant example of this form marked by a Colonial American silversmith, this dish ring is also a personal statement made by Myer Myers at the height of his career as the

79.1

leading silversmith in New York. Dish rings were used on dining tables to support bowls or plates containing hot foods, probably more as a decorative element than as a means of protecting the table, which would have been covered with a tablecloth when hot foods were served. The form was uncommon in the American Colonies; not only is Myers's the only American example, but no Irish or English silver dish rings with American histories of ownership are known. The "Pewter Ring Stand" reported stolen from Isaac Seixas of New York in 1754 is a rare documentary reference to this form.[2]

Dish rings were never popular in England, where dish stands assumed a similar function (cat. 92). The rare dish rings made in England were lower and less elaborately ornamented than their Irish counterparts.[3] Some were fitted with spirit lamps like a dish stand: in 1771 the Earl of Carlisle ordered a "dish ring & lamp" from Parker and Wakelin at a cost of £10.16.9; a surviving example made in 1773–74 by Boulton and Fothergill of Birmingham has an integral lamp and wooden handle.[4]

The distinctive tall, spool-shape dish ring first appeared in Ireland in the 1730s, with the great majority of the surviving examples made in Dublin after 1760.[5] Published Irish dish rings fall primarily into two distinct groups: those with Rococo designs of scrollwork, garlands of flowers, and Chinese or shepherd figures that are entirely chased over the pierced work; and those with geometric patterns with limited areas of chased ornament.[6] Only a few Dublin dish rings of the 1770s exhibit the type of abstract, scrolling pattern found on Myers's dish ring, and then usually as a border or subsidiary pattern rather than as the dominant motif.[7]

Like the Cornells' bread basket, the dish ring was made using the saw-piercing technique. The piercer's lack of skill is evident in some roughly shaped areas and unfinished edges. Nevertheless, the dish ring's unique design undoubtedly was intended to match the Cornells' bread basket. Quatrefoils, S-curves, and interlaced lozenges appear as motifs on both objects. The openwork design scatters light across the ring's surface, creating a glittering effect, and also makes it seem delicate and airy, despite its large size. The use of these and other techniques to diminish the overall mass of forms was typical of the later Rococo style. The large S-curves repeated around the dish ring's midsection may also have been a witty allusion to the names of Samuel and Susannah Cornell, whose initials were engraved on a heart at the center of the design; an upside-down heart shape appears at center of each pair of S's. The interlaced lozenge motif may also have functioned as a kind of signature on the dish ring, since it appeared in Myers's written signature in 1744 as well as on a porringer handle made in his workshop (cat. 46).[8]

Myers also marked the dish ring in a very personal way. By striking his surname mark twice, he not only signed the work but also reinforced the identity of his surname as the double of his given name, something more characteristic of Ashkenazic Jews, who lacked conventional English family names (p. 27). Moreover, by placing his surname mark on the small reserves flanking the Cornells' monogram—that is, on the "front" where anyone looking at this dish ring would see them— Myers claimed this exceptional object as his own creation and asserted his equality, as a Jew and as a "mechanic," with the wealthy patrons of his labor. Other objects made in his workshop that were exceptional either as unusual forms or for extraordinary ornament feature his surname mark in promi-

nent locations (cats. 38, 56), although none with such proximity to the owner's name or initials.

1 Cornell 1902, p. 381; Reynolds 1914, I, p. 14; II, pp. 846–47, III, p. 1105; Barrett 1872, II, pp. 169–73; Justine V.R. Hooper to Francis Hill Bigelow, November 20, 1929, and Roger F. Hooper to Francis P. Garvan, December 31, 1936, accession file 1936.136, American Arts Office, YUAG.

2 *The New-York Gazette or Weekly Post-Boy*, March 18, 1754, p. 4. John Marshall Phillips referred to "numerous references to them in advertisements of imported plate," but the present author has been unable to locate these references; Phillips 1949, p. 98.

3 Clayton 1971, fig. 243; Ticher 1972, pls. 66, 67, 93.

4 Rowe 1965, fig. 54; what seems to be the same object is reprod. in Delieb/Roberts 1971, facing p. 89.

5 Jackson 1911, II, pp. 933–39.

6 See the dish rings illustrated in Jackson 1911, II, figs. 1248–56; Hackenbroch 1969, no. 188; Ticher 1972, pls. 68–83, 89–92; Bennett 1976, fig. 10; Teahan 1979, pl. 38; Teahan 1982, nos. 37, 43; Davis 1992, no. 38; Lomax 1992, nos. 87, 88.

7 Jackson 1911, II, fig. 1252; Ticher 1972, pls. 82, 83, 89; Teahan 1982, no. 43.

8 Reprod. in Rosenbaum 1954A, p. 28.

80

Pair of Bottle Stands, 1770–76

Silver and mahogany with wool felt, h. 2 (5), diam. base 5 (12.6) each

MARK 9 once on back of central reserve

INSCRIPTION: "SSC" (script) engraved on front

PROVENANCE: Samuel Cornell (1731–1781) and Susannah Mabson (1732–1778); to their daughter Sarah (1762–1803), who in 1792 married Matthew Clarkson (1758–1825), the son of David and Elizabeth (French) Clarkson (cat. 27); by descent in the family to John Jay Pierrepont (b. 1958), by whom sold at auction in 1996.[1]

Collection of Ruth J. Nutt

Bottle stands first appeared in England in the mid-1750s, accommodating both the introduction of straight-sided wine bottles as well as the new custom of removing the tablecloth before the dessert course.[2] The wool felt or other fabric applied to the undersides allowed the stands to slide, or "coast," on the uncovered table; hence the terms "coaster" or "bottle slides" advertised in 1783 by Myers's former partner Benjamin Halsted.[3] One of the earliest American references to the form was an advertisement by the Philadelphia silversmith Edmund Milne, who in 1764 imported from London "neat pierced and polished silver coasters or bottle stands."[4] What may be a bottle in a bottle stand appears at the center of the table in George Roupell's drawing of a drinking scene in South Carolina in about 1760 (8-9.1). The New York merchant Isaac Gouverneur, Jr., owned "6 do. [silver] bottle stands" in 1786.[5]

This pair of bottle stands is identical to the pair made for the Schuyler family (cat. 81), except for the original twist base moldings, which have been replaced on the Schuyler pair. The

two pairs are the only extant versions of the form marked by an American silversmith in the Colonial period. As noted (p. 56), these bottle stands were made by a more accomplished craftsman than the bread basket or dish ring (cats. 78, 79). His pierced work is more delicate and very carefully finished, with no saw marks easily visible. It is possible that the bottle stands may have been executed by a different piercer in Myers's shop, and that the Cornells acquired them at a different date from cats. 78 and 79, although the "SSC" monograms were executed by the same engraver as the dish ring.

Myers may also have imported them from England for resale, although no traces of English hallmarks appear on either pair of bottle stands, and Myers's mark is struck only once on each object. These bottle stands are similar to English pierced work of the late 1760s and 1770s, and the quality of their execution more closely resembles that of London work than the bread basket or dish ring. A London cruet frame of 1769–70 exhibits a very similar piercing pattern, wavy rim, and twist molding at the base.[6] Closely related bottle stands were made in London in 1772–73 by Charles Aldridge and Henry Green and in 1774–75 by Robert Hennell.[7] A cream pail with similar pattern was marked Philip Freeman in 1773–74.[8]

1 Christie's 1996, lot 125.

2 Brown 1996, pp. 525–26.

3 *The Pennsylvania Gazette*, August 27, 1783, p. 3.

4 *The Pennsylvania Journal*, November 8, 1764, as cited in Prime 1929, p. 82.

5 NYCIR-1, box 12, Gouverneur file.

6 Jackson 1911, II, p. 843.

7 Wees 1997, no. 56; Clayton 1985, p. 233, fig. 8.

8 Clayton 1985, p. 222, fig. 10.

81

Bottle Stand
ONE OF A PAIR, 1770–76

Silver and mahogany with wool felt, h. 2⅛ (5.4), diam. rim 5 1/16 (12.9)

MARK 9 once on back of shield

ARMORIAL: Schuyler crest (a falcon close) engraved on front of shield[1]

PROVENANCE: probably Philip Schuyler (1733–1804) and Catherine Van Rensselaer (1734–1803), who were married in 1755; by descent to their grandson, George Lee Schuyler (1811–1890) or great-granddaughter Eliza (Hamilton) Schuyler (1811–1863), first cousins who married in 1835; by bequest in Eliza Schuyler's will: "In division of silver which shall be equally divided in value, those pieces which belonged to their [her children's] great-grandfather General Philip Schuyler shall be placed by my executors in the share of my son Philip"; to their son, Philip Schuyler (1836–1906), the donor.[2]

The New-York Historical Society; Bequest of Major Philip Schuyler

Like the preceding examples, the silver elements of this object were composed of three identical, openwork sections pierced with a fretsaw and finished with files. The careful finishing of

this bottle stand and its mate, as well as the design of the piercing, is identical to the Cornell pair (cat. 80). The provenance of this bottle stand and its mate suggests that they belonged to General Philip Schuyler and his wife, Catherine Van Rensselaer of New York and Albany. They had been patrons of Halsted and Myers in 1760 (see Appendix II, no. 1), although these stands were made about a decade later. Their wavy, gadrooned rims and flowering foliate patterns relate closely to English bottle stands and other pierced objects of the late 1760s and early 1770s (cats. 110, 123).

1 Bolton 1964, p. 145.
2 Westchester County Probate Records, liber 47, p. 103, Westchester County Archives, Elmsford, New York; Cunningham 1955, pp. 140–41; Christoph 1987, pp. 151–52; Christoph 1992, pp. 146–47.

82

Waiter, 1772–76

Silver, h. 1 (2.5), diam. 7 11/16 (19.5), wt. 9 oz. 19 dwt. (310g)

MARK 9 once on underside

INSCRIPTION: "Lucretia Brinckerhoff" (script) added on underside, probably in the nineteenth century

PROVENANCE: Lucretia (Brinckerhoff) Lefferts (1747–1800); by gift or bequest to her niece, Lucretia Lefferts Brinckerhoff; by descent in her family, together with cat. 84; sold in the twentieth century to the antiques dealer Harry Arons of Ansonia, Connecticut; sold at auction by his widow's estate in 1988.[1]

Private collection

On April 21, 1772, Lucretia Brinckerhoff married Jacobus Lefferts, Jr., a wealthy merchant and business associate of Henry Remsen, whose niece Dorothea Remsen would marry Lucretia's brother Abraham in December 1772. This plain waiter, a form made in considerable quantity in Myers's workshop during the later 1760s and 1770s (cat. 58), probably was purchased at this time. As Jacobus and Lucretia Lefferts had no children, Lucretia made her brother and sister-in-law's children, two of whom were named for their aunt and uncle, the principal beneficiaries of her will of May 17, 1800.[2] Several specific bequests of silver were made:

to the said Maria [(Brinckerhoff)] *Remsen, my two silver sauceboats marked M B* [presumably for her mother, Maria (Van Deursen) Brinckerhoff], *and to the said Lucretia Lefferts Brinckerhoff, my silver tea-pot marked L B and to my nephew James Lefferts Brinckerhoff, my silver tankard and silver castor marked with the name of my deceased husband; the residue of my plate I give to my said three nieces Maria Remsen*[,] *Lucretia Lefferts Brinckerhoff and Jane Brinckerhoff, to be equally divided among them.*[3]

This waiter may well be part of the "residue of plate" that

Lucretia Lefferts Brinckerhoff inherited from her aunt and namesake, and the name engraved on it memorialized this relationship. Lucretia also inherited the waiter with her father's monogram (cat. 83).

1 Christie's 1988, lot 74.
2 Bergen 1878, p. 60.
3 NYCPR-1, IV, liber 43, pp. 252–55.

83

Waiter, 1772–76

Silver, h. 1 1/4 (3.2), diam. 8 1/2 (21.6), wt. 14 oz. 9 dwt. (449g) (scratch wt. 14 oz. 17 dwt.)

MARK 9 twice on underside

INSCRIPTION: "AB" (script) engraved on front

PROVENANCE: Abraham Brinckerhoff (1745–1823); to his daughter Lucretia (1786–1851), who married John S. Schermerhorn (1776–1844); by descent in the Schermerhorn family to the present owner.

Collection of Mrs. Sheila Schermerhorn Scott

Abraham Brinckerhoff (cat. 137) and his elder sister, Lucretia (cat. 82), married within eight months of each other in 1772. They apparently purchased the same model of waiter from Myers at about the same time, perhaps using some of their shares of the estate of their father, Joris (George) Brinckerhoff, who died in 1768.[1] Abraham chose to have an elaborate script monogram (fig. 26) engraved on the front of his waiter, thereby customizing a routine form and also identifying the family whose wealth had purchased it. A small beaker marked by Myers engraved with an "AB" monogram in Rococo foliage may also have been made for him.[2]

The craftsman who executed the waiter's monogram and its Rococo frame also executed the monogram on the bread basket made contemporaneously in Myers's workshop (cat. 78). In comparison to the engraving on the Van Wyck waiter (cat. 56), the frame surrounding this monogram is stiffly symmetrical in design, and the execution features uniform lines with short rows of dots used as accents in both the letters and frame. The frame's design is strikingly similar to the frame enclosing the scene of a peace treaty at the top of a presentation certificate engraved in Philadelphia for Sir William Johnson in 1770 by the London-trained engraver Henry Dawkins (fig. 27). Dawkins had returned to New York by 1774, and it is possible that he was the craftsman who engraved this waiter.[3]

1 NYCPR-1, liber 26, pp. 381–83.
2 Sotheby's 2000, lot 135.
3 Heckscher/Bowman 1992, p. 39.

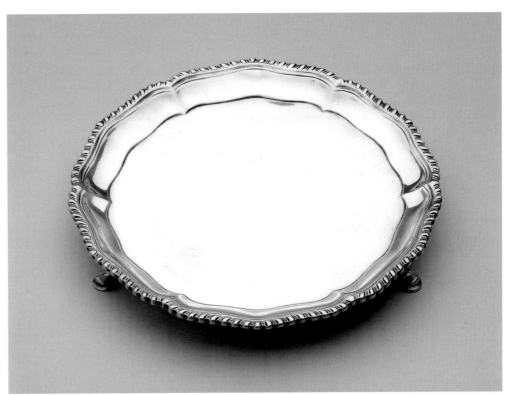

82

83

84

84

Pair of Sauceboats, 1772–76

Silver, h. 3¾ (9.5), w. 7⅛ (18.1), d. 3⅝ (9.2), wt. 8 oz. 4 dwt. (255g) each

MARK 9 once on underside of each

INSCRIPTION: "ABR:ᴹ BRINCKERHOFF" engraved in a semicircle on underside of each

PROVENANCE: Abraham Brinckerhoff (1745–1823); by descent in the family, together with cat. 82; by sale in the twentieth century to the antiques dealer Harry Arons of Ansonia, Connecticut; sold at auction by his widow's estate in 1988.[1]

Collection of Barbara and Roy Zuckerberg

None of the surviving silver owned by Abraham and Dorothea Brinckerhoff was engraved with both their names or initials. There was a clear distinction between the objects each of them brought to the marriage. Abraham's father, George, had died in 1768, four years before his son's wedding, and his will had directed: "all my Plate I bequeath to be equally divided among my Wife and Children, each one fourth Part, and if they cannot agree upon the Distribution, I order that also to be sold at a public vendue."[2] It is possible that Abraham

received these sauceboats in this division of property, but given the presence of Myers's MARK 9, they probably were commissioned at the time of his marriage in 1772.

Although distinct from Myers's sauceboats of the later 1750s (cat. 18), the Brinckerhoff sauceboats are stylistically conservative. English sauceboats with the same handle design were made in England as early as 1736–37 by Peter Archambo I and in 1739–40 by David Willaume II.[3] By the 1760s, London sauceboats with the same handle were more delicate in appearance, with smaller bodies, gadrooned rims, and shell feet; Pieter de Riemer marked a striking sauceboat of this design in New York after 1765.[4] Brinckerhoff apparently preferred the more substantial bodies and solid appearance of earlier versions of the form.

1 Christie's 1988, lot 75.
2 NYCPR-1, liber 26, p. 381.
3 Hartop 1996, nos. 35, 38; McFadden/Clark 1989, no. 18.
4 Jackson 1911, II, p. 824; Davis 1976, no. 164; Buhler/Hood 1970, II, no. 687.

85

Sugar Dish, 1772–76

Silver, h. 6¾ (17.1), diam. base 3¹⁄₁₆ (9.2), diam. rim 3 (7.6), wt. 8 oz. 19 dwt. (278.7g)

MARK 9 twice on underside of bowl, one double-struck

INSCRIPTIONS: "DR" (script) engraved within cartouche on front

PROVENANCE: Dorothea (Remsen) Brinckerhoff (1750–1834); by descent in the family to the present owners.

Collection of David M. Brinckerhoff, Nelson F. Brinckerhoff, Peter R. Brinckerhoff, and Robert W. Brinckerhoff, and their families; on long-term loan to The Metropolitan Museum of Art, New York

86

ATTRIBUTED TO MYER MYERS

Milk Pot, 1772–76

Silver, h. 5⁹⁄₁₆ (13.5), w. 4¹³⁄₁₆ (12.2), diam. base 2¼ (5.7), wt. 5 oz. 9 dwt. (169.8g)

Unmarked

INSCRIPTIONS: "DR" (script) engraved within cartouche on front

PROVENANCE: Dorothea (Remsen) Brinckerhoff (1750–1834); by descent in the family to the present owners.

Collection of David M. Brinckerhoff, Nelson F. Brinckerhoff, Peter R. Brinckerhoff, and Robert W. Brinckerhoff, and their families; on long-term loan to The Metropolitan Museum of Art, New York

Engraved with Dorothea Remsen's (cat. 136) maiden initials, this matching sugar dish and milk pot probably were acquired at the time of her marriage with a legacy from her father, who had died the previous year. In his will, Peter Remsen specified, "when any of my children are married or come of age, my wife may give to them such an outset and sums of money as may put them into a way of Business."[1] The two objects were used with an English coffeepot made a decade earlier (cat. 122), thereby creating a coffee service out of objects with similar chased ornament by the addition of identical engraved monograms. As noted (p. 164), there clearly was an interest in having matching silver tea equipage during the early 1770s. An unlocated ladle marked by Myers was engraved with the same "DR" monogram and presumably was purchased from his workshop at the same time.[2]

This milk pot and sugar dish are one of only two sets with chased ornament made in Myers's workshop that can be connected to their original owners. The set differs markedly from the other milk pot and sugar dish sets produced by Myers, such as that made for William and Anna Sackett (cats. 71, 72), which represent an earlier form updated with chasing. Unlike the low covers and ring handles on the other sugar dishes, the Remsen sugar dish has taller proportions, a high domed cover, and a finial. Its design is closer to English Rococo models, including a sugar dish by Christopher Makemeid of 1759–60, and presages the domed covers popular in New York after the Revolutionary War (cat. 117).[3]

Unlike the Sackett set, the Remsen sugar dish and milk pot were chased and engraved by different craftsmen. This may be explained by a rush order, for which different workmen in Myers's shop were used to help meet a deadline. It is also possible, however, that the two objects were not made or acquired at same time. Although unmarked, the milk pot probably was made in Myers's workshop, as its engraving and chasing were executed by Myers's preferred specialist craftsmen, and its spiral handle is identical to those found on other milk pots by Myers. Another indication that the two were made in the same workshop at the same time is that the more skilled craftsmen executed the engraved and chased decoration on the milk pot, which was more likely to be handled by its users than the sugar dish. The same distinction between the quality of the chasing is present in the set by William Gilbert (cats. 112, 113).

1 NYCPR-1, liber 28, p. 31.
2 Sotheby's 1983, lot 130.
3 The present pinecone finial is a replacement, although the chased decoration around the hole in the cover indicates that a finial of this type originally was present. The Makemeid sugar dish is reprod. Sotheby's 1991, lot 292; I am grateful to Robert B. Barker for this reference. A typical English sugar dish with a domed cover was made in 1759–60 by Samuel Taylor; Banister 1965, p. 93.

87

Cann, 1765–76

Silver, h. 5³⁄₁₆ (13.2), w. 5½ (14), diam. base 3⅝ (9.2), diam. rim 3⅜ (8.6), wt. 14 oz. 3 dwt. (439g) (scratch weight 14 oz. 5 dwt. [5 crossed out])

MARK 9 twice on underside

INSCRIPTIONS: "JS" (script) engraved on front; "JS" scratched on underside

PROVENANCE: John Stevenson (1735–1810) and Magdalena Douw (1750–1817), who were married about 1771; to their daughter Anne (1774–1821), who in 1813 became the second wife of Major General Pierre Van Cortlandt II (1762–1831); by descent to their great-great-granddaughter Catherine (Mason) Browne (b. 1911), the donor in 1995.[1]

Albany Institute of History and Art; Gift of Mrs. Robert P. Browne

The great majority of Myers's canns have the bellied shape and double-scroll handle seen on this example. Its owner, John Stevenson, was a neighbor in Albany of Philip Livingston (cat. 129), and the two were joint tenants of property on the Mohawk River. Stevenson may have emulated the Livingstons' patronage of Myers in purchasing this cann, although his own patronage of Myers was limited to smaller, relatively simple forms (see cat. 119). After Stevenson's death, it was noted in that he "had a valuable collection of silver, among which were several tankards of great age."[2]

1 Pearson 1872, p. 106; Reynolds 1914, III, pp. 1404–05.
2 Kinnear 1903, pp. 7–9; a portrait of John Stevenson faces p. 8.

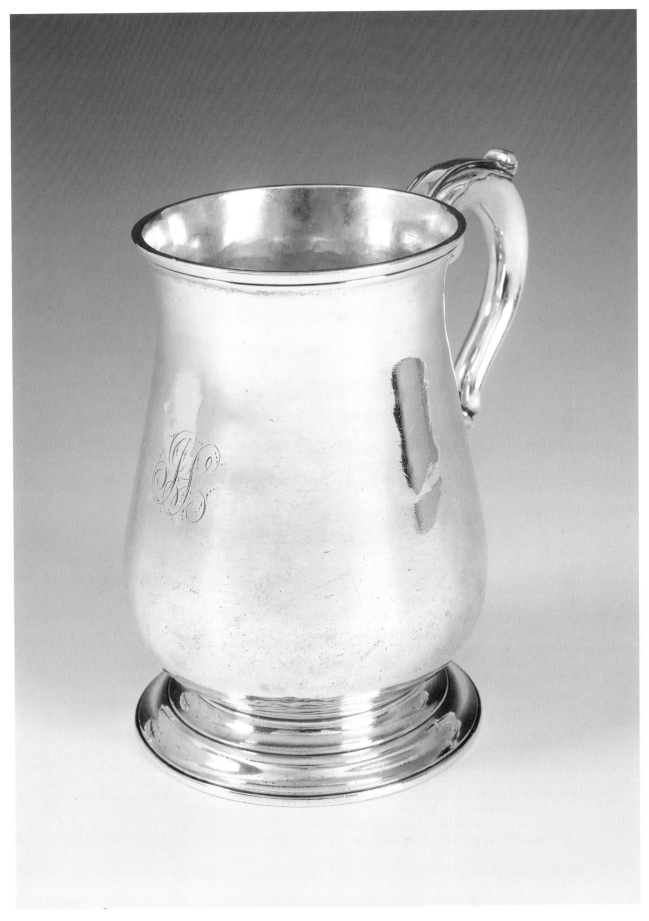

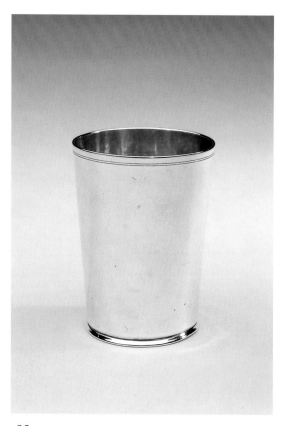

88

89

88
Beaker

FROM A SET OF SIX, 1770–76 or 1784–95

Silver, h. 4¹⁄₁₆ (10.3), diam. base 2½ (6.4), diam. rim 3⅛ (7.9), wt. 5 oz. 6 dwt. (165g)

MARK 9 once on underside

INSCRIPTION: "M/I R" engraved on underside; "SM" scratched on underside; "Lionel Moses./FROM/UNCLE ISAAC/April 16th 1871." added later on outside (not shown)

PROVENANCE: Isaac Moses (1742–1818) and Reyna Levy (1753–1824), who were married in 1770; together with cats. 89 and 90, to their son Solomon Moses ("SM"; 1774–1857); to his son Isaac (1807–1847); to his nephew Lionel Moses (1825–1895); subsequent ownership unknown prior to acquisition before 1954 by the Boston collector Mark Bortman; to his daughter, Jane (Bortman) Larus, by whom sold to the present owner.[1]

Collection of Eric Noah

1 Stern 1991, pp. 209, 264; Rosenbaum 1954A, p. 102; "Early American" 1954, no. 33.

89
Two Beakers

FROM A SET OF SIX, 1770–76 or 1784–95

Silver, h. 4 (10.2), diam. base 2½ (6.4), diam. rim 3³⁄₁₆ (8.1) each, wt. A. 5 oz. 6 dwt. (165.2g), B. 5 oz. 9 dwt. (169.6g)

MARK 9 once on underside of both, double-struck on A

INSCRIPTION: "M/I R" engraved on underside of both; "SM" scratched on underside of B

PROVENANCE: Isaac Moses (1742–1818) and Reyna Levy (1753–1824), who were married in 1770; to their son Solomon Moses ("SM"; 1774–1857) together with cats. 88 and 90; subsequent ownership unknown until purchase in 1949 by Henry Francis du Pont from the dealers Ginsburg and Levy of New York.[1]

Henry Francis du Pont Winterthur Museum, Delaware; Gift of H.F. du Pont, 1965

1 Quimby/Johnson 1995, p. 270.

90

90

Three Beakers

FROM A SET OF SIX, 1770–76 or 1784–95

Silver, h. 4¹⁄₁₆ (10.3), diam. base 2½ (6.4), diam. rim 3⅛ (7.9), wt. 5 oz. 9 dwt. (170g) each

MARK 9 once on underside on each

INSCRIPTION: "M/I R" engraved on underside of all three; "SM" scratched on underside of one; "Keep for Sally for her only" scratched on underside of one

PROVENANCE: Isaac Moses (1742–1818) and Reyna Levy (1753–1824), who were married in 1770; to their son Solomon Moses ("SM"; 1774–1857) together with cats. 88 and 89; to his son Isaac (1807–1847); to his nephew, Lionel Moses (1825–1895); to his son, Lionel Moses, Jr. (1870–1931), by whom sold or given to an architectural client, Josephine (Ettlinger) McFadden; to her son, the donor.[1]

The Metropolitan Museum of Art, New York; Gift of Mr. and Mrs. Louis E. McFadden, 1980

Made for Myers's niece and her husband, Reyna and Isaac Moses (cat. 141), the simple design and small size of these beakers is characteristic of the silver Myers produced for his family and fellow Jews. Their utilitarian quality makes it difficult to date them with certainty. In both Europe and America, beakers had been a traditional drinking vessel during the seventeenth and eighteenth centuries, but went out of fashion during the third quarter of the eighteenth century.[2] Low beakers of this type became popular again in America after the Revolutionary War, when they gradually replaced canns and mugs as the most common drinking vessel in silver; another example by Myers may have been made for Abraham Brinckerhoff (see cat. 83).

1 Obituary for Lionel Moses, Jr., *The New York Times*, February 20, 1931, p. 21; curatorial file 1980.501.1–3, The Metropolitan Museum of Art, New York.
2 Rosenbaum 1954A, p. 101.

188 MYER MYERS

91

Cruet Stand, 1765–76

Silver, h. 9¼ (23.5), w. 7⅝ (19.4), d. 7⅝ (19.4), wt. 22 oz. 13 dwt. (705g)

MARK 9 four times: twice on handle and twice on upper surface of bottom

PROVENANCE: unknown prior to 1987, when acquired by The Metropolitan Museum of Art from the dealers Bernard and S. Dean Levy of New York, by whom advertised as from the "Ludlow-Van Buren family of New York."[1]

The Metropolitan Museum of Art, New York; Gift of Mr. and Mrs. Robert G. Goelet, 1987

Cruet stands holding two cruets (or bottles) and three casters for such condiments as oil, vinegar, pepper, and dry mustard became an indispensable accouterment of dining in England by the middle of the eighteenth century. As James Lomax has observed, they probably were kept on side tables or sideboards and passed by servants during the meal.[2] The form was a smaller and less formal version of the elaborate silver centerpiece with casters and other implements that had been popular at the beginning of the eighteenth century, such as the "Warwick" cruet supplied in 1715 by the London silversmith Anthony Nelme to Baron Brooke of Warwick Castle.[3]

This is the only extant cruet stand by Myers. In July 1760, Halsted and Myers sold Catherine (Van Rensselaer) Schuyler "1 polish'd Silver cruit stand with casters & Cruits" weighing 44 oz. 17 dwt., together with "2 fine cut glass cruits & mustard glass" (see Appendix II, no. 1). It is not known whether the silver components of the Schuyler cruet were made by Halsted and Myers or imported together with the cut-glass cruets. The large-scale production of English specialists such as Samuel Wood (cat. 121) would have left Colonial American makers with less incentive to create their own versions of this form. On the few surviving examples, including one by Daniel Christian Fueter (cat. 106), only the frames were marked by the American silversmith, whereas the casters and silver fittings for the cruets were made in London. Only a few inverted pyriform casters with pierced covers have survived with Myers's mark.[4]

Myers's cruet stand is simpler and less accomplished than the versions by Wood and Fueter. The scrolled vertical supports have been attached almost at right angles to the handle, diminishing the lively silhouette seen on the others. The cast Rococo cartouche, feet, and handle are also less sophisticated, although they may have been taken from a less distinguished English cruet stand. The same handle design, with better quality chasing, was found on cruet stands made in London in 1762–63 by Jabez Daniell and in Philadelphia after 1755 by John David.[5]

1 Levy/Levy 1988, p. 109.
2 Lomax 1992, p. 95.
3 Buttery 1989, p. 142.
4 An example examined by the author was most recently sold at auction in 1991; Sotheby's 1991, lot 126. Unverified examples that have been published are listed in Rosenbaum 1954A, p. 107.
5 Christie's 1990, lot 112; Quimby/Johnson 1995, no. 334. I am grateful to Robert Barker for the former reference and his suggestion that Daniell is the maker of this stand.

92

Dish Stand, 1770–76 or 1784–95

Silver, h. 3 1/16 (7.8), outside w./d. 10 13/16 (27.5), wt. 11 oz. 3 dwt. (347g)

MARK 9 five times, once on each leg just above foot, and once on one scrolled dish support

ARMORIAL: crest (a winged spur) engraved on one arm; repeatedly published as the Bancker family crest, but also used in New York by the Johnston family (cat. 98)[1]

PROVENANCE: unknown prior to acquisition before 1954 by the collector Vincent D. Andrus of New York City; by sale to Walter M. Jeffords, the donor in 1960.[2]

Yale University Art Gallery, New Haven; John Marshall Phillips Collection

Few dish stands have survived with the marks of American silversmiths working before the Revolutionary War; among these rare examples is the one by William Hollingshead of Philadelphia.[3] The form was imported into America as early as 1763, when Edmund Milne advertised "ex's, with sliders and lamps for dish stands."[4] Robert and Catherine (McPhaedres) Livingston (cat. 38) owned a "cross" weighing 9 oz. 9 dwt. that

probably was imported, like much of their plate.[5] Myers's dish stand, now lacking its lamp, is identical to English examples of the 1760s and 1770s by London makers who specialized in pierced work, such as Samuel Herbert and William Plummer.[6] It is possible that Myers made this object using castings from an imported English dish stand, but given the marks on each foot, it is also possible that he simply overstruck the hallmarks on an English piece. The date that Myers made or sold this dish stand is uncertain. Although the closest English prototypes date to the 1770s, a pair of tankards engraved with the same crest was made in the 1780s or early 1790s for David and Magdalen Johnston (cat. 98) and the dish stand may have been acquired by them at the same time.

1 For identification of the crest with Bancker, see Rosenbaum 1954A, p. 112, and Buhler/Hood 1970, II, p. 103. For identification with Johnston, see Bolton 1964, p. 93, and Fairbairn 1992, pl. 59, no. 1.
2 Rosenbaum 1954A, p. 112.
3 Eberlein/Hubbard 1940, p. 12.
4 The Pennsylvania Journal and Weekly Advertiser, December 15, 1763, p. 1.
5 New York Supreme Court of Probates Records, box 10, Inventories and Accounts, 1666–1822, NYSA.
6 Clayton 1985, p. 204, fig. 3; Jackson 1911, II, pp. 939–40, fig. 1257.

93

Teaspoon, 1776–79

Norwalk, Connecticut

Silver, l. 4 1/4 (10.8), wt. 5 dwt. (7.7g)

MARK 7 twice on underside of handle

INSCRIPTION: "B/HF" engraved on underside of handle

PROVENANCE: Hannah Finch (1730–1782), who married Stephen Benedict (1731–1809) as his second wife in 1763; to their daughter, Jemima (1774–1859), who married Luke Keeler in 1793; to their great-great-granddaughter, the donor in 1982.[1]

Yale University Art Gallery, New Haven; Gift of Katharine Atwater Folds in memory of Josephine Setze

This teaspoon is the only object so far identified as being made during Myers's three-year residence in Norwalk, Connecticut, during the Revolutionary War. Both Stephen and Hannah Benedict were lifelong residents of the Canaan Society of Norwalk (now New Canaan), where Stephen worked as a surveyor and tax collector.[2] The three initials engraved on the back of this spoon atypically refer to Hannah (Finch) Benedict by both her maiden and married initials, although this arrangement usually featured the initials of a married couple.

Myers was active as a silversmith during his exile; in 1779, after Tryon's raid left Norwalk in ruins, he and his brother Asher were reported to have lost "a very considerable part of their tools" (p. 63). Like most of Myers's extant flatware, this teaspoon is in the simple pattern known today as "Hanover-

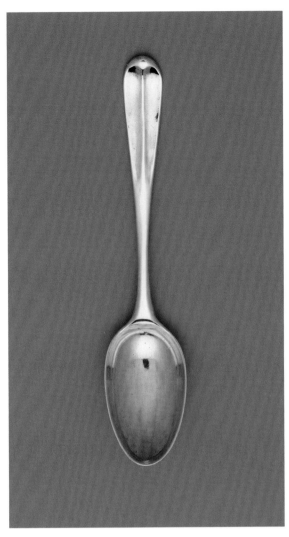

93

Tankard, 1779–83
Stratford, Connecticut

Silver, h. 6⁹⁄₁₆ (16.7), w. 7¼ (18.4), diam. base 5⅛ (13), diam. rim 4 (10.2), wt. 27 oz. 13 dwt. (860g) (scratch wt. 28 oz.)

MARK 9 twice on underside of body and once on underside of cover

INSCRIPTION: "DS" (script) engraved on cover; "JS" added later on handle flanking drop below hinge; "DDH" scratched on underside after 1926

PROVENANCE: Daniel Shelton ("DS"; 1737–1813), who married Mehitable Shelton (1747–1812) in 1760; to their daughter Jane ("JS"; 1761–1830), who in 1781 married Samuel Edwards (1758–1838) of Fairfield, Connecticut; by descent to their great-great-grandson, Appleton Glanius, by whom sold in 1926 to the silver collector Paul Mascarene Hamlen (1874–1939) of Wayland, Massachusetts; to his widow, Dorothy (Draper) Hamlen Gannett ("DDH"), by whom sold at auction in 1946, when purchased by the Boston collector Mark Bortman; by descent to his daughter, Jane (Bortman) Larus, by whom sold to the donors in 1979.[1]

Toledo Museum of Art, Ohio; Gift of Mr. and Mrs. Stanley K. Levison

As the only piece of hollow ware that can be stated with certainty to have been made during Myers's residence in Connecticut during the Revolutionary War, this tankard exemplifies the kind of objects he produced without the specialist craftsman who worked with him in New York. He apparently had at least one trained silversmith, John Burger, working with him in Stratford (cat. 117), and he may have had other assistants. Myers clearly was able to work with most techniques, including casting the thumbpiece and drop on the handle, and drawing the base molding. As noted (p. 63), however, the "DS" monogram (fig. 34) engraved on the tankard's cover is simple and somewhat old-fashioned in comparison to much of the engraving found on Myers's late Colonial silver. It may reflect Myers's own efforts at a task he formerly had assigned to specialists.

The tankard also reflects the influence of a New England patron on a New York craftsman. It is unique among Myers's versions of this popular form: although its broad proportions and lack of midband are typical of New York tankards, its domed cover undoubtedly reflects the influence of local taste for New England tankards with this feature. Elias Pelletreau was called upon to make tankards with "high tops" in Southampton, Long Island, which was settled largely by families from Connecticut.[2] A similar shift in style was seen fifty years earlier in silver made by Cornelius Kierstede of New York after his move to New Haven in 1724.[3]

This tankard was made for Daniel Shelton, a merchant who lived at Booth's Hill near the town of Huntington, Connecticut, about eight miles north of Stratford. His grandfather of the same name had emigrated from Yorkshire to Stratford and became a prominent merchant, marrying Elizabeth Welles,

ian" (see cat. 4). This style apparently appealed to Myers's New England clients; a tablespoon possibly made during his subsequent residence in Stratford, Connecticut, is in this same pattern.[3]

1 Benedict 1870, pp. 30–31; Bailey 1899, p. 23; Allen 1907, pp. 173, 213.
2 Benedict 1870, p. 30.
3 Collection of Mrs. Todd Lovell; see p. 63.

192 MYER MYERS

the daughter of Governor Samuel Welles. The distribution of the elder Shelton's estate after his widow's death in 1747 amounted to over £8,000.[4]

1 *Reunion* 1877, pp. 64–65; Appleton Glanius, Statement of Provenance, October 6, 1926, Toledo Museum of Art curatorial files; *NCAB* 1958, p. 165; Parke-Bernet 1946, lot 175.
2 Failey 1971, pp. 77–81.
3 Bohan/Hammerslough 1970, pp. 12–13; Puig et al. 1989, p. 140.
4 Cutter et al. 1911, IV, pp. 2152–53.

95

Milk Pot, 1784–85

Silver, h. 5 1/16 (12.9), w. 3 3/4 (9.6), d. 2 7/8 (7.3), wt. 4 oz. 8 dwt. (136g)

MARK 9 once on underside

INSCRIPTION: "M*C" engraved on underside

PROVENANCE: Mary Cornell (d. 1786), who in 1780 married Elijah Pell (d. 1798); by descent in the family to their great-great-granddaughter, Evelyn (Foster) Olds, the donor's wife.[1]

Yale University Art Gallery, New Haven; Gift of Irving S. Olds, B.A. 1907, in memory of Evelyn Foster Olds, for the John Marshall Phillips Collection.

If the family history of ownership is correct, this milk pot would have been one of the earliest productions of Myers's workshop after his return to New York in December 1783, as Mary (Cornell) Pell died prior to May 2, 1786.[2] The daughter of Richard and Phebe (Doughty) Cornell of Flushing, Long Island, Mary was the first cousin of Samuel Cornell (cat. 131) and Martha (Cornell) Thorne (cat. 13). The style of her milk pot is remarkably conservative, essentially the same as milk pots made thirty years earlier, including one possibly made for her cousin Martha (cats. 11, 13). It is the only extant example of this form struck with MARK 9. The milk pot may have been a leftover piece of prewar stock that Myers had retained or recovered after he returned to New York.

1 Cornell 1902, pp. 169–70; Underhill 1874, p. 187; Pierce 1899, pp. 622–23, 668.
2 Mary apparently had died by the time her mother Phebe Cornell's will was signed on May 2, 1786, as it mentions only Phebe's daughters Phebe and Anne and her granddaughter Mary Pell; NYCPR-1, liber 40, pp. 12–15.

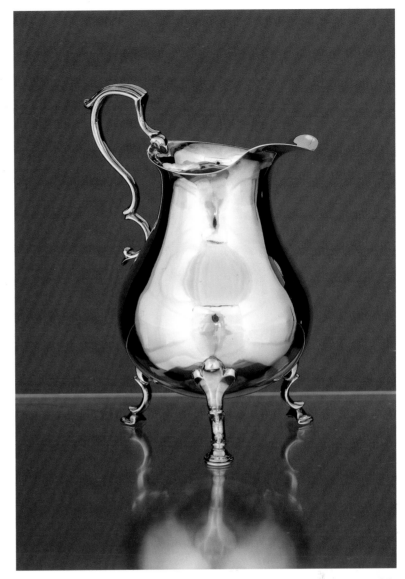

95

96

Soup Ladle, c. 1784

Silver with wood handle, l. 14⅞ (37.8), diam. bowl 4 (10.2)

MARK 9 once on underside of bowl, double-struck

PROVENANCE: probably Judith Myers (1762–1796), who married Jacob Mordecai (1762–1838) in 1784; to Eliza Kennon Mordecai (1809–1861), Jacob's daughter by his second wife (and Judith's half-sister), Rebecca Myers (1776–1863), who in 1827/28 married her cousin Samuel Hays Myers (1799–1849), the son of Samuel Myers (cat. 140); by descent in their family to their great-great-grandson, McDonald Wellford (b. 1913), the donor in 1981.[1]

Virginia Museum of Fine Arts, Richmond; Gift of McDonald Wellford

This simple ladle is one of the only pieces of silver by Myers that can be connected to any of his nine children who reached adulthood. Although intermarriage within the family has left uncertain the identity of the original owner, he most likely made it for his daughter Judith in 1784, when she married Jacob Mordecai of Philadelphia, whom she had met in that city during the Revolutionary War (p. 63). Mordecai later wrote, "it was during her residence in Philadelphia (the place of my birth) that the union of our hearts commenced."[2] The silversmith would have been likely to make a gift of a simple silver ladle to one of his daughters, just as his brother-in-law, Moses Michael Hays, did for his daughter Sarah after her marriage to Moses Mears Myers, when he sent "a little present" that

included several pieces of furniture and "one dozen teaspoons and one soup ladle."[3]

After their marriage, Mordecai worked as an auctioneer in New York, where he was declared insolvent in November 1786. What probably is this ladle was included in the inventory taken of his property in a group of silver objects marked "A present to Mrs. Mordecai" and apparently exempted from seizure:

1 Silver Teapot
1 dᵒ Sugar Box
1 Milk Pot
1 Doz Soup Spoons
1 Soup Ladle
1 Dozⁿ Tea Spoons
1 Sugar Tongs
1 pap pan & Spoon
1 Silver Punch Ladle & Strainer
2 Small Salvers
1 Set Castors, Silver Mounted[4]

The ladle descended in the family together with a set of six teaspoons and pair of sugar tongs of the same date by the Philadelphia silversmith Joseph Richardson, Jr., which also may be the ones in this inventory. Since Mordecai's family was

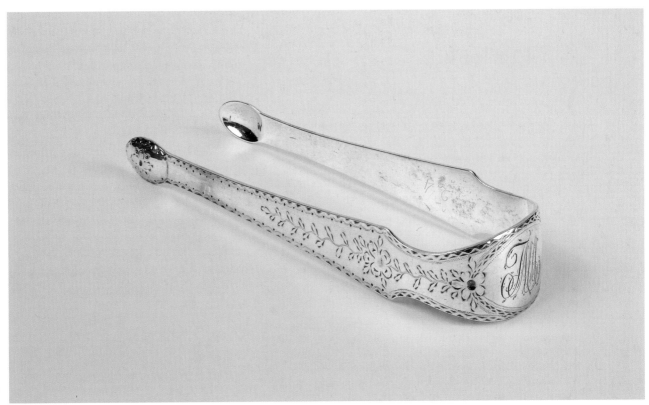

97

from Philadelphia, these may have been wedding gifts from members of the family.[5]

1 Stern 1991, p. 217.
2 Mordecai 1796, n.p.
3 Moses Michael Hays to "Sally" (Sarah [Hays] Myers), April 24, 1797, Mss. m9924.a6HS, Virginia Historical Society, Richmond.
4 NYCIR-2, box 1786–87, file 42.
5 The sugar tongs are in the Virginia Museum of Fine Arts and were published in *Early American* 1953, no. 52. An English or Dutch beaker of c. 1600 that belonged to Edward T.D. Myers and may have descended from Eliza Kennon (Mordecai) Myers is at YUAG, inv. 1968.56.3.

97

Sugar Tongs, 1784–86

Silver, l. 5 15/16 (15.1), w. 1 13/16 (4.6), wt. 2 oz. 2 dwt. (65g) (scratch wt. 2 oz. 4 dwt.)

MARK 9 once inside bow

INSCRIPTION: "TMA" (script) engraved on outside of bow

PROVENANCE: Thomas Arden (d. 1834) and his wife, Mary Boyle (d. 1786), who were married in 1773; to their daughter Sally, who in 1796 married Philip Verplanck; by descent in the family to the donor.[1]

The New-York Historical Society; Gift of John B. Morris, Jr.

Like cat. 95, these sugar tongs can be dated to the first two years after Myers's return to New York, as Mary Arden died on October 2, 1786. This time frame places the tongs among the earliest dated examples of bright-cut engraving in New York (p. 65). Myers marked several sugar tongs, tablespoons, teaspoons, and other flatware with this type of decoration.[2] The techniques vary significantly, suggesting not only that different craftsman engraved these objects, but also that Myers may have acquired them for resale from different craftsmen or merchants. Thomas and Mary Arden also owned a cann with a mark attributed to John Burger (cat. 117) in partnership with William Pritchard, and a three-piece tea set in the Neoclassical style made by the partnership of Thomas Underhill and John Vernon, all engraved with the same monogram as the tongs.[3]

1 Verplanck 1892, pp. 211, 214.
2 YUAG, inv. 1985.85.440; Skirball Cultural Center, Los Angeles, inv. 14.317; Buhler/Hood 1970, II, no. 665.
3 Waters/McKinsey/Ward 2000, II, nos. 141, 249.

Pair of Tankards, 1784–95

A. Silver, h. 6⅝ (16.8), diam. base 4⅞ (12.4), diam. rim 4⁵⁄₁₆ (11), wt. 38 oz. 7 dwt. (1193g)

MARK 9 twice on underside of body, once on exterior of body on right side

ARMORIAL: Johnston crest (a winged spur argent) engraved on cover

B. Silver, h. 6¾ (17.1), diam. base 4¹⁵⁄₁₆ (12.5), diam. rim 4⁷⁄₁₆ (11.3), wt. 37 oz. 15 dwt. (1174g)

MARK 9 twice on underside of body

ARMORIAL/INSCRIPTION: Johnston crest engraved on cover, as above; "David Johnston/1750" (script) engraved on underside, probably in the twentieth century; Johnston arms quartering an unidentified arms, Johnston crest and motto above "Johnston" engraved on side of body, probably in the late nineteenth or early twentieth century (not shown)[1]

PROVENANCE: David Johnston (1724–1809) and Magdalen Walton, who were married in 1753; by descent to their great-granddaughter Euphemia Fenno (1814–1884), who in 1834 married Frederic Tudor (1783–1864). Tankard A. given to their son William (1848–1923), whose wife loaned it to the Massachusetts exhibition at the Jamestown Tercentennial Exposition in 1907; subsequent ownership unknown prior to acquisition by the present owner. Tankard B. given by Frederic and Euphemia (Fenno) Tudor to their son, Frederic Tudor (b. 1845); to his daughter Marie Louise, who in 1893 married James Albert Garland (1870–1906) and was recorded as the owner in 1910; subsequent ownership unknown until sale at auction in 1994.[2]

Collection of Paul and Elissa Cahn

This pair of tankards reveals Myers's rapid adoption of the Neoclassical style after the Revolutionary War as well as new techniques for fabrication. The tapered bodies were formed from flat sheets of metal seamed vertically under handle. Such sheets would have been made using a rolling or "flatting" mill. Little evidence for this technology survives from eighteenth-century New York, although the "Rolers" sent in 1763 from New York to Elias Pelletreau in Southampton may have been for such a device.[3] The hoops encircling the body, each with nine reeds, were formed by the technique traditionally used for simple moldings—pulling strips of silver through a drawing swage. One pair of pint tankards marked by Myers has similar drawn hoops with nine reeds.[4]

This form is based on vessels designed to imitate the appearance of barrels, with chased vertical lines simulating wooden staves encircled by horizontal bands imitating metal hoops. A covered jug of this type appears in the pattern book of 1770–75 used at Matthew Boulton's Soho Manufactory in Birmingham.[5] On most American objects, as well as on many English tankards and mugs of the last quarter of the eighteenth century, the vertical lines were eliminated.[6] Hooped tankards were not common in New York; the majority of American versions of this form appear to have been made in Philadel-

phia, including the pair commissioned by John Penn from Joseph Anthony in 1788.[7] Myers made one pair of hooped tankards for the Hamilton family of Philadelphia (cat. 99).

David Johnston enjoyed considerable wealth and political connections. His father John Johnston was the Speaker of the New Jersey Assembly; his mother, Elizabeth Jamison, was the daughter of David Jamison, the Chief Justice of New Jersey between 1711 and 1723 and also Attorney General of New York.[8] Johnston's marriage to Magdalen Walton further increased his wealth and political connections. She was the daughter of the New York merchant Jacob Walton and his wife, Maria Beekman, who gave her a dowry of £1,000, and a niece and heir of the merchant William Walton.[9] David and Magdalen Johnston may have patronized Myers prior to the Revolutionary War, as their crest is engraved on an otherwise undocumented dish stand marked by him (cat. 92).

1 Arms, quarters 1 and 4: Argent a saltire sable, on a chief gules three cushions or (Johnston); quarters 2 and 3: Or an anchor gules. Motto: "Nunquam non paratus" ("Never unprepared"). See Bolton 1964, p. 93.
2 "Jamison and Johnston" 1874, pp. 172–74; Savary 1902, pp. 247–49; Savary 1903, p. 34; Tudor 1896, pp. 21–25; *Fourth Report* 1910, pp. 93–94; *Eleventh Report* 1921, pp. 176–77; "Memoirs" 1926, pp. 98–99; Jamestown 1907, p. 17, no. 170; Rosenbaum 1954A, p. 134; Sotheby's 1994, lot 116.
3 Failey 1971, p. 44.
4 Rosenbaum 1954A, p. 134; now in the Burrows Collection, on loan to the Sterling and Francine Clark Art Institute, Williamstown, Massachusetts, inv. TR1987.28.
5 Delieb/Roberts 1971, p. 132.
6 Stratton 1975, pp. 29–30; Jackson 1911, II, p. 773.
7 *Philadelphia* 1976, no. 120.
8 ""Jamison and Johnston" 1874, pp. 171–72; Savary 1902, p. 248.
9 *Abstracts* 1892–1906, VII, p. 179, XI, pp. 116–17.

Pair of Pint Tankards, 1784–95

Silver, h. 4⅝ (11.7), w. 5¾ (14.6), diam. base 3⅝ (9.2), diam. rim 3³⁄₁₆ (8.4) each, wt. A. 14 oz. 8 dwt. (448g), B. 15 oz. (466g) (scratch wt. "Both together/29 oz 16 penyweight")

MARK 9 twice on underside of body and once on underside of lid on each

ARMORIAL: on each, Hamilton arms (gules, a mullet pieced between three cinquefoils argent) engraved on front of body; Hamilton crest (out of a ducal coronet or, on a mound vert an oak tree transversed by a frame-saw proper) and motto ("Through") engraved on cover[1]

PROVENANCE: probably William Hamilton (1745–1813) of Philadelphia; by gift to his niece, Ann Hamilton (1769–1798), who in 1792 married James Lyle (1765–1826); by descent to their great-grandson, Cornelius Hartman Kuhn (b. 1854), by whom sold to the Philadelphia Museum in 1922.[2]

Philadelphia Museum of Art; Purchased with Membership and Joseph E. Temple Funds

The tankards made in Myers's workshop after the Revolution-

99.1

5 The double portrait is at the Historical Society of Pennsylvania, Philadelphia; Von Erffa/Staley 1986, no. 634.

100

Pair of Torah Finials, 1784–95

Silver and gilded brass

A. h. 14⅜ (36.5), diam. base 1¼ (3.2), gross wt. 24 oz. 12 dwt. (765g)

MARK 9 once on shaft and once on lowest sphere

B. h. 13⅞ (35.2), diam. base 1¼ (3.2), gross wt. 23 oz. 9 dwt. (730g)

MARK 9 once on shaft

INSCRIPTION: "Hays & Myers" (script) engraved around shaft on each

PROVENANCE: apparently Samuel Myers (cat. 140) and his second wife, Judith Hays, of Richmond, Virginia; to their granddaughter Caroline (Myers) Cohen, by whom donated to the Touro Synagogue in 1892.

Touro Synagogue, Congregation Jeshuat Israel, Newport, Rhode Island

This pair of Torah finials closely follows the same form as three other pairs by Myers dating from about 1765 to 1776 (cats. 63–65). The original crown that survives on one of the present pair was cast from one of the crowns on the other pairs, and the bases have the same moldings and openwork beading.[1] As a model to copy, Myers presumably would have had access to the pair in New York (cat. 63). Moreover, an entry in the accounts of Congregation Yeshuat Israel for 1786–87, recorded *parnas* Moses Seixas paying 12 shillings to "Myer Myers mending Romonim," so perhaps the earlier pair he made (cat. 64) was returned to him in New York.[2]

Instead of pierced and chased ornament in the Rococo style found on the three earlier pairs of finials, the present pair is lavishly decorated with bright-cut engraving in the Neoclassical style (fig. 36). This engraving was executed in New York by the same specialist engraver who executed the bright-cut ornament on the sugar dish by John Burger (cat. 117). Myers presumably chose this form of ornament since he had no specialist chasers or piercers working in his workshop after the Revolutionary War, when such ornament was no longer fashionable.

The subsequent ownership of this pair of Torah finials suggests that it belonged originally to Myers's sister Rachel and her husband, Moses Michael Hays, who were married in 1766 (cat. 42). The Hays family moved from New York to Newport about 1770, and in 1773 Moses Hays's sister Reyna married the *hazan* of Yeshuat Israel, Isaac Touro.[3] Moses and Rachel Hays remained in Rhode Island until 1782, when they settled in Boston, where they were the only Jewish family for many years. As noted (cats. 63–65), Torahs and sets of silver finials

ary War used new techniques of silver fabrication to create an entirely new version of the form. Another pair of pint tankards marked by Myers in this style was made with hooped moldings and handles different from the Hamilton pair but with coats of arms executed by the same specialist engraver.[3]

Ann (Hamilton) Lyle, from whom these tankards descended, was the daughter of Andrew and Abigail (Franks) Hamilton III and the granddaughter of David and Margaret (Evans) Franks, who had been early patrons of Myer Myers (cat. 4). Beatrice B. Garvan has proposed that this pair of tankards was originally made for Andrew's unmarried brother, William Hamilton, who is known to have traveled to New York from Philadelphia in August 1789.[4] Ann (Hamilton) Lyle was his favorite niece, with whom he had his portrait painted by Benjamin West in London in 1785, and she would have been a likely heir for these tankards bearing her family's coat of arms (fig. 35).[5]

1 Bolton 1964, pp. 74–75.

2 *Pennsylvania Museum* 1913, pp. 18, 24; *Pennsylvania Museum* 1923, p. 22; Stern 1991, pp. 75, 79–80.

3 Rosenbaum 1954A, p. 134. The tankards are in the Burrows Collection, on loan to the Sterling and Francine Clark Art Institute, Williamstown, Massachusetts, inv. TR1987.28.

4 I am indebted to Beatrice B. Garvan for this information from her forthcoming catalogue of the American silver at the Philadelphia Museum of Art.

were owned by a few wealthy American Jews, and it is not unlikely that the Hays family had a Torah.

The later engraved inscription "Hays & Myers" may refer to the 1796 marriage of Moses and Rachel's daughter Judith to her first cousin, Myers's son Samuel (cat. 140). It is possible that Samuel and Judith Myers inherited these ornaments and deposited them at a synagogue, perhaps Beth Shalom in Richmond, necessitating the identifying inscription. In 1892, their granddaughter Caroline (Myers) Cohen offered to donate to the recently-reconsecrated Touro Synagogue two sets of silver ornaments for Torah scrolls.[4] In addition to this pair marked by Myers, the Touro Synagogue now owns a pair of Torah finials of Mediterranean origin with the same engraved inscription, and it seems likely that these two pairs were those donated by Caroline Cohen.[5]

1 Both finials retained their original crowns when the pair was photographed as part of the synagogue's silver for Jones 1913, pl. XCVI. One had a replacement crown by 1954; Rosenbaum 1954A, p. 100.
2 "The Holy Sedeka of Yeshuat Israel in Newport Rhode Island with Moses Seixas," p. 2v, box 3, file 185, Lyons Collection, AJHS. The date on the document is 5547.
3 Gutstein 1936, p. 117; Stern 1991, p. 104.
4 Gutstein 1936, pp. 266–67.
5 Jones 1913, p. 320.

101

Tablespoon

ONE OF THREE, 1788–95

Silver, l. 6⅞ (17.5), wt. 19 dwt. (30g)

MARK 9 once on back of handle

ARMORIAL / INSCRIPTION: Livingston crest (a ship of three masts, top sails set) and motto ("Spero meliora" ["I hope for the best"]) engraved on front of handle; "EML" (script) engraved below crest

PROVENANCE: Edward Livingston (1764–1836) and Mary McEvers (d. 1801), who were married on April 10, 1788; subsequent ownership unknown until acquisition prior to 1958 by the West Hartford, Connecticut, collector Philip H. Hammerslough; by private sale to the donor.[1]

Harvard University Art Museums, Cambridge, Massachusetts; Bequest of David Berg

The spoon's downturned end and pointed bowl are characteristic of flatware marked by Myers after the Revolutionary War. Its original owners, the statesman Edward Livingston and his first wife, were both relatives of Myers's patrons: Edward's parents were Robert R. and Margaret (Beekman) Livingston (cats. 124, 125); Mary was daughter of Charles and Mary (Verplanck) McEvers and the sister of Gulian McEvers (cat. 8).

1 Livingston 1910, p. 398; Hammerslough 1958, p. 118.

102

Punch Ladle, 1784–95

Silver, l. 14¾ (37.5), diam. bowl 4 (10.2), wt. 5 oz. 3 dwt. (160g)

MARK 9 once on back of handle

INSCRIPTION: "DLF[or T]" (script) engraved on front of handle

PROVENANCE: unknown prior to purchase by the present owner.

Collection of Barbara and Roy Zuckerberg

The majority of Myers's flatware made after the Revolutionary War was in the "Old English" pattern with a more pointed end on the handle. Like this ladle, much of the later flatware was also ornamented with bright-cut engraving, which first appeared in England about 1775. The earliest dated example of bright-cut engraving on a surviving American object is found on the gold boxes ornamented by Peter Maverick in 1784 (cat. 115). Myers was not slow to adopt this style, however, as bright-cut decoration appears on a pair of sugar tongs marked by his workshop in 1784–86 (cat. 97). With the significant exception of one pair of Torah finials made after 1783 (cat. 100), Myers's use of bright-cut engraving was restricted to flatware. Elias Pelletreau also limited bright-cut engraving to flatware.[1]

1 Livingston 1910, p. 398; Hammerslough 1958, p. 118.

102

103

103

Sugar Tongs, 1784–95

Silver, l. 5½ (14), w. 1½ (3.8), wt. 1 oz. 3 dwt. (35g)

MARK 7 once inside bow

ARMORIAL: Goelet crest (a swan) engraved on outside of bow[1]

PROVENANCE: unknown prior to purchase by the present owner.

Private collection

This is one of the few surviving objects by Myers datable after the Revolutionary War but not struck with his second surname mark, MARK 9. The similar engraving of the Goelet crest suggests that these tongs may have been made to accompany the following sugar dish (cat. 104). They are smaller and have bright-cut ornament executed by a different craftsman than the Arden tongs (cat. 97), which suggests that Myers may have been retailing flatware drawn from a variety of sources.

1 Bolton 1964, p. 68.

104

Sugar Dish, 1784–95

Silver, h. 8¾ (22.2), w. base 2¹³⁄₁₆ (7.1), diam. rim 4⅜ (11.1), wt. 12 oz. 11 dwt. (391g)

MARK 9 once on side of base

ARMORIAL: Goelet crest (a swan) engraved on outside of bowl[1]

PROVENANCE: unknown prior to sale in 1953 to the donor, the silver dealer Stephen Ensko, by a "Mrs. J.T. Phillips," apparently a typographical error for A.T. (Annette Thompson) Phillips of Newport, Rhode Island, a relation of the Goelet family.[2]

Brooklyn Museum of Art, New York; Gift of Stephen G.C. Ensko

The Goelet family was among those that had purchased silver from Myers's workshop prior to the American Revolution and continued its patronage afterwards. At both times, the patron probably went to Myers because of his ability to supply objects in the latest style: a curvilinear waiter with Rococo engraving (cat. 58) or this sugar dish in a severely Neoclassical style, the crest engraved without any surrounding embellishment. Although the urn shape was adapted to a variety of forms in English silver after about 1770, it was not commonly used for sugar dishes. The type made in England to match helmet-shape milk jugs and other tewares in the Neoclassical taste usually had a low oval shape, frequently conceived as an open basket with a swing handle.[3] A covered oval sugar dish of this type made in 1789–90 by Hester Bateman was owned in New York by Francis Lewis.[4] However, most American patrons at this time preferred the tall, covered urn-shape sugar dish, and many New York silversmiths made examples between 1783 and 1800. Versions marked by William Van Buren and Ephraim Brasher featured the same broad shoulders and narrow taper seen on the cover and base of Myers's dish.[5] Myers's dish also exhibits a familiarity with the latest technology, since the beaded borders on the bowl and cover were applied strips produced by die-rollers.

1 Bolton 1964, p. 68.
2 Adolph S. Cavallo to Josephine Setze, Brooklyn, April 1, 1954, silversmith research files, American Arts Office, YUAG.
3 De Castres 1977, pp. 63–64, pl. 28; Jackson 1911, II, pp. 981–83.
4 Waters/McKinsey/Ward 2000, II, no. 281.
5 Quimby/Johnson 1995, no. 276; Buhler/Hood 1970, II, no. 692.

104

New York *and* London Silver

Cats. 105–123

105

PETER VAN DYCK (1684–1751)

Teapot, 1725–50

Silver with wood handle, h. 7 (17.8), diam. base 3¼ (8.3), diam. rim 2¹¹⁄₁₆ (6.8), gross wt. 20 oz. 1 dwt. (622g)

Yale University Art Gallery, New Haven; Mabel Brady Garvan Collection

Myers's early teapot (cat. 1) must have been influenced by examples of this popular form made by the previous generation of New York makers, most notably Peter Van Dyck. His superb teapot has a subtle rhythm of convex and concave outlines. Van Dyck's career underscores the ethnic complexity of the silversmith's trade in New York. Although of Dutch ancestry, Van Dyck was apprenticed to the Huguenot Bartholomew Le Roux I, who himself was born in Amsterdam but may have trained in London. Van Dyck also married Bartholomew's daughter Rachel in 1711. He was financially successful, consistently receiving the second-highest tax assessments of any silversmith (after Benjamin Wynkoop) between 1715 and 1733, due in some part to his advantageous second marriage to a wealthy widow. He presumably trained his son Richard but was not recorded as taking other apprentices.[1]

1 Waters/McKinsey/Ward 2000, I, pp. 18–22, 30.

106

DANIEL CHRISTIAN FUETER (1720–1785)

Cruet Stand, 1754–65

Silver, h. 8¾ (22.2), w. 9⅞ (25.1), d. 9 (22.9), wt. 36 oz. 13 dwt. (1140g)

Historic Deerfield, Inc., Deerfield, Massachusetts; Gift of Helen Geier Flynt

This cruet stand is associated with three casters by Samuel Wood dated 1752–53, which Fueter may have acquired during his residence in London in those years and brought to New York in 1754. It is not known if he also imported the stand or made it using an English example for the casting patterns. Details of his stand, particularly the cast cartouche and handle, are identical to an example by Wood that was owned in New York (cat. 121). Robert Barker has also noted the close similarity of the feet on Fueter's stand to the lower handle mount on one of Myers's covered jugs (cat. 27), which suggests that the two craftsmen shared the casting pattern.

The original patron for Fueter's cruet stand is unknown; the crest may be for the Van Voorhis family.[1]

1 The Van Voorhis crest is a tower argent; Bolton 1964, p. 170.

105

106

107

107

DANIEL CHRISTIAN FUETER (1720–1785)

Whistle and Bells, 1761–65

Gold and coral, l. 5³⁄₁₆ (13.2), gross wt. 2 oz. 6 dwt. (72g)

Yale University Art Gallery, New Haven; Gift of Mrs. Francis P. Garvan, James R. Graham, Walter M. Jeffords, and Mrs. Paul Moore

This spectacular object was made as a child's toy, a rattle with a whistle at one end and coral for teething at the other. Like other forms marked by Fueter, "Whisels & Bells" were rarely made by Colonial American silversmiths, but rather imported from specialist makers in London.[1] This example's embellishments of spiral fluting, Rococo shellwork, and a cherub, as well as the superb quality of its execution demonstrate the chaser's fluency with European designs and gold-chasing techniques. Fueter himself may have created the decoration, although he employed at least one specialist gold chaser from Switzerland, John Anthony Beau (p. 53). This whistle and bells predates Beau's documented presence in New York in 1769. It was presented by Mary (Thong) Livingston (cat. 128), who died in 1765, to her granddaughter and namesake, Mary Duane (1761–1813), the daughter of James Duane and Maria Livingston, who were married in 1759.[2]

1 Heckscher/Bowman 1992, pp. 115–17.
2 Livingston 1910, p. 545; Walworth 1982, p. 69. In 1787, Mary Duane married General William North, who during the Revolutionary War had served as an aide-de-camp to Major General Baron Frederick von Steuben. North later inherited Steuben's gold box by Samuel Johnson (cat. 115).

108

DANIEL CHRISTIAN FUETER (1720–1785)

Tankard, 1754–69

Silver, h. 7½ (19.1), w. 8 (20.3), diam. base 5¾ (19.6), diam. rim 4⅜ (11.1), wt. 36 oz. 10 dwt. (1135g)

Columbia University in the City of New York

In contrast to the European-influenced design of Fueter's cruet stand and whistle (cats. 106, 107), this tankard responded to local style preferences in New York. Tankards had declined in popularity in England by the second quarter of the eighteenth century, and this form of tankard, with its plain, tapered body, flat cover, and double-scroll handle, was a type made almost exclusively in New York during this period, exemplified by Halsted and Myers's contemporary tankard for Wessel and Maria Van Schaick (cat. 15).[1] It is possible that Myer Myers or another New York silversmith supplied Fueter with this tankard for resale.

William Samuel Johnson (fig. 32), who also patronized Myers at this time (p. 58), was the original owner of Fueter's tankard. It descended to his great-great-grandson and namesake, who presented it in 1934 to Frank Cheney Farley, Jr., the son of his stepdaughter Eloise (Beers) Farley (see cat. 24), from whom it was acquired on behalf of Columbia University in 1959.

1 Clayton 1971, pp. 292–95; Montgomery/Kane 1976, pp. 56–57; Ward/Ward 1979, pp. 125–27.

208 MYER MYERS

109

109

JOHN HEATH (DATES UNKNOWN)

Waiter, 1765–70

Silver, h. 1⅝ (4.1), diam. 15³⁄₁₆ (38.6), wt. 45 oz. 11 dwt. (1417g)

Henry Francis du Pont Winterthur Museum, Winterthur, Delaware;
Gift of H.F. du Pont, 1965

Very little information survives for John Heath's career as a silversmith, and only a small number of extant objects bear his
mark, including cat. 110. He registered as a Freeman on March
3, 1761, without paying a fee, which indicates that he had
served his apprenticeship in New York.[1] Heath's shop on Wall
Street was mentioned in a newspaper advertisement of January 1763.[2] Nothing is known of Heath's subsequent career as a
silversmith; he never was included in the New York City directories that were issued beginning in 1786. However, he may be

109.1

the same John Heath who was listed together with William Gilbert on March 21, 1788, as a creditor of the insolvent Philip Lott for £5.8.0; a John "Heaths" appeared as a debtor for £2.15.6/2 to the drygoods merchant Joseph Henry on January 14, 1793.[3]

The Schuyler coat of arms (vert issuing from the sinister an arm vested holding on the hand a falcon close all proper) and crest (on a helm a falcon of the field) were engraved by the same craftsman who executed similar work for Myer Myers, including the Smith arms on a punch bowl (cat. 55).[4] Like Myers, John Heath did not rely exclusively on this one craftsman for the engraved ornament on his silver. A different craftsman using a much simpler technique, consisting of thin outlines filled with uniform shading strokes, executed the Van Cortlandt coat of arms on a punch bowl Heath made for Pierre Van Cortlandt.[5] The precise history of this waiter in the Schuyler family is uncertain.[6]

1 De Lancey 1885, p. 198.
2 *The New-York Mercury*, January 3, 1763, as cited in Gottesman 1936, p. 50.
3 NYCIR-1, box 21, Lott file; box 13, Henry file.
4 Bolton 1964, pp. 145–46.
5 Buhler/Hood 1970, II, no. 724.
6 Provenance unknown prior to sale by a Mrs. William Anderson of Pittsburgh to the dealer Robert Ensko in 1932; see Quimby/Johnson 1995, p. 244.

110

JOHN HEATH (DATES UNKNOWN)

Pair of Salts, 1767–71

Silver with glass inserts, h. 2⁵⁄₁₆ (5.9), w. 3⁹⁄₁₆ (9.0), d. 2¹⁵⁄₁₆ (7.5) each, wt. (without insert) A. 2 oz. 16 dwt. (87g), B. 2 oz. 19 dwt. (91g)

Wadsworth Atheneum Museum of Art, Hartford, Connecticut; Philip H. Hammerslough Collection

A silversmith with as small a surviving production as John Heath would have been unlikely to make such labor-intensive objects as pierced salts in his workshop. He may have relied on a skilled, specialist piercer in New York to produce these objects, perhaps the same specialist who executed the bottle stands for Myer Myers (cats. 80, 81). Like the bottle stands, these salts are closely related to English models. Beth Carver Wees has observed that another, almost identical pair of pierced salts marked by Heath are strikingly similar to examples made in London by the 1763–72 partnership of David Hennell I and Robert Hennell I; this particular design was introduced by the Hennells in 1767–68 and was discontinued by 1771.[1] Subtle differences exist between the present pair of salts and those by the Hennells, most notably the absence of a reserve for engraving a monogram or crest; what appear to be the eighteenth-century initials "EVAS" are engraved on their

underside. Again like Myers's bottle stands, the salts exhibit no traces of English hallmarks and only one strike of the American silversmith's mark.

Despite these anomalies, it is nevertheless possible that these salts were imported from England for resale. As objects for export they may have been unmarked, or Heath could have filled or hammered over the hallmarks, particularly at a time of rising hostility to English imports. Other American silversmiths are known to have imported pierced salts: in November 1769, Joseph Richardson, Sr., of Philadelphia ordered from London "4 Silver ovel Peirced Salts of the Neatest Pattern with Glasses to them" and ordered four more one year later.[2] Such salts were produced in enormous quantities in England during the 1770s, particularly by Birmingham manufacturers such as Matthew Boulton.[3] As with many London makers who produced pierced objects, the Hennells specialized in making this one form; Robert I's fourth mark was registered in 1773 as a "saltmaker."[4]

1 Burrows Collection; on loan to the Sterling and Francine Clark Art Institute, Williamstown, Massachusetts, inv. TR 56/86. I am greatly indebted to Beth Wees for sharing this observation with me and to Robert B. Barker for his thoughts on the Hennell salts. See Hennell 1986, pp. 60, 64, 70, figs. 40A-B.
2 Fales 1974, p. 253.
3 Delieb/Roberts 1971, pp. 76–79.
4 Grimwade 1990, p. 543.

111

OTTO PAUL DE PARISIEN (DATES UNKNOWN; ACT. IN NEW YORK 1756–97)

Porringer, 1756–76

Silver, h. 2 (5.1), l. 7 in (17.8), diam. rim 5⅛ (13), wt. 8 oz. 10 dwt. (264.4g)

The Minneapolis Institute of Arts; The James S. Bell Memorial Fund

The handle of this porringer was cast using the same pattern as examples marked by Halsted and Myers and Myers alone (cats. 45, 46), although the loop at the tops of those two has been removed from this example, most likely because it had been damaged. Although the porringer marked by Parisien has no history of ownership, a script monogram "PCM" engraved on the side of the bowl is similar to monograms executed for Myers's workshop during the mid-1750s to mid-1760s, when Parisien seems to have been associated with Myers and may have retailed objects supplied by him (p. 58). Other objects marked by Parisien related to examples by Myers include a waiter very similar to the coffeepot stand of 1756–58 by Halsted and Myers (cat. 21).[1]

1 Known to the author only through undated photographs from Helen Burr Smith, silversmith research files, American Arts Office, YUAG.

110

III

112

WILLIAM GILBERT (1746–1832)

Sugar Dish, 1770–76

Silver, h. 5¼ (13.3), diam. base 2¹⁵⁄₁₆ (7.5), diam. rim 4¼ (10.8), wt. 9 oz. 6 dwt. (290g)

The Currier Gallery of Art, Manchester, New Hampshire; Gift of Frances H. and Laura E. Dwight

113

WILLIAM GILBERT (1746–1832)

Milk Pot, 1770–76

Silver, h. 5⅛ (13), w. 4¾ (12.1), diam. base 2⁵⁄₁₆ (5.9), wt. 5 oz. 6 dwt. (165g)

The Currier Gallery of Art, Manchester, New Hampshire; Gift of Frances H. and Laura E. Dwight

As noted (p. 171), sets of chased milk pots and sugar dishes appear to have been a specialty of Myers's workshop. The craftsman who executed the superb flat-chased ornament on the sets by Myers also ornamented the milk pot from this set by William Gilbert. Characteristic details of his work include a very fine fish-scale pattern, subtly textured shell surrounds, and rounded, curling leaves flanking cartouches. The milk pot's handle appears to be cast from the same pattern used in Myers's workshop.

As an independent silversmith whose energies appear to have been focused on retail sales (pp. 57–58), Gilbert would have been less likely to produce objects with chased ornament. It would have been easier and less expensive to purchase them from a large workshop such as Myers's, which was set up with specialist craftsmen. Like cat. 85, Gilbert's sugar dish was chased to match the milk pot by a different, less skilled craftsman, perhaps an apprentice or assistant to the other chaser.

According to the donors, the set marked by Gilbert had belonged to forebears in the Kirkland family, but the correct provenance seems to be from the Van Kleeck family of New York. The donors, Laura Emmott Dwight and Frances Howe Dwight, were the great-great-granddaughters of Hannah Van Kleeck, who in 1797 married Leonard Davis of New York City; the milk pot and sugar dish presumably belonged to the previous generation of Hannah's family.[1]

1 In the eighteenth century, the Kirkland family was based in Massachusetts and Connecticut rather than New York; see Chapman 1860 and Sanborn 1894.

113.1

114

WILLIAM GILBERT (1746–1832)

Bowl, 1770–76

Silver, h. 3¹⁄₁₆ (7.8), diam. base 3 (7.6), diam. rim 5¹⁵⁄₁₆ (15.1), wt. 8 oz. 4 dwt. (254.7g)

Henry Francis du Pont Winterthur Museum, Winterthur, Delaware; Gift of H.F. du Pont, 1965

Apart from a small difference in size, this bowl is very similar to an example marked by Myer Myers (cat. 53): their feet are the same casting, the scalloped rims follow precisely the same pattern, and both were decorated by the same engraver. A second, identical bowl by Gilbert is at the Museum of the City of New York.[1] It is possible that Gilbert made all the bowls and supplied one to Myers for resale, but given Gilbert's later career as a merchant, it seems more likely that they were made in Myers's workshop, where Gilbert probably also acquired the sugar dish and milk pot (cats. 112, 113).

The original owner of Gilbert's bowl was Elizabeth Codwise, who married Major Ezra Starr in the First Presbyterian Church of New York on April 24, 1781.[2] Her maiden initials "EC" engraved on the underside suggest that this bowl had been purchased before Gilbert left New York in 1776 to serve in the militia with his brother-in-law, Ephraim Brasher.

1 Waters/McKinsey/Ward 2000, II, no. 193.
2 "Presbyterian Church Marriages" 1756–1813.

112–113

114

115

1 *MCCNY*-2, I, p. 73.
2 Ibid., p. 99.
3 Stephens 1950, p. 95.
4 *The New-York Packet and the American Advertiser*, March 16, 1786, p. 3; Sotheby's 1991, lot 125.
5 *The New-York Packet and the American Advertiser*, July 12, 1784, p. 3.

115

SAMUEL JOHNSON (1720–1796),
ENGRAVED BY PETER MAVERICK (1755–1811)

Freedom Box, 1784

Gold, h. ¾ (1.9), w. 3¼ (8.3), d. 1¹⁵⁄₁₆ (4.9), wt. 2 oz. 12 dwt. (80g)

Yale University Art Gallery, New Haven; Mabel Brady Garvan Collection

On September 11, 1784, the New York City Common Council voted "that five respectful Addresses from this Corporation be presented with the freedom of this City in Gold Boxes" to Governor George Clinton of New York, George Washington, John Jay, the Marquis de Lafayette, and the Baron von Steuben. A committee composed of Daniel Phoenix and the two silversmiths who were members of the council, William Gilbert and Samuel Johnson, was appointed to "direct the making of the Gold Boxes."[1] Dividing the commissions between them, Johnson made one for Jay and this example for von Steuben, and Gilbert the remainder. Johnson was paid £58.17.0 on November 11, 1784 for "2 Golden Boxes."[2] Surprisingly, given what must have been a fifty-year career, very little silver by Johnson has survived, most of it dating to after the Revolutionary War.

Stephen Stephens was the first to point out that the engraving on this Freedom box was the earliest documented usage in America of bright-cut engraving (p. 65).[3] This technique may have been what Peter Maverick called in 1786 "the most elegant manner and in the newest fashion, resembling the flat chasing, as neat as in Europe."[4] From the beginning of his career, he advertised engraving on silver: "Gentlemen may have their coats of arms, crests or cyphers done in the neatest manner, Ladies may have their tea-table plate ornamented in the newest fashion, with elegance and dispatch."[5] Maverick did other work for the New York Common Council, although the Freedom box was his only commission to engrave precious-metal objects.

116

WILLIAM GILBERT (1746–1832)

Teapot, 1785–95

Silver with wood handle and finial, h. 5½ (14), w. 9⅛ (23.2), diam. base 4⁹⁄₁₆ (11.6), gross wt. 15 oz. 18 dwt. (495g)

The Burrows Collection; on long-term loan to the Sterling and Francine Clark Art Institute, Williamstown, Massachusetts

The silver in the Neoclassical style marked by Gilbert forms a more diverse group than objects from the Colonial period, suggesting that he drew on a larger number of different makers to supply a growing retail business. This teapot's raised body, applied borders, and engraved monogram is completely different from a seamed oval teapot with bright-cut decoration that bears the same mark.[1] The engraved decoration on this teapot appears to be by the same craftsman responsible for the Winthrop arms on a pair of canns made by Lewis Fueter before 1783, although these arms may be later additions.[2] The "WMP" monogram was for William Popham of Fishkill, New York, in whose family it descended.[3]

1 Christie's 1994, lot 123.
2 Buhler/Hood 1970, II, no. 748.
3 Provenance: by descent to Popham's great-grandson Charles P. Hidden; by sale to the dealers Firestone and Parson in 1972; see *Antiques*, 102 (October 1972), p. 573.

117

JOHN BURGER (C. 1745–1828)

Sugar Dish, 1784–1795

Silver, h. 8⁵⁄₁₆ (21.1), w./d. (base) 2⅞ (7.3), diam. rim 4³⁄₁₆ (10.6), wt. 9 oz. 16 dwt. (304g)

Yale University Art Gallery, New Haven; Mabel Brady Garvan Collection

This sugar dish's high, domed cover reflected a local taste that apparently was inspired by late Colonial examples, such as Myer Myers's sugar dish made in the early 1770s for Dorothea (Remsen) Brinckerhoff (cat. 85). The bright-cut engraving was executed by the same specialist craftsman who ornamented the pair of Torah finials made by Myer Myers between 1784

and 1795 (cat. 100). Almost every motif on this dish is repeated on the Torah finials, including the quatrefoils alternating with tapering dots on the outside edge of the cover and the tightly spaced husk garlands with pendant trails of dots and zigzags.

Very little hollow ware in the early Neoclassical style by Burger has survived.[1] He may have had some difficulty in finding commissions, as a 1786 advertisement indicates:

He will thankfully receive any orders from the public in the GOLD and SILVERSMITH'S BUSINESS, especially for large plate. He respectfully informs those who may be pleased to favour him with their custom, that any work which is not executed to their expectation either in goodness of metal, workmanship, or moderation of charge, he will not insist on their taking.[2]

This sugar dish also indicates that Burger may have worked primarily as a wholesale supplier to retail silversmiths or jewelers such as William Gilbert or Benjamin Halsted, who may have marked the wares sold in their stores. Burger's urn was part of a tea service assembled, presumably by the retailer, from different makers; the teapot, marked by Jabez Halsey, was engraved to match by the same specialist.[3]

1 Waters/McKinsey/Ward 2000, I, no. 139.
2 *The New-York Packet*, April 13, 1786, p. 3.
3 Buhler/Hood 1970, II, no. 729.

118

BENJAMIN HALSTED (1734–1817)

Plateau, 1790–95

Silver, sheet copper, and glass, h. 2⅛ (5.4), w. 17³⁄₁₆ (43.7), d. 21¹⁄₁₆ (53.5)

Private collection

During the Federal period, Benjamin Halsted worked as a retail jeweler or smallworker. Most of the Neoclassical silver marked by him was flatware: a range of forms similar to those listed in his advertisements survives, including punch ladles, salt spoons, teaspoons, and sugar tongs, with bright-cut ornament similar to that seen on this plateau.[1] He marked only a few small pieces of hollow ware in the Neoclassical style.[2]

This plateau is the most sophisticated piece of silver from this period to survive with Halsted's mark. The form is extremely rare in American silver: at the time George Washington ordered a plated plateau from France in 1789, his secretary reported, "Mr. [Robert] Morris & Mr. [William] Bingham have them, and the French & Spanish Ministers . . . but I know no one else who has."[3] A more elaborate American example was made about 1825 by John W. Forbes of New York.[4]

The construction of Halsted's plateau is very simple. The cast feet are soldered to the solid copper bottom; the flat strips of the border are pinned to the bottom; the glass is secured by an inner molding that is also pinned in place. The pattern of the bright-cut engraving is identical to the decoration on a sugar urn by William Garret Forbes and may have been engraved by the same craftsman.[5] Halsted easily could have made the components, or he could have acquired them separately and assembled them. The twist handles are a later addition, probably of the early twentieth century.

According to family tradition, this plateau was made for Daniel Crommelin Verplanck and his second wife, Ann Walton, who were married in 1790. Verplanck owned an extensive collection of both new and inherited silver, including the covered jug by Myer Myers (cat. 26).

1 Halsted flatware in public collections include a salt spoon at the Albany Institute of History and Art, inv. 1981.54.8; a punch ladle at Historic Deerfield, Inc., inv. 98.16.1; and teaspoons (inv. 1985.84.503, 1999.49.20), tablespoons (inv. 1985.86.233.1-2), sugar tongs (inv. 1985.85.345-46), and a punch ladle (1988.93.42) at YUAG; see also Buhler/Hood 1970, II, no. 814.

2 For a sauceboat, see Sotheby's 1976, lot 591. Other Neoclassical hollow ware by Halsted includes an urn-shape milk pot (Christie's 1983A, lot 64A) and a pap boat (Buhler/Hood 1970, II, no. 815).

3 Tobias Lear to Clement Biddle, cited in Buhler 1957, p. 49.

4 "American Rarity" 1961; Waters 2000, pp. 355–58.

5 Buhler/Hood 1970, II, no. 700.

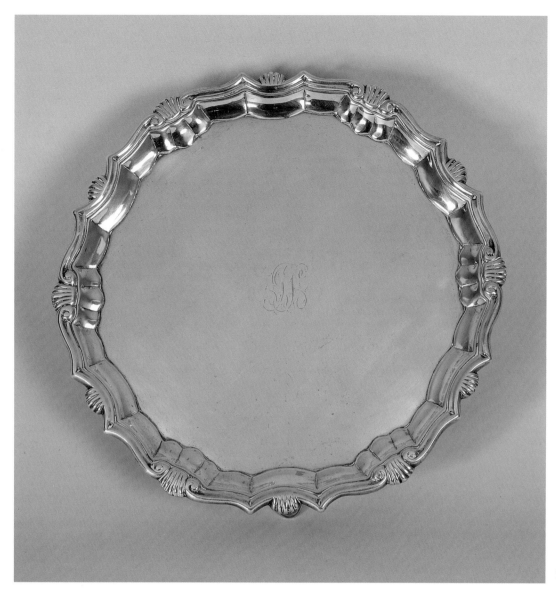

119

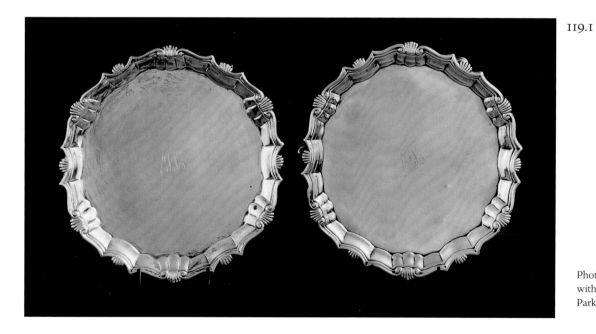

119.1

Photograph of cat. 119 (right)
with waiter by Myer Myers (left),
Parke-Bernet Galleries, New York, 1941.

119

WILLIAM PEASTON (ACT. 1746–78)
London, England

Waiter, 1747–48

Sterling silver, h. 1³⁄₁₆ (3), diam. 8⅝ (21.9), wt. 12 oz. 17 dwt. (400g) (scratch wt. 13 oz. 18 dwt.)

Historic Hudson Valley, Tarrytown, New York; Gift of Paul Mellon

This waiter exemplifies the routine production of a large London workshop that produced waiters as one of its specialties; two almost identical examples by Peaston of 1753–54 and 1754–55 were owned in Williamsburg, Virginia, by Peyton Randolph.[1] As the product of a specialist manufacturer who sold them to wholesalers and retailers, this type of silver object was easily available to American customers or their agents and less expensive than bespoke commissions.

This waiter is also an important document for the transmission of style from London to the Colonies, albeit with a significant time lag. Like Myers's cann (cat. 87), it was owned by John Stevenson and his wife Magdalena Douw of Albany, who married about 1771.[2] It is not known if John Stevenson purchased this object directly from London or bought it secondhand, but he could not have owned it until at least a decade after it was made. Stevenson evidently liked this object's style, or perhaps the waiter's restrained decoration made it less obviously old-fashioned at a time when the narrow gadrooned borders were more popular (cat. 58).

Stevenson apparently ordered a second waiter as a copy of Peaston's from Myer Myers, who may have had the Peaston waiter for sale in his store. Unfortunately, Myers's waiter remains unlocated, but photographs taken at Parke-Bernet when it was auctioned in 1941 (119.1) document its mark as MARK 9, indicating a date of manufacture of 1765–76.[3] Since Stevenson did not marry until about 1771, it seems likely that the two waiters were acquired by him at that date, Myers's being commissioned as a copy of the English model, which may well have supplied the requisite casting patterns. Myers may have used the patterns to make at least one other waiter with a nearly identical border.[4]

1 Davis 1976, pp. 133–34, no. 136. Another similar example is reprod. in Wees 1997, no. 336.
2 Provenance: to their daughter Anne, who in 1813 became the second wife of Major General Pierre Van Cortlandt II; to their great-granddaughters, Catherine Van Cortlandt Matthews and Isabel Rutherford (Matthews) Mason; by sale at auction in 1941 (Parke-Bernet 1941, lot 464); subsequently purchased by Paul Mellon, the donor in 1958.
3 Parke-Bernet 1941, lot 463. A photograph of the mark was sent to YUAG curator John Marshall Phillips at the time of the sale; silversmith research files, American Arts Office, YUAG.
4 Christie's 2000, lot 325; see also cat. 11.

120

WILLIAM GRUNDY (C. 1720–C. 1779)
London, England

Punch Bowl (Monteith), 1754–55

Sterling silver, h. 8¾ (22.2), diam. rim 10⅜ (26.4), diam. base 6¹⁵⁄₁₆ (17.6), wt. 64 oz. 14 dwt. (2013g) (scratch wt. 64 oz. 18 dwt.)

Museum of Fine Arts, Boston; Gift of Mrs. St. John Morgan

The sumptuous combination of cast, chased, and engraved Rococo ornament on this bowl was rarely found in American silver but was routine for large London workshops such as Grundy's.[1] Ellenor Alcorn concluded that the bowl's relatively small size indicated its use as a punch bowl rather than as a monteith for chilling glasses, a form that was out of fashion by the middle of the eighteenth century.[2] The bowl descended in the family of Robert Gilbert Livingston (1749–1787), the oldest surviving son of Robert Gilbert Livingston and his wife Catherine McPheadres.[3] Although no silver bowl of this size appears in Catherine's 1792 estate inventory, she and husband probably were the original owners, since their son was only six years old at the time the bowl was made.[4] Moreover, Robert and Catherine Livingston were fond of silver with rich Rococo ornament—they owned a substantial number of such pieces that probably are contemporary with the bowl, including the equally ornate candle snuffers and tray by Myer Myers (cat. 38).

1 Grimwade 1990, p. 529.
2 Alcorn 2000A, p. 181.
3 Livingston 1910, p. 547; Lawrence 1932, p. 33; Kinkead 1953, pp. 6–8, 99–101. For the punch bowl's descent, see Alcorn 2000A, p. 180.
4 New York Supreme Court of Probates Records, box 10, Inventories and Accounts, 1666–1822, NYSA

121

SAMUEL WOOD (C. 1704–1794)
London, England

Cruet Stand with Casters and Bottles, 1754–55

Sterling silver with glass bottles, (stand) h. 9¼ (23.5), w. 9¾ (24.8), d. 9¾ (24.8), wt. 33 oz. 15 dwt. (1049g)

Museum of the City of New York; Gift of Honoria Livingston McVitty 1996 Trust

This cruet set belonged to David Clarkson, Jr., and his wife, Elizabeth French (cat. 27); in the 1782 inventory of Clarkson's plate, the "Cruet-stand" weighing 58 troy oz. and 18 dwt. was valued at £24.3.7.[1] Each piece of this set had the Clarkson crest

120

121

of a griffin's head engraved on it, probably by the silversmith from whom it was purchased, just as Clarkson ordered a silver bread basket from London "with the crest, a griffin's head, upon it" (p. 62). Like the other London silver owned by Myers's New York patrons, this form was a specialty of its maker, who probably worked exclusively as a wholesale supplier to retail silversmiths.[2] Wood also made the casters associated with the cruet frame by Daniel Christian Fueter (cat. 106), as well as a cruet frame of 1752–53 owned by Munford family of Virginia.[3]

1 *Clarksons* 1876, p. 281. Provenance: by descent in the family to the donor, a great-great-great-granddaughter of David and Elizabeth (French) Clarkson. See Spooner 1907, p. 281, and Lawrence 1932, pp. 71, 100–01.
2 Grimwade 1990, p. 709.
3 Davis 1976, p. 154.

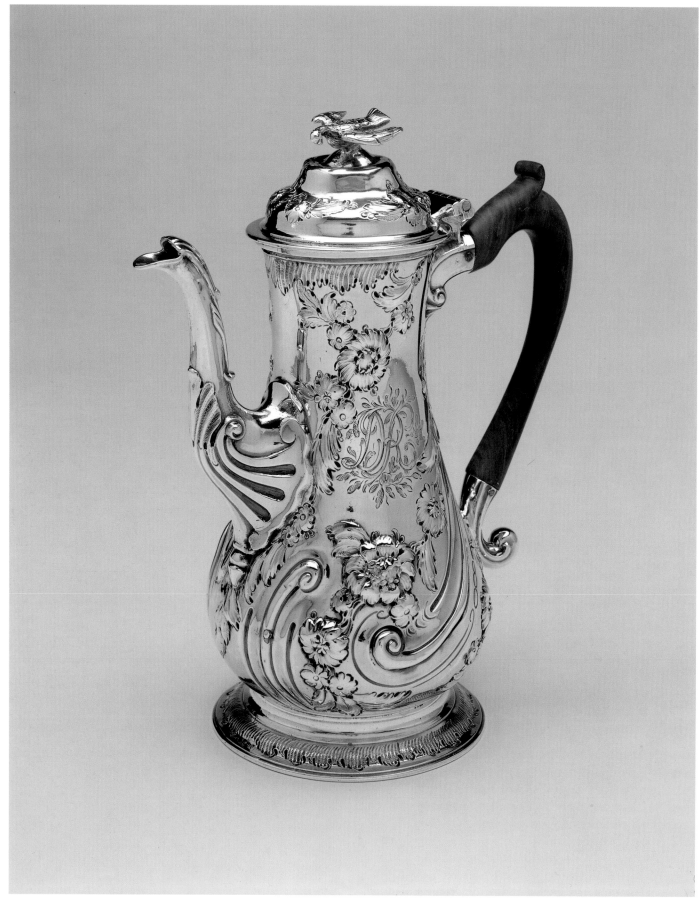

122

222 MYER MYERS

123

122

ROBERT PEASTON (ACT. 1756–66)
AND WILLIAM PEASTON (ACT. 1746–78),
IN PARTNERSHIP 1756–63
London, England

Coffeepot, 1761–62

Sterling silver with wood handle, h. 9¼ (23.5), w. 8⅛ (20.6), diam. base 4⁵⁄₁₆ (11), diam. rim 3 (7.6), gross wt. 26 oz. 4 dwt. (815g)

Collection of David M. Brinckerhoff, Nelson F. Brinckerhoff, Peter R. Brinckerhoff, and Robert W. Brinckerhoff, and their families; on long-term loan to The Metropolitan Museum of Art, New York

Chased ornament of scrolls and foliage was popular in New York during the 1760s, when this coffeepot may have arrived in the city, perhaps as part of a shipment such as the one of "neat chas'd silver coffee pots with cases" that Captain Jacobson imported from London in 1765 (p. 51). About a decade after its manufacture, the Peastons' coffeepot was acquired by Dorothea (Remsen) Brinckerhoff and engraved with her maiden initials, as were a chased sugar dish and milk pot supplied by Myers (cats. 85, 86). Like the Stevenson waiter (cat. 119), this adoption of an older object may signify conservative taste, or that a decade-old coffeepot was purchased second-hand, at a lower price. A similar coffeepot made by the Peastons in 1762–63 descended from John Stevenson's daughter Ann.[1]

Myer Myers possibly may have offered this coffeepot for sale in his store, perhaps as a secondhand object. The spout of the Peaston coffeepot is very similar to a spout Myers used on coffeepots during the 1770s (see discussion in cat. 47), and he may have taken his casting pattern from an imported version such as this as it passed through his hands, for resale or repair, or perhaps when it was engraved to match the objects made in his workshop.

1 Butler 1967, p. 83.

123

THOMAS NASH I (ACT. 1759–82)
London, England

Pair of Bottle Stands, 1770–71

Sterling silver and mahogany with wool felt, h. 2⅛ (5.4), diam. 4¾ (12.1) each

Museum of the City of New York; Gift of a descendant, Estelle de Peyster Hosmer, in memory of her sister, Justina de Peyster Martin

Thomas Nash is typical of the specialist craftsmen who produced pierced objects in eighteenth-century London; he registered marks as a smallworker and bucklemaker.[1] Like Myer Myers's bottle stands, these were made in three sections pierced with a small fretsaw before being joined together.

The initials "H/S*H" engraved on the front of each bottle stand were for Samuel Hake and his wife Helena Livingston, who married in 1769. Helena was the youngest child of Robert Gilbert Livingston and Catherine McPheadres (cats. 38, 120).[2] Like her parents, Helena Hake owned other stylish English silver, including two sets of candle snuffers and matching trays made in London in 1765–66.[3]

1 Grimwade 1990, p. 605.
2 Provenance: to their son Samuel, who in 1805 married Eva Margareta Elizabeth de Peyster; to the family of their nephew, Frederick de Peyster, Jr.; to the donors. See Lawrence 1932, pp. 33–34; Belknap 1956, pp. 76–77.
3 The Metropolitan Museum of Art, New York; Gift of Frederic Ashton de Peyster, 46.33.2-5. The maker's mark is W.T in an oval, which may be a mark of the London silversmith William Tuite; Grimwade 1990, p. 276, nos. 3901–02.

Paintings, Documents, *and* Prints

Cats. 124–149

124

JOHN WOLLASTON (ACT. 1742–75)

Robert R. Livingston, 1749–52

Oil on canvas, 50 x 40 (127 x 101.6)

Clermont State Historic Site, New York State Parks, Recreation, and Historic Preservation, Clermont, New York

Not exhibited

125

JOHN WOLLASTON (ACT. 1742–75)

Margaret (Beekman) Livingston, 1749–52

Oil on canvas, 50 x 40 (127 x 101.6)

Clermont State Historic Site, New York State Parks, Recreation, and Historic Preservation, Clermont, New York

Not exhibited

Robert R. Livingston (1718–1775) was a grandson of the first Robert Livingston through the latter's third son, Robert (1688–1775), who had received 13,000 acres at the southern end of Livingston Manor as the estate of Clermont. While his father resided at Clermont, Robert R. Livingston pursued a career in New York City as a lawyer, receiving appointments as judge of the Admiralty Court in 1760 and judge of the Supreme Court in 1763. He was chairman of the Stamp Act Congress in 1765 and drew up the petition to be presented to the House of Commons. In 1742, he married his second cousin Margaret Beekman (1724–1800), who was the daughter of Henry and Janet (Livingston) Beekman and the first cousin of Margaret Livingston, who married Peter R. Livingston (cats. 32, 34).

These portraits were painted in New York by the English-trained painter John Wollaston, who had operated a studio in London for about six years before moving to New York in 1749. During the three years he remained in the city, he produced almost one hundred portraits of New York's leading families in a highly conventional, Rococo manner derived from the leading London portrait painter Thomas Hudson.[1] Wollaston's elegant and graceful presentation of his sitters contrasts with the sober images of other Livingston family members by McIlworth and Delanoy (cats. 127–30). Robert and Margaret Livingston's preference for elegant Rococo design is evidenced not only by the engraving on their tankard by Myers (cat. 28), but also by their set of side chairs with pierced splats, whose pattern forms a mirror cypher of their initials.[2]

1 Craven 1986, pp. 304–08.
2 Hawley 1989.

124   125

126

126

THOMAS MCILWORTH (ACT. C. 1757–70)

The Reverend Samuel Johnson, c. 1761

Oil on canvas, 30 x 24¾ (76.2 x 62.9)

Columbia University in the City of New York; Bequest of Geraldine W. Carmalt, 1967

The Reverend Samuel Johnson (1696–1772) and his first wife, Charity (Floyd) Nicoll were among Myer Myers's most important patrons; they owned or commissioned at least eight pieces from his workshop (p. 000; cats. 20–26). This portrait of Samuel Johnson in his later years is a one of a group of four family portraits, including a pendant female portrait identified as Johnson's second wife, Sarah (Hull) Beach, whom he married after Charity's death in 1758. It seems likely that the portraits were painted in celebration of Samuel and Sarah's marriage on June 2, 1761; presumably they were completed before her death two years later. The related pair of portraits of Johnson's son William Samuel Johnson (fig. 32) and his wife, Ann Beach, who was Sarah's daughter, appears to have been executed at the same time.[1] The artist, Thomas McIlworth, worked in New York for about four years between 1757 and 1761. He apparently charged £10 for each likeness, including the frame, although as Johnson's 1761 letter to his son William indicates, his portraits failed to please:

Your Reflexions on the pictures are but too just & truly they are the language of just Resentment. Indeed I was truly sorry to send them. Yours indeed is a shocking thing. I wish it here again to be blotted out & Kilburn try when you come to do it better, as he did Mr. Holland's for 40 sh. Your wife's I think a good likeness, & only wants better Colours & Drapery, but I don't think that 10£ lost & the frames are worth the money: So that only the 10£ for yours is lost which is indeed worse than nothing.[2]

Johnson's reference is to the London-trained artist Lawrence Kilburn, who had arrived in New York from England in 1754.[3]

1 Thomas 1939, p. 218. Sarah (Hull) Johnson's portrait is owned by Columbia University, Archives and Columbiana Collection; Ann (Beach) Johnson's portrait is owned by the Munson-Williams-Proctor Institute, Utica, New York; Muehlig 1999, p. 23. The standard references for Johnson's life are Beardsley 1874 and Schneider/Schneider 1929.
2 Samuel Johnson to William Samuel Johnson, New York, July 27, 1761, Samuel Johnson Papers, vol. 3, Rare Book and Manuscript Library, Columbia University, New York.
3 Saunders/Miles 1987, pp. 254–55.

127   128

127

THOMAS MCILWORTH (ACT. C. 1757–70)

Robert Livingston, Jr., 1764

Oil on canvas, 49¾ x 40 (126.4 x 101.6)

The New-York Historical Society; Gift of Goodhue Livingston

128

THOMAS MCILWORTH (ACT. C. 1757–70)

Mary (Thong) Livingston, 1764

Oil on canvas, 49¾ x 40 (126.4 x 101.6)

The New-York Historical Society; Gift of Goodhue Livingston

Robert Livingston, Jr. (1708–1790) was the third and last Lord of Livingston Manor, consisting of 160,000 acres in what are now Columbia and Dutchess Counties. The manor had been confirmed to his grandfather Robert Livingston in 1686 and subsequently was inherited by his father, Philip Livingston,

who was also the father of Philip (cat. 129) and Catherine (cats. 35, 36). Like his father and grandfather, Robert, Jr., married into the established Dutch oligarchy. His first wife, Mary Thong, was the granddaughter of Governor Rip Van Dam; his second wife, Gertrude (Van Rensselaer) Schuyler, was the daughter of the patroon Kiliaen Van Rensselaer.

Aristocratic hauteur and a certain conservatism of are evident in these portraits, especially Mary Livingston's. As Susan Sawitzky first pointed out, the portrait was influenced in both composition and even the details of costume and lighting by John Wollaston's 1752 portrait of Mary's mother-in-law, Catharina (Van Brugh) Livingston, which probably was hanging in the Livingston manor house when McIlworth was painting there in November and December 1764, en route to Albany and eventually Montreal.[1] The only significant difference between Wollaston's and McIlworth's portraits is that the title of Mary's Bible is in English rather than Dutch, reflecting the change in the 1760s to English as the language of the Reformed Dutch Church (see cat. 59).[1]

1 Sawitzky 1951, pp. 122–26; Piwonka 1986, pp. 40–41.
2 *Catalogue of American Portraits* 1974, I, p. 479.

129

129

ATTRIBUTED TO ABRAHAM DELANOY
(1742–1795)

Philip Livingston, c. 1771

Oil on canvas, 50 x 40 (127 x 101.6)

Clermont State Historic Site, New York State Parks, Recreation, and Historic Preservation, Clermont, New York

Exhibited in New Haven only

130

ATTRIBUTED TO ABRAHAM DELANOY
(1742–1795)

Christina (Ten Broeck) Livingston, c. 1771

Oil on canvas, 50 x 40 (127 x 101.6)

Clermont State Historic Site, New York State Parks, Recreation, and Historic Preservation, Clermont, New York

Exhibited in New Haven only

130

Philip Livingston (1717–1778) was a younger brother of Robert Livingston, Jr. Cynthia Kierner has characterized him as the archetypal late Colonial gentleman, combining public service with a successful career as a merchant. Philip was educated at Yale (class of 1737) and served as a New York City alderman, member and later Speaker of the General Assembly, and signed the Declaration of Independence as a delegate to the Second Continental Congress.[1] He also wrote several pamphlets in support of the Presbyterian-Whig party espoused by his younger brother William (pp. 4–5).

Like his father and brother Robert, in 1740 Philip married into the Dutch establishment; his wife, Christina (1718–1801), was the daughter of Dirck Ten Broeck, Mayor of Albany, and Margarita Cuyler; her paternal grandfather, Dirck Wesselse Ten Broeck, had also served as Mayor of Albany.[2] Her brother Abraham Ten Broeck was a representative to the First Continental Congress and a brigadier general in the American army during the Revolutionary War.[3]

William and Susan Sawitzky attributed these portraits to Abraham Delanoy. Born in New York, Delanoy briefly studied in London with Benjamin West in 1766 before returning to his native city to paint portraits of the gentry.[4] He depicted Philip as an educated man in his library, standing with an open book, whereas Christina was shown seated with her arms folded demurely, next to a basket with sewing implements.

1 Kierner 1992, p. 8.
2 Reynolds 1911, II, pp. 763–64; Blackburn/Piwonka et al. 1988, p. 277.
3 Runk 1897, p. 59.
4 Sawitzky 1957, pp. 204–05; Evans 1980, p. 33.

131

131

UNIDENTIFIED ARTIST

Samuel Cornell, c. 1770

Oil on canvas, 14⅝ x 12⅝ (37.1 x 32.1)

Tryon Palace Historic Sites and Gardens, New Bern, North Carolina

This modest portrait is the only known image of Samuel Cornell (1731–1781).[1] Together with his wife, Susannah Mabson (1732–1778), Cornell commissioned six pieces of silver from Myers (cats. 19, 77–80), an extraordinary collection of unique or unusual forms as well as the largest group of pierced silver made in the American Colonies. As noted (p. 60), these objects may have been purchased after Cornell's appointment in 1770 to the Provincial Council in North Carolina. Governor William Tryon wrote to the Earl of Hillsborough, then Secretary of State for the Colonies:

Mr. Cornell is a Merchant of the first Credit and Fortune in the Province, a Native of New York, about forty Years of Age, of a very gen-teel Publick Spirit; as an Evidence of the latter, He lent Me for the use of the Publick, Six Thousand Pounds to carry on the Governors House at Newbern; without whose Assistance the Building must have been greatly retarded.[2]

Cornell's support for Tryon extended beyond financing the construction of his residence. In 1771, Cornell not only contributed £1,000 toward fighting the Regulators, a radical revolt by residents of western counties against British taxation, but he also outfitted some of the troops and personally served under Tryon as a lieutenant colonel, suffering a minor wound at the Battle of Alamance on May 16, 1771.[3]

1 Provenance: to Cornell's daughter Hannah (Cornell) LeRoy (see cat. 19); by descent to Robert Emmett (Cornell 1902, p. 215, pl. facing p. 190); subsequent ownership uncertain; purchased in 1997 by Tryon Palace together with a portrait of Catherine (LeRoy) Newbold.
2 Powell 1981, pp. 422–23.
3 Dill 1955, pp. 128–54; Powell 1981, pp. 661, 740.

132

SAMUEL KING (1749–1819)
Boston, Massachusetts

Rabbi Haim Isaac Carigal, 1782

Oil on canvas, 30 x 25 (76.2 x 63.5) (sight)

Private collection

This is a posthumous portrait of Raphael Haim Isaac Carigal (1733–1777), one of the few ordained rabbis to visit what is now the United States during the Colonial period. Born in Hebron in Palestine, he studied for the rabbinate in Jerusalem and traveled throughout the Near East, North Africa, and Europe before journeying to Curaçao in 1761 to serve two years as substitute rabbi for the congregation there. He then returned to Europe and the Near East, but went to Jamaica in 1771 and the following year visited Philadelphia and New York before arriving in Newport in 1773. After about six months in Newport, he sailed for Suriname; on June 19, 1774, he was elected the rabbi of Congregation Nidhe Israel in Bridgetown, Barbados. Carigal died in Bridgetown on May 5, 1777.[1]

Unlike Isaac Pinto (cat. 144) or Gershom Mendes Seixas (fig. 5), Carigal had been ordained as a rabbi and was a native speaker of Hebrew. His visit to America excited great interest, particularly on the part of Ezra Stiles (cat. 133), then pastor of Newport's Second Congregational Church. On the eve of Purim on March 8, 1773, Stiles attended a service at the Touro Synagogue and noted that Carigal "was dressed in a red Garment with the usual Phylacteries and habiliments, the white silk Surplice; he wore a high brown furr Cap, had a long Beard."[2] Stiles quickly made Carigal's acquaintance and discussed languages, including Hebrew and Arabic: "I suppose I then for the first Time heard the true pronunciation of Arabic," he recorded after one meeting, and after another: "We conversed much and freely—he is learned and truly modest, far more so than I ever saw a Jew."[3]

Carigal preached a sermon on the first day of Shavuot (Sivan 6, 5533/May 28, 1773), which Governor Joseph Wanton and two judges attended, as well as Stiles, who wrote in his diary:

At reading the Law the Rabbi was desired and read the Ten Commandments. But before reading the Law and the prophets the Rabbi went to the Desk or Taubah [tebah] and preached a Sermon about 47 minutes long, in Spanish. It was interspersed with Hebrew. His Oratory, Elocution and Gestures were fine and oriental. It was very animated. . . . The Affinity of the Spanish and Latin enabled me to understand something of the Discourse—but after all I have but an imperfect Idea of it. . . . The Jews intend to print it.[4]

Carigal's sermon was translated into English by Abraham Lopez and printed by July 1773 by Solomon Southwick, publisher of the *Newport Mercury*, making it the first sermon by a rabbi to be delivered and printed in America.

After Carigal's departure from Newport, Stiles maintained a regular correspondence with him, noting in December 1773 that he had "finished a Hebrew Letter of 22 pages to R. Haijm Isaac Karigal."[5] After becoming president of Yale College, Stiles wrote to the former *parnas* (president) of Yeshuat Israel, Aaron Lopez:

The affectionate Respect I bear to the Memory of that great & eminent Hocham, the Rabbi Karigal, has made me wish that his Picture might be deposited in the Library of this College. I remember it was taken in Crayons. . . . You can employ Mr. King to copy it in oyl colours, which will be durable & much preferable to the Chalk of Crayons. . . . I shd think it would be honorable to your Nation as well as ornamental to this University.[6]

Stiles's choice of Samuel King, a Newport native who also worked as a gilder and carriage and sign painter, undoubtedly stemmed from his acquaintance with King while both men lived in Newport. Stiles had officiated at King's marriage in 1770, and in the same year King began his portrait of Stiles (cat. 133).[7] Following Stiles's suggestion, Carigal's portrait was commissioned from King in 1781 and donated to Yale in 1782 by Lopez's father-in-law, Jacob Rodrigues de Rivera of Newport.[8] At the time of Stiles's death in 1795, however, the portrait was in his possession. It was inherited by his daughter Emilia (Stiles) Leavitt and descended in the family to the present owner.

1 Biographical information on Carigal is taken from Friedman 1940.
2 Dexter 1901, I, p. 354.
3 Ibid., pp. 358, 361.
4 Ibid., pp. 376–77.
5 Ibid., p. 423; Morgan 1962, pp. 143–44.
6 Ezra Stiles to Aaron Lopez, May 31, 1781, cited in Friedman 1940, pp. 29–30.
7 Little 1976, p. 146.
8 Friedman 1940, pp. 30–33.

133

SAMUEL KING (1749–1819)
Newport, Rhode Island

The Reverend Ezra Stiles, 1770–71

Oil on canvas, 33½ x 27½ (85.1 x 69.9)

Yale University Art Gallery, New Haven; Bequest of Dr. Charles Jenkins Foote, B.A. 1883, M.D. 1890

Ezra Stiles (1727–1795) received a B.A. from Yale College in 1746 and an M.A. in 1749. After practicing law in New Haven, he was called as the minister of the Second Congregational Church in Newport, Rhode Island, where this portrait was

132

painted.[1] Stiles remained in Newport until the outbreak of the Revolutionary War, and served as the president of Yale College from 1778 until his death.

Stiles had a lifelong enthusiasm for Jewish religion and history and for the Hebrew language in particular, which he claimed to have taught himself. His knowledge of Judaism and Hebrew texts is commemorated in the "Emblems" of this portrait, which he apparently designed himself and had Samuel King add in the summer of 1771 to the canvas King had begun the previous year. At the upper left is a globe that Stiles called "an Emblem of the Universe or intellectual World"; at its center is the Hebrew word *Yahweh*, a transliteration of the four Hebrew letters that form one of the names of God. Judaism was one of the four religions that Stiles chose to encapsulate in his history of the world, as represented by the four folio books at the lower right. The other three are: pagan (the Roman historian Livy, presumably his *Historia Romanae*); Christian (Eusebius's *Historia Ecclesiae*); and Chinese, "being one Third or more of the human Race & different from all the rest of the Orientals" (Jean-Baptiste du Halde's *Description géographique, historique, chronologique, politique, et physique de l'empire de la Chine et de la Tartarie chinoise* of 1735, translated on the spine as *History of China*). Stiles chose to represent the Jews by a volume of the Talmud, with the names on the spine of the eleventh- and twelfth-century Sephardic biblical commentators Abraham ibn Ezra and Solomon ben Isaac in Hebrew, and the name of the twelfth-century philosopher Moses Maimonides and the title of his *Moreh Nevukhim* ("Guide of the Perplexed") in Aramaic. In his diary, Stiles went into detail on his choice of the last volume:

[It shows] *the Rabbin. Learng party in the two most eminent Periods of it; the first before & at the Time of Christ containg the Decisions of the house of R. Eleazer at Babylon, and those of the Houses Hillel & Shammai at Jerusalem; the second period was at the Revival of the Hebrew Learning in the XIth & Twelfth Centuries, when arose those Lights of the Captivity, Jarchi* [i.e. Rashi, an acrostic form of

133

Solomon ben Isaac's name], *Maimonides &c. I prize this Learng only for the scattered Remains of the antient Doctrine of the Trinity, & a suffering Messiah, preserved in the Opinions of some of the Rabbins before Christ—the very Labors of the modern Rabbins to obviate or interpret them into another sense & Application evincing their Genuiness & Reality. The Moreh Nevochim [sic] which was originally written in Arabic, is curious for many Reasons; it was a capital Work, & became an Occasion of the greatest literary Dispute among the Jews since the days of Hillel—it contains great Concessions, which have recommended it to Xtian [Christian] Divines.*[2]

After becoming president of Yale College, Stiles instituted the mandatory study of Hebrew by all freshmen, but discontinued it after 1790 because "this has proved very disagreeable to a Number of the Students."[3]

There is one remote connection between Myer Myers and Ezra Stiles. On October 8, 1789, Stiles climbed Pinnacle Rock above Lake Waramug in Connecticut to examine a "Hebrew Inscription" at the summit. He recorded: "The Characters are

good Hebrew well engraved, I believe by some Jews who have been visiting the Kent & New Milfd. [Milford] Mountains for Gold Mines for 30 y. past. I took them off accurately. . . . The Incision was made with a Chizel as on Tombstones."[4] These carvings subsequently have been interpreted as two sets of names: "Abram/Isaac" and "Moses/Adam."[5] Stiles's reference to Jews searching for gold mines thirty years earlier undoubtedly represented an imperfect recollection by local residents of Myers and his partners' investment in the Spruce Hill Lead Mine, less than ten miles south (p. 45). It is possible that someone connected with the lead mine was responsible for the inscriptions Stiles copied.

1 For further information on the portrait, see Dexter 1901, I, pp. 131–33; Setze 1957.
2 Dexter 1901, I, p. 131.
3 Ibid., III, p. 397.
4 Ibid., III, p. 368.
5 Trento 1997, p. 188.

134   135

134

UNIDENTIFIED ARTIST

William Gilbert, c. 1795–1805

Pastel on paper, 9¼ x 6¼ (23.5 x 15.9) (sight)

Private collection

135

UNIDENTIFIED ARTIST

Mrs. William Gilbert, c. 1795–1805

Pastel on paper, 9¼ x 6¼ (23.5 x 15.9) (sight)

Private collection

This modest rendering of William Gilbert is one of the only images of a New York silversmith active during the Colonial

period, although it was executed after he had ceased to work or refer to himself as a craftsman. The identity of the companion portrait is uncertain; a later inscription on the back states that she was Gilbert's first wife, Catherina Cosine, who died in 1801. But the portraits could also have been made to celebrate Gilbert's marriage in 1802 to his second wife, Elizabeth Hawley.[1]

When the pastel of Gilbert was lent to the Museum of the City of New York in 1937, it was attributed to the English pastel portraitist James Sharples, who made his first visit to America between 1796 and 1801; he lived in New York City between 1797 and 1798.[2] His work was greatly admired and became extremely popular, spawning a number of imitators. The Gilbert portraits lack the complexity and subtlety of Sharples's documented works, and probably were done by another artist.

1 Provenance: to the sitters' great-great grandson, Henry Varick Gilbert, Jr.; by sale to the collector Andrew Varick Stout; to his son, Gardiner Stout; by sale to the dealers Ginsburg and Levy; from whom the present owner acquired them.
2 For Sharples, see Knox 1930.

136

137

136

JOHN TRUMBULL (1756–1843)

Dorothea (Remsen) Brinckerhoff, 1804–08

Oil on canvas, 28¾ x 23¾ (73 x 60.3) (sight)

Collection of Robert W. Brinckerhoff

Exhibited in New Haven only

137

GILBERT STUART (1755–1828)

Abraham Brinckerhoff, 1793–94

Oil on canvas, 28¾ x 23¾ (73 x 60.3) (sight)

Collection of Robert W. Brinckerhoff

Exhibited in New Haven only

Abraham Brinckerhoff (1745–1823) and his wife, Dorothea Remsen (1750–1834) purchased a significant number of objects from Myers around the time of their marriage in 1772 (cats.

83–86). Both portraits were painted much later. Gilbert Stuart depicted the fifty-year-old Brinckerhoff while briefly residing in New York, having returned from Dublin in the spring of 1793; Stuart moved to Philadelphia in November 1794. William Dunlap later recalled that Stuart "opened an *attelier* [*sic*] in Stone-street, near William-street, where all who admired the art or wished to avail themselves of the artist's talents, daily resorted."[1] Trumbull's portrait of Dorothea Brinckerhoff was painted about a decade later, when the artist had returned to New York City after six years in England.[2] Its rectangular format and cool, monochromatic tonality indicates that Trumbull did not intend to match Stuart's oval canvas and vivid colors, although the two paintings were later framed as pendants. Dorothea's portrait resembles other paintings of older women that Trumbull executed at this time, particularly his c. 1806 portrait of *Hannah (Lindley) Murray*, where the pose of the hands is similar, as is the lace cap and thinly painted drapery in the background.[3]

1 Dunlap 1834, I, pp. 195–96.
2 Sizer 1967, p. 21.
3 Caldwell/Johnson/Roque 1994, pp. 221–22.

138

138

CHARLES PEALE POLK (1767–1822)
Baltimore, Maryland

Barnard Gratz, c. 1792

Oil on canvas, 40 x 35 (101.6 x 88.9)

Collection of E. Norman Flayderman

Barnard Gratz (1738–1801) emigrated from Silesia to Philadelphia in 1755. Together with his brother Michael, David Franks (cat. 4), and Joseph Simon (cat. 139), he established himself as a leading merchant, fur trader, and investor in western lands.[1] Within about two years of his arrival, Gratz had business dealings with Myer Myers, which may have included trade silver for Indians (p. 61). The two men's connection was strengthened on December 10, 1760, when the twenty-two-year-old Barnard married twenty-nine-year-old Richea Myers Cohen,

the sister of Myers's first wife, Elkaleh. As a founding trustee of Congregation Mikveh Israel in Philadelphia, Gratz was also closely involved with the acquisition of Torah finials from Myers (cat. 65).

Charles Peale Polk was the nephew and namesake of Charles Willson Peale, with whom he trained. His portrait of Gratz apparently was painted about 1792 in Baltimore, where the widowed Gratz had moved to be with his daughter Rachel (Gratz) Etting. Polk also painted Rachel Etting's mother-in-law, Shinah (Solomon) Etting, in the same year.[2] Gratz's portrait presents him as a man of learning as well as a devout Jew, since books with titles in Hebrew are included on the shelves behind him.

1 For the Gratz brothers, see Fish 1994.
2 Brilliant/Smith 1997, no. 50.

139

139

GILBERT STUART (1755–1828)
Philadelphia, Pennsylvania

Miriam (Simon) Gratz, 1802

Oil on canvas, 28½ x 23¼ (72.4 x 59.1) (sight)

Private collection

Miriam (Simon) Gratz (1749–1808) was the daughter of Joseph Simon and Rose Bunn, who was a first cousin of Myers's wife, Elkaleh.[1] Joseph Simon had settled in Lancaster, Pennsylvania, about 1740 but had many business interests in common with David Franks (cat. 4) and the brothers Barnard (cat. 138) and Michael Gratz of Philadelphia, particularly in the fur trade along the Ohio River. Simon was also a leader of the Jewish community in Philadelphia. These economic and religious connections were strengthened by his daughter's marriage on June 20, 1769 to Michael Gratz.

Miriam Gratz sat for this portrait in 1803, near the end of Gilbert Stuart's decade-long residence in Philadelphia. During these years, and particularly while Philadelphia was the capital of the United States, he painted the leaders of the "Republican Court," the wealthy Federalists who led society, and was celebrated for his elegant images of such women as Anne (Willing) Bingham.[2] The more modest depiction of Miriam Gratz shows her in a simple black dress, her head covered with a linen cap and her hands folded in her lap.

1 Stern 1991, pp. 223, 271.
2 Garvan 1987, fig. 13.

140

140

GILBERT STUART (1755–1828)
Boston, Massachusetts

Samuel Myers, 1805–10

Oil on panel, 27¾ x 22½ (70.5 x 57.2) (sight)

Collection of Helen and Peter Du Bois

Samuel Myers (1755–1836) was the second son of Myer and Elkaleh Myers. Although at age eleven he signed a receipt for payment of repair work done by his father's workshop (Appendix II, no. 4), Samuel did not train as a silversmith. As a teenager, he began what became a lifelong career as a merchant. By the 1790s, he was involved in trading West Indies staples (rum, coffee, and sugar) for North American products

(wheat, flour, and tobacco), as well as importing such exotic goods as "Holland Gin," brandy, "Hyson tea," and textiles.[1] Samuel first was based in the Caribbean but had relocated to Amsterdam by the time of the Revolutionary War, when he worked in partnership with his cousin by marriage Isaac Moses (cat. 141) and Moses Myers (1753–1835) to import European goods through the British blockade.[2] After the war, Moses Myers moved to Norfolk, Virginia, and Samuel eventually settled in Petersburg and later Richmond, Virginia, at which point his business expanded thanks to family connections made after his second marriage in 1796. In the same year, he wrote to a prospective associate:

I intend to hold a Vessel or Two in the St. Domingo Trade and will occasionelly require your services in the commission line at Aux Cayes

140.1. William Barksdale Myers, *Gustavus Adolphus Myers*, Richmond, Virginia, 1868. Oil on composition board. The Virginia Historical Society, Richmond; Gift of Mrs. Edward R. Wardwell.

[Haiti]. . . . *I have established my Two young Brothers in Petersburg Virginia under my former firm of Samuel Myers and Brothers.*[3]

The "Brothers" were his younger half-brothers, Moses Mears Myers and Samson Mears Myers.[4]

Like his father, Samuel Myers benefited throughout his life from the closely intertwined business and kinship networks that existed among American Jews in the eighteenth century. In the year that he established his brothers in Petersburg, Samuel married his second wife, his cousin Judith Hays, the eldest child of Moses Michael Hays and Rachel Myers (cat. 42). On the same day, September 21, 1796, Judith's sister Sarah married Samuel's half-brother and partner, Moses Mears Myers. Cousins from these families continued to marry in the next generation (cat. 96).

This portrait of Samuel Myers in his early fifties was painted by Gilbert Stuart in Boston, where the artist had moved in 1805. Myers made frequent visits to Boston in his capacities as a merchant and son-in-law of Moses and Rachel Hays. His granddaughter Caroline Cohen noted that "his cold and dignified demeanor created an impression of severity which has become a tradition amongst his descendants," an impression belied by the "tenderest feeling" of his letters to his sister Judith.[5] The austerity of his image seems consistent with sentiments Samuel expressed in a letter to Moses Myers of Norfolk in 1796: "My state of mediocrity pleases me more than the appearance of opulence that many make and are oblig'd to support at an expence that proves fatal in the end."[6] Although no portrait of Myer Myers is known, it is tempting to seek a suggestion of his features in the strong resemblance between his son Samuel and his grandson Gustavus Adolphus (140.1). Gustavus Adolphus Myers was a leading figure in economic, political, and cultural circles of antebellum Virginia. Although he served on the board of the Beth Shalom Synagogue in Richmond, he married a Christian, Anne Augusta (Giles) Conway, the daughter of Governor William Giles. Their only child, William Barksdale Myers, was raised as a Christian and became an artist.[7]

1 Myers 1796–98, pp. 34–36, 43–45, 82–84.
2 Ibid., p. 6; Cohen 1913, p. 1; Mordecai 1796, n.p.; Berman 1979, pp. 65–70.
3 Myers 1796–98, p. 3.
4 Stern 1991, p. 217.
5 Cohen 1913, p. 6.
6 Myers 1796–98, pp. 50–51.
7 Rosenbaum 1954A, p. 62.

141

141

JOHN WESLEY JARVIS (1780–1840)

Isaac Moses, c. 1815

Oil on canvas, 30 x 24⅞ (76.2 x 63.2)

Museum of the City of New York, Presented by a Group of Friends of the Museum

Born in Hanover, Germany, Isaac Moses (1742–1818) arrived in New York about 1761 and became closely connected to Myer Myers. In 1770, Moses married his first cousin, Reyna Levy, the daughter of his maternal uncle, Hayman Levy and Sloe Myers, the silversmith's sister.[1] On April 25, 1771, Moses was naturalized, with Myer Myers testifying as to his required residency.[2] Moses served together with both Levy and Myers as an elder of Shearith Israel both before and after the American Revolution (cat. 145); during the war, he was the business partner of Myers's son Samuel (cat. 140). In 1787, Myer Myers engraved the pair of brass candlesticks Moses donated to the burial society at Shearith Israel (cat. 142).

This portrait was painted when Moses was about seventy-three years old and had become wealthy through a variety of enterprises, including shipping, privateering during the Revolutionary War, real estate investments, and banking.[3] He contributed £3,000 toward provisioning the American army in 1780 and paid the highest rate of £12 for his seat in the Mill Street Synagogue in 1792.[4] The artist John Wesley Jarvis seems to have been engaged during the early nineteenth century by a number of prominent Jewish sitters, including the Hendricks and Isaacs families of New York and the Etting family of Baltimore.[5]

1 Stern 1991, p. 159, 217.
2 Oppenheim 1926, p. 2; Pool 1952, p. 385, states that Moses first petitioned for naturalization in 1768, but it was not granted until 1771.
3 Pool 1952, pp. 385–90.
4 *The Pennsylvania Gazette*, July 5, 1780, p. 1; "Sales of the Mens Seats in Synagogue," August 26, 1792, box 2, file 113; Lyons Collection, AJHS.
5 Brilliant/Smith 1997, nos. 73–74, 76, 80.

142

MAKER UNIDENTIFIED
Probably England

ENGRAVED BY MYER MYERS

Pair of Candlesticks, 1770–87

Brass with later silver plating

A. h. 15⅝ [originally 14⅜] (39.7 [36.5]), w. 5¼ (13.3), d. 5¼ (13.3)

B. h. 16¼ [originally 14¹⁵⁄₁₆] (41.3 [37.9]), w. 5⁵⁄₁₆ (13.5), d. 5⁵⁄₁₆ (13.5)

INSCRIPTION: In Hebrew: "This candelabrum is a gift of the honorable gentleman Yitzhak son of Moshe David for the use of the holy society Gemiluth Hasadim in New York in the year 5547"[1]

Congregation Shearith Israel, New York

Exhibited in New Haven only

The *Hebra Gemiluth Hasadim* ("Society of doing acts of personal service") was a short-lived charitable organization formed in 1785 by men of Shearith Israel, including Myer Myers, to carry out the proper rituals for burial of the dead. Members would bring these candlesticks to the home of the deceased to provide illumination for dressing the corpse and keeping a vigil over it until the funeral. Trustee Israel Baer Kursheedt's instructions for attending the dead included the directive "remove everything offensive from the Corpse, Cover it with the Black Cloth, & Place a lighted Candle at the Head."[2] A candle was supposed to burn for seven days following a death.[3] According to *hazan* Jacques Judah Lyons, in the 1870s the pair of candlesticks was "still devoted to its original purposes at the hour of death and in the Synagogue on the evening of Tishabeab," the fast on the 9th of Ab commemorating the destruction of the Temple.[4]

The candlesticks were presented to the *Hebra Gemiluth Hasadim* in 1787 by member Isaac Moses (cat. 141). Myers was paid 16 shillings by the society for engraving the dedication.[5] Since knowledge of Hebrew would have been important for properly recording these inscriptions, Myers himself may have done the engraving (142.3). Two years later, he was paid 2 shillings for engraving the society's name in Hebrew on a copper cistern, now known only through a photograph of the early 1870s (142.1).[6] Lyons described it as "a copper vase or fountain (as it was called in olden times) used as yet on the Beth haim [burial ground] for the washing of hands after interment."[7]

The square bases, sharply tapered shafts, and unmolded surface of the candlesticks are typical features of the Neoclassical style. Documented examples include a pattern illustrated in a Birmingham brass founder's catalogue of c. 1780 and candlesticks marked by Thomas Warner of London between 1782 and 1798.[8] The high bases and attenuated proportions suggest that the Shearith Israel candlesticks probably are of provincial English origin. They may well have been imported by one of

the members of the congregation involved in the copper and brass trades, including Myers's brother Asher or the Hendricks family. One of the candlesticks bears a shield-shaped mark (142.2), atypical of eighteenth-century brass-founder's marks but related to the shield-shape surround of London city hallmarks found on silver between 1739 and 1756.[9]

When the *Hebra Gemiluth Hasadim* was disbanded about 1802, the candlesticks became the property of the successor burial society, the *Hebra Hased Va-Amet* ("Society of kindness and truth"). At some point after Lyons had them photographed in the 1870s, larger drip pans were added to the tops. The candlesticks have been electroplated with silver, probably when these drip pans were added, although electroplating could have taken place earlier. Lyons recorded that four eighteenth-century brass "nobs" used to hold the *tebah* (reader's desk) cloth in place had been "plated" in 1842, and perhaps the candlesticks were also plated at this time.[10]

1 I am indebted to Rabbi Marc Angel of Congregation Shearith Israel for recording this inscription and providing the translation.
2 *Lyons Collection* 1920, p. 230.
3 Kanof 1975, p. 51.
4 Jacques Judah Lyons, Notebook no. 1, p. 32, Lyons Collection, AJHS.
5 Ibid., p. 34.
6 Ibid., p. 34.
7 Ibid., pp. 32–33. The cistern apparently has not survived.
8 Gentle/Feild 1975, p. 123; Fennimore 1996A, p. 207.
9 Gentle/Feild 1975, pp. 75–76; Burks 1986, pp. 28–29, 96, 104; Fennimore 1996A, pp. 41–47. I am indebted to Donald Fennimore for his observations on the style of these candlesticks and their mark.
10 "Inventory of Property in 1805," p. IV, Lyons Collection, box 6, AJHS.

142.1. Photograph of cat. 142 with cistern (detail), New York, c. 1870. American Jewish Historical Society, New York City and Waltham, Massachusetts.

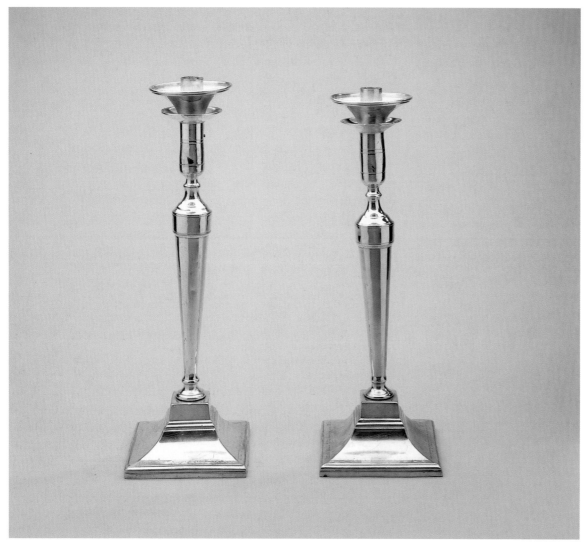

142

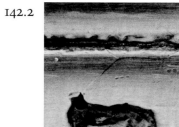

142.2

142.3

143

DAVID GRIM (1737–1826)

A Plan of the City and Environs of New York as they were in the Years 1742, 1743 & 1744, 1813

(illustrated in color on p. xvi)

Pen and ink with watercolor on paper, 22⅛ x 21⅞ (56.2 x 55.6)

The New-York Historical Society, Collection of the Library

Exhibited in New Haven only

Myer Myers was a child of seven when Congregation Shearith Israel erected the first synagogue in Mill (now South William) Street. It was dedicated on April 8, 1730, and demolished in 1833.[1] The New York historian William Smith observed in 1757, "The Jews, who are not inconsiderable for their numbers, worship in a synagogue erected in a very private part of the town, plain without, but very neat within."[2] The only contemporary rendering of the Mill Street Synagogue, David Grim's sketch at the upper right of this map, records this plain appearance and relatively small scale.

Both these features followed the pattern of synagogue buildings established in England during the eighteenth century. As Edward Jamilly has noted, unlike the Great Portuguese Synagogue of 1671–75 in Amsterdam, which towered over its neighborhood, London synagogue buildings of the Georgian era were more modestly scaled structures of relatively low height, with severely plain exteriors that often were not visible from the street.[3] The Mill Street Synagogue was only 21 feet high and set back from the street within a courtyard. The building's square plan (35 x 35 feet) may have been based on the original Great Synagogue in Duke's Place in London, a square structure 63 x 60 feet used by the Ashkenazic Jewish community. Jamilly pointed out that the brick exteriors and tall rounded windows found in most English synagogues (as well as Mill Street) were similar to the design of Christian non-conformist houses of worship.[4] On Grim's map, the Mill Street Synagogue is particularly close in scale and style to the Baptist and Quaker meeting houses depicted to the left. This exterior simplicity, however, was also a feature of Anglican church architecture in the Colonies after 1720, as Dell Upton has demonstrated for eastern Virginia.[5]

The thumbnail images of buildings across the top of the map—ten houses of worship framed by civic structures and fortifications—provide one of the most vivid illustrations of the religious and ethnic pluralism of Colonial New York City, a pluralism that had few counterparts in British North America (pp. 2–3). David Grim, who drew this map at the age of seventy-six from his "perfect and correct" memory, would have

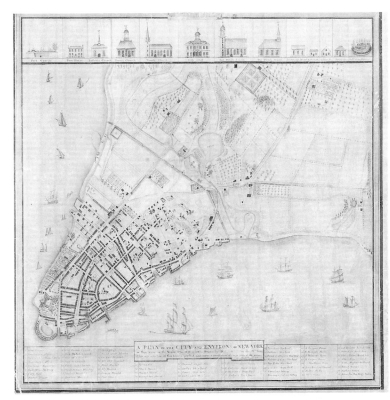

143

been as keenly conscious as Myer Myers of the benefits of New York's pluralistic environment. Born in Zweibrücken, Bavaria, he was brought to New York as a child by his parents in 1739. He always identified with the German community: a lifelong member of the Lutheran, or "German Evangelical," church, he was active in both church offices and the German Society of New York, and succeeded the war hero Baron von Steuben (cat. 115) as president of the society.[6]

1 For a detailed account of the synagogue building and its history, see Pool/Pool 1955, pp. 40–52.
2 Smith/Kammen 1972, I, p. 208.
3 Jamilly 1999, pp. 1–10.
4 Ibid., p. 16.
5 Upton 1997, pp. 158–59.
6 Eickhoff 1884, pp. 97, 135–36.

PRAYERS

FOR

SHABBATH, ROSH-HASHANAH, AND KIPPUR,

OR

The SABBATH, the BEGINNING of the YEAR,

AND

The DAY of ATONEMENTS;

WITH

The AMIDAH and MUSAPH of the MOADIM.

OR

SOLEMN SEASONS.

According to the Order of the Spanish and Portuguese Jews.

TRANSLATED BY ISAAC PINTO.

And for him printed by JOHN HOLT, in New-York,
A. M. 5526.

144

144

ISAAC PINTO (1720–1791), TRANSLATOR

Prayers for Shabbath, Rosh-Hashanah, and Kippur, 1766

New York: John Holt

Printed book, 7¼ x 5⅝ (18.4 x 14.3)

Beinecke Rare Book and Manuscript Library, Yale University, New Haven

No published English translation of Jewish prayers or services existed until the appearance of Isaac Pinto's books in New York.[1] Services at synagogues in England and America were conducted in Hebrew, with a few prayers in Spanish or Portuguese, and prayerbooks with translations allowed participants unfamiliar with Hebrew to understand the service.[2] Sephardic Jews had published Spanish translations of Jewish

services and prayers in Italy as early as the mid-sixteenth century, in Amsterdam by the third quarter of the seventeenth century, and in London by the first decade of the eighteenth century—even though the London rabbinical authorities prohibited English translations.[3] No such prohibitions were carried to the Colonies, however, and Pinto's 1766 translation answered the needs of a small New York congregation with its mixture of Sephardic and Ashkenazic Jews. In his preface, Pinto observed:

A Veneration for the Language, sacred by being that in which it pleased Almighty God to reveal himself to our Ancestors, and a desire to preserve it, in firm Persuasion that it will again be re-established in Israel; are probably leading Reasons for our performing divine Service in Hebrew: But that being imperfectly understood by many, by some, not at all; it has been necessary to translate our Prayers. . . . In Europe, the Spanish and Portuguese Jews have a Translation in Spanish, which as they generally understand, may be sufficient; but that not being the Case in the British Dominions in America, has induced me to attempt a Translation in English. . . .

After the Revolutionary War, Shearith Israel's *hazan* (cantor-reader), Gershom Mendes Seixas (fig. 5), began chanting the old Portuguese prayers in English, since he was "unacquainted with the Spanish and Portuguese languages which have ever been used since the first establishment of the synagogue"; he also preached sermons in English.[4] The first English translation of Jewish prayers to be published in London appeared in 1770, and a number of versions were available in the United States by 1792, when Sheftall Sheftall, then resident in Philadelphia, wrote his father, Mordecai Sheftall, in Savannah:

By Collin's Sloop I Sent Some Hebrew books. . . . also a book Intirely in English With all the Ceremonies of our Religion—Several had been Imported, by Mr. Josephson—The Christians purchas'd them as Well as the Jews—Mr. David Levi the Translator.[5]

Isaac Pinto was eldest brother of silversmith Joseph Pinto (p. 36).[6] In the later 1780s and into the early 1790s he advertised that he taught Spanish, and his obituary stated: "He was well versed in several of the foreign languages."[7] As indicated in his preface to the 1766 translation, Pinto based part of his prayerbooks on the "Elegant Spanish" translation done by Rabbi Isaac Nieto of London in 1740. Pinto's literary efforts went beyond translation. Under the name "Isaac the Scribe," he published a travel narrative in 1769, and he corresponded with Rabbi Haim Carigal (cat. 132) concerning the interpretation of Arabic words in Talmudic commentaries by Abraham ibn Ezra.[8] Ezra Stiles (cat. 133) referred to Pinto as the "learned Jew at New York."[9]

1 Karp 1976–77, pp. 15–16.
2 Pool/Pool 1952, pp. 83, 87.
3 Mintz/Rotmil 1992, esp. pp. 20, 72–76, 90, 99, 101; Jacobs/Wolf 1888, p. 174.
4 Pool/Pool 1955, p. 87; Pool 1952, pp. 363–67.

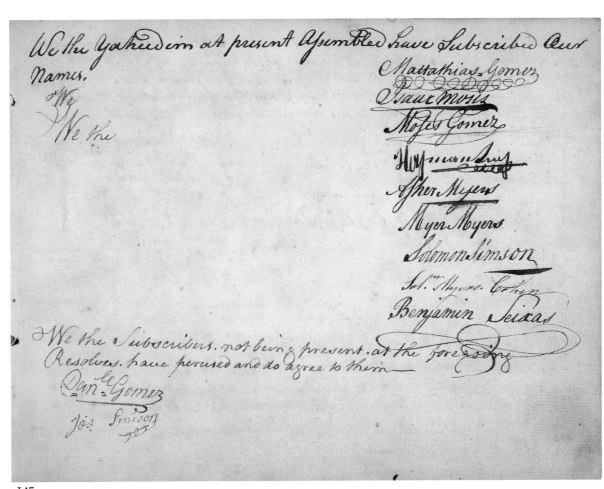

145

5 Sheftall Sheftall to Mordecai Sheftall, Philadelphia, July 8, 1792, Sheftall Papers, AJHS; for English translations, see Jacobs/Wolf 1888, pp. 174–75.

6 Stern 1991, p. 251.

7 The New-York Journal and Patriotic Register, December 9, 1790, p. 1; Pool 1952, pp. 260–62.

8 Pool 1952, p. 261.

9 Dexter 1901, III, p. 392.

145

Second Minute Book of Kahal Kadosh Shearith Israel, 1760–86

Manuscript book, 7½ x 10 (19.1 x 25.4)

American Jewish Historical Society, New York City and Waltham, Massachusetts; Jacques Judah Lyons Collection

Myer Myers's life is better documented than most New York silversmiths because of his active role as an elder of Shearith Israel. Among the many congregational records that have survived are two eighteenth-century minute books recording quarterly meetings of the senior officers. On Tevet 8, 5535 (December 8, 1774), the newly elected (mostly reelected) "Yahudim" (*yehidim*), members serving as trustees, signed this page of the second minute book.

This group of trustees vividly illustrates the ethnic complexity and close family relationships that characterized Shearith Israel in the eighteenth century. Despite the congregation's adherence to Sephardic ritual, six of the nine trustees were Ashkenazic Jews who were closely interrelated by blood or marriage, sometimes both. Myers served together with his younger brother Asher as well as his brothers-in-law Hayman Levy and Solomon Simson (p. 27). Another trustee, Isaac Moses (cat. 141), was married to Hayman Levy's daughter and Myers's niece, Reyna. Solomon Myers Cohen was a first cousin of Myers's first wife, Elkaleh. Nine months after this election, Solomon's younger sister, Elkaleh, married *hazan* Gershom Mendes Seixas (fig. 5), a Sephardic Jew and the older brother of Benjamin Seixas. Benjamin in 1779 would marry Zipporah Levy, another daughter of Hayman Levy and niece of Myer Myers, thereby becoming Isaac Moses's brother-in-law as well.

The first and third to sign as trustees were Matthias Gomez, *parnas*, or president, and his first cousin Moses Gomez, long-time clerk of the congregation. They were from a wealthy Sephardic mercantile family whose patriarch, their grandfather Luis Moses Gomez, had been born in Spain and lived in the West Indies before arriving in New York.[1] Beginning a family tradition of service to Shearith Israel, Luis Gomez made many contributions to the congregation, including acting as the agent for the purchase of additional land for the cemetery.[2] Perhaps because of their wealth and Sephardic background, the Gomez family remained somewhat removed from the rest of the community. Luis's five sons all married women from Sephardic families in the West Indies rather than New York, and there was a separate enclosed section for female family members in the women's gallery of the Mill Street Synagogue (p. 16).

1 Stern 1991, p. 85.
2 Pool 1952, pp. 217–23.

146

JACOB RAPHAEL COHEN (1738–1811)
AND POSSIBLY A.A. VAN OETTINGEN
(DATES UNKNOWN)

Prayer for the United States, 1784

Ink on paper, 14 x 8½ (35.6 x 21.6)

American Jewish Historical Society, New York City and Waltham, Massachusetts

The overwhelming majority of American Jews sided with the Colonists' cause during the Revolutionary War. Members of Shearith Israel suffered considerable hardships, abandoning their homes and businesses in New York during the British occupation and living as refugees in Connecticut, Pennsylvania, and elsewhere. Much like the address of "the Antient Congregation of Israelites, lately returned from Exile" that Myer Myers and his relatives were chosen to present to Governor Clinton in January 1784 (p. 64), this prayer was an unambiguous statement of the Jews' political allegiance to the American Republic, linking the new government to ancient Jewish history.[1] It asked God to bestow David's glory and Solomon's wisdom on "our lords, the rulers of these thirteen states, to judge the people, yea also to the commanding general, Governor Clinton," and to give the strength of Samson to "our lord and commanding general George Washington."[2] The prayer was written early in 1784 by Jacob Cohen, the acting *hazan* in Gershom Mendes Seixas's absence, who had been born in North Africa and became the *hazan* in Montreal before serving Shearith Israel in that capacity when he was stranded in New York during the war.[3] Credited as co-author in a notation on the document was a "Rabbi Hendla Jochanan Van Oettingen," possibly the *shohet* A.A. van Oettingen, who taught Hebrew, sold Hebrew books, and was learned in Jewish law.[4]

Similar patriotic prayers were written for other American congregations. After moving to Philadelphia during the Revolutionary War, Gershom Mendes Seixas invoked divine protection for Congress, George Washington, and the American forces among his prayers at the dedication of Mikveh Israel's synagogue in 1782.[5] A prayer created in 1789 for the Jewish congregation in Richmond, Virginia, was composed as an acrostic, the first letters of each line spelling the name of George Washington.[6]

1 *Lyons Collection* 1920, pp. 32–34.
2 A full translation of the prayer was published in Ibid., pp. 34–37.
3 Pool/Pool 1955, p. 170.
4 *Lyons Collection* 1920, p. 34; Pool 1952, p. 385; Pool/Pool 1955, pp. 187, 272. For the role of the *shohet*, see pp. 27–28.
5 Lyons Collection, box 2, file 87, AJHS; a translation was published in *Lyons Collection* 1920, pp. 126–27. See also Wolf/Whiteman 1957, pp. 120–21.
6 Mittelman 1998, pp. 17, 64. The prayer is signed "Jacob, son of R. Joshua Cohen." This may be Jacob I. Cohen (1744–1823) of Philadelphia, son of Joshua Cohen (1720–1771) of Oberdorf, Germany; Jacob's brother Israel (1751–1803) had moved to Richmond in 1787; see Stern 1991, p. 32.

אָנוּ לְיָהּ וּלְיָהּ עֵינֵינוּ

בָּרוּךְ ה' אֲשֶׁר טוֹב גְּמָלָנוּ בְּרַחֲמָיו וּבְרוֹב חֲסָדָיו הִגְדִּיל לָנוּ וּבְרוּחַ פִּיו בָּרָא שָׁמַיִם וָאָרֶץ תֵּבֵל וְיוֹשְׁבֶיהָ וְהוּא הַמֵּאִיר לָאָרֶץ וְלַדָּרִים עָלֶיהָ הוּא בָּרָא כָל הַנִּבְרָאִים וְהוֹצִיא יֵשׁ מֵאַיִן כָּל הַנִּמְצָאִים מֶלֶךְ עוֹלָמִים לוֹ הַמְּלוּכָה וּמַמְלֵיכֵהּ מְלָכִים הוּא אֲשֶׁר נָטַע שָׁלוֹם בְּלֵב מְלָכִים וְשָׂרִים וּלְהָשִׁיב חֶרֶב אֶל נְדָנָהּ אָמַר ה' שָׁלוֹם לָרָחוֹק וְלַקָּרוֹב נוֹדֶה לַהּ בְּמַקְהֵלוֹת עַל חֲסָדָיו אֲשֶׁר הֵיטַב עִמָּנוּ צַעֲקוּ אֵלֶה הַצַּר לָנוּ וּבְכֹחַ צִוְקוֹתֵינוּ הוֹצִיאָנוּ וְאֶת הָעָם הָרַפֶּה יוֹשְׁבֵי הָאָרֶץ הִצְלִיחַ בְּטוֹבוֹ מִלְחַמְתֵּנוּ וּמִיְדֵי צָרִים וְנָכְרִים לָנוּ הַשֵּׁבַח נַחֲלָתֵנוּ וְהֶחֱזִירָנוּ מֵשׁוֹשׁ לִבֵּנוּ:

וְעַתָּה בָּאנוּ מֶלֶךְ רָם עַל רָמִים לִשְׁפּוֹךְ נַפְשֵׁנוּ לְפָנֶיךָ שְׁמַע צ' תְּפִלָּה בְּכָךְ בְּכוֹרֵךְ עִם סְגֻלָּתֶךָ הַבּוֹטְחִים עַל שְׁלֹשׁ עֶשְׂרֵה מְדִינוֹתֶיךָ שֶׁאֵינָם חוֹזְרִים רֵיקָם מִלְּפָנֶיךָ אֲמוּנִים בְּנֵי מַאֲמִינִים בִּשְׁלֹשׁ עֶשְׂרֵה עִיקְרֵי דָתֶיךָ:

בְּשֵׁם שֶׁחַלַּקְתָּ מִכְּבוֹדְךָ לְדָוִד בֶּן יִשַׁי וְלִבְנוֹ שְׁלֹמֹה נָתַתָּ חָכְמָה מִכָּל אָדָם כֵּן תַּחֲלֵק כָּבוֹד שֶׁכֶּל בִּינָה וָמַדָּע לְשׁוֹפֵט אֶת הָעָם לַאֲדוֹנֵינוּ שַׂר שְׁלֹשׁ עֶשְׂרֵה מְדִינוֹת הָאֵלּוּ וּבְתוֹכָם שַׂר הַצָּבָא גוֹרְנֵר קלינטן עִם יוֹעֲצֵיהֶם וְשָׂרֵיהֶם הַפְּרַפְמֵיס הַפְּחוֹת וְהַסְּגָנִים אִישׁ עַל מַחֲנֵהוּ וְאִישׁ עַל דִּגְלוֹ אֲשֶׁר שִׁכַּת הַמִּשְׂרָה עַל שִׁכְמוֹ יִתְגַּשֵּׂא וְיָרוּם הוֹדוֹ וְיִהְיֶה כַּזַּיִת רַעֲנָן וְיִפְרַח כְּשׁוֹשַׁנַּת הָעֲמָקִים וּכְחֲבַצֶּלֶת הַשָּׁרוֹן וְהָיָה כְּעֵץ שָׁתוּל עַל פַּלְגֵי מַיִם אֲשֶׁר פִּרְיוֹ יִתֵּן בְּעִתּוֹ וְעָלֵהוּ לֹא יִבּוֹל וְכָל אֲשֶׁר יַעֲשֶׂה יַצְלִיחַ וְכַאֲשֶׁר בְּחַסְדָּם הַגְּדוֹלִים מְטִיבִים עִמָּנוּ וּבְצִילָם אֲנַחְנוּ יוֹשְׁבִים שְׁלֵוִים וּשְׁקֵטִים כֵּן תְּשַׁלֵּם לָהֶם גְּמוּלָם וְתֵן לָהֶם מִשְׁאֲלוֹת לִבָּם וְיֵיטִיבוּ עִמָּנוּ עַד אַחֲרִיתָם וְתִתְּנֵם לְחֵן וּלְחֶסֶד בְּעֵינֵיהֶם וּבְחוֹתָם עַל לִבָּם יְשִׂימוּנוּ וְכֵן יְהִי רָצוֹן וְנֹאמַר אָמֵן:

בְּשֵׁם שֶׁנָּתַתָּ כֹּחַ לְשִׁמְשׁוֹן בֶּן מָנוֹחַ וְשֶׁסַע כְּפִיר בִּגְבוּרָתוֹ כֵּן תְּגַבֵּר וּתְחַזֵּק מָגֵן יִשְׁעֵנוּ הָעָה לַאֲדוֹנֵינוּ רֹאשׁ וְשַׂר הַצָּבָא דִּשְׁיָארְדִּישׁ וָאשִׁנְגְטוֹן מְשׁוֹחַ מִלְחָמָה בַּיָּם בִּיַּבָּשָׁה וּבְמַדְרֵגָה עִם כָּל הַחַיָּילִים נָתָן רִכְבּוֹ וּבְפָרָשָׁיו וּבְעֵת מָצוֹא יְדַבֵּר עֲמָיִים תַּחַת רַגְלָיו עַד יִפְנוּ אֵלָיו עוֹרֶךְ וְלֹא פָנִים יִפְּלוּ וְלֹא יוֹסִיפוּ קוּם וְהוּא יִרְדּוֹף אוֹיְבָיו וְיַשִּׂיגֵם וְלֹא יָשׁוּב עַד כַּלּוֹתָם אָנָּא ה' הוֹשִׁיעָה נָא אָנָּא ה' הַצְלִיחָה נָא אַךְ טוֹב וּמַה נָּעִים אִם תְּחַזֵּק שָׁלוֹם בְּלֵב מְלָכִים וְשָׂרִים כַּאֲשֶׁר נָטַעְתָּ וְכִתְּתוּ חַרְבוֹתָם לְאִתִּים וַחֲנִיתוֹתֵיהֶם לְמִזְמָרוֹת

לְמִזְמָרוֹת וְלֹא יִשָּׂא גוֹי אֶל גּוֹי חֶרֶב וְלֹא יִלְמְדוּ עוֹד מִלְחָמָה וִיקַיְּים בָּנוּ מִקְרָא שֶׁכָּתוּב וְנָתַתִּי שָׁלוֹם בָּאָרֶץ וּשְׁכַבְתֶּם וְאֵין מַחֲרִיד שָׁלוֹם רַב לְאוֹהֲבֵי תּוֹרָתֶךָ וְאֵין לָמוֹ מִכְשׁוֹל יְהִי שָׁלוֹם בְּחֵילֵךְ שַׁלְוָה בְּאַרְמְנוֹתָיִךְ וְתֵן בְּלִבָּם רַחֲמָנוּת לַעֲשׂוֹת טוֹבוֹת עִמָּנוּ וְעִם כָּל יִשְׂרָאֵל בִּזְכוּת אַהֲבַת הַקַּדְמוֹנִים כְּדִכְתִיב וְזָכַרְתִּי אֶת בְּרִיתִי יַעֲקוֹב וְאַף אֶת בְּרִיתִי יִצְחָק וְאַף אֶת בְּרִיתִי אַבְרָהָם אֶזְכּוֹר וְהָאָרֶץ אֶזְכּוֹר וְכֵן יְהִי רָצוֹן וְנֹאמַר אָמֵן:

בְּשֵׁם שֶׁנָּתַתָּ שְׁלֹשׁ עֶשְׂרֵה מְדִינוֹת אַמֶעריקא הָאֵלֶּה לְחֵירוּת עוֹלָם כֵּן תּוֹצִיאֵנוּ שֵׁנִית מֵעַבְדוּת לְחֵירוּת וְתִתְקַע בְּשׁוֹפָר גָּדוֹל לְחֵירוּתֵנוּ כְּמָה שֶׁנֶּאֱמַר וְהָיָה בַּיּוֹם הַהוּא יִתָּקַע בְּשׁוֹפָר גָּדוֹל וּבָאוּ הָאוֹבְדִים בְּאֶרֶץ אַשּׁוּר וְהַנִּדָּחִים בְּאֶרֶץ מִצְרַיִם וְהִשְׁתַּחֲווּ לַה' בְּהַר הַקֹּדֶשׁ בִּירוּשָׁלַיִם וְיִתְנַעֲרוּ מֵעָפָר לָשֶׁבֶת לָאֵל לְיוֹם נָקָם מַהֵר פְּדִיּוֹנֵינוּ כִּי אַתָּה הַגּוֹאֵל וְאָז נָשִׁיר שִׁיר חָדָשׁ לָהּ אֱלֹקֵי יִשְׂרָאֵל וְשָׁם נַעַבְדֵהוּ בְּיִרְאָה כִּימֵי עוֹלָם וּבְשָׁנִים קַדְמוֹנִיּוֹת וְיִרְאֵינוּ נִפְלָאוֹת כִּימֵי קֶדֶם וְיָשׁוּב הַקָּדוֹשׁ בָּרוּךְ הוּא שְׁכִינָתוֹ לְצִיּוֹן וְסֵדֶר הָעֲבוֹדָה לִירוּשָׁלַיִם וְנִזְכֶּה לַחֲזוֹת בְּנוֹעַם ה' וּלְבַקֵּר בְּהֵיכָלוֹ וְיִשְׁלַח לָנוּ כֹּהֵן צֶדֶק וְהוּא יוֹלִיכֵנוּ קוֹמְמִיּוּת לְאַרְצֵנוּ וִיהִי נוֹעַם ה' עָלֵינוּ וּבָא לְצִיּוֹן גּוֹאֵל בִּמְהֵרָה בְּיָמֵינוּ וְכֵן יְהִי רָצוֹן וְנֹאמַר אָמֵן:

146

147

EZRA STILES (1727–1795)
Newport, Rhode Island

"Dedication of the Synagogue in Newport," from Stiles, "Journal or Diary of Silkworms," 1763

Ink on paper, 8¼ x 6½ (21 x 16.5)

Ezra Stiles Papers, Beinecke Rare Book and Manuscript Library, Yale University, New Haven

Exhibited in New Haven only

Begun in 1759 and completed in 1763, the Touro Synagogue in Newport, Rhode Island, is the only surviving synagogue building from eighteenth-century America. It was designed by the English-born mariner Peter Harrison, who had settled in Newport but made return trips to England to gather English architectural books and designs. Carl Bridenbaugh discovered that Harrison based his design for the synagogue's interior (fig. 3) on a chapel designed by John Webb, published in 1727.[1] Its exterior was entirely in the Anglo-American synagogue tradition (see cat. 143), with a brick exterior, rounded windows, and small pedimented porch.[2]

In this journal entry, Stiles copied a notice from the *Newport Mercury* and added his own observations on the building and the Ark:

Dedication of the Synagogue in Newport 1763. Dec' 2, 1763. Friday. "In the Afternoon was the Dedication of the new Synagogue in this Town. It began by a handsom procession in which were carried the Books of the Law, to be deposited in the Ark. Several Portions of Scripture, & of their Service with a Prayer for the Royal Family, were read & finely sung by the priest & People. There were present many Gentlemen & Ladies. The Order & Decorum, the Harmony & Solemnity of the Musick, together with a handsom Assembly of People, in an Edifice the most perfect of the Temple kind perhaps in America, & splendidly illu-minated, could not but raise in the Mind a faint Idea of the Majesty & Grandeur of the ancient Jewish Worship mentioned in Scripture. Dr Isaac de Abraham Touro performed the Service."

The Synagogue is about perhaps fourty foot long & 30 wide, of Brick on a Foundation of free Stone: it was begun about two years ago, & is now finished except the Porch & the Capitals of the Pillars. The Front representation of the holy of holies, or its Partition Veil, consists only of wainscotted Breast Work on the East End, in the lower part of which four long Doors cover an upright Square Closet the depth of which about a foot or the Thickness of the Wall, & in this Apartment (vul-garly called the Ark) were deposited three Copies & Rolls of the Penta-teuch, written on Vellum or rather tanned Calf Skin; one of these Rolls, I was told by Dr Touro was presented from Amsterdam & is Two Hun-dred years old; the Letters have the Rabbinical Flourishes.

Stiles's thumbnail sketch of the Ark recorded a less elaborate architectural facade than the ark presently in the synagogue, and it has been suggested that the current ark may be a post-Revolutionary War or even nineteenth-century restoration.[3]

1 Bridenbaugh 1949, p. 100.
2 Jamilly 1999, pp. 24–25.
3 Schwartz 1959, pp. 118–24.

Dedication of the Synagogue in Newport 1763

Decr 2. 1763 Friday. "In the Afternoon was the Dedication of the new
„ Synagogue in this Town — It began by a handsom procession,
„ in which were carried the Books of the Law, to be deposited in
„ the Ark. Several Portions of Scripture, & of their Service
„ with a Prayer for the Royal Family were read & finely sung
„ by the Priest & People. There were present many Gentlemen
„ & Ladies. The Order & Decorum, the Harmony & Solemnity of the
„ Musick, together with a handsom Assembly of People, in an
„ Edifice the most perfect of the Temple kind perhaps in
„ America, & splendidly illuminated, could not but raise in
„ the Mind a faint Idea of the Majesty & Grandeur of the
„ antient Jewish Worship mentioned in Scripture

„ Dr Isaac ^{de} Abraham Touro performed the Service"

The Synagogue is about perhaps fourty foot long & 30
wide, of Brick on a foundation of free Stone: it was
begun about two years ago, & is now finished except the
Porch & the Capitals of the Pillars. The Front representation of the holy of holies, or it Partition Veil, consists only of
wainscotted Breast Work on the East End, in the lower part
of which four long Doors cover an upright Square Closet the
depth of which about a foot or the Thickness of the Wall, &
in this Apartment (vulgarly called the Ark) were deposited
three Copies & Rolls of the Pentateuch written on Vellum or rather
tanned Calf Skin; one of these Rolls, I was told by Dr Touro
was presented from Amsterdam & is Two Hundred years
old; the Letters have the Rabbinical Flourishes.

ARK

10 feet

UNIDENTIFIED ARTIST AND PUBLISHER
London, England

A Prospect of the New Jerusalem, 1753

Engraving, 12⅛ x 9⅛ (30.8 x 23.2)

Lewis Walpole Library, Farmington, Connecticut, a department of Yale University Library

Jews had been expelled from England by Edward I in 1291; they were not legally permitted to live there until readmission under Oliver Cromwell in 1656. Even then, they lacked many basic rights. Unlike immigrants to British colonies, foreign Jews who settled to England could not become naturalized subjects, although they could apply for the lesser status of endenization, which allowed them residency.[1] Bills permitting the naturalization of Jews resident in England had been submitted to Parliament since the beginning of the eighteenth century but did not pass until June 1753, under the influence of the Duke of Newcastle in the House of Lords and his younger brother, Henry Pelham, in the Commons.[2]

Passage of the "Jew Bill," as it was called, inspired such widespread popular outrage that it was repealed on December 4, 1753, and Parliament was dissolved. A principal point of opposition was the unfounded belief that naturalized Jews would buy hereditary estates, which frequently controlled such ecclesiastical appointments as parish churches or hospitals, with the intention of appointing Catholic priests to these posts in order to destablize the established Church of England. The poem attached to this anonymously published print reflected the popular view that the Catholic Church had instigated the naturalization of Jews as a plot to destabilize the Church of England and restore the Stuart pretenders to the English throne: "These can't be English, these are Romish works:/Some Popish Plot to bring in the Pretender." Twelve years earlier, on April 27, 1741, official suspicions of Jewish support for the Catholic Jacobites had forced Myers's father, Solomon Myers, and twenty other naturalized Jews in New York to sign a loyalty oath to George II. They pledged to abjure "that damnable Doctrine & position, that princes excommunicated or deprived by the pope, or any authority of the See of Rome, may be deposed or murthered by their Subjects" and declared the succession to the British throne "is & stands limitted to the Princess Sophia, Electoress & Dutchess Dowager of Hannover [the Protestant granddaughter of James I and grandmother of George II], & the Heirs of her body, being protestants." An additional seven Jews signed the document the following January.[3]

A large number of caricatures were created in England as part of the backlash against the Jew Bill. Many of them pandered to fears of a Jewish takeover by predicting forced circumcisions of Christian males, or ridiculed Jewish dietary laws by depicting Jews secretly seeking meals of pork.[4] This print, which was also issued as a woodcut broadside, had a subtler if no less anti-Semitic theme: that the political and mercantile support for the bill had been bought with bribes from wealthy Jewish merchants, symbolized here by the devil holding a bag containing £500,000. The bearded Jews are advancing to take possession of the City of London, dominated by St. Paul's Cathedral, having bribed the "Two Brothers" (i.e. the Duke of Newcastle and Henry Pelham), seen in the background at the extreme left, as well as Sir William Calvert, Lord Mayor and Alderman of London, the robed figure at the right.[5]

1 Lipman 1972, pp. 15–17.
2 Hyamson 1912.
3 Loyalty oath, April 27, 1741, N.Y. Oaths, manuscript collection, NYHS.
4 Rubens 1954, pp. 34–40; Stephens/Hawkins 1978, pp. 862–63, nos. 3208–09.
5 See Stephens/Hawkins 1978, pp. 859–61, nos. 3204–06. In the broadside version (no. 3206), this print was paired with *The Circumcised Gentiles, or A Journey to Jerusalem* (no. 3205).

Why, Friend, 'tis here in Print, the year too, See,   The Devil, Infidels, Hereticks, and Turks!
One Thousand Seven hundred Fifty Three,   These can't be English, these are Romish works:
Christ Save us from his Enemies the Jews!   Some Popish Plot to bring in the Pretender;
What's this made free and true born English Jews!   Pray Heaven guard our glorious Faith's Defender!

Numb.ˢ Chap. XXXII . Let this land, be given unto thy Servants, for a Possession:

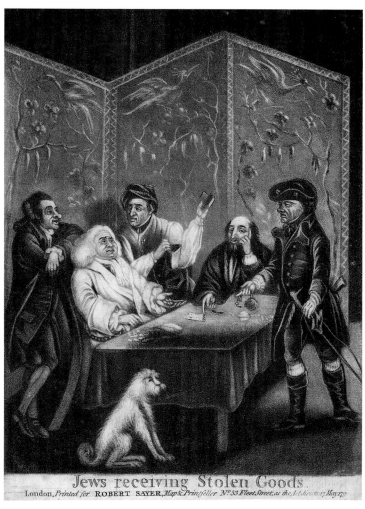

149

149

ROBERT SAYER (1725–1794)
London, England

Jews Receiving Stolen Goods, c. 1778

Mezzotint, 5⅝ x 4½ (14.3 x 11.4)

Lewis Walpole Library, Farmington, Connecticut, a department of Yale University Library

This mezzotint was issued, together with a companion piece, *One of the Tribe of Levi, Going to Brakefast with a Young Christian*, in at least two different sizes; this example is the smaller, called a "small mezzotinto" and priced at 6 pence.[1] The bald, bearded figure at the end of the table is the same man seen entertaining a prostitute in the companion image, with the implication that his ill-gotten wealth was used to debauch Christian women, a common theme in English literature as well as caricature.[2] The fact that these prints were conceived as a pair and offered in different sizes implies usage as decorative images on a wall, with the option of different scale and symmetry. Such twinned images of the Jews' supposed rapaciousness and lasciviousness clearly had appeal in a majority Protestant culture in which prejudice against Jews was deeply ingrained, and they stand in stark contrast to the more enlightened understanding of the Jews and their culture found in such figures as Ezra Stiles (cat. 133).

The traditional association of Jews with usury and other amoral means of gaining wealth had great currency in England during the later seventeenth and early eighteenth centuries, when the most visible Jews in London were wealthy Sephardic merchants from Amsterdam, who profited in the rapidly expanding economy.[3] Even in the American Colonies, it was difficult for Jews to escape the suspicion of illegal practices for financial gain. In August 1789, Myer Myers, together with Solomon Simons and his brother-in-law Solomon Simson, testified unsuccessfully on behalf of a Samuel Israel, who had been accused of receiving stolen goods and was sentenced to a month's imprisonment and a fine of £10.[4]

1 *Sayer and Bennett* 1970, p. 28. *One of the Tribe of Levi* is illustrated in Felsen-stein/Mintz 1995, p. 67.
2 Ibid., pp. 65–67.
3 Lipman 1972, pp. 17–21.
4 Weeks 1898, p. 78. This Samuel Israel apparently was the same man who married his first wife in 1794 and died in 1835. He was the son of the Philadelphia innkeeper Israel Israel (1744–1822) and his wife, Hannah Erwin (1757–1813); see Stern 1991, p. 128.

Appendix I: Marks

During his fifty-year career, Myer Myers used at least nine different marks that can be securely attributed to him, as well as two additional marks for his partnership with Benjamin Halsted. All but two of Myers's nine marks were struck on objects that can be dated before 1770. MARK 9 was Myers's primary mark after about 1765 until his death in 1795, and MARK 7 was used on flatware and jewelry during and after the Revolutionary War. One additional mark, MARK 10, is here attributed to Myers with the reservation that it so far has not been found on an object with a firmly documented provenance to a likely patron of Myers's.

Marks on eighteenth-century Anglo-American silver did not necessarily indicate authorship. The so-called "workers' marks" or maker's marks in England were in fact the marks of those individuals who presented finished objects to the Goldsmith's Company for assay and guaranteed that the metal met the traditional sterling alloy of 92.5 percent silver alloyed with 7.5 percent copper.[1] By the eighteenth century, these individuals tended to be the masters of large workshops or the retailers of finished goods rather than the makers.[2] As there were no assay offices in the Colonies, marks were not required on American-made silver, although most colonial silversmiths used them. As in England, what was called the "stamp" or mark on an object was described as the "maker's name," but again tended to be the mark of the master of the workshop or the retailer.

Like most Colonial American silversmiths, Myers followed the English tradition of marking silver made in his workshop as a guarantee of the alloy's quality. However, over the course his career, he came to use marks differently. After about 1750, he began using marks that spelled out his surname, a break with English tradition that was as much self-promotion as a guarantee. Moreover, on a few important commissions, Myers placed his surname marks in prominent locations where they functioned as a kind of signature.

Myers's Initials Marks

Maker's marks had been required on silver made in England since 1363, and marks composed of the initials of a silversmith's first and last names were in use by the middle of the sixteenth century and eventually mandated in 1739 by an Act of Parliament.[3] Although these regulations did not apply to craftsmen working in the Colonies, most American silversmiths used marks composed of two or three initials, the latter being popular in New York for silversmiths such as Charles Le Roux (CLR) and Peter Van Dyck (PVD). Myer Myers used initials marks from the beginning of his career in 1746, but after about 1765 they were supplanted almost completely by surname MARK 9. The sole exception, MARK 7, is the only instance of an initials mark used after 1776.

All of Myers's initials marks were simple block capitals with no pellets or other devices. The collector Hollis French, who owned a mote spoon with the distinctive mark of two script M capitals in an oval, misidentified it as a mark of Myers's in 1917.[4] Based on French's study, this mark repeatedly was published as Myers's in many subsequent guides to American silver, although both Kathryn Buhler and Phillip M. Johnston declined to attribute it to Myers.[5] The mark in fact was registered in 1782 by the Dutch smallworker Matthijs Matthijsen, who worked in Amsterdam between 1782 and 1809.[6]

MARK 1 (c. 1746–55)

"MM" in a shield-shape surround with an indented top center and rounded center drop. MARK 1 is found on the earliest documented object to survive from Myers's workshop, the teapot made for Nicoll and Tabitha Floyd before 1755 (cat. 1). It is also found on a small group of stylistically early objects: a tankard (cat. 2), a waiter made for David and Margaret (Evans) Franks (fig. 10), a cann (fig. 12), and a set of six tablespoons.[7] Ernest Currier first published this mark in 1938.[8]

1   2

MARK 2 (c. 1746–55)

"MM" in a long, narrow rectangle. The best-documented object with this mark is a tankard made for the New York merchant Ennis Graham and his first wife, Sarah Man, between their marriage in 1747 and Sarah's death prior to 1763.[9] This mark also appears on a stylistically early waiter (cat. 3), probably made for the Bocking family, and a salt shovel (cat. 4) that may have been made for David and Margaret (Evans) Franks. Jeanette Rosenbaum first published this mark in 1954.[10]

3

4

on only one other object, an undocumented sugar dish.[14] The mark does not seem to have been published previously.

17

MARK 3 (c. 1746–60)

"MM" in a shieldshape surround with a pointed top center and an indented bottom center; the lower serifs of the first M and the serif of the left downstroke of the second M form a continuous line. Two sugar dishes struck with this mark closely resemble New York sugar dishes of the 1730s and 1740s; such stylistically conservative objects may have been made during the earliest years of Myers's career.[11] A pair of sauceboats (cat. 18) with this mark is identical to a pair made in 1756–58 (cat. 17); a bowl (cat. 7) with MARK 3 was made prior to Thomas Barnes's death in 1763. Hollis French first published this mark in 1917.[12]

MARK 6 (c. 1755–70)

"MM" in a rectangle; the letters touch each other but are not conjoined. This small mark was in use as early as about 1755, when it was struck on the four candlesticks (cats. 35, 36) made for Catherine (Livingston) Lawrence. It also appears on a waiter (cat. 10) with similar cast and chased elements. It was used to mark all Myers's surviving works in gold (cats. 48–51), of which the documented examples date to 1764. A small, hexagonal waiter with a narrow, gadrooned border of the type made in Myers's shop after about 1765 (see cat. 58) is struck with MARK 6.[15] Kathryn Buhler and Graham Hood first published this mark in 1970.[16]

7

18

39

10

35

36

MARK 4 (c. 1755–65)

"MM" conjoined in a rectangle. This mark is by far the most common of Myers's initial marks; it appears on wide variety of objects, including tankards (cat. 28), waiters, milk pots (cat. 11), ladles, and spoons (fig. 33). Its use is documented as early as 1757, when it was struck on the sword made for Lieutenant David Jones (cat. 16); it was also stuck on a set of tablespoons made for the Bush-Sheftall family (fig. 33) that could date after 1764. Jeanette Rosenbaum first published this mark in 1954.[13]

48

49

50

51

11

16

28

MARK 7 (c. 1776–95)

"MM" in a long, narrow rectangle; thin lines connect the serifs on the inside edges of each letter. The author has found this mark only on flatware and a pair of silver shoe buckles.[17] One teaspoon (cat. 93) appears to date from Myers's residence in Norwalk, Connecticut, between 1776 and 1779. The buckles and a pair of sugar tongs (cat. 103) are decorated with bright-cut engraving that indicates a date of manufacture after Myers's return to New York in December 1783. The mark does not seem to have been published previously.

MARK 5 (c. 1756–58)

"MM" conjoined in a rectangle. Although very similar to MARK 4 in appearance, this mark is considerably smaller, only about two-thirds the size of MARK 4. The right downstroke of the second M is raised higher than the other downstrokes, and the left serif of the first M is very faint. This mark is struck once on each of the sauceboats made between 1756 and 1758 for presentation to Nathaniel Merserve (cat. 17). The author has found it

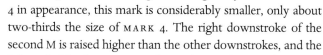

93

103

Myers's Surname Marks

Silversmith's marks using the craftsman's full surname were an American innovation, since the 1739 Act of Parliament required English silversmiths to use only their initials. As Patricia Kane demonstrated in her study of Colonial Massachusetts, the Boston silversmith John Burt apparently introduced the surname mark; the earliest extant example is struck on a two-handled cup dated 1724. By 1730, at least six of Burt's fellow silversmiths in Boston had also adopted surname marks. Kane observed that these craftsmen probably represented the more aggressive marketers of their work.[18]

A generation passed before silversmiths in New York followed the Bostonians' example.[19] Myer Myers was the first New York silversmith to use a surname mark; the earliest documented instances of his surname MARK 8 are struck on a coffeepot, stand, and cann (cats. 20–22) made between 1754 and 1758. His adoption of a surname mark is consistent with his other innovative strategies in the mid-1750s, such as forming the partnership with Benjamin Halsted (p. 33). These marks clearly gave him name recognition. A set of six tablespoons stolen from Rebecca Hays in 1767 were identified in the newspaper as having the "Maker's Name *Myers*," and another group of spoons stolen during the British occupation in 1779 were described as "all made by Myers, late of New-York, and marked as well with his mark as with the owner's crest."[20]

Once he adopted the surname mark, Myers clearly favored it over the smaller, more traditional initials marks. At least 207 of his 380 extant objects are struck with either MARK 8 or MARK 9; none of the initials marks were used with the same frequency as the surname marks. Myers used his second surname mark, MARK 9, almost exclusively after 1765. By this date, several other New York silversmiths were using surname marks. Charles Oliver Bruff advertised in 1767: "I design to put the stamp of my name, in full, on all my works."[21] Other New York silversmiths using surname marks in the 1760s included Ephraim Brasher, Cary Dunn, William Gilbert, Otto Paul de Parisien, John Heath, Samuel Johnson, and John Burt Lyng. As noted (pp. 57–58), the first four silversmiths had close associations with Myers. All but Heath and Lyng became members of the Gold and Silver Smith's Society. After the Revolutionary War, Society members Daniel Bloom Coen, William Forbes, and John Burger also used surname marks, which by the 1790s became the standard format for most postwar silversmiths.

Unlike John Burt and Jacob Hurd in Boston, or several of his New York colleagues, Myers never adopted either a surname mark that included the initial of his first name or a full-name mark.[22] Instead, he apparently made a play on his unusual name and struck his surname mark twice as a substitute for a full-name mark. His earlier surname mark, MARK 8, is only rarely struck twice; the earliest instance is on the coffeepot stand (cat. 21) of 1756–58 that is also marked by Halsted and

Fig. 1. Myer Myers, *Coffeepot*, New York, 1765–76 (detail of marks). Silver. Saint Louis Art Museum, Missouri; Purchase, Funds given by Charles H. Stix in memory of his mother, Mrs. Henry Stix.

Myers. Other instances include the set of candlesticks (cats. 8, 9), the snuffers tray (cat. 38), and a ladle.[23] The later surname mark, MARK 9, is frequently found with two strikes, and on one coffeepot they were overlapped deliberately to create an impression of the craftsman's name (fig. 1).

On most examples of Colonial American silver, including Myers's own work, the marks are located on the undersides or in positions at the "back" of the object, like the handle of a tankard (cat. 2). After Myers adopted a surname mark, however, on some major commissions he struck his mark where someone viewing the object from the "front" could not fail to notice it. The earliest instance is the single strike of MARK 8 on the snuffers made for Robert Gilbert Livingston (cat. 38). More significant are the single strike of MARK 9 on the front of the waiter made for Theodorus Van Wyck (cat. 56) and the two strikes of MARK 9 on the dish ring (cat. 79) made for Samuel and Susannah Cornell. In both instances, Myers's surname mark is deliberately placed in close association with the waiter's engraved inscription and the monogram of the dish ring's owners, as a signature or statement of pride in the importance of his work.

MARK 8 (c. 1750–65)

"Myers" script in a partially conforming surround. The second vertical stroke of the M is flared at the top, and the lower end of this downstroke and the tail of the y overlap. A long stroke connects the r and the s. This mark appears on stylistically early objects, including the covered cup (fig. 9), milk pot (cat. 5), and set of candlesticks (cats. 8, 9). It was also struck on the coffeepot, stand, and cann (cats. 20–22) made for Charity (Floyd) Johnson, who died in 1758. It was the primary mark on objects with cast ornament made in the later 1750s, and its usage seems to have been discontinued by the middle 1760s. Ernest Currier first published this mark in 1938.[24]

5

6

8

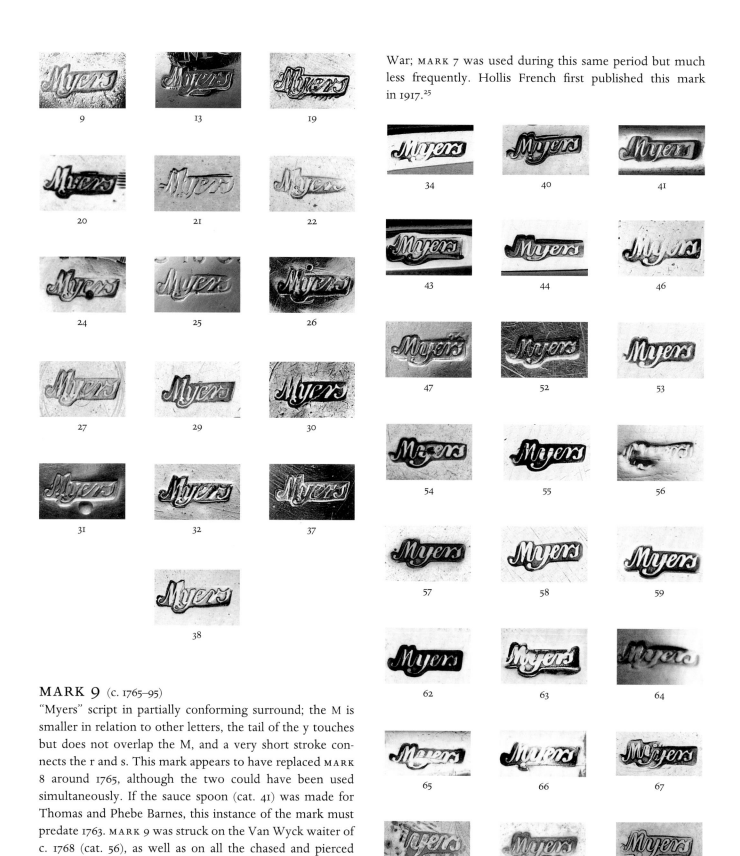

War; MARK 7 was used during this same period but much less frequently. Hollis French first published this mark in 1917.[25]

MARK 9 (c. 1765–95)

"Myers" script in partially conforming surround; the M is smaller in relation to other letters, the tail of the y touches but does not overlap the M, and a very short stroke connects the r and s. This mark appears to have replaced MARK 8 around 1765, although the two could have been used simultaneously. If the sauce spoon (cat. 41) was made for Thomas and Phebe Barnes, this instance of the mark must predate 1763. MARK 9 was struck on the Van Wyck waiter of c. 1768 (cat. 56), as well as on all the chased and pierced objects made in the later 1760s and early 1770s. MARK 9 was Myers's principal mark during and after the Revolutionary

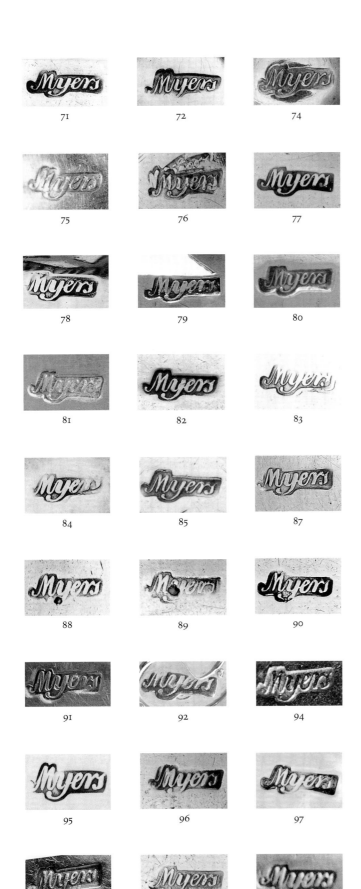

MARK 10 (c. 1755–65)

The author has located this mark on four undocumented objects: a ladle, pepper box, pipe lighter, and tablespoon (cat. 33).[26] The last object bears the initials "M/RL" in a distinctive arrangement also found on the tankard (cat. 30) made by Myers for Robert and Mary (Thong) Livingston. Myers also made tablespoons of the same pattern for Robert and Mary's son Peter R. Livingston (cat. 34). It seems logical to assume that cat. 33 was made for the Livingstons, and that the mark can therefore be attributed to Myers's workshop. The pipe lighter is very similar to another example from Myers's workshop that is struck with MARK 8, which suggests that MARK 10 was used during the same time period.[27] One possible explanation for the rarity of this mark is that it might have been used by Myer Myers's brother Joseph, who was identified as a silversmith and had business associations with his brother (p. 35). However, as discussed above, the overwhelming evidence in the eighteenth century is that the marks on a piece of silver signified the master who functioned as the public identity for the workshop, and there is no evidence that Joseph Myers worked independently as a craftsman in New York. This mark has not been published previously.

33

Halsted and Myers Marks

The partnership of Benjamin Halsted and Myer Myers (pp. 33–35) used two different "H&M" marks (11–12). Confusion over the identity of Myers's partner has plagued the literature on early American silver since the first attempts to identify the partnership's marks. MARK 11 was first published by Hollis French in 1917 as the mark of "Hays & Myers" of New York and Newport, c. 1765.[28] French apparently based his identification on the entry for the Torah finials at the Touro Synagogue (cat. 100) in E. Alfred Jones's *The Old Silver of American Churches* of 1913, which stated that the finials were by Myer Myers and engraved with the inscription "Hays & Myers."[29]

This information was repeated four years later by Francis Hill Bigelow, who noted, "They are engraved on the stems Hays and Myers from whom perhaps they were a gift."[30] French's identification of MARK 11 with the names in the inscription was taken up by Stephen G.C. Ensko in 1927 and repeated in two later editions of his book, as well as in other sources.[31] With the publication of Rita Susswein Gottesman's *Arts and Crafts in New York* in 1936, the two newspaper advertisements of the Halsted and Myers partnership entered the literature. However, James Graham in 1936 and Ernest Currier in 1938 specifically named Myers's partner as Andrew Hays, who had registered as a Freeman in 1769; bolstered by the names engraved on the Torah finials, this misidentification has persisted.[32] Given the absence of any objects by Andrew Hays or other evidence that he worked independently as a silversmith (p. 36), it seems very unlikely that he had a formal partnership with Myers. The H&M mark and Myers's partner were not definitively identified as Halsted and Myers until Rosenbaum's monograph on Myers was published in 1954.[33]

MARK 11 (c. 1756–66)

"H&M" in a rectangle; the letters fill the rectangle and the lower serifs of the ampersand and M are conjoined; the upper inside serifs of the H and M extend over the ampersand. As noted (p. 33), this single mark combining the initials of the partners' surnames was the earliest instance in America of this type of mark.[34] MARK 11 is found on two objects also struck with Myers's surname marks. The coffeepot stand (cat. 21) made for Charity Johnson between 1756 and 1758 has both MARK 11 and Myers's surname MARK 8; it is the earliest documented usage of both marks. On a cann that apparently was owned by Barnard and Richea Gratz (cat. 40), MARK 11 is overstruck with Myers's surname MARK 9, perhaps because the cann was made as a stock item but not sold or given away until after the partnership had ceased.

MARK 11A (c. 1756–70)

"N-York" script in a rectangle with tapered, rounded ends. This mark has not been published previously. It appears on at least three extant objects marked by the Halsted and Myers partnership: a milk pot (cat. 12) struck with MARK 11 and a teapot (cat. 60) and covered jar (cat. 61) struck with MARK 12. On the jar, MARK 11A is struck on its drawn base molding, a highly unconventional location. Presumably the mark was struck on this molding before it was soldered in place.

The use of a mark spelling out the city's name was an innovation of the mid-1750s in New York that the Halsted and Myers partnership either invented themselves or adopted; the earliest instances of a "N-York" mark appear on their silver and on objects marked by Daniel Christian Fueter (cats. 106–108). From the fifteenth century onward, assay offices in England were required to mark all gold and silver objects with symbols that identified their location, such as the leopard's head for London.[35] No silversmiths in other American cities, including Boston, seem to have adopted marks with their city's name until after the Revolutionary War. Fueter may have originated the idea of a city mark, given both his prior activity in London and the fact that he consistently used a "N:York" mark on his American silver. Halsted and Myers, on the other hand, apparently used it more selectively, and neither Myers nor Halsted struck it on any surviving objects they marked independently.

This usage of a city mark in Colonial New York implies that silver so marked was being marketed outside the locality where the silversmiths' initials marks would have been recognized. Halsted and Myers's covered jar (cat. 61) was made for a client in Pennsylvania, but no documented histories of ownership are known for other objects. Most of the younger New York silversmiths who used a city mark in the Colonial period tended to be the same craftsmen who used surname marks— Ephraim Brasher, Cary Dunn, William Gilbert (cat. 114), John Burt Lyng, and Samuel Tingley—and the city marks probably complemented their surname marks as a marketing tool.[36] As noted (pp. 57–58), Halsted, Dunn, and Gilbert may have worked as retailers rather than craftsmen, and as such were more likely to sell silver outside of New York. City marks became common after the Revolutionary War, as the market became national rather than local; at that time, John Burger (cat. 117) used a script "NYork" mark very similar in appearance to that used by Halsted and Myers.

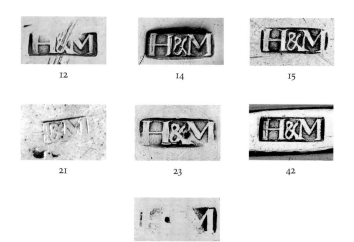

12

14

15

21

23

42

45

12

60

61

MARK 12 (c. 1766–70)

"H&M" in a rectangle with canted corners; this mark is much smaller than MARK 11. MARK 12 was struck on a covered jar (cat. 61) in conjunction with the same "N-York" MARK 11A that appears on a milk pot with MARK 11 and therefore can be presumed to be a second mark of the Halsted and Myers partnership. Both the covered jar and a teapot (cat. 60) with MARK 12 can be dated, either stylistically or by provenance, to the late 1760s or early 1770s. As noted (p. 34), these objects provide the primary evidence that the Halsted and Myers partnership continued in some fashion after Halsted's move to New Jersey in 1766. This mark has not been published previously.

60

61

NOTES

1 Jackson 1921, pp. 54–55; Alcorn 2000A, pp. 13–14.

2 Hare/Snodin/Clifford 1990, p. 24.

3 Jackson 1921, pp. 55–57; Forbes 1998, pp. 19, 203–04.

4 French 1917, p. 86.

5 Rosenbaum 1954A, p. 127; Johnston 1994, p. 103.

6 Citroen 1975, p. 133.

7 The tablespoons are in the Wadsworth Atheneum Museum of Art, Hartford, inv. 1977.73A–F.

8 Currier 1938, p. 103.

9 Rosenbaum 1954B, p. 127.

10 Rosenbaum 1954A, p. 66, no. 3.

11 The sugar dishes by Myers, both unpublished, are in private collections. They resemble sugar dishes made in New York between 1730 and 1750 by Adrian Bancker (Buhler/Hood 1970, II, no. 629) and George Ridout (Hammerslough 1958, p. 30).

12 French 1917, p. 86.

13 Rosenbaum 1954A, p. 66, no. 2.

14 The Burrows Collection, on long-term loan to the Sterling and Francine Clark Art Institute, Williamstown, Massachusetts, inv. TR 85/27.

15 Collection of Ruth J. Nutt; the waiter is unpublished.

16 Buhler/Hood 1970, II, p. 283, no. 657–658.

17 Other objects struck with this mark include a pair of teaspoons in The Metropolitan Museum of Art, New York, inv. 52.210.1-2, and the pair of buckles at the Daughters of the American Revolution Museum, Washington, D.C., inv. 62.142A–B; see also "Jewish Community" 1980, p. 16.

18 Kane 1998, p. 78.

19 Ibid., p. 78. A surname mark published in Darling 1964, p. 108, as the mark of a John Jackson who registered as a Freeman in New York on April 6, 1731 (De Lancey 1885, p. 117), is in fact the mark used by the Nantucket silversmith of the same name; Kane 1998, pp. 626–27.

20 The New-York Gazette, April 6–13, 1767, p. 4; The Royal Gazette, November 13, 1779, p. 2.

21 The New-York Mercury, April 20, 1767, as cited in Gottesman 1936, p. 33.

22 Kane 1998, pp. 78–80.

23 The ladle is in the collection of Barbara and Roy Zuckerberg.

24 Currier 1938, p. 103.

25 French 1917, p. 85.

26 The ladle, in the Hanoverian pattern, is in the Harvard University Art Museums, inv. 1999.306.23. The pepper box and pipe lighter are in the collection of Paul and Elissa Cahn; Sotheby's 1991, lot 125, and Sotheby's 1995, lot 1435.

27 Christie's 1993, lot 124.

28 French 1917, p. 61.

29 Jones 1913, p. 320.

30 Bigelow 1917, pp. 428–29.

31 Ensko 1927, p. 184; Ensko 1937, p. 40; Ensko 1948, p. 186; see also Wyler 1937, p. 295; Thorn 1949, p. 106.

32 Graham 1936, p. 36; Currier 1938, p. 70; see also Kovel/Kovel 1961, p. 134; Hamilton 1995, p. 184.

33 Rosenbaum 1954A, pp. 34, 66. Currier 1938, p. 70, listed MARK 11 under "Hays & Myers" but noted the existence of the "Myers and Halsted" partnership.

34 A tankard at YUAG bearing the marks of both Everardus Bogardus and Henricus Boelen II probably was not the product of a partnership, but has a body marked by Bogardus and a later cover made as a repair by the younger craftsman; Buhler/Hood 1970, II, no. 577.

35 Jackson 1921, pp. 7–8; Forbes 1998, pp. 45–47.

36 Buhler/Hood 1970, II, nos. 689–90, 752–54, 727–28, 716–19; Waters/McKinsey/Ward 2000, I, p. 131; Quimby/Johnson 1995, p. 241; Darling 1964, p. 177. Darling 1964, p. 164, also reproduces an "N:York" mark with a script "SS" mark as belonging to Simeon Soumaine, but these marks are too late in style for Soumaine's working dates.

1. Receipted bill from Halsted and Myers to Catherine (Van Rensselaer) Schuyler, New York, July 1, 1760. Philip Schuyler Papers, Manuscripts and Archives Division, The New York Public Library.

2. Receipted bill from Halsted and Myers to an unidentified Mrs. Livingston, New York, October 24, 1760. Philip Schuyler Papers, Manuscripts and Archives Division, The New York Public Library.

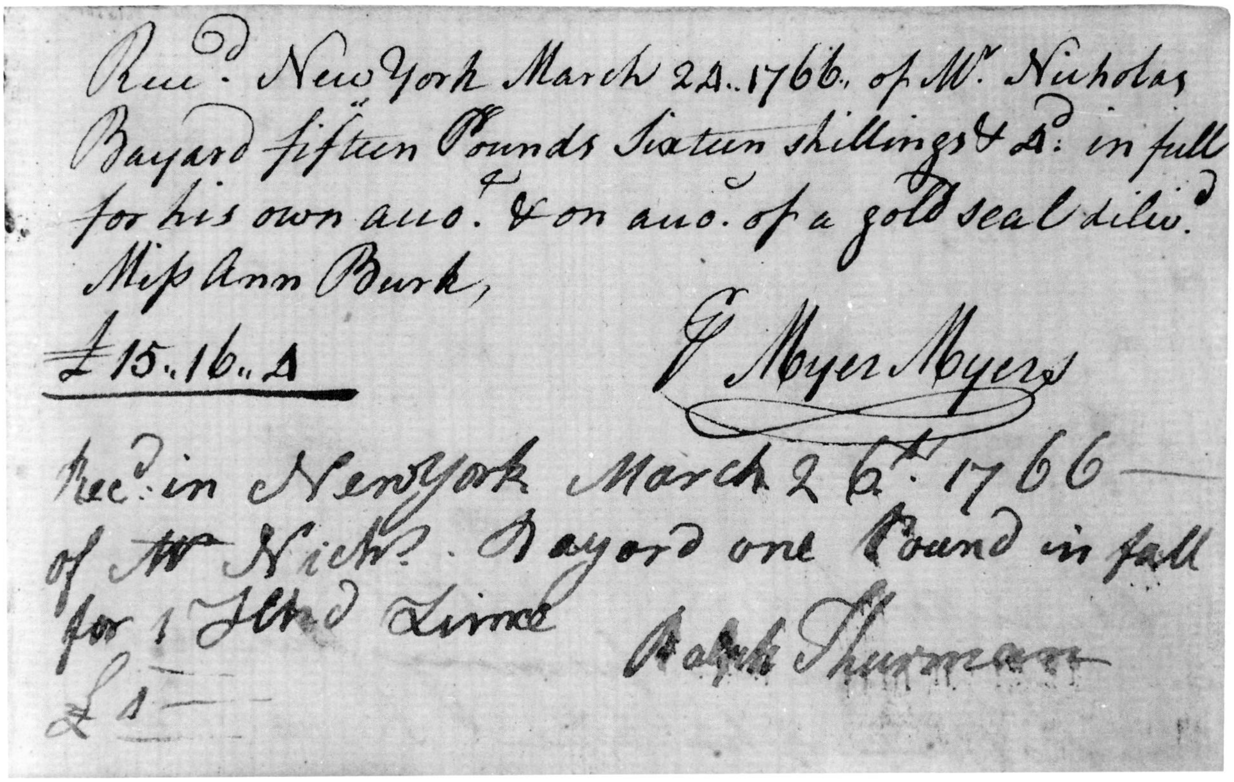

Rec.d New York March 24. 1766. of Mr. Nicholas
Bayard fifteen Pounds Sixteen shillings & d.: in full
for his own acc.t & on acc. of a gold seal deliv.d
Miss Ann Burk,

£15..16..Δ

& Myer Myers

Rec.d in New York March 26.t 1766 —
of Mr. Nich.s Bayard one Pound in full
for 1 Hhd Lime

£ 1 —

Ralph Thurman

3. Entry in the Receipt Book of Nicholas Bayard, New York, March 24, 1766. Bayard Papers, The New-York Historical Society.

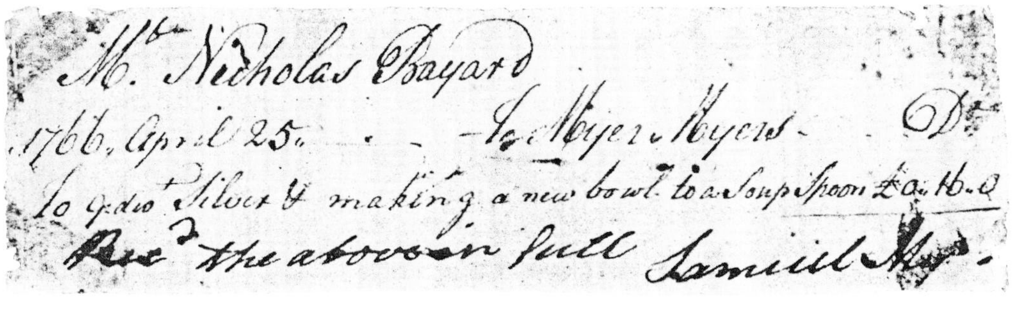

Mr. Nicholas Bayard
1766, April 25. _____ & Myer Myers _____ Dr
To 9 dw.t Silver & making a new bowl to a Soup Spoon £o. 16. 0
Rec.d the above in full Samuel Myers.

4. Receipted bill from Myer Myers to Nicholas Bayard, New York, April 25, 1766. Private collection.

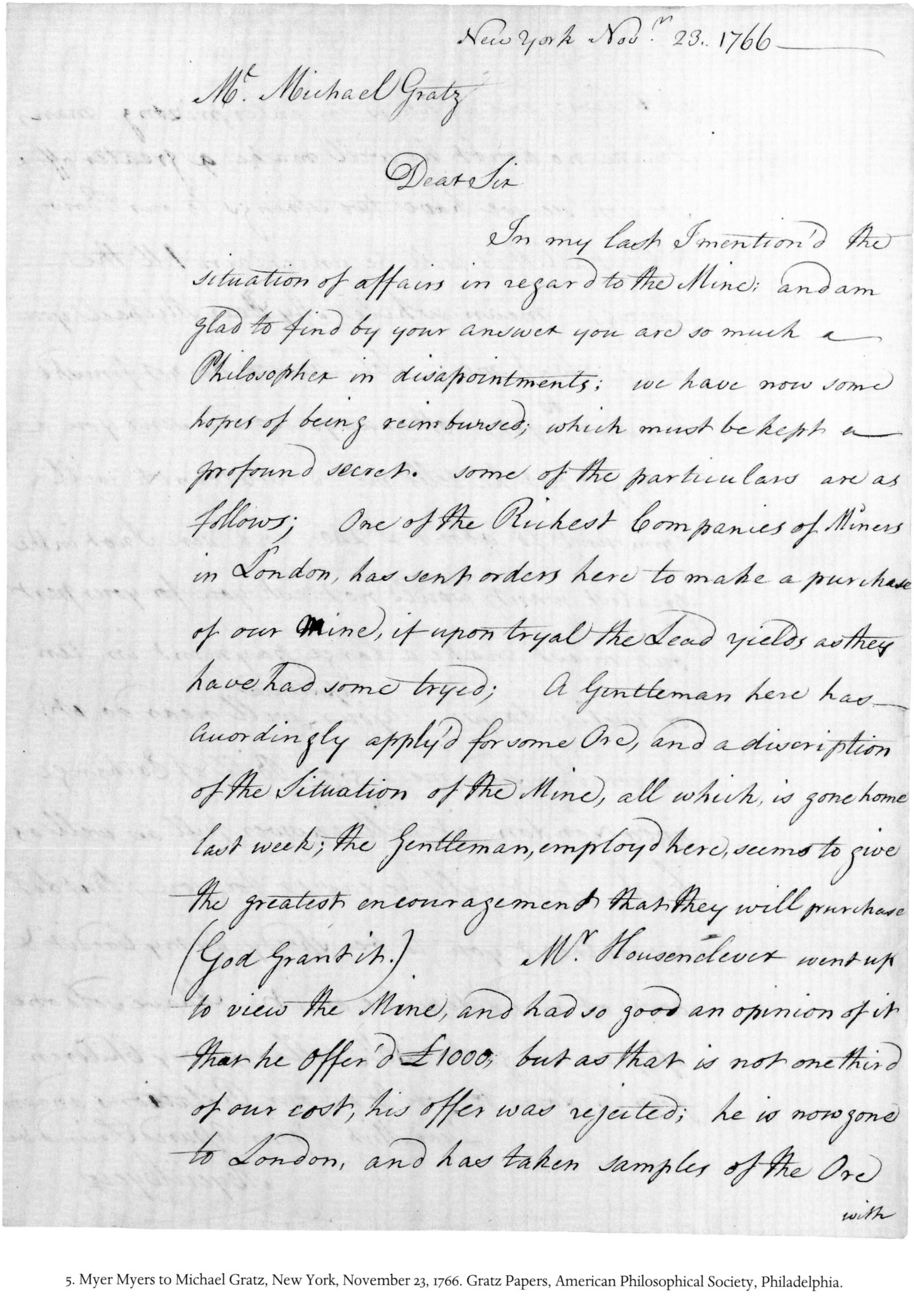

New York Nov.r 23. 1766

M.r Michael Gratz

Dear Sir

In my last I mention'd the
situation of affairs in regard to the Mine; and am
glad to find by your answer you are so much a
Philosopher in disapointments; we have now some
hopes of being reimbursed; which must be kept a
profound secret. some of the particulars are as
follows; One of the Richest Companies of Miners
in London, has sent orders here to make a purchase
of our Mine, if upon tryal the Lead yields as they
have had some tryed; A Gentleman here has
accordingly apply'd for some Ore, and a discription
of the Situation of the Mine, all which, is gone home
last week; the Gentleman, employ'd here, seems to give
the greatest encouragement that they will purchase
(God Grant it.) M.r Housenclever went up
to view the Mine, and had so good an opinion of it
that he offer'd £1000; but as that is not one third
of our cost; his offer was rejected; he is now gone
to London, and has taken samples of the Ore
with

5. Myer Myers to Michael Gratz, New York, November 23, 1766. Gratz Papers, American Philosophical Society, Philadelphia.

with him; and as he is an enterprizing man,
I make no doubt he will make a greater offer
so you see we have two strings to our Bow,

But all this will be uncertain till the ___
Spring; mean while My Dear Michael you
must assist me; Sol.n Simson has not finish'd
the Auo.to yet; other ways would send you a
coppy, but he tells me a Sixteenth will,
ammount to about £240: and were I not in the
greatest want, would not ask you for your part
but must make a large payment in ten
or twelve days; your assistance will near do it;
if you can send me a good Bill of Exchange
upon London, it will answer full as well as
Cash, if it will be easier for you, But let
me entreat you to be speedy as my Credit &
ease of mind depends on it; I have sold one
of your rings for 20½ dollars; my Children
join in Love to you & all our Relations, and am
Dear Mich.l Your Assured Friend &c
Myer Myers

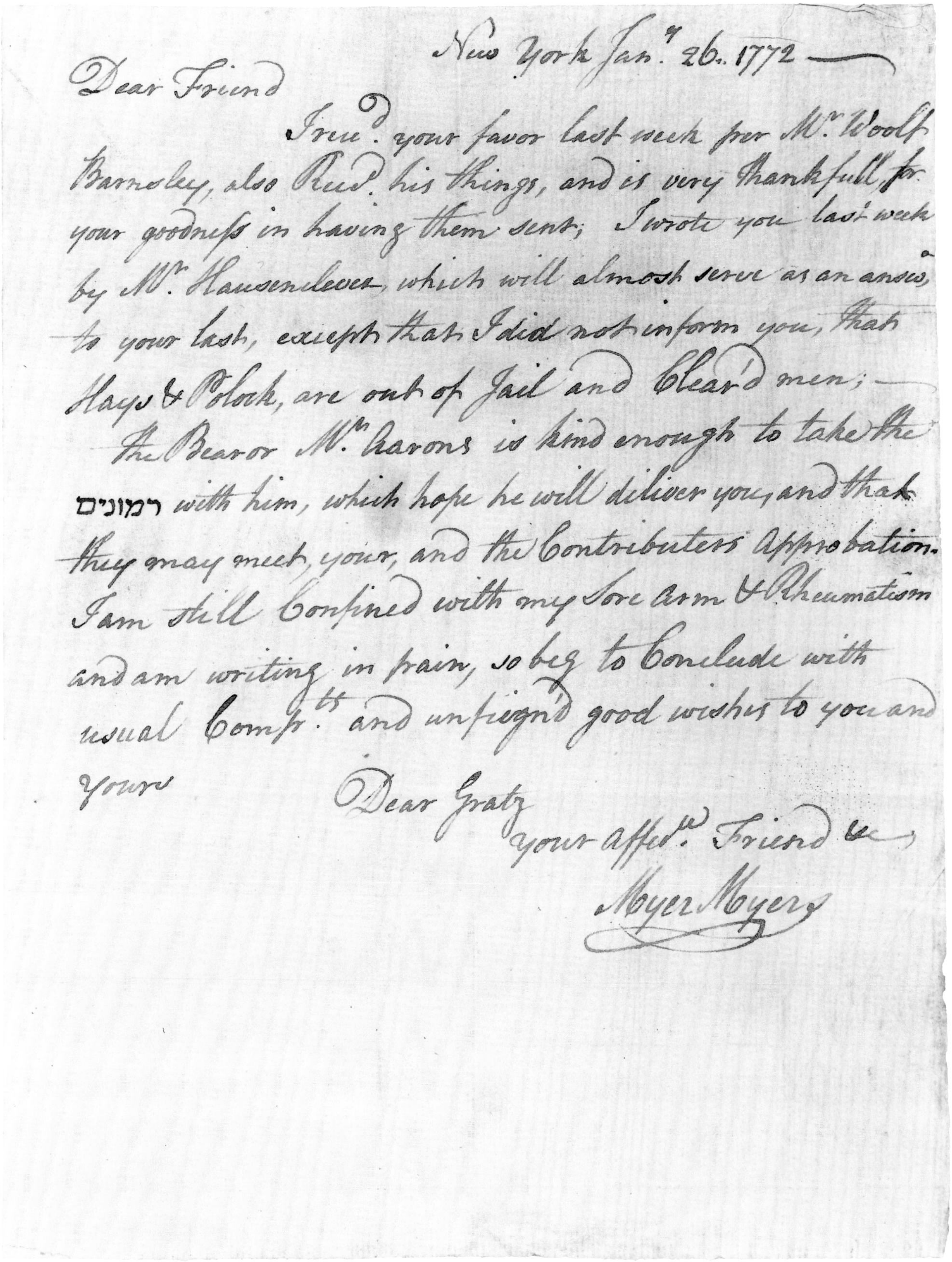

New York Jany. 26. 1772 —

Dear Friend

Recd. your favor last week per Mr. Woolf Barnsley, also Recd. his things, and is very thankfull for your goodness in having them sent; I wrote you last week by Mr. Hausendever, which will almost serve as an answer to your last, except that I did not inform you, that Hays & Polock, are out of Jail and Clear'd men; —

the Bearer Mr. Aarons is kind enough to take the רמונים with him, which hope he will deliver you, and that they may meet, your, and the Contributers Approbation. I am still Confined with my Sore Arm & Rheumatism and am writing in pain, so beg to Conclude with usual Compts. and unfeign'd good wishes to you and yours

Dear Gratz

your affecte. Friend &c

Myer Myers

6. Myer Myers to Michael Gratz, New York, January 26, 1772. Etting Collection, The Historical Society of Pennsylvania, Philadelphia.

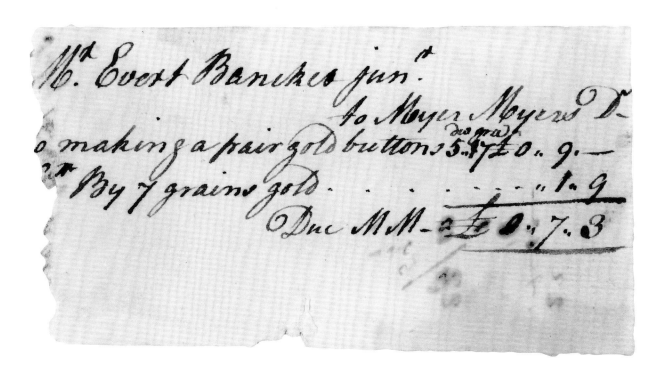

7. Bill from Myer Myers to Evert Bancker, Jr., New York, undated. Bancker Papers, The New-York Historical Society.

Bibliographical Abbreviations

Abrahams 1756–81
Abrahams, Abraham. "Register of Circumcisions, 5516–41 [1756–81]." Lyons Collection, AJHS.

Abstracts 1892–1906
Abstracts of Wills on File in the Surrogate's Office, City of New York (Collections of The New-York Historical Society, 25–39). 15 vols. New York: The New-York Historical Society, 1892–1906.

Ahlstrom 1972
Ahlstrom, Sydney E. *A Religious History of the American People.* New Haven: Yale University Press, 1972.

AJHS
American Jewish Historical Society, New York, and Waltham, Massachusetts.

Alcorn 2000A
Alcorn, Ellenor. *English Silver in the Museum of Fine Arts, Boston.* Volume II. *Silver from 1697 Including English and Irish Silver.* Boston: MFA Publications, 2000.

Alcorn 2000B
Alcorn, Ellenor. "London-made Silver in the American Colonies." *Antiquesamerica.com* (website), article no. 305, March 2000.

Allen 1894
Allen, Charles Dexter. *American Book-Plates.* New York: Macmillan, 1894.

Allen 1907
Allen, Orrin Peer. *The Allen Memorial, Second Series: Descendants of Samuel Allen of Windsor, Conn., 1607–1907.* Palmer, Massachusetts: 1907.

"American Rarity" 1961
"An American Rarity." *Antiques,* 80 (October 1961), p. 340.

American Silver 1960
American Silver and Art Treasures: An Exhibition Sponsored by the English-Speaking Union and Held at Christie's Great Rooms, London. Exhibition catalogue. London: English-Speaking Union, 1960.

Antiquarian Society 1977
The Antiquarian Society of The Art Institute of Chicago: The First One Hundred Years. Exhibition catalogue. Chicago: The Art Institute of Chicago, 1977.

Appleby 1984
Appleby, Joyce Oldham. *Capitalism and a New Social Order: The Republican Vision of the 1790s.* New York: New York University Press, 1984.

Archdeacon 1983
Archdeacon, Thomas J. *Becoming American: An Ethnic History.* New York: Free Press, 1983.

Argentum 1986
Argentum, the Leopard's Head: Catalogue Fall, 1986, Supplement. San Francisco: Argentum, 1986.

Ashton 1997
Ashton, Dianne. *Unsubdued Spirits: Rebecca Gratz and Women's Judaism in America.* Detroit: Wayne State University Press, 1997.

Avery 1920
Avery, C. Louise. *American Silver of the XVII & XVIII Centuries: A Study Based on the Clearwater Collection.* New York: The Metropolitan Museum of Art, 1920.

Avery 1925
Avery, C. Louise. "European Silver: The Alfred Duane Pell Bequest." *Bulletin of The Metropolitan Museum of Art,* 20 (March 1925), pp. 69–72.

Avery 1930
Avery, C. Louise. *Early American Silver.* New York and London: The Century Company, 1930.

Bailey 1899
Bailey, Frederic W., ed. *Early Connecticut Marriages as Found on Ancient Church Records Prior to 1800. Fourth Book.* New Haven: Bureau of American Ancestry for Family Researches, 1899.

Balmer 1989
Balmer, Randall H. *A Perfect Babel of Confusion: Dutch Religion and English Culture in the Middle Colonies.* New York: Oxford University Press, 1989.

Baltimore 1912
Baltimore: Its History and Its People. 3 vols. New York and Chicago: Lewis Historical Publishing Company, 1912.

Banister 1965
Banister, Judith. *English Silver.* London and Sydney: Ward Lock, 1965.

Barker 1996
Barker, Robert B. "Exports of English Silver—A Factor Affecting the Transmission of Style to Colonial Silversmiths, 1730–1769." Typescript of paper, April 19, 1996, Museum of Fine Arts, Boston.

Barnard 1931
Barnard, Ella K. "'Mount Royal' and Its Owners." *Maryland Historical Magazine,* 26 (December 1931), pp. 311–15.

Barnett 1931
Barnett, Lionel D., ed. and trans. *El Libro de los Acuerdos.* Oxford: Oxford University Press, 1931.

Barnett 1974
Barnett, R.D., ed. *Catalogue of the Permanent and Loan Collections of the Jewish Museum, London.* London: Harvey Miller, 1974.

Barr 1980
Barr, Elaine. *George Wickes, 1698–1761: Royal Goldsmith*. New York: Rizzoli, 1980.

Barrett 1889
Barrett, Walter [Joseph Alfred Scoville]. *The Old Merchants of New York City*. 5 vols. New York: Worthington Company, 1889.

Barter et al. 1998
Barter, Judith A., et al. *American Arts at The Art Institute of Chicago: From Colonial Times to World War I*. Chicago: The Art Institute of Chicago, 1998.

Batchellor 1895
Batchellor, Albert S. *The New Hampshire Grants: Being Transcripts of the Charters of Townships*. Volume III. Concord, New Hampshire: Edward N. Pearson, 1895.

Beam 1901
Beam, Jacob N., ed. "Lancaster in 1772." *Journal of the Lancaster County Historical Society*, 5 (1901), pp. 106–12.

Beardsley 1874
Beardsley, E. Edwards. *Life and Correspondence of Samuel Johnson, D.D.* New York: Hurd and Houghton, 1874.

Beinart 1992
Beinart, Haim, ed. *Moreshet Sepharad: The Sephardi Legacy*. 2 vols. Jerusalem: Magnes Press, Hebrew University, 1992.

Belden 1967
Belden, Louise C. "The Verplanck Cup." *Antiques*, 92 (December 1967), pp. 840–42.

Belden 1980
Belden, Louise C. *Marks of American Silversmiths in the Ineson-Bissell Collection*. Charlottesville: University Press of Virginia, 1980.

Belknap 1956
Belknap, Waldron Phoenix, Jr. *The De Peyster Genealogy*. Boston: 1956.

Benedict 1870
Benedict, Henry Marvin. *The Genealogy of the Benedicts in America*. Albany, New York: Joel Munsell, 1870.

Benjamin 1956
Benjamin, I.J. *Three Years in America*. Trans. Charles Reznikoff. Philadelphia: The Jewish Publication Society of America, 1956.

Bennett 1972
Bennett, Douglas. *Irish Georgian Silver*. London: Cassell, 1972.

Bennett 1976
Bennett, Douglas. *Irish Silver*. The Irish Heritage Series, no. 7. Dublin: Eason and Sons, 1976.

Berman 1979
Berman, Myron. *Richmond's Jewry, 1769–1976: Shabbat in Shockoe*. Charlottesville: University Press of Virginia, 1979.

Bigelow 1917
Bigelow, Francis Hill. *Historic Silver of the Colonies and Its Makers*. New York: The Macmillan Company, 1917.

Blackburn/Piwonka et al. 1988
Blackburn, Roderic H., Ruth Piwonka, et al. *Remembrance of Patria: Dutch Arts and Culture in Colonial America, 1609–1776*. Albany, New York: Albany Institute of History and Art, 1988.

Blau/Baron 1963
Blau, Joseph L., and Salo W. Baron. *The Jews of the United States 1790–1840: A Documentary History*. New York: Columbia University Press, 1963.

Bloom 1934
Bloom, Herbert I. "A Study of Brazilian Jewish History 1623–1654, Based Chiefly Upon the Findings of the Late Samuel Oppenheim." *PAJHS*, 33 (1934), pp. 43–125.

Bloom 1937
Bloom, Herbert I. *The Economic Activities of the Jews in Amsterdam in the 17th and 18th Centuries*. Williamsport, Pennsylvania: Bayard Press, 1937.

Bodian 1985
Bodian, Miriam. The *Escamot* of the Spanish-Portuguese Jewish Community of London, 1664." *Michael*, 9 (1985), pp. 9–26.

Bohan 1963
Bohan, Peter J. *American Gold 1700–1860*. Exhibition catalogue. New Haven: Yale University Art Gallery, 1963.

Bohan/Hammerslough 1970
Bohan, Peter J., and Philip Hammerslough. *Early Connecticut Silver, 1700–1840*. Middletown, Connecticut: Wesleyan University Press, 1970.

Bolton 1964
Bolton, Charles Knowles. *Bolton's American Armory: A Record of Coats of Arms Which Have Been in Use Within the Present Bounds of the United States*. 2nd ed. 1927. Reprint, Baltimore: Heraldic Book Company, 1964.

Bonomi 1971
Bonomi, Patricia U. *A Factious People: Politics and Society in Colonial New York*. New York: Columbia University Press, 1971.

Bonomi 1986
Bonomi, Patricia U. *Under the Cope of Heaven: Religion, Society and Politics in Colonial New York*. New York: Oxford University Press, 1986.

Bortman 1954
Bortman, Jane. "Moses Hays and His Revere Silver." *Antiques*, 66 (October 1954), pp. 304–05.

Breen 1994
Breen, T.H. "'Baubles of Britain': The American and Consumer Revolutions of the Eighteenth Century." In Cary Carson, Ronald Hoffman, and Peter J. Albert, eds. *Of Consuming Interests: The Style of Life in the Eighteenth Century*. Charlottesville: University Press of Virginia, 1994, pp. 444–82.

Brener 1976
Brener, David. "Lancaster's First Jewish Community 1715 to 1804: The Era of Joseph Simon." *Journal of the Lancaster County Historical Society*, 80 (1976), pp. 211–321.

Bridenbaugh 1938
Bridenbaugh, Carl. *Cities in the Wilderness: The First Century of Urban Life in America, 1625–1742*. New York: The Ronald Press, 1938.

Bridenbaugh 1949
Bridenbaugh, Carl. *Peter Harrison: First American Architect*. Chapel Hill: University of North Carolina Press, 1949.

Bridenbaugh 1955
Bridenbaugh, Carl. *Cities in Revolt: Urban Life in America, 1743–1776*. New York: Alfred A. Knopf, 1955.

Bridenbaugh 1960
Bridenbaugh, Carl. *Cities in the Wilderness: The First Century of Urban Life in America, 1625–1742*. New York: Knopf, 1960.

Brilliant/Smith 1997
Brilliant, Richard, and Ellen Smith. *Facing the New World: Jewish Portraits in Colonial and Federal America*. Exhibition catalogue. New York: The Jewish Museum, 1997.

Broches 1942
Broches, S. *Jews in New England, Six Monographs: II. Jewish Merchants in Colonial Rhode Island*. New York: Bloch Publishing Company, 1942.

Brown 1995
Brown, Peter B. *In Praise of Hot Liquors: The Study of Chocolate, Coffee and Tea-Drinking, 1600–1850*. Exhibition catalogue. York, England: Fairfax House, 1995.

Brown 1996
Brown, Peter B. "Stands, Coasters, Wagons, and Chariots for the Table." *Antiques*, 150 (October 1996), pp. 524–33.

Brown/Day 1997
Brown, Peter B., and Ivan Day. *Pleasures of the Table: Ritual and Display in the European Dining Room, 1600–1900*. Exhibition catalogue. York, England: Fairfax House, 1997.

Brown/Schwartz 1996
Brown, Peter B., and Marla H. Schwartz. *Come Drink the Bowl Dry: Alcoholic Liquors and Their Place in 18th Century Society*. Exhibition catalogue. York, England: Fairfax House, 1996.

Buck 1888
Buck, J.H. *Old Plate, Ecclesiastical, Decorative, and Domestic: Its Makers and Marks*. New York: The Gorham Manufacturing Company, 1888.

Buhler 1956
Buhler, Kathryn C. *Colonial Silversmiths, Masters & Apprentices*. Exhibition catalogue. Boston: Museum of Fine Arts, 1956.

Buhler 1957
Buhler, Kathryn C. *Mount Vernon Silver*. Mount Vernon, Virginia: The Mount Vernon Ladies' Association of the Union, 1957.

Buhler 1960
Buhler, Kathryn C. *Masterpieces of American Silver*. Exhibition catalogue. Richmond: Virginia Museum of Fine Arts, 1960.

Buhler 1972
Buhler, Kathryn C. *American Silver 1655–1825 in the Museum of Fine Arts, Boston*. 2 vols. Greenwich, Connecticut: New York Graphic Society, 1972.

Buhler/Hood 1970
Buhler, Kathryn C., and Graham Hood. *American Silver: Garvan and Other Collections in the Yale University Art Gallery*. 2 vols. New Haven and London: Yale University Press, 1970.

Bullock 1996
Bullock, Steven C. *Revolutionary Brotherhood: Freemasonry and the Transformation of the American Social Order, 1730–1840*. Chapel Hill: University of North Carolina Press for the Institute of Early American History and Culture, 1996.

Burke 1979
Burke, Ellin M. *The Jewish Community in Early New York, 1654–1800*. Exhibition catalogue. New York: Fraunces Tavern Museum, 1979.

Burke's 1975.
Burke's Peerage and Baronetage. 105th ed. London: Burke's Peerage, 1975.

Burks 1986
Burks, Jean M. *Birmingham Brass Candlesticks*. Charlottesville: University Press of Virginia, 1986.

Burrows/Wallace 1999
Burrows, Edwin G., and Mike Wallace. *Gotham: A History of New York City to 1898*. New York: Oxford University Press, 1999.

Burton 1991
Burton, E. Milby. *South Carolina Silversmiths, 1690–1860*. 3rd rev. ed., Warren Ripley, ed. Charleston, South Carolina: The Charleston Museum, 1991.

Butler 1967
Butler, Joseph T. *The Family Collections at Van Cortlandt Manor*. Tarrytown, New York: Sleepy Hollow Restorations, 1967.

Butler 1983A
Butler, Jon. *The Huguenots in America: A Refugee People in New York Society*. Cambridge, Massachusetts: Harvard University Press, 1983.

Butler 1983B
Butler, Joseph T. *Sleepy Hollow Restorations: A Cross-Section of the Collection*. Tarrytown, New York: Sleepy Hollow Press, 1983.

Butler 1990
Butler, Jon. *Awash in a Sea of Faith: Christianizing the American People*. Cambridge, Massachusetts: Harvard University Press, 1990.

Butler 2000
Butler, Jon. *Becoming American: The Revolution Before 1776*. Cambridge, Massachusetts: Harvard University Press, 2000.

Buttery 1989
Buttery, David. "Nelme's Masterpiece: The Warwick Cruet." *Country Life*, 183 (April 13, 1989), p. 142.

Caldwell/Johnson/Roque 1994
Caldwell, John, Dale T. Johnson, and Oswaldo Rodriguez Roque. *American Paintings in The Metropolitan Museum of Art*. Volume I. *Artists Born by 1815*. New York: The Metropolitan Museum of Art, 1994.

Calendar 1941
Calendar of Wills, Archives of the State of New Jersey, 1st series, 36. Trenton: 1941.

Campbell 1747
Campbell, Robert. *The London Tradesman* (1747). Reprint, London: David and Charles, 1969.

Carlson 1983
Carlson, Janice H. "The Stevens Institute Silver Collection."

Analytical Laboratory Report, 1372, April 22, 1983. Henry Francis du Pont Winterthur Museum, Winterthur, Delaware.

Carman 1935
Carman, Albert P. *Thomas C. Carman and Phebe Pruden Carman.* Urbana, Illinois: Twin City Printing Company, 1935.

Carré 1931
Carré, Louis. *A Guide to Old French Plate.* London: Chapman and Hall, 1931.

Carson/Hoffman/Albert 1994
Carson, Cary, Ronald Hoffman, and Peter J. Albert, eds. *Of Consuming Interests: The Style of Life in the Eighteenth Century.* Charlottesville: University Press of Virginia, 1994.

Catalogue of American Portraits 1974
Catalogue of American Portraits in The New-York Historical Society. 2 vols. New Haven and London: Yale University Press, 1974.

Channing 1868
Channing, George G. *Early Recollections of Newport, R.I. from the Year 1793 to 1811.* Boston: Nichols and Noyes, 1868.

Chapman 1860
Chapman, Rev. F.W. "Genealogical Notes of the Kirtland Family in the United States." *New England Historical and Genealogical Register,* 14 (July 1860), pp. 241–45.

Checklist 1968
Checklist of American Silversmiths' Work, 1650–1850, in Museums in the New York Metropolitan Area. New York: The Metropolitan Museum of Art, 1968.

Christie's 1982
Important American Furniture, Silver and Decorative Arts. Auction catalogue. New York: Christie's, June 12, 1982.

Christie's 1983A
Important American Furniture, Silver and Decorative Arts Auction catalogue. New York: Christie's, June 2, 1983.

Christie's 1983B
Important American Furniture, Silver and Decorative Arts. Auction catalogue. New York: Christie's, October 13, 1983.

Christie's 1986
Important American Furniture, Silver, Folk Art and Decorative Arts. Auction catalogue. New York: Christie's, October 18, 1986.

Christie's 1988
Important American Furniture, Silver, Prints, Folk Art and Decorative Arts. Auction catalogue. New York: Christie's, June 4, 1988.

Christie's 1990
Silver and Objects of Vertu. Auction catalogue. London: Christie's, November 28, 1990.

Christie's 1991
Silver and Objects of Vertu. Auction catalogue. London: Christie's, May 23, 1991.

Christie's 1992
Important American Furniture, Silver, Prints, Folk Art and Decorative Arts. Auction catalogue. New York: Christie's, January 17–18, 1992.

Christie's 1993
Important American Silver: The Collection of James H. Halpin. Auction catalogue. New York: Christie's, January 22, 1993.

Christie's 1994
Important American Furniture, Silver, Prints, Folk Art and Decorative Arts. Auction catalogue. New York: Christie's, January 21–22, 1994.

Christie's 1996
Important American Furniture, Silver, Prints, Folk Art, and Decorative Arts. Auction catalogue. New York: Christie's, January 27, 1996.

Christie's 1998
Highly Important American Furniture, Silver, Paintings, Prints, Folk Art and Decorative Arts. Auction catalogue. New York: Christie's, January 16, 1998.

Christie's 1999
Important American Furniture, Silver, Prints, Folk Art and Decorative Arts. Auction catalogue. New York: Christie's, January 15–16, 1999.

Christie's 2000
Important American Furniture, Silver, Prints, Folk Art and Decorative Arts. Auction catalogue. New York: Christie's, January 21, 2000.

Christie's 2001
Important American Furniture, Silver, Prints, Folk Art and Decorative Arts. Auction catalogue. New York: Christie's, January 18–19, 2001.

Christoph 1987
Christoph, Florence A. *Schuyler Genealogy: A Compendium of Sources Pertaining to the Schuyler Families in America Prior to 1800.* Albany, New York: The Friends of Schuyler Mansion, 1987.

Christoph 1992
Christoph, Florence A. *Schuyler Genealogy.* Volume II. *The Schuyler Families in America Prior to 1900.* Albany, New York: The Friends of Schuyler Mansion, 1992.

Chyet 1970
Chyet, Stanley F. *Lopez of Newport: Colonial American Merchant Prince.* Detroit: Wayne State University Press, 1970.

Citroen 1975
Citroen, K.A. *Amsterdam Silversmiths and Their Marks.* Volume I. *North-Holland Studies in Silver.* Amsterdam and Oxford: North-Holland Publishing Company, 1975.

Clarksons 1876
The Clarksons of New York: A Sketch. 2 vols. New York: Bradstreet Press, 1876.

Clayton 1971
Clayton, Michael. *The Collector's Dictionary of the Silver and Gold of Great Britain and North America.* New York and Cleveland: World Publishing Company, 1971.

Clayton 1985
Clayton, Michael. *Christie's Pictorial History of English and American Silver.* Oxford: Phaidon-Christie's, 1985.

Coen 1954–55
Coen, Davis. "Pioneer Jewish Masons in New York." *Transactions of the American Lodge of Research, Free and Accepted Masons,* 6 (1954–55), pp. 158–60.

Cohen 1913

Cohen, Caroline. *Records of the Myers, Hays and Mordecai Families from 1707 to 1913*. 1913.

Cohen n.d.

Cohen, Judah. "Documents Concerning the Jews of the Virgin Islands." N.d., private collection.

Conger / Rollins 1991

Conger, Clement E., and Alexandra W. Rollins. *Treasures of State: Fine and Decorative Arts in the Diplomatic Reception Rooms of the U.S. Department of State*. New York: Harry N. Abrams, 1991.

Conrad 1900

Conrad, Henry C. *Gunning Bedford, Junior* (Papers of The Historical Society of Delaware, 26). Wilmington: The Historical Society of Delaware, 1900.

Conradsen 1999

Conradsen, David H. *Useful Beauty: Early American Decorative Arts from St. Louis Collections*. Exhibition catalogue. Saint Louis: The Saint Louis Art Museum, 1999.

Conroy 1995

Conroy, David W. *In Public Houses: Drink and the Revolution of Authority in Colonial Massachusetts*. Chapel Hill: University of North Carolina Press for the Institute of Early American History and Culture, 1995.

Cornell 1902

Cornell, John. *Genealogy of the Cornell Family: Being an Account of the Descendants of Thomas Cornell of Portsmouth, R.I.* New York: T.A. Wright, 1902.

Corwin 1901–16

Corwin, Edward T., ed. *Ecclesiastical Records, State of New York*. 7 vols. Albany: J.B. Lyon, 1901–16.

Cothren 1854

Cothren, William. *History of Ancient Woodbury, Connecticut, from the First Indian Deed in 1659 to 1854*. Waterbury, Connecticut: Bronson Brothers, 1854.

Countryman 1981

Countryman, Edward. *A People in Revolution: The American Revolution and Political Society in New York, 1760–1790*. Baltimore: The Johns Hopkins University Press, 1981.

Cox 1912

Cox, Rev. Henry Miller. *The Cox Family in America*. New York: Unionist Gazette Association, 1912.

Craven 1971

Craven, Wayne. "Painting in New York City, 1750–1775." In Ian M.G. Quimby, ed., *American Painting to 1776: A Reappraisal*. Winterthur, Delaware: Henry Francis du Pont Winterthur Museum, 1971, pp. 251–97.

Craven 1986

Craven, Wayne. *Colonial American Portraiture*. Cambridge: Cambridge University Press, 1986.

Crosby 1886

Crosby, Ernest H. "The Rutgers Family of New York." *NYGBR*, 17 (April 1886), pp. 82–93.

Cunningham 1955

Cunningham, Anna K. *Schuyler Mansion: A Critical Catalogue of the Furnishings and Decorations*. Albany, New York: New York State Education Department, 1955.

Currier 1938

Currier, Ernest M. *Marks of Early American Silversmiths, with Notes on Silver, Spoon Types, and List of New York City Silversmiths 1815–1841*. Portland, Maine: The Southworth-Anthoensen Press, 1938.

Curtis 1913

Curtis, George Munson. *Early Silver of Connecticut and Its Makers*. Meriden, Connecticut: International Silver Company, 1913.

Curtiss 1903

Curtiss, Frederic Haines. *A Genealogy of the Curtiss Family*. Boston: Rockwell and Churchill Press, 1903.

Cutten 1952

Cutten, George Barton. *The Silversmiths of Virginia (Together with Watchmakers and Jewelers) from 1694 to 1850*. Richmond, Virginia: The Dietz Press, 1952.

Cutten 1958

Cutten, George Barton. *The Silversmiths of Georgia, together with Watchmakers & Jewelers—1733 to 1850*. Savannah, Georgia: The Pigeonhole Press, 1958.

Cutter et al. 1911

Cutter, William Richard, et al. *Genealogical and Family History of the State of Connecticut*. 4 vols. New York: Lewis Historical Publishing Company, 1911.

Cutter 1913

Cutter, William Richard. *Genealogical and Family History of Southern New York and the Hudson River Valley*. 3 vols. New York: Lewis Historical Publishing Company, 1913.

Cutting n.d.

Cutting, Mrs. W. Bayard. "Bayard Genealogy and Bayard Family Notes." Manuscript collection, NYHS.

DAB

Dictionary of American Biography. 21 vols. New York: Charles Scribner's Sons, 1943–44.

Darling 1964

Darling, Herbert F. *New York State Silversmiths*. Eggertsville, New York: The Darling Foundation of New York State Early American Silversmiths and Silver, 1964.

Davis 1976

Davis, John D. *English Silver at Williamsburg* (The Williamsburg Decorative Arts Series, Graham Hood, ed.). Williamsburg, Virginia: The Colonial Williamsburg Foundation, 1976.

Davis 1985

Davis, Thomas J. *A Rumor of Revolt: The 'Great Negro Plot' in Colonial New York*. New York: Free Press, 1985.

Davis 1992

Davis, John D. *The Genius of Irish Silver: A Texas Private Collection*. Exhibition catalogue. Williamsburg, Virginia: The Colonial Williamsburg Foundation, 1992.

Day 1909
Day, Richard E. *Calendar of the Sir William Johnson Manuscripts in the New York State Library.* Albany, New York: University of the State of New York, 1909.

Daybook 1755–69
Unidentified merchant, Daybook, 1755–69. Etting Collection, AJHS.

De Castres 1977
De Castres, Elizabeth. *A Collector's Guide to Tea Silver, 1670–1900.* London: Frederick Muller, 1977.

Decatur 1941
Decatur, Stephen. "William Gilbert, Silversmith of New York." *American Collector,* 10 (July 1941), pp. 8–9, 20.

Delafield 1952
Delafield, John Ross. "Walter Thong of New York and His Forefathers." *NYGBR,* 83 (October 1952), pp. 196–204.

De Lancey 1876
De Lancey, Edward F. "Original Family Records, *Morris* of Morrisania, Westchester Co, New York." *NYGBR,* 8 (January 1876), pp. 16–18.

De Lancey 1885
De Lancey, Edward F. *The Burghers of New Amsterdam and The Freemen of New York* (Collections of The New-York Historical Society, 18). New York: The New-York Historical Society, 1885.

Delaplaine 1753–56.
Joshua Delaplaine, Daybook, 1753–56. Delaplaine Papers, NYHS.

Delieb/Roberts 1971
Delieb, Eric, and Michael Roberts. *Matthew Boulton: Master Silversmith, 1760–1790.* New York: Clarkson N. Potter, 1971.

De Lorm 2000
De Lorm, Jan Rudolph. *Amsterdams Goud en Zilver.* Amsterdam: Rijksmuseum, 2000.

Den Blaauwen 1979
Den Blaauwen, A.L. *Nederlands zilver/Dutch Silver.* Exhibition catalogue. Amsterdam: Rijksmuseum, 1979.

Dennis 1968
Dennis, Jessie McNab. "Franks Family Silver by Lamerie." *Antiques,* 93 (May 1968), pp. 636–41.

Dexter 1885–1912
Dexter, Franklin Bowditch. *Biographical Sketches of the Graduates of Yale College with Annals of the College History.* 6 vols. New York: H. Holt and Company, 1885–1912.

Dexter 1901
Dexter, Franklin Bowditch, ed. *The Literary Diary of Ezra Stiles.* 3 vols. New York: Charles Scribner's Sons, 1901.

Dill 1955
Dill, Alonzo Thomas. *Governor Tryon and His Palace.* Chapel Hill: The University of North Carolina Press, 1955.

Disosvray 1865
Disosvray, Gabriel P. *The Earliest Churches of New York and Its Vicinity.* New York: J.G. Gregory, 1865.

Doty 1912
Doty, Ethan Allen. "The Doughty Family of Long Island." *NYGBR,* 43 (July 1912), pp. 273–87.

Downs 1952
Downs, Joseph. *American Furniture: Queen Anne and Chippendale Periods in The Henry Francis du Pont Winterthur Museum.* New York: Macmillan, 1952.

Duncan 1791
Duncan, William. *The New-York Directory and Register for the Year 1791.* New York: T. and J. Swords, 1791.

Duncan 1792
Duncan, William. *The New-York Directory and Register for the Year 1792.* New York: T. and J. Swords, 1792.

Duncan 1793
Duncan, William. *The New-York Directory and Register for the Year 1793.* New York: T. and J. Swords, 1793.

Duncan 1794
Duncan, William. *The New-York Directory and Register for the Year 1794.* New York: T. and J. Swords, 1794.

Duncan 1795
Duncan, William. *The New-York Directory and Register for the Year 1795.* New York: T. and J. Swords, 1795.

Dunlap 1834
Dunlap, William. *A History of the Rise and Progress of the Arts of Design in the United States.* 2 vols. New York, G.P. Scott and Company, 1834.

Duyckinck 1908
Duyckinck, Whitehead Cornell. *The Duyckinck and Allied Families.* New York: Tobias A. Wright, 1908.

Dwight 1873
Dwight, Benjamin W. "The Descendants of Rev. Benjamin Woolsey, of Dosoris (Glen Cove), L.I." *NYGBR,* 4 (July 1873), pp. 143–55.

Dwight 1903
Dwight, Rev. Melatiah E. "Anthony Bleecker." *NYGBR,* 34 (October 1903), pp. 231–34.

"Early American" 1953
"Early American Jewish Portraits and Silver." Exhibition checklist. Boston: Museum of Fine Arts, 1953.

Eberlein/Hubbard 1940
Eberlein, Harold Donaldson, and Cortlandt van Dyke Hubbard. "The Morris Foundation: A Family Trust of Heirlooms." *American Collector,* 9 (October 1940), pp. 12–13, 18.

Eickhoff 1884
Eickhoff, Anton. *In den Neuen Heimath: Geschichtliche Mittheilungen über die Deutschen Einwanderer in allen Theilen der Union.* New York: E. Steiger and Company, 1884.

Elazar/Sarna/Monson 1992
Elazar, Daniel J., Jonathan D. Sarna, and Rela G. Monson, eds. *A Double Bond: The Constitutional Documents of American Jewry.* Lanham, Maryland: University Press of America, 1992.

Eleventh Report 1921
Eleventh Report of the Class of 1871 of Harvard College. Cambridge, Massachusetts: Riverside Press, 1921.

Emmanuel 1955
Emmanuel, Isaac S. "New Light on Early American Jewry." *American Jewish Archives,* 7 (January 1955), pp. 3–64.

Emmanuel 1962

Emmanuel, Isaac S. "Seventeenth-Century Brazilian Jewry: A Critical Review." *American Jewish Archives*, 14 (1962), p. 41.

Emmanuel/Emmanuel 1970

Emmanuel, Isaac S., and Suzanne A. Emmanuel. *History of the Jews of the Netherlands Antilles*. 2 vols. Cincinnati: American Jewish Archives, 1970.

Endelman 1979

Endelman, Todd. *The Jews of Georgian England 1714–1830*. Philadelphia: The Jewish Publication Society of America, 1979.

Engerman/Gallman 1996

Engerman, Stanley L., and Robert E. Gallman, eds. *The Cambridge Economic History of the United States: The Colonial Era*. New York: Cambridge University Press, 1996.

Ensko 1927

Ensko, Stephen G.C. *American Silversmiths and Their Marks*. New York: 1927.

Ensko 1937

Ensko, Stephen G.C. *American Silversmiths and Their Marks II*. New York: Robert Ensko, 1937.

Ensko 1948

Ensko, Stephen G.C. *American Silversmiths and Their Marks III*. New York: Robert Ensko, 1948.

Evans 1901

Evans, Thomas Grier, ed. *Records of the Reformed Dutch Church in New Amsterdam and New York*. Volume II. *Baptisms from 25 December, 1639, to 27 December, 1730*. New York: The New–York Genealogical and Biographical Society, 1901.

Evans 1980

Evans, Dorinda. *Benjamin West and His American Students*. Exhibition catalogue. Washington, D.C.: National Portrait Gallery, 1980.

Exhibition 1929

Exhibition of American Eighteenth Century Art Owned In and Near Worcester. Exhibition catalogue. Worcester, Massachusetts: Worcester Art Museum, 1929.

"Exhibition" 1954

"Exhibition of Works in Silver and Gold by Myer Myers: A Checklist of Objects Exhibited at the Brooklyn Museum." Exhibition checklist. New York: Brooklyn Museum, 1953.

Ezekiel/Lichtenstein 1917

Ezekiel, Herbert T., and Gaston Lichtenstein. *The History of the Jews of Richmond from 1769 to 1917*. Richmond, Virginia: H.T. Ezekiel, 1917.

Faber 1992

Faber, Eli. *A Time for Planting: The First Migration, 1654–1820*. Volume I. *The Jewish People in America*, Henry L. Feingold, ed. Baltimore: The Johns Hopkins University Press, 1992.

Failey 1971

Failey, Dean F. "Elias Pelletreau, Long Island Silversmith." M.A. thesis. Newark: University of Delaware, 1971.

Failey 1976

Failey, Dean F. *Long Island Is My Nation: The Decorative Arts and Craftsmen, 1640–1830*. Setauket, New York: Society for the Preservation of Long Island Antiquities, 1976.

Fairbairn 1992

Fairbairn, James. *Fairbairn's Crests of the Families of Great Britain and Ireland*. Rev. ed., Laurence Butters, ed. New York: Dorset Press, 1992.

Fales 1958

Fales, Martha Gandy. *American Silver in the Henry Francis du Pont Winterthur Museum*. Winterthur, Delaware: Henry Francis du Pont Winterthur Museum, 1958.

Fales 1970

Fales, Martha Gandy. *Early American Silver*. Rev. ed. Excalibur Books, 1970.

Fales 1974

Fales, Martha Gandy. *Joseph Richardson and Family: Philadelphia Silversmiths*. Middletown, Connecticut: Wesleyan University Press for The Historical Society of Pennsylvania, 1974.

Fales 1995

Fales, Martha Gandy. *Jewelry in America 1600–1900*. Woodbridge, England: Antique Collectors' Club, 1995.

"Family Register" 1975

"Family Register: Lispenard—Bleecker." *NYGBR*, 106 (October 1975), pp. 233–35.

Felsenstein/Mintz 1995

Felsenstein, Frank, and Sharon Liberman Mintz. *The Jew as Other: A Century of English Caricature, 1730–1830*. Exhibition catalogue. New York: The Library of The Jewish Theological Seminary of America, 1995.

Fennimore 1984

Fennimore, Donald L. *Silver and Pewter*. New York: Alfred A. Knopf, 1984.

Fennimore 1996A

Fennimore, Donald L. *Metalwork in Early America: Copper and Its Alloys*. Winterthur, Delaware: Henry Francis du Pont Winterthur Museum, 1996.

Fennimore 1996B

Fennimore, Donald L., comp. *Henry Will Account Book: A Record of His Pewtering and Related Activities in New York City and Albany from 1763 to 1800*. Morgantown, Pennsylvania: Masthof Press, 1996.

Feuer 1987

Feuer, Lewis S. *Jews in the Origins of Modern Science and Bacon's Scientific Utopia: The Life and Work of Joachim Gaunse, Mining Technologist and First Recorded Jew in English-Speaking North America* (Brochure Series of the American Jewish Archives, 6) Cincinnati: American Jewish Archives, 1987.

Fielding 1926

Fielding, Mantle. *Dictionary of American Painters, Engravers and Sculptors*. Philadelphia: 1926.

Fifty Years 1986

Fifty Years on 57th Street. Exhibition catalogue. New York and London: S.J. Shrubsole, 1986.

Finlay 1956
Finlay, Ian. *Scottish Gold and Silver Work*. London: Chatto and Windus, 1956.

Fish 1929
Fish, Stuyvesant B. *Ancestors of Hamilton Fish and Julia Ursin Niemcewicz Kean, His Wife*. New York: The Evening Post Job Printing Office, 1929.

Fish 1994
Fish, Sidney M. *Barnard and Michael Gratz: Their Lives and Times*. Lanham, Maryland: University Press of America, 1994.

Flick 1927
Flick, Alexander C., ed. *The Papers of Sir William Johnson*. Volume V. Albany, New York: The University of the State of New York, 1927.

Floyd-Jones 1906
Floyd-Jones, Thomas. *Thomas Jones, Fort Neck, Queens County, Long Island, 1695, and His Descendants, The Floyd-Jones Family*. New York: 1906.

Flynt/Fales 1968
Flynt, Henry N., and Martha Gandy Fales. *The Heritage Foundation Collection of Silver, with Biographical Sketches of New England Silversmiths, 1625–1825*. Old Deerfield, Massachusetts: The Heritage Foundation, 1968.

Forbes 1998
Forbes, J.S. *Hallmark: A History of the London Assay Office*. London: The Goldsmiths' Company, 1998.

Fourth Report 1910
Fourth Report of the Harvard College Class of 1893. Cambridge, Massachusetts: Harvard University Press, 1910.

Fox 1926
Fox, Dixon Ryan. *Caleb Heathcote, Gentleman Colonist: The Story of a Career in the Province of New York, 1692–1721*. New York: Charles Scribner's Sons, 1926.

Franklin 1964
Franklin, Benjamin. *The Autobiography of Benjamin Franklin*. Leonard W. Labaree, Ralph L. Ketcham, Helen C. Boatfield, and Helene H. Fineman, eds. New Haven: Yale University Press, 1964.

Franks 1786
Franks, David. *The New-York Directory*. New York: Shepard Kollock, 1786.

Franks 1787
Franks, David. *The New-York Directory*. New York: The Editor, 1787.

French 1917
French, Hollis. *A List of Early American Silversmiths and Their Marks*. New York: 1917.

French 1939
French, Hollis. *Jacob Hurd and His Sons Nathaniel & Benjamin, Silversmiths: 1702–1781*. Cambridge, Massachusetts: The Walpole Society, 1939.

French 1940
French, Mansfield Joseph. *Ancestors and Descendants of Samuel French the Joiner of Stratford, Connecticut*. Ann Arbor, Michigan: Edwards Brothers, 1940.

Freudenheim 1965
Freudenheim, Tom L. *Myer Myers: American Silversmith*. Exhibition catalogue. New York: The Jewish Museum, 1965.

Friedman 1940
Friedman, Lee M. *Rabbi Haim Isaac Carigal: His Newport Sermon and His Yale Portrait*. Boston: D.B. Updike, The Merrymount Press, 1940.

Friedman 1946
Friedman, Lee M. "The Newport Synagogue." *Old-Time New England*, 36 (January 1946), pp. 48–57.

Friedman 1975
Friedman, Terry F. "Two Eighteenth-Century Catalogues of Ornamental Pattern Books." *Furniture History*, 11 (1975), pp. 66–75.

Garvan 1959
Garvan, Anthony N.B. "The New England Porringer: An Index of Custom." *Annual Report of the Board of Regents of the Smithsonian Institution* (Publication 4354). Washington, D.C.: U.S. Government Printing Office, 1959, pp. 543–52.

Garvan 1987
Garvan, Beatrice B. *Federal Philadelphia, 1785–1825: The Athens of the Western World*. Exhibition catalogue. Philadelphia: Philadelphia Museum of Art, 1987.

Gentle/Feild 1975
Gentle, Rupert, and Rachael Feild. *English Domestic Brass, 1680–1810, and the History of Its Origins*. New York: E.P. Dutton, 1975.

Gerber 1992
Gerber, Jane S. *The Jews of Spain*. New York: Free Press, 1992.

Gerlach 1964
Gerlach, Don R. *Philip Schuyler and the American Revolution in New York, 1733–1777*. Lincoln: University of Nebraska Press, 1964.

Gerstell 1972
Gerstell, Vivian S. *Silversmiths of Lancaster, Pennsylvania 1730–1850*. Lancaster, Pennsylvania: Lancaster Historical Society, 1972.

Gilchrist 1967
Gilchrist, James. *Anglican Church Plate*. London: The Connoisseur and Michael Joseph, 1967.

Gilje/Rock 1992
Gilje, Paul A., and Howard B. Rock. *Keepers of the Revolution: New Yorkers at Work in the Early Republic*. Ithaca, New York: Cornell University Press, 1992.

Glenn 1900
Glenn, Thomas Allen. *Some Colonial Mansions and Those Who Lived in Them*. 2nd ser. Philadelphia: Henry T. Coates and Company, 1900.

Glen-Sanders Collection 1966
The Glen-Sanders Collection from Scotia, New York. Exhibition catalogue. Williamsburg, Virginia: Colonial Williamsburg, 1966.

Godfrey/Godfrey 1995

Godfrey, Sheldon S., and Judith C. Godfrey. *Search Out the Land: The Jews and the Growth of Equality in British Colonial America, 1740–1867*. Montreal: McGill-Queen's University Press, 1995.

Goldman 1993A

Goldman, Karla A. "Beyond the Gallery: The Place of Women in the Development of American Judaism." Ph.D. dissertation. Cambridge, Massachusetts: Harvard University, 1993.

Goldman 1993B

Goldman, Shalom, ed. *Hebrew and the Bible in America*. Hanover, New Hampshire: University Press of New England, 1993.

Goldsborough 1983

Goldsborough, Jennifer Faulds. *Silver in Maryland*. Exhibition catalogue. Baltimore: Museum and Library of Maryland History, Maryland Historical Society, 1983.

Goldstein 1930

Goldstein, Israel. *A Century of Judaism in New York: B'nai Jeshurun, 1825–1925*. New York: Congregation B'nai Jeshurun, 1930.

Goodfriend 1975

Goodfriend, Joyce D. "'Too Great a Mixture of Nations': The Development of New York City Society in the Seventeenth Century." Ph.D. dissertation. Los Angeles: University of California at Los Angeles, 1975.

Goodfriend 1991

Goodfriend, Joyce D. *Before the Melting Pot: Society and Culture in Colonial New York City, 1664–1730*. Princeton: Princeton University Press, 1991.

Gordon 1919

Gordon, William Seton. "Gabriel Ludlow (1663–1736) and His Descendants." *NYGBR*, 50 (April 1919), pp. 139–49.

Gottesman 1936

Gottesman, Rita Susswein. *The Arts and Crafts in New York, 1726–1776: Advertisements and News Items from New York City Newspapers* (Collections of The New-York Historical Society, 69). New York: The New-York Historical Society, 1936.

Gottesman 1954

Gottesman, Rita Susswein. *The Arts and Crafts in New York, 1777–1799: Advertisements and News Items from New York City Newspapers*. New York: The New-York Historical Society, 1954.

Graham 1936

Graham, James, Jr. *Early American Silver Marks*. New York: James Graham, Jr., 1936.

Grafman/Mann 1996

Grafman, Rafi, and Vivian B. Mann. *Crowning Glory: Silver Torah Ornaments of The Jewish Museum, New York*. New York: The Jewish Museum, 1996.

Gratz 1757–62A

Gratz, Barnard. Account Book, 1757–1762. Etting Collection, Historical Society of Pennsylvania, Philadelphia.

Gratz 1757–62B

Gratz, Barnard. Memorandum Book, 1757–1762. Etting Collection, Historical Society of Pennsylvania, Philadelphia.

Gratz/Gratz 1768–72

Gratz, Barnard, and Michael Gratz. Letterbook, 1768–1772. Etting Collection, Historical Society of Pennsylvania, Philadelphia.

Gray 1908

Gray, George Arthur. *The Descendants of George Holmes of Roxbury, 1594–1908*. Boston: 1908.

Green 1977

Green, Robert Alan. *Marks of American Silversmiths*. Harrison, New York: Robert Alan Green, 1977.

Grimwade et al. 1951

Grimwade, Arthur G., et al. *Treasures of a London Temple: A Descriptive Catalogue of the Ritual Plate, Mantles and Furniture of the Spanish and Portuguese Jews' Synagogue in Bevis Marks*. London: Taylor's Foreign Press, 1951.

Grimwade 1955

Grimwade, Arthur G. *Anglo-Jewish Silver*. London: The Jewish Historical Society of England and The Jewish Museum, 1955.

Grimwade 1990

Grimwade, Arthur G. *London Goldsmiths, 1697–1837: Their Marks and Lives*. 3rd rev. ed. London: Faber and Faber, 1990.

Grinstein 1945

Grinstein, Hyman B. *The Rise of the Jewish Community of New York, 1654–1860*. Philadelphia: The Jewish Publication Society of America, 1945.

Groce 1937

Groce, George C., Jr. *William Samuel Johnson: A Maker of the Constitution*. New York, 1937.

Grogan 1997

The November Auction. Auction catalogue. Boston: Grogan and Company, November 22–23, 1997.

GRSNS

Genealogical Records of Saint Nicholas's Society.

Gutstein 1936

Gutstein, Morris A. *The Story of the Jews of Newport: Two and a Half Centuries of Judaism, 1658–1908*. New York: Bloch Publishing Company, 1936.

Hackenbroch 1969

Hackenbroch, Yvonne. *English and Other Silver in the Irwin Untermyer Collection*. 1963. Rev. ed. New York: The Metropolitan Museum of Art, 1969.

Hagy 1993

Hagy, James William. *This Happy Land: The Jews of Colonial and Antebellum Charleston*. Tuscaloosa: University of Alabama Press, 1993.

Hall 1977

Hall, Peter Dobkin. "Family Structure and Economic Organization: Massachusetts Merchants, 1700–1850." In Tamara K. Hareven, ed. *Family and Kin in Urban Communities, 1700–1930*. New York and London: New Viewpoints, 1977, pp. 38–61

Halsey/Buck 1906

Halsey, R.T.H., and J.H. Buck. *American Silver: The Work of the Seventeenth and Eighteenth Century Silversmiths*. Exhibition catalogue. Boston: Museum of Fine Arts, 1906.

Hamilton 1995
Hamilton, Martha Wilson. *Silver in the Fur Trade, 1680–1820.* Chelmsford, Massachusetts: Martha Hamilton Publishing, 1995.

Hammerslough 1958
Hammerslough, Philip H. *American Silver Collected by Philip H. Hammerslough.* Hartford, Connecticut: 1958.

Hammerslough 1960
Hammerslough, Philip H. *American Silver Collected by Philip H. Hammerslough.* Volume II. Hartford, Connecticut: 1960.

Hammerslough 1965
Hammerslough, Philip H. *American Silver Collected by Philip H. Hammerslough.* Volume III. Hartford, Connecticut: 1965.

Hammerslough/Feigenbaum 1973
Hammerslough, Philip H., and Rita F. Feigenbaum. *American Silver Collected by Philip H. Hammerslough.* Volume IV. Hartford, Connecticut: 1973.

Handlin 1949
Handlin, Oscar. *This Was America: True Accounts of People and Places, Manners and Customs, As Recorded by European Travelers to the Western Shore in the Eighteenth, Nineteenth and Twentieth Centuries.* Cambridge, Massachusetts: Harvard University Press, 1949.

Hare/Snodin/Clifford 1990
Hare, Susan, Michael Snodin, and Helen Clifford. *Paul de Lamerie: At the Sign of The Golden Ball.* Exhibition catalogue. London: The Goldsmiths' Company, 1990.

Harrison 1980
Harrison, Richard A. *Princetonians, 1769–1775: A Biographical Dictionary.* Princeton: Princeton University Press, 1980.

Hartop 1996
Hartop, Christopher. *The Huguenot Legacy: English Silver 1680–1760 from the Alan and Simone Hartman Collection.* Exhibition catalogue. New York: Exhibitions International, 1996.

Harvard Class 1934
Class of 1884, Harvard College: Fiftieth Anniversary Report of the Secretary. Cambridge: Harvard Unviersity Press, 1934.

Harvard Class 1966
Harvard Class of 1916 Fiftieth Anniversary Report. Cambridge: Harvard University, 1966.

Harvard College 1899
Harvard College: Report of the Secretary, No. V. New York: The Evening Post Job Printing Office, 1899.

Hawley 1989
Hawley, Henry. "A Livingston Chair." *The Bulletin of The Cleveland Museum of Art,* 76 (November 1989), pp. 326–31.

Hayward 1959
Hayward, J.F. *Huguenot Silver in England, 1688–1727.* London: Faber and Faber, 1959.

Heckscher 1979
Heckscher, Morrison H. "Lock and Copland: A Catalogue of the Engraved Ornament." *Furniture History,* 15 (1979), pp. 1–23.

Heckscher/Bowman 1992
Heckscher, Morrison H., and Leslie G. Bowman. *American Rococo, 1750–1775: Elegance in Ornament.* Exhibition catalogue. New York: The Metropolitan Museum of Art, 1992.

Hennell 1986
Hennell, Percy. *Hennell Silver Salt Cellars, 1736 to 1876.* London: Hennell, 1986.

Herr 1995
Herr, Donald M. *Pewter in Pennsylvania German Churches.* Birdsboro, Pennsylvania: The Pennsylvania German Society, 1995.

Hershkowitz 1964
Hershkowitz, Leo. "The Mill Street Synagogue Reconsidered." *PAJHS,* 53 (1964), pp. 404–10.

Hershkowitz 1966A
Hershkowitz, Leo. "Wills of Early New York Jews (1704–1740)." *PAJHS,* 55 (March 1966), pp. 319–63.

Hershkowitz 1966B
Hershkowitz, Leo. "Wills of Early New York Jews (1743–1774)." *PAJHS,* 56 (September 1966), pp. 62–122.

Hershkowitz 1969
Hershkowitz, Leo. "Another Abigail Franks Letter and a Geneaological Note." *PAJHS,* 59 (1969), p. 223–26.

Hershkowitz 1976
Hershkowitz, Leo. "Some Aspects of the New York Jewish Merchant and Community, 1654–1820." *PAJHS,* 66 (September 1976), pp. 10–34.

Hershkowitz 1981
Hershkowitz, Leo. "Powdered Tin and Rose Petals: Myer Myers, Goldsmith and Peter Middleton, Physician." *American Jewish History,* 70 (1981), pp. 462–67.

Hershkowitz 1990
Hershkowitz, Leo. "Asser Levy and the Inventories of Early New York Jews." *American Jewish History,* 80 (Autumn 1990), pp. 21–55.

Hershkowitz 1993
Hershkowitz, Leo. "New Amsterdam's Twenty-Three Jews: Myth or Reality?" In Shalom Goldman, ed. *Hebrew and the Bible in America.* Hanover, New Hampshire: University Press of New England, 1993, pp. 171–83.

Hershkowitz/Meyer 1968
Hershkowitz, Leo, and Isidor S. Meyer, eds. *Letters of the Franks Family (1733–1748): The Lee Max Friedman Collection of American Jewish Correspondence.* Waltham, Massachusetts: American Jewish Historical Society, 1968.

Hinman 1842
Hinman, Royal R. *Historical Collection, from Official Records, Files, & c., of the Part Sustained by Connecticut, during the War of the Revolution.* Hartford, Connecticut: E. Gleason, 1842.

Hoffman 1899
Hoffman, Eugene A. *Genealogy of the Hoffman Family.* New York: Dodd, Mead and Company, 1899.

Hollan 1994
Hollan, Catherine B. *Three Centuries of Alexandria Silver.* Exhibition catalogue. Alexandria, Virginia: The Lyceum, 1994.

Hollander 1897

Hollander, J.H. "The Naturalization of Jews in the American Colonies Under the Act of 1740." *PAJHS*, 5 (1897), pp. 103–17.

Holloway 1946

Holloway, H. Maxson. "American Presentation Silver." *NYHSQ*, 30 (October 1946), pp. 215–33.

Hood 1971

Hood, Graham. *American Silver: A History of Style*. New York: Praeger, 1971.

Horsmanden 1971

Horsmanden, Daniel. *The New York Conspiracy*. Thomas J. Davis, ed. Boston: Beacon Press, 1971.

Hühner 1900

Hühner, Leon. "Asser Levy: A Noted Jewish Burger of New Amsterdam." *PAJHS*, 8 (1900), pp. 9–23.

Hühner 1903

Hühner, Leon. "The Jews of New England (Other than Rhode Island) Prior to 1800." *PAJHS*, 11 (1903), pp. 75–99.

Hühner 1905

Hühner, Leon. "Naturalization of Jews in New York Under the Act of 1740." *PAJHS*, 13 (1905), pp. 1–6.

Hull 1966

Hull, Daniel R. *Bewitched Mine Hill: The Silver-Lead-Iron Mine of Roxbury, Connecticut*. Stonington, Connecticut: The Pequot Press for The Old Woodbury Historical Society, 1966.

Hyamson 1912

Hyamson, Albert M. "The Jew Bill of 1753." In *Transactions of the Jewish Historical Society, Sessions 1908–1910*. London: Ballantyne, Hanson and Company, 1912, pp. 156–77.

Indentures 1909

Indentures of Apprentices, Otober 21, 1718 to August 7, 1727 (Collections of The New-York Historical Society, 42). New York: The New-York Historical Society, 1909, pp. 111–19.

Israel 1989

Israel, Jonathan. "Menasseh Ben Israel and the Dutch Sephardic Colonization Movement of the Mid-Seventeenth Century (1645–1657)." In Yosef Kaplan, Henry Mechoulan, and Richard H. Popkin, eds. *Menasseh Ben Israel and His World*. Leiden: E.J. Brill, 1989, pp. 139–63.

Jackson 1911

Jackson, Charles James. *An Illustrated History of English Plate, Ecclesiastical and Secular*. 2 vols. London: B.T. Batsford, 1911.

Jackson 1921

Jackson, Charles James. *English Goldsmiths and Their Marks*. 2nd rev. ed. London: Macmillan, 1921.

Jackson 1995

Jackson, Kenneth, ed. *The Encyclopedia of New York City*. New Haven: Yale University Press, 1995.

Jacobs/Wolf 1888

Jacobs, Joseph, and Lucien Wolf. *Bibliotheca Anglo-Judaica: A Bibliographical Guide to Anglo-Jewish History*. (Publications of the Anglo-Jewish Historical Exhibition, 3). London: The Jewish Chronicle, 1888.

Jacobus 1930

Jacobus, Donald Lines. *History and Genealogy of the Families of Old Fairfield*. 3 vols. Fairfield, Connecticut: The Eunice Dennie Burr Chapter, Daughters of the American Revolution, 1930.

Jameson 1909

Jameson, J. Franklin, ed. *Narratives of New Netherland, 1609–1664*. New York: Charles Scribner's Sons, 1909.

Jamestown 1907

The Massachusetts Colonial Loan Exhibit at the Jamestown Ter-Centennial Exposition, 1607–1907. Exhibition catalogue. Boston: Wright and Potter, 1907.

Jamilly 1999

Jamilly, Edward. *The Georgian Synagogue: An Architectural History*. London: The Working Party on Jewish Monuments in the UK and Ireland and the Jewish Memorial Council, 1999

"Jamison and Johnston" 1874

"Jamsion and Johnston of New York and New Jersey." *NYGBR*, 5 (October 1874), pp. 171–74.

Jewish Art 1955

Jewish Art from the Hebrew Union College and Other Collections. Exhibition catalogue. Hartford, Connecticut: Wadsworth Atheneum, 1955.

"Jewish Community" 1980

"The Jewish Community in Early America." Exhibition checklist. Washington, D.C.: Daughters of the American Revolution Museum, 1980.

Johnson 1754

Johnson, Samuel. *A Dictionary of the English Language* (1754). Reprint, London: Times Books, 1983.

Johnson 1939

Johnson, Monroe. "The Gouverneur Genealogy." *NYGBR*, 70 (April 1939), pp. 134–38.

Johnston 1994

Johnston, Phillip M. *Catalogue of American Silver: The Cleveland Museum of Art*. Cleveland: The Cleveland Museum of Art, 1994.

Jones 1907

Jones, John H. *The Jones Family of Long Island: Descendants of Major Thomas Jones (1665–1726) and Allied Families*. New York: Tobias A. Wright, 1907.

Jones 1913

Jones, E. Alfred. *The Old Silver of American Churches*. Letchworth, England: National Society of the Colonial Dames of America, 1913.

Kaellgren 2000

Kaellgren, Peter. "English Silver Baskets." *Antiques*, 157 (June 2000), pp. 940–47.

Kammen 1975

Kammen, Michael. *Colonial New York: A History*. New York: Charles Scribner's Sons, 1975.

Kane 1998

Kane, Patricia E., ed. *Colonial Massachusetts Silversmiths and Jewelers: A Biographical Dictionary Based on the Notes of Francis Hill Bigelow & John Marshall Phillips*. New Haven: Yale University Art Gallery, 1998.

Kanof 1975
    Kanof, Abram. *Ceremonial Art in the Judaic Tradition.* Exhibition catalogue. Raleigh: North Carolina Museum of Art, 1975.

Kaplan 1986
    Kaplan, Yosef. "The Portuguese Community in Amsterdam in the 17th Century: Between Tradition and Change." *Divre Ha-Akademya Ha-Leumit Ha-Yisraelit Le-Mada'im,* 7, (1986), pp. 161–81.

Kaplan 1989
    Kaplan, Yosef. "The Portuguese Community in 17th-Century Amsterdam and the Ashkenazi World." *Dutch Jewish History,* 2 (1989), pp. 23–45.

Kaplan 1992
    Kaplan, Yosef. "The Jewish Profile of the Spanish-Portuguese Community of London During the Seventeenth Century." *Judaism,* 41 (Summer 1992), pp. 229–40.

Kaplan 1993
    Kaplan, Yosef. "Deviance and Excommunication in the Eighteenth Century: A Chapter in the Social History of the Sephardi Community of Amsterdam." *Dutch Jewish History,* 3 (1993), pp. 103–15.

Kaplan/Mechoulan/Popkin 1989
    Kaplan, Yosef, Henry Mechoulan, and Richard H. Popkin, eds. *Menasseh Ben Israel and His World.* Leiden: E.J. Brill, 1989.

Karp 1976–77
    Karp, Abraham J. "America's Pioneer Prayerbooks." *Jewish Book Annual,* 34 (5737, 1976–77), pp. 15–25.

Kauffman 1966
    Kauffman, Henry J. *Early American Ironware: Cast and Wrought.* Rutland, Vermont: The Charles E. Tuttle Company, 1966.

Keen 1991
    Keen, Michael E. *Jewish Ritual Art in the Victoria & Albert Museum.* London: Her Majesty's Stationers' Office, 1991.

Kernan 1961
    Kernan, John D. "Some New York Silver of Exceptional Interest: Johnson Silver by Myer Myers." *Antiques,* 80 (October 1961), pp. 338–39.

Kessler/Rachlis 1959
    Kessler, Henry H., and Eugene Rachlis. *Peter Stuyvesant and His New York.* New York: Random House, 1959.

Kierner 1992
    Kierner, Cynthia A. *Traders and Gentlefolk: The Livingstons of New York, 1675–1790.* Ithaca, New York: Cornell University Press, 1992.

Kim 1978
    Kim, Sung Bok. *Landlord and Tenant in Colonial New York: Manorial Society, 1664–1775.* Chapel Hill: University of North Carolina Press for the Institute of Early American History and Culture, 1978.

Kinkead 1953
    Kinkead, George B. "Gilbert Livingston and Some of His Descendants." *NYGBR,* 84 (January 1953), pp. 4–15; (April 1953), pp. 99–107; (July 1953), pp. 170–78; (October 1953), pp. 239–45.

Kinkead 1954
    Kinkead, George B. "Gilbert Livingston and Some of His Descendants." *NYGBR,* 85 (January 1954), pp. 20–34; (April 1954), pp. 107–13; (July 1954), pp. 172–80; (October 1954), pp. 230–39.

Kinnear 1903
    Kinnear, Peter. *Historical Sketch of St. Andrew's Society of the City of Albany.* Albany, New York: Weed-Parsons Printing Company, 1903.

Kirby 1970
    Kirby, John B. "Early American Politics—The Search for an Ideology: An Historiographical Analysis and Critique of the Concept of Deference." *Journal of Politics,* 32 (1970), pp. 808–38.

Kirshenblatt-Gimblett 1982
    Kirshenblatt-Gimblett, Barbara. "The Cut That Binds: The Western Ashkenazic Torah Binder as Nexus Between Circumcision and Torah." In Victor Turner, ed. *Celebration: Studies in Festivity and Ritual.* Washington, D.C.: Smithsonian Institution Press, 1982.

KKMI-MB
    Kahal Kadosh Mikveh Israel. Minute Book. Congregation Mikveh Israel, Philadelphia.

KKSI-MB1
    Kahal Kadosh Shearith Israel. First Minute Book, 5488–5519 (1728–59). Transcr. Jacques Judah Lyons. Lyons Collection, AJHS.

KKSI-MB2
    Kahal Kadosh Shearith Israel. Second Minute Book, 5520–5546 (1760–86). Lyons Collection, AJHS.

Klein 1963
    Klein, Milton M., ed. *The Independent Reflector: or Weekly Essay on Sundry Important Subjects More particularly adapted to the Province of New-York, by William Livingston and others.* Cambridge, Massachusetts: Belknap Press of Harvard University Press, 1963.

Klett 1996
    Klett, Joseph, ed. *Genealogies of New Jersey Families.* Baltimore: Genealogical Publishing Company, 1996.

Kline et al. 1983
    Kline, Mary-Jo, ed., et al. *Political Correspondence and Public Papers of Aaron Burr.* 2 vols. Princeton: Princeton University Press, 1983.

Knapp 1909
    Knapp, Shepherd. *A History of the Brick Presbyterian Church in the City of New York.* New York: The Trustees of the Brick Presbyterian Church, 1909.

Knight 1901
    Knight, Erastus C., comp. *New York in the Revolution as Colony and State Supplement.* Albany, New York: Oliver A. Quayle, 1901.

Knox 1930
    Knox, Katharine McCook. *The Sharples: Their Portraits of George Washington and His Contemporaries.* New Haven: Yale University Press, 1930.

Koke 1973
    Koke, Richard J. *Accomplice in Treason: Joshua Hett Smith and the*

Arnold Conspiracy. New York: The New-York Historical Society, 1973.

Korn 1976

Korn, Bertram W. *A Bicentennial Festschrift for Jacob Rader Marcus*. New York: Ktav, 1976.

Kouwenhoven 1972

Kouwenhoven, John A. *The Columbia Historical Portrait of New York: An Essay in Graphic History*. New York: Harper and Row, 1972.

Kovel/Kovel 1961

Kovel, Ralph M., and Terry H. Kovel. *A Directory of American Silver, Pewter and Silver Plate*. New York: Crown Publishers, 1961.

Krauskopf 1906

Krauskopf, Joseph. "The Jewish Pilgrim Fathers." *PAJHS*, 14 (1906), pp. 121–30.

Krinsky 1985

Krinsky, Carol Herselle. *Synagogues of Europe: Architecture, History, Meaning*. Cambridge, Massachusetts: The MIT Press, 1985.

Labaree 1943

Labaree, Leonard W., ed. *The Public Records of the State of Connecticut*. Volume V. *For the Years 1783 and 1784*. Hartford: The State of Connecticut, 1943.

Laidlaw 1988

Laidlaw, Christine Wallace. "Silver by the Dozen: The Wholesale Business of Teunis D. DuBois." *Winterthur Portfolio*, 23 (Spring 1988), pp. 25–50.

Langdon 1960

Langdon, John Emerson. *Canadian Silversmiths and Their Marks, 1667–1867*. Lunenburg, Vermont: The Stinehour Press, 1960.

Langdon 1968

Langdon, John Emerson. "New Light on Charles Oliver Bruff, Tory Silversmith." *Antiques*, 93 (June 1968), pp. 768–69.

Langdon 1970

Langdon, John Emerson. *American Silversmiths in British North America*. Toronto: 1970.

Larus n.d.

Larus, Jane Bortman. *Myer Myers, Silversmith: 1723–1795*. Exhibition catalogue. Washington, D.C.: Klutznick Exhibit Hall, B'nai B'rith, n.d.

Lawrence 1858

Lawrence, Thomas. *Historical Genealogy of the Lawrence Family*. New York: Edward O. Jenkins, 1858.

Lawrence 1932

Lawrence, Ruth. *Genealogical Histories of Livingston and Allied Families*. New York: National Americana Society, 1932.

Le Corbeiller 1966

Le Corbeiller, Clare. *European and American Snuff Boxes, 1730–1830*. New York: Viking Press, 1966.

Leehey et al. 1988

Leehey, Patrick M., et al. *Paul Revere—Artisan, Businessman, and Patriot: The Man Behind the Myth*. Boston: The Paul Revere Memorial Association, 1988.

Levy/Levy 1988

Levy, Bernard and S. Dean Levy. *Sales catalogue*, Volume VI. New York: Bernard & S. Dean Levy, 1988.

Lewis 1972

Lewis, Lesley. "English Commemorative Sculpture in Jamaica." *The Jamaican Historical Review*, 9 (1972).

Lindsey 1999

Lindsey, Jack L. *Worldly Goods: The Arts of Early Pennsylvania, 1680–1758*. Exhibition catalogue. Philadelphia: Philadelphia Museum of Art, 1999.

Lipman 1972

Lipman, Vivian. "England." In Geoffrey Wigoder, ed. *Jewish Art and Civilization*. Volume II. New York: Walker and Company, 1972, pp. 8–51.

Lipson 1977

Lipson, Dorothy Ann. *Freemasonry in Federalist Connecticut, 1789–1832*. Princeton: Princeton University Press, 1977.

Little 1976

Little, Nina Fletcher. *Paintings by New England Provincial Artists, 1775–1800*. Exhibition catalogue. Boston: Museum of Fine Arts, 1976.

Livingston 1909

Livingston, Noel B. *Sketch Pedigrees of Some of the Early Settlers in Jamaica*. Kingston, Jamaica: The Educational Supply Company, 1909.

Livingston 1910

Livingston, Edwin Brockholst. *The Livingstons of Livingston Manor*. New York: The Knickerbocker Press, 1910.

"Livro dos Miseberagh"

"Livro dos Miseberagh Ascaboth & Diversas outras Cerimonias quese uzas no kahal kados de *Shearith Israel* de New York," 5519–30 [1758–69]. Shearith Israel Papers, box 1, file 1, AJHS.

Loker 1991

Loker, Zvi. *Jews in the Caribbean*. Jerusalem: Misgav Yerushalayim, 1991.

Lomax 1992

Lomax, James. *British Silver at Temple Newsam and Lotherton Hall: A Catalogue of the Leeds Collection*. Leeds: Leeds Art Collections Fund, 1992.

Longworth's 1797

Longworth's American Almanack, New-York Register, and City Directory. New York: T. and J. Swords, 1797.

Loring 1862

Loring, James S. "Will of Gen. John Bradstreet." *New England Historical and Genealogical Register*, 16 (October 1862), pp. 315–16.

Low 1796

Low, John. *The New-York Directory and Register for the Year 1796*. New York: John Buel and John Bull, 1796.

Lynd 1962

Lynd, Staughton. *Anti-Federalism in Dutchess County, New York: A Study of Democracy and Class Conflict in the Revolutionary Era*. Chicago: Loyola University Press, 1962.

Lynd 1968
Lynd, Staughton. *Intellectual Origins of American Radicalism.* New York: Pantheon Books, 1968.

Lyons Collection 1913
The Lyons Collection. Volume I. *PAJHS*, 21 (1913).

Lyons Collection 1920
The Lyons Collection. Volume II. *PAJHS*, 27 (1920).

McCusker/Menard 1985
McCusker, John J., and Russell R. Menard. *The Economy of British America, 1607–1789.* Chapel Hill: University of North Carolina Press for the Institute of Early American History and Culture, 1985.

McFadden/Clark 1989
McFadden, David Revere, and Mark A. Clark. *Treasures for the Table: Silver from the Chrysler Museum.* Exhibition catalogue. New York: The American Federation of Arts, 1989.

McKinsey 1984
McKinsey, Kristan Helen. "New York City Silversmiths and Their Patrons, 1687–1750." M.A. thesis. Newark: University of Delaware, 1984.

McLachlan 1976
McLachlan, James. *Princetonians, 1748–1768: A Biographical Dictionary.* Princeton: Princeton University Press, 1976.

Maimonides 1990
Maimonides. *Mishneh Torah: Hilchot Tefillin UMezuzah V'Sefer Torah, Hilchot Tzitzit.* Trans. Rabbi Eliyahu Touger. New York and Jerusalem: Moznaim Publishing, 1990.

Marcus 1949
Marcus, Jacob Rader. "Light on Early Connecticut Jewry." *American Jewish Archives*, 1 (January 1949), pp. 3–52.

Marcus 1951
Marcus, Jacob Rader. *Early American Jewry: The Jews of New York, New England and Canada, 1649–1794.* Volume I. Philadelphia: The Jewish Publication Society of America, 1951.

Marcus 1959
Marcus, Jacob Rader. *American Jewry: Documents Eighteenth Century.* Cincinnati: Hebrew Union College Press, 1959.

Marcus 1969
Marcus, Jacob Rader. *Studies in American Jewish History.* Cincinnati: Hebrew Union College Press, 1969.

Marcus 1970
Marcus, Jacob Rader. *The Colonial American Jew, 1492–1776.* 3 vols. Detroit: Wayne State University Press, 1970.

Marcus 1989–93
Marcus, Jacob Rader. *United States Jewry 1776–1985.* 4 vols. Detroit: Wayne State University Press, 1989–93.

Marcus 1990
Marcus, Jacob Rader, comp. *This I Believe: Documents of American Jewish Life.* Northvale, New Jersey: J. Aronson, 1990.

Marcus 1996
Marcus, Jacob Rader. *The Jew in the American World: A Source Book.* Detroit: Wayne State University Press, 1996.

Marriage Licenses 1860
Names of Persons for Whom Marriage Licenses were Issued by the Secretary of the Province of New York, Previous to 1784. Albany, New York: Weed, Parsons and Company, 1860.

Mason 1966
Mason, Bernard. "Entrepreneurial Activity in New York During the American Revolution." *Business History Review*, 40 (1966), pp. 190–212.

"Matricula" 1754–57
"The Matricula or Register of Admissions & Graduations, & of Officers employed in King's College at New York." Typescript of manuscript original. Archives and Columbiana Collection, Columbia University, New York.

Matson 1996
Matson, Cathy. "The Revolution, the Constitution, and the New Nation." In Stanley L. Engerman and Robert E. Gallman, eds. *The Cambridge Economic History of the United States: The Colonial Era.* New York: Cambridge University Press, 1996, pp. 337–62.

Matthews 1965
Matthews, John. *Complete American Armoury and Blue Book.* Louis R. Sosnow, ed. New York: Heraldic Publishing Company, 1965.

MCCNY-1
Minutes of the Common Council of the City of NY, 1675–1776. 8 vols. New York: Dodd, Mead and Company, 1905.

MCCNY-2
Minutes of the Common Council of the City of NY, 1784–1831. 21 vols. New York: The City of New York, 1917.

MCNY
Museum of the City of New York.

Means 1971
Means, E.D. "Sephardim." In *Encyclopaedia Judaica.* Volume XIV. Jerusalem: Keter Publishing, 1971, cols. 1164–78.

Medicus 1944
Medicus, Philip. "American Silver-Hilted Swords, Part II." *Antiques*, 46 (December 1944), pp. 342–44.

"Memoirs" 1926
"Memoirs." *New England Historical and Genealogical Register*, 80 (1926), pp. 98–99.

Metcalf 1965
Metcalf, George. *Royal Government and Political Conflict in Jamaica, 1729–1783.* London: Longmans for the Royal Commonwealth Society, 1965.

Metropolitan 1909
The Hudson-Fulton Celebration: Catalogue of an Exhibition Held at The Metropolitan Museum of Art. Exhibition catalogue. 2 vols. New York: The Metropolitan Museum of Art, 1909.

Meyer 1988
Meyer, Michael A. *Response to Modernity: A History of the Reform Movement in Judaism.* New York: Oxford University Press, 1988.

Michman-Melkman 1972
Michman-Melkman, Jozeph. "Netherlands." In Geoffrey

Wigoder, ed. *Jewish Art and Civilization*. Volume II. New York: Walker and Company, 1972, pp. 54–82.

Miller 1912

Miller, Henry. *The Cox Family in America*. New York: Unionist Gazette Association, 1912.

Miller 1937

Miller, V. Isabelle. *Silver by New York Makers, Late 17th Century to 1900*. Exhibition catalogue. New York: Museum of the City of New York, 1937.

Mintz/Deitsch 1997

Mintz, Sharon Liberman and Elka Deitsch. *Kehillat Ha-Kodesh, Creating the Sacred Community: The Roles of the Rabbi, Cantor, Mohel and Shohet in Jewish Communal Life*. Exhibition catalogue. New York: The Library of the Jewish Theological Seminary of America, 1997.

Mintz/Rotmil 1992

Mintz, Sharon Liberman, and Lisa Rotmil. *Text and Context: The Development and Dissemination of Medieval Sephardic Culture*. Exhibition catalogue. New York: The Library of the Jewish Theological Seminary of America, 1992.

Mishnah 1987

A.H. Abramowitz, ed., Roy Abramowitz, trans. *The Mishnah: Seder Nezikin, Avodah Zarah*. Jerusalem: Eliner Library, Department for Torah Education and Culture in the Diaspora of the World Zionist Organization, 1987.

Mittelman 1998

Mittelman, Karen S., ed. *Creating American Jews: Historical Conversations about Identity*. Philadelphia: National Museum of American Jewish History, 1998.

Moffat 1904

Moffat, R. Burnham. *The Barclays of New York: Who They Are and Who They Are Not,—and Some Other Barclays*. New York: Robert Grier Cooke, 1904.

Montgomery 1978

Montgomery, Charles F. *A History of American Pewter*. Rev. ed. New York: E.P. Dutton, 1978.

Montgomery/Kane 1976

Montgomery, Charles F., and Patricia E. Kane, eds. *American Art 1750–1800: Towards Independence*. Exhibition catalogue. New Haven: Yale University Art Gallery, 1976.

Morais 1894

Morais, Henry Samuel. *The Jews of Philadelphia: Their History from the Earliest Settlements to the Present Time*. Philadelphia: The Levytype Company, 5654 (1894).

Mordecai 1796

Mordecai, Jacob. "Memoir of Judith Mordecai," 1796. Virginia Historical Society, Richmond.

Mordecai 1847

Mordecai, Julia. "Family Register collected by Julia Mordecai October 1847 and copied for her brother Alfred February 1848." Alfred Mordecai Papers, Library of Congress, Washington, D.C.

Morgan 1962

Morgan, Edmund S. *The Gentle Puritan: A Life of Ezra Stiles, 1727–1795*. Chapel Hill: University of North Carolina Press, 1962.

Morgenstein/Levine 1981–82

Morgenstein, Susan W., and Ruth E. Levine. *The Jews in the Age of Rembrandt*. Exhibition catalogue. Washington, D.C.: Judaic Museum of the Jewish Community Center of Greater Washington, 1981–82.

Muehlig 1999

Muehlig, Linda, ed. *Masterworks of American Painting and Sculpture from the Smith College Museum of Art*. Northampton, Massachusetts: Smith College Museum of Art, 1999.

Murrin 1990

Murrin, John. "The Menacing Shadow of Louis XIV and the Rage of Jacob Leisler: The Constitutional Order of Seventeenth-Century New York." In Stephen Schechter and Richard Bernstein, eds. *New York and the Union*. Albany, New York: New York State Commission on the Bicentennial of the United States Constitution, 1990, pp. 29–71.

Muster and Pay Rolls 1915

Muster and Pay Rolls of the War of the Revolution, 1775–1783. Volume II. (Collections of The New-York Historical Society, 48). New York: The New-York Historical Society, 1915.

Myers 1796–98

Myers, Samuel. Letterbook, May 25, 1796–December 25, 1798, Henry E. Huntington Library, Museum and Gardens, San Marino, California.

Nahon 1992

Nahon, Gerard. "From New Christians to the Portuguese Jewish Nation in France." In Haim Beinart, ed. *Moreshet Sepharad: The Sephardi Legacy*. 2 vols. Jerusalem: Magnes Press, Hebrew University, 1992.

Nash 1979

Nash, Gary. *The Urban Crucible: Social Change, Political Consciousness, and the Origin of the American Revolution*. Cambridge, Massachusetts: Harvard University Press, 1979.

NCAB 1958

National Cyclopedia of American Biography. Volume XLII. New York: James T. White, 1958.

Newman 1990

Newman, Eric P. *The Early Paper Money of America*. 3rd ed. Iola, Wisconsin: Krause Publications, 1990.

New-York Directory 1789

The New-York Directory and Register for the Year 1789. New York: Hodge, Allen, and Campbell, 1789.

New-York Directory 1790

The New-York Directory and Register for the Year 1790. New York: Hodge, Allen, and Campbell, 1790.

Nooter/Bonomi 1988

Nooter, Eric, and Patricia U. Bonomi, eds. *Colonial Dutch Studies: An Interdisciplinary Approach*. New York and London: New York University Press, 1988.

Norman-Wilcox 1954

Norman-Wilcox, Gregor. "American Silver, 1690–1810, in California Collections." *Antiques*, 65 (January 1954), pp. 48–51.

NYCIR-1

New York City Insolvency Records. New York State Archives, Albany.

NYCIR-2
New York City Insolvency Records. Municipal Archives, New York.

NYCLR
New York City Land Records. City Register's Office, New York.

NYCMCMB
Mayor's Court Minute Books, 1674–1821. 62 vols. Division of Old Records, New York County Clerk, New York.

NYCMCR
Mayor's Court Records. Division of Old Records, New York County Clerk, New York.

NYCPR-1
New York City Probate Records. New York State Archives, Albany.

NYCPR-2
New York City Probate Records. Surrogate's Court, New York.

NYGBR
New York Genealogical and Biographical Record.

NYHS
The New-York Historical Society, New York.

NYHSQ
New-York Historical Society Quarterly.

NYPL
The New York Public Library, New York.

NYSA
New York State Archives, Albany, New York.

O'Callahan 1849–51
O'Callahan, Edmund B., ed. *The Documentary History of the State of New York.* 4 vols. Albany, New York: Weed, Parsons & Co., 1849–51.

Old English 1962
Old English and Early American Silver Work: Early Silver in California Collections. Exhibition catalogue. Los Angeles: Los Angeles County Museum of Art, 1962.

Oles 1958
Oles, M. Arthur. "The Henry Joseph Collection of the Gratz Family Papers at the American Jewish Archives: A Survey of the Yiddish Material." In *Essays in American Jewish History.* Cincinnati: American Jewish Archives, 1958, pp. 99–122.

Oman 1947
Oman, Charles. *English Domestic Silver.* 2nd ed. London: Adam and Charles Black, 1947.

Oman 1965
Oman, Charles. *English Silversmiths' Work, Civil and Domestic: An Introduction.* London: Her Majesty's Stationery Office, 1965.

Oman 1970
Oman, Charles. *Caroline Silver, 1625–1688.* London: Faber and Faber, 1970.

Oman 1978
Oman, Charles. *English Engraved Silver, 1150 to 1900.* London: Faber and Faber, 1978.

Oppenheim 1907
Oppenheim, Samuel. "An Early Jewish Colony in Western Guiana, 1658–1666 and Its Relation to the Jews in Surinam, Cayenne, and Tobago." *PAJHS,* 16 (1907), pp. 95–186.

Oppenheim 1909
Oppenheim, Samuel. "The Early History of the Jews in New York, 1654–1664. Some New Matter on the Subject." *PAJHS,* 18 (1909), pp. 1–91.

Oppenheim 1913
Oppenheim, Samuel. "A Philadelphia Jewish Merchant's Day Book." Typescript of paper, February 12, 1913. Etting Family Papers, AJHS.

Oppenheim 1926
Oppenheim, Samuel. "Isaac Moses and His Services Rendered During the American Revolution." Typescript of paper, October 23, 1926. Moses Papers, AJHS.

Orcutt 1886
Orcutt, Rev. Samuel. *A History of the Old Town of Stratford and the City of Bridgeport, Connecticut.* 2 vols. New Haven: Fairfield County Historical Society, 1886.

PAJHS
Publications of the American Jewish Historical Society. Since the 1960s, published as *American Jewish History Quarterly.*

Palmer 1984
Palmer, Gregory. *Biographical Sketches of Loyalists of the American Revolution.* Westport, Connecticut: Meckler Publishing, 1984.

Pargellis 1933
Pargellis, Stanley McCrory. *Lord Loudon in North America.* New Haven: Yale University Press, 1933.

Parke-Bernet 1941
Fine Early American Silver, Jewelry and Other Heirlooms. Auction catalogue. New York: Parke-Bernet, February 6–8, 1941.

Parke-Bernet 1946
An Important Collection of Early American Miniatures and Silver. Auction catalogue. New York: Parke-Bernet, November 30, 1946.

Parke-Bernet 1949
American Furniture, Paintings, and Silver. Auction catalogue. New York: Parke-Bernet, January 13–15, 1949.

Parke-Bernet 1961
American and English Furniture and Decorative Objects Belonging to Philip Peckerman, Danbury, Connecticut, and Other Owners. Auction catalogue. New York: Parke-Bernet, February 10–11, 1961.

Parke-Bernet 1969
English, American & Continental Silver. Auction catalogue. New York: Parke-Bernet, May 20, 1969.

Patterson 1978
Patterson, Jerry E. *The City of New York: A History Illustrated from the Collections of the Museum of the City of New York.* New York: Harry N. Abrams, 1978.

Pearce 1961
Pearce, John N. "New York's Two-handled Paneled Silver Bowls." *Antiques,* 80 (October 1961), pp. 341–45.

Pearson 1872

Pearson, Jonathan. *Contributions for the Geneaologies of the First Settlers of the Ancient County of Albany from 1630 to 1800 (1872).* Reprint, Baltimore: Genealogical Publishing Company, 1976.

Pelletreau 1907

Pelletreau, William S. *Historic Homes and Institutions and Genealogical and Family History of New York.* 4 vols. New York and Chicago: The Lewis Publishing Company, 1907.

Pennsylvania Museum 1913

Pennsylvania Museum and School of Industrial Art Annual Report. Philadelphia: Pennsylvania Museum and School of Industrial Art, 1913.

Pennsylvania Museum 1923

Pennsylvania Museum and School of Industrial Art Annual Report. Philadelphia: Pennsylvania Museum and School of Industrial Art, 1923.

Philadelphia 1976

Philadelphia: Three Centuries of American Art. Exhibition catalogue. Philadelphia: Philadelphia Museum of Art, 1976.

Philipson 1929

Philipson, David. *Letters of Rebecca Gratz.* Philadelphia: The Jewish Publication Society of America, 1929.

Phillips 1934

Phillips, John Marshall. "Two Copley Portraits." *Bulletin of the Associates in Fine Arts at Yale University,* 6 (June 1934), pp. 31–33.

Phillips 1937

Phillips, John Marshall. "Additions to the Garvan Collection of Silver." *Bulletin of the Associates in Fine Arts at Yale University,* 8 (June 1937), pp. 3–10.

Phillips 1949

Phillips, John Marshall. *American Silver.* New York: Chanticleer Press, 1949.

Phillips/Parker/Buhler 1955

Phillips, John Marshall, Barbara N. Parker, and Kathryn C. Buhler, eds. *The Waldron Phoenix Belknap, Jr., Collection of Portraits and Silver, with a Note on the Discoveries of Waldron Phoenix Belknap, Jr. Concerning the Influence of the English Mezzotint on Colonial Painting.* Cambridge, Massachusetts: Harvard University Press, 1955.

Phillips/Phillips 1894

Phillips, U. Taylor, and Rosalie S. Phillips. "The Old Cemetery of the Congregation Shearith Israel in the City of New York, situated on New Bowery near Chatham Square, New York, N.Y., as it existed in the Year 1894—with Diagram thereof and copies of the Tombstones therein." Manuscript ledger. Shearith Israel Papers, AJHS.

Pierce 1899

Pierce, Frederick Clayton. *Foster Genealogy.* Chicago: W.B. Conkey, 1899.

Pigler 1956

Pigler, A. *Barockthemen: Eine Auswahl von Verzeichnissen zur Ikonographie des 17. und 18. Jahrhunderts.* 2 vols. Budapest: Verlag der Ungarischen Akademie der Wissenschaften, 1956.

Pine 1904

Pine, John B. *Gifts and Endowments with the Names of Benefactors 1754–1904.* New York: Columbia University in the City of New York, 1904.

Piwonka 1986

Piwonka, Ruth. *A Portrait of Livingston Manor 1686–1850.* Clermont, New York: Friends of Clermont, 1986.

Pleasants/Sill 1930

Pleasants, J. Hall, and Howard Sill. *Maryland Silversmiths, 1715–1830.* Baltimore: Lord Baltimore Press, 1930.

Pleasants/Sill 1941

Pleasants, J. Hall, and Howard Sill. "Charles Oliver Bruff, Silversmith." *Antiques,* 39 (June 1941), pp. 309–11.

Plumb 1893

Plumb, Henry Blackman. *The Plumbs, 1635–1800.* Peely, Pennsylvania: 1893.

Pocock 1976

Pocock, J.A. "The Classical Theory of Deference." *American Historical Review,* 81 (1976), pp. 516–23.

Pointer 1988

Pointer, Richard W. *Protestant Pluralism and the New York Experience: A Study of Eighteenth-Century Religious Diversity.* Bloomington: Indiana University Press, 1988.

Pool 1930

Pool, David de Sola. *The Mill Street Synagogue (1730–1817) of the Congregation Shearith Israel.* New York: 1930.

Pool 1952

Pool, David de Sola. *Portraits Etched in Stone: Early Jewish Settlers, 1682–1831.* New York: Columbia University Press, 1952.

Pool/Pool 1955

Pool, David de Sola, and Tamara de Sola Pool. *An Old Faith in the New World: Portrait of Shearith Israel, 1654–1954.* New York: Columbia University Press, 1955.

Powell 1981

Powell, William S., ed. *The Correspondence of William Tryon and Other Selected Papers.* Volume II. *1768–1818.* Raleigh, North Carolina: Division of Archives and History, Department of Cultural Resources, 1981.

"Presbyterian Church Marriages" 1756–1813

"First and Second Presbyterian Church, New York: Marriages, 1756–1813." Genealogical Department, Church of Jesus Christ of Latter-day Saints, familysearch.com (website).

Prime 1929

Prime, Alfred Coxe. *The Arts and Crafts in Philadelphia, Maryland, and South Carolina, 1721–1785: Gleanings from Newspapers.* Topsfield, Massachusetts: The Walpole Society, 1929.

Prime 1956

Prime, Phoebe Phillips. *Philadelphia Silver, 1682–1800.* Exhibition catalogue. Published as *The Philadelphia Museum Bulletin,* 60 (Spring 1956).

Prince 1899

Prince, Frank A. *Genealogy of the Prince Family.* Danielson, Connecticut: J.H. Briggs, 1899.

Prown 1966
Prown, Jules David. *John Singleton Copley*. 2 vols. Cambridge, Massachusetts: Harvard University Press for the National Gallery of Art, 1966.

Puig et al. 1989
Puig, Francis J., et al. *English and American Silver in the Collection of The Minneapolis Institute of Arts*. Minneapolis: The Minneapolis Institute of Arts, 1989.

Pulos/Schwartz 1959
Pulos, Arthur J., and Marvin D. Schwartz. *Elias Pelletreau, Long Island Silversmith, and His Sources of Design*. Exhibition catalogue. New York: The Brooklyn Museum, 1959.

Pulse of the People 1976
The Pulse of the People: New Jersey 1763–1789. Exhibition catalogue. Trenton: New Jersey State Museum, 1976.

Purple 1890
Purple, Samuel S., ed. *Records of the Reformed Dutch Church in New Amsterdam and New York*. Volume I. *Marriages from 11 December, 1639, to 26 August, 1801*. New York: The New-York Genealogical and Biographical Society, 1890.

Putík et al. 1994
Putík, Alexandr, et al. *Jewish Customs and Traditions*. Trans. Till Gottheinerová. Prague: The Jewish Museum, 1994.

Quimby/Johnson 1995
Quimby, Ian M.G., and Dianne Johnson. *American Silver at Winterthur*. Winterthur, Delaware: Henry Francis du Pont Winterthur Museum, 1995.

Randolph/Hastings 1941
Randolph, Howard S.F., and Mrs. Russell Hastings. "Jacob Boelen, Goldsmith, of New York and His Family Circle." *NYGBR*, 72 (October 1941), pp. 265–94.

Ranlet 1986
Ranlet, Philip. *The New York Loyalists*. Knoxville: University of Tennessee Press, 1986.

Rasmussen 1991
Rasmussen, James A. "Gilbert Family of Albany and New York." *NYGBR*, 122 (April 1991), pp. 65–74.

Reich 1953
Reich, Jerome R. *Leisler's Rebellion: A Study of Democracy in New York, 1664–1720*. Chicago: University of Chicago Press, 1953.

Reid 1938–39
Reid, Robert W. "Some Early Masonic Engravers in America." *Transactions of the American Lodge of Research, Free and Accepted Masons*, 3 (1938–39), pp. 97–125.

Reunion 1877
Reunion of the Descendants of Daniel Shelton at Birmingham, Conn. Newburgh, New York: E.M. Ruttenberg and Son, 1877.

Reynolds 1911
Reynolds, Cuyler, ed. *Hudson-Mohawk Genealogical and Family Memoirs*. 4 vols. New York: Lewis Historical Publishing Company, 1911.

Reynolds 1914
Reynolds, Cuyler. *Genealogical and Family History of Southern New York and the Hudson River Valley*. 3 vols. New York: Lewis Historical Publishing Company, 1914.

Rice 1964
Rice, Norman S. *Albany Silver 1652–1825*. Exhibition catalogue. Albany, New York: Albany Institute of History and Art, 1964.

Rink 1994
Rink, Oliver A. "Private Interest and Godly Gain: The West India Company and the Dutch Reformed Church in New Netherland, 1624–1664." *New York History*, 75 (July 1994), pp. 245–64.

Ripa 1988
Ripa, Cesare. *Iconologia* (1644). Piero Buscaroli, ed. 2 vols. Turin, Fògola, 1988.

Rivkind 1937
Rivkind, Isaac. "Early American Hebrew Documents." *PAJHS*, 34 (1937), pp. 51–74.

Robison/Bartlett 1917
Robison, Jeannie F-J., and Henrietta C. Bartlett, eds. *Genealogical Records: Manuscript Entries of Births, Deaths, and Marriages, Taken from Family Bibles, 1581–1917*. New York: The Colonial Dames of the State of New York, 1917.

Rococo 1984
Rococo: Art and Design in Hogarth's England. Exhibition catalogue. London: Victoria and Albert Museum, 1984.

Rodrigues-Pereira 1992
Rodrigues-Pereira, Miriam. "Abraham Lopes de Oliveira, Silversmith." *The Jewish Museum Annual Report*, 60 (1991–92), pp. 10–14.

Roney 1940
Roney, Lila James. "An Echo of a Romance of Early New York." *NYGBR*, 71 (April 1940), pp. 120–28.

Rosenbach 1909
Rosenbach, A.S.W. *Dedication of the New Synagogue of the Congregation Mikve Israel*. Philadelphia: Congregation Mikveh Israel, 1909.

Rosenbaum 1954A
Rosenbaum, Jeanette Whitehill. *Myer Myers, Goldsmith, 1723–1795*. Philadelphia: The Jewish Publication Society of America, 1954.

Rosenbaum 1954B
Rosenbaum, Jeanette Whitehill. "Myer Myers, Early New York Goldsmith." *Antiques*, 65 (February 1954), pp. 124–27.

Rosendale 1893
Rosendale, Simon W. "An Act Allowing Naturalization of Jews in the Colonies." *PAJHS*, 1 (1893), pp. 93–98.

Rosenwaike 1960
Rosenwaike, Marcus. "An Estimate and Analysis of the Jewish Population of the United States in 1790." *PAJHS*, 50 (1960), pp. 23–67.

Rothschild 1990
Rothschild, Nan A. *New York City Neighborhoods: The 18th Century*. San Diego: Academic Press, 1990.

Rowe 1965

Rowe, Robert. *Adam Silver, 1765–1795*. New York: Taplinger, 1965.

Rubens 1954

Rubens, Alfred. *A Jewish Iconography*. London: The Jewish Museum, 1954.

Rubin 1983

Rubin, Saul J. *Third to None: The Saga of Savannah Jewry, 1733–1983*. Savannah, Georgia: Mickve Israel, 1983.

Runk 1897

Runk, Emma Ten Broeck. *The Ten Broeck Genealogy*. New York: The DeVinne Press, 1897.

Rutledge 1945

Rutledge, Anna Wells. "A Hand-list of Miniatures in the Collections of the Maryland Historical Society." *Maryland Historical Magazine*, 40 (1945), pp. 119–36.

Sabine 1958

Sabine, William, ed. *Historical Memoirs of William Smith, Historian of the Province of New York, Member of the Governor's Council, and Last Chief Justice of that Province Under the Crown; Chief Justice of Quebec*. 2 vols. New York, 1958.

Sack 1987

Sack, Albert. "Regionalism in Early American Tea Tables." *Antiques*, 131 (January 1987), pp. 248–63.

Safford 1983

Safford, Frances Gruber. "Colonial Silver in The American Wing." *The Metropolitan Museum of Art Bulletin*, 41 (Summer 1983) .

St. Patrick's Lodge 1966

St. Patrick's Lodge No. 4, F. & A.M. 200th Anniversary: Johnstown, New York, 1766–1966. Johnstown, New York: 1966.

Salomon 1979

Salomon, Herman P. "Joseph Jesurun Pinto (1729–1782): A Dutch Hazan in Colonial New York." *Studia Rosenthaliana*, 13 (January 1979), pp. 18–29.

Salomon 1995

Salomon, Herman P. "K.K. Shearith Israel's First Language: Portuguese." *Tradition*, 30 (Fall 1995), pp. 74–84.

Samuel 1992

Samuel, Edgar. *The Portuguese Jewish Community in London (1656–1830)*. London: The Jewish Museum, 1992.

Sanborn 1894

Sanborn, V.C. "The Kirtland or Kirkland Family." *New England Historical and Genealogical Register*, 48 (January 1894), pp. 66–70.

Sarna 1981

Sarna, Jonathan D. "The Impact of the American Revolution on American Jews." *Modern Judaism*, 1 (1981), pp. 149–60.

Sarna 1991

Sarna, Jonathan D. "Seating and the American Synagogue." In Philip R. Vandermeer and Robert P. Swierenga, eds. *Belief and Behavior: Essays in the New Religious History*. New Brunswick, New Jersey: Rutgers University Press, 1991, pp. 189–94.

Sarna/Dalin 1997

Sarna, Jonathan D., and David G. Dalin. *Religion and State in the American Jewish Experience*. Notre Dame, Indiana: University of Notre Dame Press, 1997.

Sarna/Smith 1995

Sarna, Jonathan D., and Ellen Smith, eds. *The Jews of Boston: Essays on the Occasion of the Centenary (1895–1995) of the Combined Jewish Philanthropies of Greater Boston*. Boston: Combined Jewish Philanthropies of Greater Boston, 1995.

Saunders 1995

Saunders, Richard H. *John Smibert: Colonial America's First Portrait Painter*. New Haven and London: Yale University Press, 1995.

Saunders/Miles 1987

Saunders, Richard H., and Ellen G. Miles. *American Colonial Portraits 1700–1776*. Exhibition catalogue. Washington, D.C.: National Portrait Gallery, 1987.

Savary 1902

Savary, A.W. "Some Annadale Johnstons in America." *NYGBR*, 33 (October 1902), pp. 246–49.

Savary 1903

Savary, A.W. "Some Annadale Johnstons in America." *NYGBR*, 34 (January 1903), pp. 33–37.

Sawitzky 1951

Sawitzky, Susan, ed. "Thomas McIlworth." *NYHSQ*, 35 (April 1951), pp. 117–39.

Sawitzky 1957

Sawitzky, Susan. "Abraham Delanoy in New Haven." *NYHSQ*, 41 (April 1957), pp. 193–206.

Sayer and Bennett 1970

Sayer and Bennett's Catalogue of Prints for the Year 1775. Reprint, London: The Holland Press, 1970.

Schappes 1971

Schappes, Morris U. *A Documentary History of the Jews of the United States, 1654–1875*. 3rd ed. New York: Schocken Books, 1971.

Schechter/Bernstein 1990

Schechter, Stephen, and Richard Bernstein, eds. *New York and the Union*. Albany, New York: New York State Commission on the Bicentennial of the United States Constitution, 1990.

"Schermerhorn" 1919

"Frederick Augustus Schermerhorn." *NYGBR*, 50 (October 1919), pp. 305–06.

Schneider/Schneider 1929

Schneider, Herbert, and Carol Schneider. *Samuel Johnson, President of King's College: His Career and Writings*. Volume I. *Autobiography and Letters*. New York: Columbia University Press, 1929.

Schoenberger 1953

Schoenberger, Guido. "The Ritual Silver Made by Myer Myers." *PAJHS*, 43 (1953), pp. 1–9.

Scholem 1973

Scholem, Gershom. *Sabbatai Sevi: The Mystical Messiah*. Princeton: Princeton University Press, 1973.

Schwartz 1959

Schwartz, Esther I. "Restoration of the Touro Synagogue." *Rhode Island Jewish Historical Notes*, 3 (October 1959), pp. 106–31.

Scott 1953

Scott, Kenneth. *Counterfeiting in Colonial New York* (Numismatic Notes and Monographs, 127). New York: The American Numismatic Society, 1953.

Scott 1969

Scott, Kenneth. *Genealogical Data from New York Administration Bonds, 1753–1799* (Collections of the New York Genealogical and Biographical Society, 10). New York: The New-York Genealogical and Biographical Society, 1969.

Scott 1975

Scott, Kenneth. *Denizations, Naturalizations, and Oaths of Allegiance in Colonial New York*. Baltimore: Genealogical Publishing Company, 1975.

Setze 1957

Setze, Josephine. "Portraits of Ezra Stiles." *Bulletin of the Associates in Fine Arts at Yale University*, 23 (September 1957), pp. 1–10.

Sheftall 1984

Sheftall, John McKay. "The Sheftalls of Savannah: Colonial Leaders and Founding Fathers of Georgia Judaism." In *Jews of the South: Selected Essays from the Southern Jewish Historical Society*. Samuel Proctor, Louis Schmier, and Malcolm Stern, eds. Macon, Georgia: Mercer University Press, 1984, pp. 65–78.

Shepard 1831

Shepard, Charles U. "Notice of the Mine of Spathic Iron (Steel Ore) of New Milford, and of the Iron Works in Salisbury, in the State of Connecticut." *The American Journal of Science and Arts*, 19 (1831), pp. 311–26.

Sias 1973

Sias, Elizabeth H. "A Soumain Bowl in the Mercer Museum." *Antiques*, 103 (Janaury 1973), pp. 126–27.

Sickels 1967

Sickels, Elizabeth Galbraith. "Thimblemakers in America." *Antiques*, 92 (September 1967), pp. 372–73.

Silvestro/Franco 1976

Silvestro, Clement M., and Barbara Franco. *Masonic Symbols in American Decorative Arts*. Exhibition catalogue. Lexington, Massachusetts: Scottish Rite Masonic Museum of Our National Heritage, 1976.

Singer/Lang 1981

Singer, Herbert T., and Ossian Lang. *New York Freemasonry: A Bicentennial History, 1781–1981*. New York: The Grand Lodge of Free and Accepted Masons of the State of New York, 1981.

Sizer 1967

Sizer, Theodore. *The Works of Colonel John Trumbull: Artist of the American Revolution*. Rev. ed. New Haven: Yale University Press, 1967.

Skerry/Sloane 1992

Skerry, Janine E., and Jeanne Sloane. "Images of Politics and Religion on Silver Engraved by Joseph Leddel." *Antiques*, 141 (March 1992), pp. 490–99.

Smith 1889

Smith, Thomas E.V. *The City of New York in the Year of Washington's Inauguration, 1789*. New York: A.D.F. Randolph & Co., 1889.

Smith 1950

Smith, Helen Burr. "Nicholas Roosevelt—Goldsmith (1715–1769)." *NYHSQ*, 34 (1950), pp. 301–18.

Smith 1966

Smith, Helen Burr. "The Bancker Silver." *NYGBR*, 97 (October 1966), pp. 192–208.

Smith 1981

Smith, Billy G. "The Material Lives of Laboring Philadelphians 1750 to 1800." *William and Mary Quarterly*, 3rd ser., 38 (1981), pp. 163–202.

Smith/Kammen 1972

Smith, William, Jr. *The History of the Province of New-York*. Michael Kammen, ed. 2 vols. Cambridge, Massachusetts: The Belknap Press of Harvard University Press, 1972.

Smith/Tatsch 1937

Smith, Harry, and J. Hugo Tatsch. *Moses Michael Hays: Merchant, Citizen, Freemason, 1739–1805*. Boston: Moses Michael Hays Lodge A.F.& A.M., 1937.

Snodin 1982

Snodin, Michael. *English Silver Spoons*. Rev. ed. London: Charles Letts Books, 1982.

Snyder 1991

Snyder, Holly. "We Have the World to Begin Againe: Jewish Life in Colonial Savannah, 1733–1783." *Proceedings of the Middle Atlantic Historical Association of Catholic Colleges and Universities*, 6 (1991), pp. 122–32.

Sotheby's 1972

Important American Silver. Auction catalogue. New York: Sotheby Parke-Bernet, October 17, 1972.

Sotheby's 1973

American, English and Continental Silver. Auction catalogue. New York: Sotheby Parke-Bernet, March 28, 1973.

Sotheby's 1974

The American Heritage Society Auction of Americana. Auction catalogue. New York: Sotheby Parke-Bernet, November 12–16, 1974.

Sotheby's 1976

The American Heritage Society Auction of Americana. Auction catalogue. New York: Sotheby Parke-Bernet, November 18–20, 1976.

Sotheby's 1978

Auction of Americana. Auction catalogue. New York: Sotheby Parke-Bernet, November 16–18, 1978.

Sotheby's 1979

The American Heritage Society Auction of Americana. Volume I. Auction catalogue. New York: Sotheby Parke-Bernet, November 27–29, 1979.

Sotheby's 1980

Fine Americana. Volume I. Auction catalogue. New York: Sotheby Parke-Bernet, January 30–February 2, 1980.

Sotheby's 1981A

Fine American Furniture and Related Decorative Arts. Auction catalogue. New York: Sotheby's, April 29–May 1, 1981.

Sotheby's 1981B

American, Continental and English Silver, Portrait Miniatures and Chess Sets. Auction catalogue. New York: Sotheby's, July 14, 1981.

Sotheby's 1981C

American Silver. Auction catalogue. New York: Sotheby's, November 17, 1981.

Sotheby's 1982A

The American Heritage Auction of Americana. Auction catalogue. New York: Sotheby's, January 27–30, 1982.

Sotheby's 1982B

American Furniture and Related Decorative Arts. Auction catalogue. New York: Sotheby's, June 30–July 1, 1982.

Sotheby's 1983

Important American Furniture and Related Decorative Arts. Auction catalogue. New York: Sotheby's, January 27 and 29, 1983.

Sotheby's 1985

Important American Furniture, Folk Art, Silver, Chinese Export Porcelain and Rugs. Auction catalogue. New York: Sotheby's, January 31–February 2, 1985.

Sotheby's 1986A

The Cornelius C. Moore Collection of Early American Silver. Auction catalogue. New York: Sotheby's, January 31, 1986.

Sotheby's 1986B

Important Americana including Furniture, Folk Art and Folk Paintings, Prints, Silver, and Chinese Export Porcelain. Auction catalogue. New York: Sotheby's, January 30–31, February 1, 1986.

Sotheby's 1988

Fine American Furniture, Folk Art, Silver and China Trade Paintings. Auction catalogue. New York: Sotheby's June 23, 1988.

Sotheby's 1991

Fine Americana: Including Furniture, Folk Art, Folk Paintings, Stoneware and Redware, Silver, Gold and Portrait Miniatures. Auction catalogue. New York: Sotheby's, June 26–27, 1991.

Sotheby's 1994

Fine Americana. Auction catalogue. New York: Sotheby's, January 28–31, 1994.

Sotheby's 1995

Important Americana. Auction catalogue. New York: Sotheby's, January 24–30, 1995.

Sotheby's 2000

Important Americana: Silver, Folk Art, and Furniture. Auction catalogue. New York: Sotheby's, October 13, 2000.

Spencer-Mounsey 1927

Spencer-Mounsey, Creighton. "The Meiser Family of New Amsterdam and Wappingers Falls, N.Y." NYGBR, 58 (April 1927), pp. 172–80.

Spooner 1907

Spooner, Walter W., ed. Historic Families of America. New York: Historic Families Publishing Association, 1907.

Statham 1920

Statham, Charles A. History of the Family of Maunsell (Mansell, Mansel). 2 vols. London: Kegan Paul Trench and Company, 1920.

Stayton 1990

Stayton, Kevin L. Dutch by Design: Tradition and Change in Two Historic Brooklyn Houses, the Schenck Houses at The Brooklyn Museum. New York: The Brooklyn Museum, 1990.

Stephens 1950

Stephens, Stephen DeWitt. The Mavericks: American Engravers. New Brunswick, New Jersey: Rutgers University Press, 1950.

Stephens/Hawkins 1978

Stephens, Frederick G., and Edward Hawkins. Catalogue of the Prints and Drawings in the British Museum. Division I: Political and Personal Satires. London: British Museum Publications, 1978.

Stern 1958

Stern, Malcolm H. "The Function of Genealogy in American Jewish History." In Essays in American Jewish History. Cincinnati: American Jewish Archives, 1958, pp. 69–97.

Stern 1963

Stern, Malcolm H. "New Light on the Jewish Settlement of Savannah." PAJHS, 52 (1963), pp. 163–99.

Stern 1965

Stern, Malcolm H. "The Sheftall Diaries: Vital Records of Savannah Jewry (1733–1808)." PAJHS, 54 (March 1965), p. 247.

Stern 1967

Stern, Malcolm H. "Two Jewish Functionaries in Colonial Pennsylvania." PAJHS, 57 (1967), pp. 24–25, 49–51.

Stern 1974

Stern, Malcolm H. "Asser Levy—A New Look at Our Jewish Founding Father." American Jewish Archives, 26 (April 1974), pp. 66–77.

Stern 1991

Stern, Malcolm H. First American Jewish Families. 1960; 3rd ed. Baltimore: Ottenheimer Publishers, 1991.

Stern/Angel 1976

Stern, Malcolm H., and Marc D. Angel. New York's Early Jews: Some Myths and Misconceptions. New York: Jewish Historical Society of New York, 1976.

Stevens 1867

Stevens, John Austin. Colonial Records of the New York Chamber of Commerce, 1768–1784, with Historical and Biographical Sketches. New York: John F. Trow and Company, 1867.

Stillinger 1980

Stillinger, Elizabeth. The Antiquers. New York: Alfred A. Knopf, 1980.

Stillwell 1903–32

Stillwell, John E. Historical and Genealogical Miscellany: Data Relating to the Settlement and Settlers of New York and New Jersey. 5 vols. New York: 1903–32.

Stone 1985

Stone, Jonathan. "Anglo-Jewish Silver: An Illegal Mark Discovered." Antique Collecting, 19 (February 1985), pp. 64–68.

Stott 1995

Stott, Richard. "Furniture." In Kenneth T. Jackson, ed. *The Encyclopedia of New York City*. New Haven: Yale University Press, 1995, p. 445.

Stow 1950

Stow, Millicent. *American Silver*. New York: M. Barrows and Company, 1950.

Stratton 1975

Stratton, Deborah. *Mugs and Tankards*. London: Souvenir Press, 1975.

Swetschinski 1980

Swetschinski, Daniel. "The Portuguese Jewish Merchants of 17th Century Amsterdam." Ph.D. dissertation. Waltham, Massachusetts: Brandeis University, 1980.

Sympson 1750

Sympson, Samuel. *A New Book of Cyphers*. London: John Bowles and Son, 1750.

Szasz 1967

Szasz, Ferenc M. "The New York Slave Revolt of 1741: A Re-Examination." *New York History*, 48 (1967), pp. 215–30.

Talcott 1883

Talcott, S.V. *Genealogical Notes of New York and New England Families*. Albany, New York: Weed, Parsons and Company, 1883.

Talcott 1984

Talcott, Alvan. *Families of Early Guilford, Connecticut*. Baltimore: Genealogical Publishing Company, 1984.

Tatum 1961

Tatum, George B. *Penn's Great Town: 250 Years of Philadelphia Architecture Illustrated in Prints and Drawings*. Philadelphia: University of Pennsylvania Press, 1961.

Teahan 1979

Teahan, John. *Irish Silver: A Guide to the Exhibition*. Exhibition catalogue. Dublin: National Museum of Ireland, 1979.

Teahan 1982

Teahan, John. *Irish Silver from the Seventeenth to the Nineteenth Century*. Exhibition catalogue. Washington, D.C.: Smithsonian Institution, 1982.

Thomas 1939

Thomas, Milton Halsey. "The Bible Record of William Samuel Johnson, D.C.L. (Oxon.), LL.D., and His Descendants." *NYGBR*, 70 (July 1939), pp. 217–22.

Thorn 1949

Thorn, C. Jordan. *Handbook of American Silver and Pewter Marks*. New York: Tudor Publishing Company, 1949.

Ticher 1972

Ticher, Kurt. *Irish Silver in the Rococo Period*. Shannon, Ireland: Irish University Press, 1972.

Todd 1878

Todd, Charles Burr. *A General History of the Burr Family in America*. New York: E. Wells Sackett and Brother, 1878.

Trachtenberg 1944

Trachtenberg, Joshua. *Consider the Years: The Story of the Jewish Community of Easton, 1752–1942*. Easton, Pennsylvania: Centennial Committee of Temple Brith Shalom, 1944.

Traquair 1940

Traquair, Ramsay. *The Old Silver of Quebec*. Toronto: The Macmillan Company of Canada, 1940.

Trento 1997

Trento, Salvatore M. *Field Guide to Mysterious Places of Eastern North America*. New York: Henry Holt and Company, 1997.

"Trinity Church Marriages" 1746–1861

"Trinity Church Parish, New York: Marriages, 1746–1861." Film 0882993, Genealogical Department, Church of Jesus Christ of Latter-day Saints, familysearch.com (website).

Tudor 1896

Tudor, William, ed. *Deacon Tudor's Diary*. Boston: 1896.

Tully 1994

Tully, Alan. *Forming American Politics: Ideals, Interests, and Institutions in Colonial New York and Pennsylvania*. Baltimore: The Johns Hopkins University Press, 1994.

Tuttle 1869

Tuttle, Charles W. "Col. Nathaniel Meserve." *New England Historical and Genealogical Register*, 23 (April 1869), pp. 201–03.

Two Hundred 1890

Two Hundred and Fiftieth Anniversary of the Settlement of the Town of Stratford, October 3rd, 1889. 1890.

Underhill 1874

Underhill, Abraham S. "Records of the Society of Friends of the City of New York and Vicinity, from 1640 to 1800." *NYGBR*, 5 (October 1874), pp. 186–90.

United States Bureau of the Census 1960

United States Bureau of the Census. *Historical Statistics of the United States, Colonial Times to 1957*. Washington, D.C.: United States Government Printing Office, 1994.

Upshur 1904

Upshur, Thomas Teakle. *The Genealogy of Henrietta Chauncey Wilson, Wife of James Whiteley of Baltimore, Maryland*. Nassawadoix, Virginia: 1904.

Upton 1997

Upton, Dell. *Holy Things and Profane: Anglican Parish Churches in Colonial Virginia*. New Haven and London: Yale University Press, 1997.

Vandermeer/Swierenga 1991

Vandermeer, Philip R., and Robert P. Swierenga, eds. *Belief and Behavior: Essays in the New Religious History*. New Brunswick, New Jersey: Rutgers University Press, 1991.

Van Pelt 1898

Van Pelt, Daniel. *Leslie's History of the Greater New York*. 3 vols. New York: Arkell Publishing Company, 1898.

Van Wyck 1979

Van Wyck, Philip. *The Story of a Dutch Colonial Family*. 1979.

Vedder 1927

Vedder, J. Van Vechten. *History of Greene County*. Volume I. *1651–1800*. 1927.

Veldman/Luijten 1993

Veldman, Ilja M., comp., and Ger Luijten, ed. *The New Hollstein: Dutch and Flemish Etchings, Engravings and Woodcuts, 1450–1700. Maarten Van Heemskerck, Part I.* Roosendaal, The Netherlands: Koninklijke Van Poll, 1993.

Ver Planck 1892

Ver Planck, William E. *History of Abraham Isaacse Ver Planck and His Male Descendants in America.* Fishkill, New York: Spaight, 1892.

Vickers 1996

Vickers, Daniel. "The Northern Colonies: Economy and Society, 1600–1755." In Stanley L. Engerman and Robert E. Gallman, eds. *The Cambridge Economic History of the United States: The Colonial Era.* New York: Cambridge University Press, 1996, pp. 234–35.

Vlessing 1991

Vlessing, Odette. "New Light on the Earliest History of the Amsterdam Portuguese Jews." *Dutch Jewish History*, 3 (1991), pp. 43–75.

Von Erffa/Staley 1986

Von Erffa, Helmut, and Allen Staley. *The Paintings of Benjamin West.* New Haven and London: Yale University Press, 1986.

Von Khrum 1978

Von Khrum, Paul. *Silversmiths of New York City, 1684–1850.* New York: 1978.

Wadsworth 1945

An Exhibition of Early American Silver. Exhibition catalogue. Hartford, Connecticut: Wadsworth Atheneum, 1945.

Walkling 1985

Walkling, Gillian. *Tea Caddies: An Illustrated History.* London: Victoria and Albert Museum, 1985.

Walworth 1982

Walworth, Reuben Hyde. *Livingston Genealogy.* Rhinebeck, New York: Friends of Clermont, 1982.

Ward 1984

Ward, Barbara McLean. "Boston Goldsmiths, 1690–1730." In Ian M.G. Quimby, ed. *The Craftsman in Early America.* Winterthur, Delaware: Henry Francis du Pont Winterthur Museum, 1984, pp. 126–57.

Ward 1988

Ward, Barbara McLean. "'In a Feasting Posture': Communion Vessels and Community Values in Seventeenth- and Eighteenth-Century New England." *Winterthur Portfolio*, 23 (Spring 1988), pp. 1–24.

Ward 1990

Ward, Barbara McLean. "Hierarchy and Wealth Distribution in the Boston Goldsmithing Trade, 1690–1760." *Essex Institute Historical Collections*, 126 (July 1990), pp. 129–47.

Ward/Ward 1979

Ward, Barbara McLean, and Gerald W.R. Ward, eds. *Silver in American Life: Selections from the Mabel Brady Garvan and Other Collections at Yale University.* Exhibition catalogue. New Haven: Yale University Art Gallery, 1979.

Warren et al. 1998

Warren, David B., et al. *American Decorative Arts and Paintings in the Bayou Bend Collection.* Houston: The Museum of Fine Arts, 1998.

Warren/Howe/Brown 1987

Warren, David B., Katherine S. Howe, and Michael K. Brown. *Marks of Achievement: Four Centuries of American Presentation Silver.* Exhibition catalogue. Houston: The Museum of Fine Arts, 1987.

Waters 1984

Waters, Deborah Dependahl. *Delaware Collections in the Museum of The Historical Society of Delaware.* Wilmington: The Historical Society of Delaware, 1984.

Waters 1994

Waters, Deborah Dependahl. *A Treasury of New York Silver.* Exhibition catalogue. New York: New York Silver Society for the Museum of the City of New York, 1994.

Waters 2000

Waters, Deborah Dependahl. "'Silver Ware in Great Perfection': The Precious-Metal Trades in New York City." In Catherine Hoover Voorsanger and John K. Howat, eds. *Art and the Empire City: New York, 1825–1861.* Exhibition catalogue. New York: The Metropolitan Museum of Art, 2000.

Waters/McKinsey/Ward 2000

Waters, Deborah Dependahl, Kristan H. McKinsey, and Gerald W.R. Ward. *Elegant Plate: Three Centuries of Precious Metals in New York City.* 2 vols. New York: Museum of the City of New York, 2000.

Weeks 1898

Weeks, Lyman Horace. *Prominent Families of New York.* New York: Historical Company, 1898.

Wees 1997

Wees, Beth Carver. *English, Irish and Scottish Silver at the Sterling and Francine Clark Art Institute.* New York: Hudson Hills Press, 1997.

Wetmore et al. 1863

Wetmore, William C., et al. *Index of Grantees: Conveyances Recorded in the Office of the Register of the City and County of New York.* New York: Commissioners of Records, 1863.

Weygant 1907

Weygant, Charles H. *The Sacketts of America: Their Ancestors and Descendants, 1630–1907.* Newburgh, New York: Journal Print, 1907.

Wheeler 1907

Wheeler, William Ogden. *The Ogden Family, Elizabethtown Branch.* Philadelphia: Lippincott Company, 1907.

Whittelsey 1902

Whittelsey, Charles Barney. *The Roosevelt Genealogy, 1649–1902.* Hartford: J.B. Burr and Company, 1902.

Wilentz 1984

Wilentz, Sean. *Chants Democratic: New York City and the Rise of the American Working Class, 1788–1850.* New York: Oxford University Press, 1984.

Williams 1949
Williams, Carl M. *Silversmiths of New Jersey, 1700–1825, with Some Notice of Clockmakers Who Were Also Silversmiths.* Philadelphia: George S. MacManus Company, 1949.

Winchester 1947
Winchester, Alice. "Some Heirloom Silver from an Old New York Family." *Antiques*, 51 (June 1947), pp. 390–91.

Winterthur 1969
Spanish, French, and English Traditions in The Colonial Silver of North America. Addresses and exhibition catalogue from the 14th Winterthur Conference. Winterthur, Delaware: Henry Francis du Pont Winterthur Museum, 1969.

Wischnitzer 1955
Wischnitzer, Rachel. *Synagogue Architecture in the United States.* Philadelphia: The Jewish Publication Society of America, 1955.

Wittmeyer 1886
Wittmeyer, Alfred V. *Registers of the Births, Marriages, and Deaths of the "Eglise Françoise à la Nouvelle York" from 1688 to 1804* (1886). Reprint, Baltimore: Genealogical Publishing Company, 1968.

Wiznitzer 1954
Wiznitzer, Arnold. "The Exodus from Brazil and Arrival in New Amsterdam of the Jewish Pilgrim Fathers, 1654." *PAJHS*, 44 (1954), pp. 80–98.

Wiznitzer 1956
Wiznitzer, Arnold. "Jewish Soldiers in Dutch Brazil (1630–1654)." *PAJHS*, 46 (1956), pp. 40–50.

Wiznitzer 1958
Wiznitzer, Arnold. "The Merger Agreement and Regulations of Congregation Talmud Torah of Amsterdam (1638–39)." *Historia Judaica*, 20 (October 1958), pp. 109–32.

Wiznitzer 1960
Wiznitzer, Arnold. *Jews in Colonial Brazil.* New York: Columbia University Press, 1960.

Wolf 1994
Wolf, Edwin, 2nd. "Torah, Trade, and Kinship." In Catherine E. Hutchins, ed. *Shaping a National Culture: The Philadelphia Experience, 1750–1800.* Winterthur, Delaware: Henry Francis du Pont Winterthur Museum, 1994, pp. 169–80.

Wolf/Whiteman 1957
Wolf, Edwin, 2nd, and Maxwell Whiteman. *The History of the Jews of Philadelphia from Colonial Times to the Age of Jackson.* Philadelphia: The Jewish Publication Society of America, 1957.

Wolfe 1963
Wolfe, Richard J. "The Colonial Naturalization Act of 1740 with a List of Persons Naturalized in New York Colony, 1740–1760." *NYGBR*, 94 (July 1963), pp. 132–47.

Woodhouse 1921
Woodhouse, Samuel Jr. "Special Silver Catalogue." *The Pennsylvania Museum Bulletin*, no. 68 (June 1921). Exhibition catalogue.

"Woolsey Bowl" 1943
"The Woolsey Bowl by Richard Van Dyck." *American Collector*, 12 (November 1943), p. 4.

Wright 1902
Wright, Tobias Alexander. *Records of the Reformed Dutch Church in New Amsterdam and New York.* Volume III. *Baptisms from 1 January, 1731, to 29 December, 1800.* New York: The New-York Genealogical and Biographical Society, 1902.

Wyler 1937
Wyler, Seymour B. *The Book of Old Silver: English, American, Foreign.* New York: Crown Publishers, 1937.

YUAG
Yale University Art Gallery, New Haven.

Yerushalmi 1982
Yerushalmi, Yosef H. "Between Amsterdam and New Amsterdam: The Place of Curaçao and the Caribbean in Early Modern Jewish History." *American Jewish History*, 72 (December 1982), pp. 172–92.

Zimm et al. 1946
Zimm, Louise Hasbrouck, A. Elwood Corning, Joseph W. Emsley, and Willitt C. Jewell. *Southeastern New York: A History of the Counties of Ulster, Dutchess, Orange, Rockland and Putnam.* 3 vols. New York: Lewis Historical Publishing Company, 1946.

Zimmels 1976
Zimmels, Hirsch J. *Ashkenazim and Sephardim* (1958). London: Marla Publications, 1976.

Index

References in **boldface** indicate catalogue-entry pages for catalogue items; in italics, photos and illustrations; and those followed by "n," notes. All works are by Myer Myers unless noted otherwise.

A

Abeel, Johanna, 132
  Porringer (1765–76) (cat. 46), 37, 49, 58, **132**, *133*
Act of Naturalization, 27
adjunta (council), 14
Adolphus, Isaac, 45, 47
Ainsworth, Bertram John Lawrence, 167
Aldridge, Charles, 178
Aldridge, Edward I, 55, 174 n 2
allegories, 145
Alms Basins, Set of Three (1761–65) (cat. 32), 5,
  116, *117*
Alsop, John, 132
Alstyne, Jeronimus, 66
American Judaism, 22–23
ampersand, 33
Amsterdam, 8, 23 n 28
  Synagogue des Juifs Portugais à Amsterdam
    (Picart), *11*
Anderson, William, 146 n 5
Andrews, Jeremiah, 57
Andrus, Vincent D., 190
Anglicans, 42
Anthony, Joseph, Jr., 90 n 6, 196
anti-Semitism, 1–2, 20
  Jews Receiving Stolen Goods (Sayer) (cat. 149),
    20, *252*, **252**
  A Prospect of the New Jerusalem (unidentified
    artist and publisher) (cat. 148), 20, 27, **250,**
    251
apprentices, 3, 35–36
Arcedeckne, Andrew, 138
Arcedeckne, Robert, 138
  Pair of Shoe Buckles (1765–70) (cat. 51), 47, 56,
    137–138, *138*
Archambo, Peter I, 182
Arden, Sally. *see* Verplanck, Philip and Sally
Arden, Thomas and Mary (Boyle), 68, 195
  Sugar Tongs (1784–86) (cat. 97), 64–65, *195*, **195**
armorials, 38. *see also* crests
  Clarkson arms, 37–38, *39*

Dunscomb arms, *39*
Hamilton arms, *65*
Livingston arms, 26, 38, *39*
Onderdonck arms, 71 n 143
Philipse arms, 49–50, *50*, 146 n 1
Schuyler arms, *209*, 210
Smith arms, 49, *49*
Van Cortlandt arms, 69 n 56
Arons, Harry, 119, 180, 182
Ash, Gilbert, 4
Ashkenazim, 2, 8, 16–17, 22, 23 n 28, 46

B

Bailey, Henry, 55
Baker, Sarah, 63
Bancker, Abraham, 56
Bancker, Adrian, 29, 55, 123, 145
Bancker, Evert, Jr., 56, *265*
Bancker crest, 190
bar Meyr, Selomo. *see* Myers, Solomon
Barclay, Andrew D., 136
Barclay, Maria (Van Beverhoudt), 136, 147
Baretti, P., 142
Barnes, Phebe, 140
Barnes, Philinda or "Philena," 58, 140
  Punch Bowl (1746–63) (cat. 7), 86, **86**
Barnes, Thomas and Phebe, 31, 85
  Punch Bowl (1746–63) (cat. 7), 86, **86**
  Sauce Spoon (1765–76) (cat. 41), *128*, **128**
Barnsley, Andrew, 48
Barwick, Mary, 80 n 1
Bateman, Hester, 202
Bateman, William, 38, 57, 110
Battle of Brooklyn, 6
Bayard, Nicholas, 35, 56, 136, 147
  receipts from Myer Myers, *261*
Bayard, William, Jr., 174
Bayard crest, 58
Bayley, Simeon, 66
Bayly, John, 48
Beach, Sarah (Hull), 226
beakers
  Beaker (1770–76 or 1784–95) (cat. 88), *186*,
    186–187
  Three Beakers (1770–76 or 1784–95) (cat. 90),
    187, **187**
  Two Beakers (1770–76 or 1784–95) (cat. 89),

186, **186–187**
Beau, John Anthony, 38–39, 53–54, 57, 207
Beckensteiner, Johann Samuel
  Torah Finials (c. 1750), **162**, *162*
Bedford, Gunning, Jr., 89
Bedford, Gunning S., Jr., 89
Bedford, Henrietta Jane, 89
Beekman, Margaret. *see* Livingston, Robert R.
  and Margaret
Beers, Caroline Ryder (Gatley), 73 n 317
Beers, William Harmon, 73 n 317
Belknap, Waldron Phoenix, Jr., 86
Bell, John, 34
bells, on Torah finials, 154, *155* (Hedges)
Bells, Whistle and (1761–65) (cat. 107) (Fueter), *207*,
  207
Benedict, Hannah (Finch), 62
  Teaspoon (1776–79) (cat. 93), 62, **190–191**, *191*
Benedict, Jemima, 190
Benedict, Stephen, 190
Bennett, James, 57
Bennett and Dixon, 33
Berdell, Elizabeth F., 104
Berg, David, 113, 200
Bergland, Julia (Whiteridge), 134
Bergh, Thauvet, 57, 78
Betts, Peter, 62
Bieaus, Blanck, 67
Billings, Andrew, 132 n 3
Birckhead, Catherine (McEvers), 87–89
Birckhead, Hugh McCullough, 87
Black Horse Tavern (New York), 5
Blanchard, Susannah, 33
Blankarn, Mr. and Mrs. Marshall P., 136
Bleecker, Leonard, 132
Bocking, Maria E., 80
bodek (searcher), 27–28
Boelen, Henricus, 29, 78, 116 n 11
Boelen, Jacob, 52
bookplates, 111, 142
  Bookplate of Jeremias Van Rensselaer (1761)
    (Gallaudet), *40*
Bortman, Mark, 97, 105, 186, 191
bottle slides, 178
bottle stands, 60
  Bottle Stand (1770–76) (cat. 81), 49, 55–56,
    178–180, *179*
  Pair of Bottle Stands (1770–71) (cat. 123)

Photographs of objects in institutional collections were supplied by the owners. Additional acknowledgments appear below. Details and mark illustrations are from the same source unless otherwise noted.

Michael Agee: cats. 23, 40, 45, 57, 72, 116; figs. 23, 29

David Allison: cat. 27

© 1999, The Art Institute of Chicago, All Rights Reserved: cat. 76; fig. 9

Gavin Ashworth: fig. 3

David L. Barquist: fig. 36; marks 24, 37, 64, 75, 100

Jay Beebe: cats. 29, 101

E. Irving Blomstrann: figs. 2, 13

Stephen Briggs: cats. 112, 113, 132

Will Brown: cats. 59, 65, 66; fig. 24

Richard Caspole: figs. 4, 5, 7; cat. illus. 62.1, 63-65.1

Christie's Images 2001: cat. 54

Alex Contreras: cat. 93

Richard Goodbody: cats. 1, 4, 5, 6, 8, 9, 15, 16, 17, 18, 20, 22, 34, 42, 44, 48, 54, 55, 58, 61, 62, 63, 67, 68, 71, 82, 84, 88, 102, 103, 108, 126, 134, 135, 139, 140, 142; figs. 21, 30; cat. illus. 44.1

Carl Kaufman: cats. 2, 35, 38, 43, 46, 51, 79, 95, 105, 107, 115, 117, 133

Suzanne Kaufman: cat. 144

Penny Leveritt: cat. 106

Joseph Levy: cat. 87

The Library of The Jewish Theological Seminary of America: cat. 144

Paul Macapia: cat. 70

Terry G. McCrea: cat. 83; fig. 26

Sanders H. Milens: cats. 136, 137

The Metropolitan Museum of Art: fig. 19

Museum of Fine Arts, Boston: cat. 64

National Museum of American History, Smithsonian Institution: cat. 83, fig. 26

© Collection of The New-York Historical Society: cat. 3, 7, 81, 97, 127, 128, 143

Paul Nurnberg: fig. 33

Thomas R. Nutt: cats. 14, 25, 37, 75, 80

Panaro & Prettyman Photography, Inc.: cat. 10

David Prencipe: cat. 24

M.S. Rau Antiques: fig. 12

St. Louis Art Museum: cats. 31, 56, 98; fig. 22

Sotheby's: cat. illus. 77.1

William Stone, 1913: cat. 100

Joseph Szaszfai: cats. 28, 53; fig. 28

Tim Thayer: cat. 95

© Virginia Museum of Fine Arts: cats. 47, 96

Katherine Wetzel: cats. 47, 96

Graydon Wood: cats. 13, 73, 74, 99; fig. 35